ALICE IN BORDERLAND

STORY AND ART BY

HARO ASO

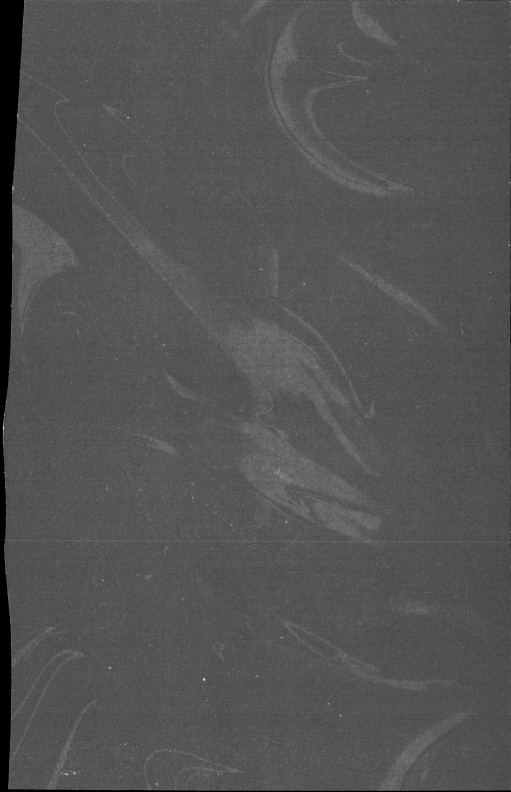

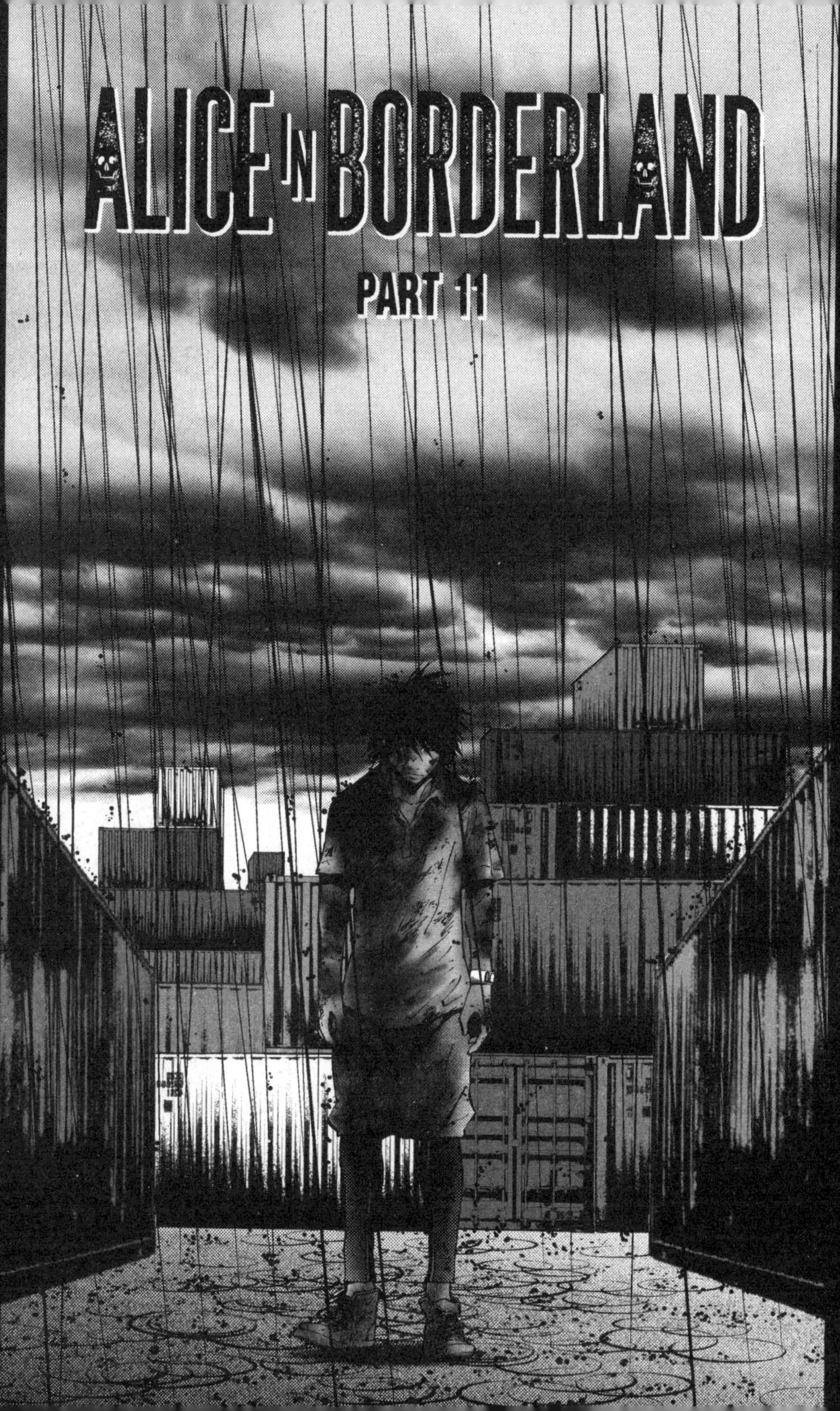
ALICE IN BORDERLAND
PART 11

ALICE IN BORDERLAND

PART 11

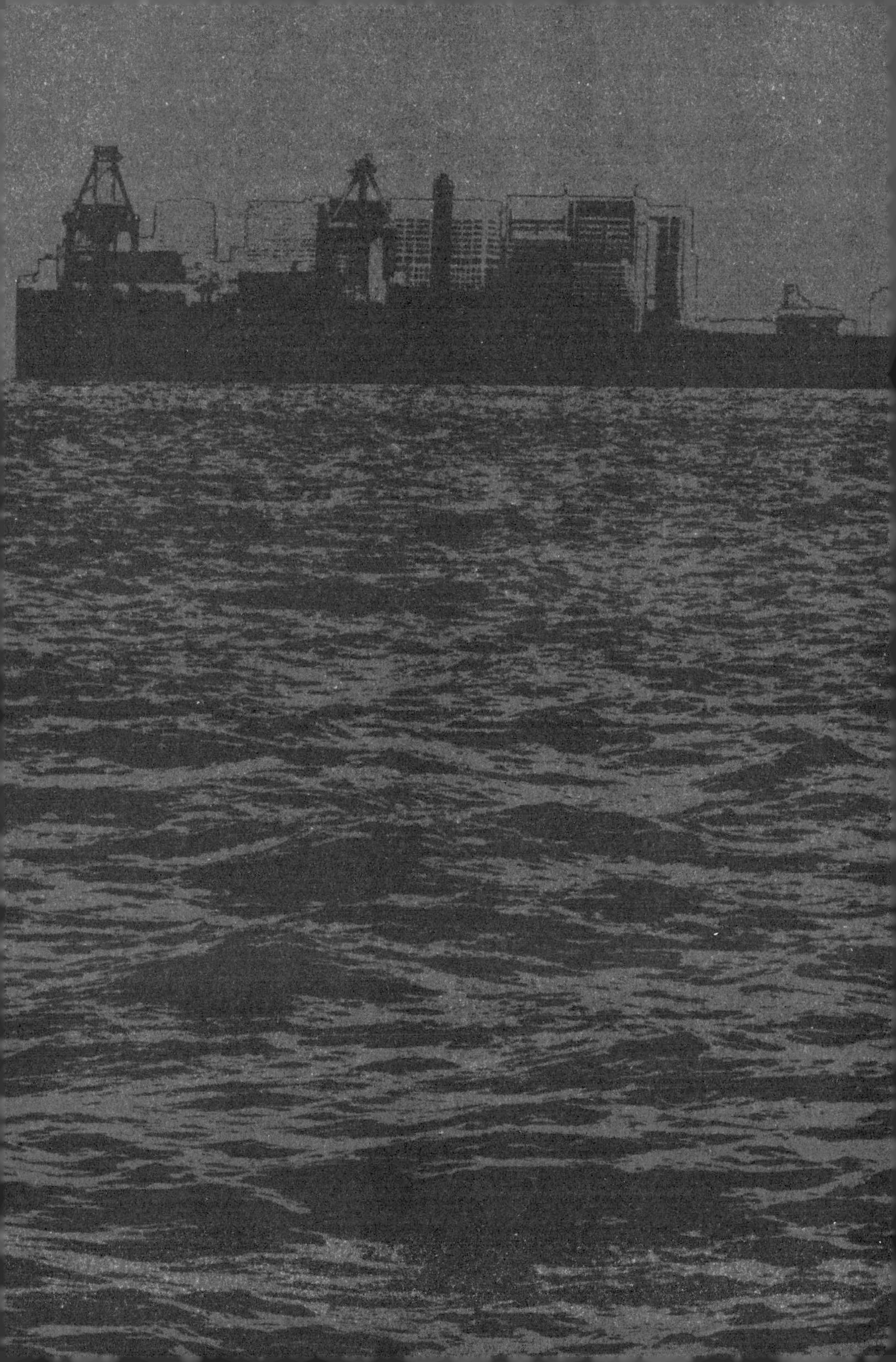

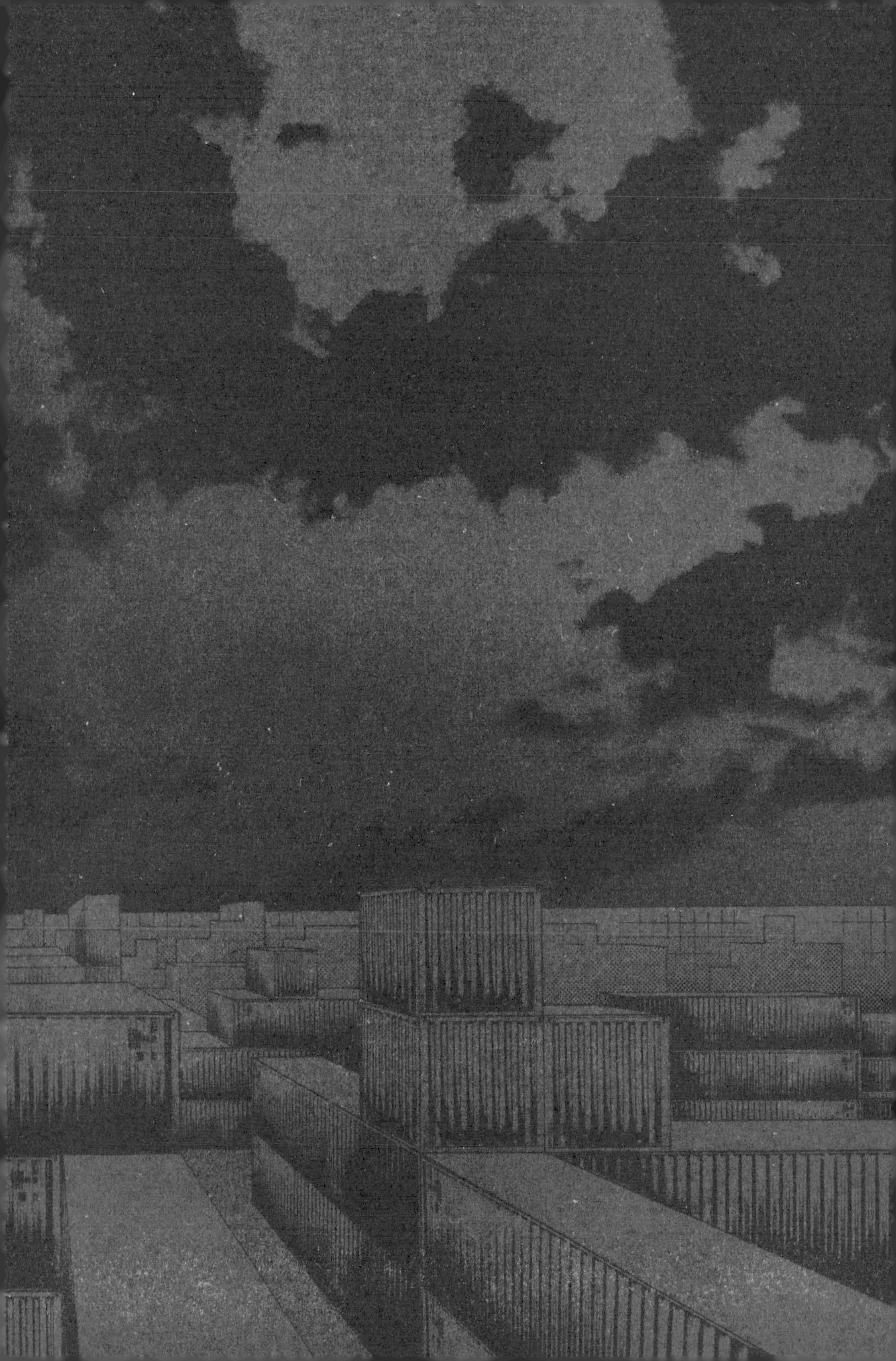

CHAPTER 38: King of Clubs, Part 6

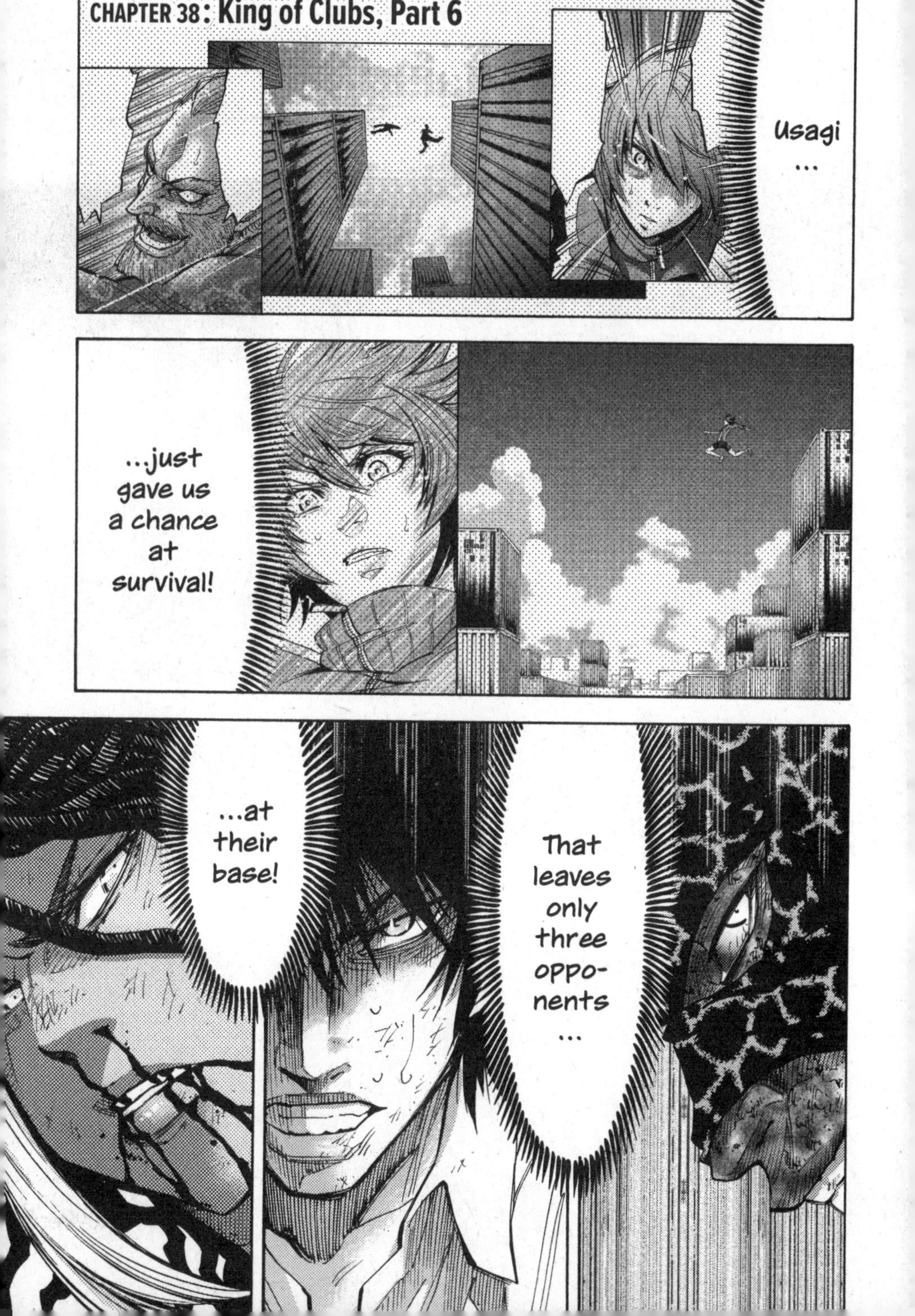
Usagi ...
...just gave us a chance at survival!
That leaves only three opponents ...
...at their base!

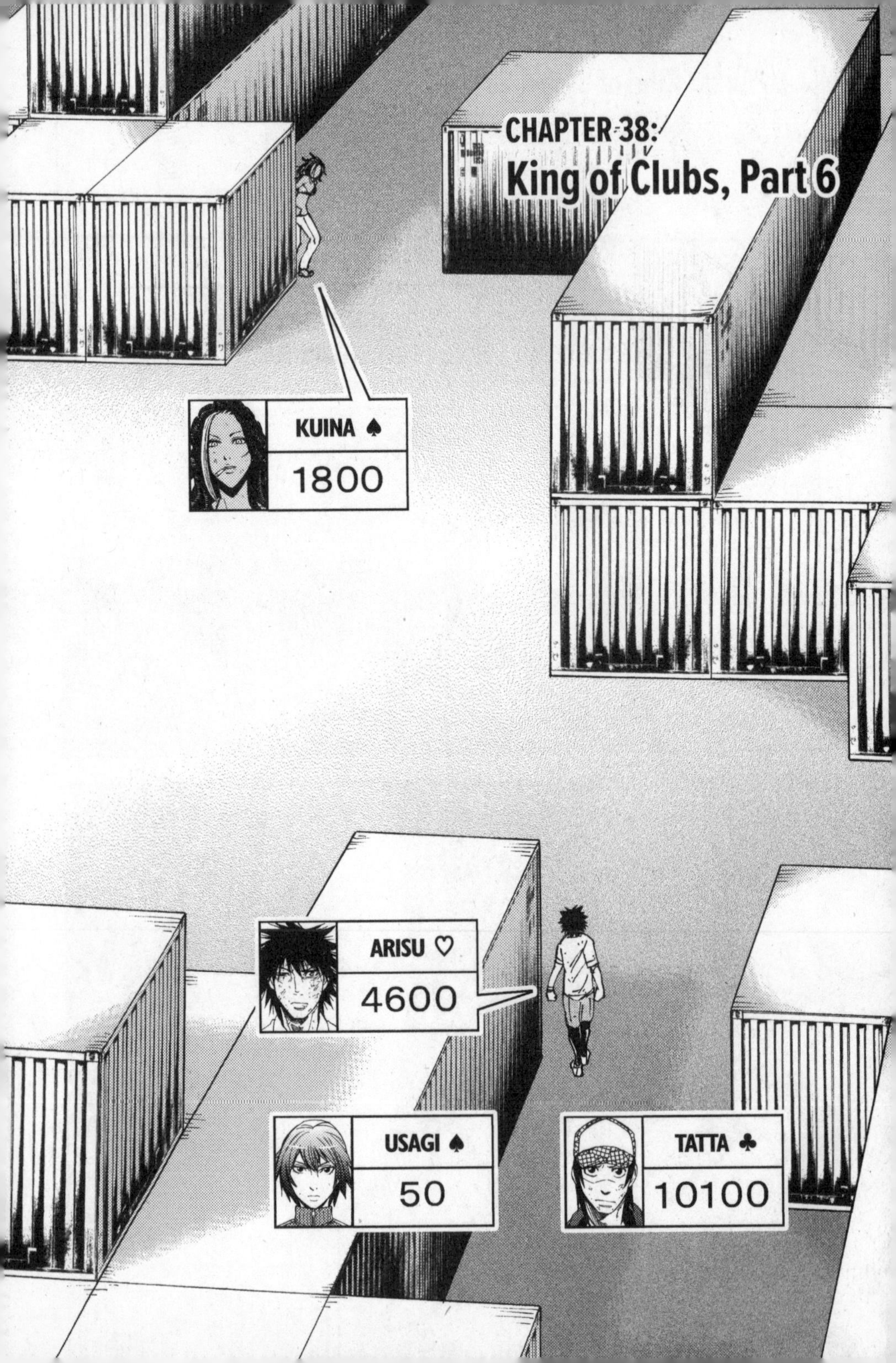
CHAPTER 38:
King of Clubs, Part 6
KUINA ♠
1800
ARISU ♡
4600
TATTA ♣
10100
USAGI ♠
50

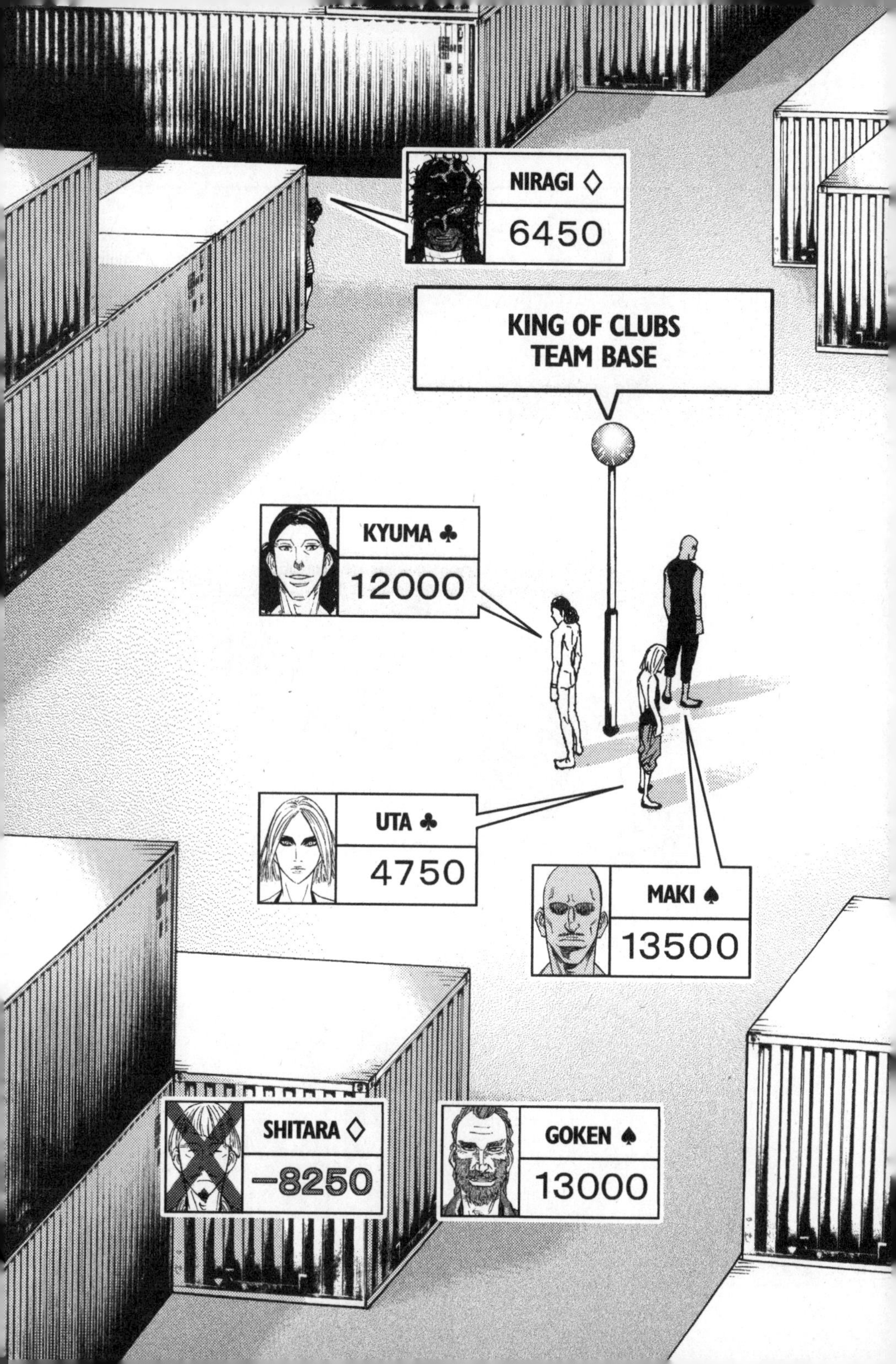
NIRAGI ◇
6450
KING OF CLUBS TEAM BASE
KYUMA ♣
12000
UTA ♣
4750
MAKI ♠
13500
GOKEN ♠
13000
SHITARA ◇
−8250

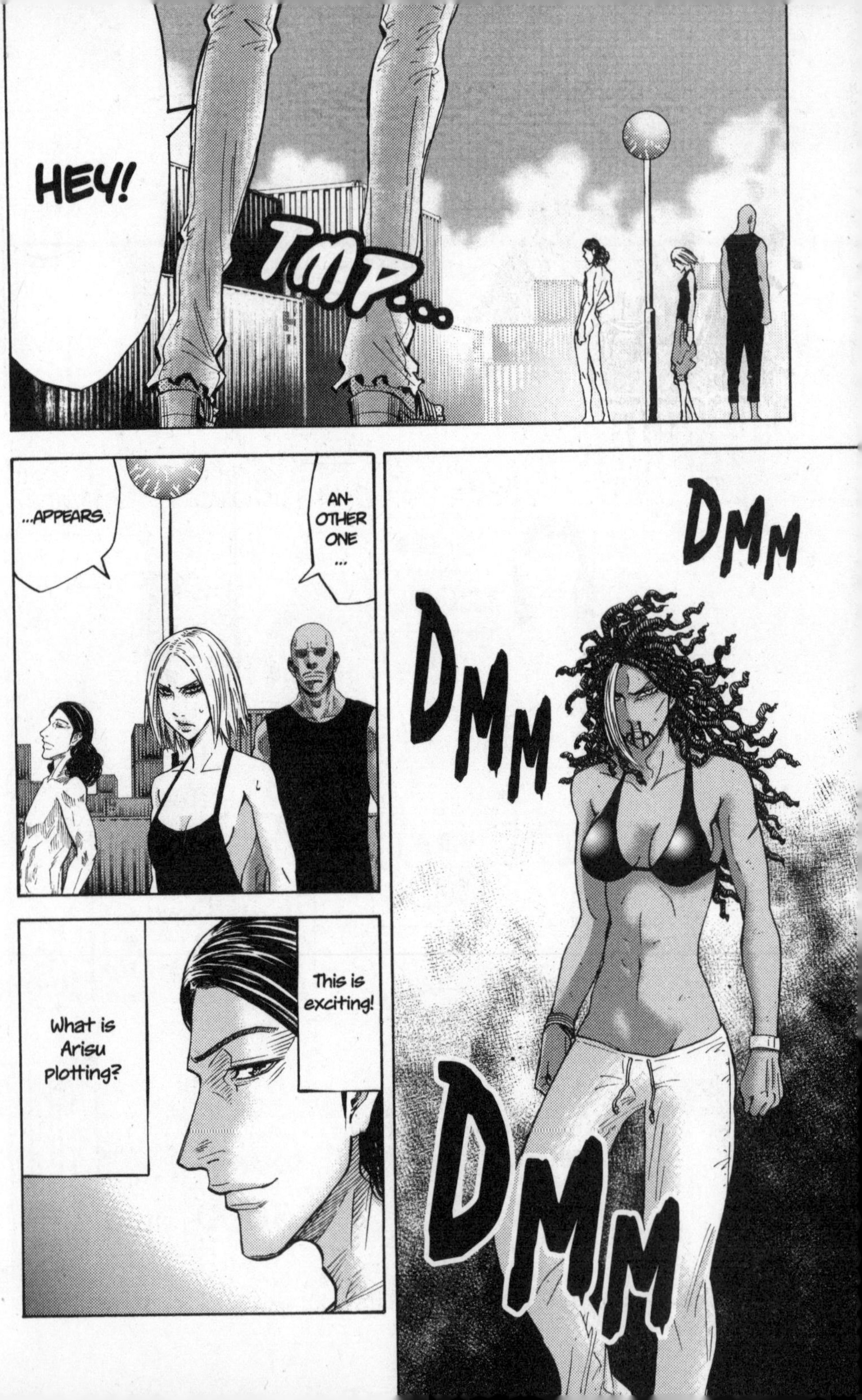
HEY!
TMP...
DMM
DMM
DMM
AN-OTHER ONE ...
...APPEARS.
This is exciting!
What is Arisu plotting?

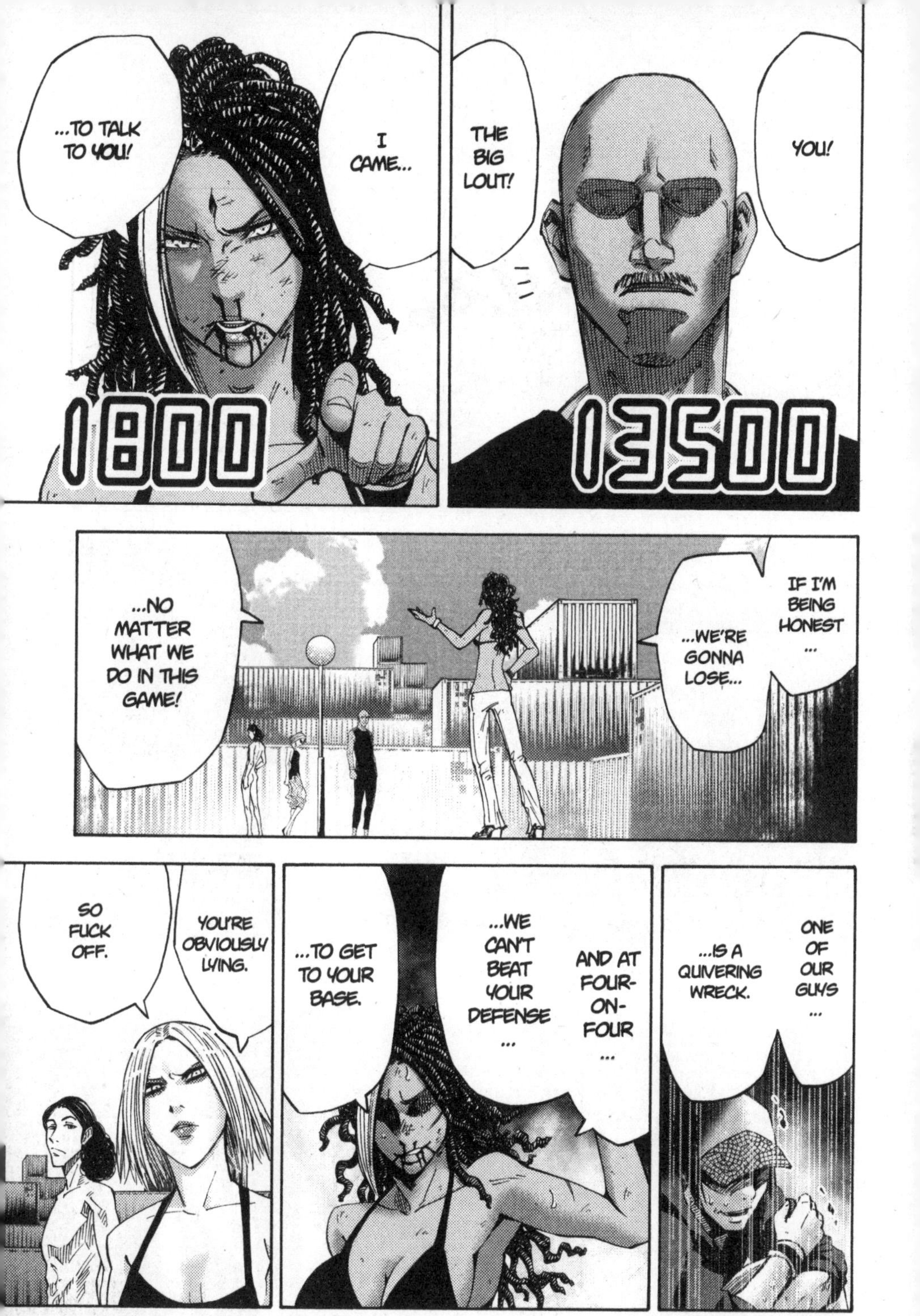
YOU!
THE BIG LOUT!
13500
I CAME...
...TO TALK TO YOU!
1800
IF I'M BEING HONEST ...
...WE'RE GONNA LOSE...
...NO MATTER WHAT WE DO IN THIS GAME!
ONE OF OUR GUYS ...
...IS A QUIVERING WRECK.
AND AT FOUR-ON-FOUR ...
...WE CAN'T BEAT YOUR DEFENSE ...
...TO GET TO YOUR BASE.
YOU'RE OBVIOUSLY LYING.
SO FUCK OFF.

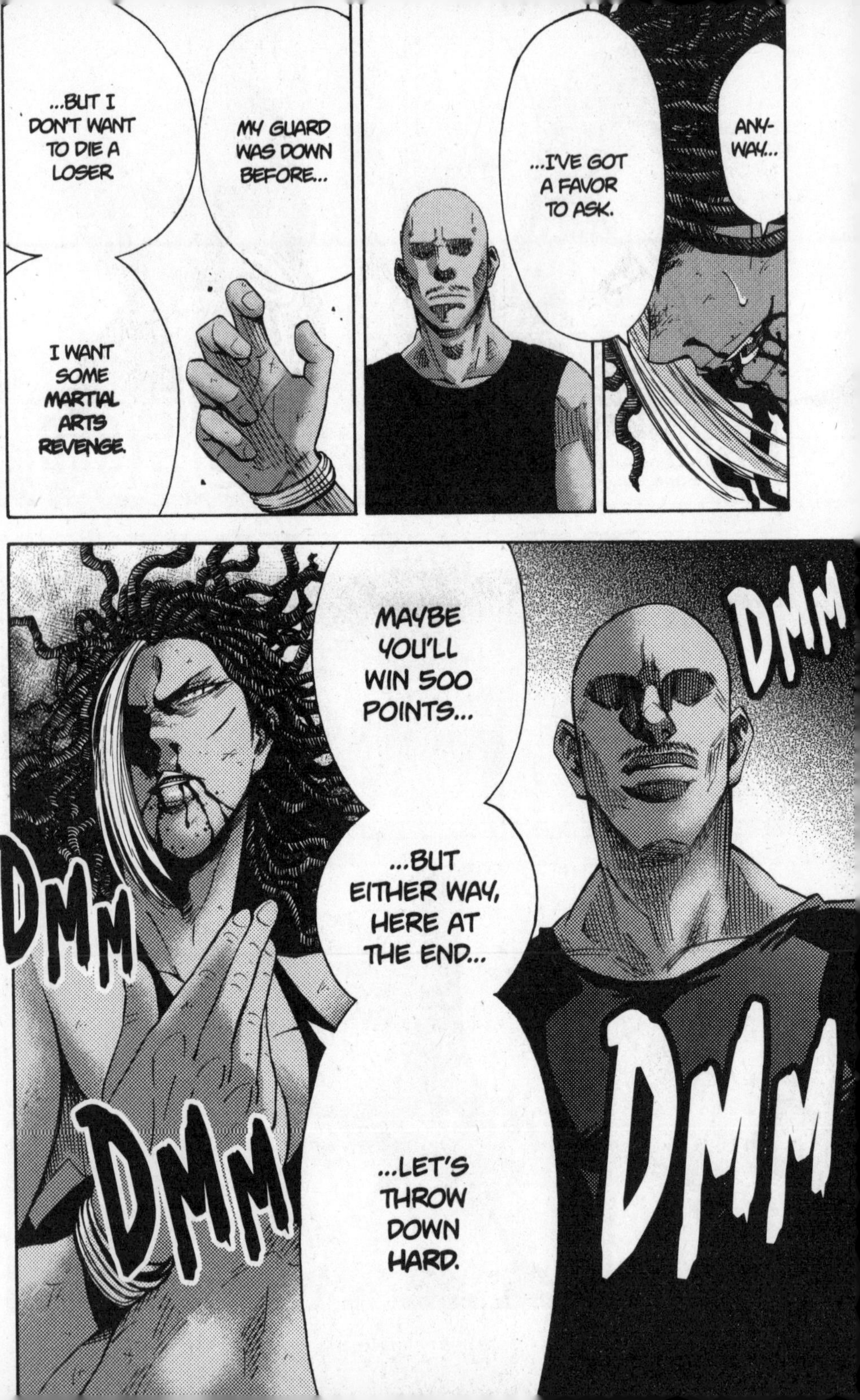
ANY-WAY...
...I'VE GOT A FAVOR TO ASK.
MY GUARD WAS DOWN BEFORE...
...BUT I DON'T WANT TO DIE A LOSER
I WANT SOME MARTIAL ARTS REVENGE.
DMM
MAYBE YOU'LL WIN 500 POINTS...
DMM
...BUT EITHER WAY, HERE AT THE END...
DMM
DMM
...LET'S THROW DOWN HARD.

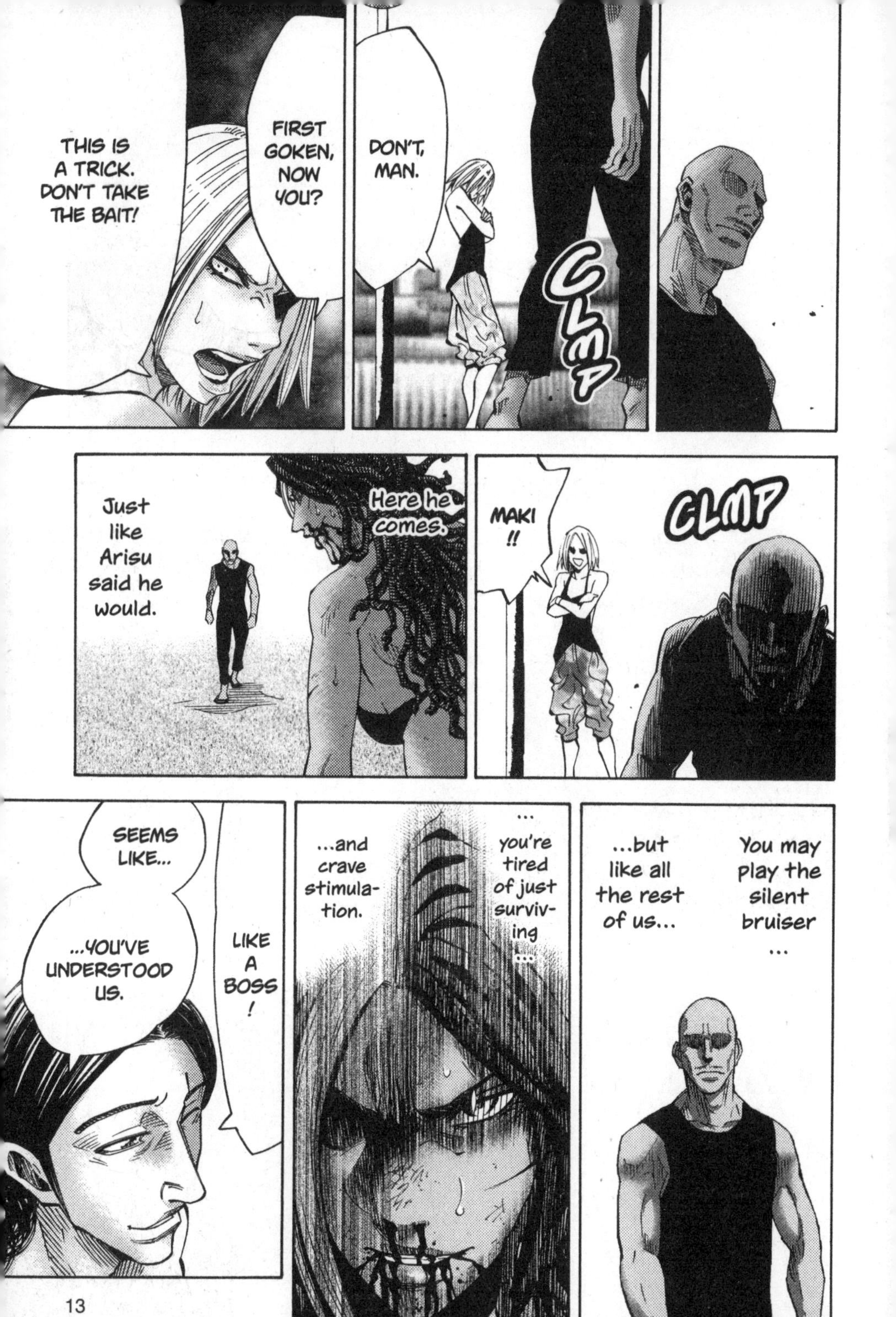
CLMP
DON'T, MAN.
FIRST GOKEN, NOW YOU?
THIS IS A TRICK. DON'T TAKE THE BAIT!
CLMP
MAKI !!
Here he comes.
Just like Arisu said he would.
You may play the silent bruiser...
...but like all the rest of us...
...you're tired of just surviving...
...and crave stimulation.
LIKE A BOSS!
SEEMS LIKE...
...YOU'VE UNDERSTOOD US.

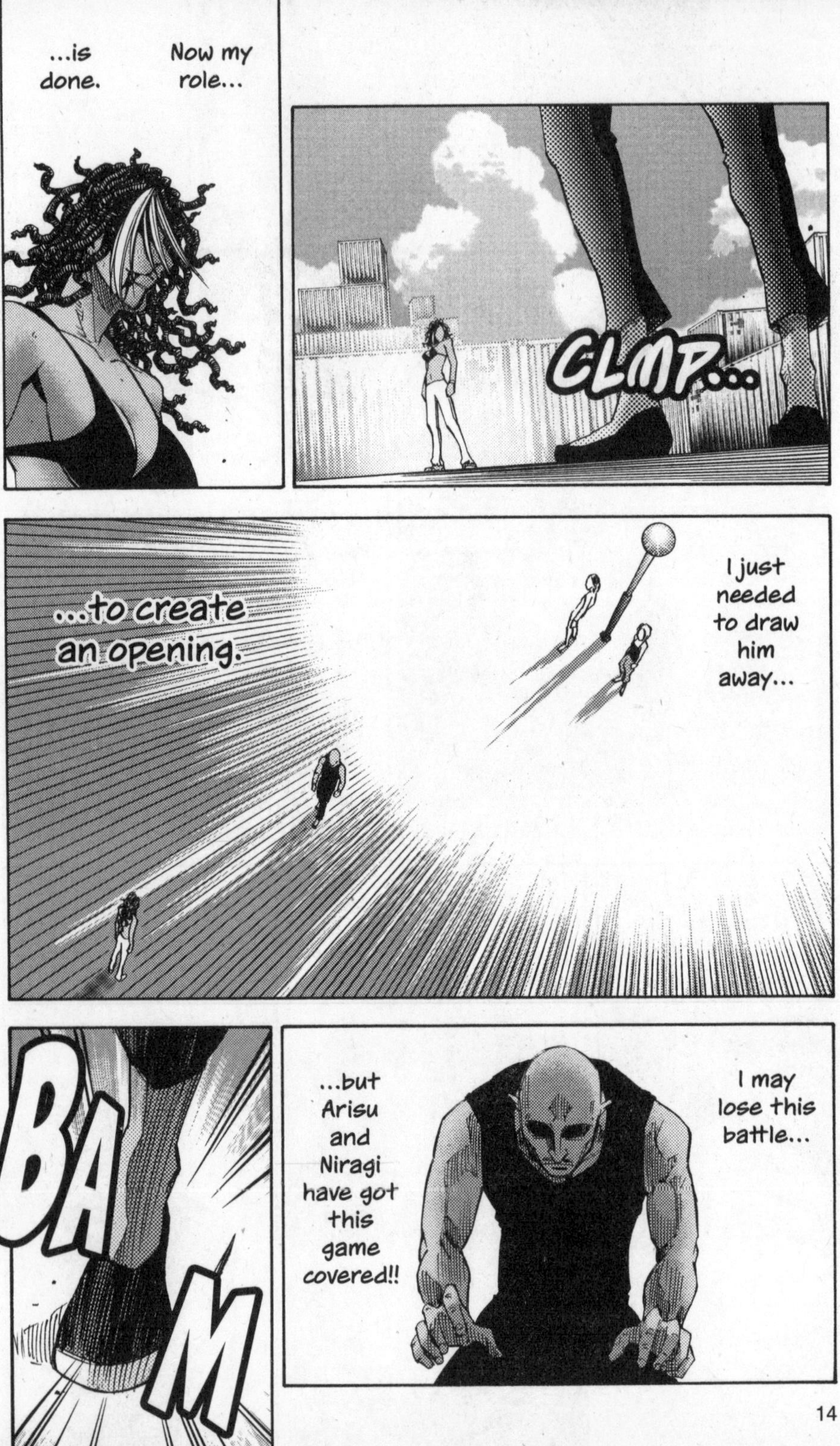
CLMP...
Now my role...
...is done.
I just needed to draw him away...
...to create an opening.
I may lose this battle...
...but Arisu and Niragi have got this game covered!!
BAM

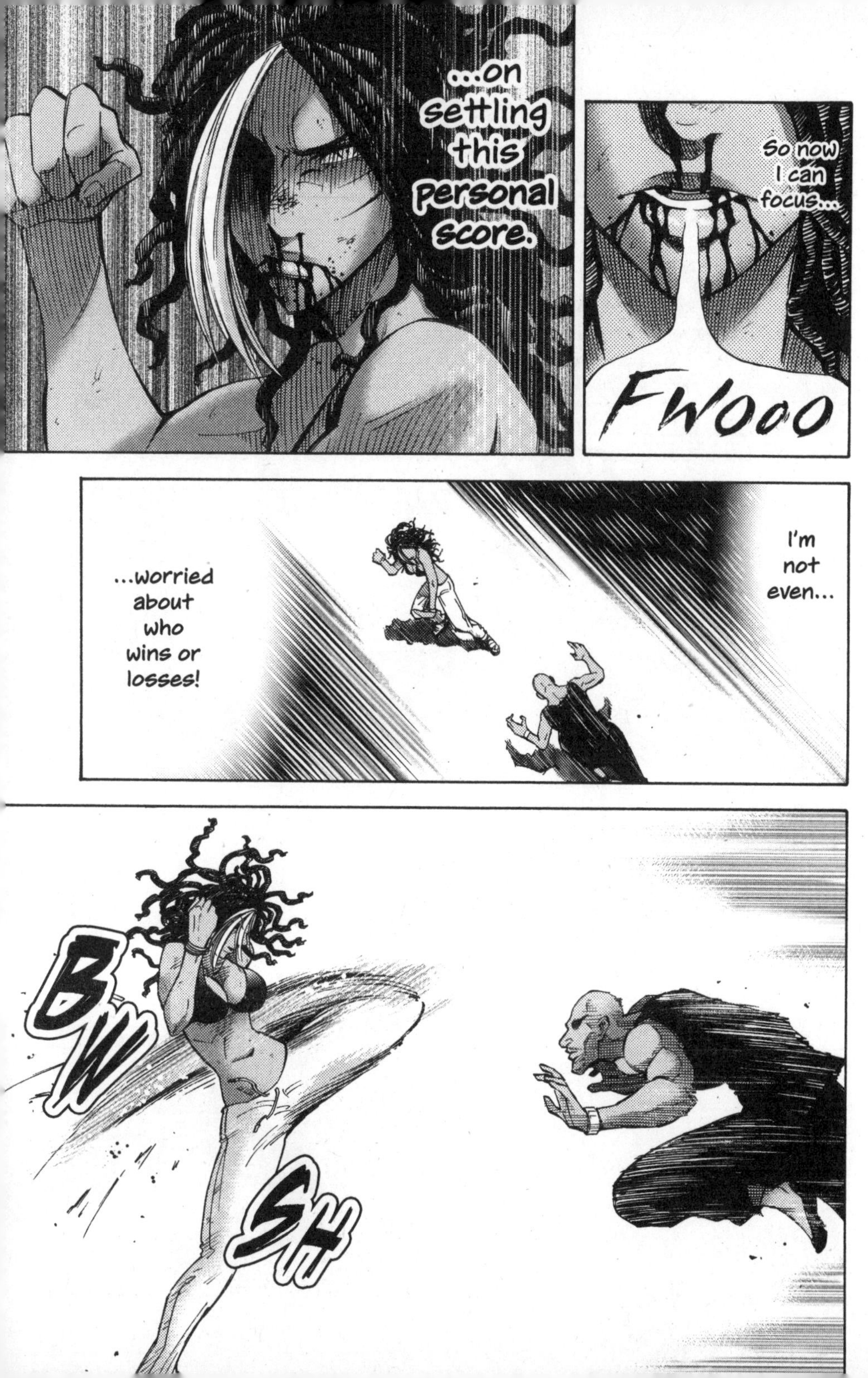
So now I can focus...
FWOOO
...on settling this personal score.
I'm not even...
...worried about who wins or losses!
BWSH

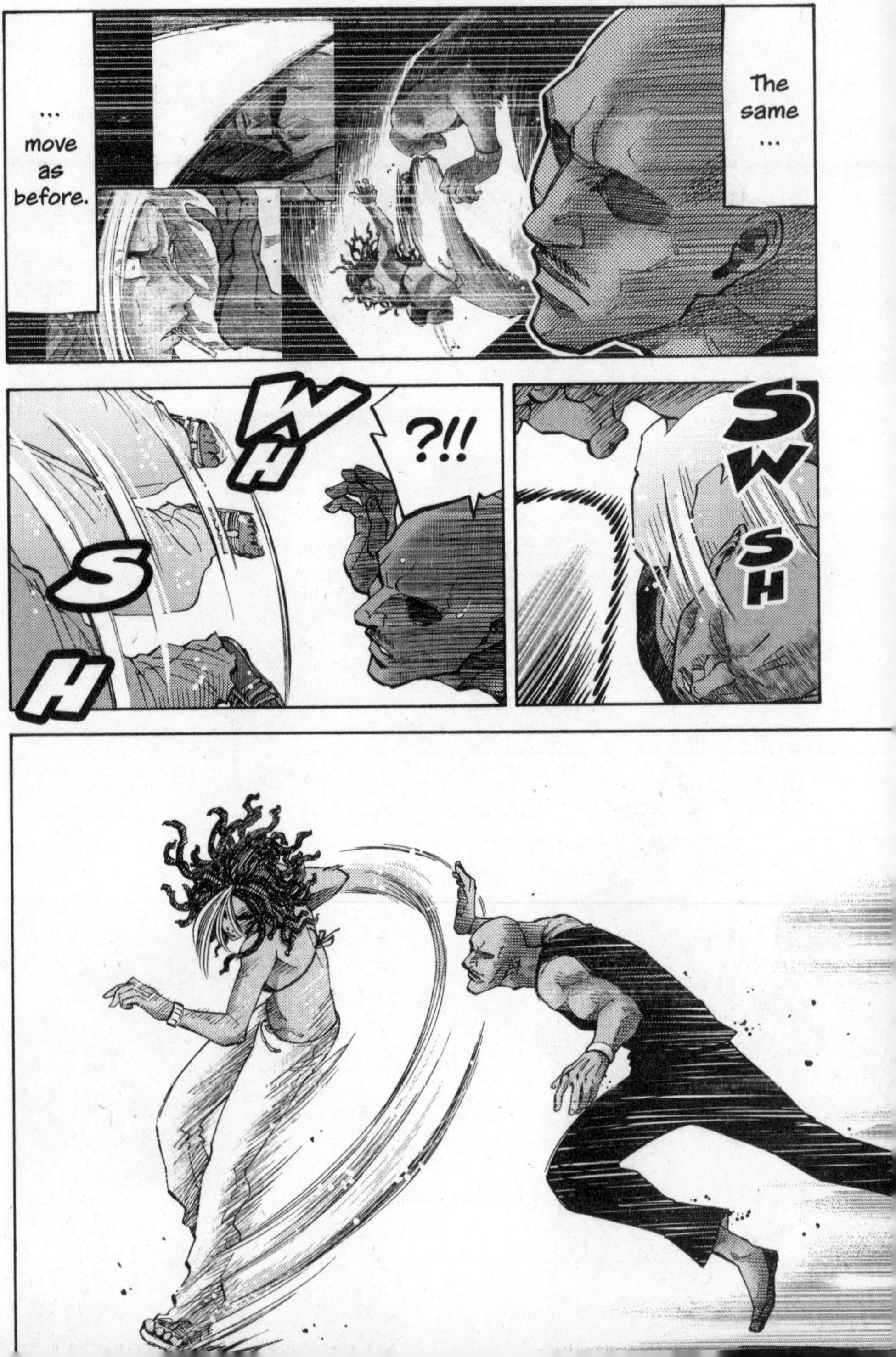
The same ...
... move as before.
SWSH
?!!
WHSH

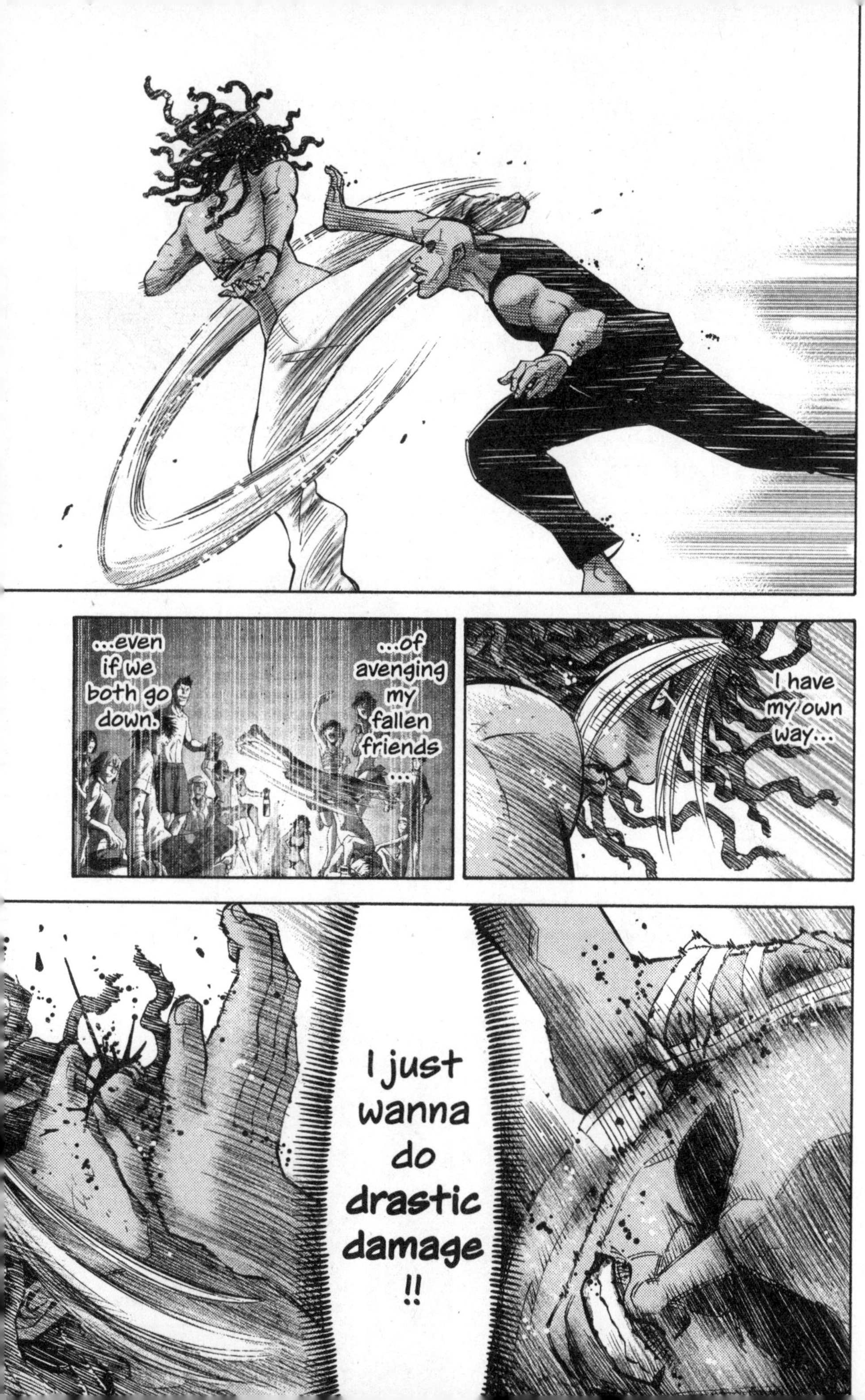
I have my own way...
...of avenging my fallen friends...
...even if we both go down.
I just wanna do drastic damage!!

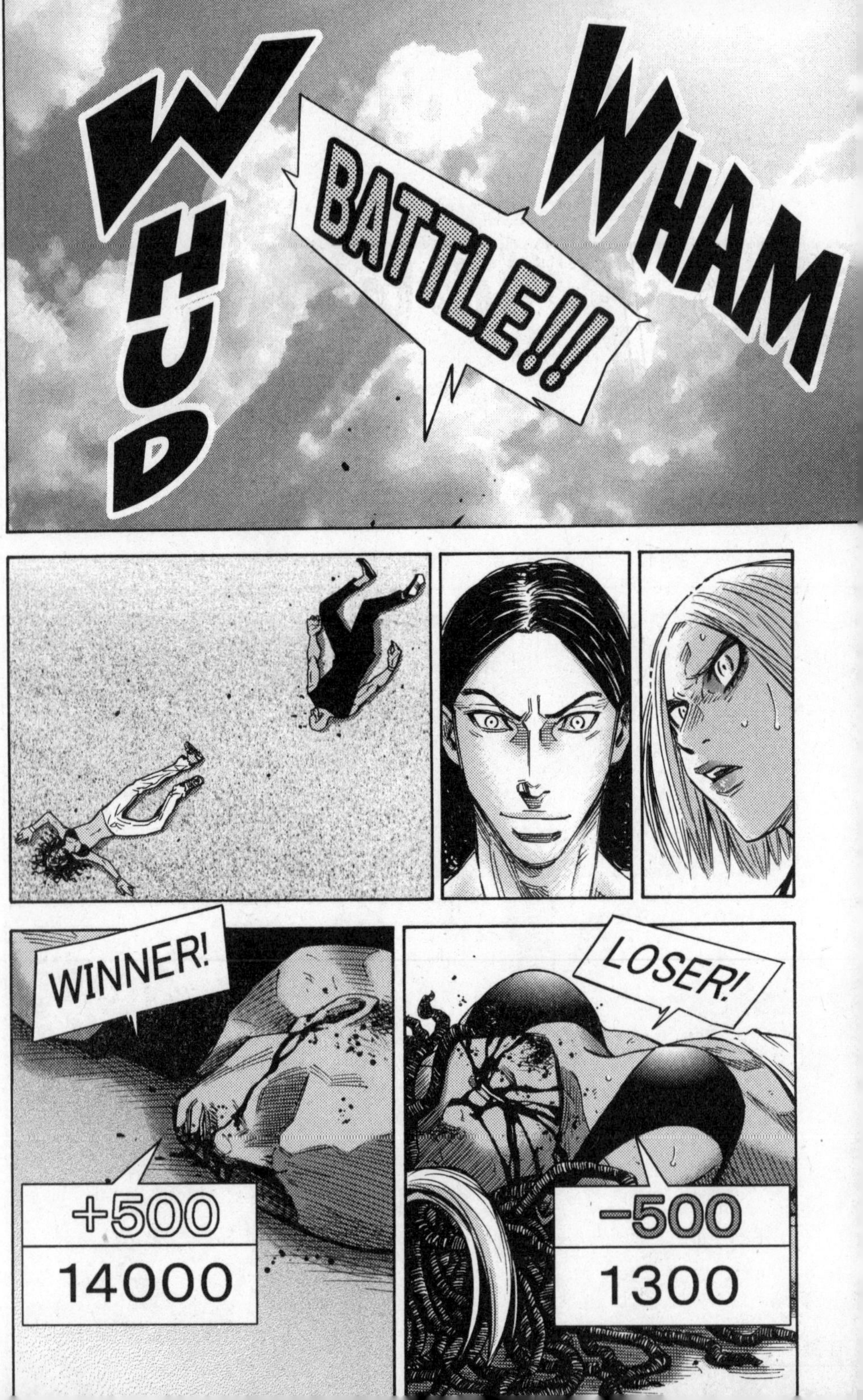
WHAM
BATTLE!!
WHUD
LOSER!
-500
1300
WINNER!
+500
14000

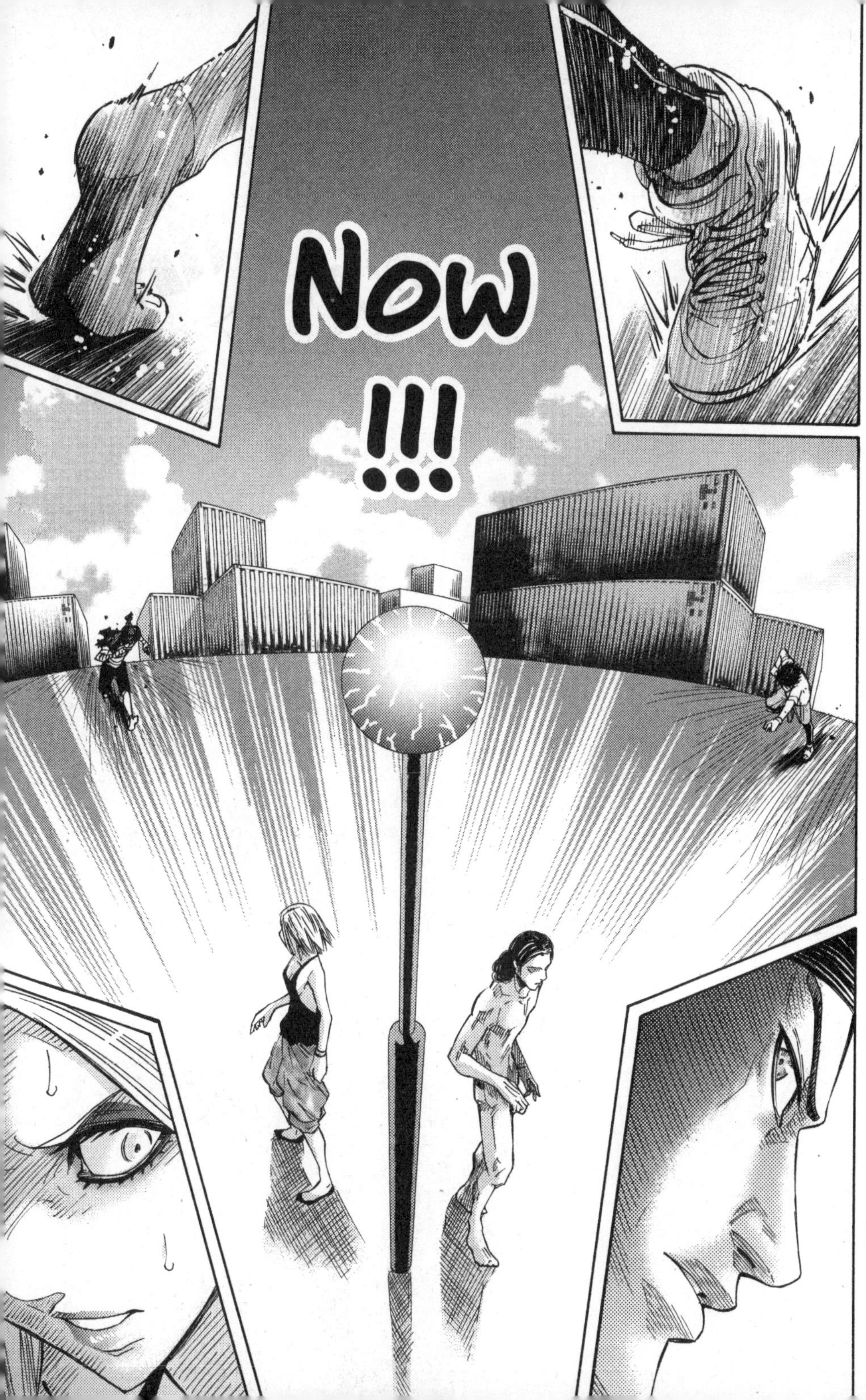
Now
!!!

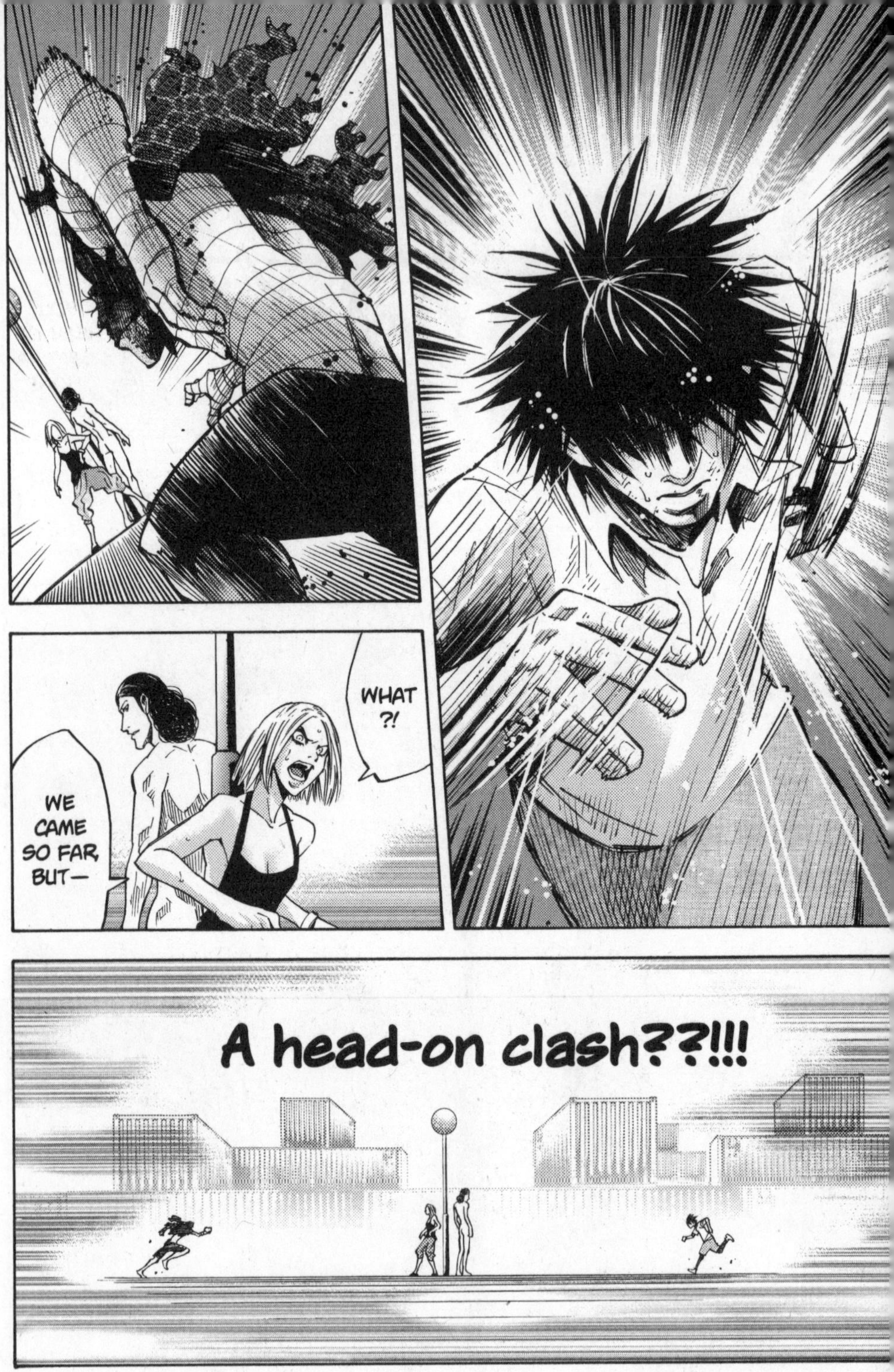
WHAT ?!
WE CAME SO FAR, BUT—
A head-on clash??!!!

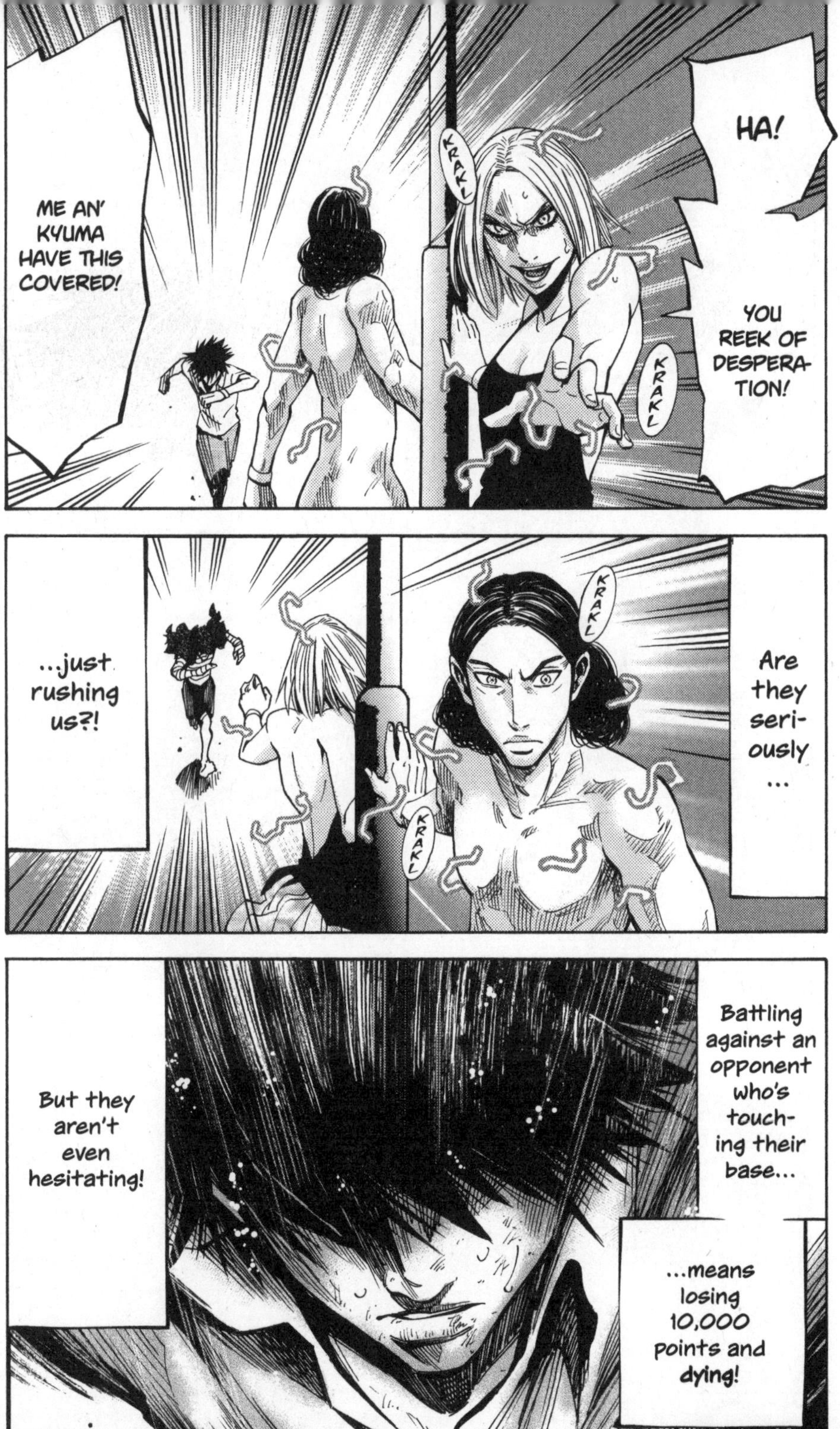
HA!
KRAKL
YOU REEK OF DESPERA-TION!
KRAKL
ME AN' KYUMA HAVE THIS COVERED!
KRAKL
Are they seri-ously ...
KRAKL
...just rushing us?!
Battling against an opponent who's touch-ing their base...
...means losing 10,000 points and dying!
But they aren't even hesitating!

WH

SH

Can that really be their plan?!

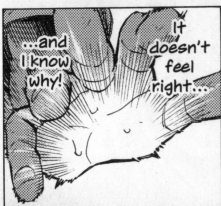

It doesn't feel right...

...and I know why!

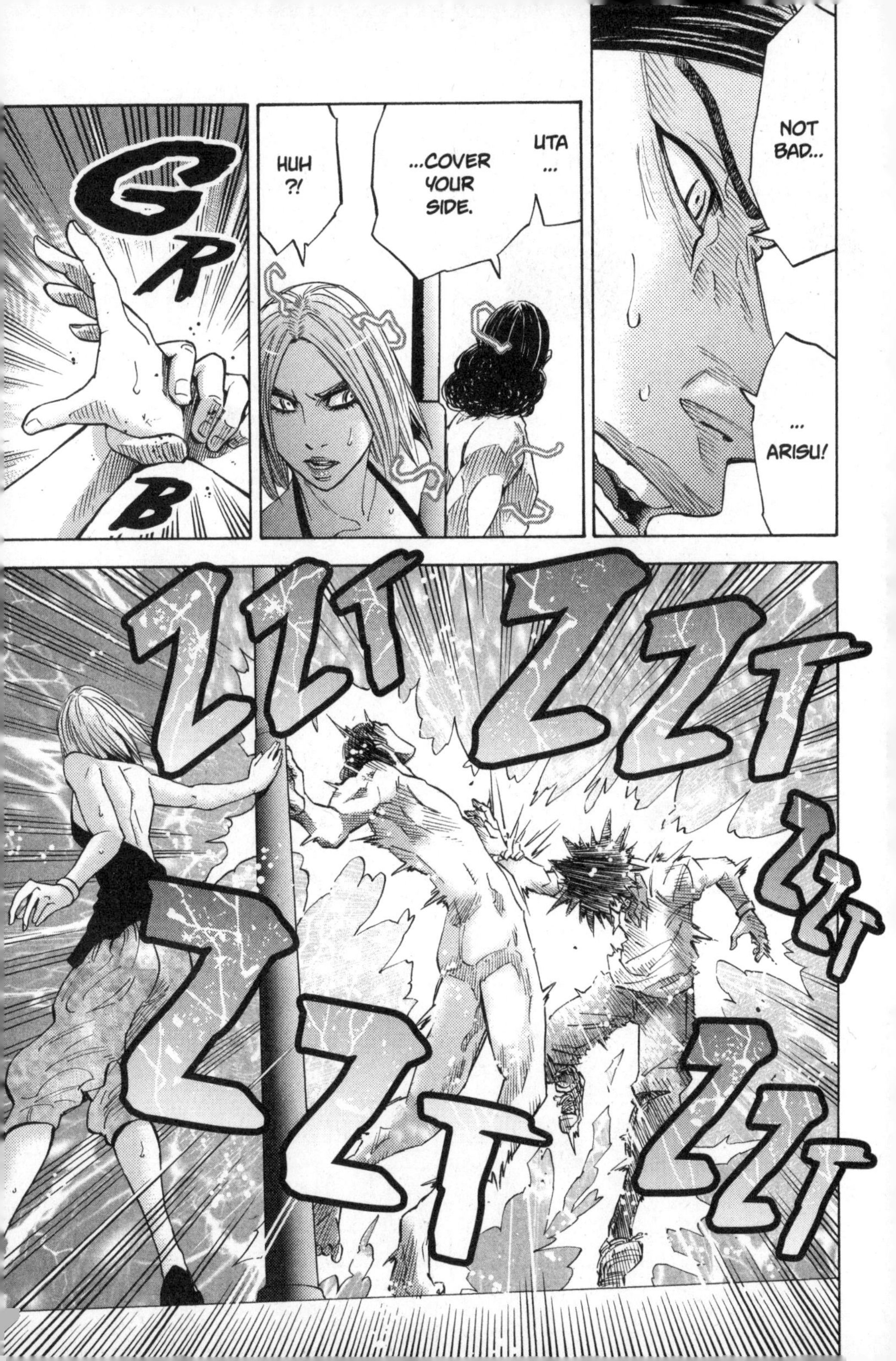
NOT BAD...
... ARISU!
UTA ...
...COVER YOUR SIDE.
HUH ?!
GRB
ZZT
ZZT
ZZT
ZZT
ZZT

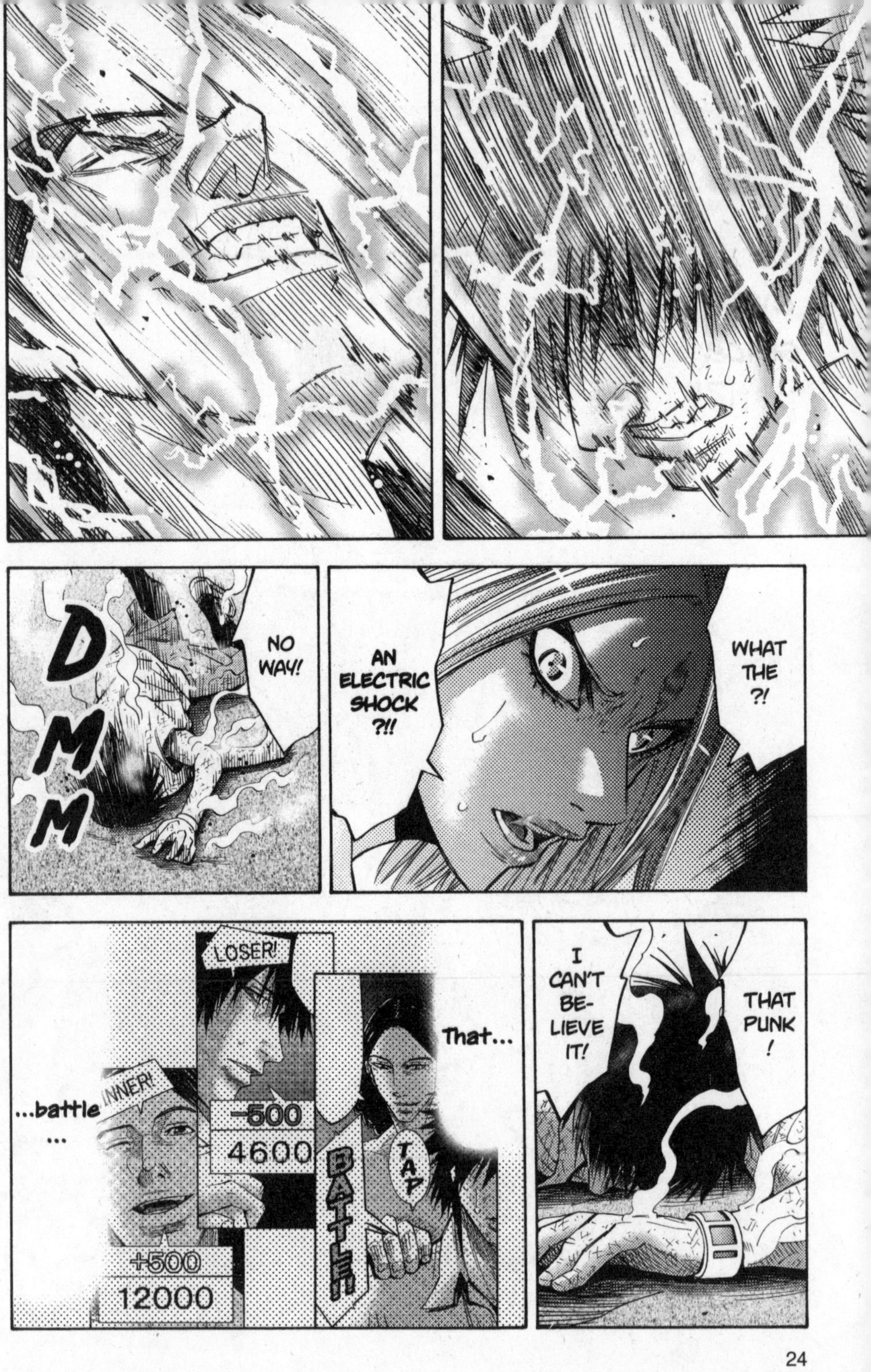
WHAT THE ?!
AN ELECTRIC SHOCK ?!!
NO WAY!
DMMM
THAT PUNK!
I CAN'T BE-LIEVE IT!
That...
LOSER!
TAP
BATTLE
-500
4600
...battle ...
+500
12000

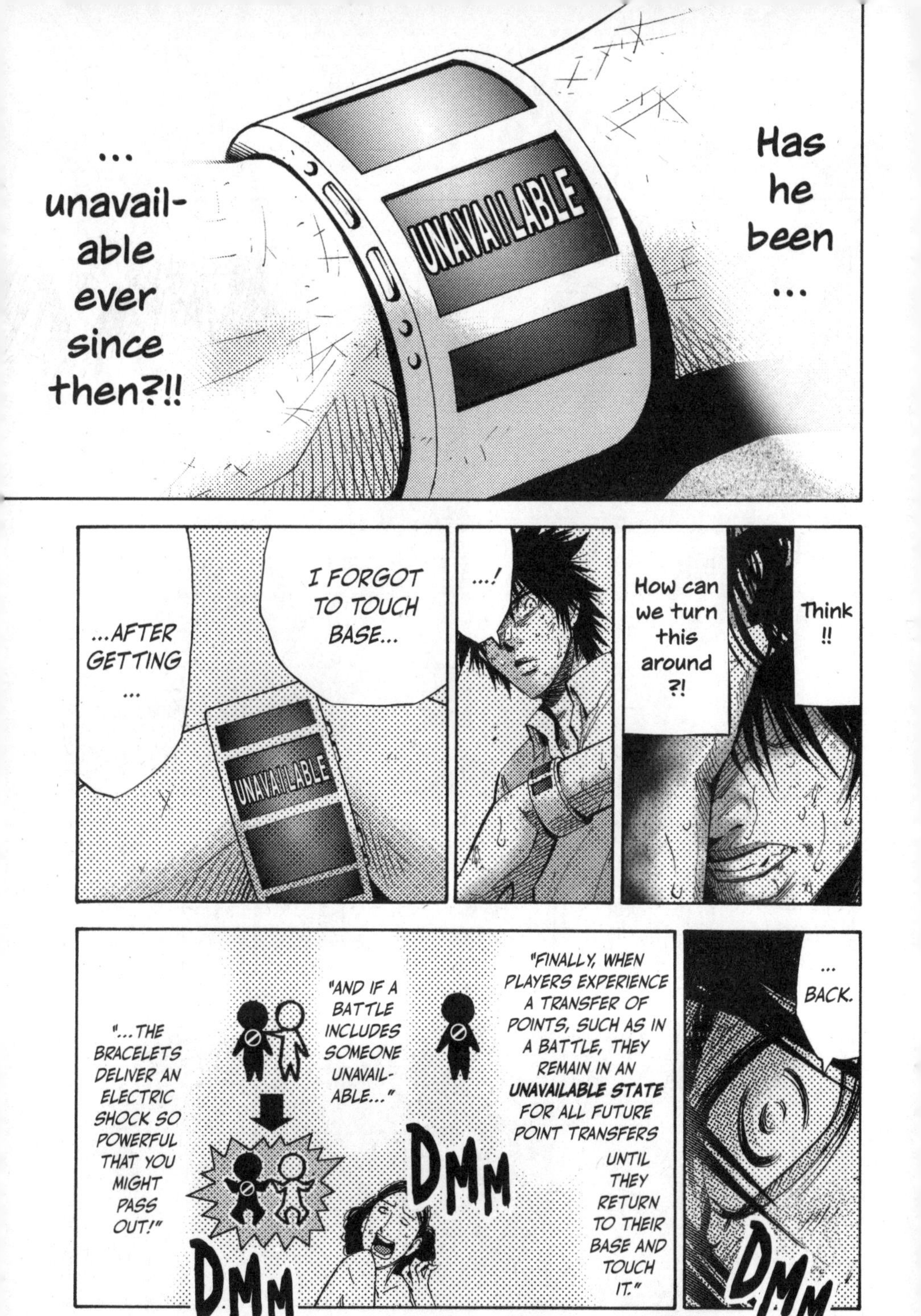
Has he been ...
... unavailable ever since then?!!
UNAVAILABLE
Think !!
How can we turn this around ?!
...!
I FORGOT TO TOUCH BASE...
...AFTER GETTING ...
UNAVAILABLE
... BACK.
DMM
"FINALLY, WHEN PLAYERS EXPERIENCE A TRANSFER OF POINTS, SUCH AS IN A BATTLE, THEY REMAIN IN AN **UNAVAILABLE STATE** FOR ALL FUTURE POINT TRANSFERS
UNTIL THEY RETURN TO THEIR BASE AND TOUCH IT."
"AND IF A BATTLE INCLUDES SOMEONE UNAVAILABLE..."
DMM
"...THE BRACELETS DELIVER AN ELECTRIC SHOCK SO POWERFUL THAT YOU MIGHT PASS OUT!"
DMM

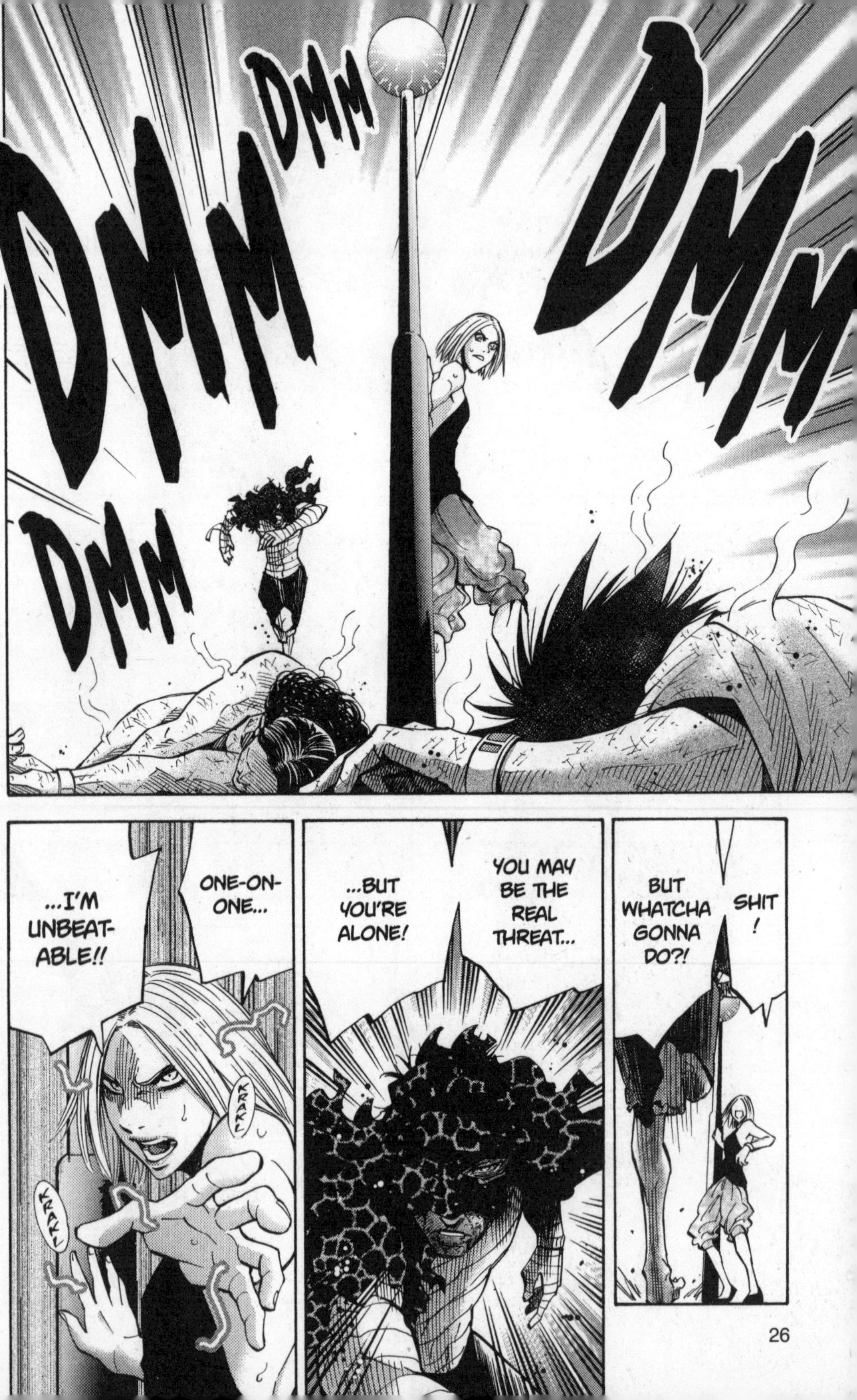
DMM
DMM
DMM
DMM
DMM
SHIT!
BUT WHATCHA GONNA DO?!
YOU MAY BE THE REAL THREAT...
...BUT YOU'RE ALONE!
ONE-ON-ONE...
...I'M UNBEATABLE!!
KRAKL
KRAKL

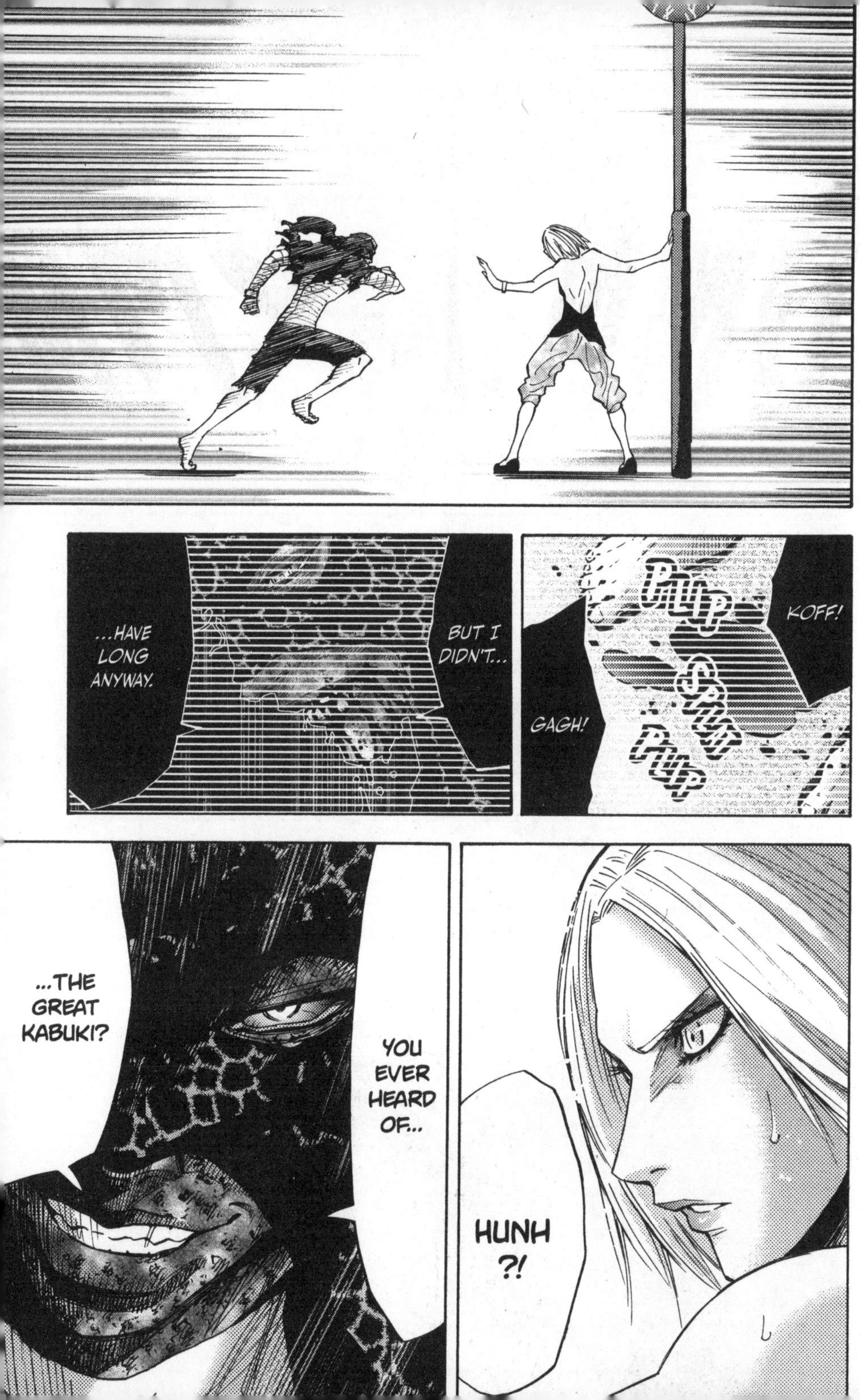
KOFF!
GAGH!
BUT I DIDN'T...
...HAVE LONG ANYWAY.
HUNH ?!
YOU EVER HEARD OF...
...THE GREAT KABUKI?

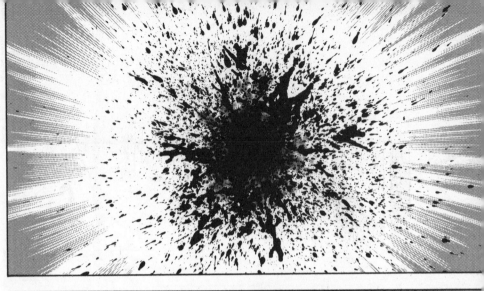

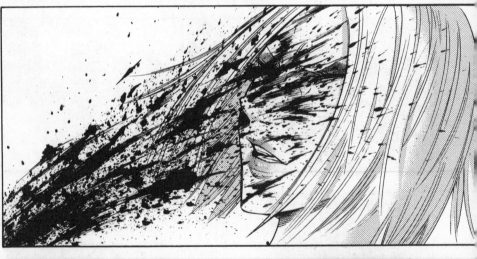

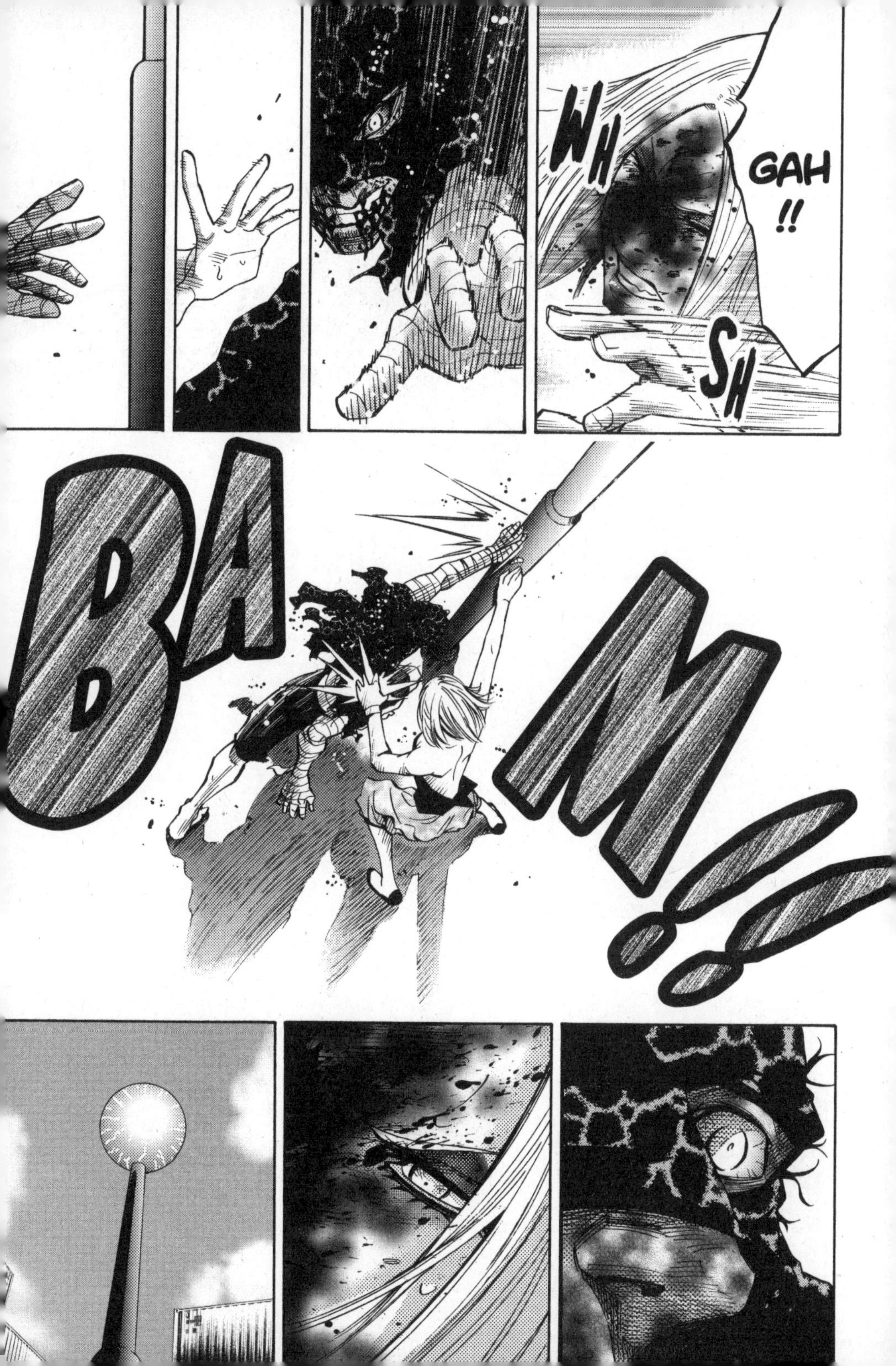
GAH !!
WHSH
BAM!!

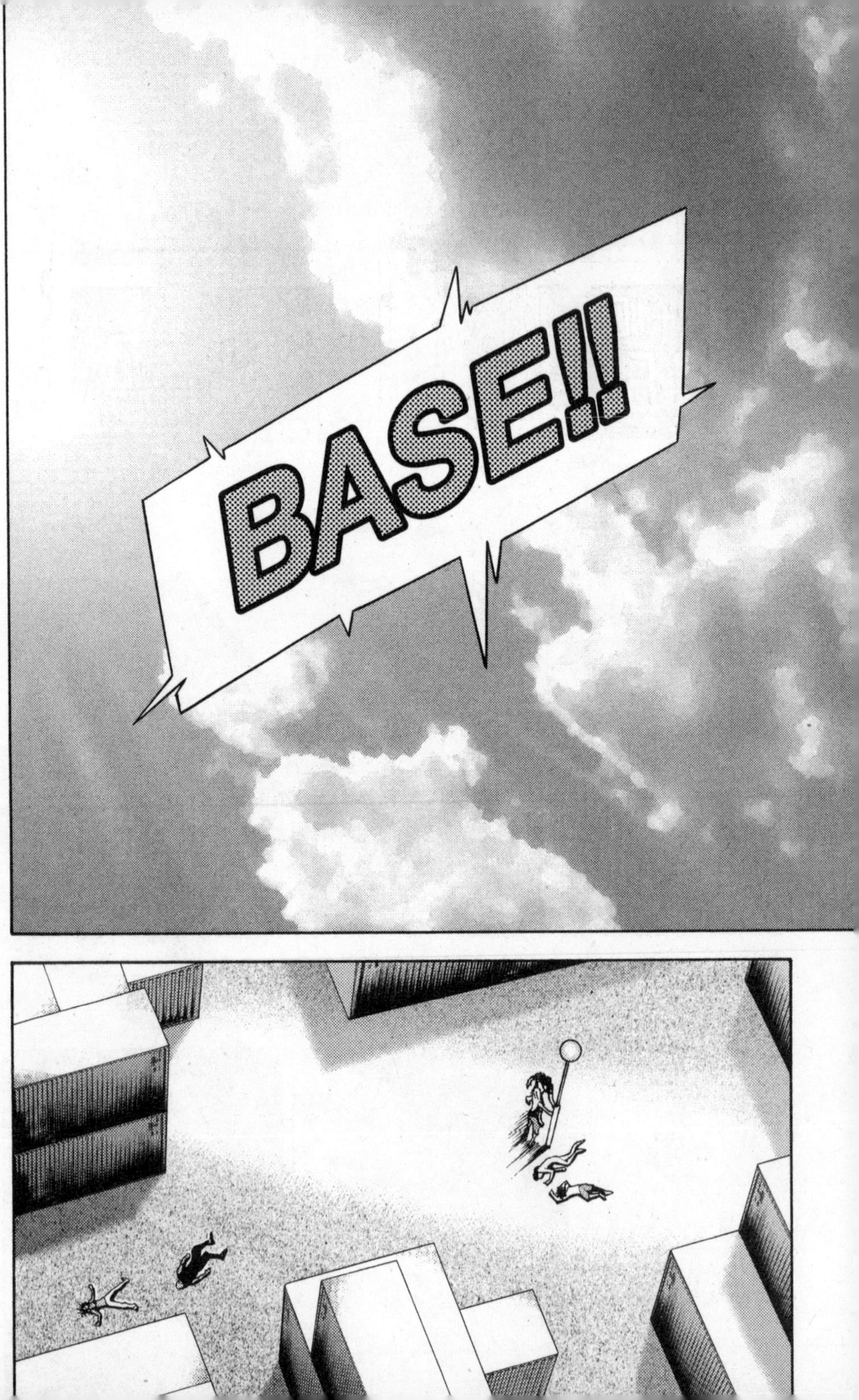
BASE!!

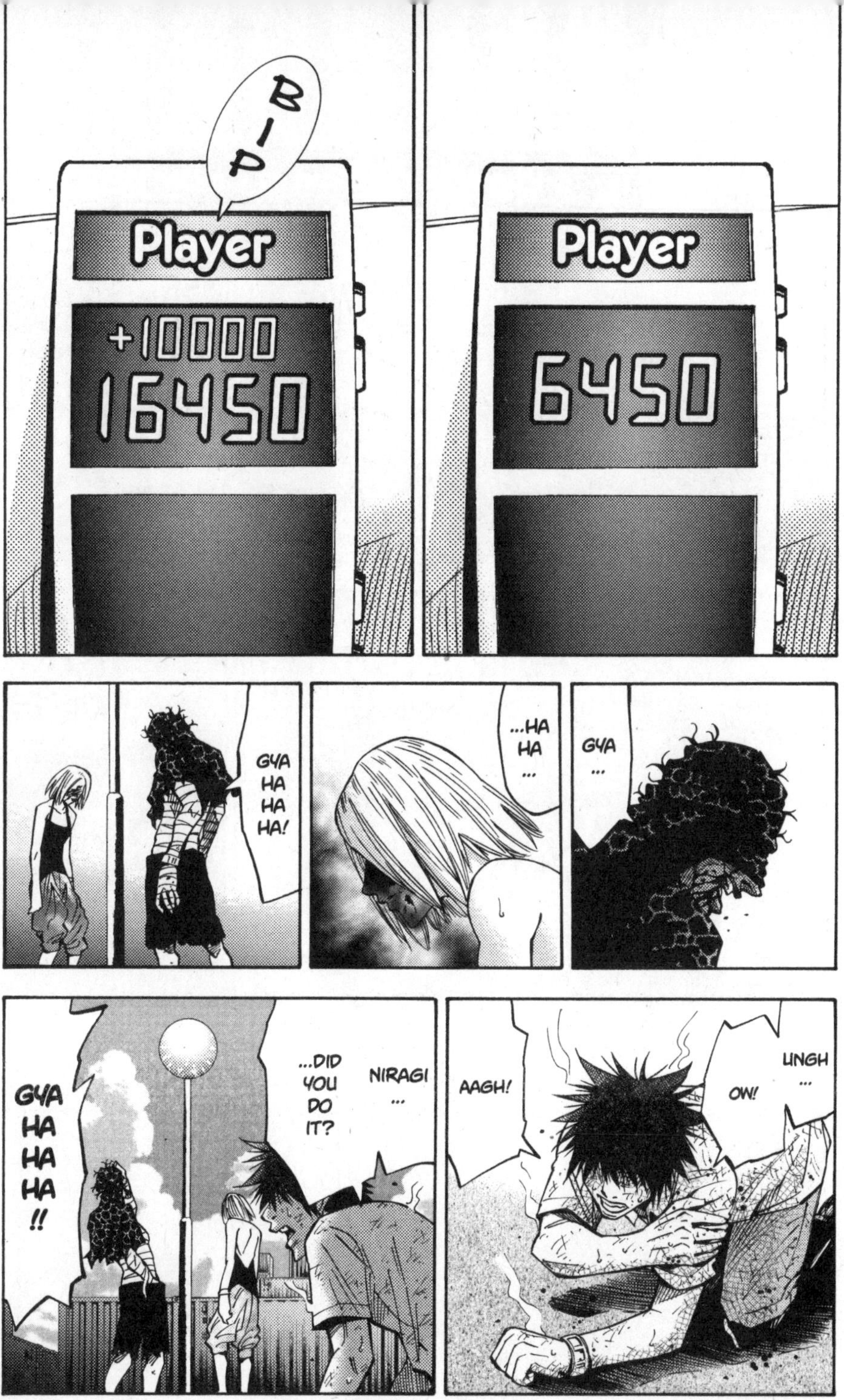
Player
6450
BIP
Player
+10000
16450
GYA ...
...HA HA ...
GYA HA HA HA!
UNGH ...
OW!
AAGH!
NIRAGI ...
...DID YOU DO IT?
GYA HA HA HA!!

...HAS GAINED POINTS.

BIP

Players	King of Clubs
+10000	
32500	35500

0:21:36

THE PLAYERS TEAM...

...TOUCH OUR BASE?

UTA, DID THEY...

HM?

THAT HURT!

OWWW!

WE GOT 10,000 POINTS.

WE...

...DID IT!

USAGI!

KUINA!

WE DID IT!

WE DID IT!

WE DID IT!

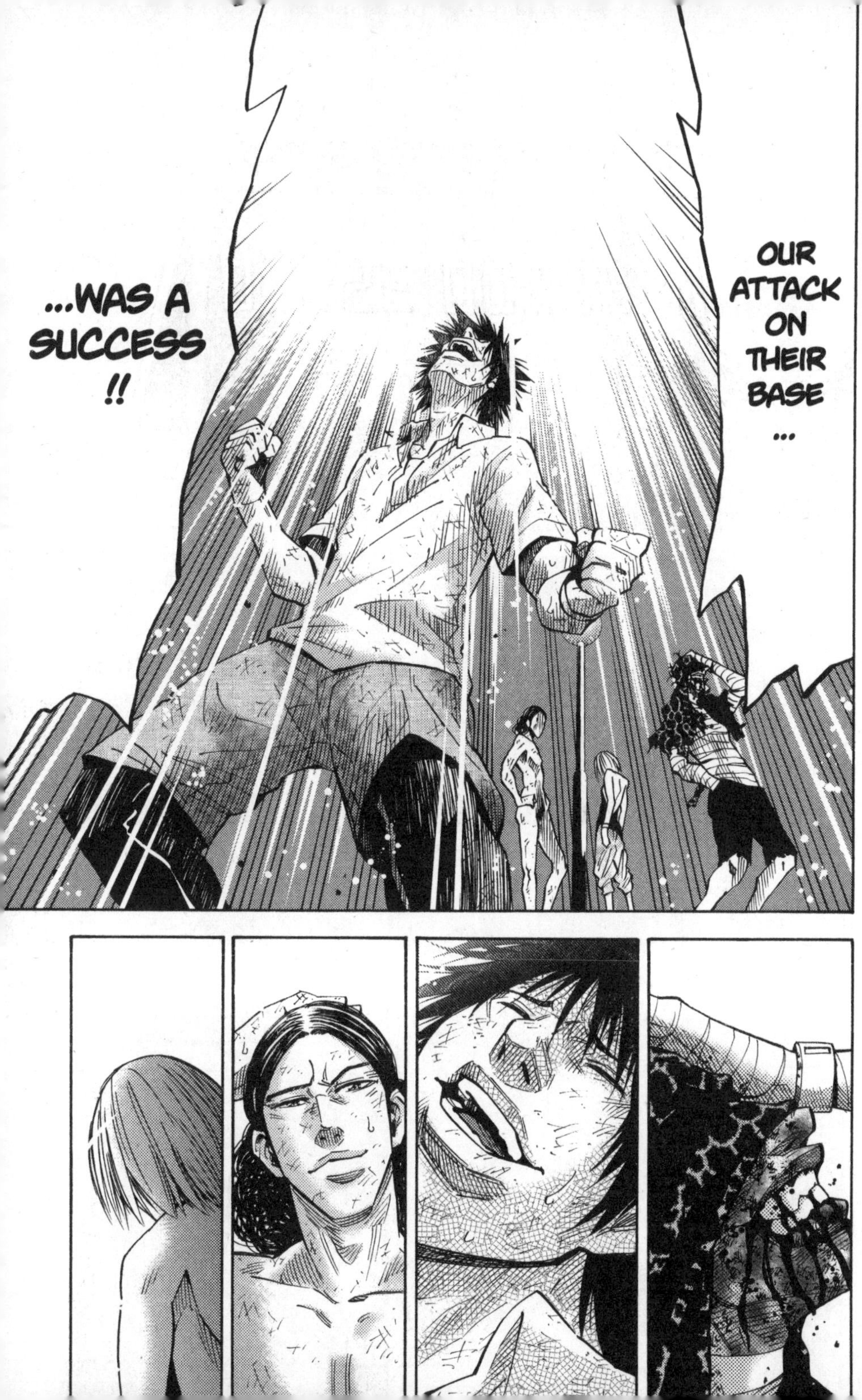
OUR ATTACK ON THEIR BASE...
...WAS A SUCCESS!!

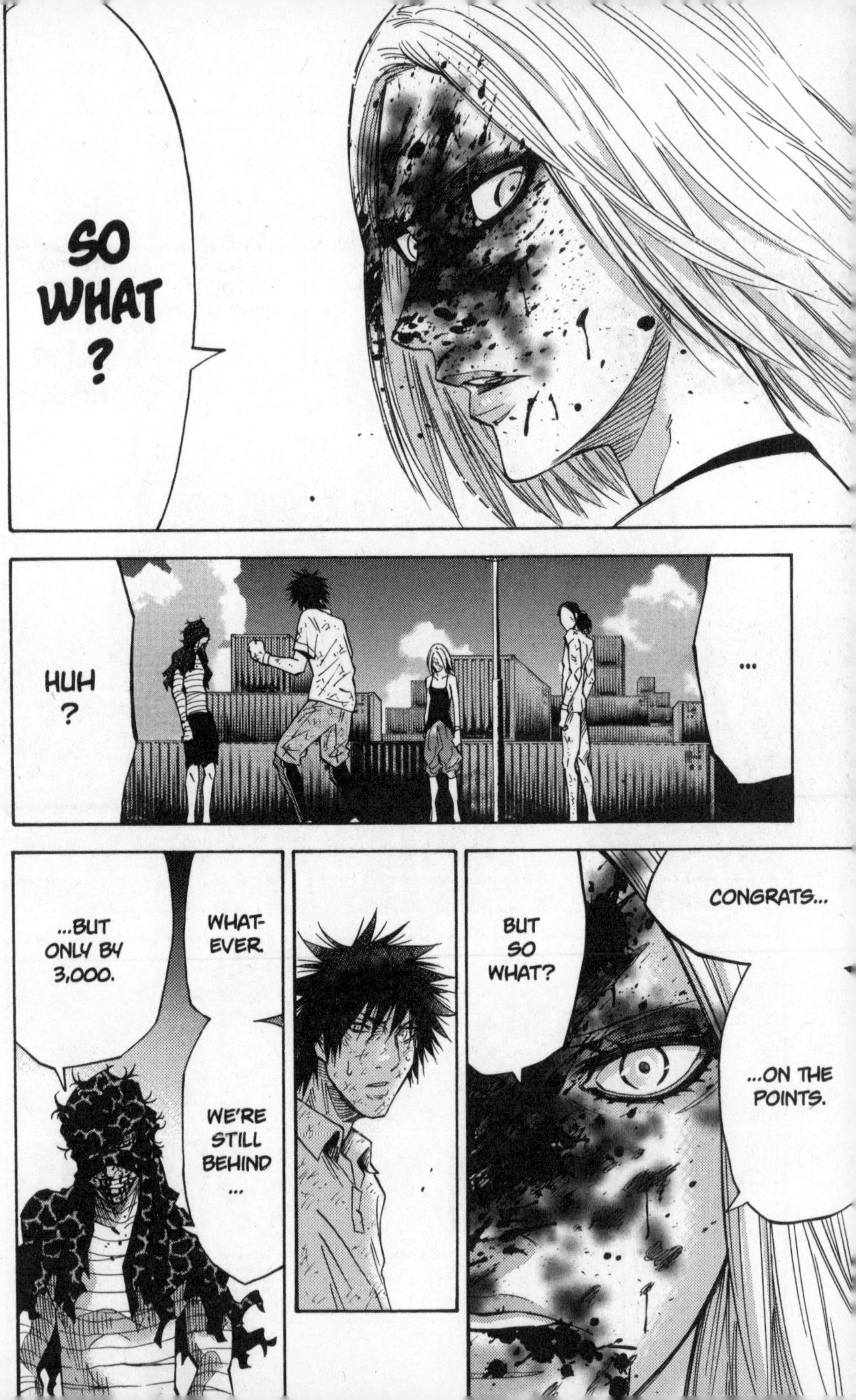
SO WHAT ?
...
HUH ?
CONGRATS...
...ON THE POINTS.
BUT SO WHAT?
WHAT-EVER.
WE'RE STILL BEHIND ...
...BUT ONLY BY 3,000.

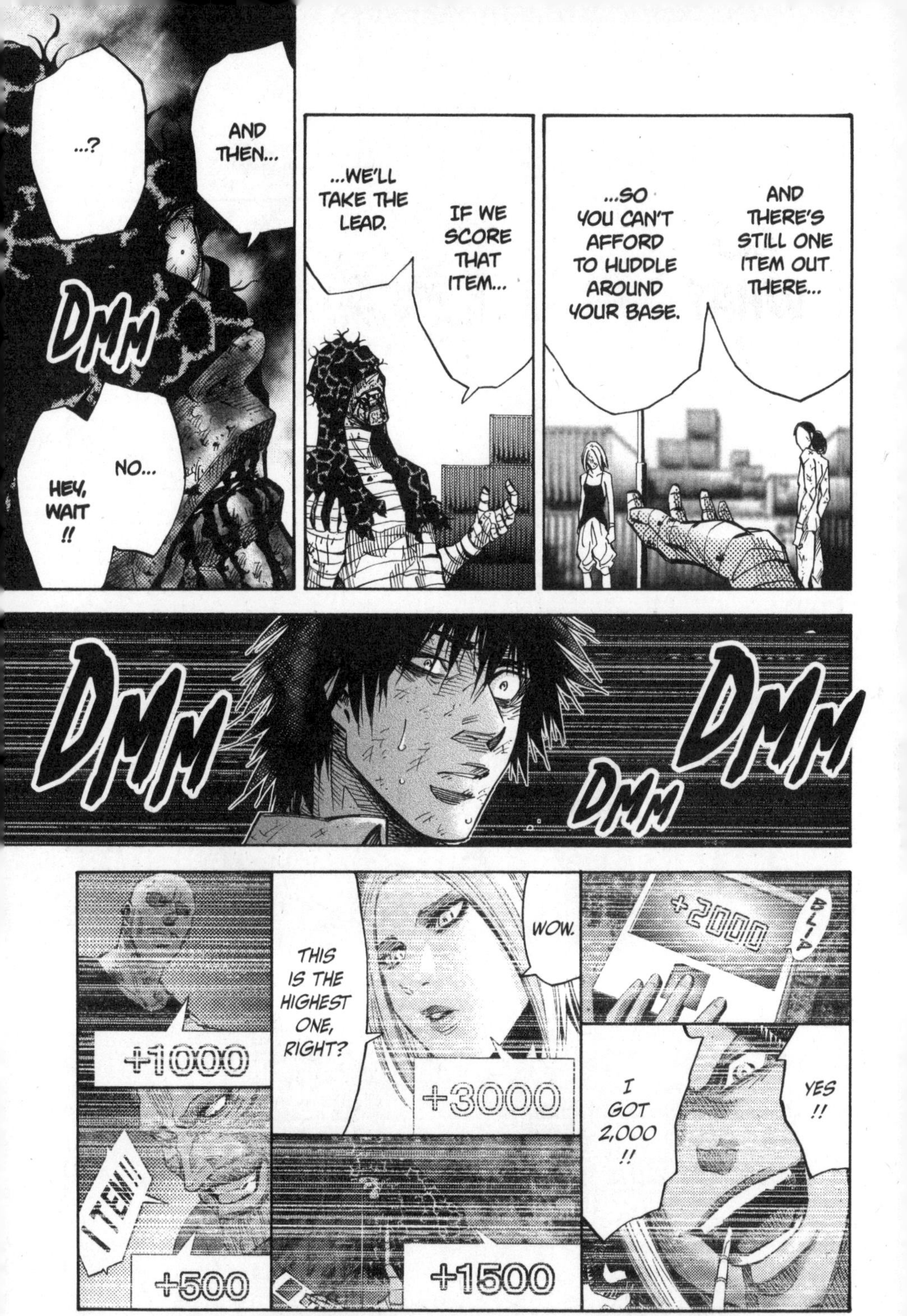
AND THERE'S STILL ONE ITEM OUT THERE...
...SO YOU CAN'T AFFORD TO HUDDLE AROUND YOUR BASE.
IF WE SCORE THAT ITEM...
...WE'LL TAKE THE LEAD.
AND THEN...
...?
DMM
NO...
HEY, WAIT!!
DMM
DMM
DMM
+2000
BLIP
YES!!
I GOT 2,000!!
WOW.
THIS IS THE HIGHEST ONE, RIGHT?
+3000
+1000
ITEM!!
+500
+1500

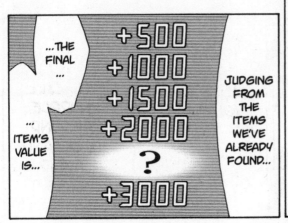

...THE FINAL...

...ITEM'S VALUE IS...

+500
+1000
+1500
+2000
?
+3000

JUDGING FROM THE ITEMS WE'VE ALREADY FOUND...

OH... I GET IT.

YEP.

...2,500.

SLMP...

...YOU'RE STILL BEHIND.

Players	King of Clubs
+2500	
35000	35500

SO EVEN IF YOU GET THE FINAL ITEM...

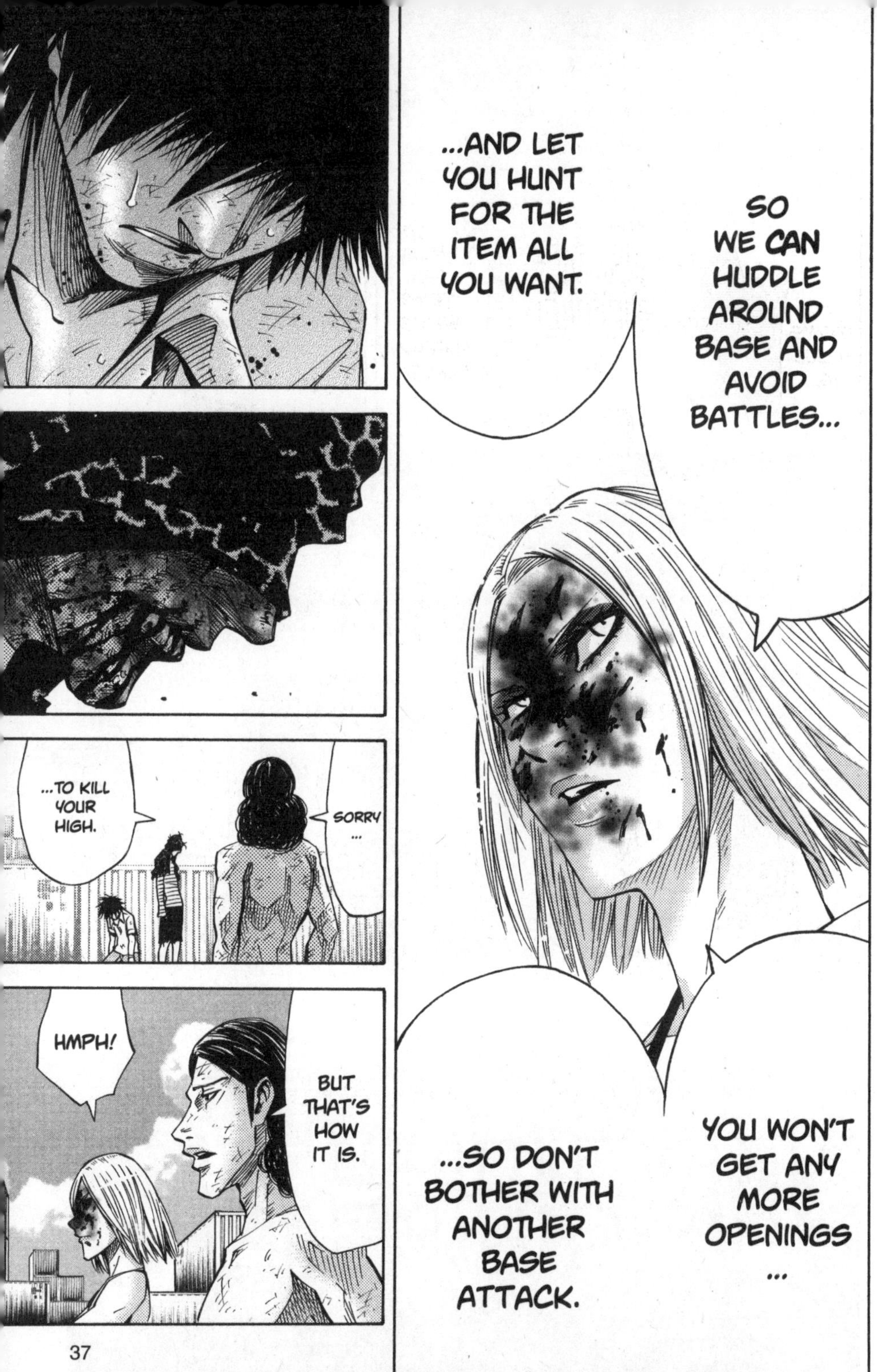
SO WE CAN HUDDLE AROUND BASE AND AVOID BATTLES...
...AND LET YOU HUNT FOR THE ITEM ALL YOU WANT.
YOU WON'T GET ANY MORE OPENINGS ...
...SO DON'T BOTHER WITH ANOTHER BASE ATTACK.
SORRY ...
...TO KILL YOUR HIGH.
BUT THAT'S HOW IT IS.
HMPH!

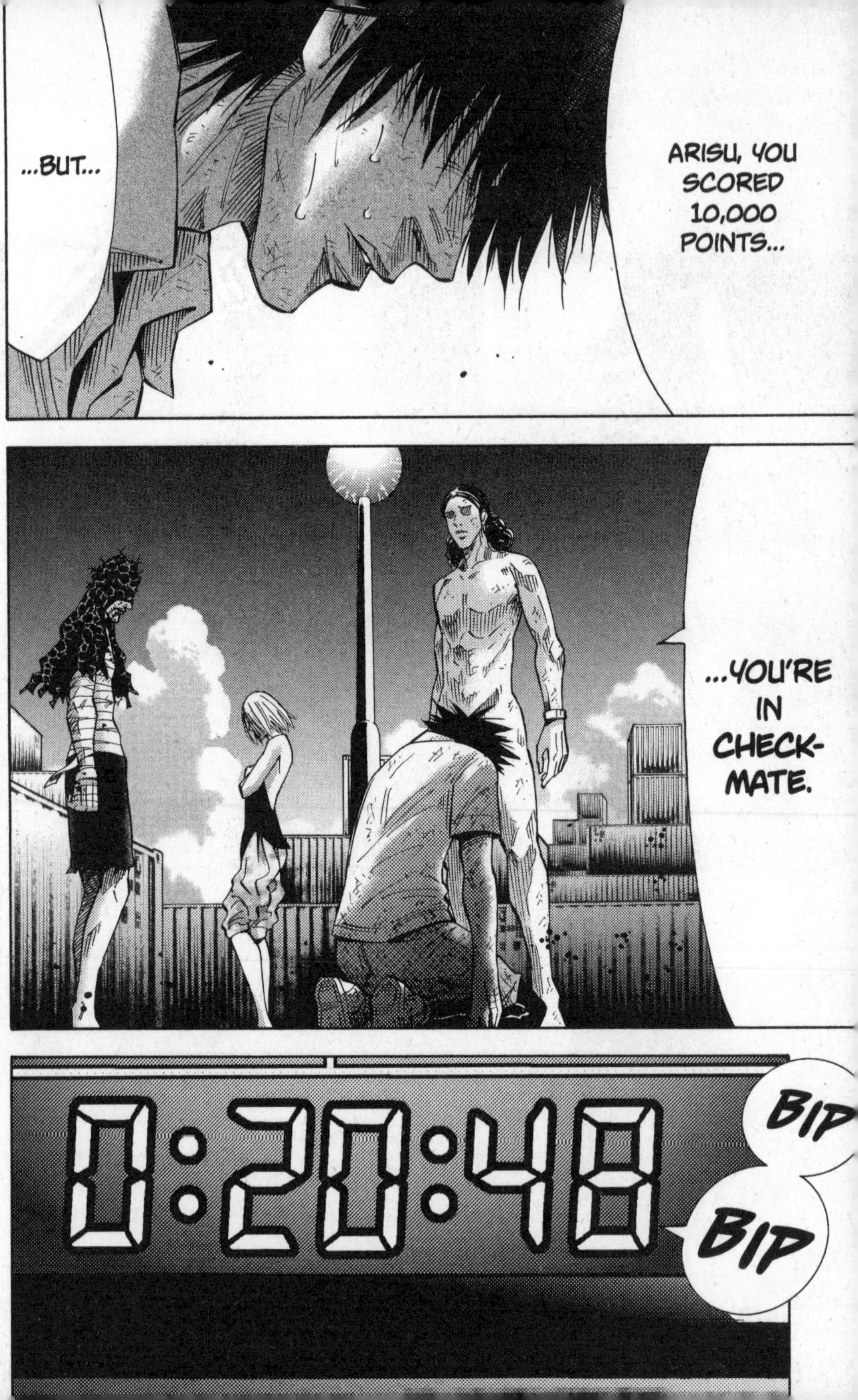
ARISU, YOU SCORED 10,000 POINTS...
...BUT...
...YOU'RE IN CHECKMATE.
BIP
BIP
0:20:48

CHAPTER 39: King of Clubs, Part 7

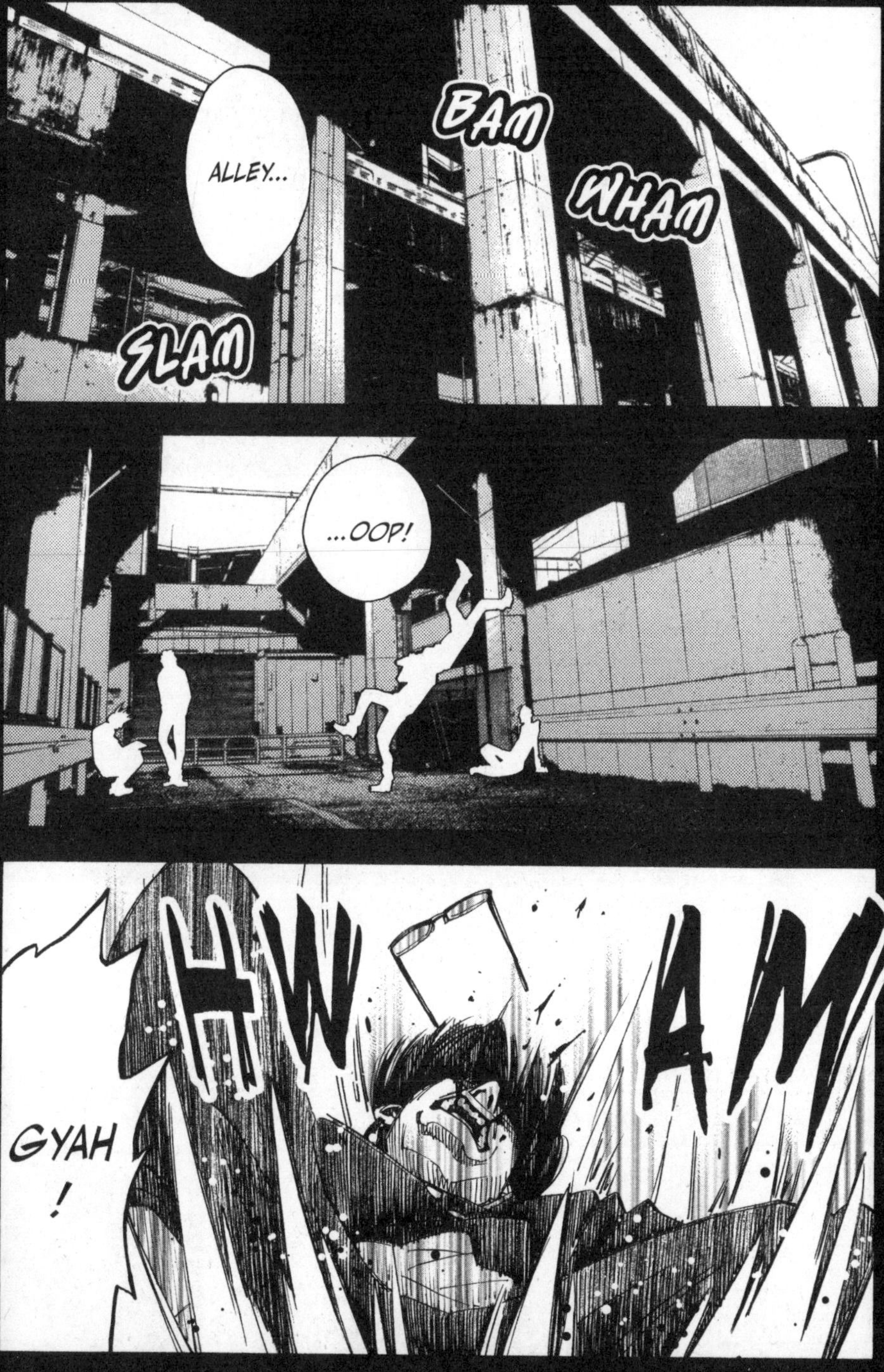
BAM
WHAM
ALLEY...
SLAM
...OOP!
HWAM
GYAH!

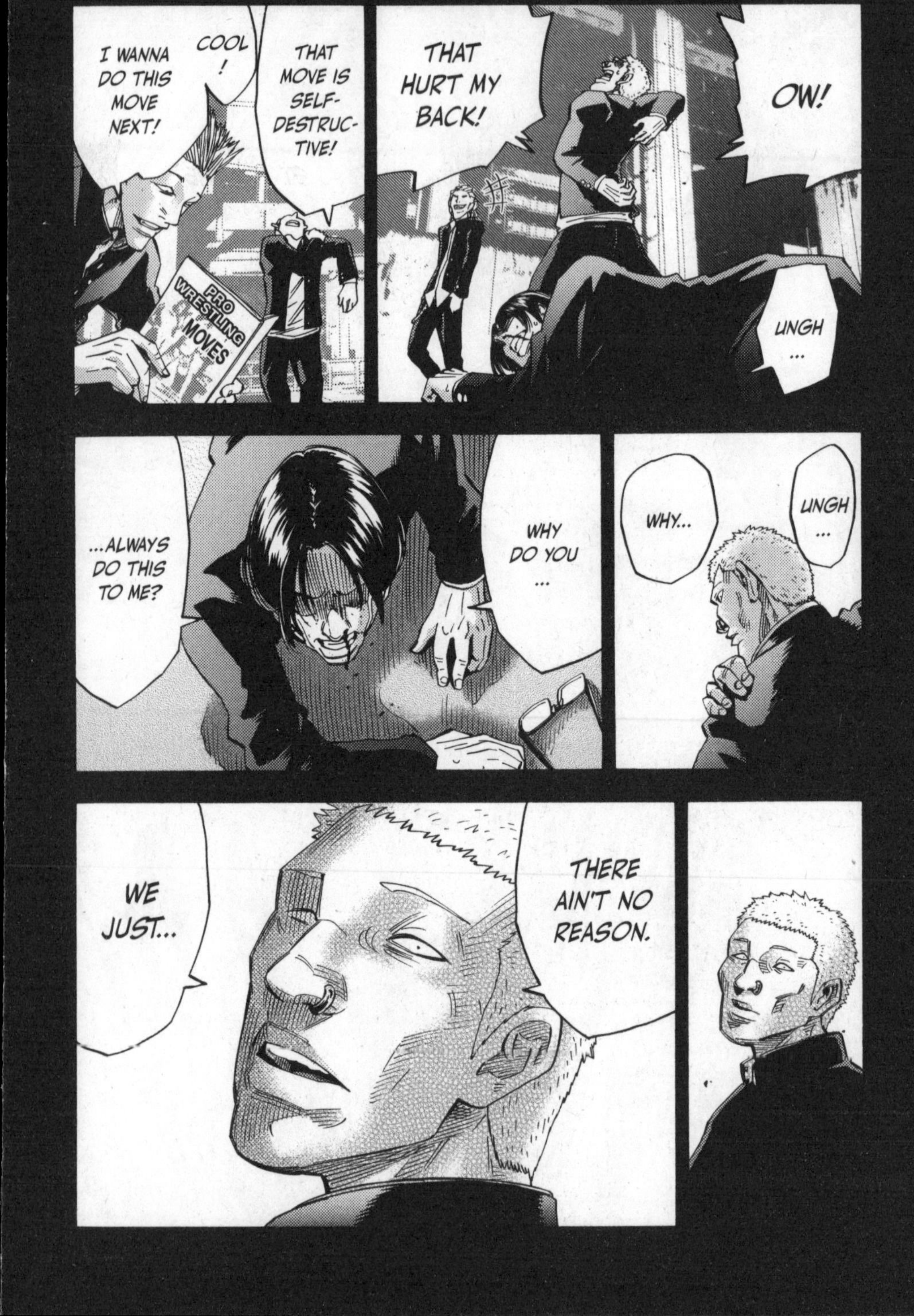
OW!
THAT HURT MY BACK!
UNGH ...
THAT MOVE IS SELF-DESTRUCTIVE!
COOL!
I WANNA DO THIS MOVE NEXT!
PRO WRESTLING MOVES
UNGH ...
WHY...
WHY DO YOU ...
...ALWAYS DO THIS TO ME?
THERE AIN'T NO REASON.
WE JUST...

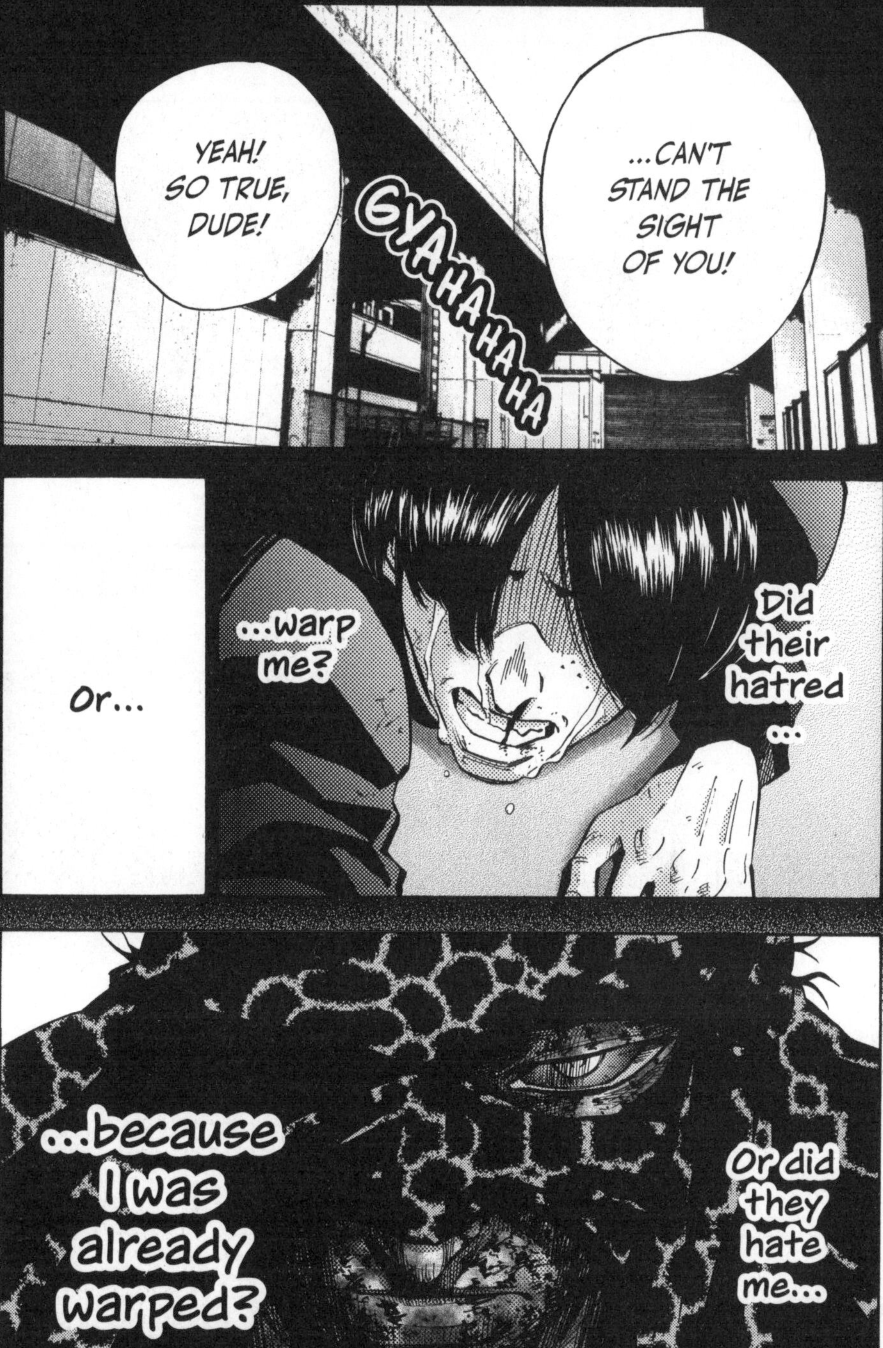
...CAN'T STAND THE SIGHT OF YOU!
GYAHAHAHAHA
YEAH! SO TRUE, DUDE!
Did their hatred...
...warp me?
Or...
Or did they hate me...
...because I was already warped?

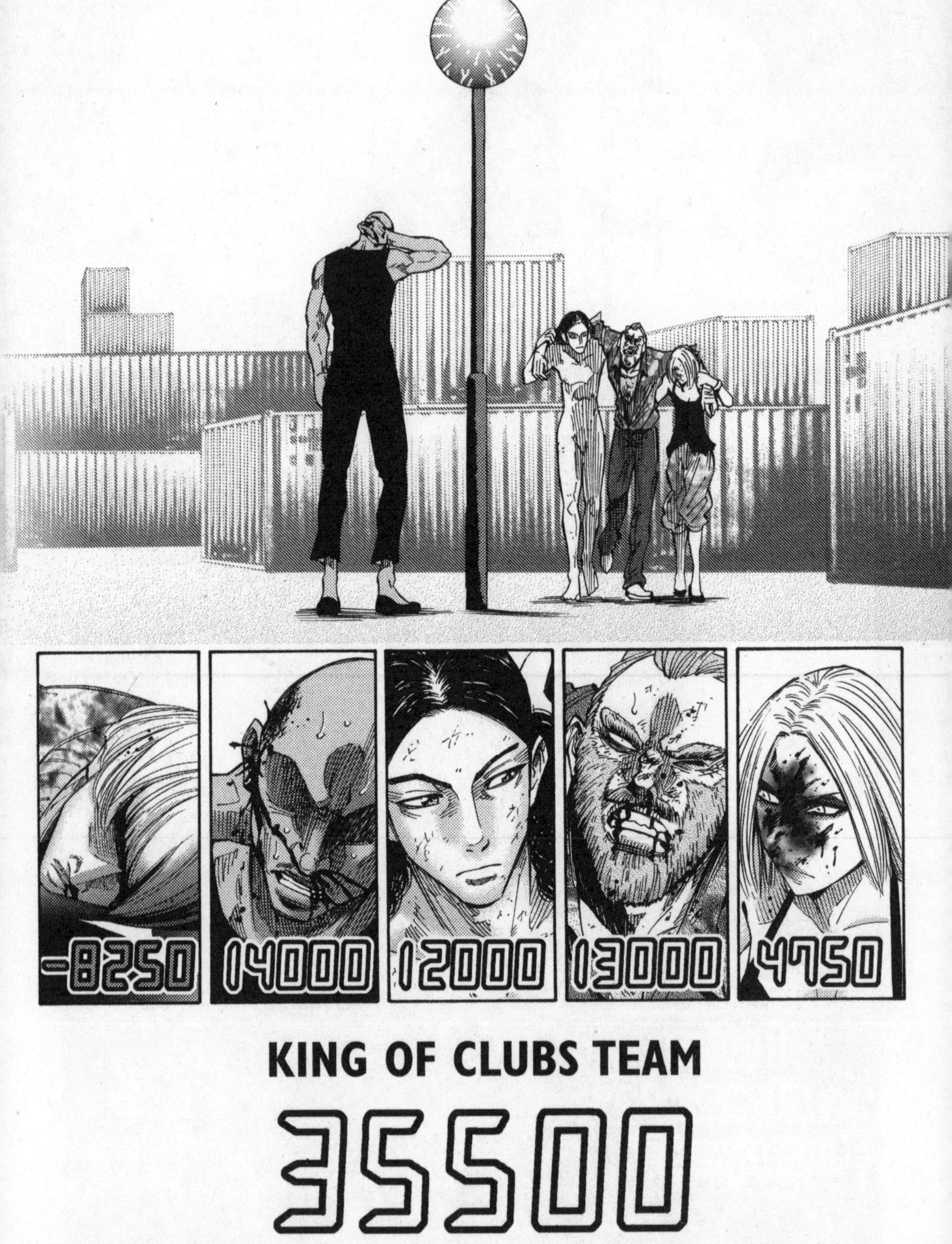
4750
13000
12000
14000
-8250
KING OF CLUBS TEAM
35500

CHAPTER 39: King of Clubs, Part 7

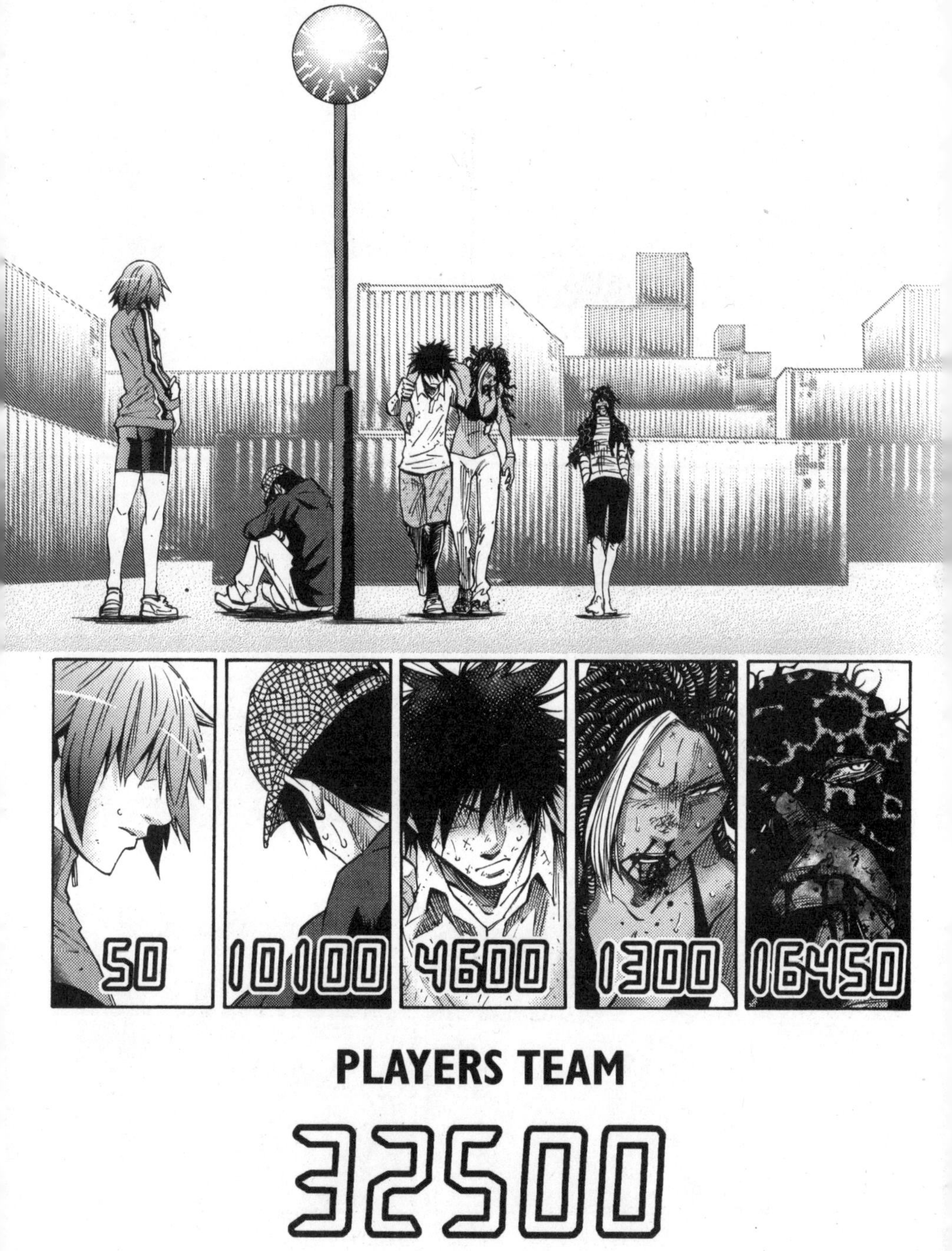
16450
1300
4600
10100
50

PLAYERS TEAM

32500

Players	King of Clubs
32500	35500

0:15:57

BIP
BIP
BIP

...15 MINUTES.

WE'VE ONLY GOT...

0:15:43

...RUN OUT OF IDEAS?

...REALLY...

HAVE WE...

IF ALL FOUR OF THEM ARE GUARDING THEIR BASE...

MIRACLES DON'T HAPPEN TWICE.

...THEN ANOTHER ATTACK IS GUARANTEED TO FAIL.

...TO SIT HERE AND WAIT FOR DEATH?

IS OUR ONLY OPTION...

ONCE A TEAM GETS EVEN THE SLIGHTEST LEAD...

BATTLE

LOSE   WIN
-500   +500

TEAM SCORES

| 9500 | 10500 |

CERTAIN VICTORY

...THEY COULD THEN AVOID ANY FURTHER POINT TRANSFERS.

WITHOUT THEM...

...THE FIRST BATTLE COULD DECIDE EVERYTHING.

...WHY THIS GAME HAS ITEMS.

NOW I REALIZE...

...THE KING OF CLUBS WILL KEEP THE LEAD.

EVEN IF WE GET THE LAST ITEM WORTH 2,500 POINTS...

Players	King of Clubs
+2500	
35000	35500

...AND THAT MEANS PARTICIPANTS HAVE TO MOVE AROUND AND BATTLE.

BUT THE ITEMS ADD AN UNPREDICTABLE ELEMENT...

ITEM!

BATTLE!

ITEM!

...ALREADY LOST THIS GAME.

WE'VE...

IT DOESN'T MATTER HOW MUCH TIME WE HAVE LEFT.

...AND WAIT FOR TIME TO RUN OUT.

...PROTECT THEIR BASE...

...AVOID BATTLES...

THEY'LL JUST...

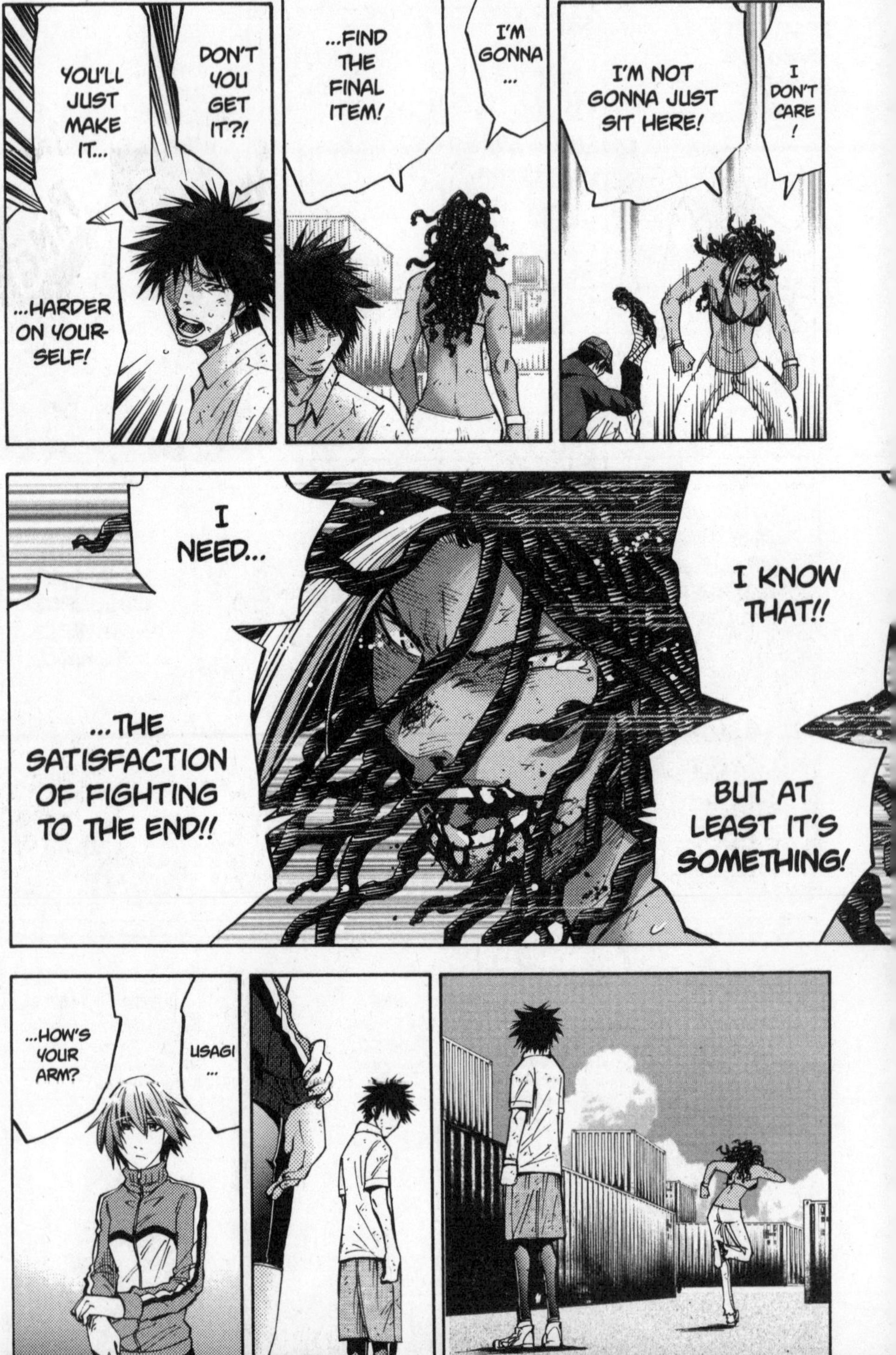
I DON'T CARE!
I'M NOT GONNA JUST SIT HERE!
I'M GONNA...
...FIND THE FINAL ITEM!
DON'T YOU GET IT?!
YOU'LL JUST MAKE IT...
...HARDER ON YOURSELF!
I KNOW THAT!!
BUT AT LEAST IT'S SOMETHING!
I NEED...
...THE SATISFACTION OF FIGHTING TO THE END!!
USAGI...
...HOW'S YOUR ARM?

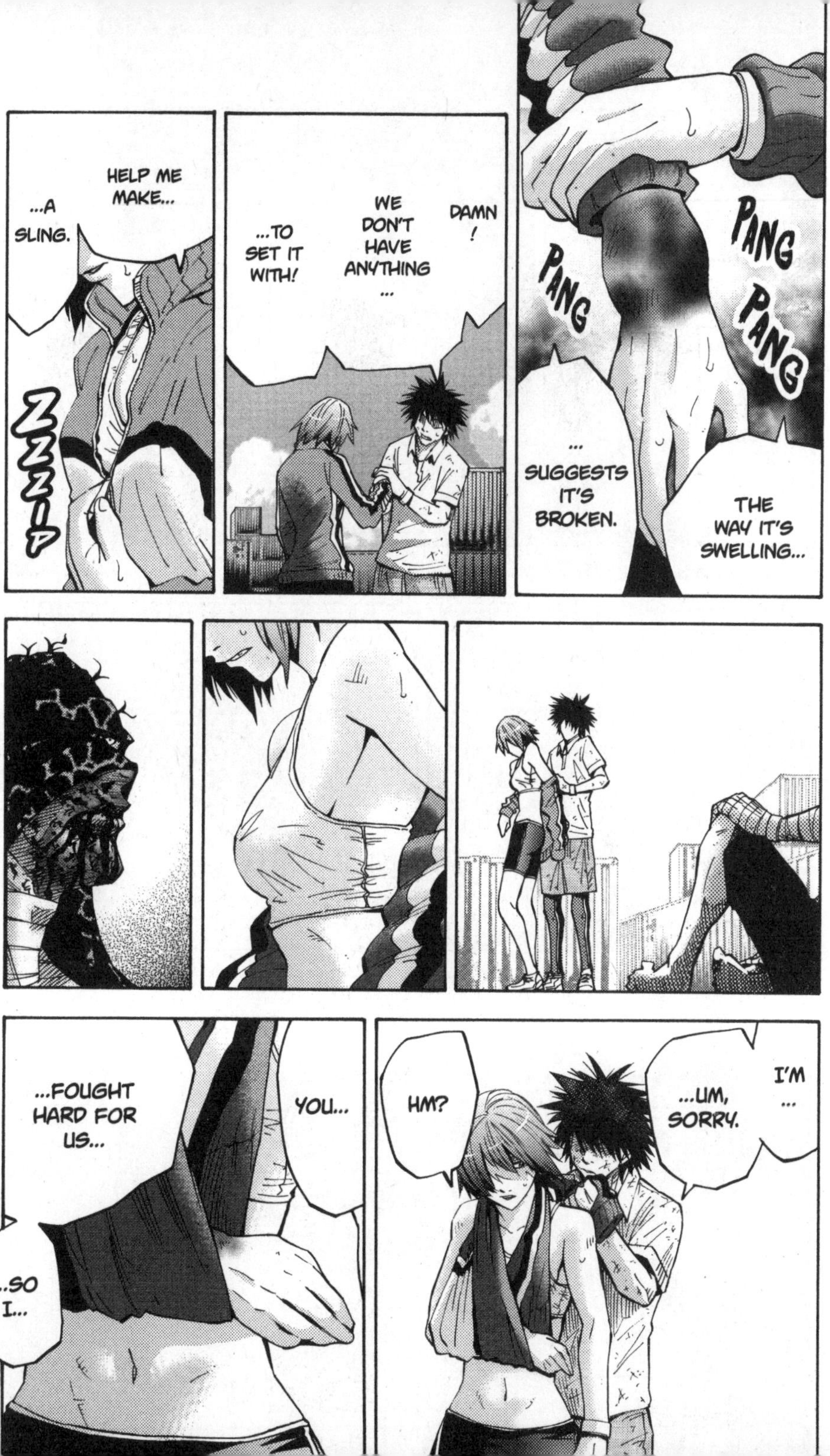
PANG
PANG
PANG
THE WAY IT'S SWELLING...
...SUGGESTS IT'S BROKEN.
DAMN!
WE DON'T HAVE ANYTHING...
...TO SET IT WITH!
HELP ME MAKE...
...A SLING.
ZZZIP
I'M ...
...UM, SORRY.
HM?
YOU...
...FOUGHT HARD FOR US...
...SO I...

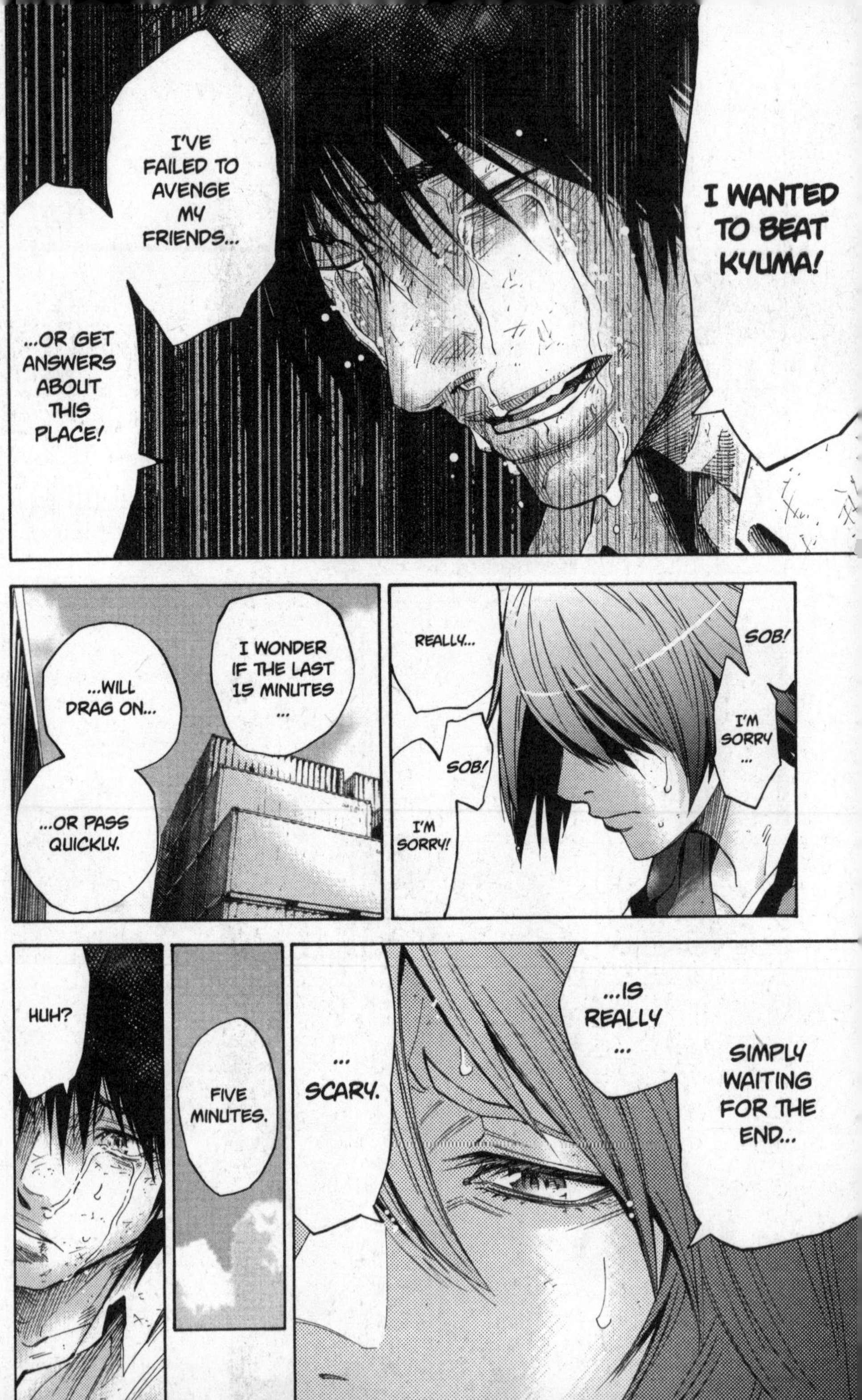
I WANTED TO BEAT KYUMA!
I'VE FAILED TO AVENGE MY FRIENDS...
...OR GET ANSWERS ABOUT THIS PLACE!
SOB!
REALLY...
I'M SORRY ...
SOB!
I'M SORRY!
I WONDER IF THE LAST 15 MINUTES ...
...WILL DRAG ON...
...OR PASS QUICKLY.
SIMPLY WAITING FOR THE END...
...IS REALLY ...
... SCARY.
FIVE MINUTES.
HUH?

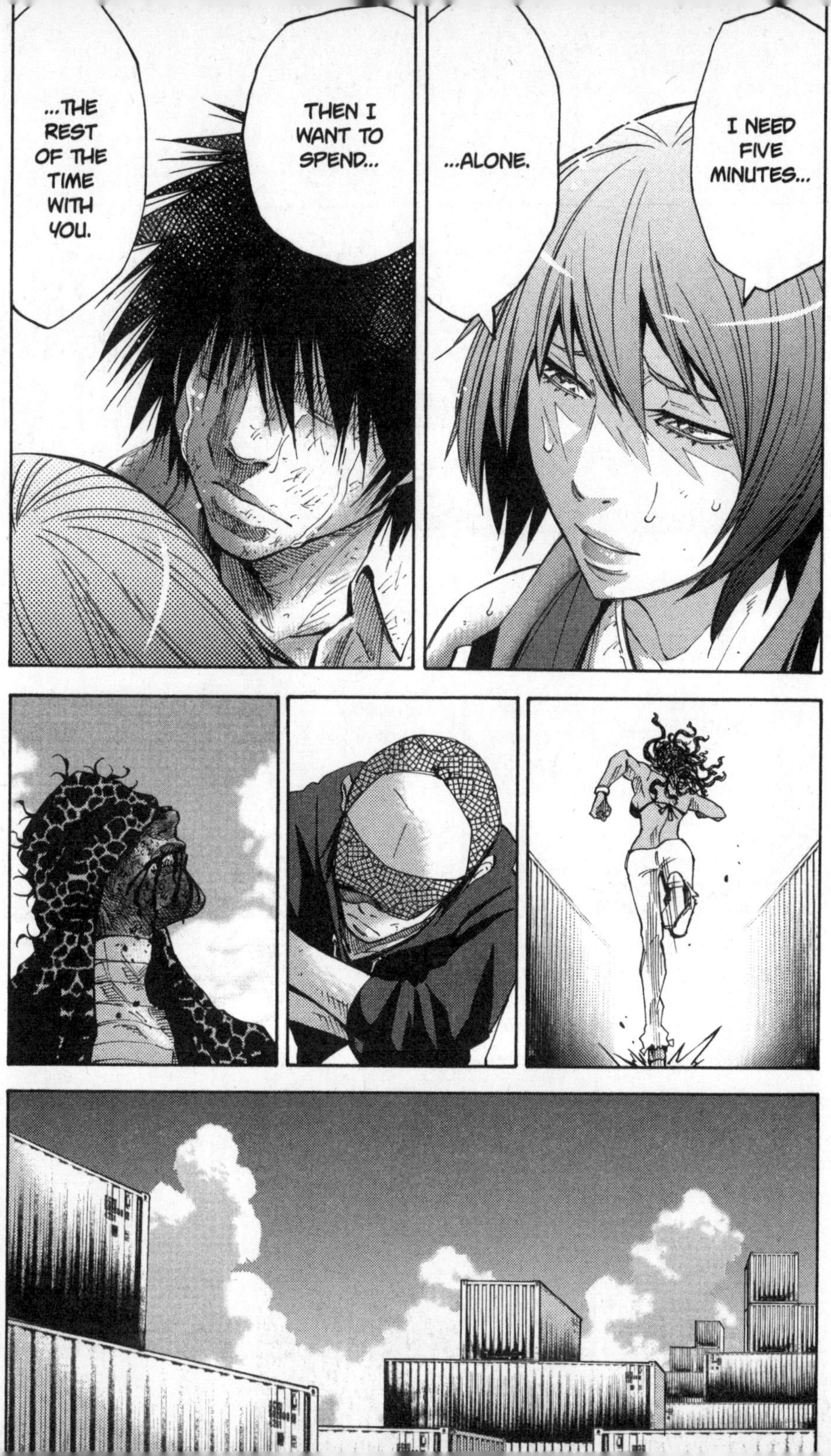
I NEED FIVE MINUTES...
...ALONE.
THEN I WANT TO SPEND...
...THE REST OF THE TIME WITH YOU.

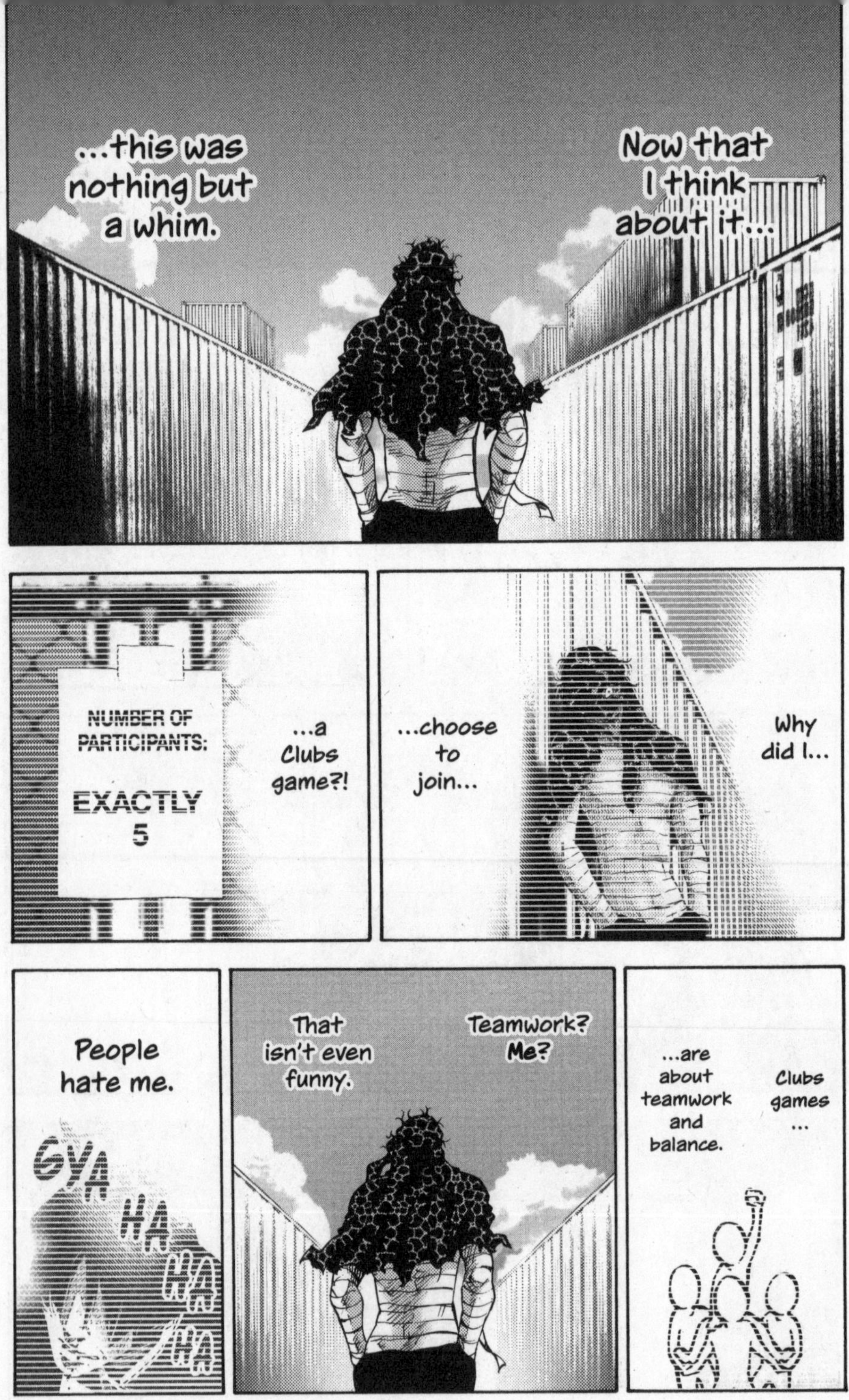
Now that I think about it...
...this was nothing but a whim.
Why did I...
...choose to join...
...a Clubs game?!
NUMBER OF PARTICIPANTS:
EXACTLY 5
Clubs games...
...are about teamwork and balance.
Teamwork? Me?
That isn't even funny.
People hate me.
GYA HA HA HA HA

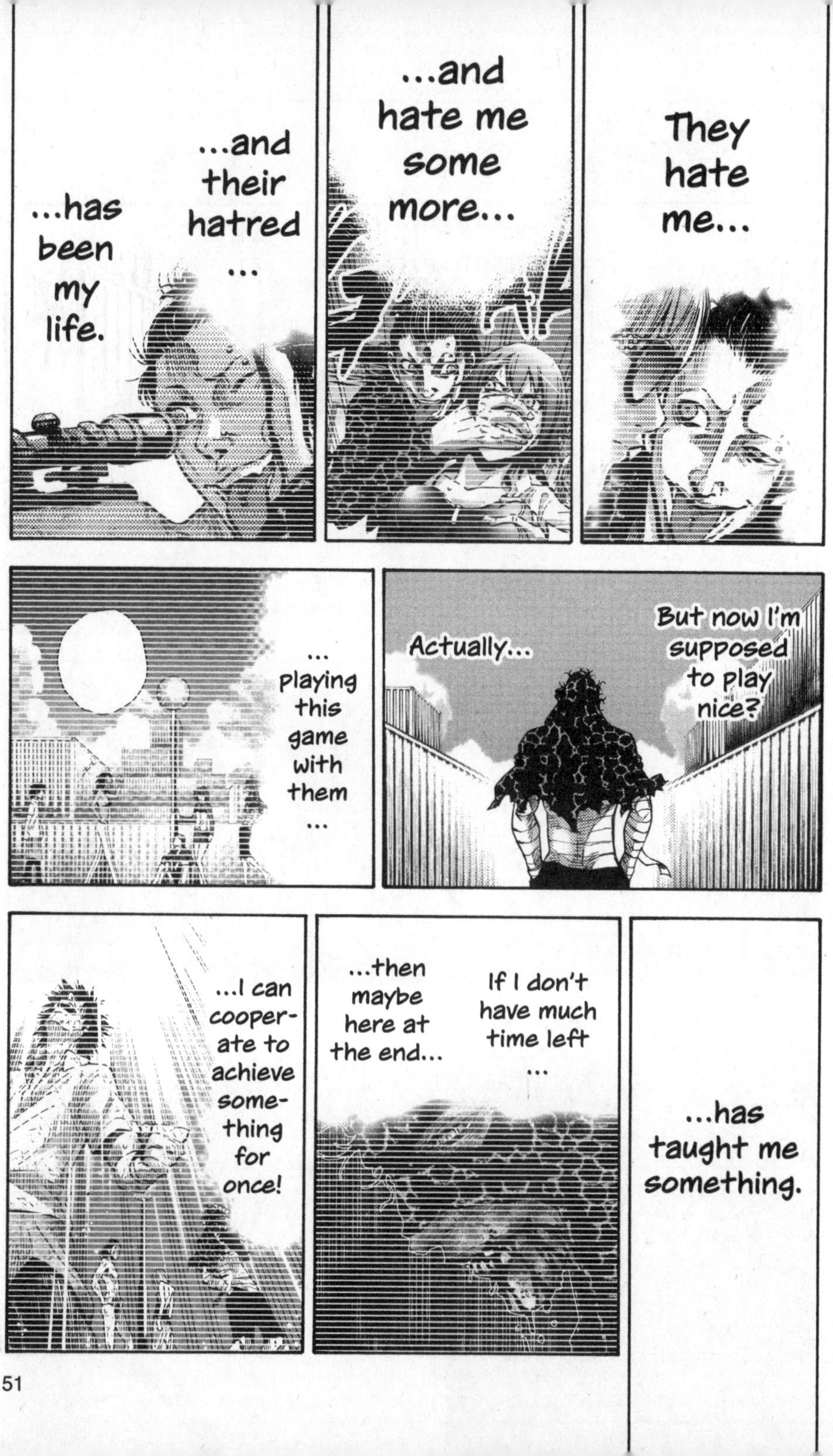
They hate me...
...and hate me some more...
...and their hatred ...
...has been my life.
But now I'm supposed to play nice?
Actually...
... playing this game with them ...
...has taught me something.
If I don't have much time left ...
...then maybe here at the end...
...I can cooperate to achieve something for once!

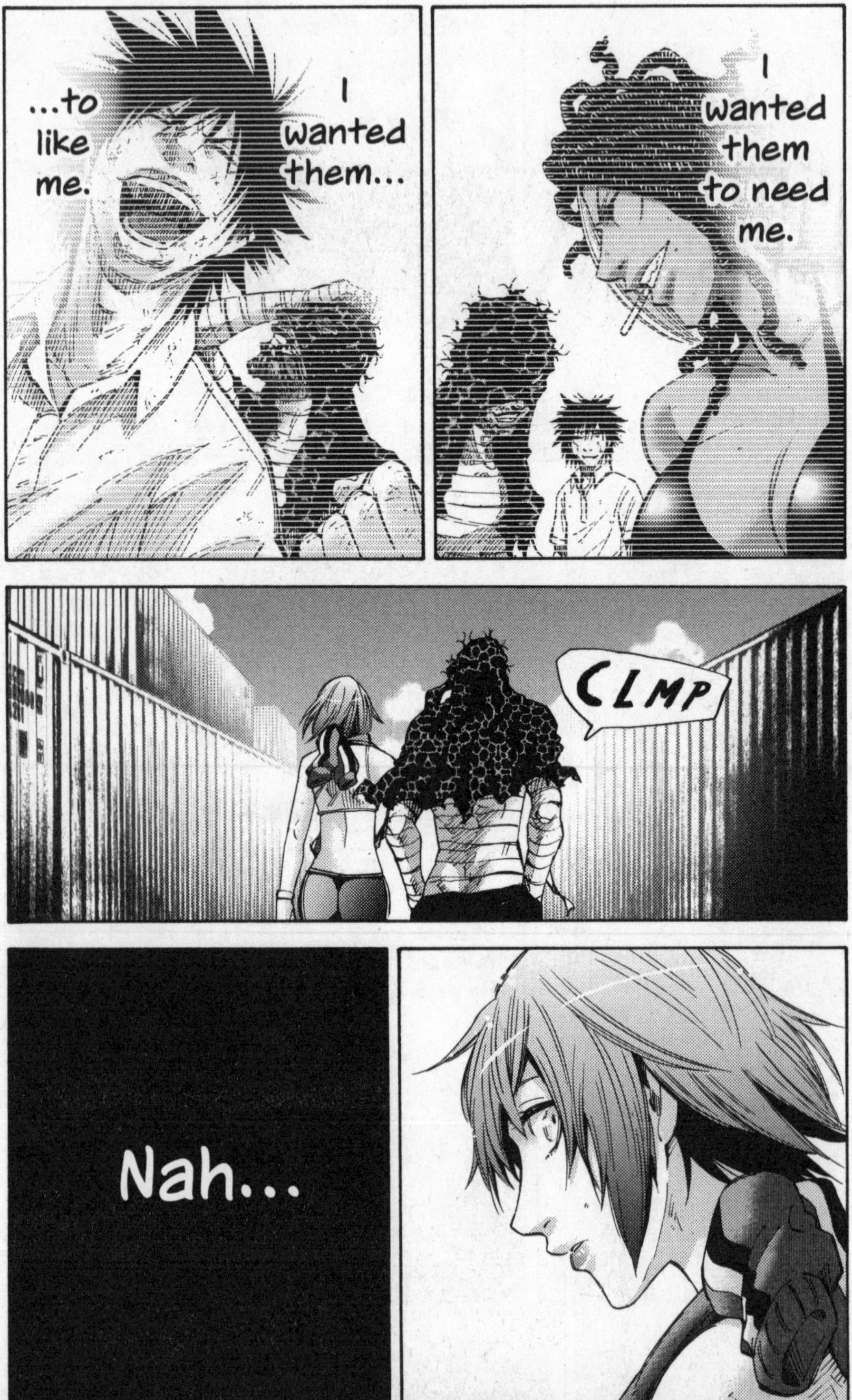
I wanted them to need me.
I wanted them...
...to like me.
CLMP
Nah...

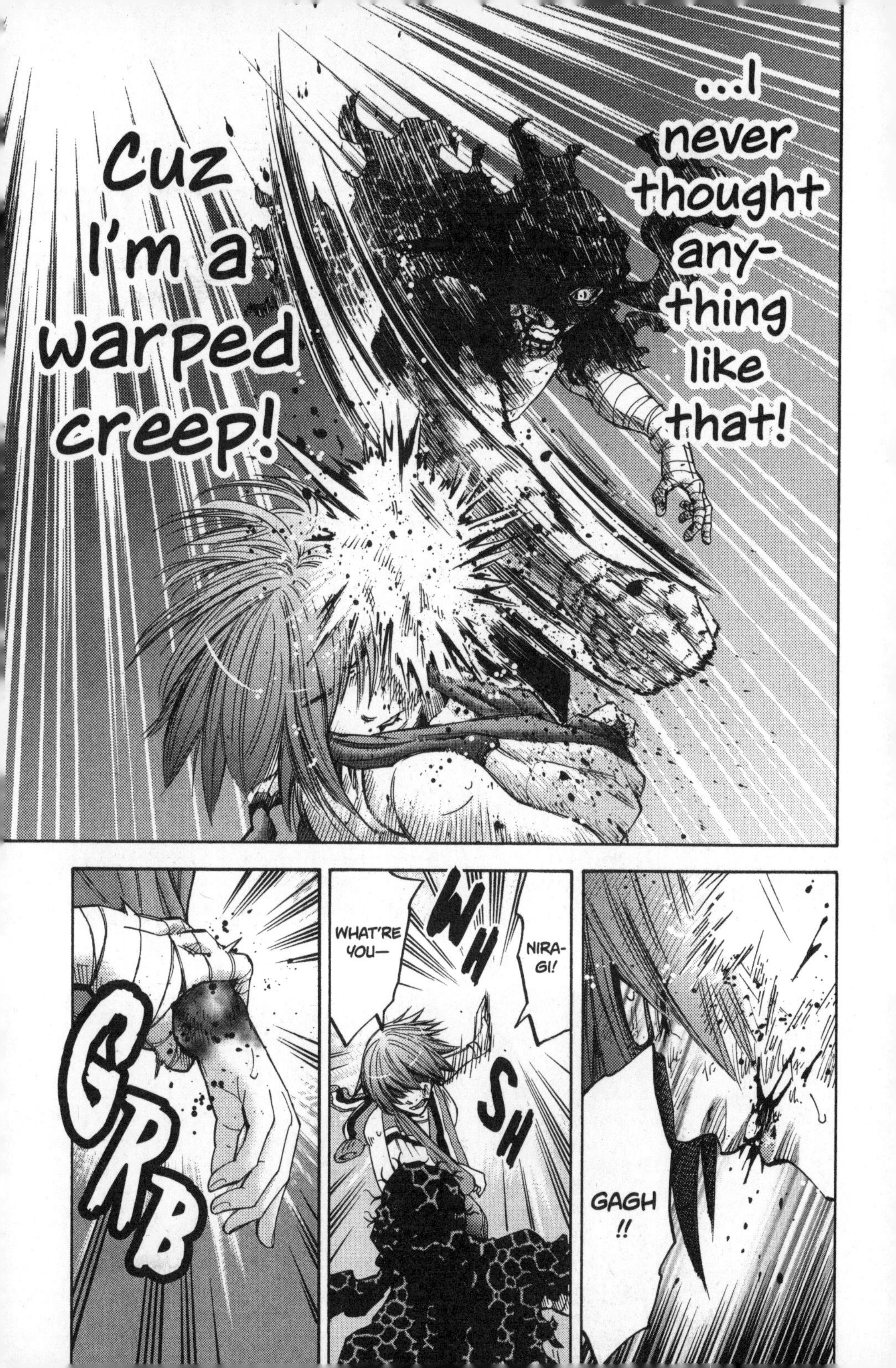
...I never thought any-thing like that!
Cuz I'm a warped creep!
GAGH !!
NIRA-GI!
WHAT'RE YOU—
WHSH
GRB

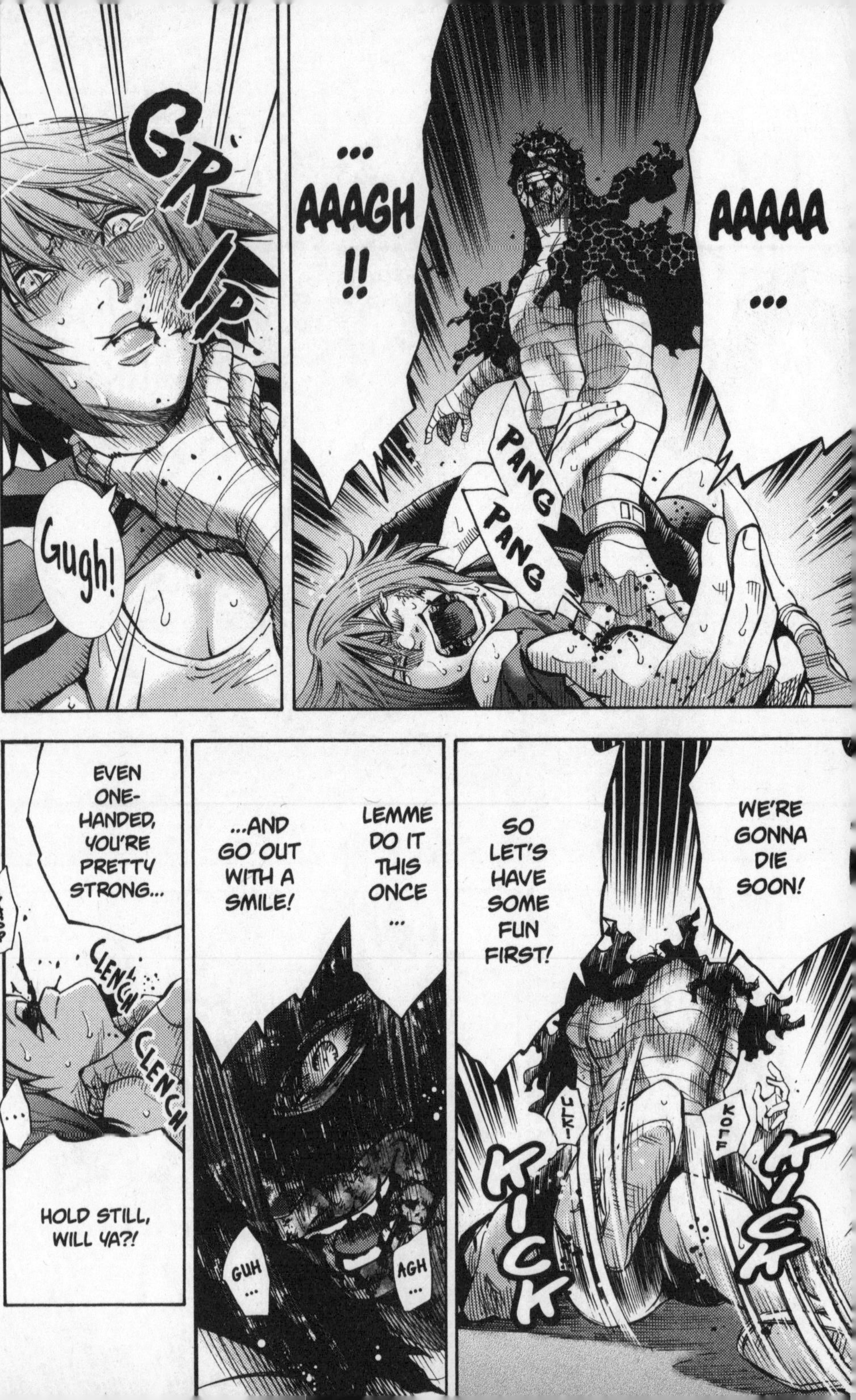
AAAAA...
...AAAGH!!
PANG PANG
GRIP
Gugh!
WE'RE GONNA DIE SOON!
SO LET'S HAVE SOME FUN FIRST!
KICK
KOFF
ULK!
KICK
LEMME DO IT THIS ONCE...
...AND GO OUT WITH A SMILE!
AGH...
GUH...
EVEN ONE-HANDED, YOU'RE PRETTY STRONG...
GASP
CLENCH
CLENCH
...
HOLD STILL, WILL YA?!

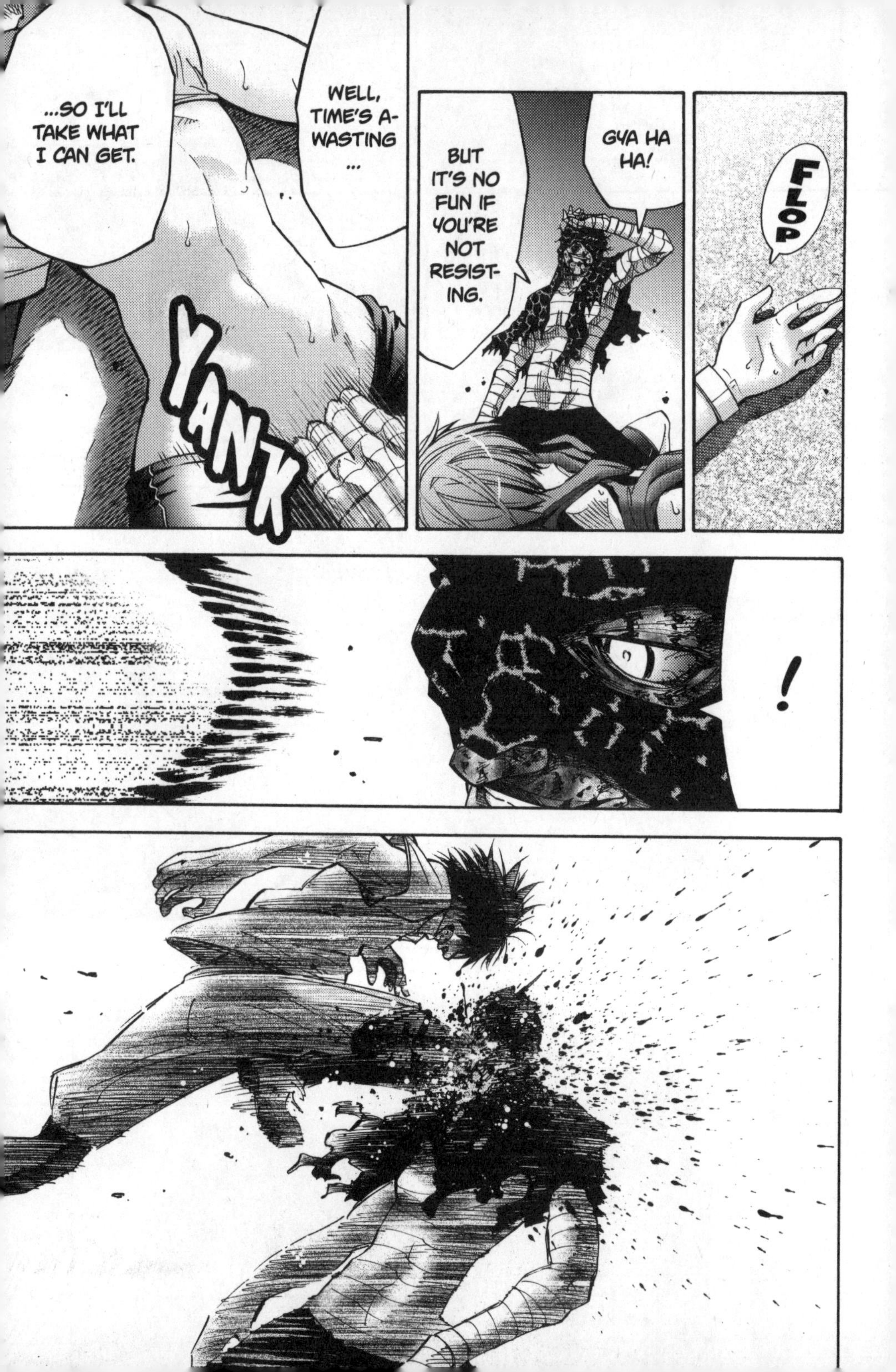
FLOP
GYA HA HA!
BUT IT'S NO FUN IF YOU'RE NOT RESISTING.
WELL, TIME'S A-WASTING ...
...SO I'LL TAKE WHAT I CAN GET.
YANK
!

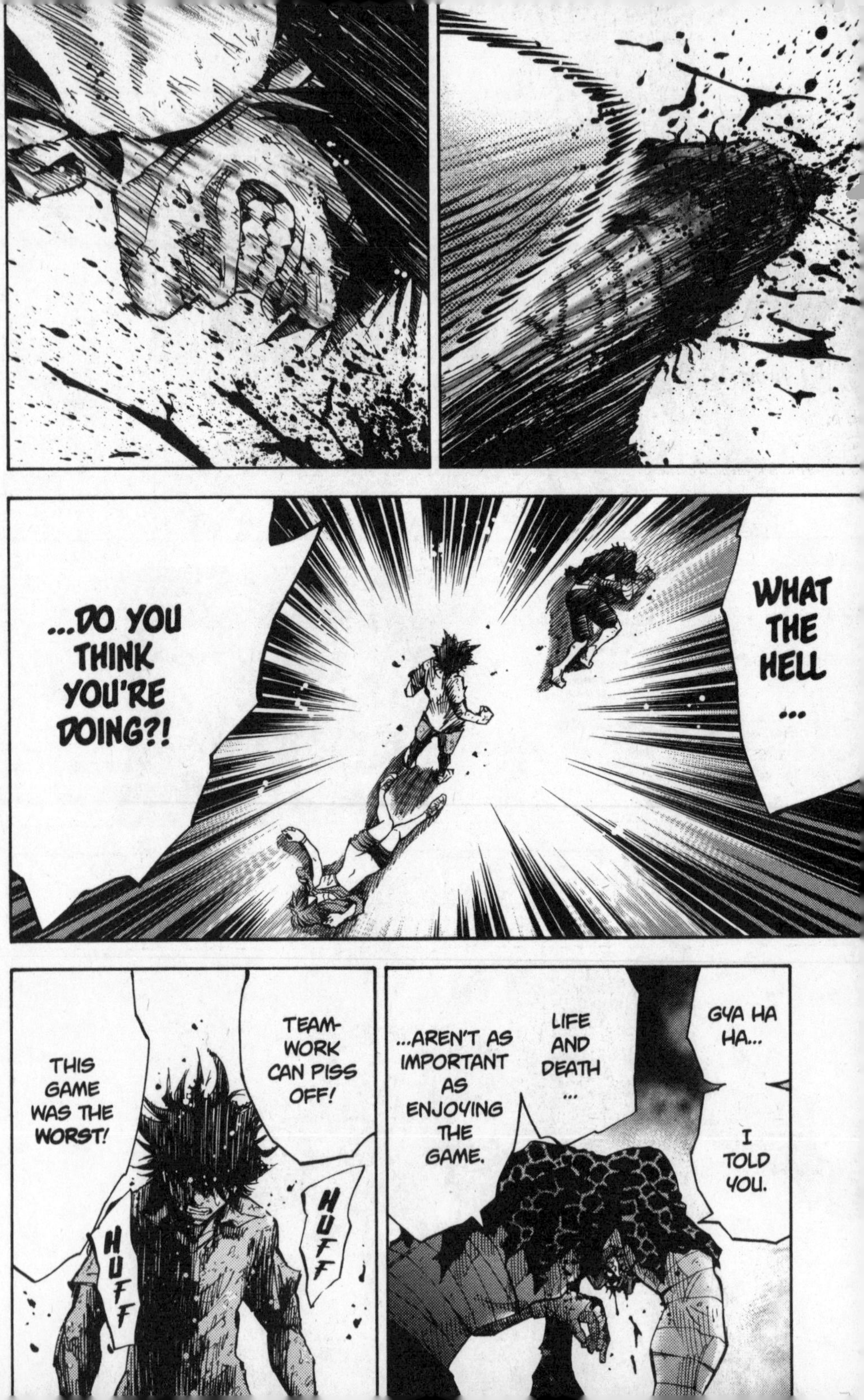
WHAT THE HELL...
...DO YOU THINK YOU'RE DOING?!
GYA HA HA...
I TOLD YOU.
LIFE AND DEATH...
...AREN'T AS IMPORTANT AS ENJOYING THE GAME.
TEAM-WORK CAN PISS OFF!
THIS GAME WAS THE WORST!
HUFF
HUFF

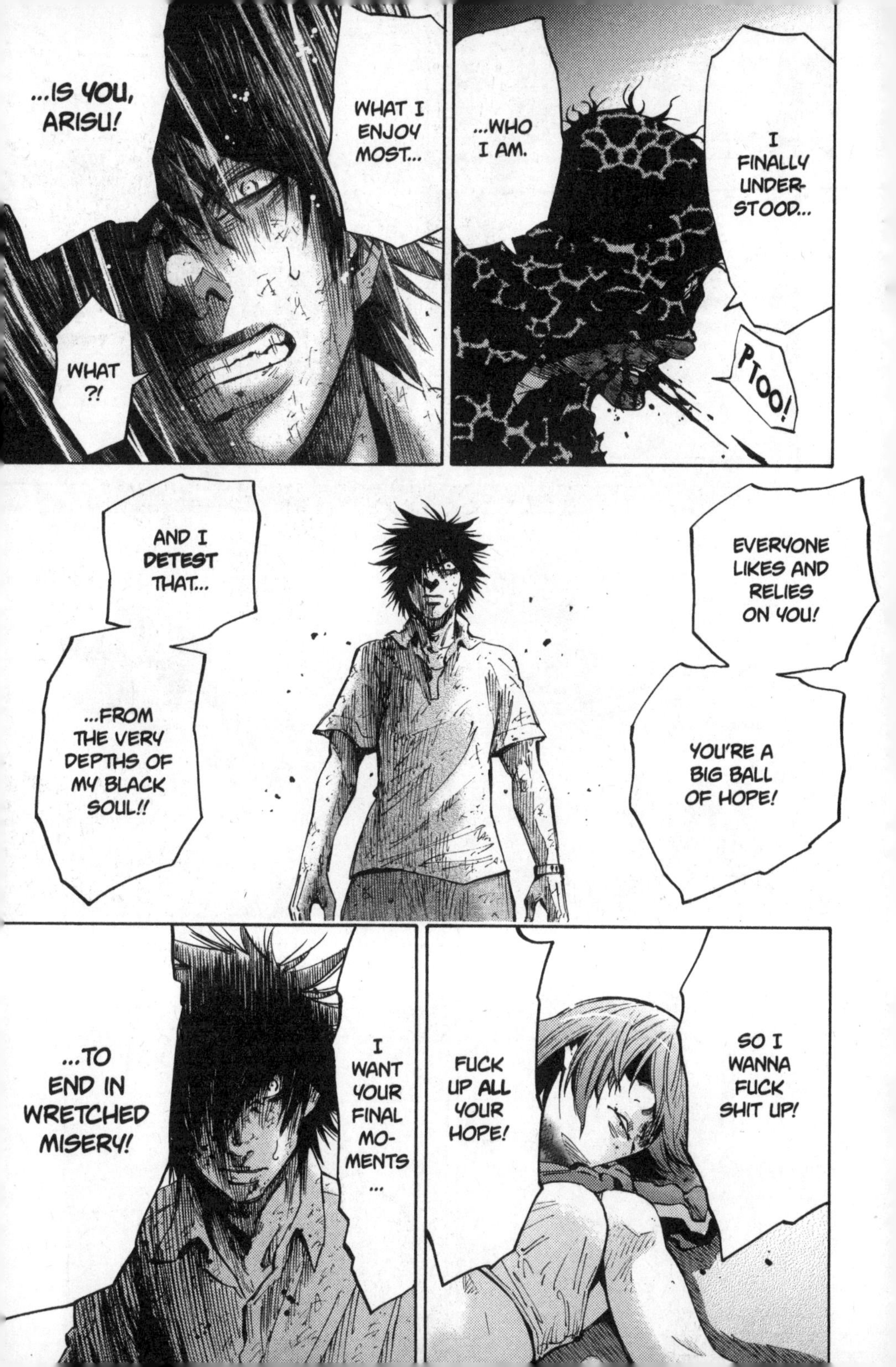
I FINALLY UNDERSTOOD...
...WHO I AM.
PTOO!
WHAT I ENJOY MOST...
...IS YOU, ARISU!
WHAT?!
EVERYONE LIKES AND RELIES ON YOU!
YOU'RE A BIG BALL OF HOPE!
AND I DETEST THAT...
...FROM THE VERY DEPTHS OF MY BLACK SOUL!!
SO I WANNA FUCK SHIT UP!
FUCK UP ALL YOUR HOPE!
I WANT YOUR FINAL MOMENTS...
...TO END IN WRETCHED MISERY!

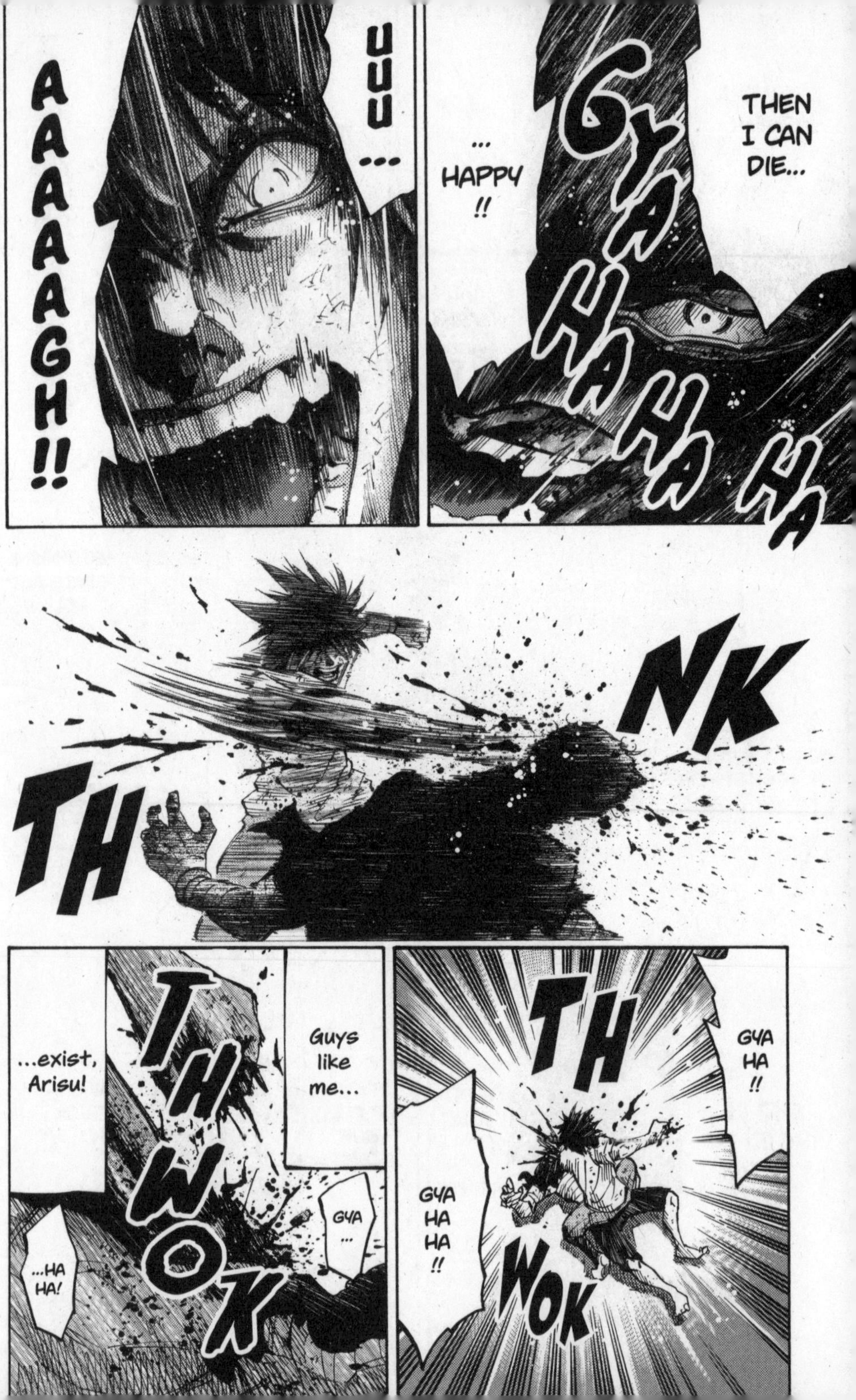
THEN I CAN DIE...
GYAHAHAHA HA HA
...HAPPY!!
UUU...
AAAAAAAGH!!
NK
TH
GYA HA!!
TH
GYA HA HA!!
WOK
Guys like me...
...exist, Arisu!
THWOK
GYA...
...HA HA!

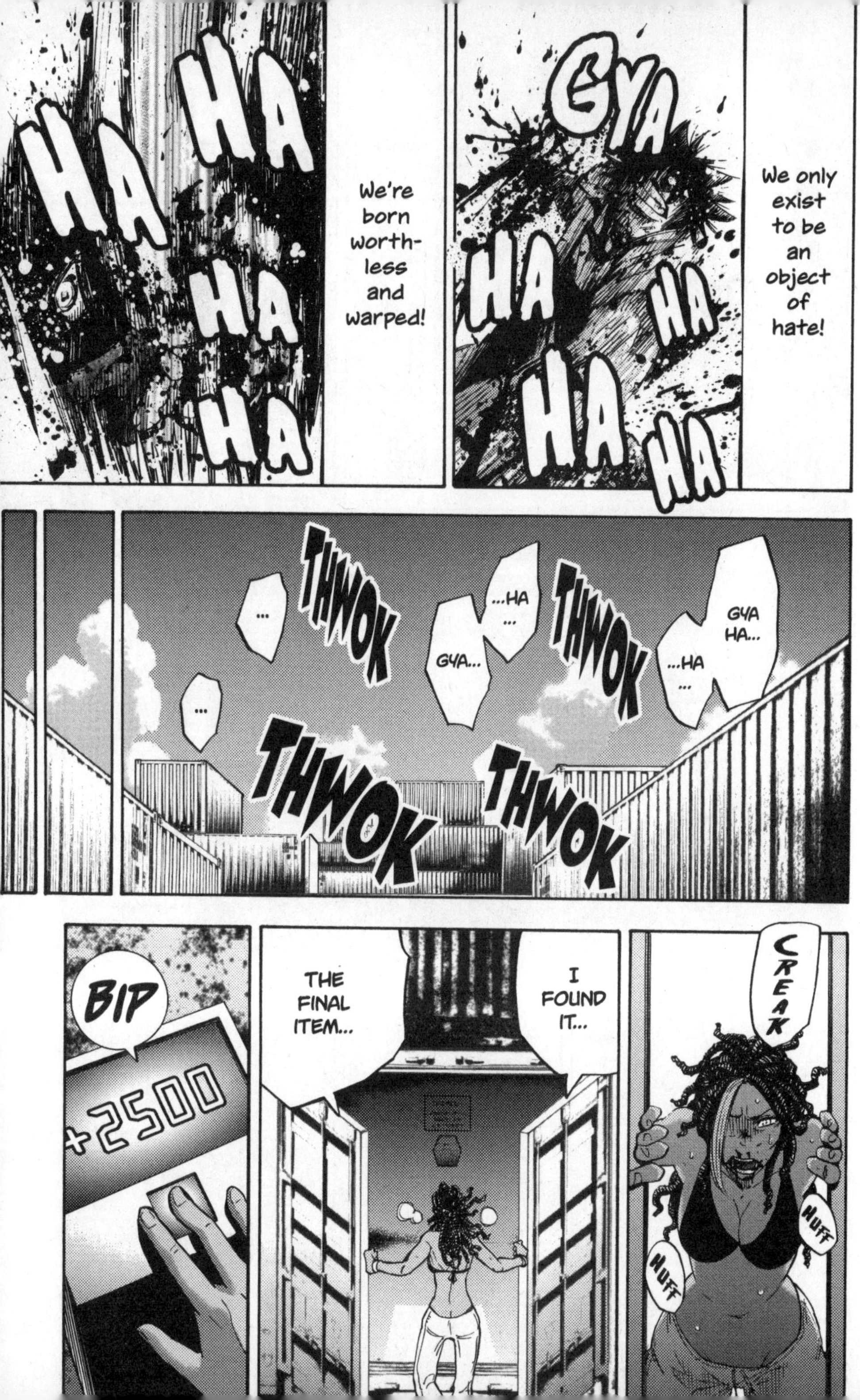
We only exist to be an object of hate!
GYA
HA HA HA HA HA
We're born worth-less and warped!
HA HA HA HA HA
GYA HA...
...HA ...
THWOK
...HA ...
GYA...
THWOK
THWOK
...
THWOK
...
CREAK
HUFF
HUFF
I FOUND IT...
THE FINAL ITEM...
BIP
+2500

...I CAN DIE...

... SATIS-FIED.

NOW...

I GOT 2,500 POINTS!

ITEM!!

HA HA...

+2500
3800

...HAVE CHANGED.

Players	King of Clubs
+2500 35000	35500

BIP

0:09:43

THE PLAYERS TEAM'S POINTS...

...I'LL TAKE A WALK.

I THINK...

KYUMA?

I'M...

... GET-TING BORED.

...

KING OF CLUBS TEAM BASE

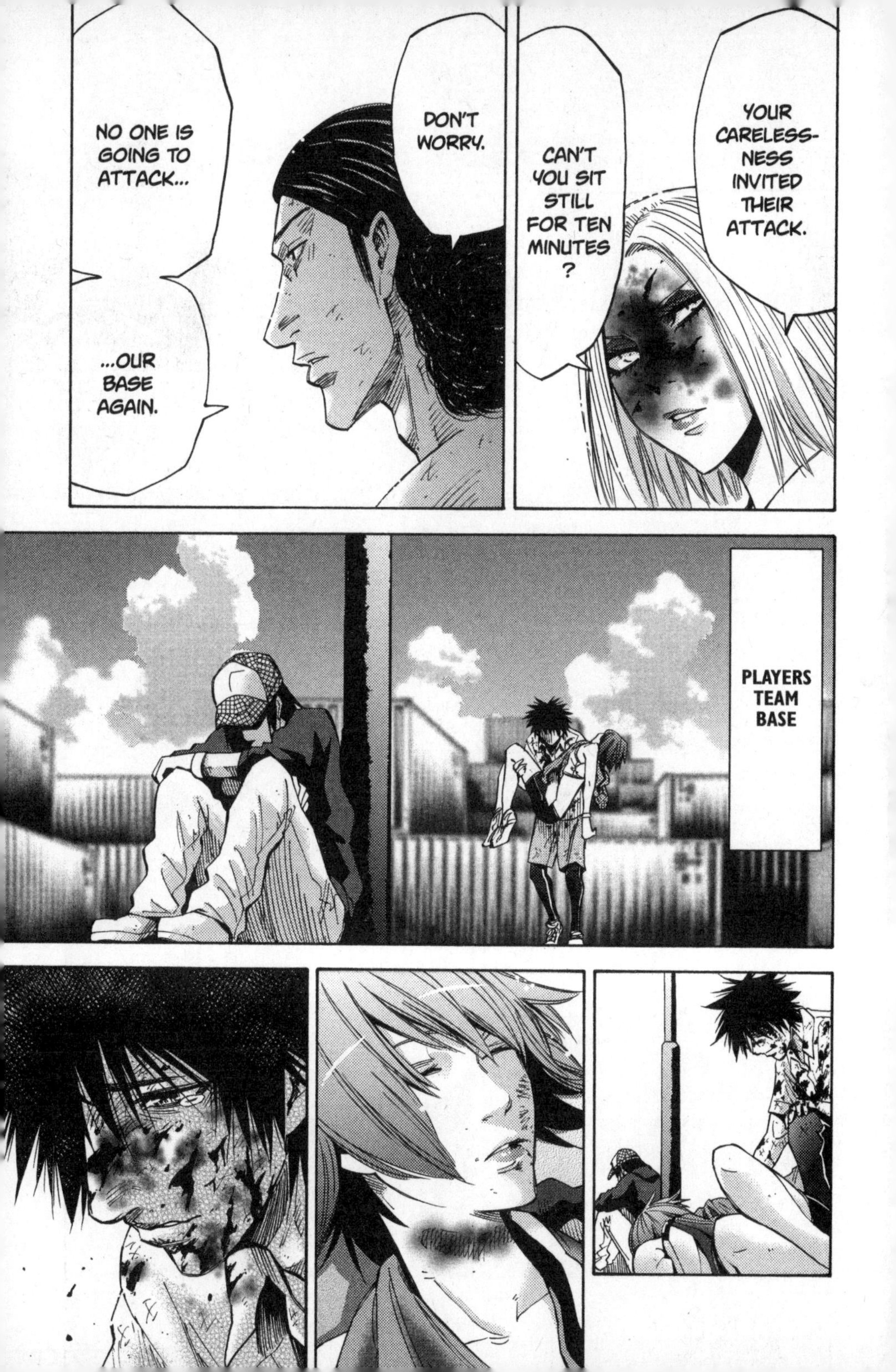
YOUR CARELESSNESS INVITED THEIR ATTACK.
CAN'T YOU SIT STILL FOR TEN MINUTES?
DON'T WORRY.
NO ONE IS GOING TO ATTACK...
...OUR BASE AGAIN.
PLAYERS TEAM BASE

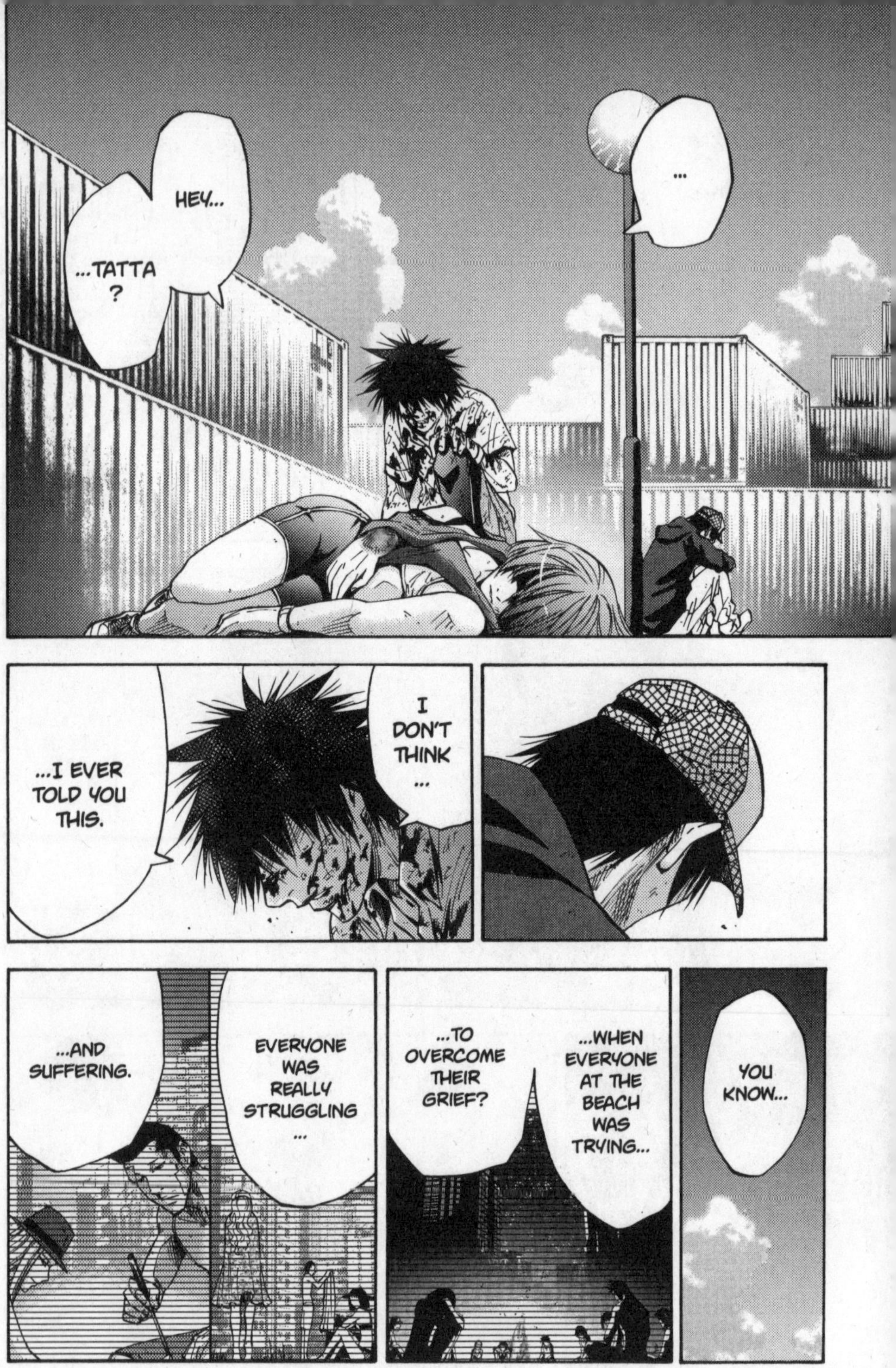
...
HEY... ...TATTA?
I DON'T THINK ...
...I EVER TOLD YOU THIS.
YOU KNOW...
...WHEN EVERYONE AT THE BEACH WAS TRYING...
...TO OVERCOME THEIR GRIEF?
EVERYONE WAS REALLY STRUGGLING ...
...AND SUFFERING.

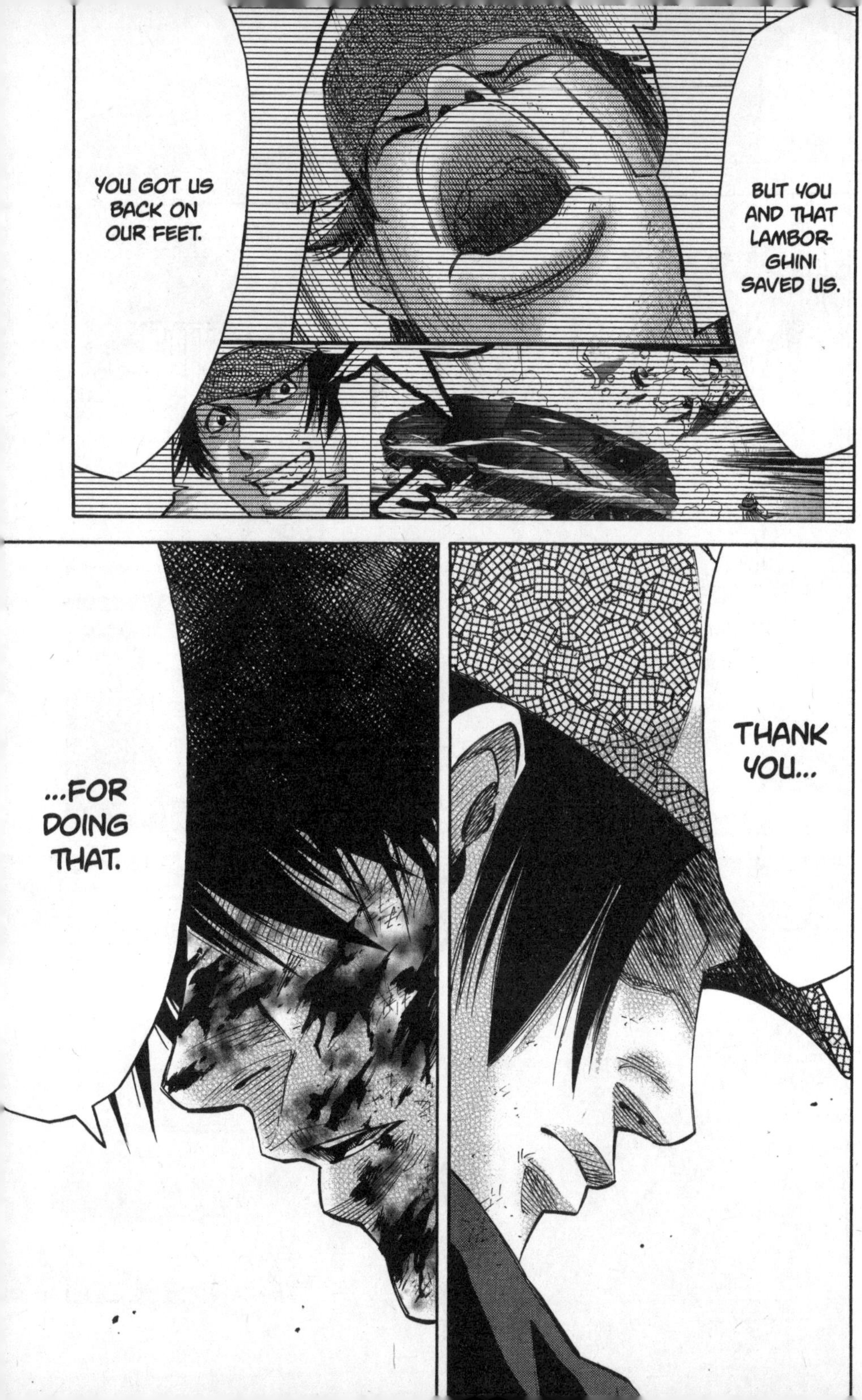
BUT YOU AND THAT LAMBOR-GHINI SAVED US.
YOU GOT US BACK ON OUR FEET.
THANK YOU...
...FOR DOING THAT.

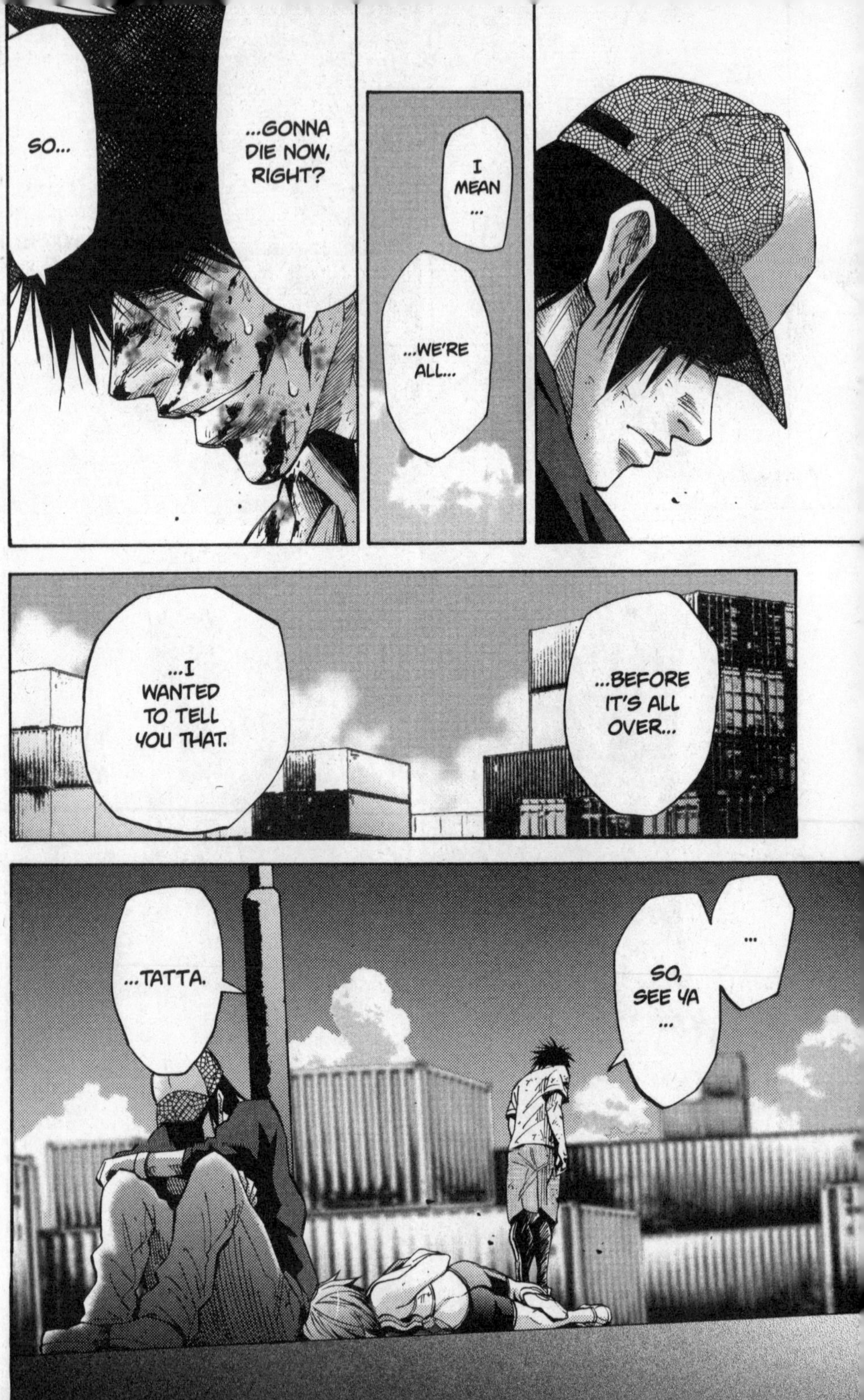
I MEAN ...
...WE'RE ALL...
...GONNA DIE NOW, RIGHT?
SO...
...BEFORE IT'S ALL OVER...
...I WANTED TO TELL YOU THAT.
... SO, SEE YA ...
...TATTA.

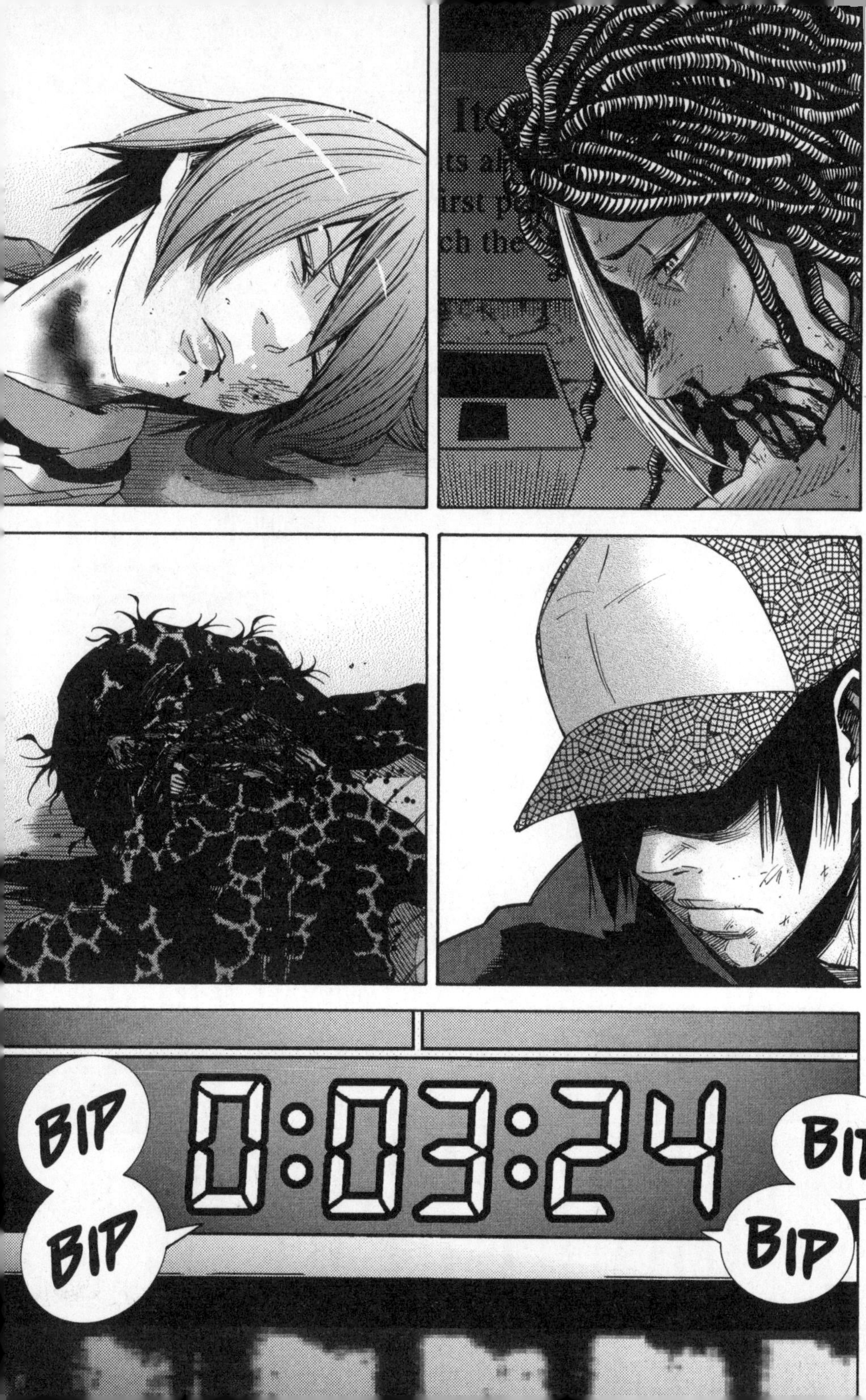
BIP
BIP
0:03:24
BIP
BIP

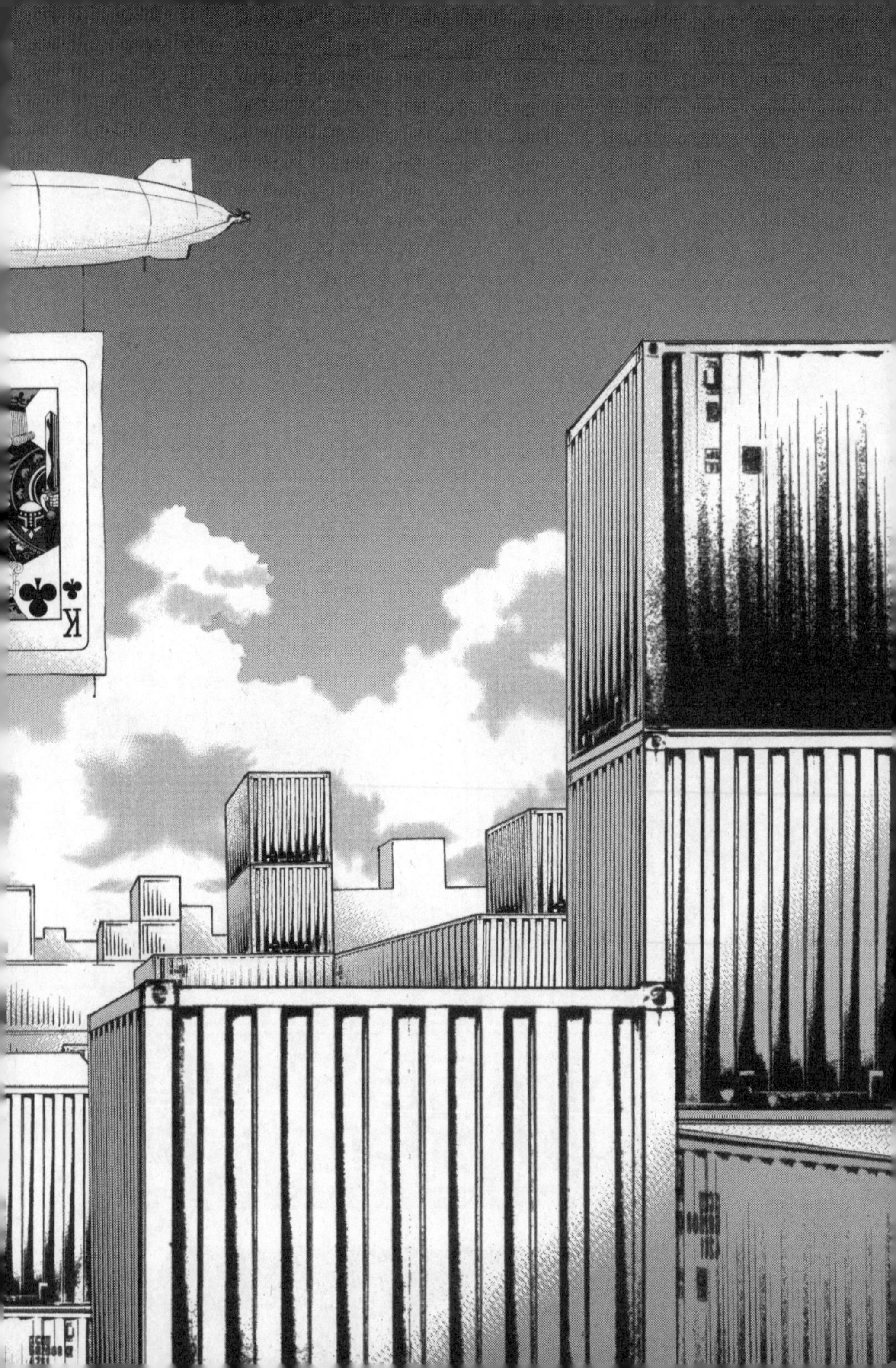

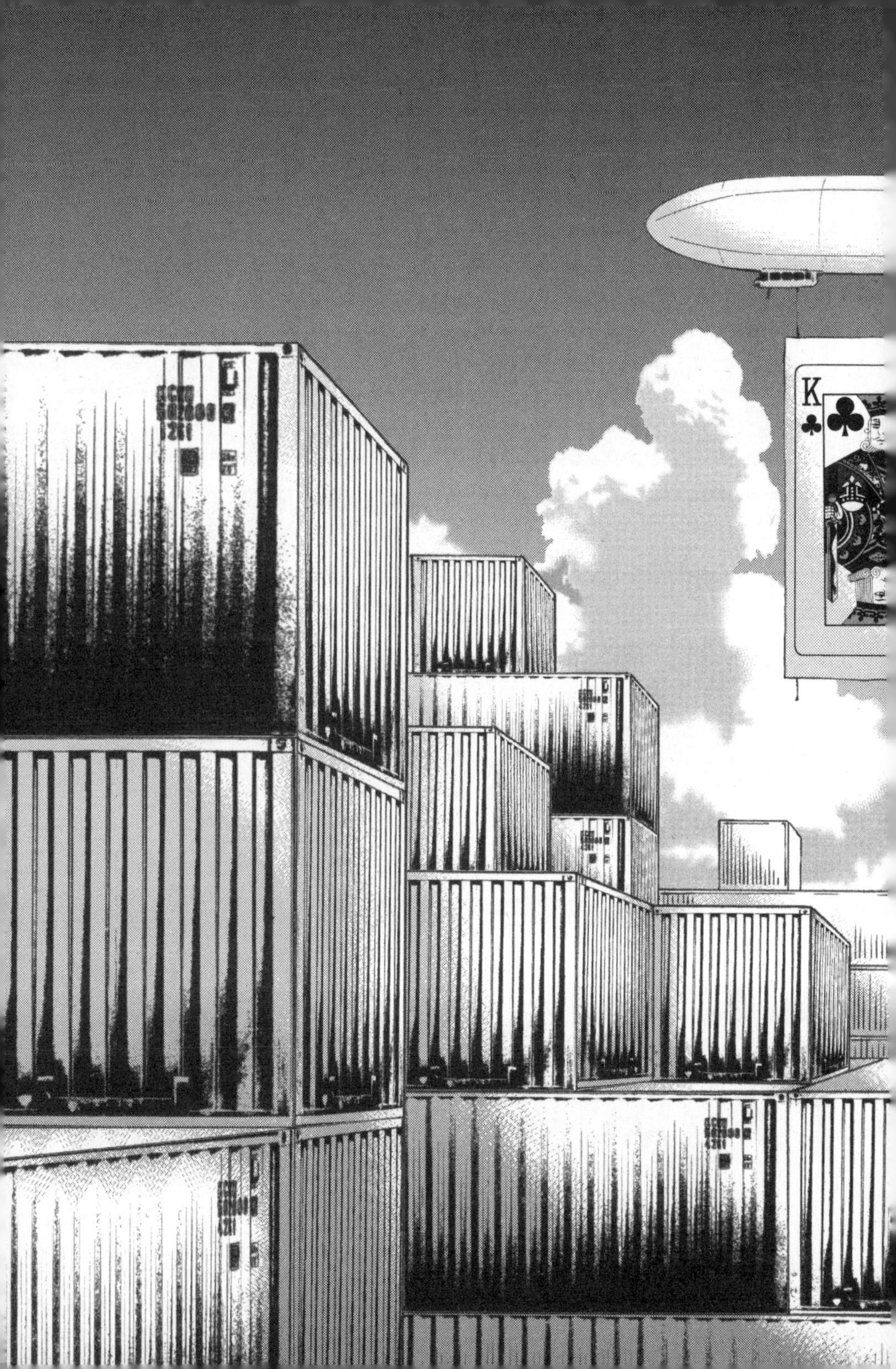
K

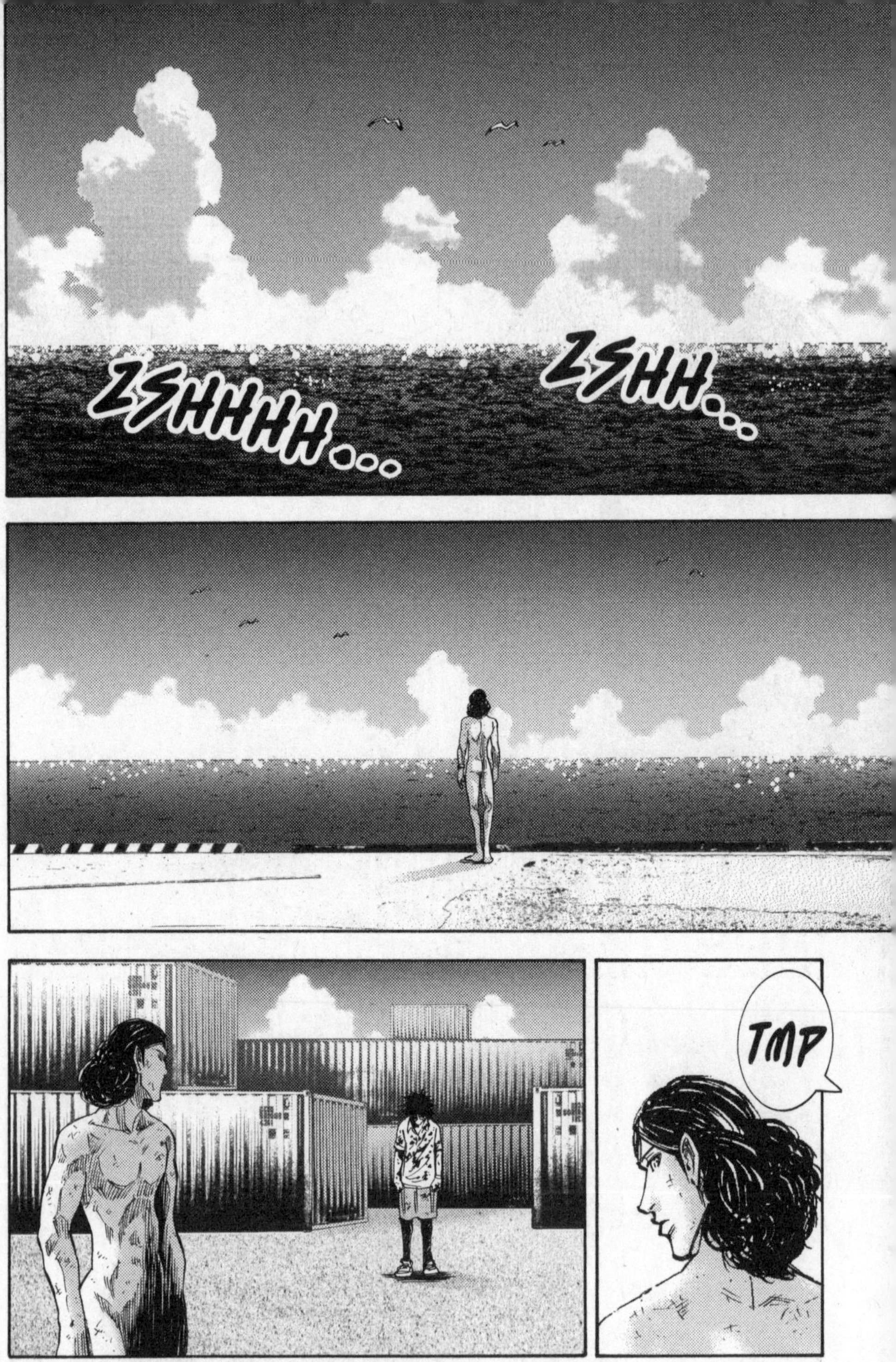
ZSHH...
ZSHHHHH...
TMP

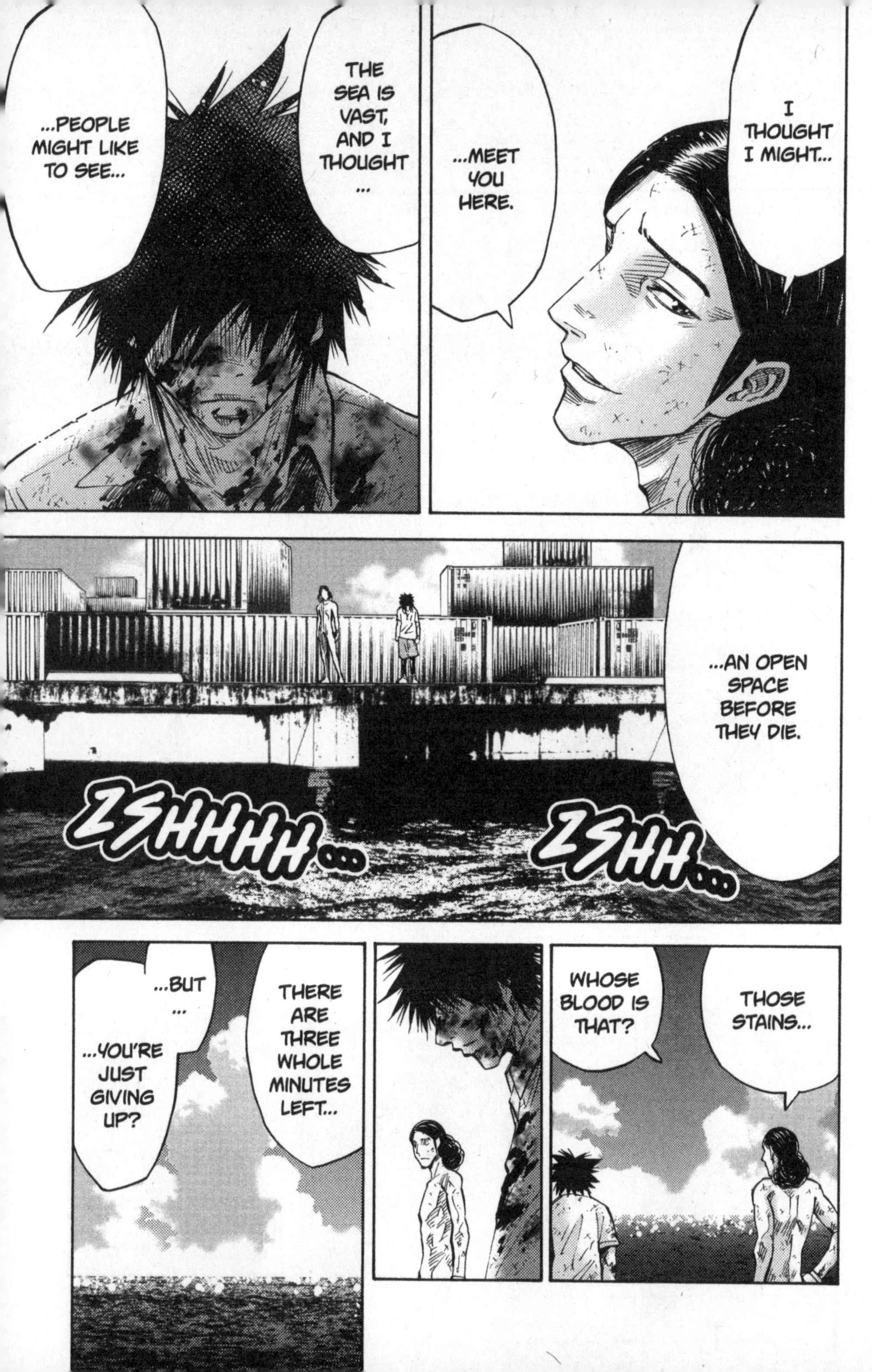
I THOUGHT I MIGHT...
...MEET YOU HERE.
THE SEA IS VAST, AND I THOUGHT ...
...PEOPLE MIGHT LIKE TO SEE...
...AN OPEN SPACE BEFORE THEY DIE.
ZSHHH...
ZSHHHHH...
THOSE STAINS...
WHOSE BLOOD IS THAT?
THERE ARE THREE WHOLE MINUTES LEFT...
...BUT ...
...YOU'RE JUST GIVING UP?

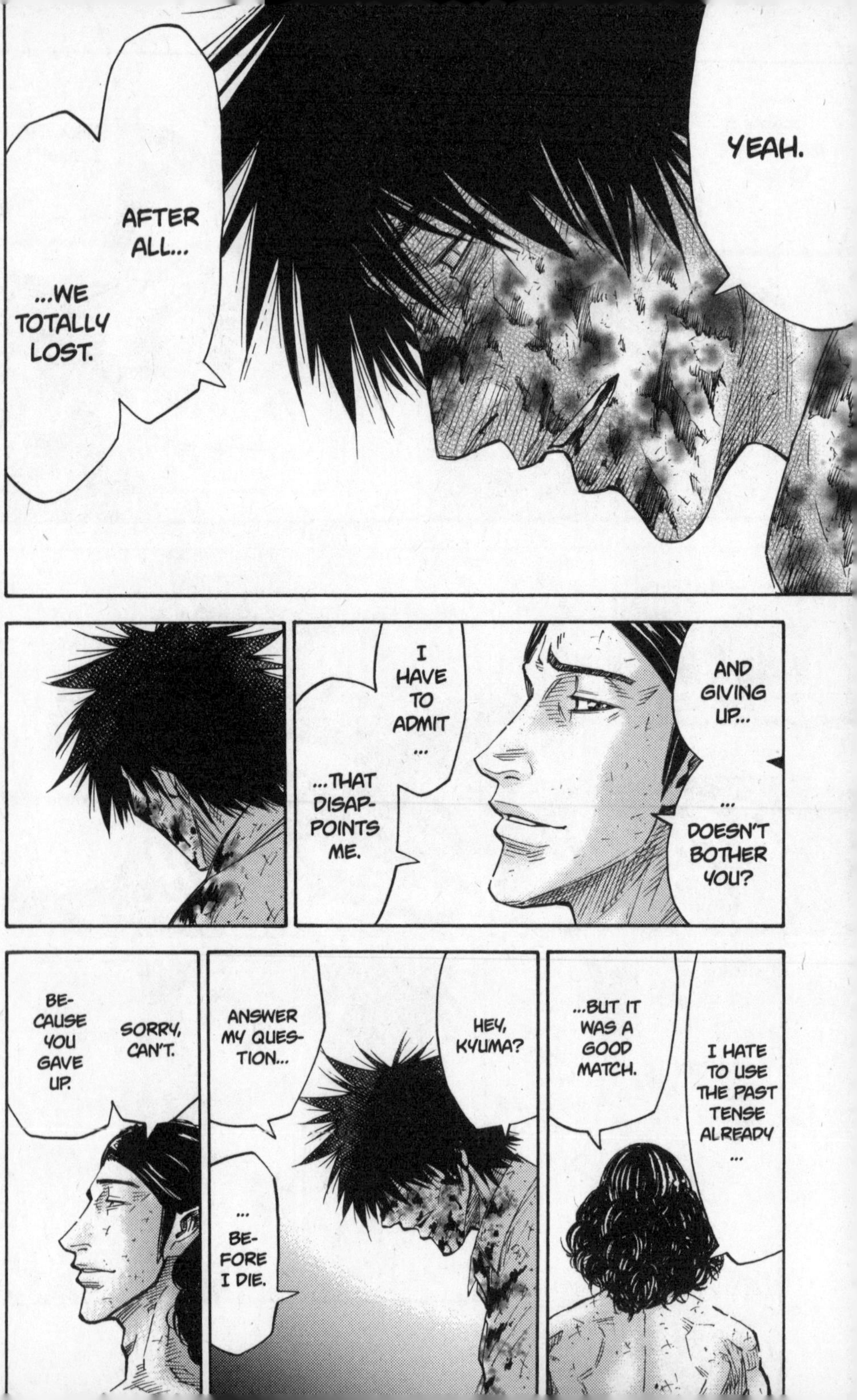
YEAH.
AFTER ALL...
...WE TOTALLY LOST.
AND GIVING UP...
...DOESN'T BOTHER YOU?
I HAVE TO ADMIT...
...THAT DISAPPOINTS ME.
I HATE TO USE THE PAST TENSE ALREADY...
...BUT IT WAS A GOOD MATCH.
HEY, KYUMA?
ANSWER MY QUESTION...
...BEFORE I DIE.
SORRY, CAN'T.
BE-CAUSE YOU GAVE UP.

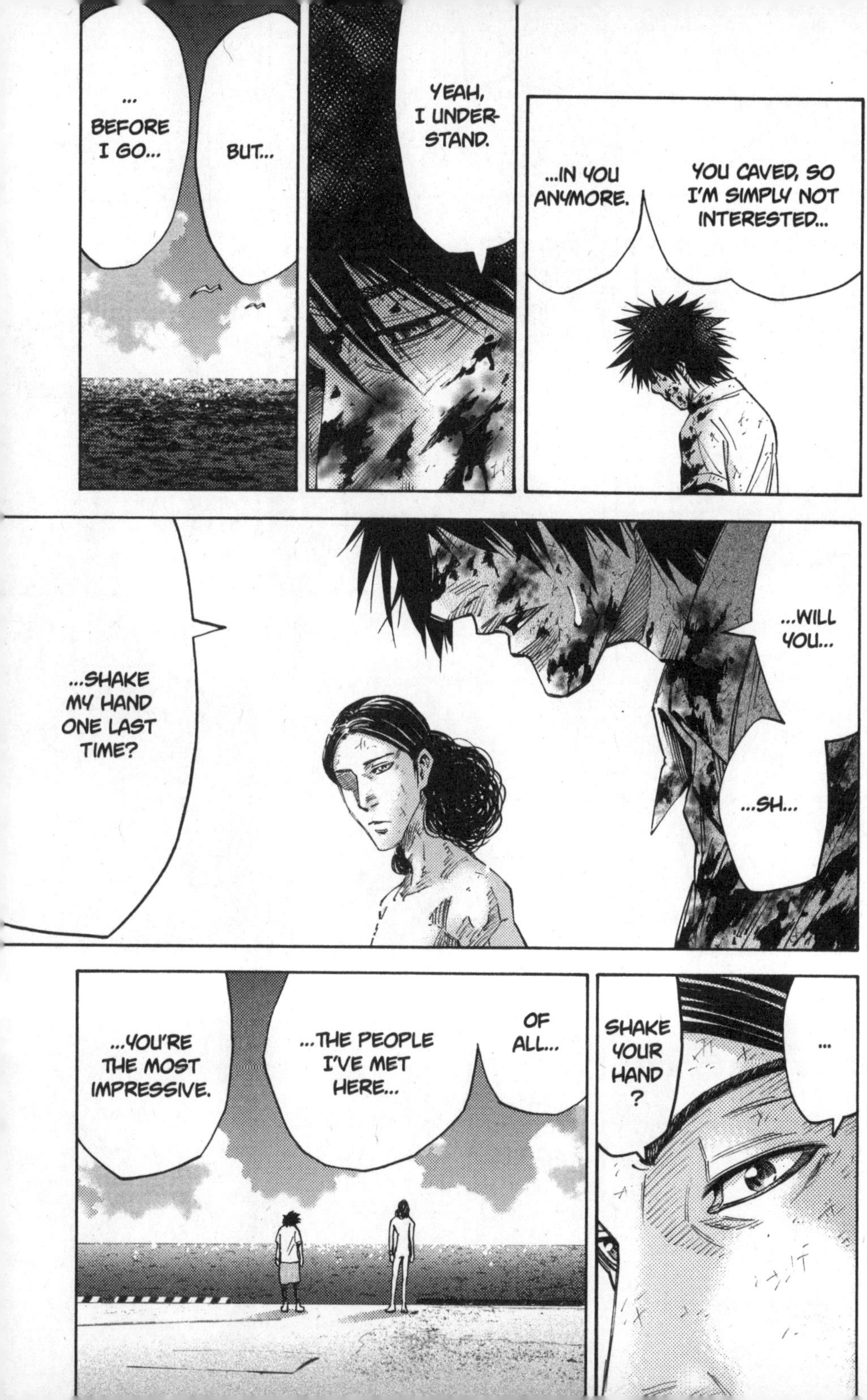
YOU CAVED, SO I'M SIMPLY NOT INTERESTED...
...IN YOU ANYMORE.
YEAH, I UNDER-STAND.
BUT...
...
BEFORE I GO...
...WILL YOU...
...SH...
...SHAKE MY HAND ONE LAST TIME?
...
SHAKE YOUR HAND ?
OF ALL...
...THE PEOPLE I'VE MET HERE...
...YOU'RE THE MOST IMPRESSIVE.

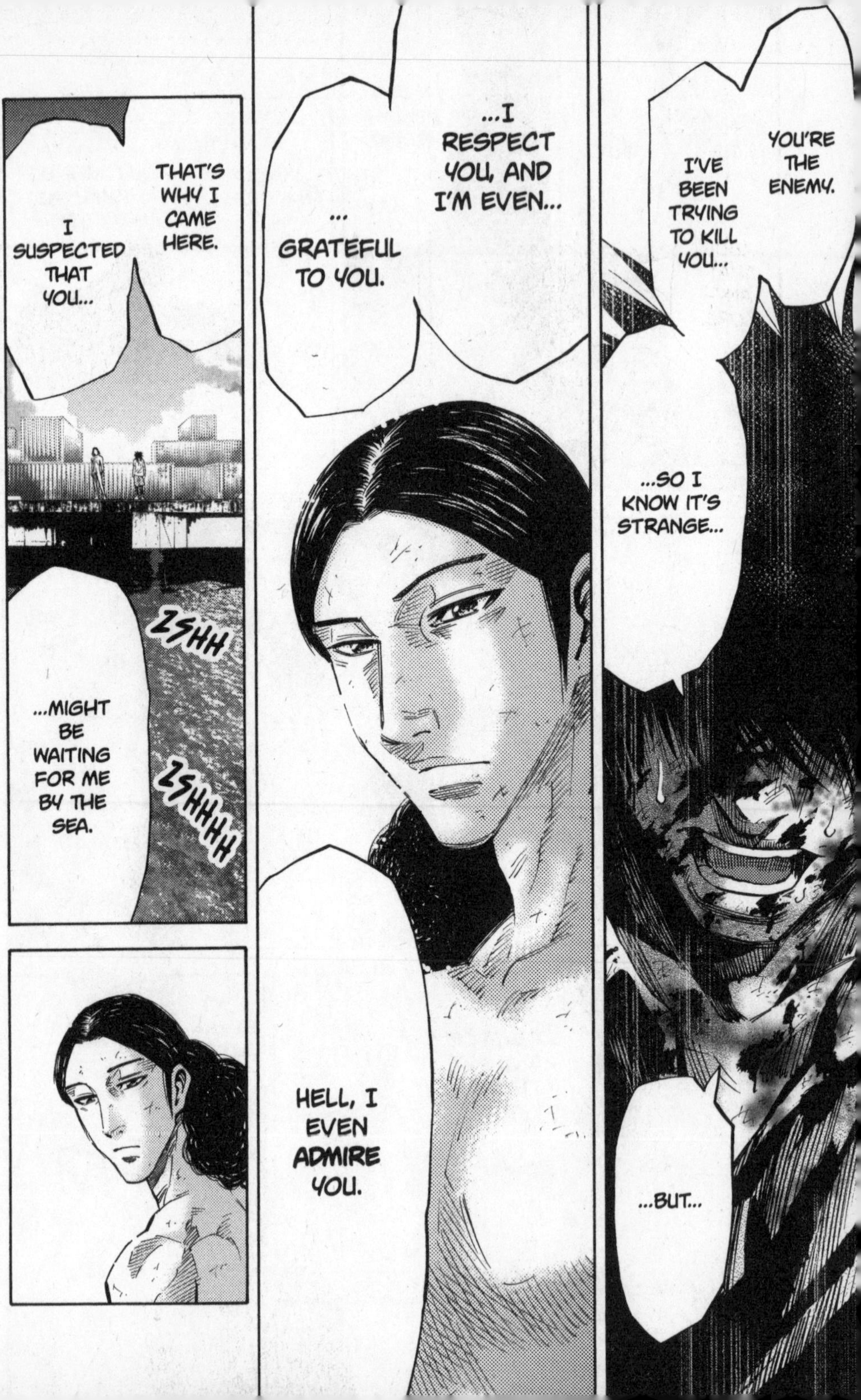
YOU'RE THE ENEMY.
I'VE BEEN TRYING TO KILL YOU...
...SO I KNOW IT'S STRANGE...
...BUT...
...I RESPECT YOU, AND I'M EVEN...
...GRATEFUL TO YOU.
HELL, I EVEN ADMIRE YOU.
THAT'S WHY I CAME HERE.
I SUSPECTED THAT YOU...
ZSHH
...MIGHT BE WAITING FOR ME BY THE SEA.
ZSHHHH

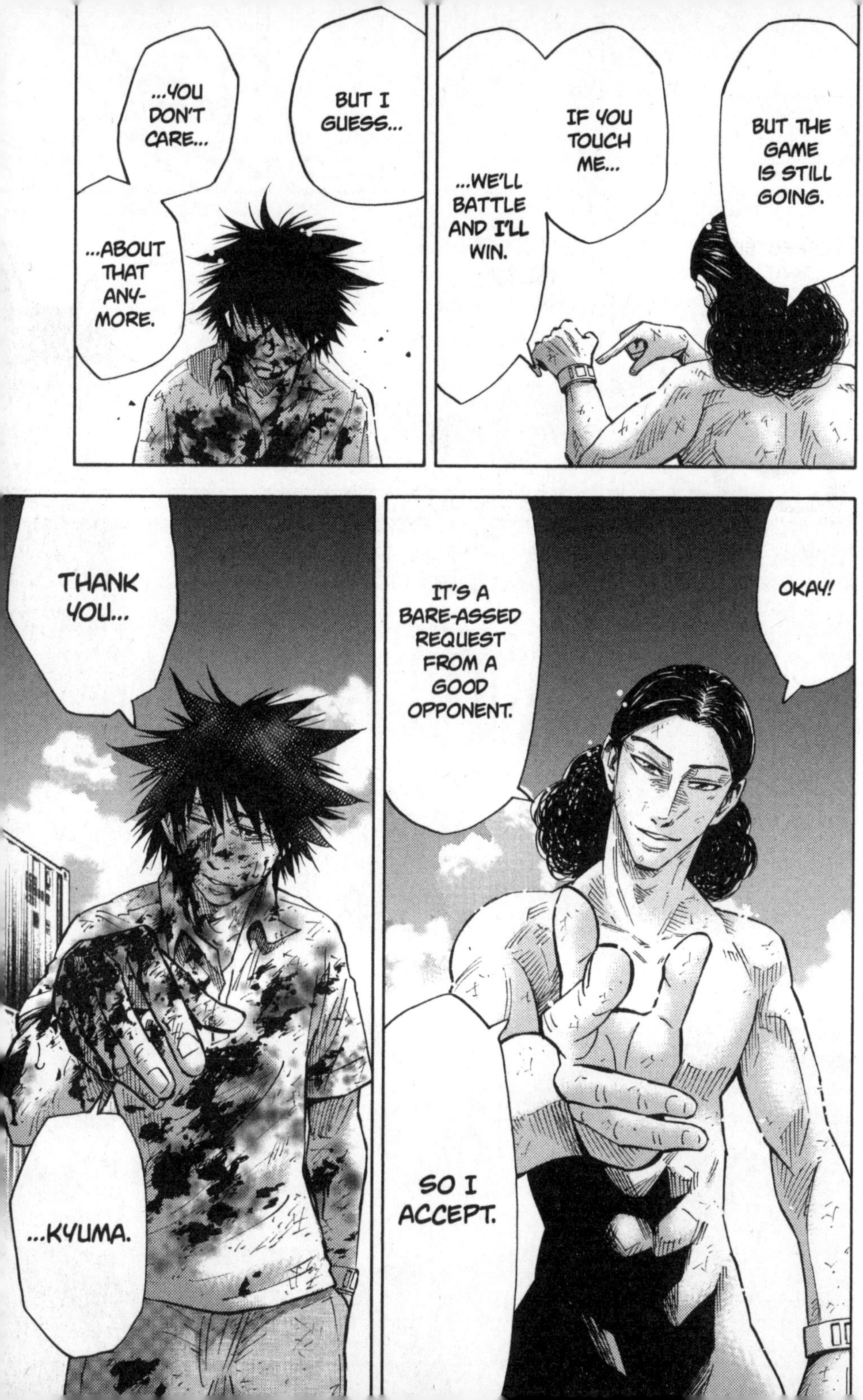
BUT THE GAME IS STILL GOING.
IF YOU TOUCH ME...
...WE'LL BATTLE AND I'LL WIN.
BUT I GUESS...
...YOU DON'T CARE...
...ABOUT THAT ANYMORE.
OKAY!
IT'S A BARE-ASSED REQUEST FROM A GOOD OPPONENT.
SO I ACCEPT.
THANK YOU...
...KYUMA.

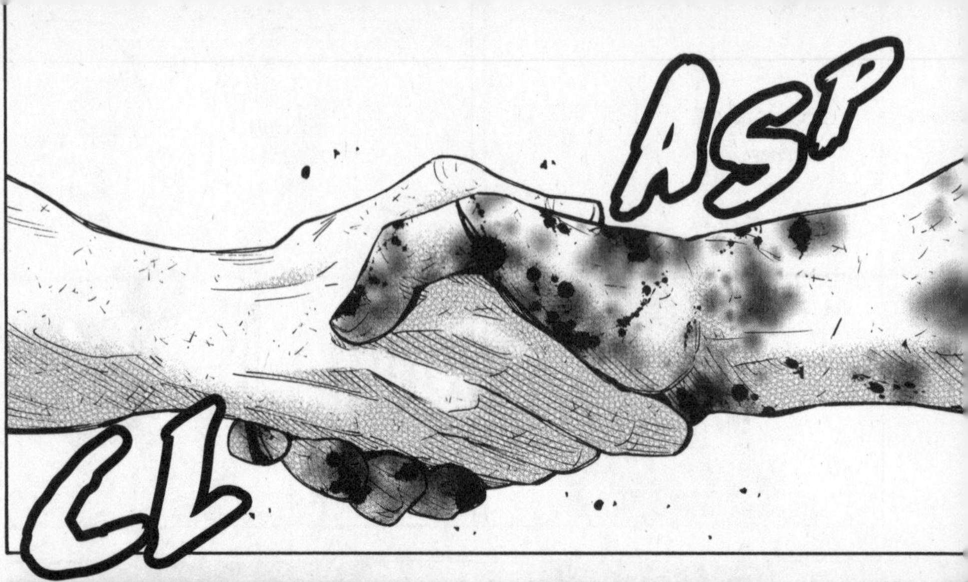
CLASP
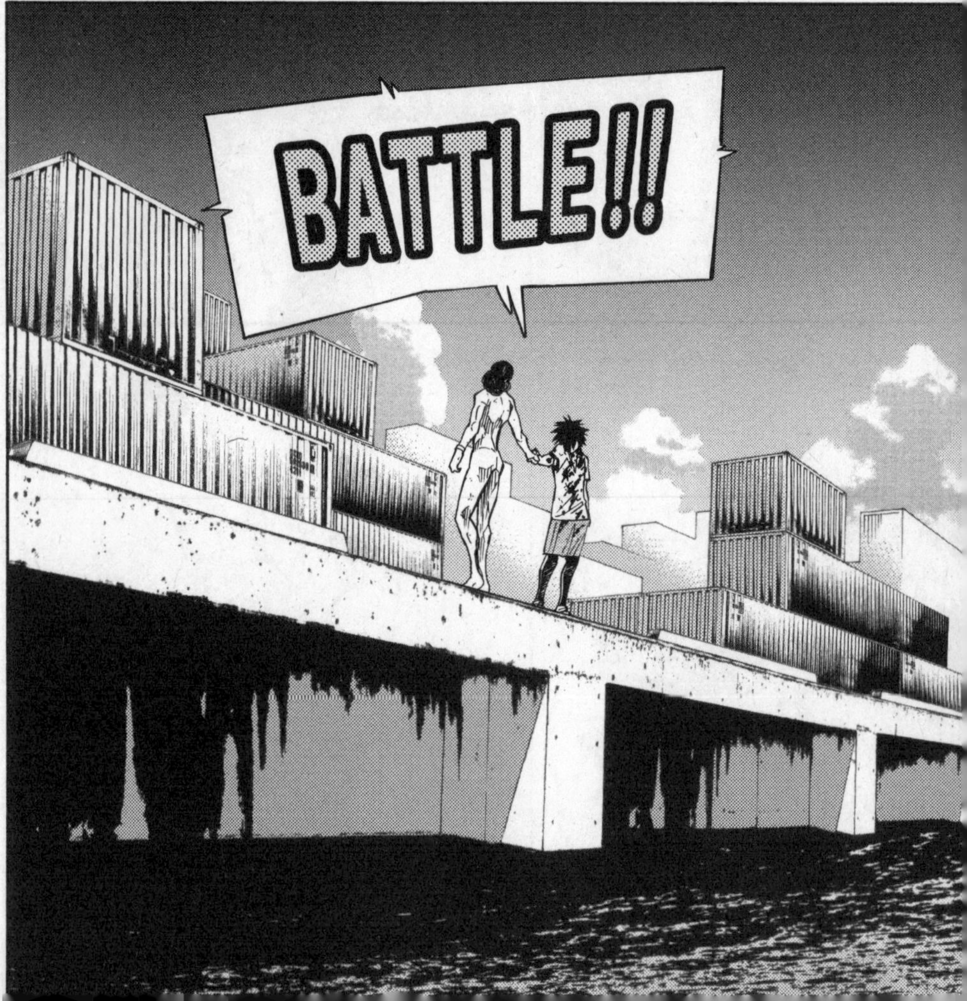
BATTLE!!

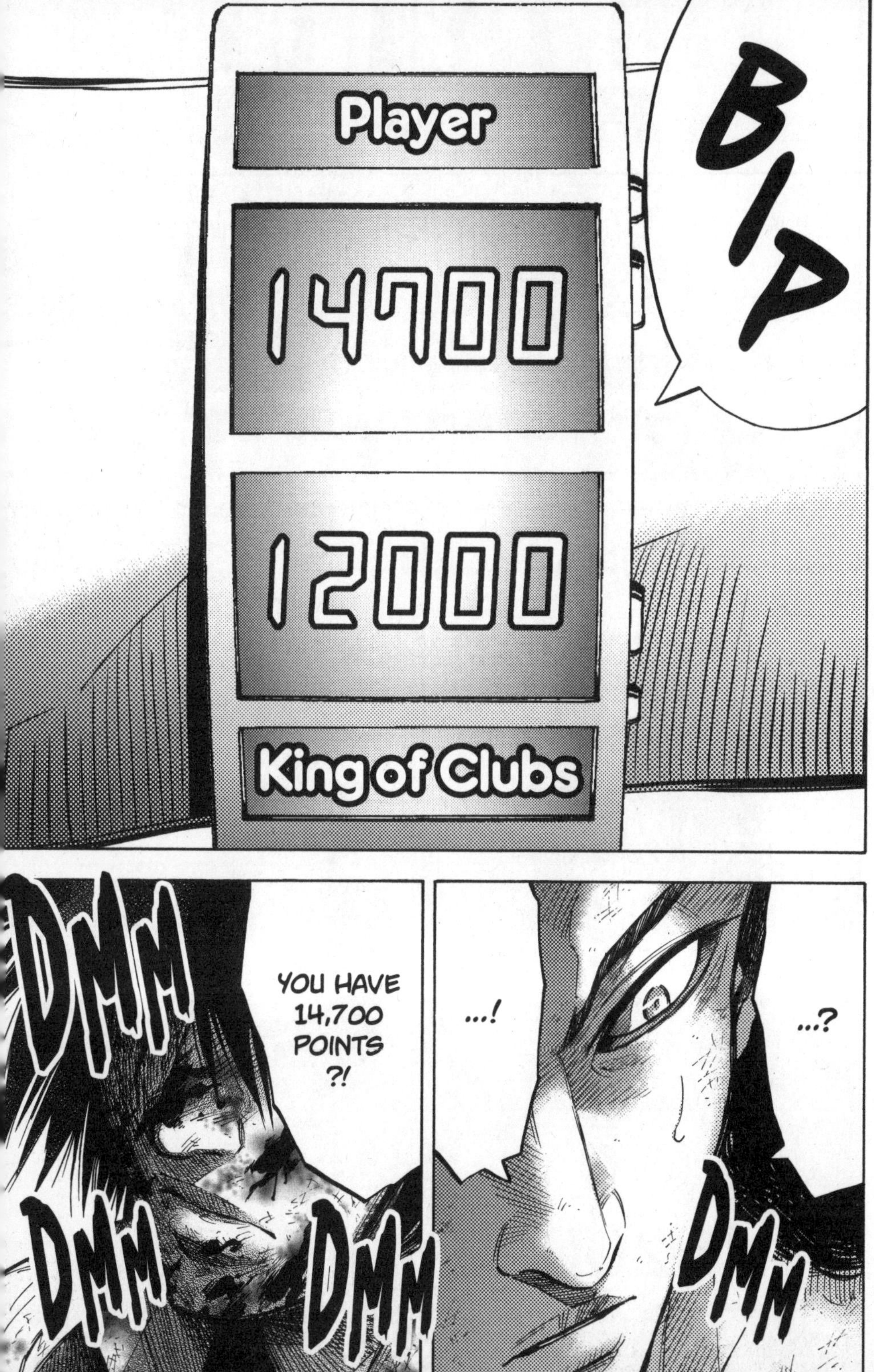
BIP
Player
14700
12000
King of Clubs
..?
...!
DMM
YOU HAVE 14,700 POINTS ?!
DMM
DMM
DMM

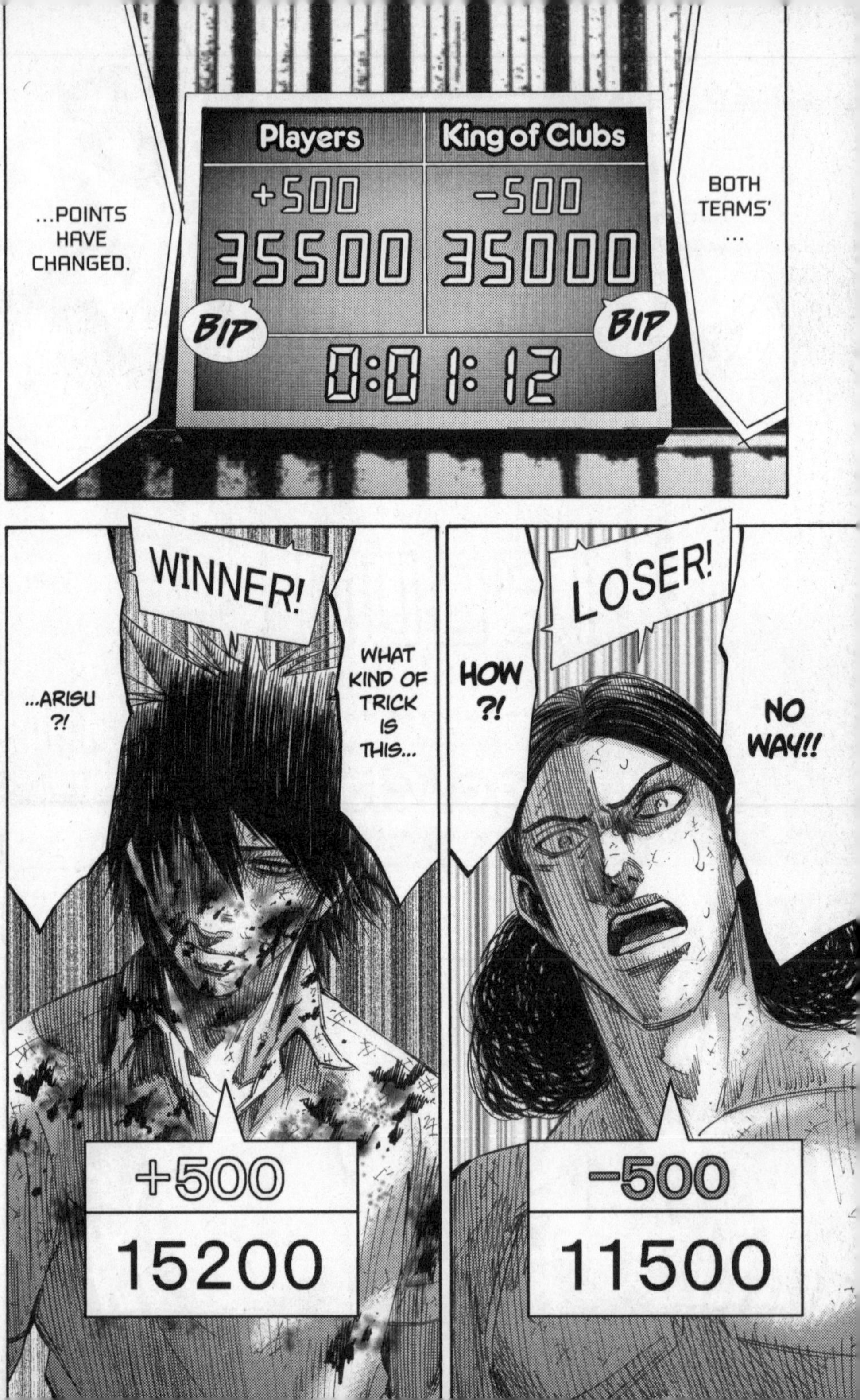
BOTH TEAMS' ...
Players
King of Clubs
+500
-500
35500
35000
BIP
BIP
0:01:12
...POINTS HAVE CHANGED.
LOSER!
NO WAY!!
HOW ?!
-500
11500
WINNER!
WHAT KIND OF TRICK IS THIS...
...ARISU ?!
+500
15200

CHAPTER 40: King of Clubs, Part 8

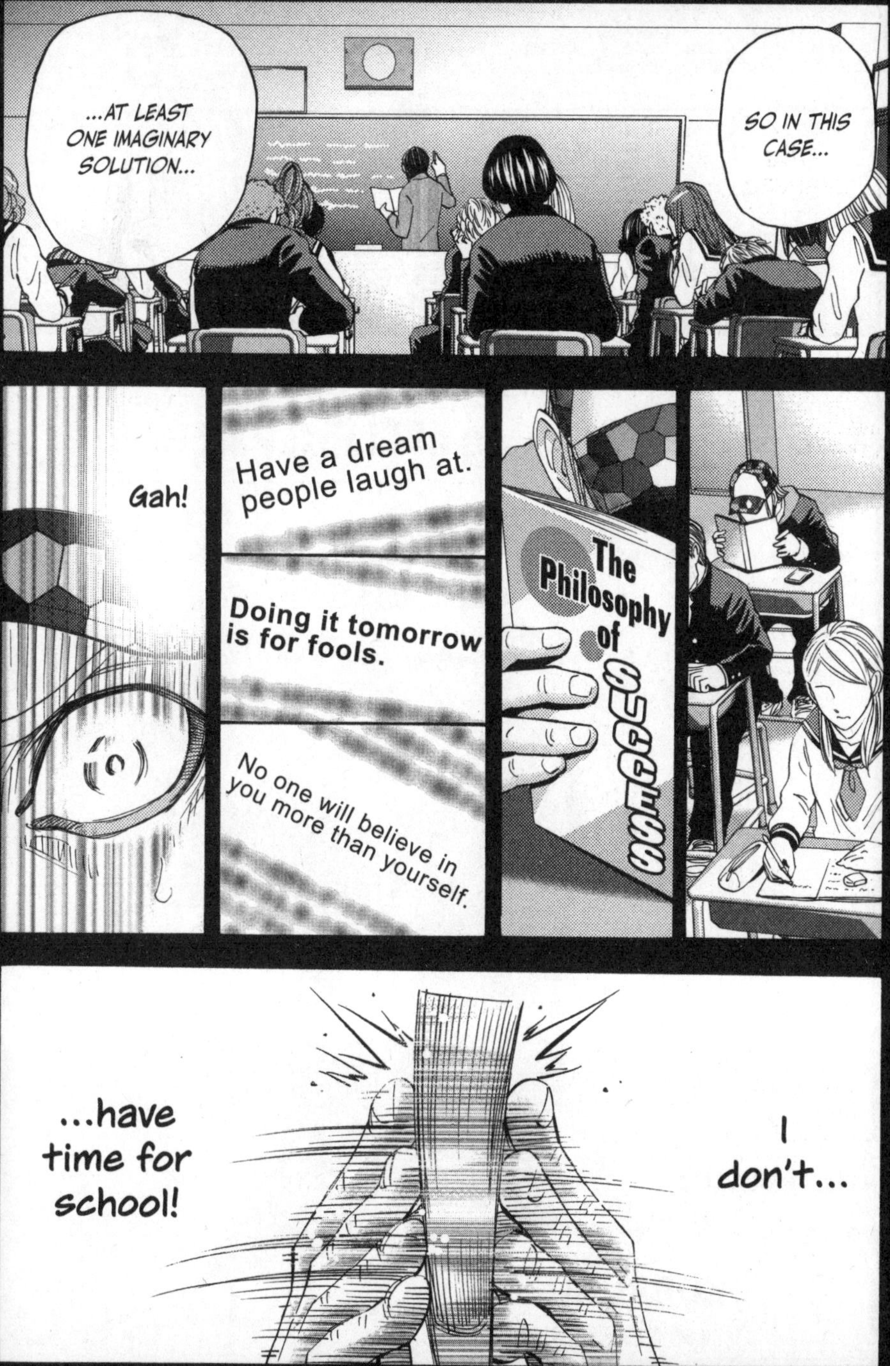

SO IN THIS CASE...
...AT LEAST ONE IMAGINARY SOLUTION...
The Philosophy of SUCCESS
Have a dream people laugh at.
Doing it tomorrow is for fools.
No one will believe in you more than yourself.
Gah!
I don't...
...have time for school!

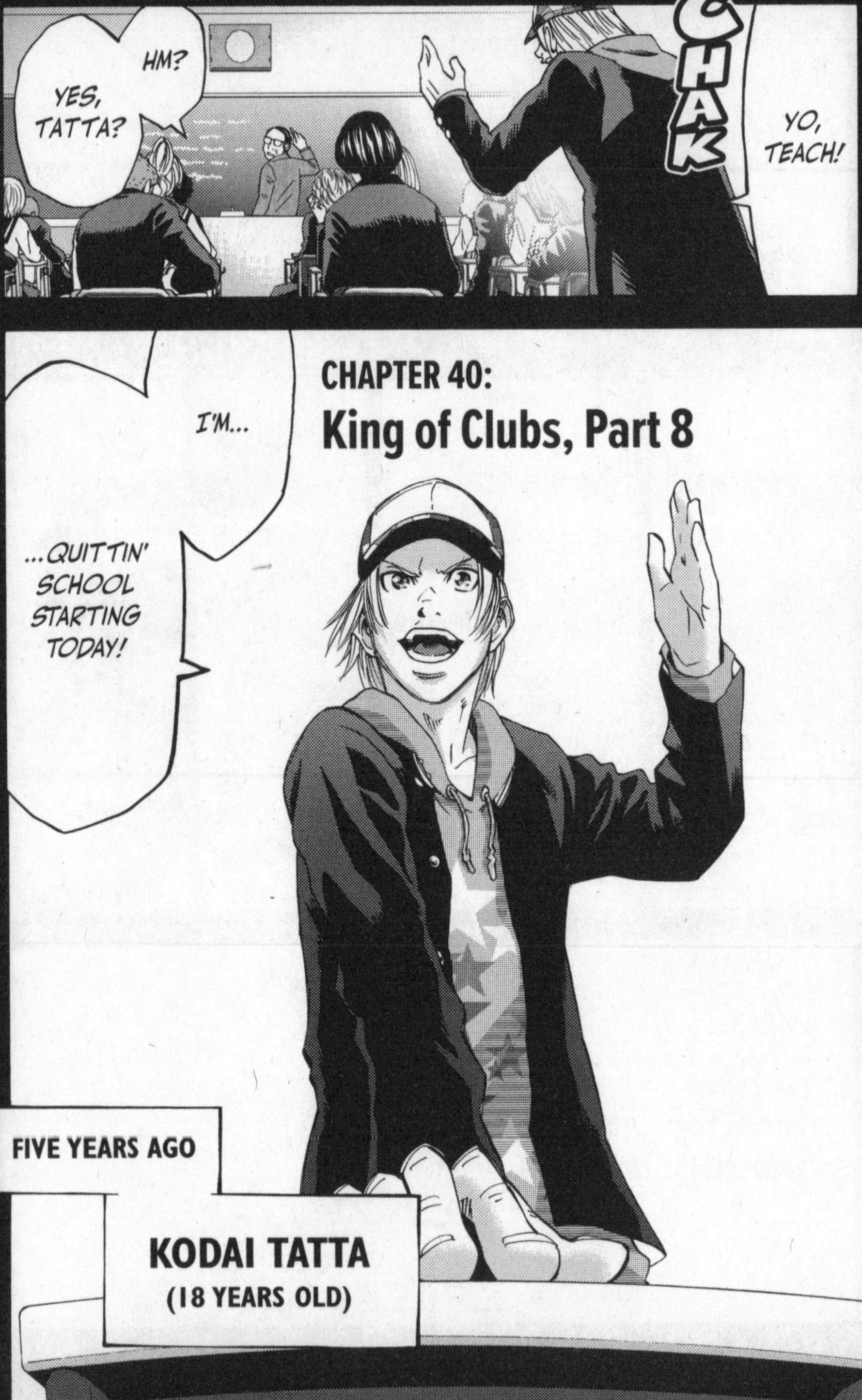
CHAK
YO, TEACH!
HM? YES, TATTA?
CHAPTER 40:
King of Clubs, Part 8
I'M...
...QUITTIN' SCHOOL STARTING TODAY!
FIVE YEARS AGO
KODAI TATTA
(18 YEARS OLD)

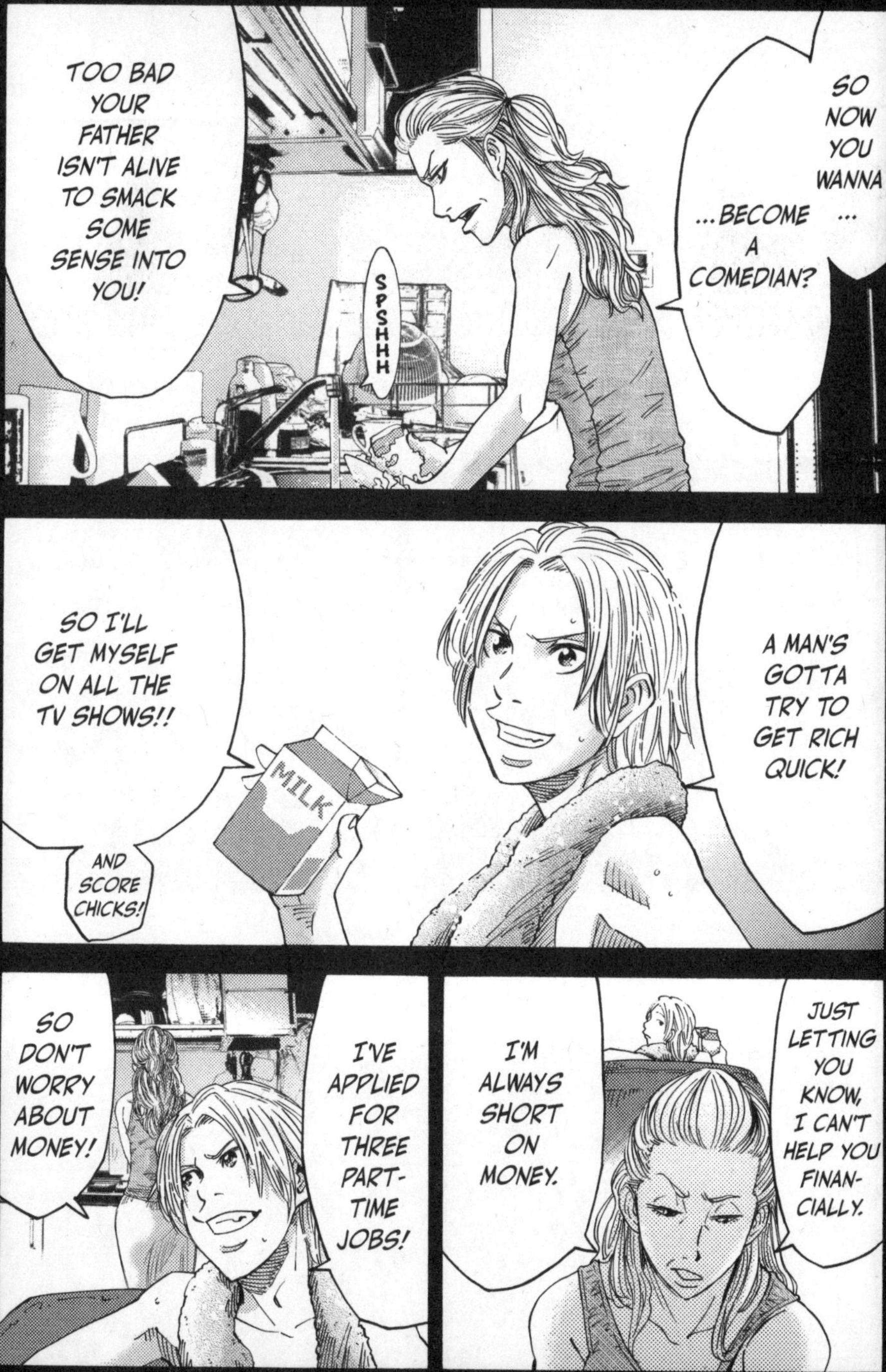
SO NOW YOU WANNA ...
...BECOME A COMEDIAN?
SPSHHH
TOO BAD YOUR FATHER ISN'T ALIVE TO SMACK SOME SENSE INTO YOU!
A MAN'S GOTTA TRY TO GET RICH QUICK!
SO I'LL GET MYSELF ON ALL THE TV SHOWS!!
AND SCORE CHICKS!
MILK
JUST LETTING YOU KNOW, I CAN'T HELP YOU FINAN-CIALLY.
I'M ALWAYS SHORT ON MONEY.
I'VE APPLIED FOR THREE PART-TIME JOBS!
SO DON'T WORRY ABOUT MONEY!

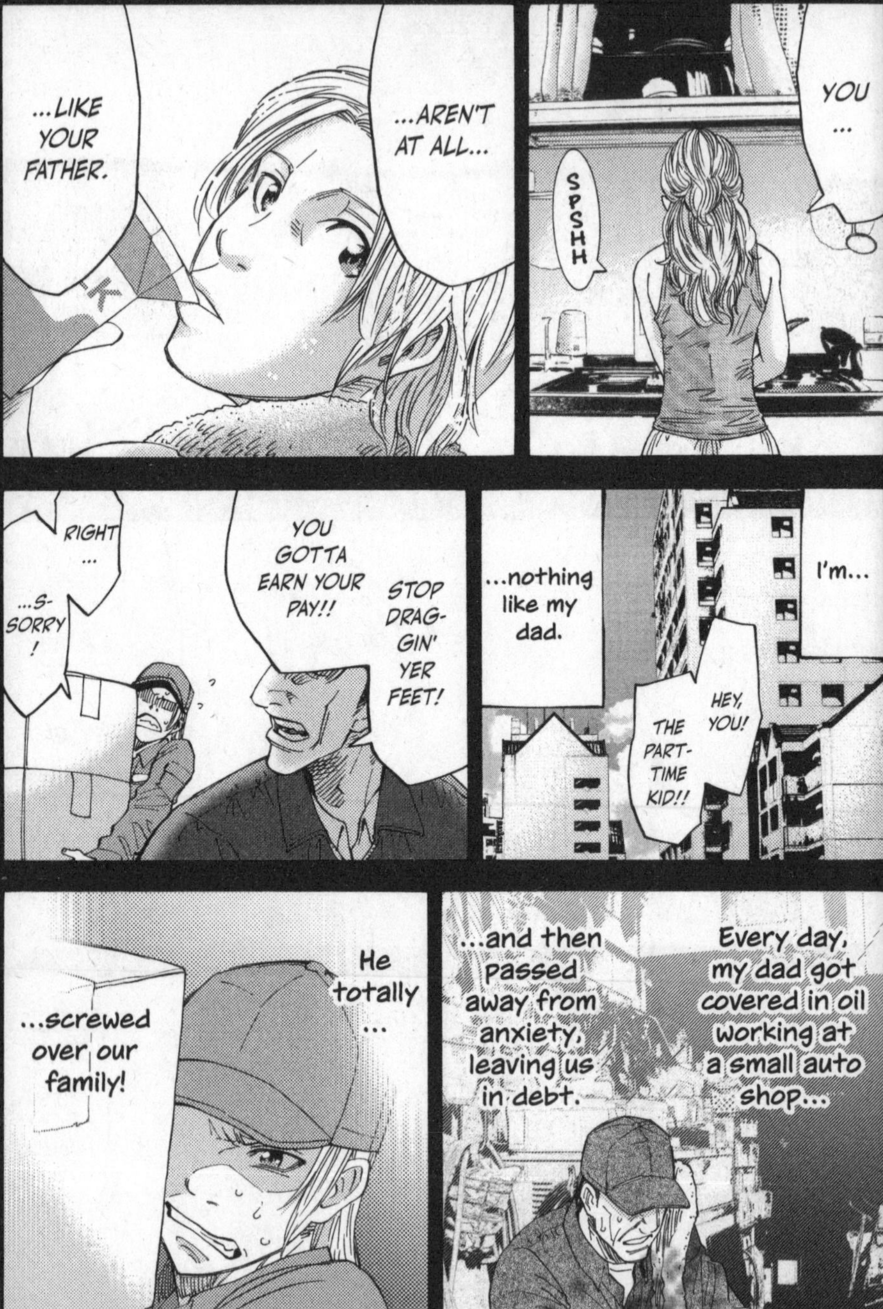
YOU ...
SPSHH
...AREN'T AT ALL...
...LIKE YOUR FATHER.
I'm...
...nothing like my dad.
HEY, YOU!
THE PART-TIME KID!!
YOU GOTTA EARN YOUR PAY!!
STOP DRAG-GIN' YER FEET!
RIGHT ...
...S-SORRY !
Every day, my dad got covered in oil working at a small auto shop...
...and then passed away from anxiety, leaving us in debt.
He totally ...
...screwed over our family!

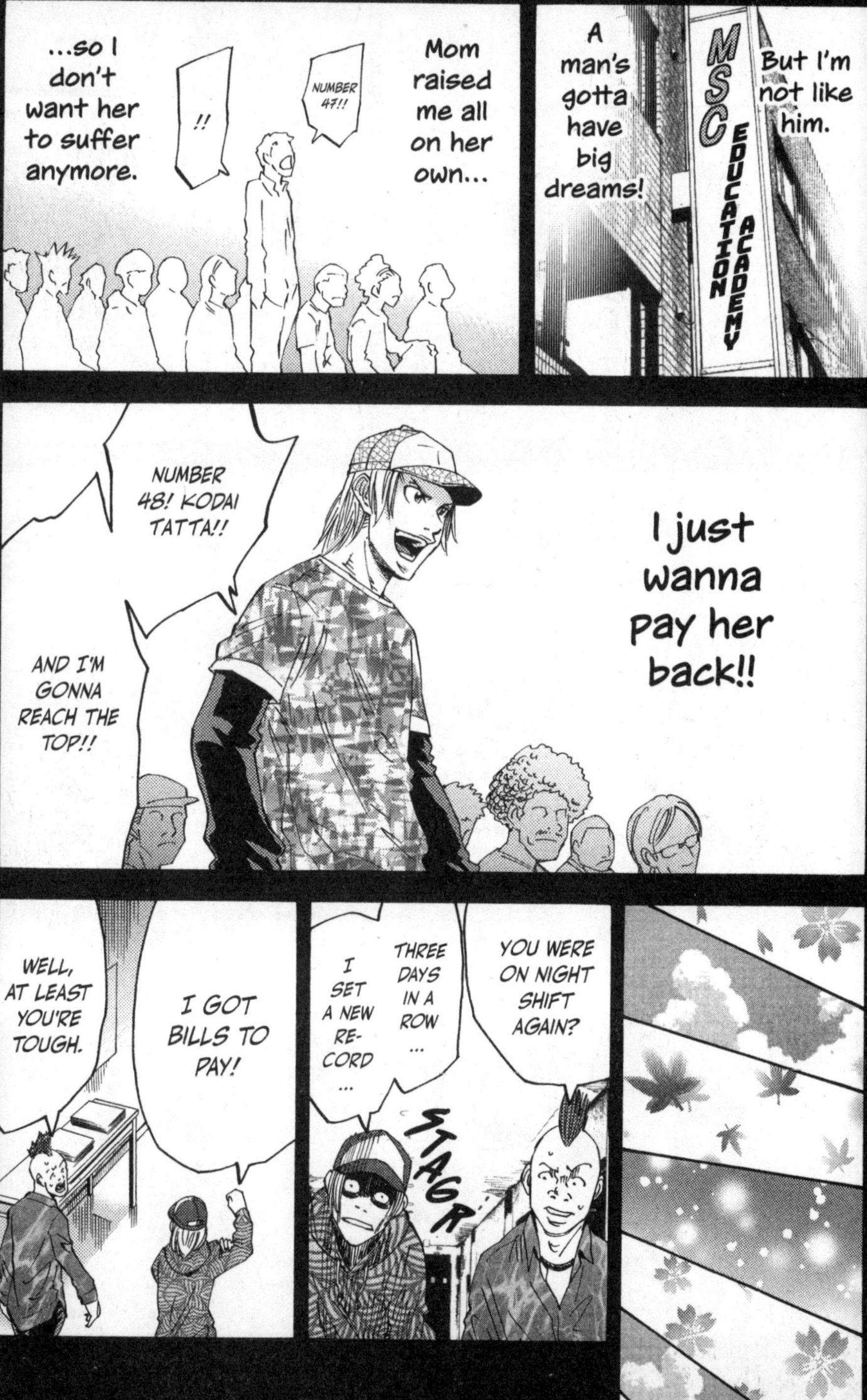
But I'm not like him.
A man's gotta have big dreams!
MSC EDUCATION ACADEMY
Mom raised me all on her own...
NUMBER 47!!
!!
...so I don't want her to suffer anymore.
I just wanna pay her back!!
NUMBER 48! KODAI TATTA!!
AND I'M GONNA REACH THE TOP!!
YOU WERE ON NIGHT SHIFT AGAIN?
THREE DAYS IN A ROW...
I SET A NEW RE-CORD...
STAGR
I GOT BILLS TO PAY!
WELL, AT LEAST YOU'RE TOUGH.

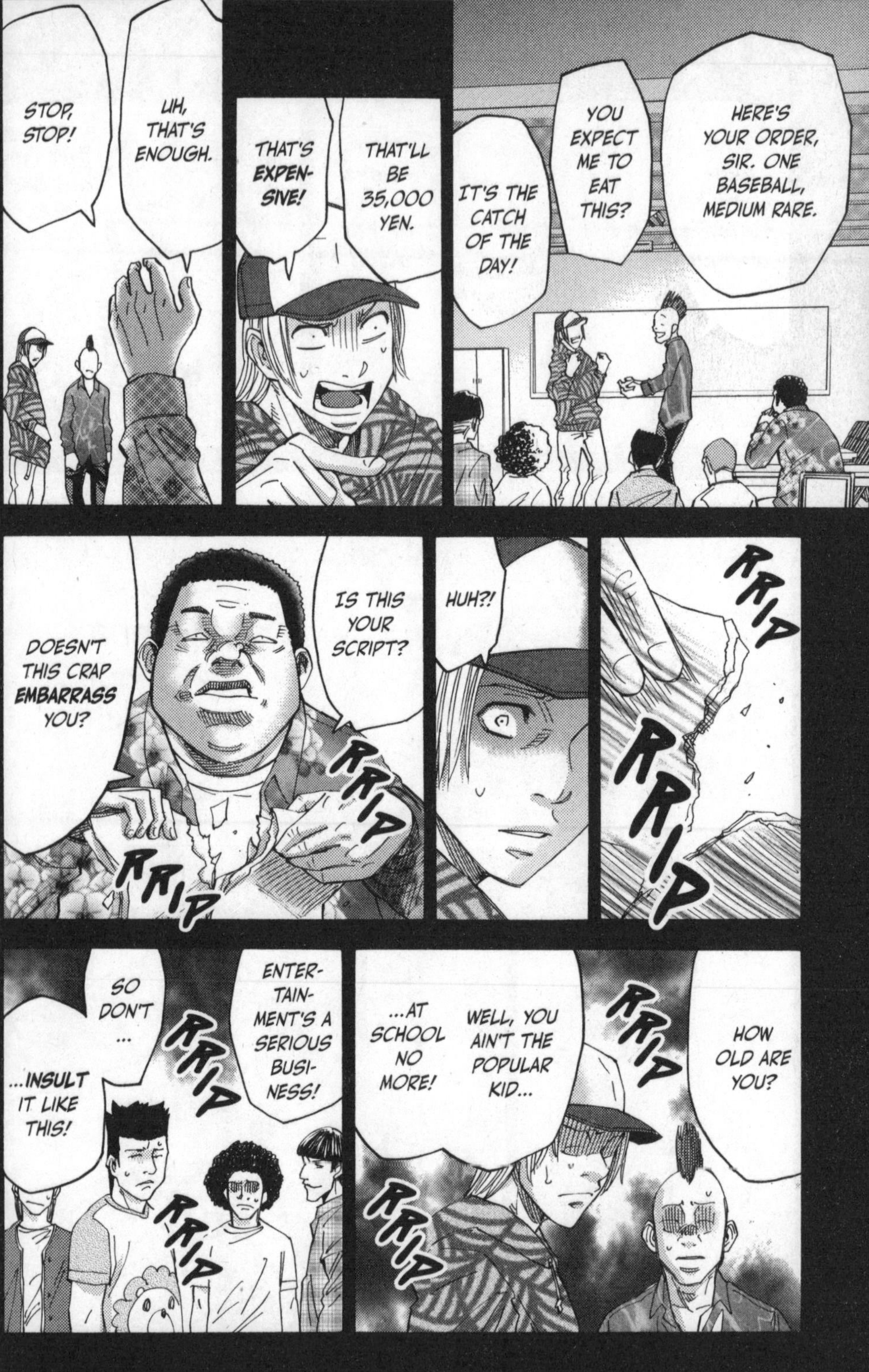
HERE'S YOUR ORDER, SIR. ONE BASEBALL, MEDIUM RARE.
YOU EXPECT ME TO EAT THIS?
IT'S THE CATCH OF THE DAY!
THAT'LL BE 35,000 YEN.
THAT'S **EXPENSIVE!**
UH, THAT'S ENOUGH.
STOP, STOP!
RRIP
RRIP
HUH?!
IS THIS YOUR SCRIPT?
DOESN'T THIS CRAP **EMBARRASS** YOU?
RRIP
RRIP
HOW OLD ARE YOU?
RRIP
WELL, YOU AIN'T THE POPULAR KID...
...AT SCHOOL NO MORE!
RRIP
ENTERTAINMENT'S A SERIOUS BUSINESS!
SO DON'T ...
RRIP
...**INSULT** IT LIKE THIS!
RRIP

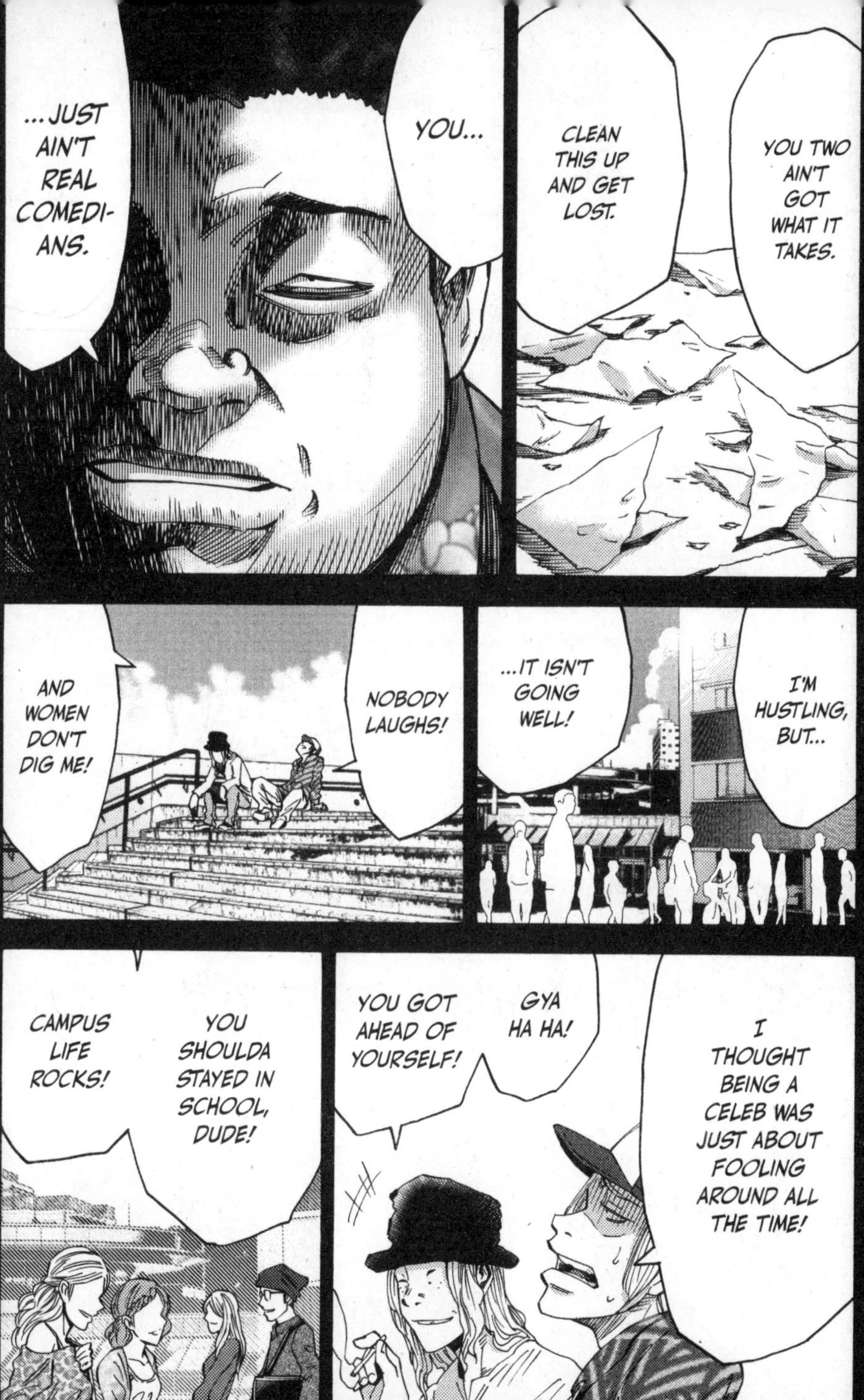
YOU TWO AIN'T GOT WHAT IT TAKES.
CLEAN THIS UP AND GET LOST.
YOU...
...JUST AIN'T REAL COMEDIANS.
I'M HUSTLING, BUT...
...IT ISN'T GOING WELL!
NOBODY LAUGHS!
AND WOMEN DON'T DIG ME!
I THOUGHT BEING A CELEB WAS JUST ABOUT FOOLING AROUND ALL THE TIME!
GYA HA HA!
YOU GOT AHEAD OF YOURSELF!
YOU SHOULDA STAYED IN SCHOOL, DUDE!
CAMPUS LIFE ROCKS!

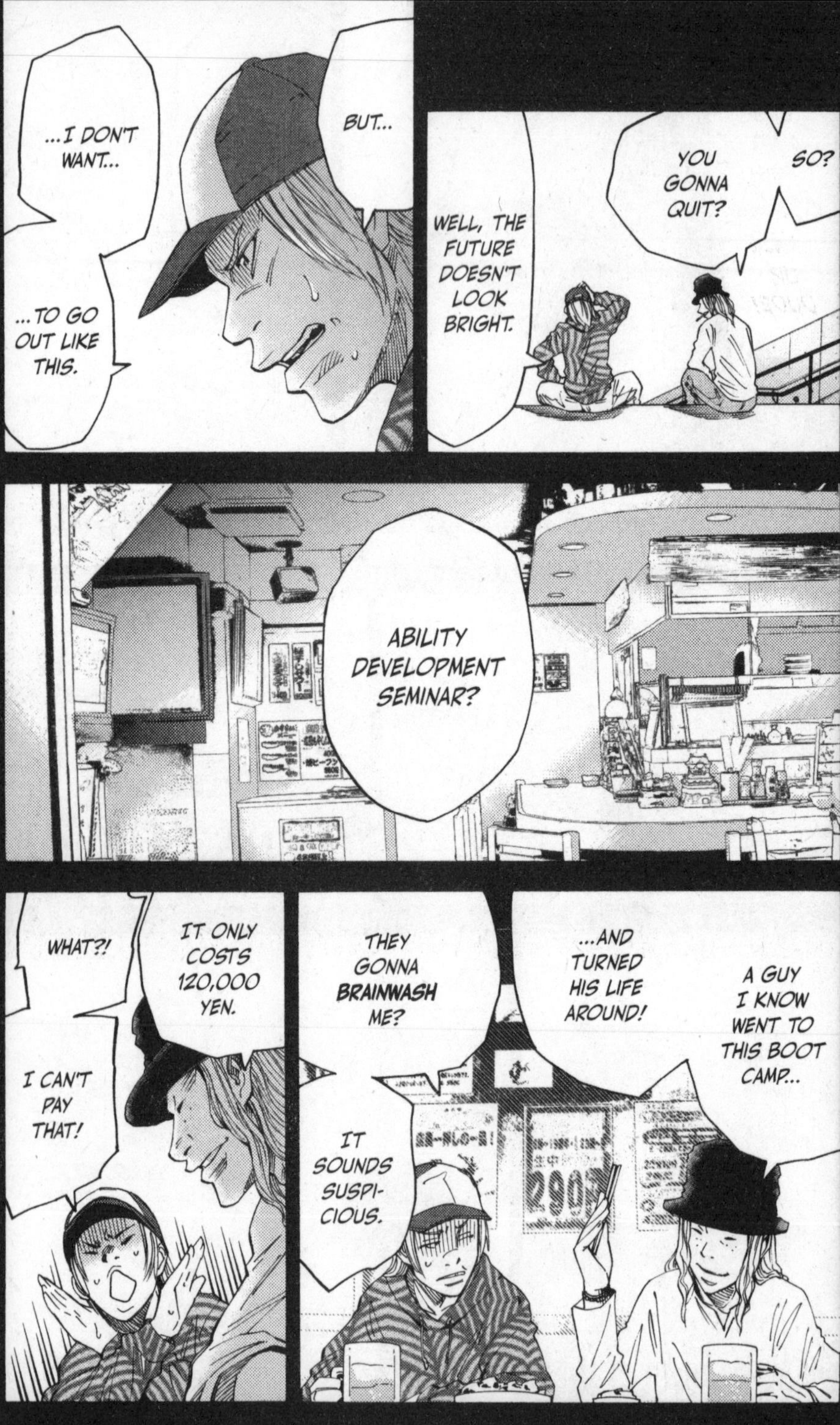
SO?
YOU GONNA QUIT?
WELL, THE FUTURE DOESN'T LOOK BRIGHT.
BUT...
...I DON'T WANT...
...TO GO OUT LIKE THIS.
ABILITY DEVELOPMENT SEMINAR?
A GUY I KNOW WENT TO THIS BOOT CAMP...
...AND TURNED HIS LIFE AROUND!
THEY GONNA **BRAINWASH** ME?
IT SOUNDS SUSPICIOUS.
IT ONLY COSTS 120,000 YEN.
WHAT?!
I CAN'T PAY THAT!

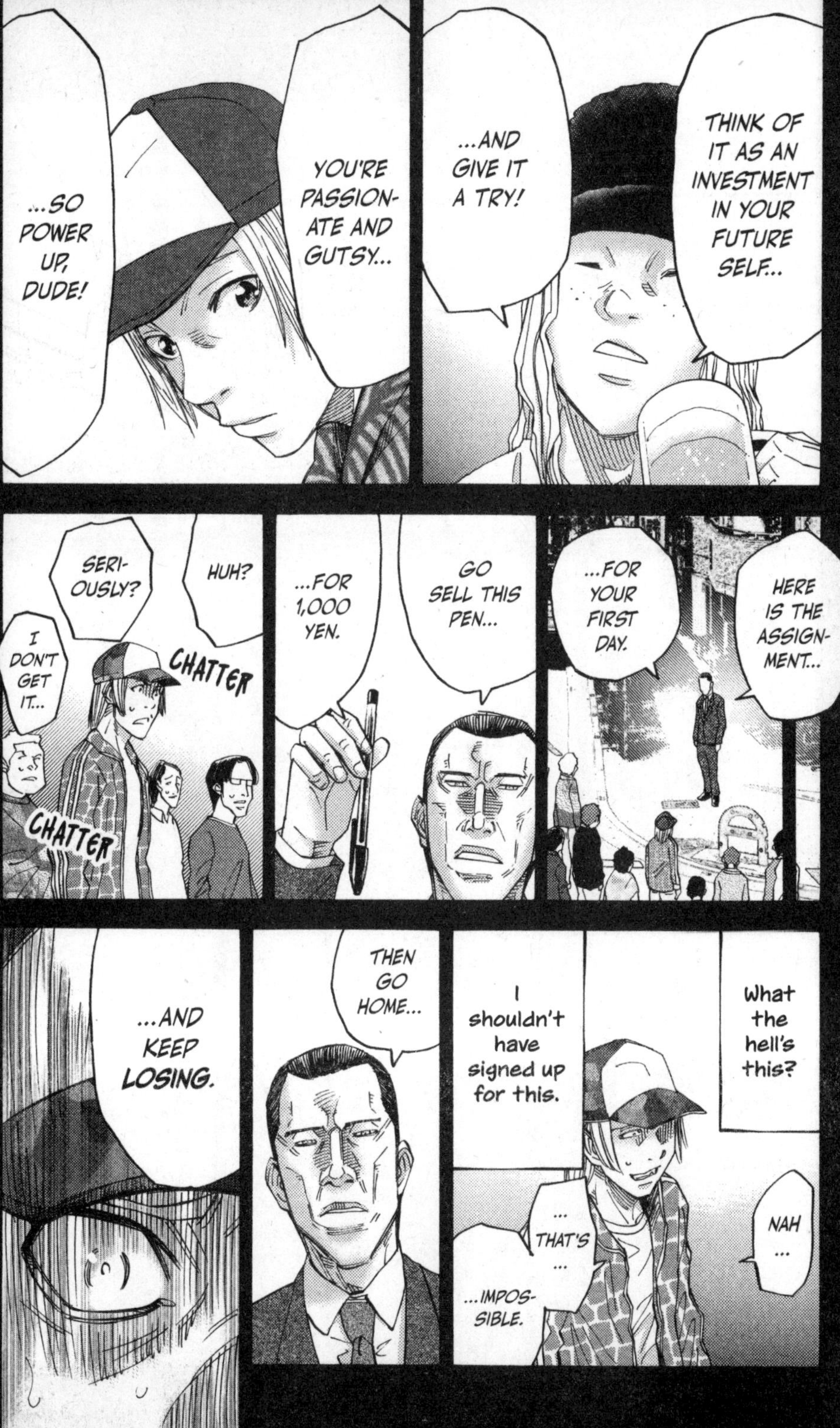
THINK OF IT AS AN INVESTMENT IN YOUR FUTURE SELF...
...AND GIVE IT A TRY!
YOU'RE PASSION-ATE AND GUTSY...
...SO POWER UP, DUDE!
HERE IS THE ASSIGN-MENT...
...FOR YOUR FIRST DAY.
GO SELL THIS PEN...
...FOR 1,000 YEN.
HUH?
SERI-OUSLY?
CHATTER
I DON'T GET IT...
CHATTER
What the hell's this?
I shouldn't have signed up for this.
NAH ...
... THAT'S ...
...IMPOS-SIBLE.
THEN GO HOME...
...AND KEEP LOSING.

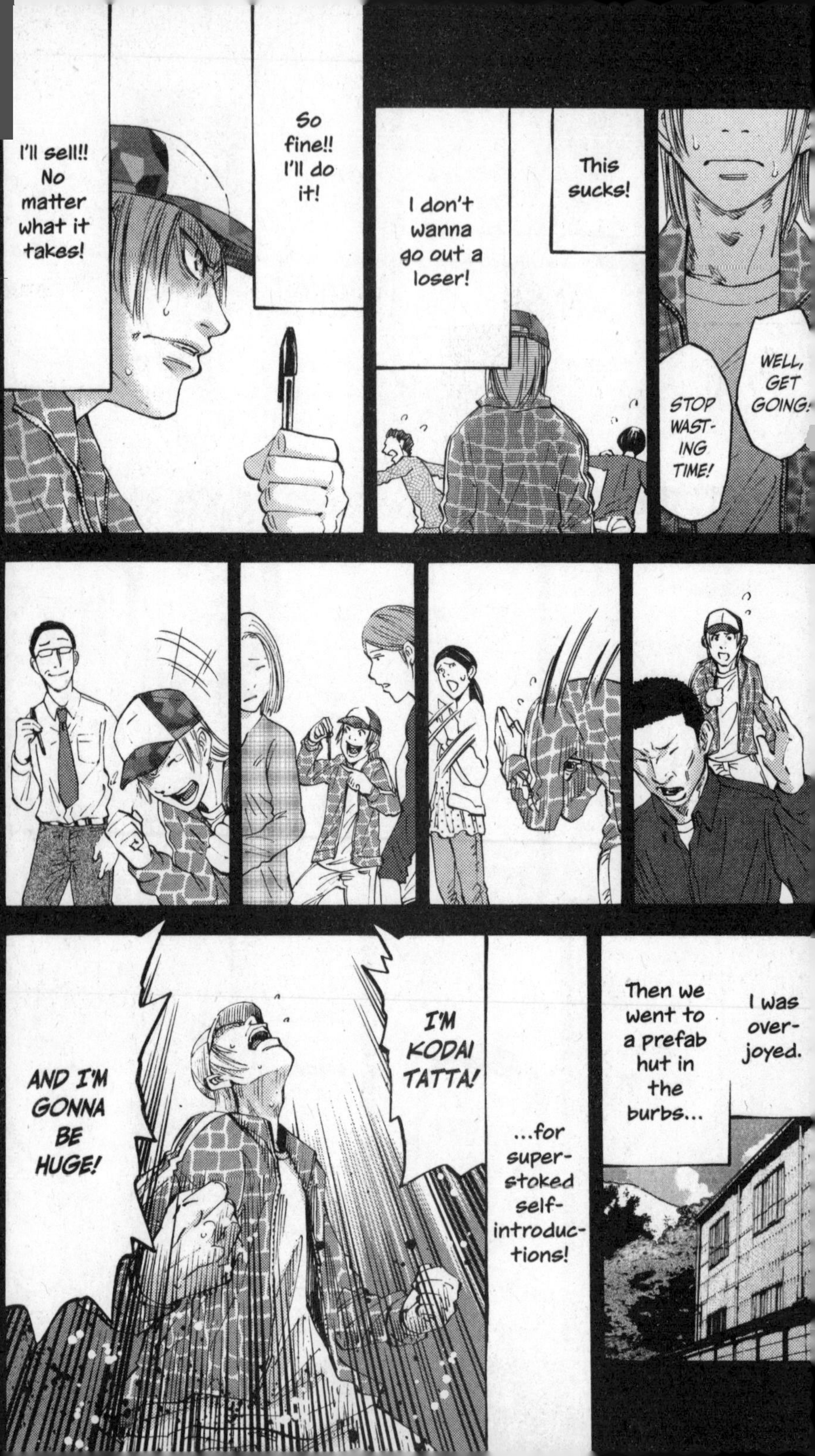
WELL, GET GOING!
STOP WASTING TIME!
This sucks!
I don't wanna go out a loser!
So fine!! I'll do it!
I'll sell!! No matter what it takes!
I was overjoyed.
Then we went to a prefab hut in the burbs...
...for super-stoked self-introductions!
I'M KODAI TATTA!
AND I'M GONNA BE HUGE!

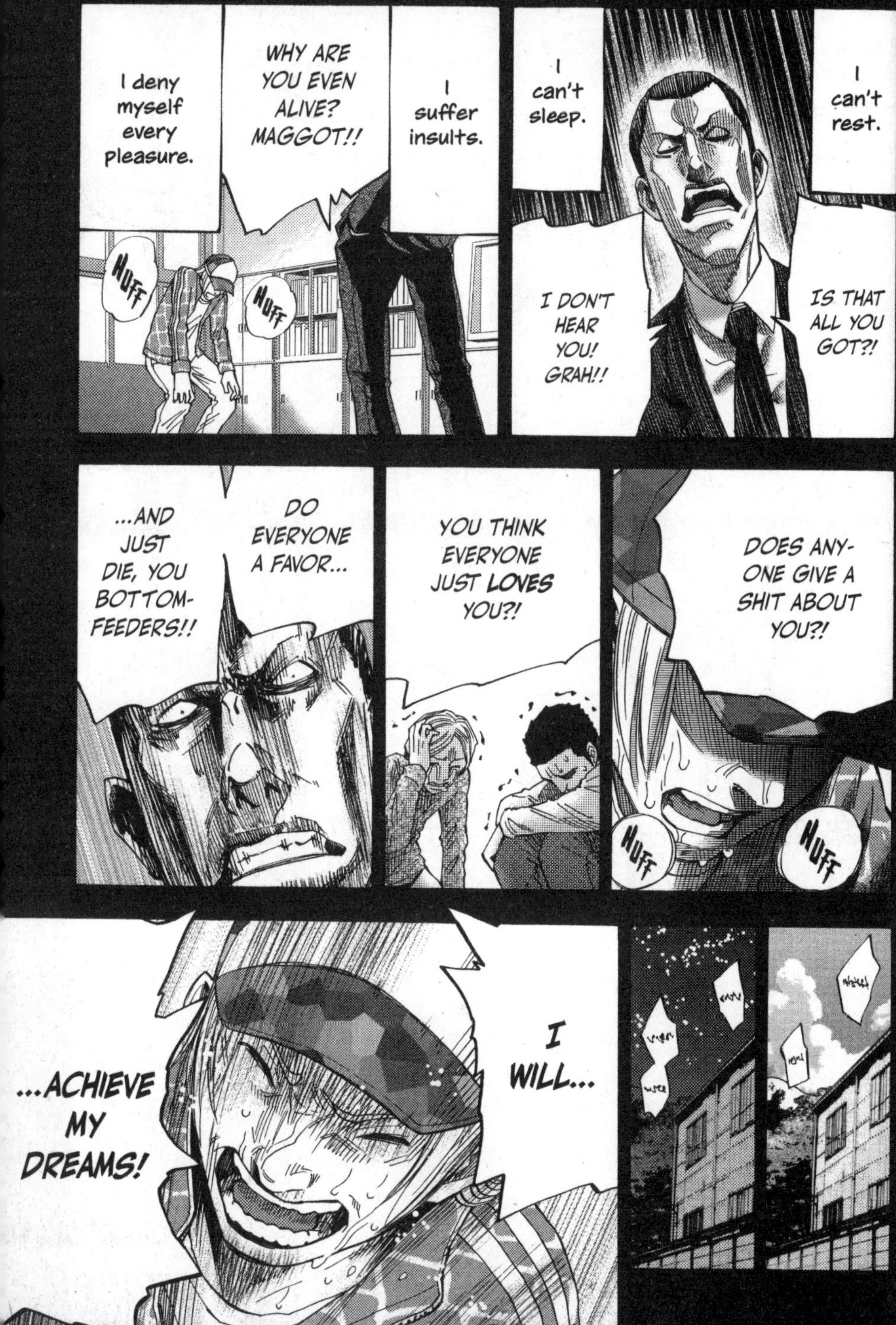

I can't rest.
IS THAT ALL YOU GOT?!
I can't sleep.
I DON'T HEAR YOU! GRAH!!
I suffer insults.
WHY ARE YOU EVEN ALIVE? MAGGOT!!
I deny myself every pleasure.
HUFF
HUFF
DOES ANY-ONE GIVE A SHIT ABOUT YOU?!
HUFF
HUFF
YOU THINK EVERYONE JUST LOVES YOU?!
DO EVERYONE A FAVOR...
...AND JUST DIE, YOU BOTTOM-FEEDERS!!
I WILL...
...ACHIEVE MY DREAMS!

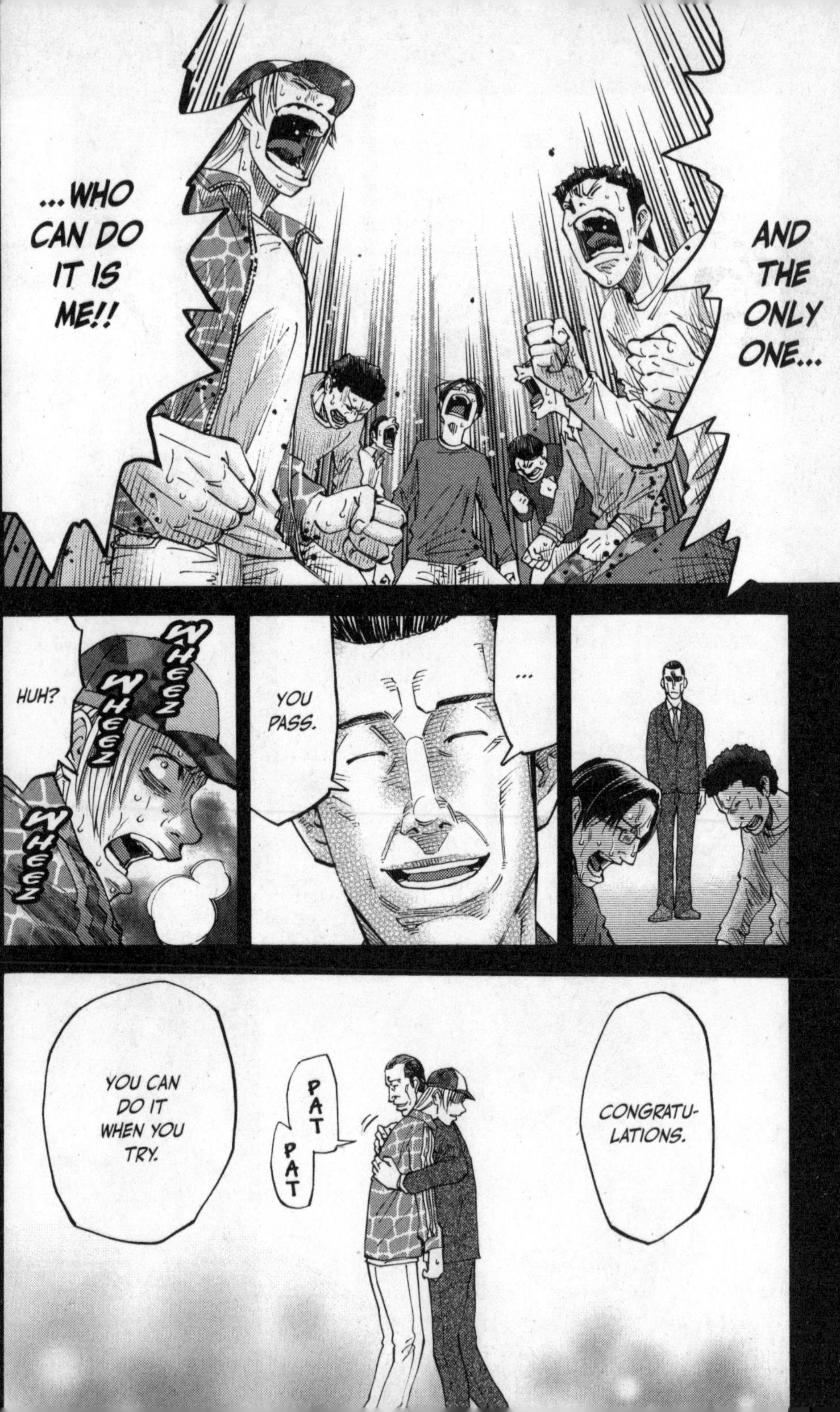
AND THE ONLY ONE...
...WHO CAN DO IT IS ME!!
...
YOU PASS.
WHEEZ
WHEEZ
HUH?
WHEEZ
CONGRATU-LATIONS.
PAT PAT
YOU CAN DO IT WHEN YOU TRY.

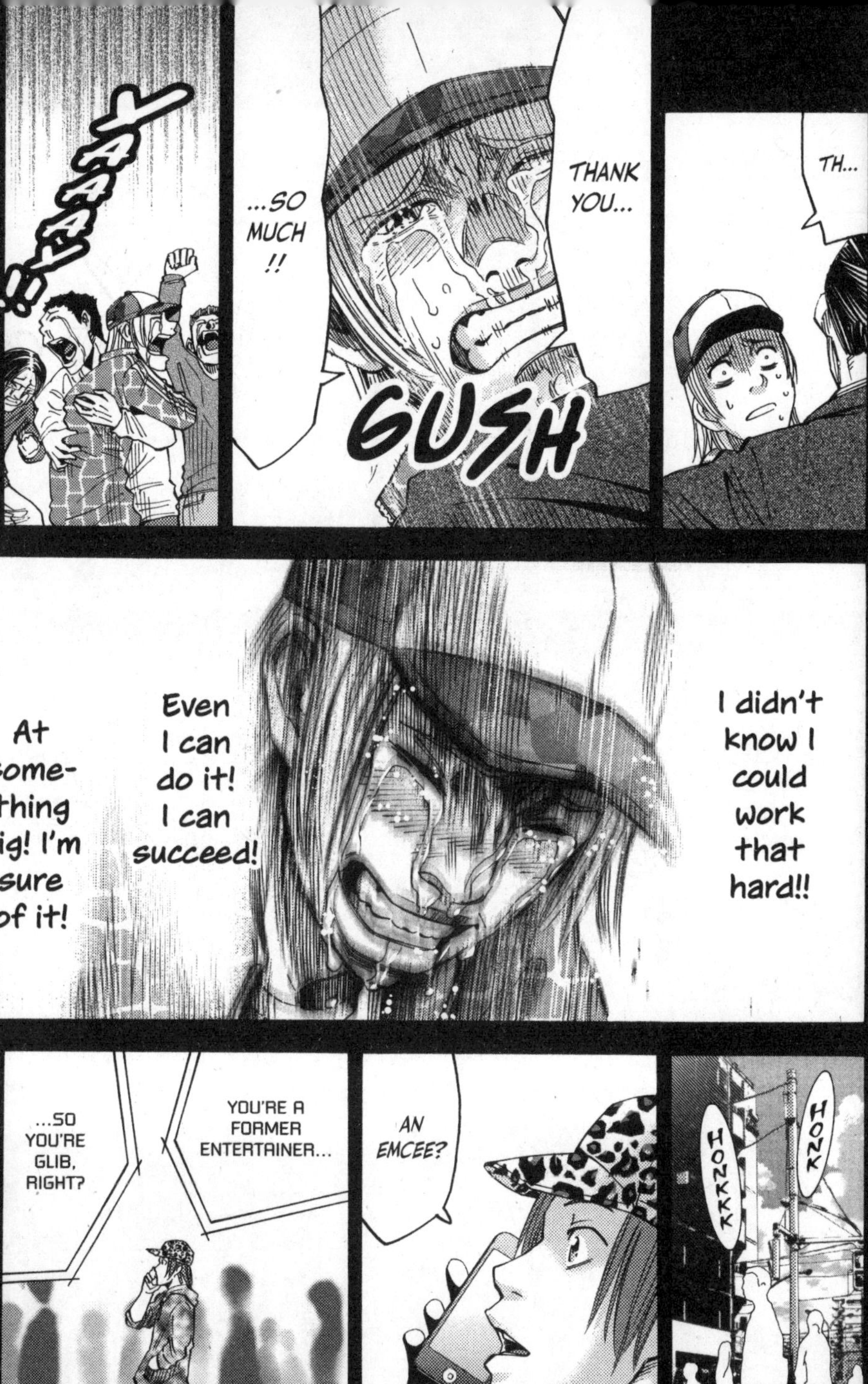
TH...
THANK YOU...
...SO MUCH !!
GUSH
YAAAAY!!
I didn't know I could work that hard!!
Even I can do it! I can succeed!
At some-thing big! I'm sure of it!
HONK
HONKKK
AN EMCEE?
YOU'RE A FORMER ENTERTAINER...
...SO YOU'RE GLIB, RIGHT?

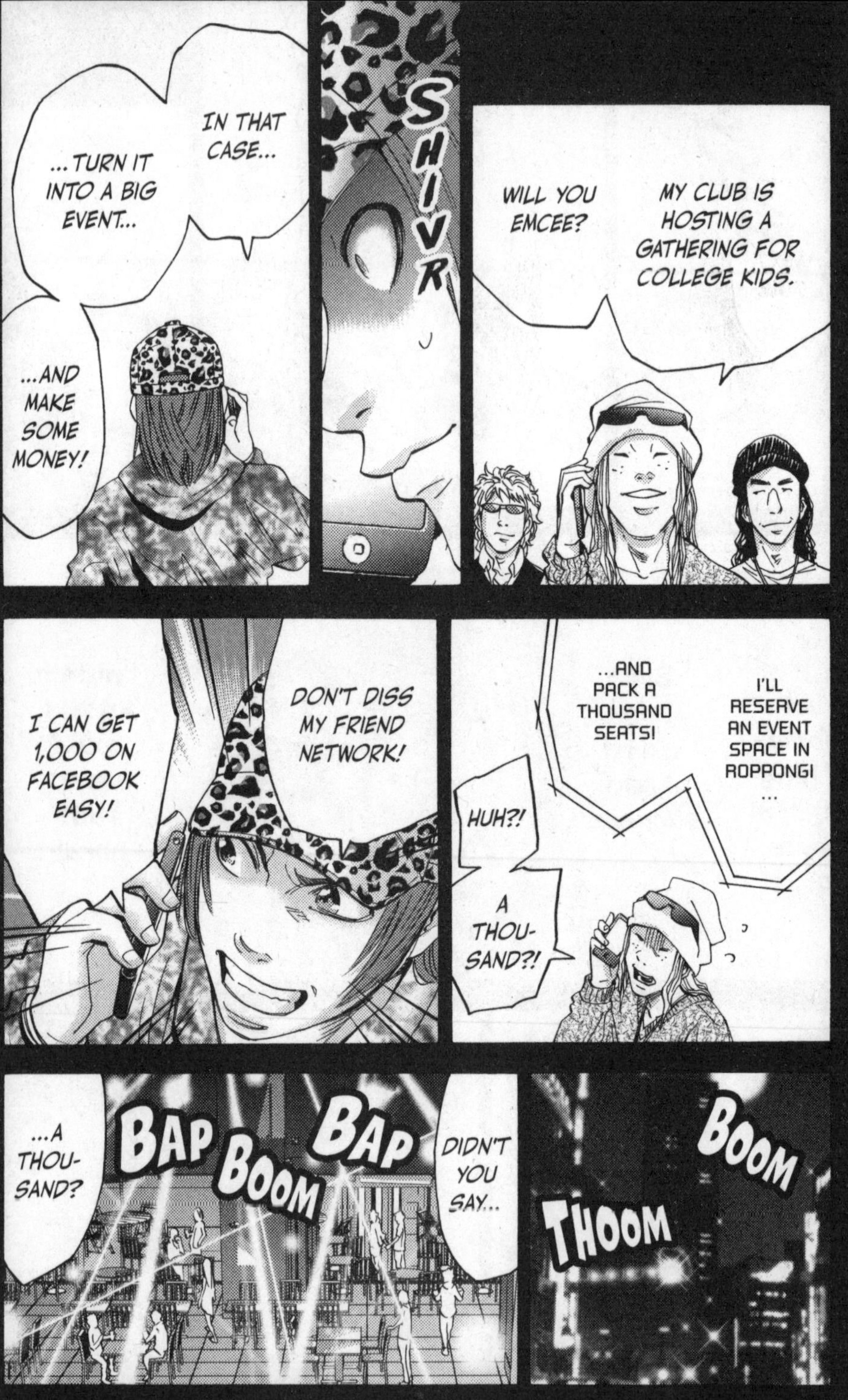
MY CLUB IS HOSTING A GATHERING FOR COLLEGE KIDS.
WILL YOU EMCEE?
SHIVR
IN THAT CASE...
...TURN IT INTO A BIG EVENT...
...AND MAKE SOME MONEY!
I'LL RESERVE AN EVENT SPACE IN ROPPONGI ...
...AND PACK A THOUSAND SEATS!
HUH?!
A THOU-SAND?!
DON'T DISS MY FRIEND NETWORK!
I CAN GET 1,000 ON FACEBOOK EASY!
BOOM
THOOM
DIDN'T YOU SAY...
BAP
BAP
BOOM
...A THOU-SAND?

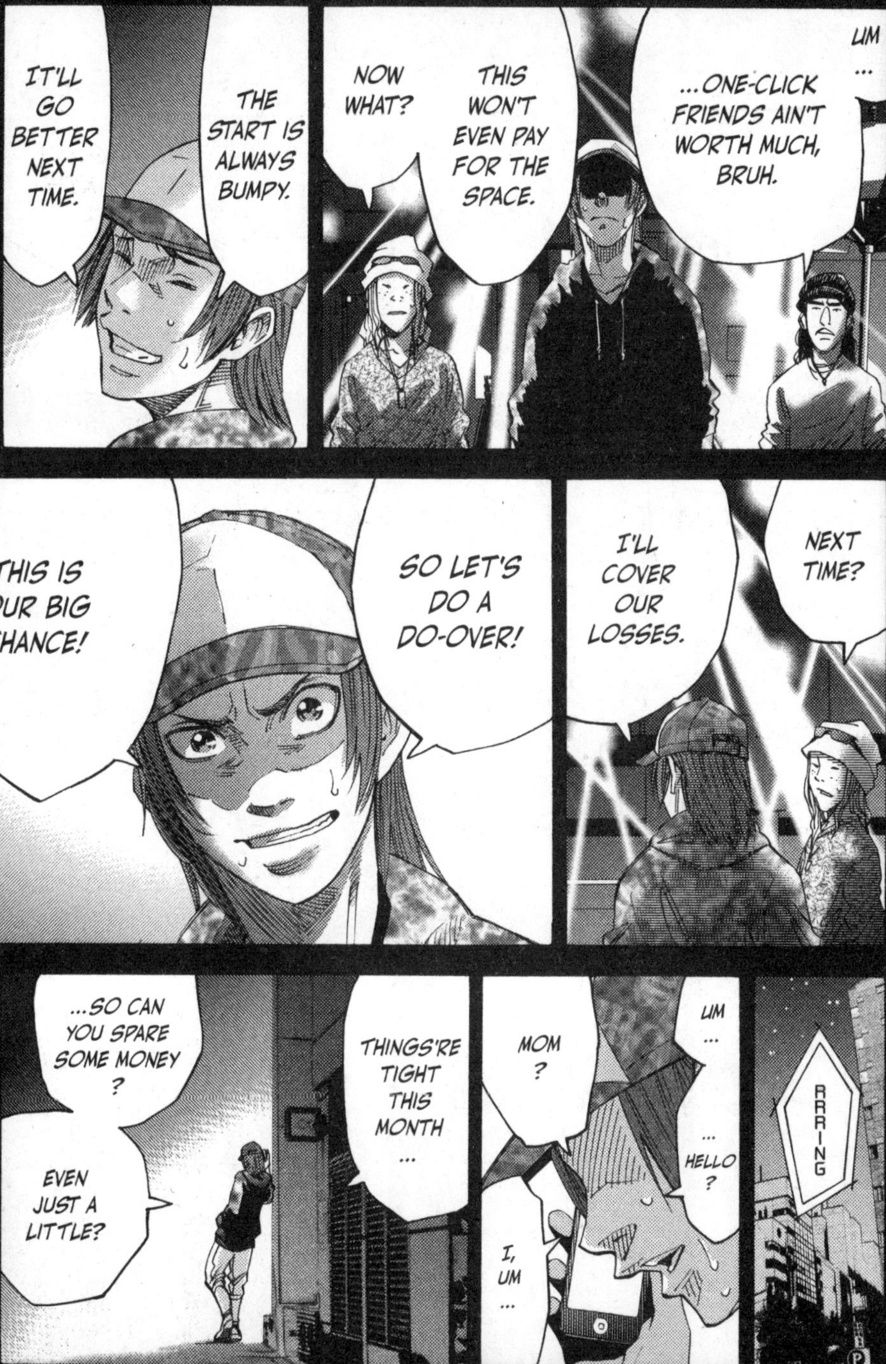
UM ...
...ONE-CLICK FRIENDS AIN'T WORTH MUCH, BRUH.
THIS WON'T EVEN PAY FOR THE SPACE.
NOW WHAT?
THE START IS ALWAYS BUMPY.
IT'LL GO BETTER NEXT TIME.
NEXT TIME?
I'LL COVER OUR LOSSES.
SO LET'S DO A DO-OVER!
THIS IS OUR BIG CHANCE!
RRRING
UM ...
... HELLO ?
MOM ?
I, UM ...
THINGS'RE TIGHT THIS MONTH ...
...SO CAN YOU SPARE SOME MONEY ?
EVEN JUST A LITTLE?

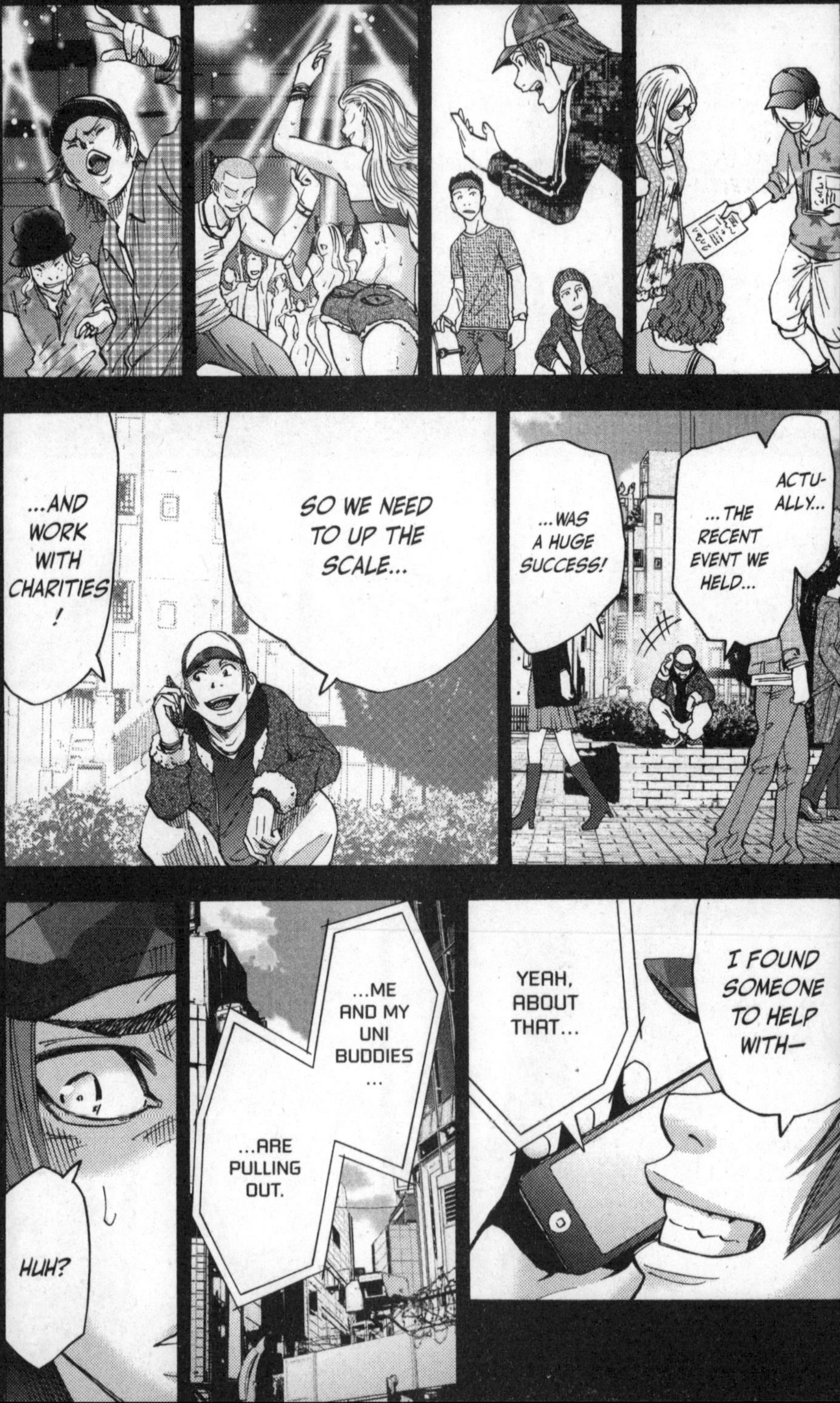
ACTUALLY...
...THE RECENT EVENT WE HELD...
...WAS A HUGE SUCCESS!
SO WE NEED TO UP THE SCALE...
...AND WORK WITH CHARITIES!
I FOUND SOMEONE TO HELP WITH—
YEAH, ABOUT THAT...
...ME AND MY UNI BUDDIES...
...ARE PULLING OUT.
HUH?

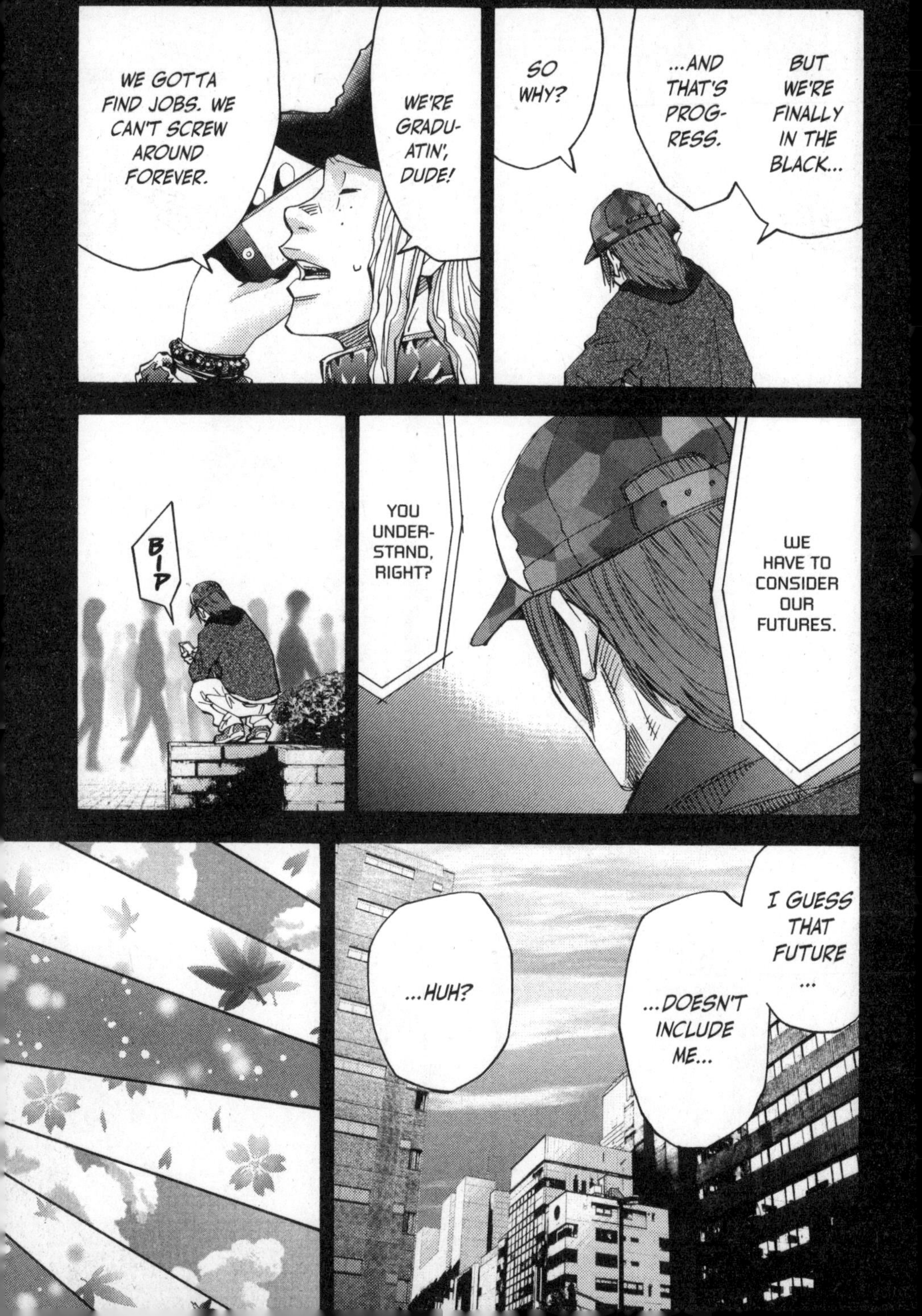
BUT WE'RE FINALLY IN THE BLACK...
...AND THAT'S PROG-RESS.
SO WHY?
WE'RE GRADU-ATIN', DUDE!
WE GOTTA FIND JOBS. WE CAN'T SCREW AROUND FOREVER.
WE HAVE TO CONSIDER OUR FUTURES.
YOU UNDER-STAND, RIGHT?
BIP
I GUESS THAT FUTURE ...
...DOESN'T INCLUDE ME...
...HUH?

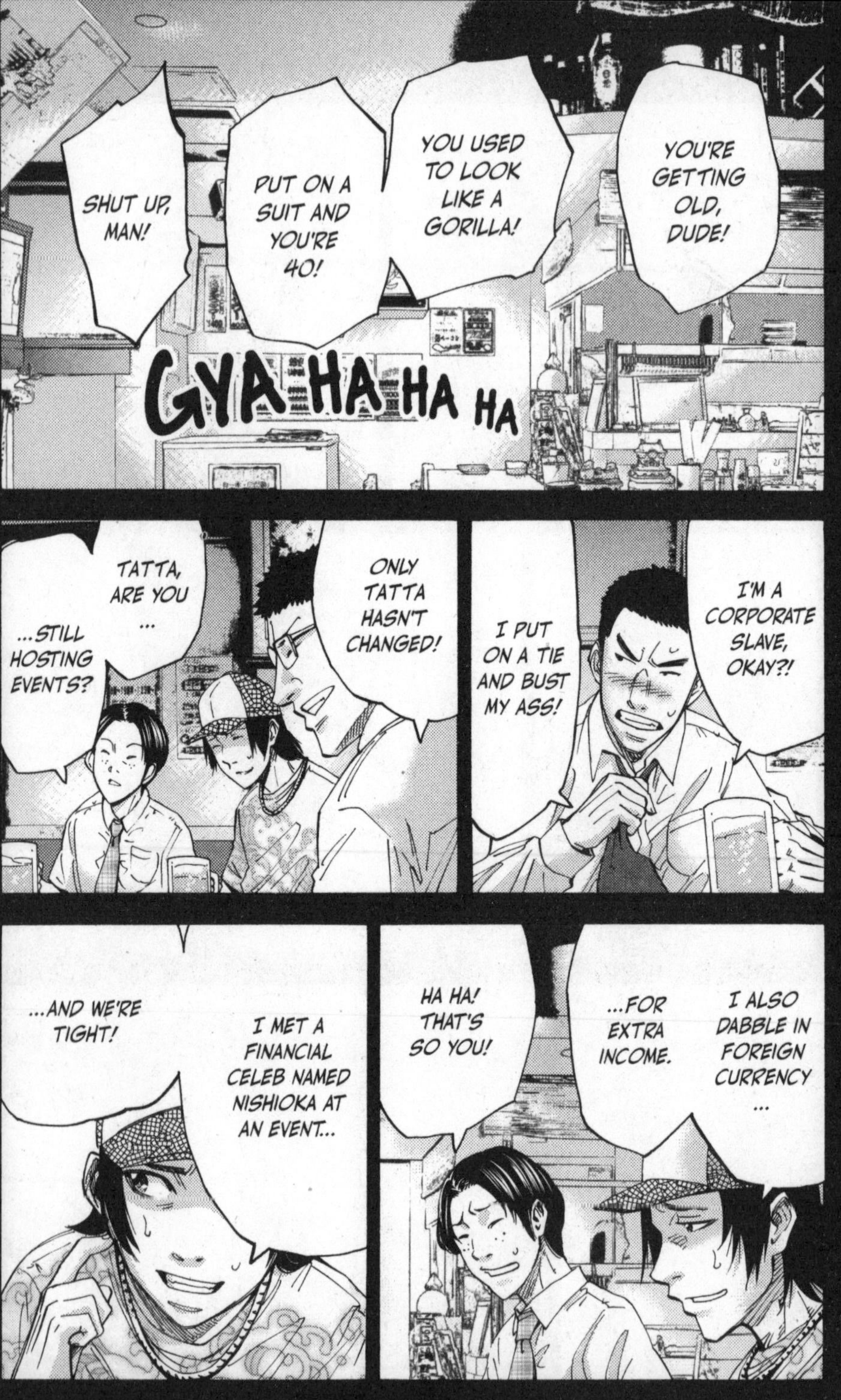

YOU'RE GETTING OLD, DUDE!
YOU USED TO LOOK LIKE A GORILLA!
PUT ON A SUIT AND YOU'RE 40!
SHUT UP, MAN!
GYA HA HA HA
I'M A CORPORATE SLAVE, OKAY?!
I PUT ON A TIE AND BUST MY ASS!
ONLY TATTA HASN'T CHANGED!
TATTA, ARE YOU ...
...STILL HOSTING EVENTS?
I ALSO DABBLE IN FOREIGN CURRENCY ...
...FOR EXTRA INCOME.
HA HA! THAT'S SO YOU!
I MET A FINANCIAL CELEB NAMED NISHIOKA AT AN EVENT...
...AND WE'RE TIGHT!

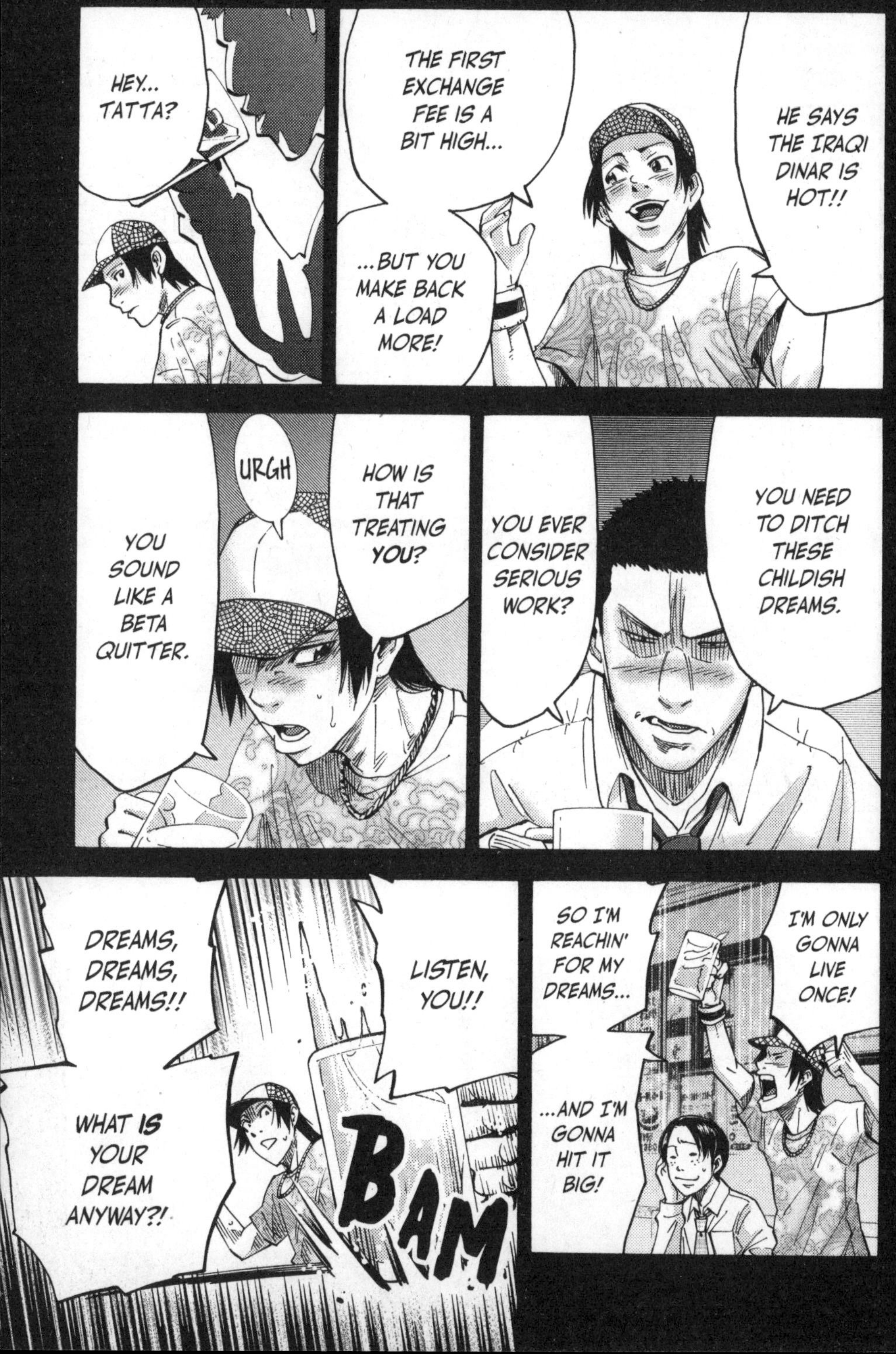
HE SAYS THE IRAQI DINAR IS HOT!!
THE FIRST EXCHANGE FEE IS A BIT HIGH...
...BUT YOU MAKE BACK A LOAD MORE!
HEY... TATTA?
YOU NEED TO DITCH THESE CHILDISH DREAMS.
YOU EVER CONSIDER SERIOUS WORK?
HOW IS THAT TREATING YOU?
URGH
YOU SOUND LIKE A BETA QUITTER.
I'M ONLY GONNA LIVE ONCE!
SO I'M REACHIN' FOR MY DREAMS...
...AND I'M GONNA HIT IT BIG!
LISTEN, YOU!!
BAM
DREAMS, DREAMS, DREAMS!!
WHAT IS YOUR DREAM ANYWAY?!

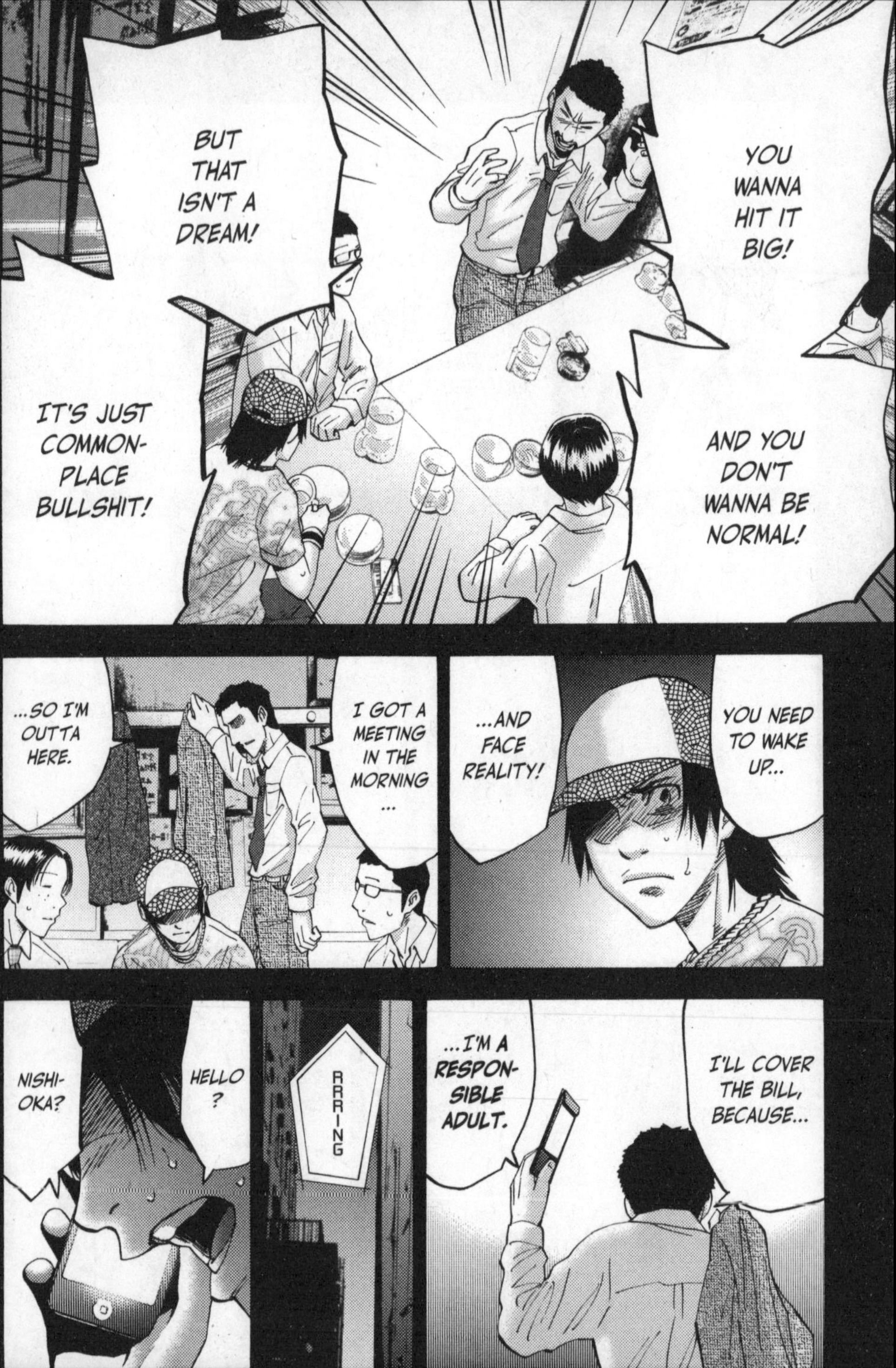
YOU WANNA HIT IT BIG!
AND YOU DON'T WANNA BE NORMAL!
BUT THAT ISN'T A DREAM!
IT'S JUST COMMONPLACE BULLSHIT!
YOU NEED TO WAKE UP...
...AND FACE REALITY!
I GOT A MEETING IN THE MORNING...
...SO I'M OUTTA HERE.
I'LL COVER THE BILL, BECAUSE...
...I'M A RESPONSIBLE ADULT.
RRRING
HELLO?
NISHIOKA?

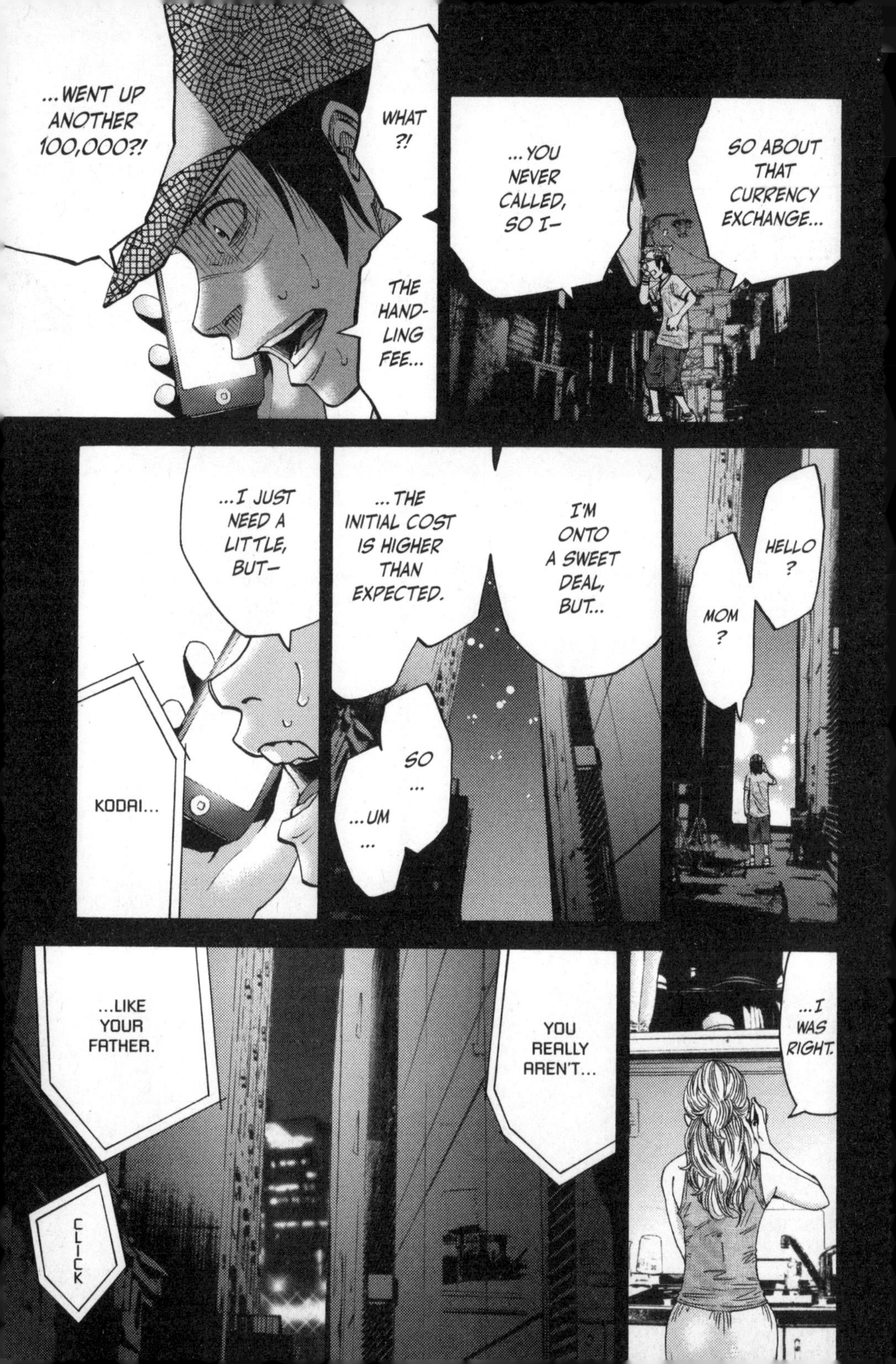
SO ABOUT THAT CURRENCY EXCHANGE...
...YOU NEVER CALLED, SO I—
WHAT ?!
THE HAND-LING FEE...
...WENT UP ANOTHER 100,000?!
HELLO ?
MOM ?
I'M ONTO A SWEET DEAL, BUT...
...THE INITIAL COST IS HIGHER THAN EXPECTED.
SO ...
...UM ...
...I JUST NEED A LITTLE, BUT—
KODAI...
...I WAS RIGHT.
YOU REALLY AREN'T...
...LIKE YOUR FATHER.
CLICK

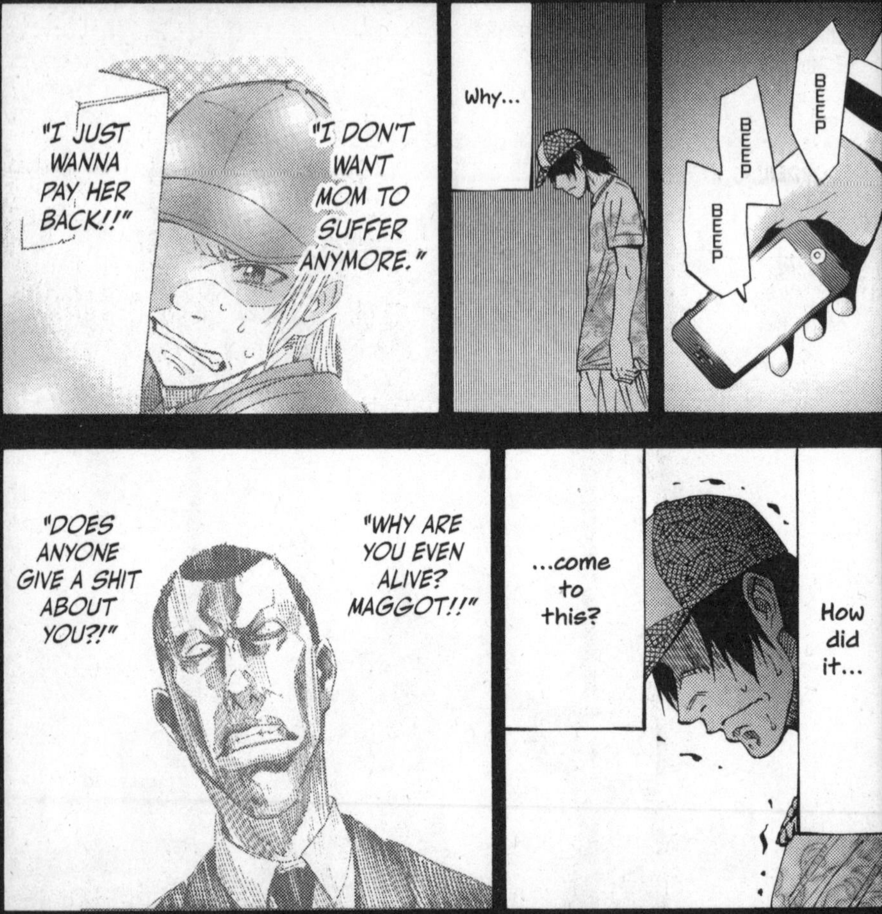
BEEP
BEEP
BEEP
Why...
"I DON'T WANT MOM TO SUFFER ANYMORE."
"I JUST WANNA PAY HER BACK!!"
How did it...
...come to this?
"WHY ARE YOU EVEN ALIVE? MAGGOT!!"
"DOES ANYONE GIVE A SHIT ABOUT YOU?!"

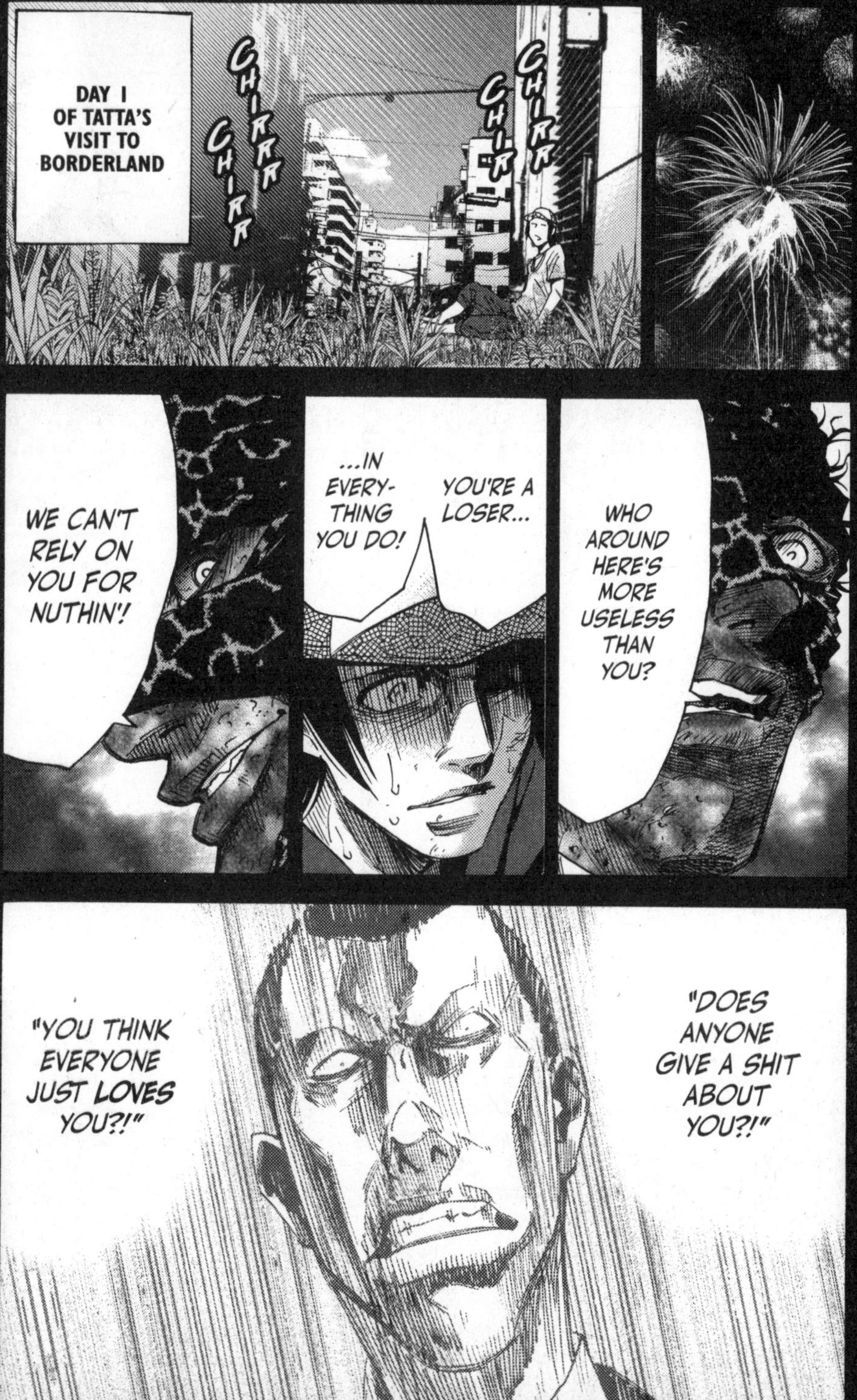
CHIRR CHIRR CHIRR
CHIRR CHIRR
DAY 1 OF TATTA'S VISIT TO BORDERLAND
WHO AROUND HERE'S MORE USELESS THAN YOU?
YOU'RE A LOSER...
...IN EVERY-THING YOU DO!
WE CAN'T RELY ON YOU FOR NUTHIN'!
"DOES ANYONE GIVE A SHIT ABOUT YOU?!"
"YOU THINK EVERYONE JUST LOVES YOU?!"

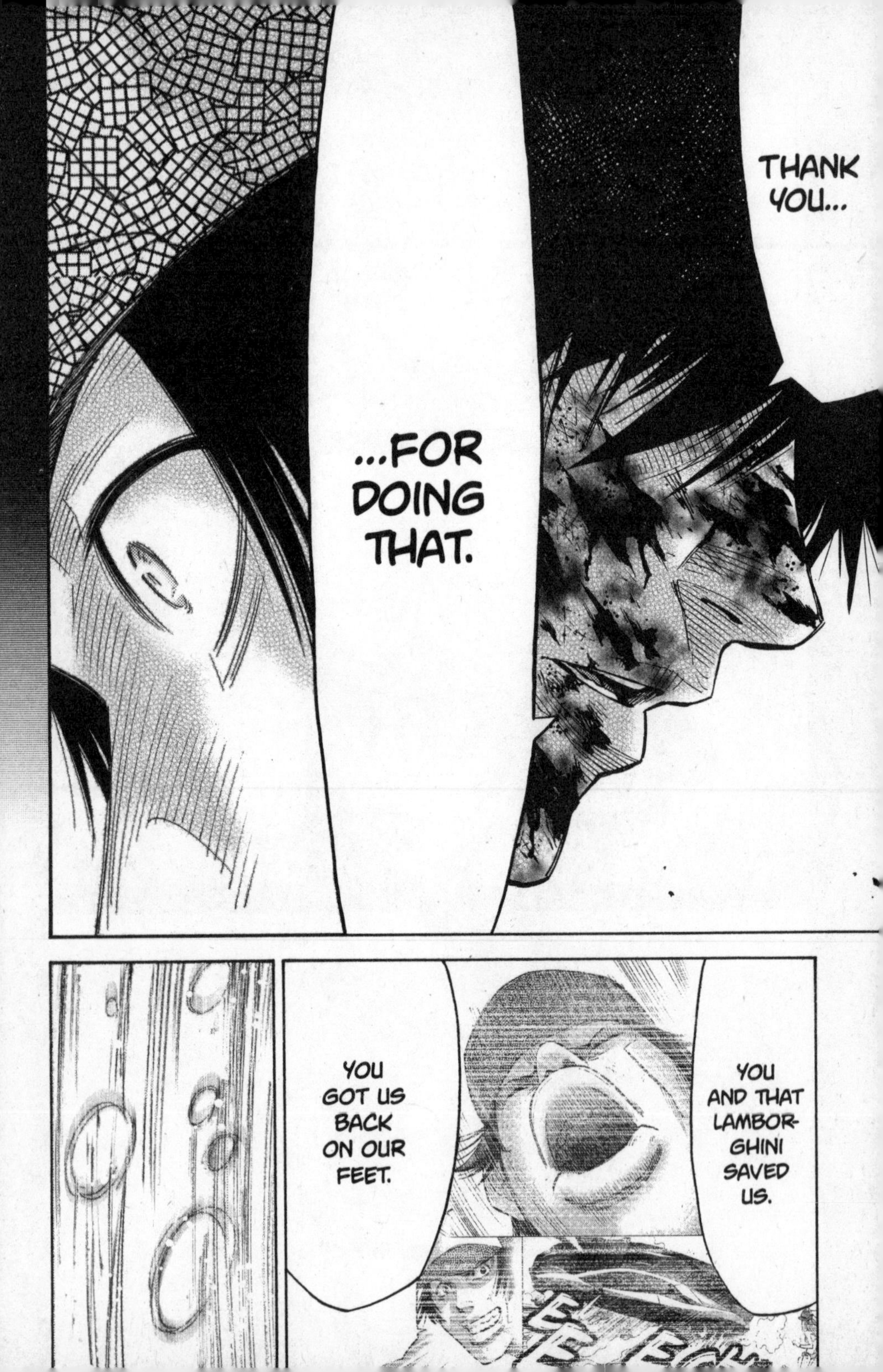
THANK YOU...
...FOR DOING THAT.
YOU AND THAT LAMBOR-GHINI SAVED US.
YOU GOT US BACK ON OUR FEET.

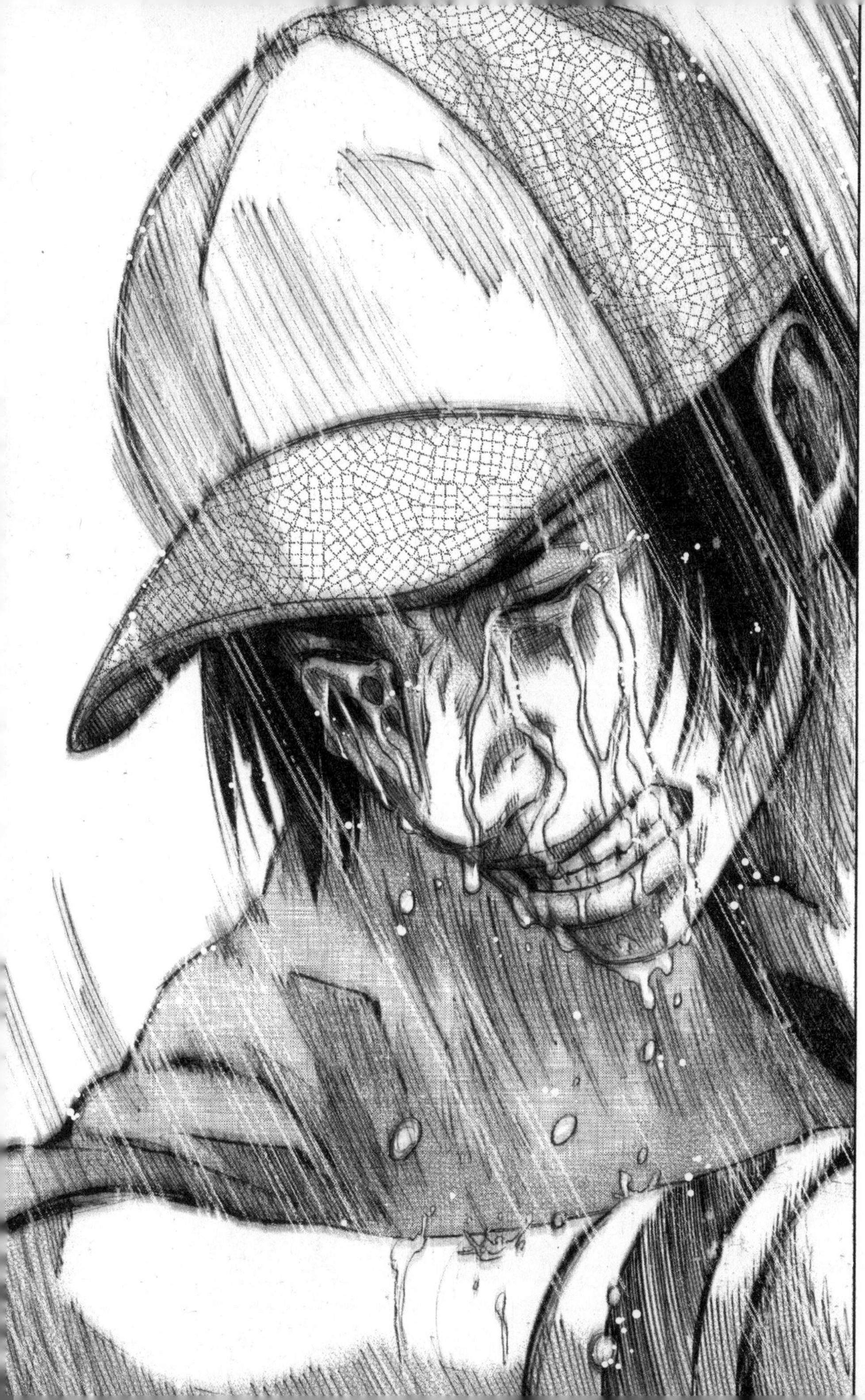

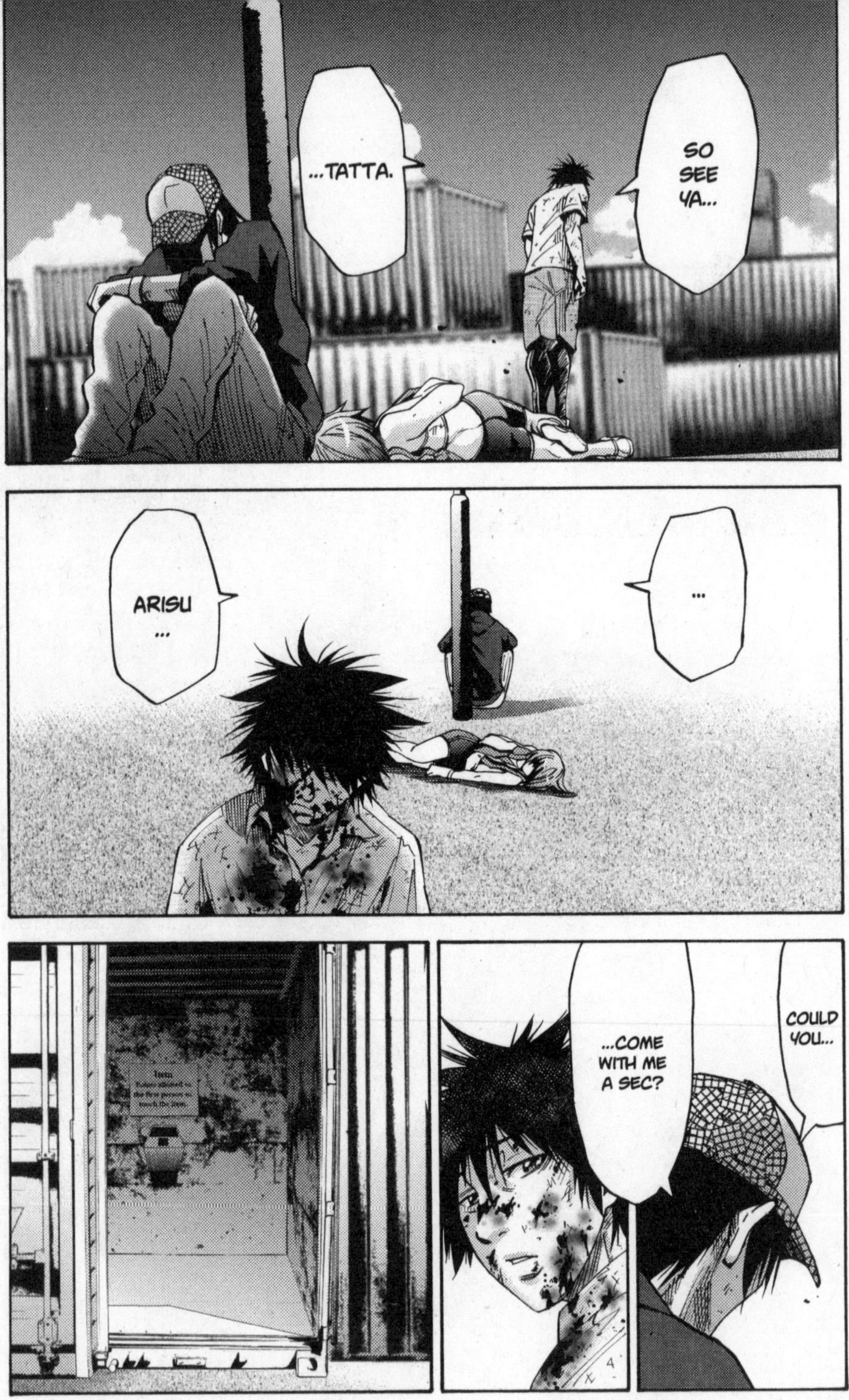
SO SEE YA...
...TATTA.
...
ARISU ...
COULD YOU...
...COME WITH ME A SEC?

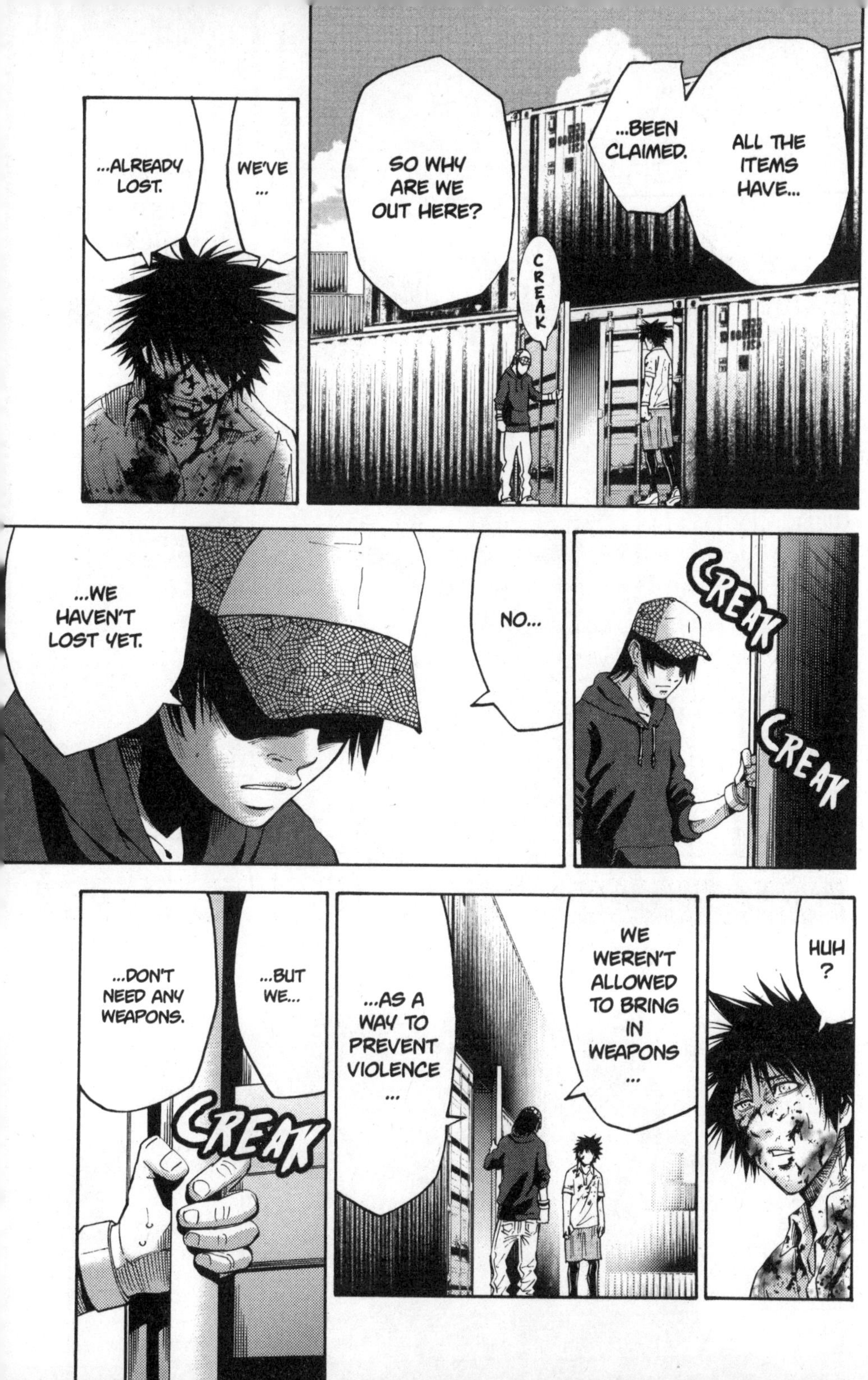
ALL THE ITEMS HAVE...
...BEEN CLAIMED.
SO WHY ARE WE OUT HERE?
CREAK
WE'VE ...
...ALREADY LOST.
CREAK
CREAK
NO...
...WE HAVEN'T LOST YET.
HUH ?
WE WEREN'T ALLOWED TO BRING IN WEAPONS ...
...AS A WAY TO PREVENT VIOLENCE ...
...BUT WE...
...DON'T NEED ANY WEAPONS.
CREAK

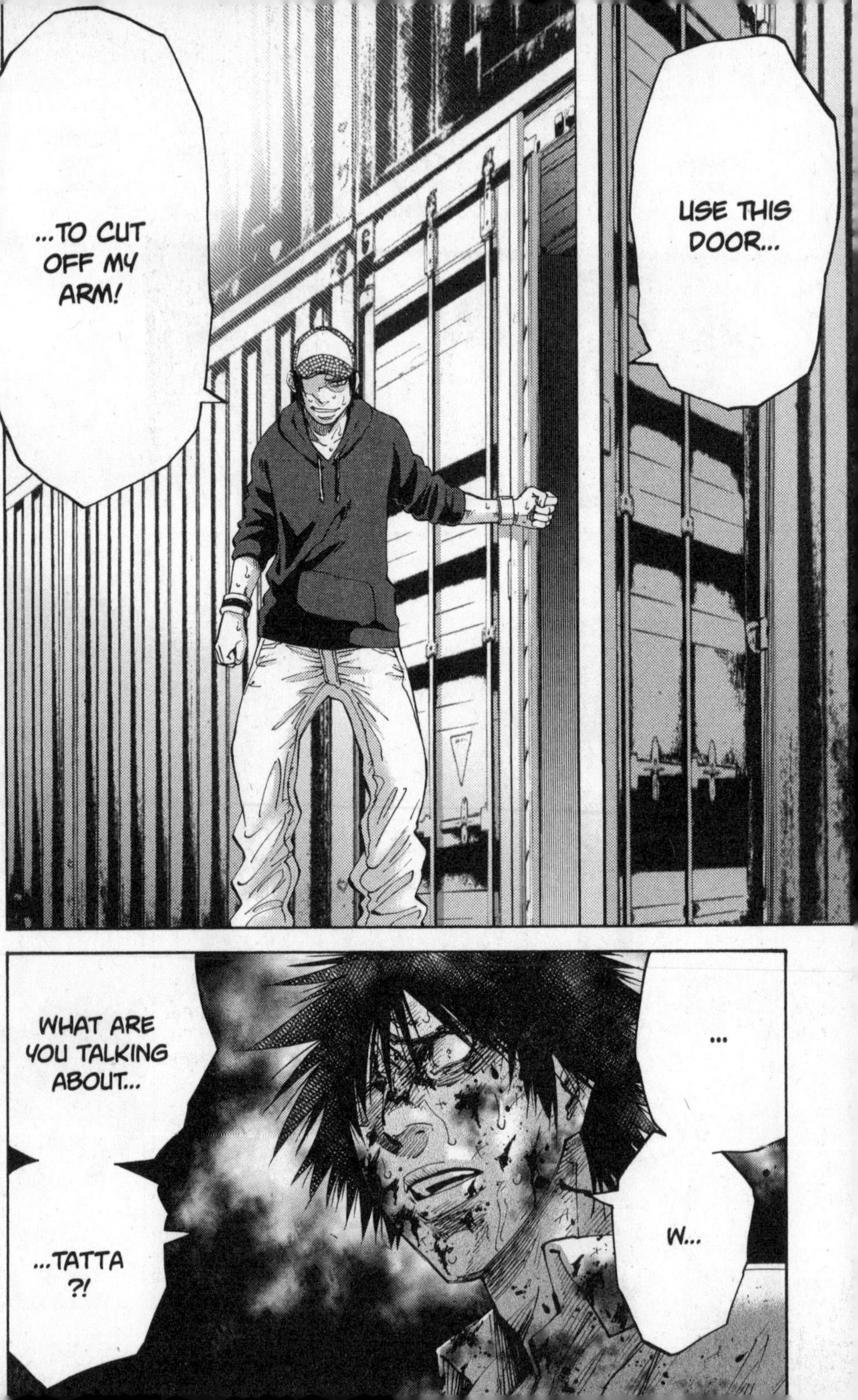
USE THIS DOOR...
...TO CUT OFF MY ARM!
...
W...
WHAT ARE YOU TALKING ABOUT...
...TATTA ?!

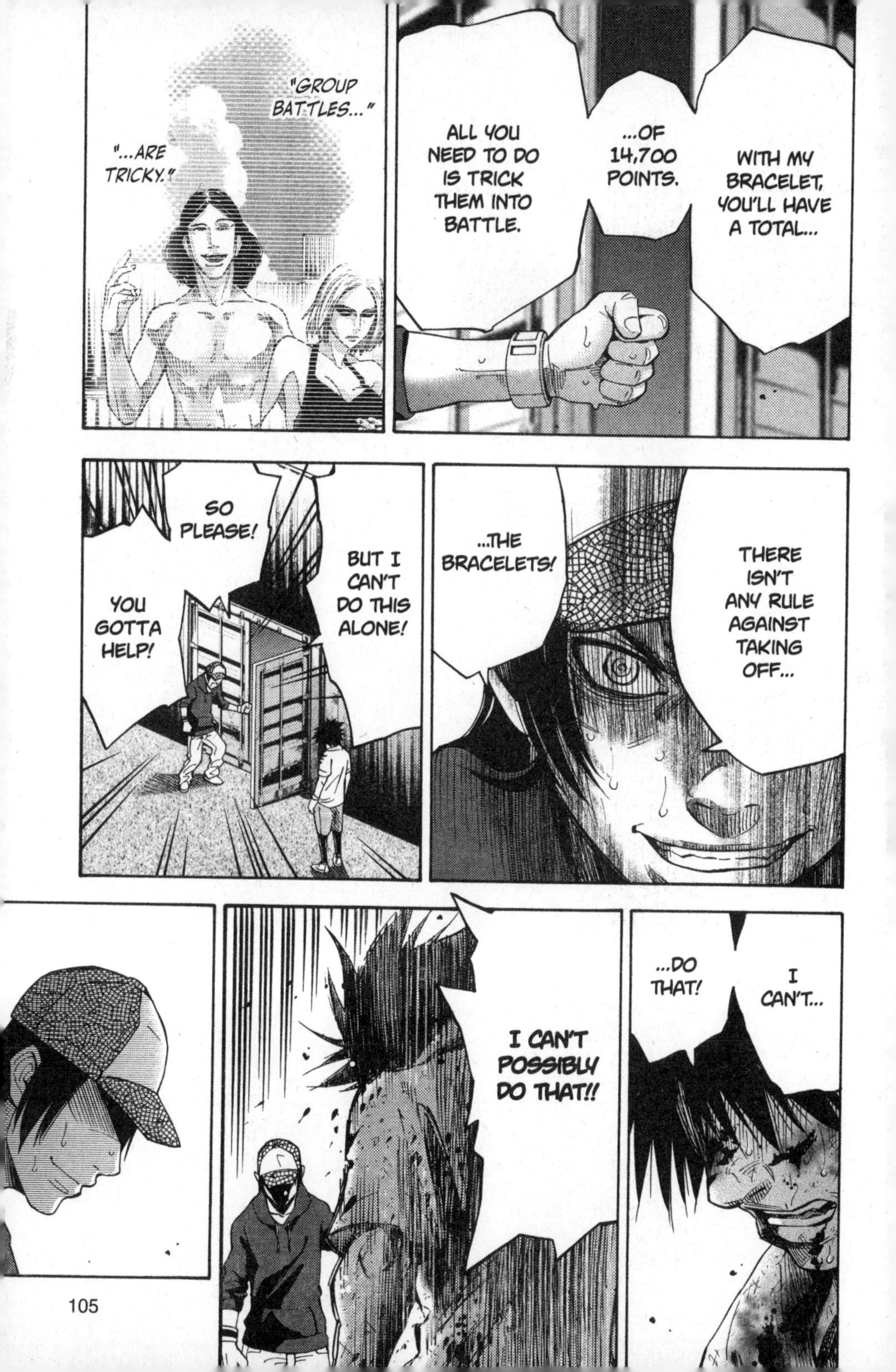
WITH MY BRACELET, YOU'LL HAVE A TOTAL...
...OF 14,700 POINTS.
ALL YOU NEED TO DO IS TRICK THEM INTO BATTLE.
"GROUP BATTLES..."
"...ARE TRICKY."
THERE ISN'T ANY RULE AGAINST TAKING OFF...
...THE BRACELETS!
BUT I CAN'T DO THIS ALONE!
SO PLEASE!
YOU GOTTA HELP!
I CAN'T...
...DO THAT!
I CAN'T POSSIBLY DO THAT!!

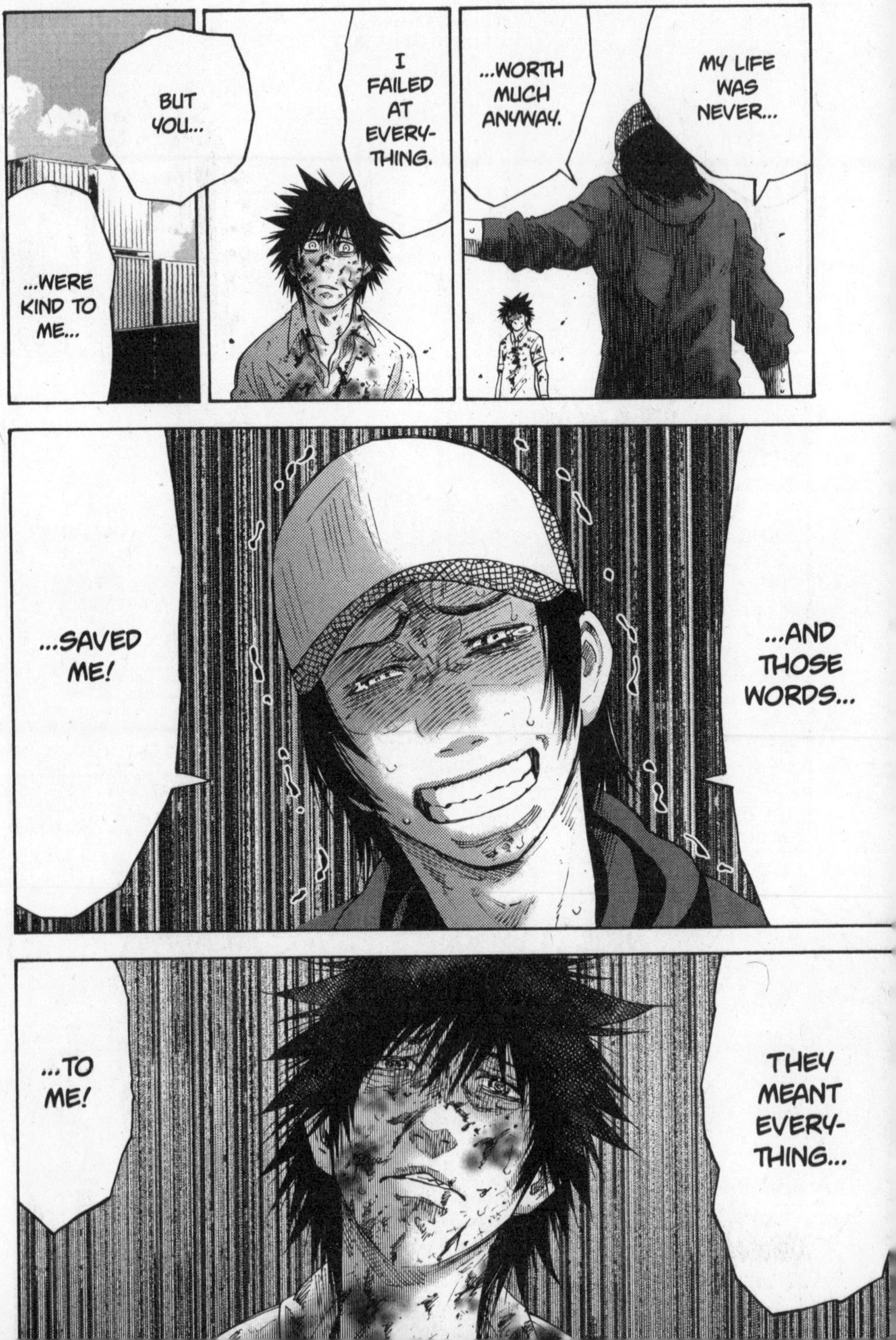
MY LIFE WAS NEVER...
...WORTH MUCH ANYWAY.
I FAILED AT EVERY-THING.
BUT YOU...
...WERE KIND TO ME...
...AND THOSE WORDS...
...SAVED ME!
THEY MEANT EVERY-THING...
...TO ME!

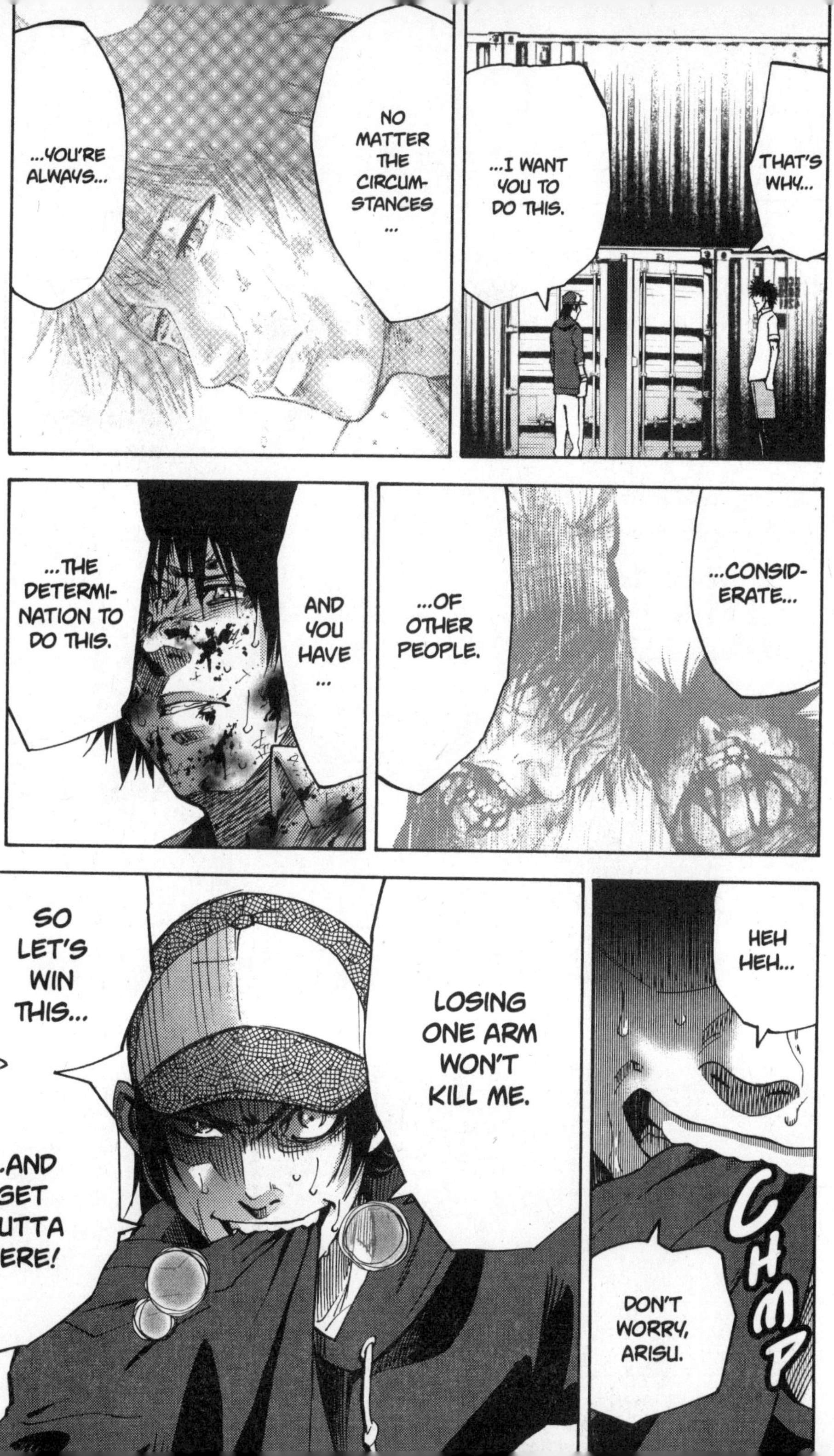
THAT'S WHY...
...I WANT YOU TO DO THIS.
NO MATTER THE CIRCUM-STANCES...
...YOU'RE ALWAYS...
...CONSID-ERATE...
...OF OTHER PEOPLE.
AND YOU HAVE...
...THE DETERMI-NATION TO DO THIS.
HEH HEH...
CHMP
DON'T WORRY, ARISU.
LOSING ONE ARM WON'T KILL ME.
SO LET'S WIN THIS...
...AND GET OUTTA HERE!

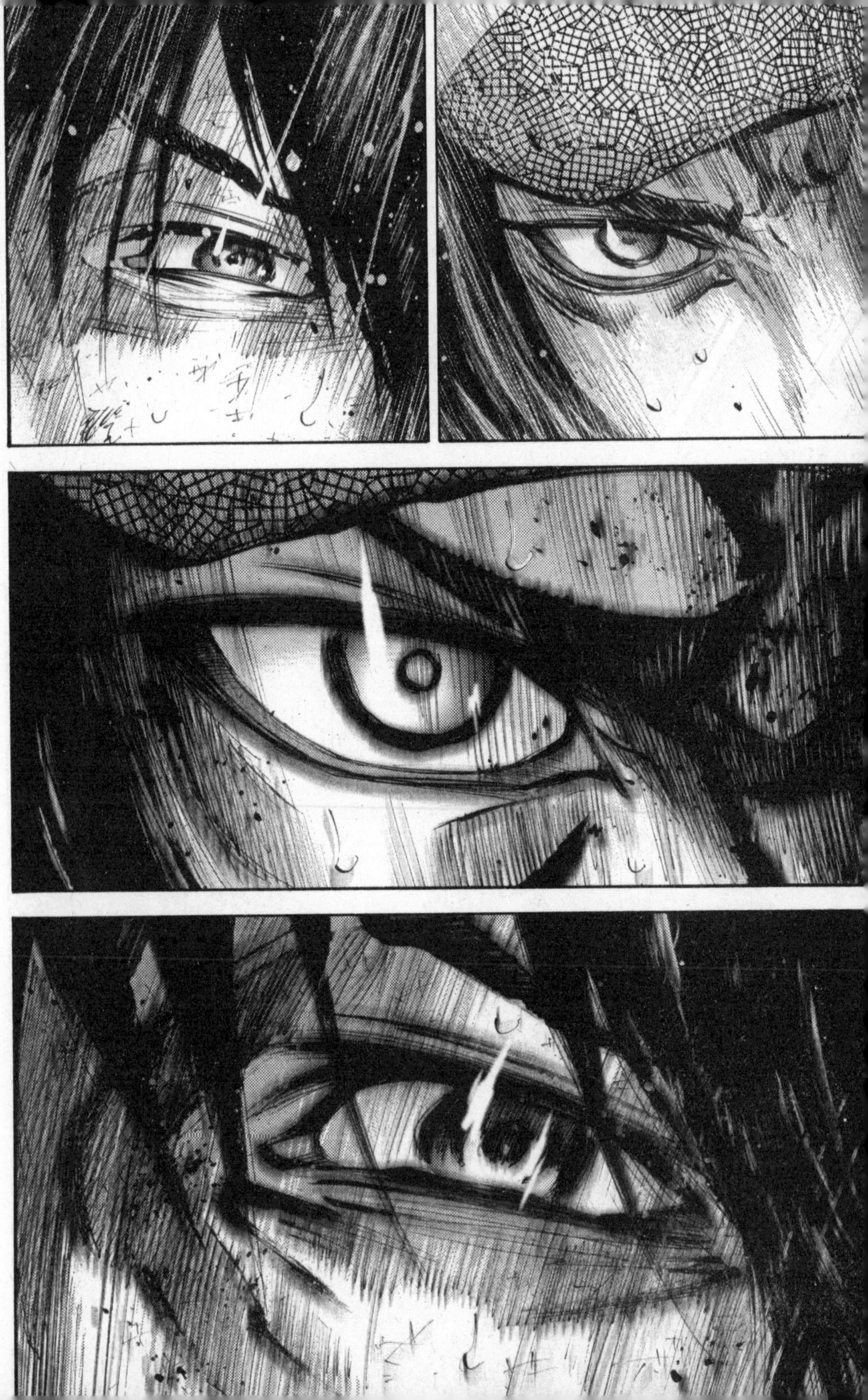

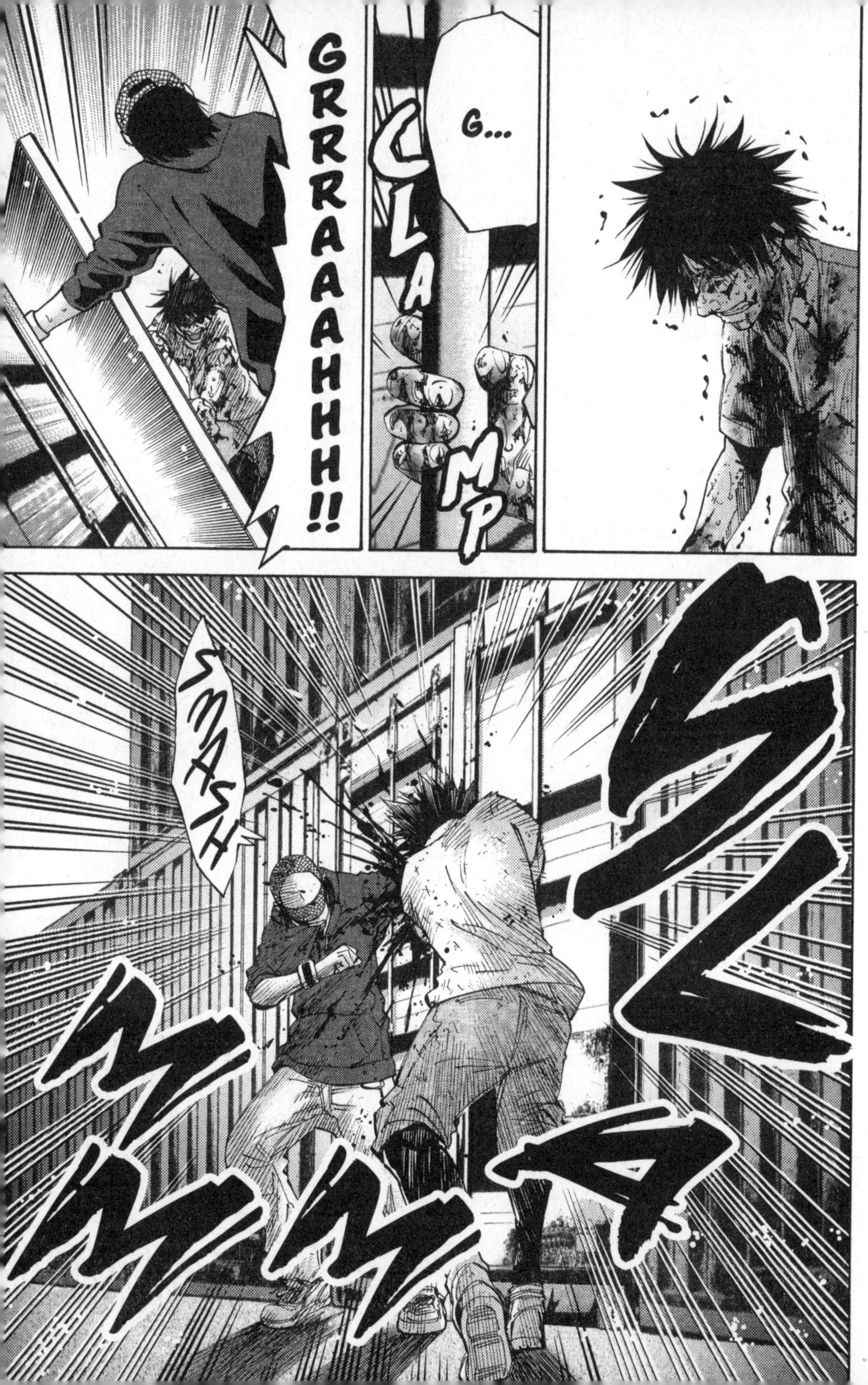
G...
CLAMP
GRRRAAAAHHHH!!
SMASH

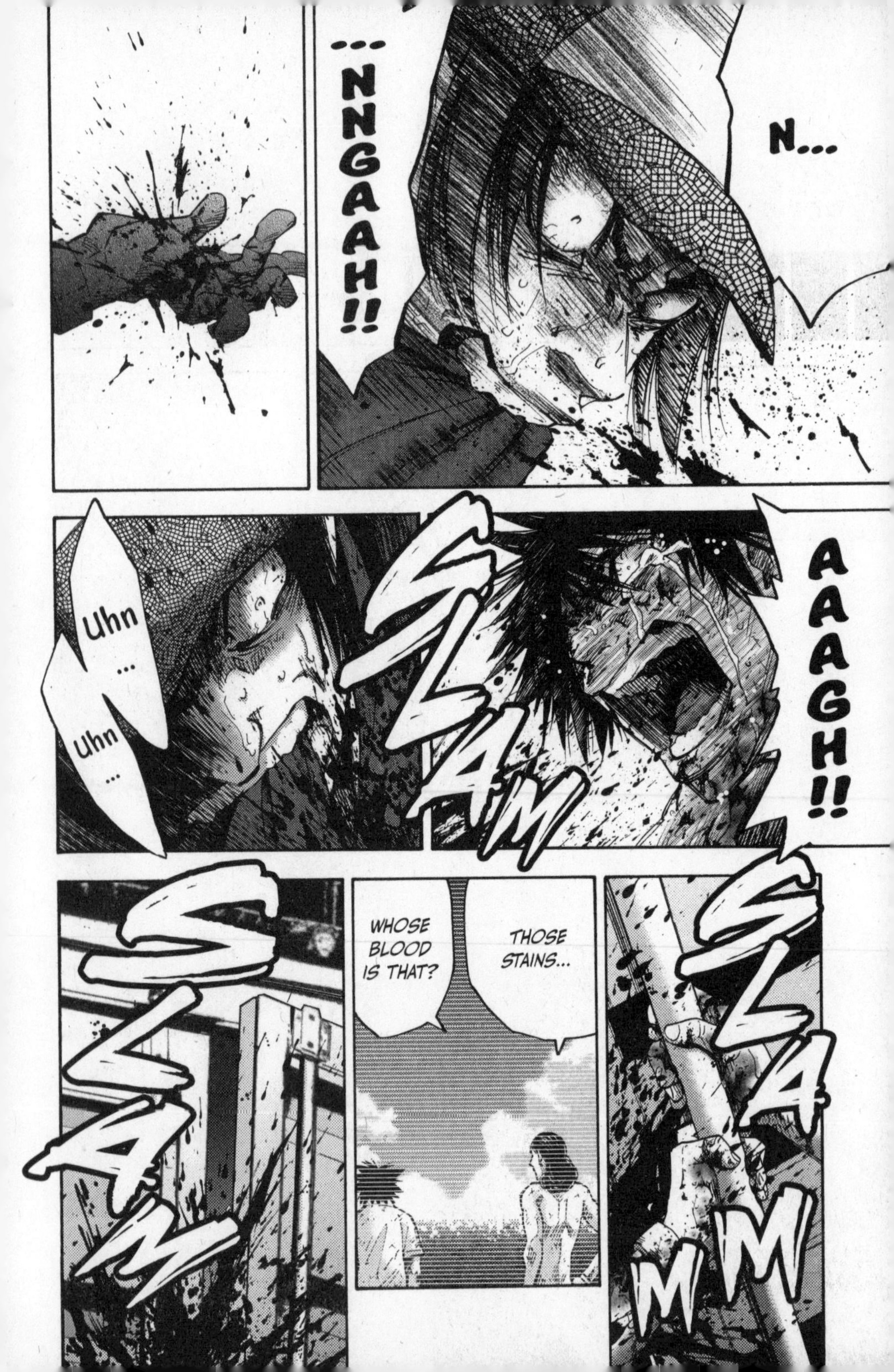
N...
...NNGAAH!!
AAAGH!!
SLAM
Uhn ... Uhn ...
SLAMMM
THOSE STAINS...
WHOSE BLOOD IS THAT?
SLAM

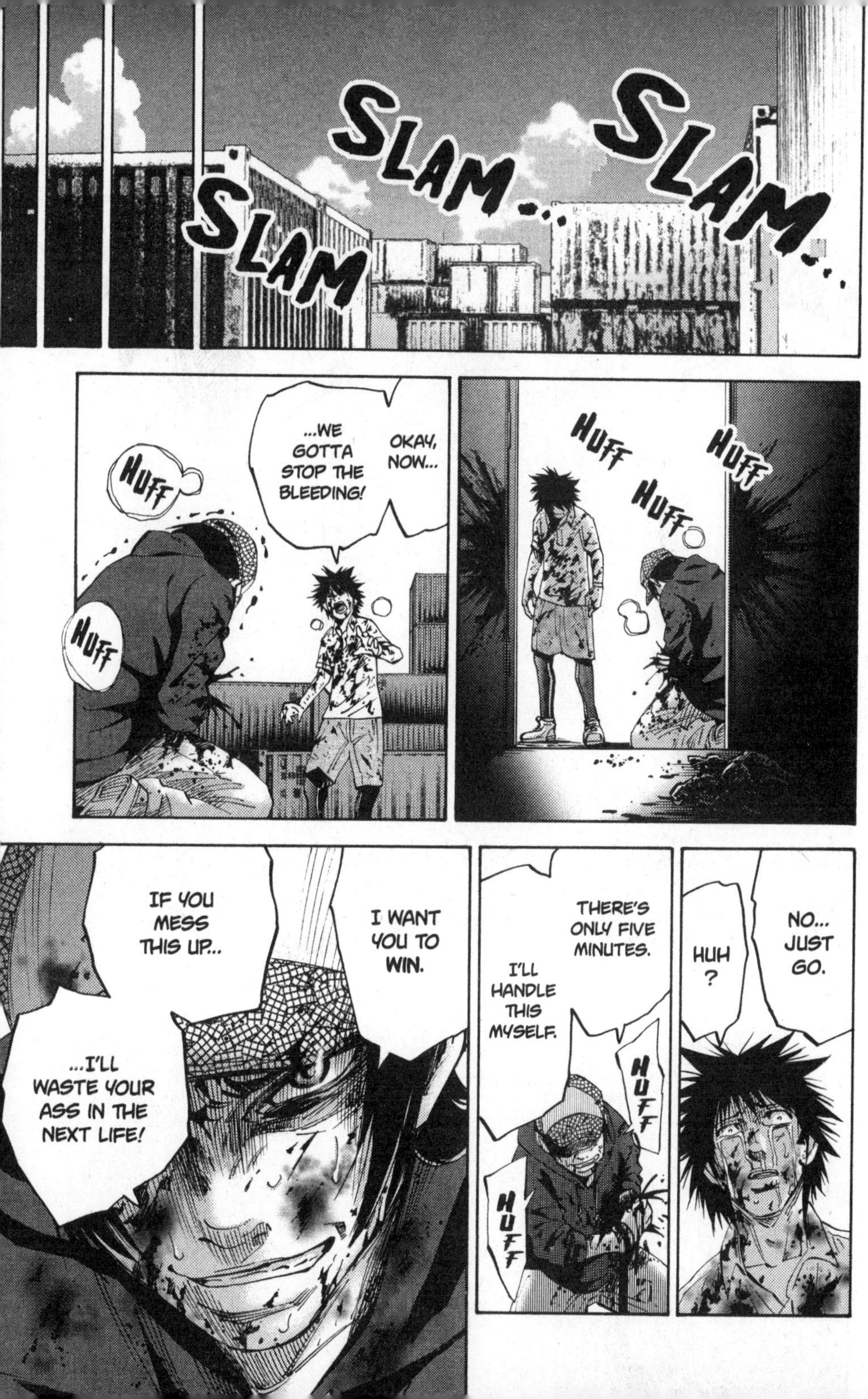
SLAM...
SLAM...
SLAM
HUFF
HUFF
HUFF
OKAY, NOW...
...WE GOTTA STOP THE BLEEDING!
HUFF
HUFF
NO... JUST GO.
HUH?
THERE'S ONLY FIVE MINUTES.
I'LL HANDLE THIS MYSELF.
HUFF
HUFF
I WANT YOU TO WIN.
IF YOU MESS THIS UP...
...I'LL WASTE YOUR ASS IN THE NEXT LIFE!

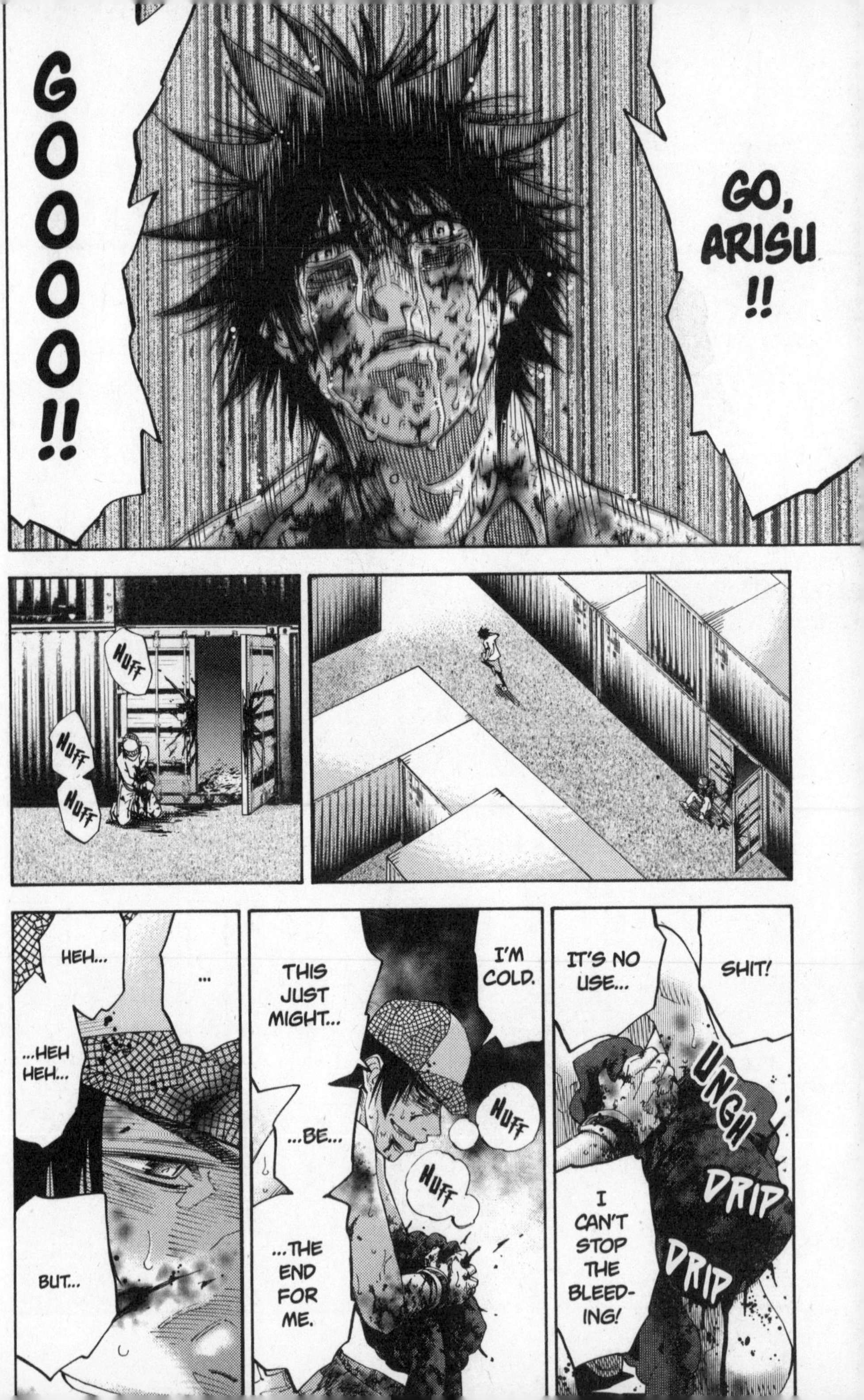
GO, ARISU!!
GOOOOO!!
HUFF
HUFF
HUFF
SHIT!
IT'S NO USE...
UNGH
DRIP
DRIP
I CAN'T STOP THE BLEED-ING!
I'M COLD.
THIS JUST MIGHT...
HUFF
HUFF
...BE...
...THE END FOR ME.
...
HEH...
...HEH HEH...
BUT...

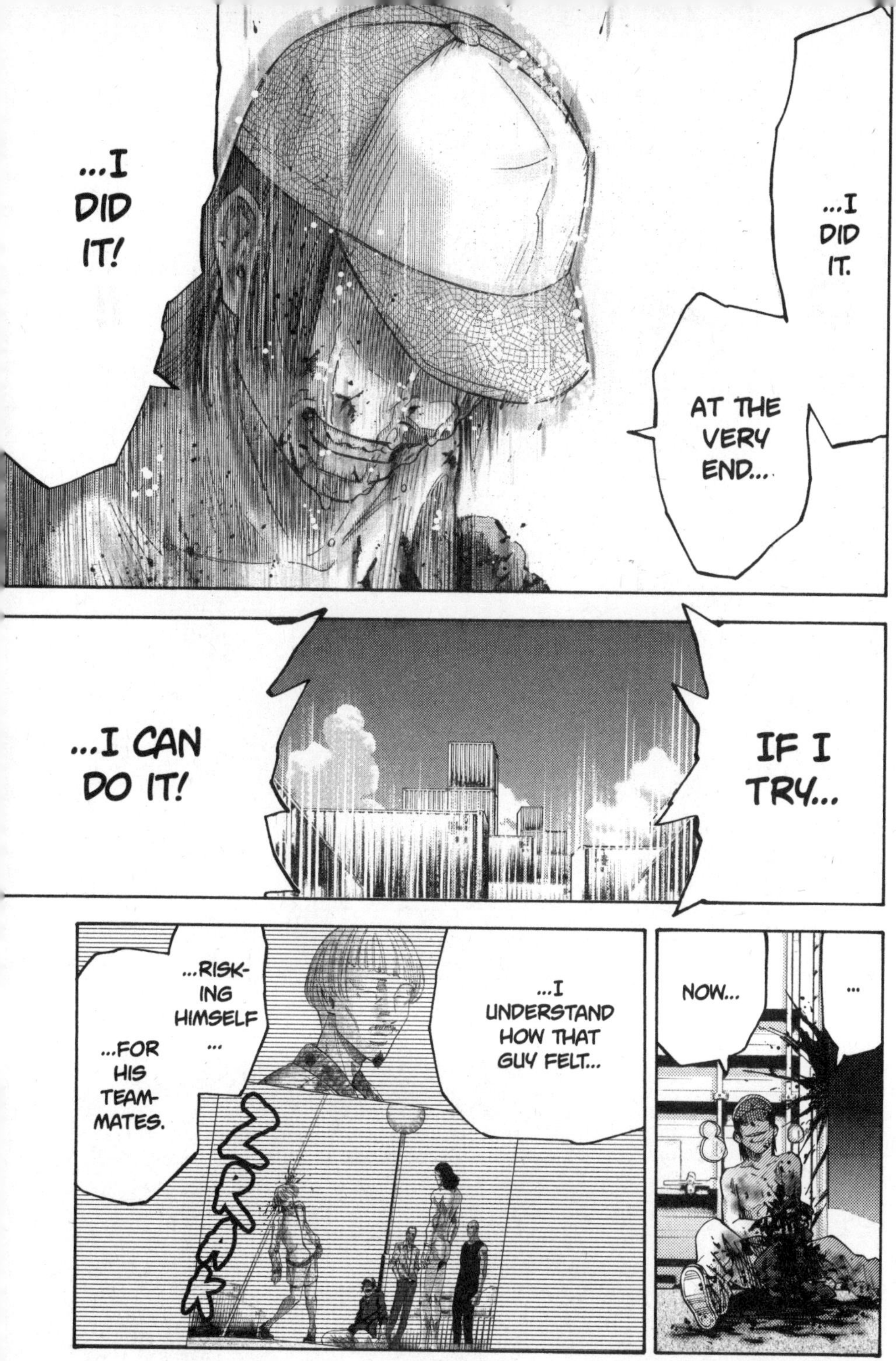
...I DID IT.
AT THE VERY END...
...I DID IT!
IF I TRY...
...I CAN DO IT!
...
NOW...
...I UNDERSTAND HOW THAT GUY FELT...
...RISKING HIMSELF...
...FOR HIS TEAMMATES.

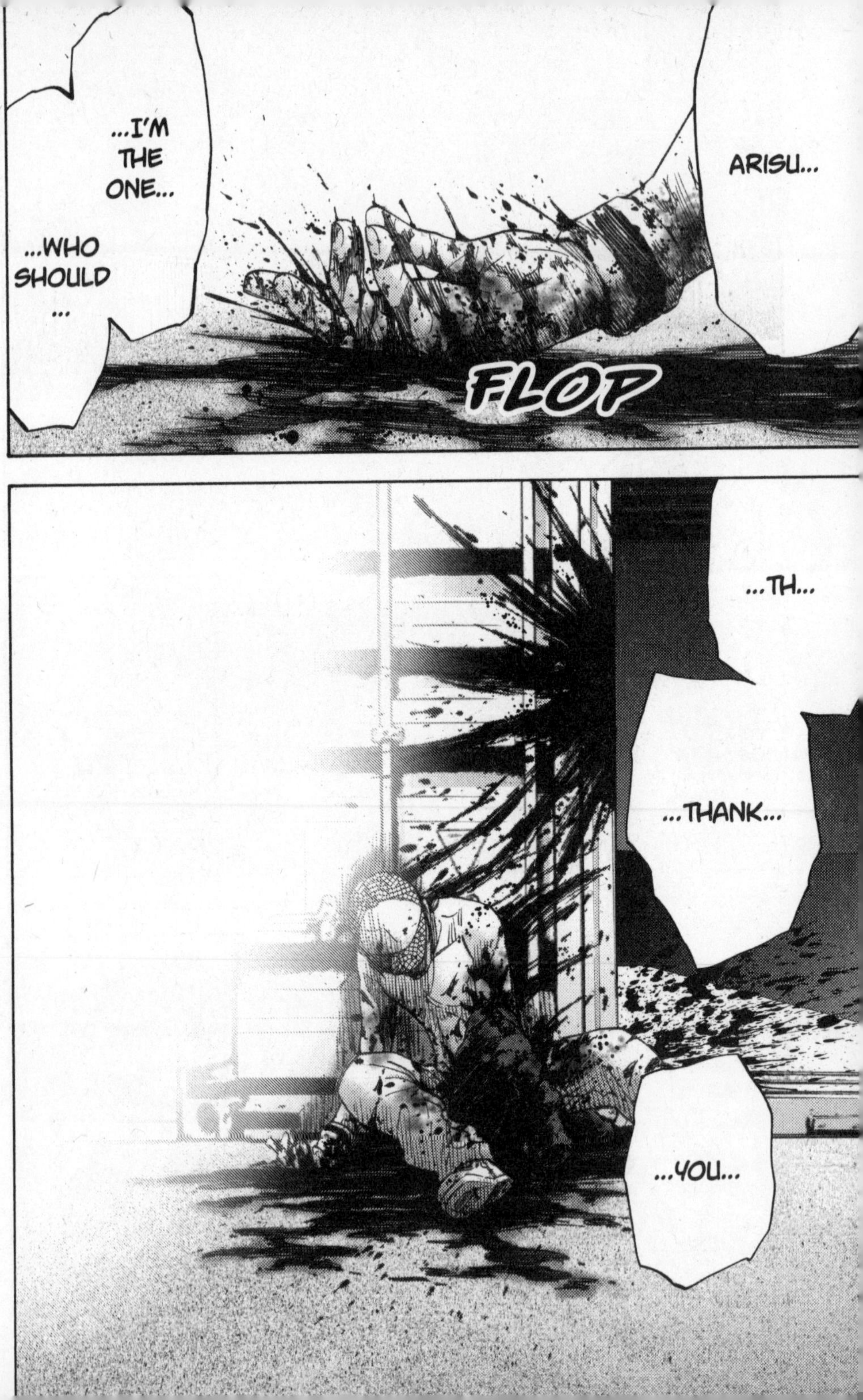
ARISU...
...I'M THE ONE...
...WHO SHOULD ...
FLOP
...TH...
...THANK...
...YOU...

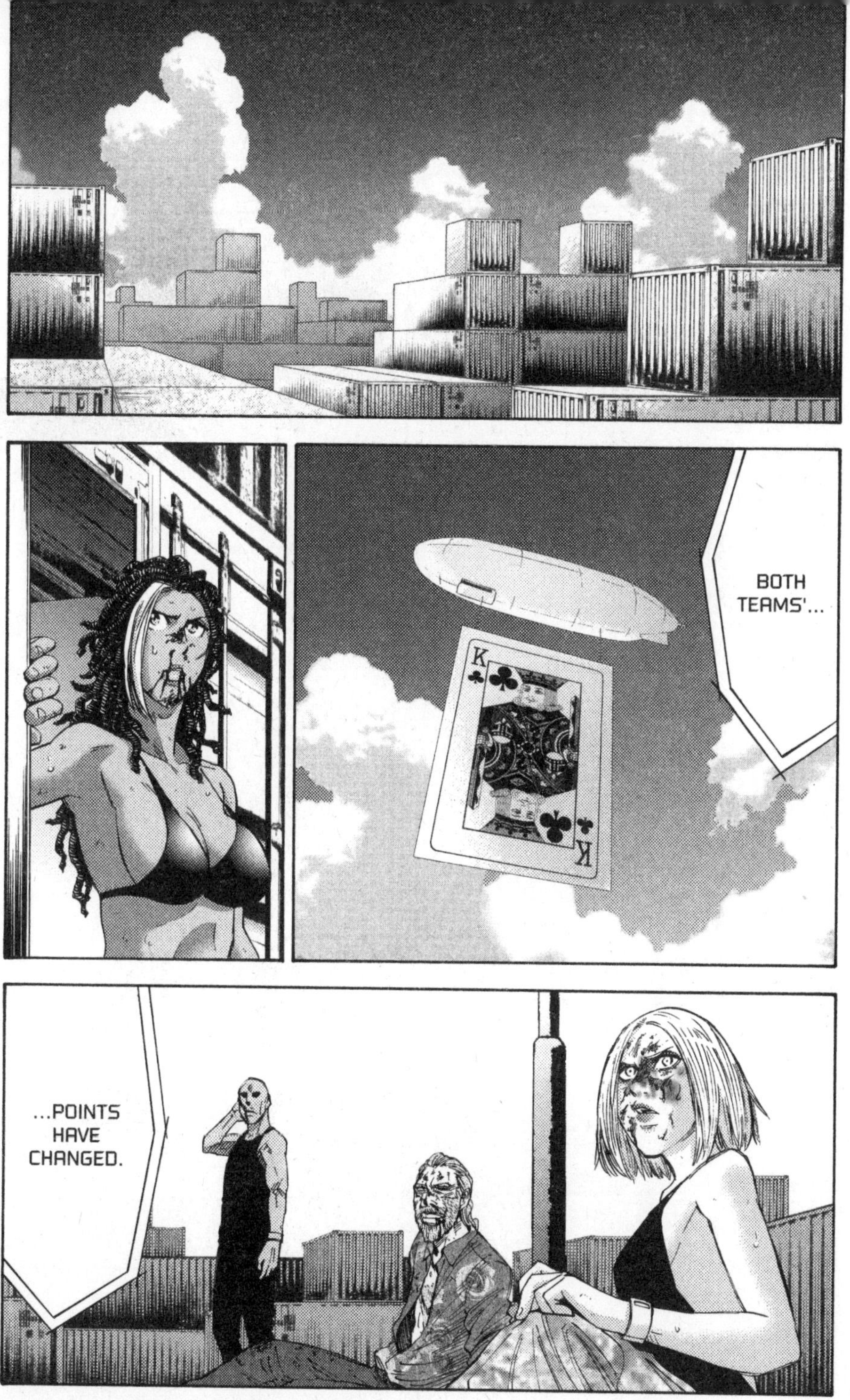
BOTH TEAMS'...
...POINTS HAVE CHANGED.

CHAPTER 41: King of Clubs, Part 9

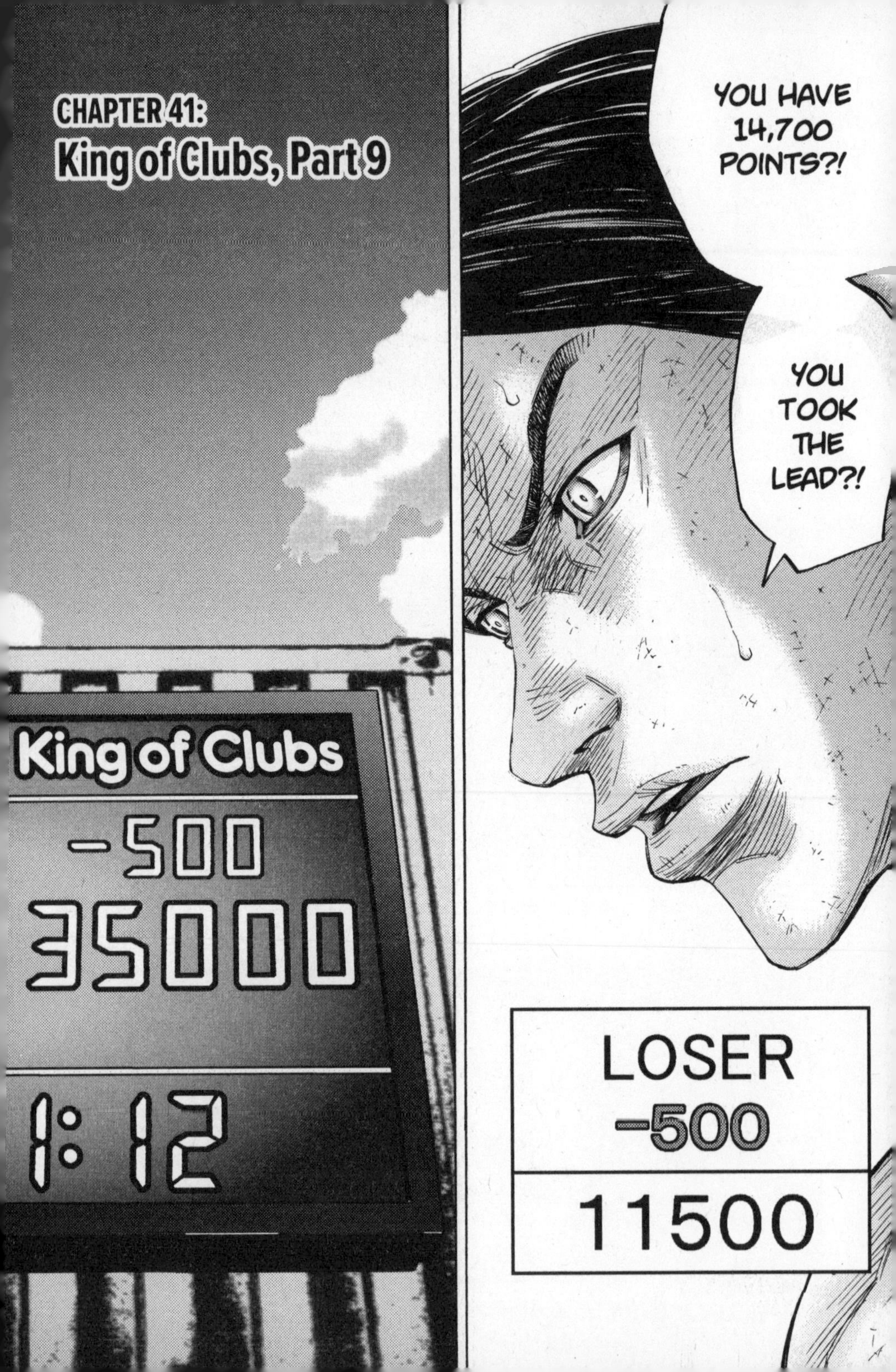
YOU HAVE 14,700 POINTS?!
YOU TOOK THE LEAD?!
LOSER
-500
11500
CHAPTER 41:
King of Clubs, Part 9
King of Clubs
-500
35000
1:12

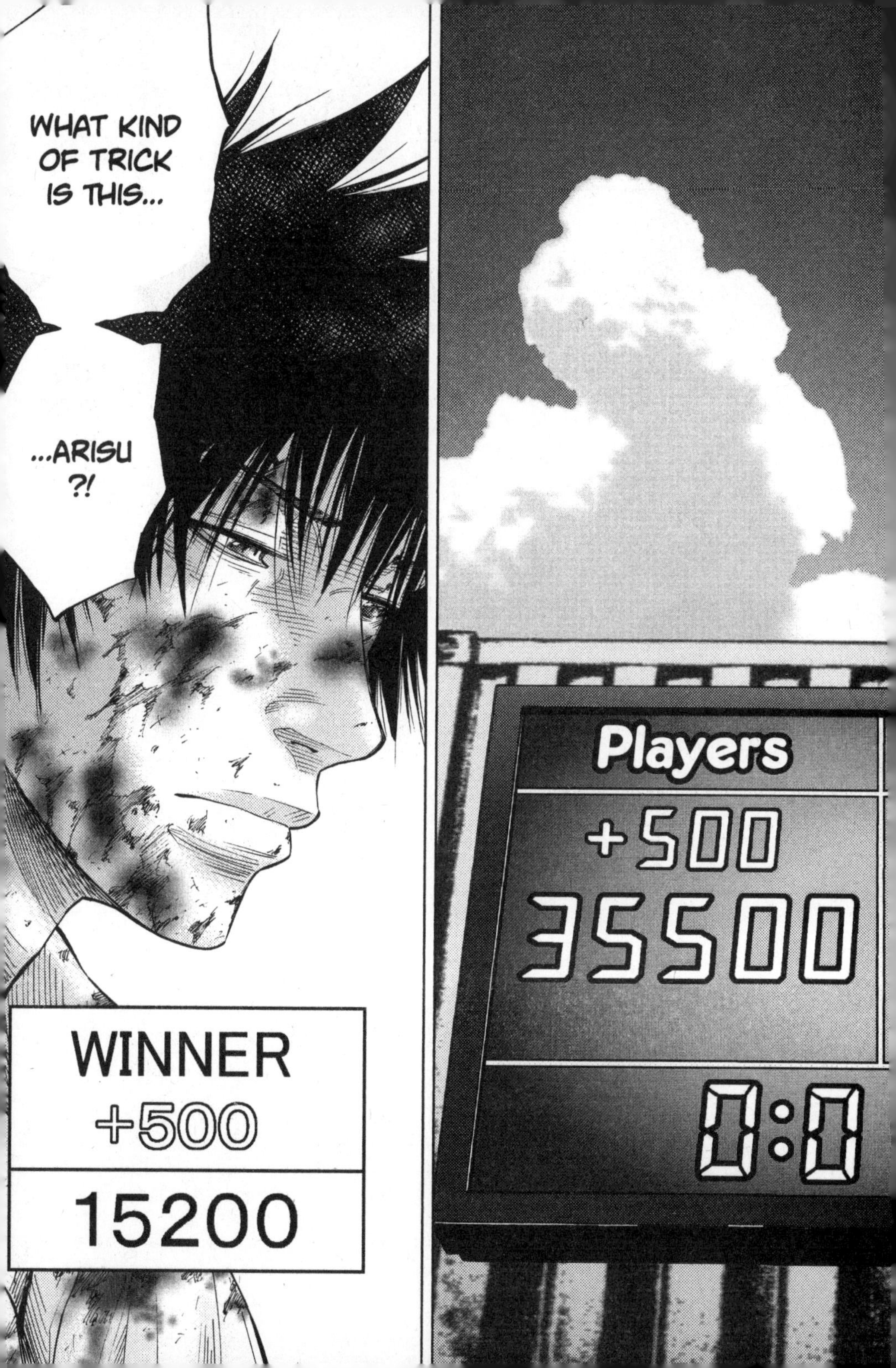
Players
+500
35500
0:0
WHAT KIND OF TRICK IS THIS...
...ARISU ?!
WINNER
+500
15200

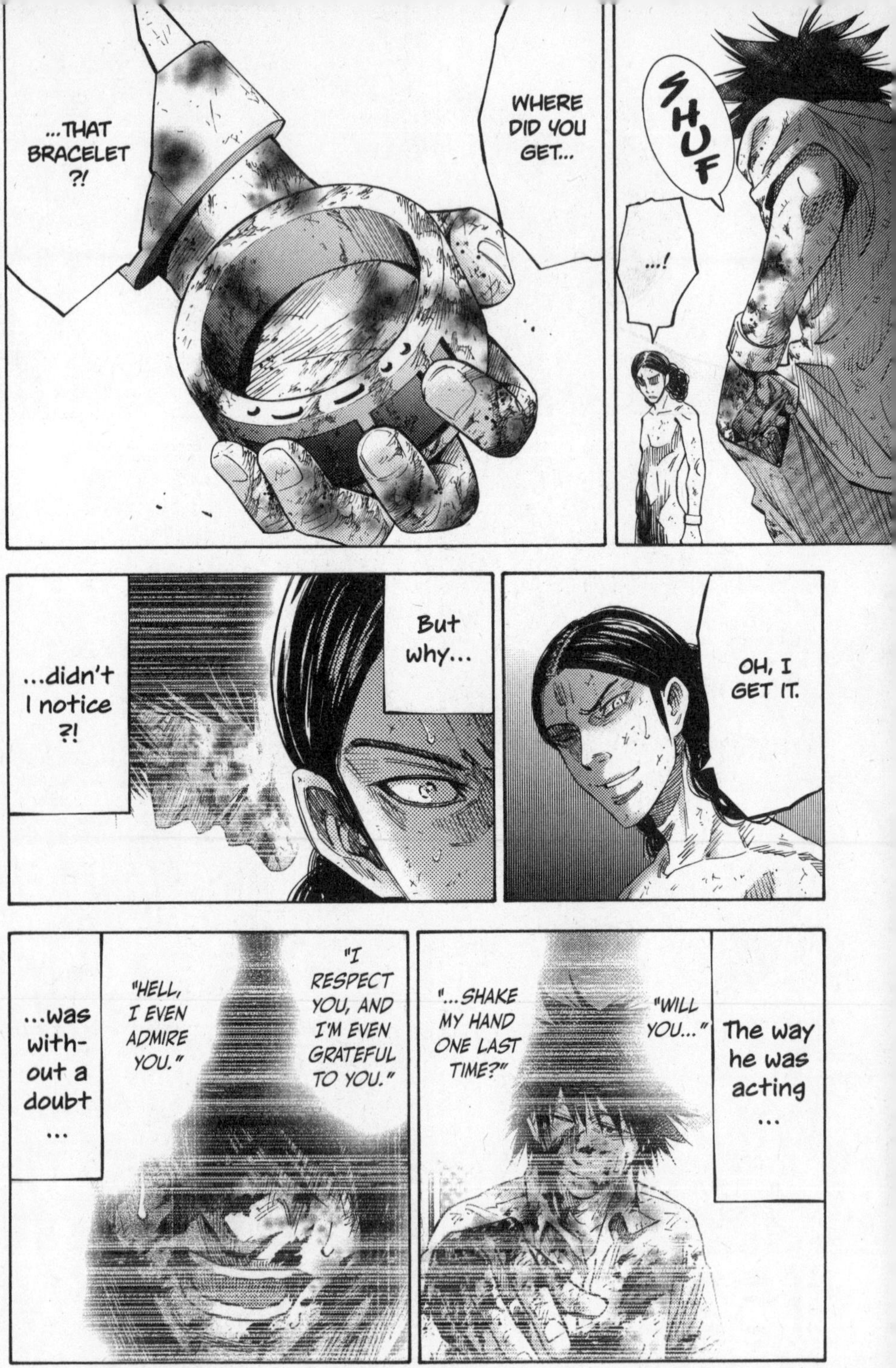
SHUF
...!
WHERE DID YOU GET...
...THAT BRACELET ?!
OH, I GET IT.
But why...
...didn't I notice ?!
The way he was acting ...
"WILL YOU..."
"...SHAKE MY HAND ONE LAST TIME?"
"I RESPECT YOU, AND I'M EVEN GRATEFUL TO YOU."
"HELL, I EVEN ADMIRE YOU."
...was with-out a doubt ...

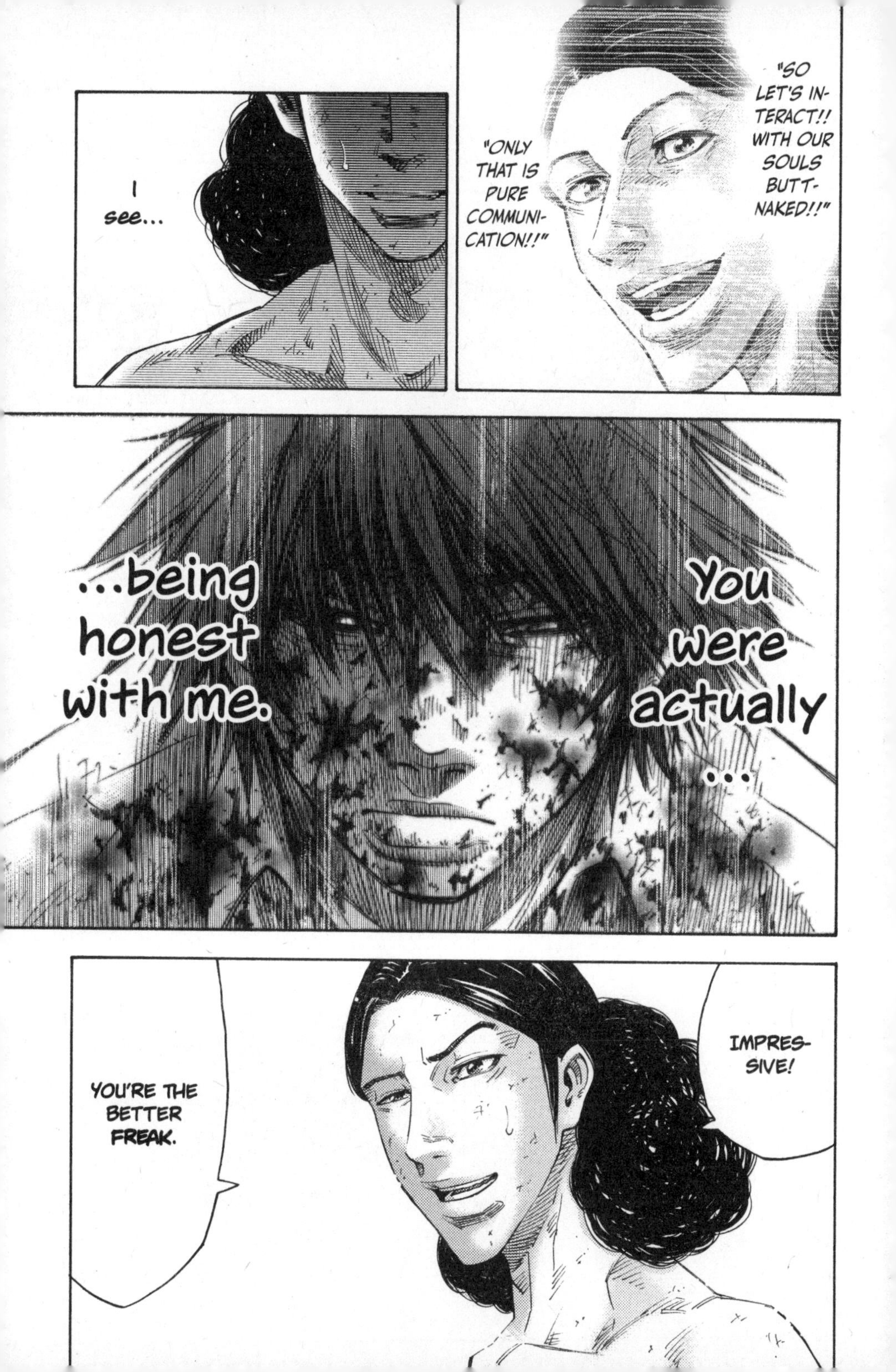
"SO LET'S INTERACT!! WITH OUR SOULS BUTT-NAKED!!"
"ONLY THAT IS PURE COMMUNICATION!!"
I see...
You were actually...
...being honest with me.
IMPRESSIVE!
YOU'RE THE BETTER FREAK.

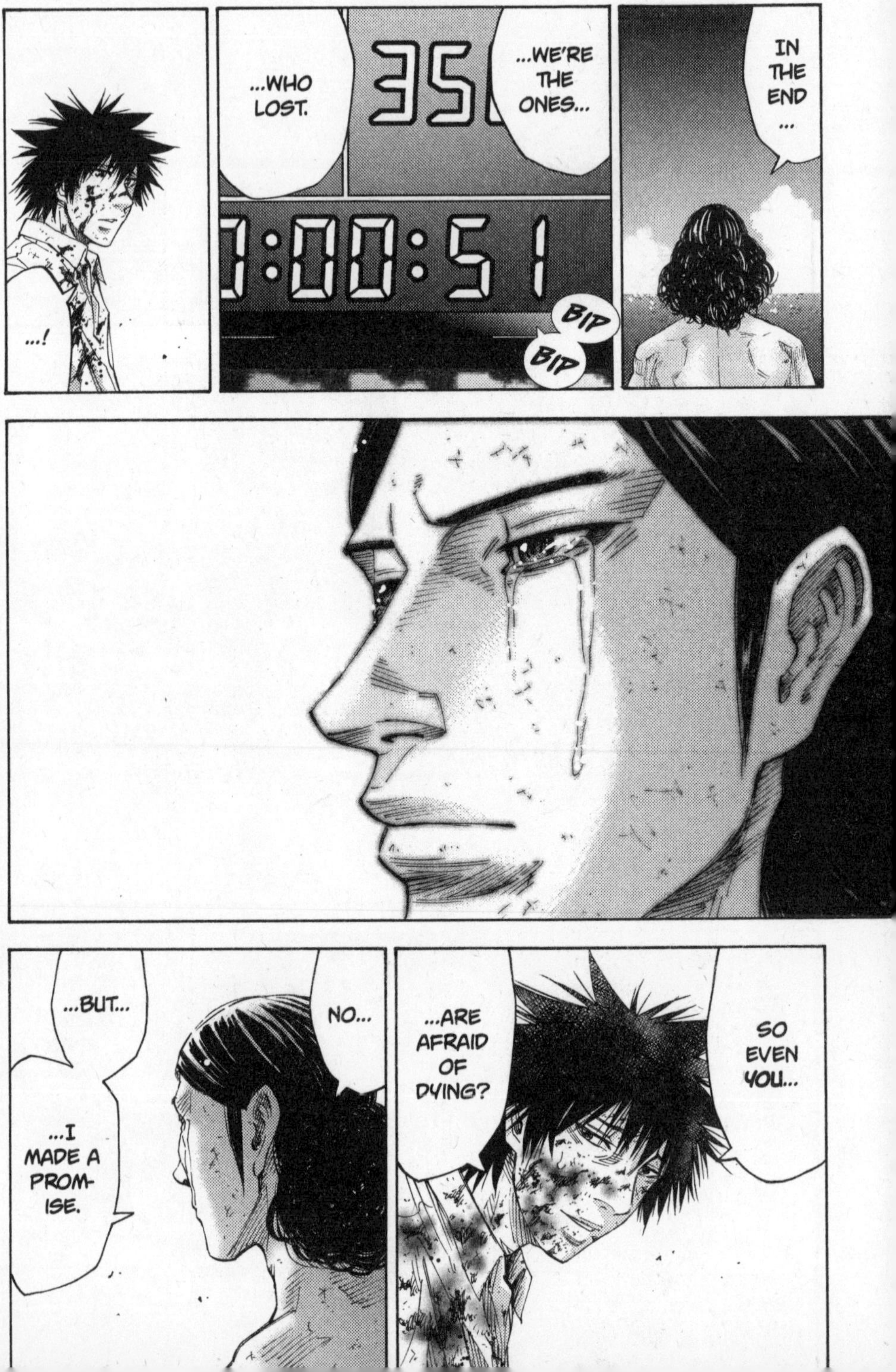
IN THE END...
...WE'RE THE ONES...
...WHO LOST.
BIP
BIP
...!
SO EVEN YOU...
...ARE AFRAID OF DYING?
NO...
...BUT...
...I MADE A PROM-ISE.

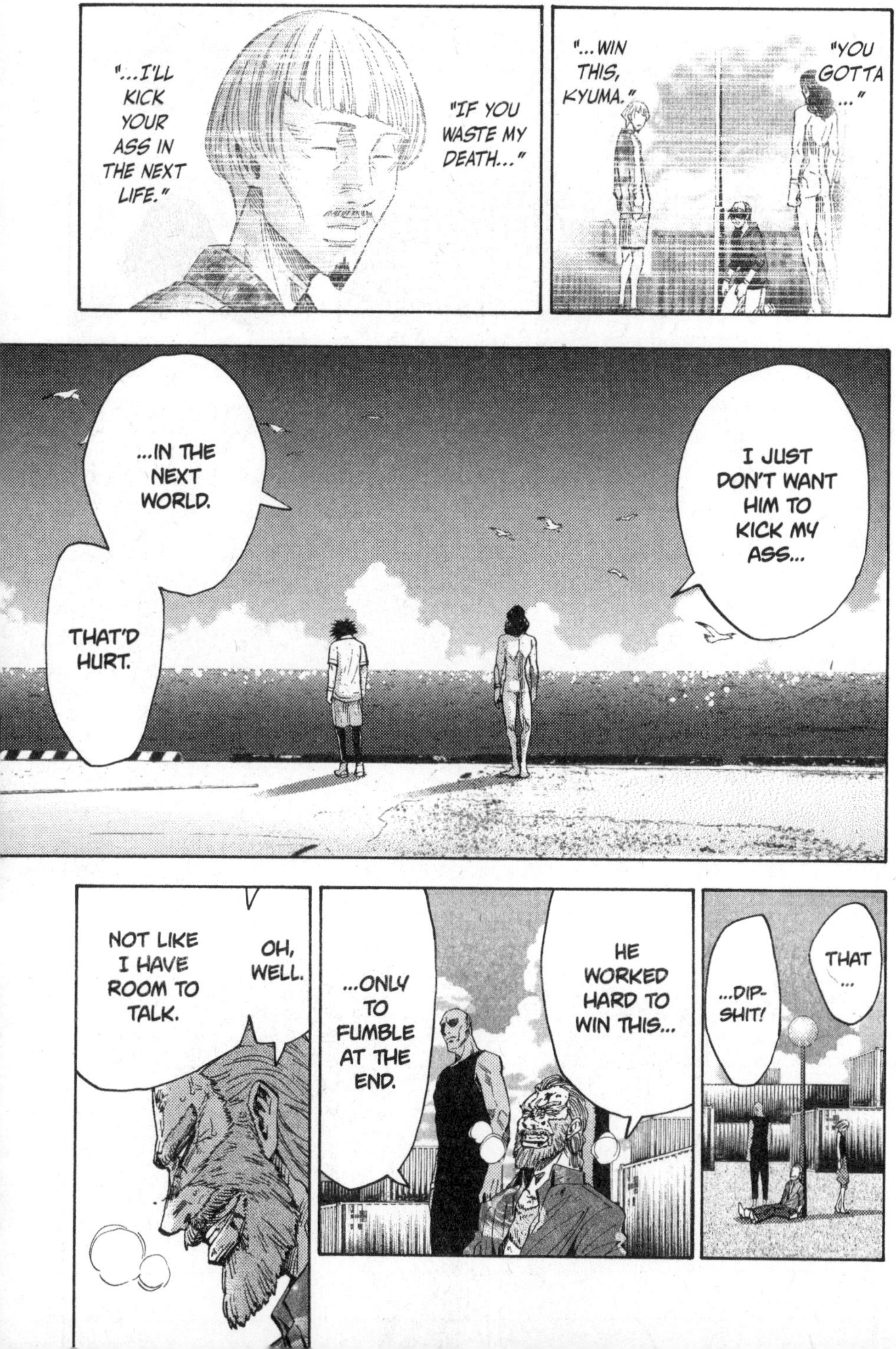
"YOU GOTTA ..."
"...WIN THIS, KYUMA."
"IF YOU WASTE MY DEATH..."
"...I'LL KICK YOUR ASS IN THE NEXT LIFE."
I JUST DON'T WANT HIM TO KICK MY ASS...
...IN THE NEXT WORLD.
THAT'D HURT.
THAT...
...DIP-SHIT!
HE WORKED HARD TO WIN THIS...
...ONLY TO FUMBLE AT THE END.
OH, WELL.
NOT LIKE I HAVE ROOM TO TALK.

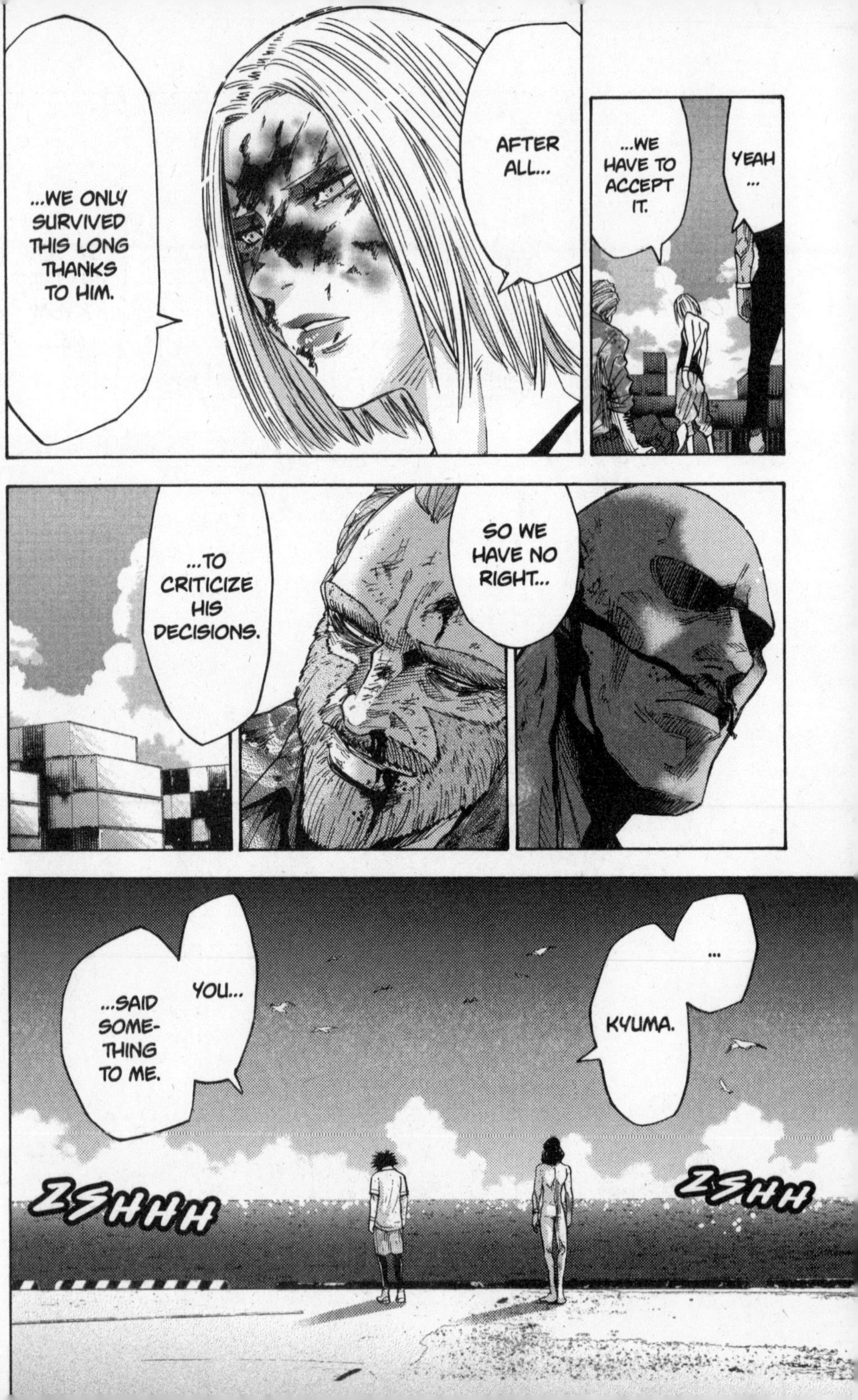
YEAH...
...WE HAVE TO ACCEPT IT.
AFTER ALL...
...WE ONLY SURVIVED THIS LONG THANKS TO HIM.
SO WE HAVE NO RIGHT...
...TO CRITICIZE HIS DECISIONS.
...
KYUMA.
YOU...
...SAID SOME-THING TO ME.
ZSHHH
ZSHHHH

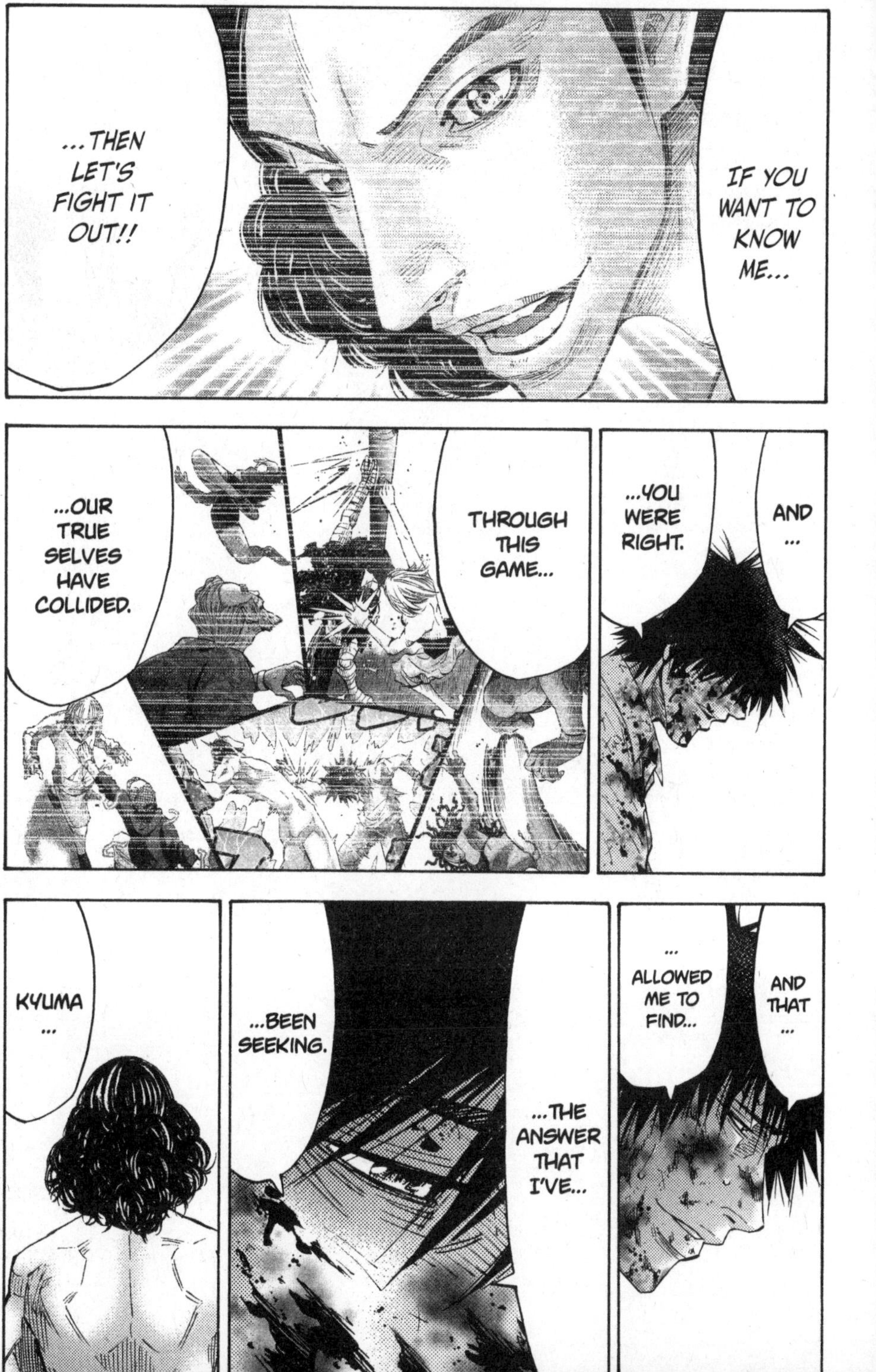
IF YOU WANT TO KNOW ME...
...THEN LET'S FIGHT IT OUT!!
AND ...
...YOU WERE RIGHT.
THROUGH THIS GAME...
...OUR TRUE SELVES HAVE COLLIDED.
AND THAT ...
... ALLOWED ME TO FIND...
...THE ANSWER THAT I'VE...
...BEEN SEEKING.
KYUMA ...

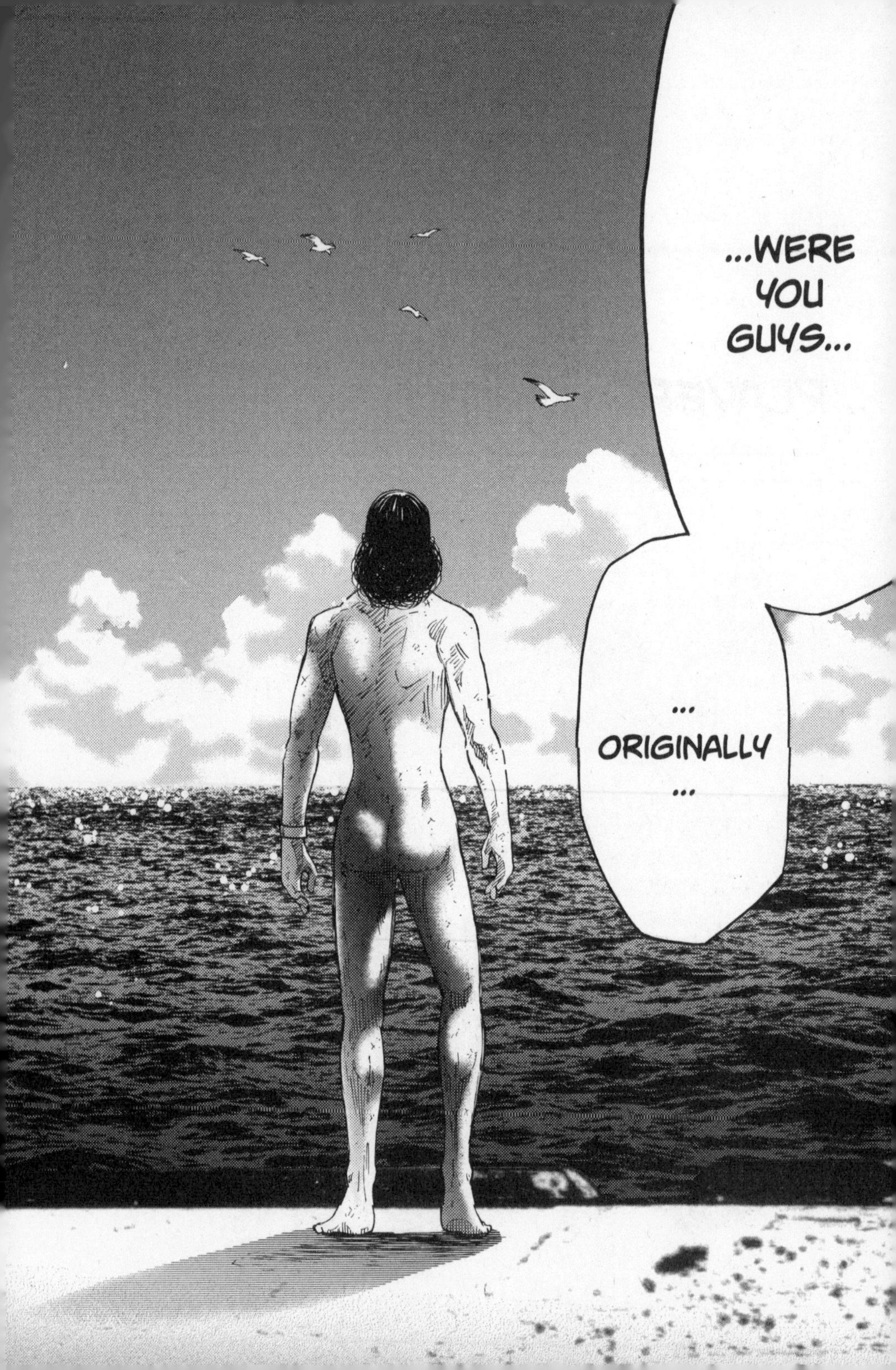
...WERE YOU GUYS...
... ORIGINALLY ...

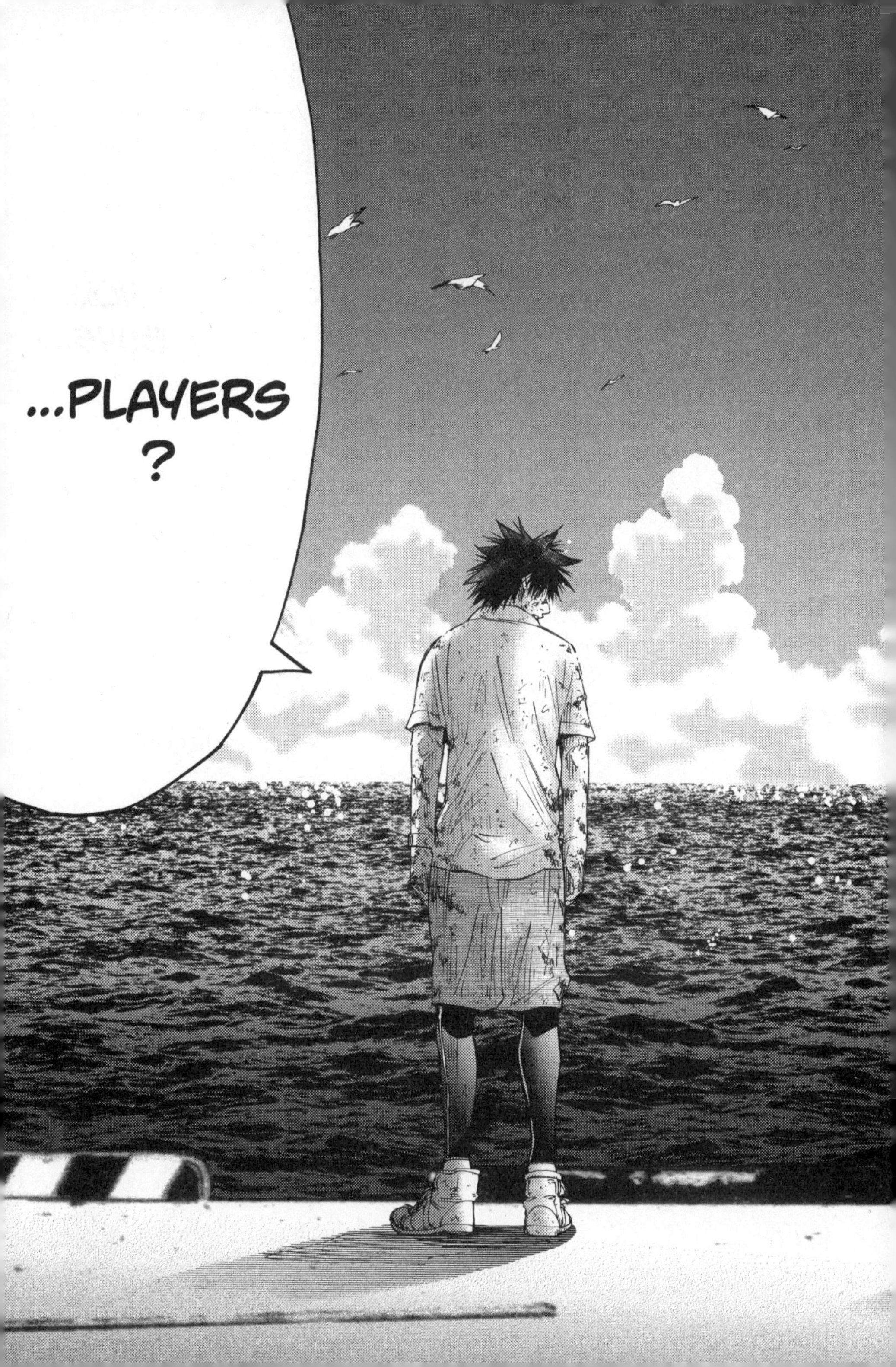
...PLAYERS ?

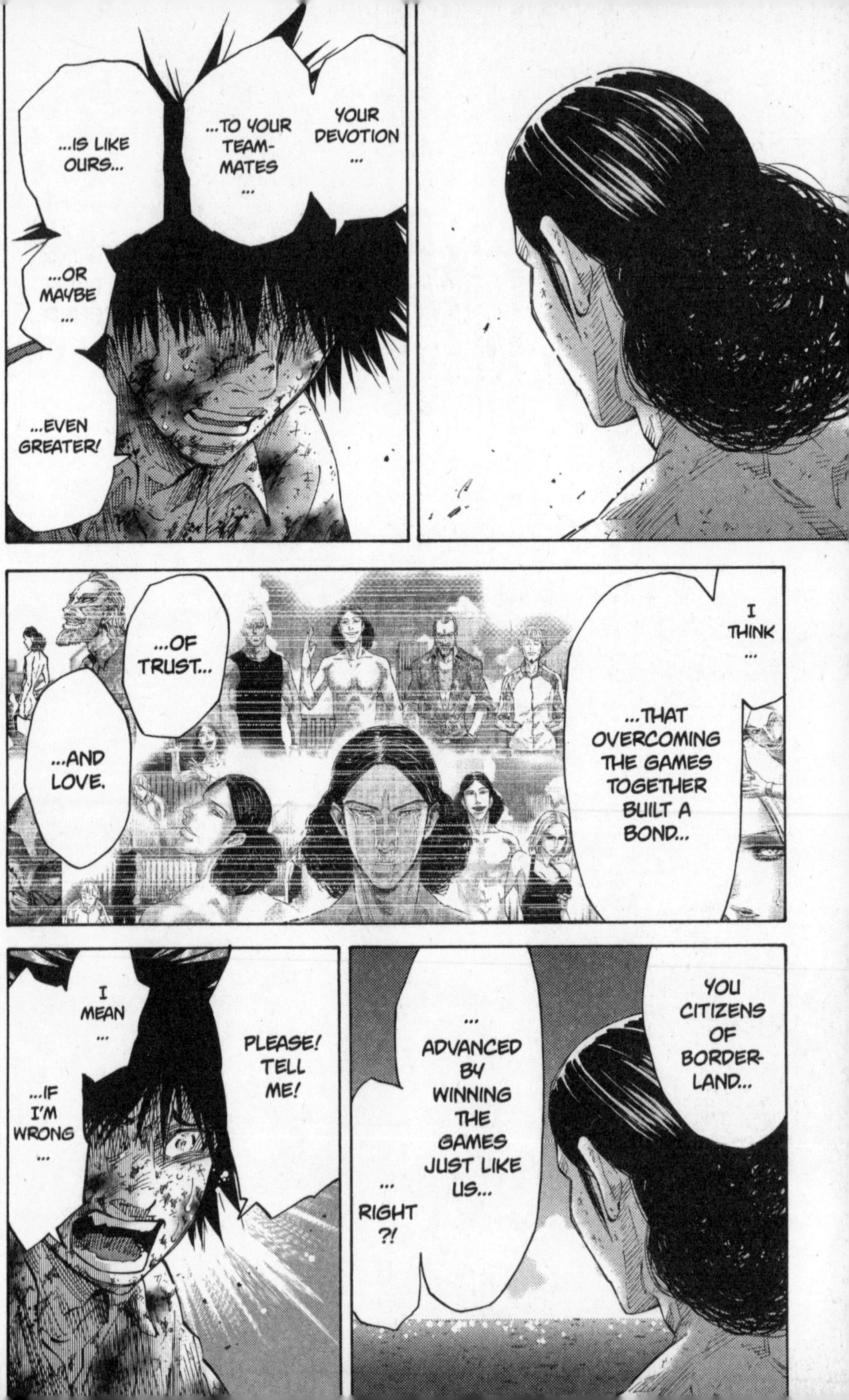
YOUR DEVOTION...
...TO YOUR TEAM-MATES...
...IS LIKE OURS...
...OR MAYBE...
...EVEN GREATER!
I THINK...
...THAT OVERCOMING THE GAMES TOGETHER BUILT A BOND...
...OF TRUST...
...AND LOVE.
YOU CITIZENS OF BORDER-LAND...
...ADVANCED BY WINNING THE GAMES JUST LIKE US...
...RIGHT?!
I MEAN...
...IF I'M WRONG...
PLEASE! TELL ME!

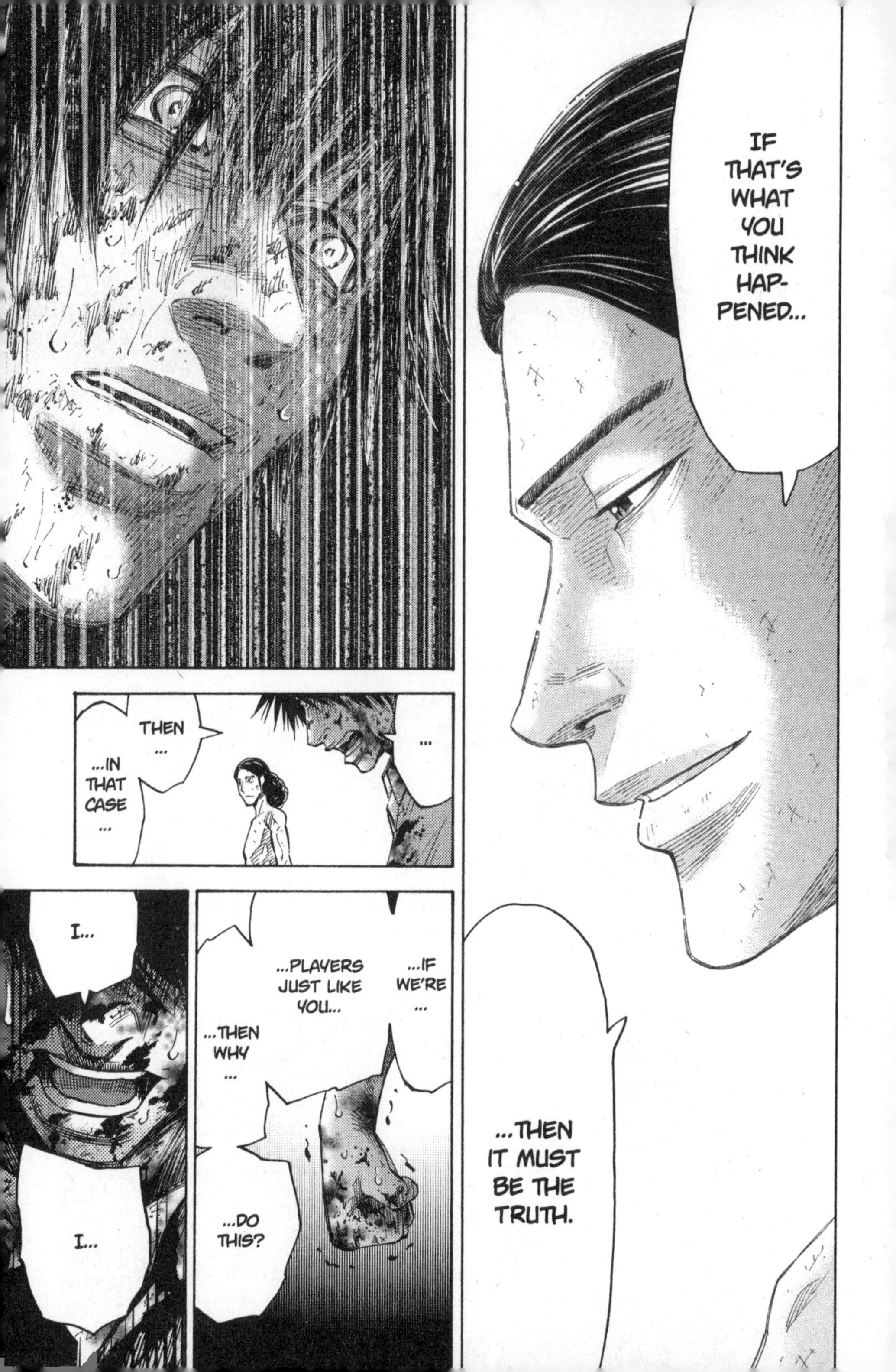
IF THAT'S WHAT YOU THINK HAP- PENED...
...THEN IT MUST BE THE TRUTH.
...
THEN ...
...IN THAT CASE ...
...IF WE'RE ...
...PLAYERS JUST LIKE YOU...
...THEN WHY ...
...DO THIS?
I...
I...

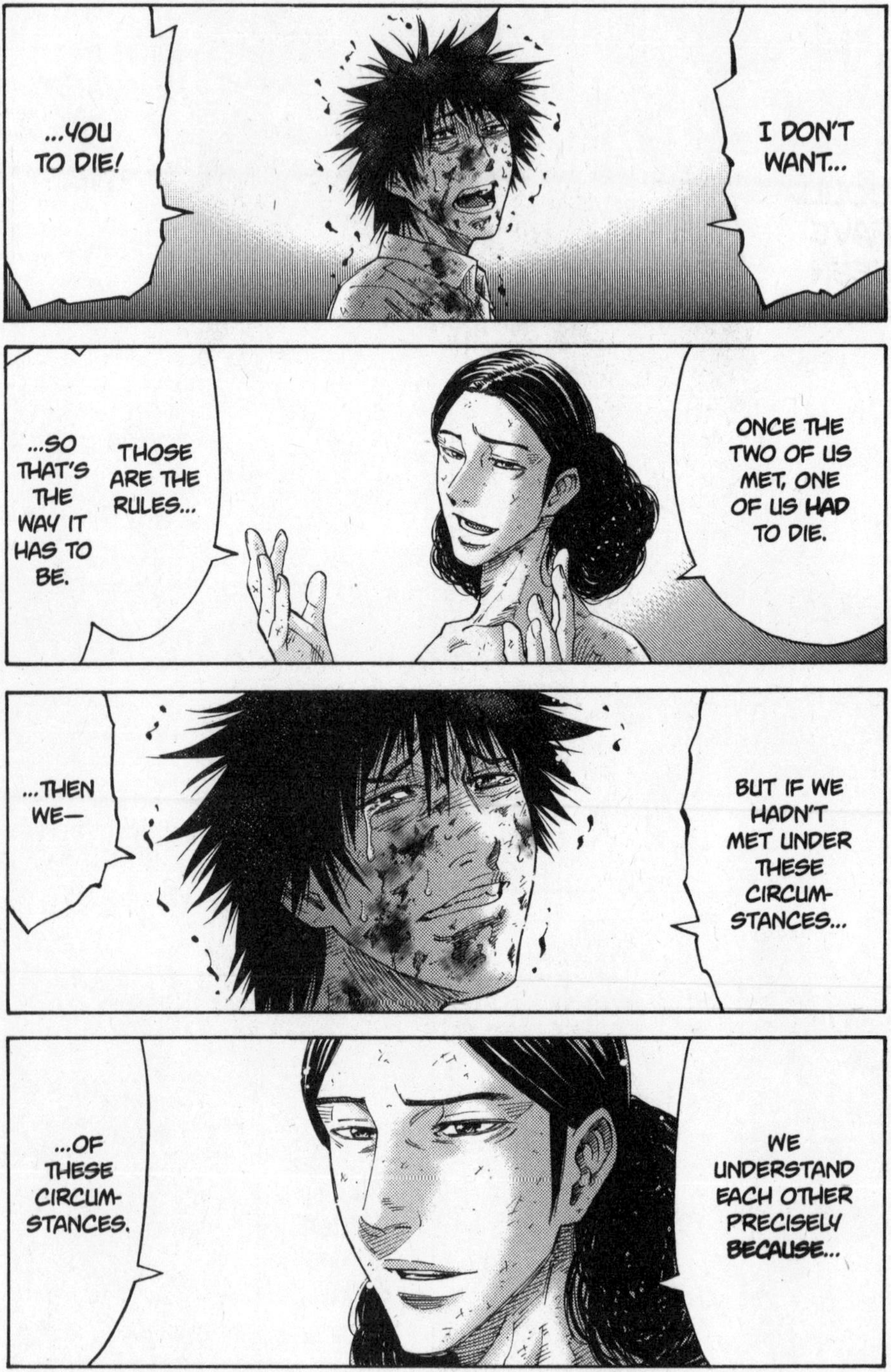
I DON'T WANT...
...YOU TO DIE!
ONCE THE TWO OF US MET, ONE OF US HAD TO DIE.
THOSE ARE THE RULES...
...SO THAT'S THE WAY IT HAS TO BE.
BUT IF WE HADN'T MET UNDER THESE CIRCUM-STANCES...
...THEN WE—
WE UNDERSTAND EACH OTHER PRECISELY BECAUSE...
...OF THESE CIRCUM-STANCES.

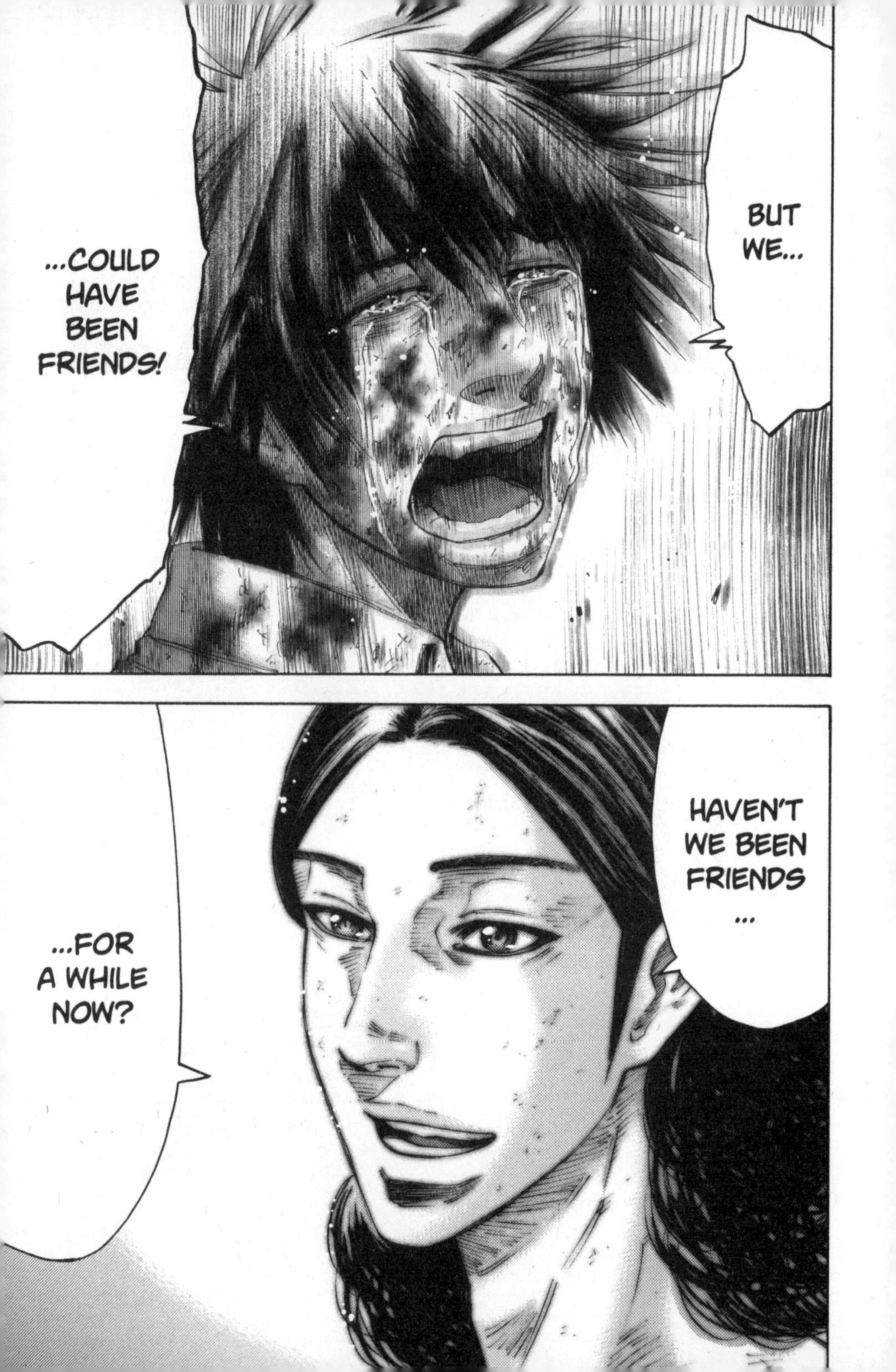
BUT WE...
...COULD HAVE BEEN FRIENDS!
HAVEN'T WE BEEN FRIENDS ...
...FOR A WHILE NOW?

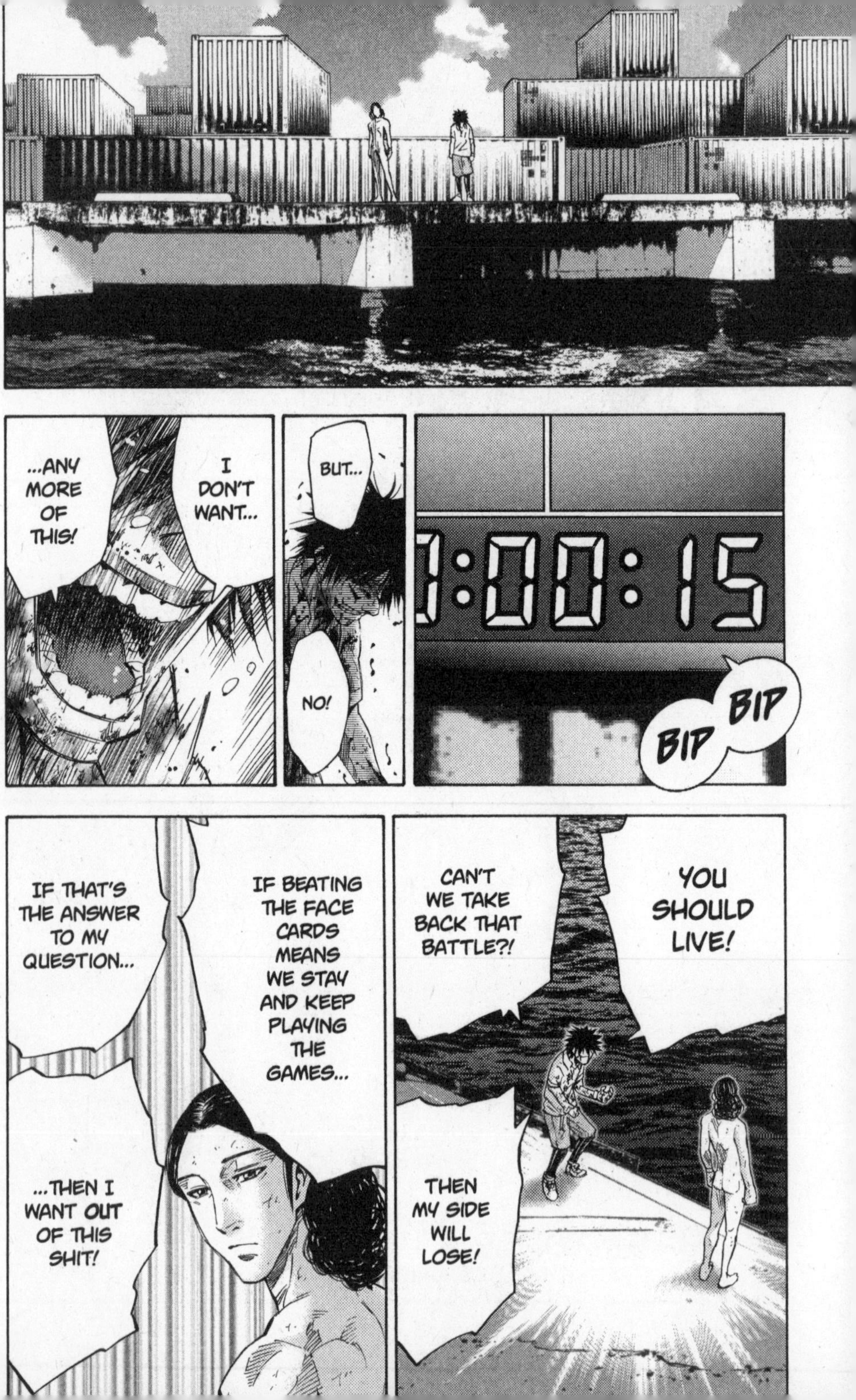
00:15
BIP
BIP
BUT...
NO!
I DON'T WANT...
...ANY MORE OF THIS!
YOU SHOULD LIVE!
CAN'T WE TAKE BACK THAT BATTLE?!
THEN MY SIDE WILL LOSE!
IF BEATING THE FACE CARDS MEANS WE STAY AND KEEP PLAYING THE GAMES...
IF THAT'S THE ANSWER TO MY QUESTION...
...THEN I WANT OUT OF THIS SHIT!

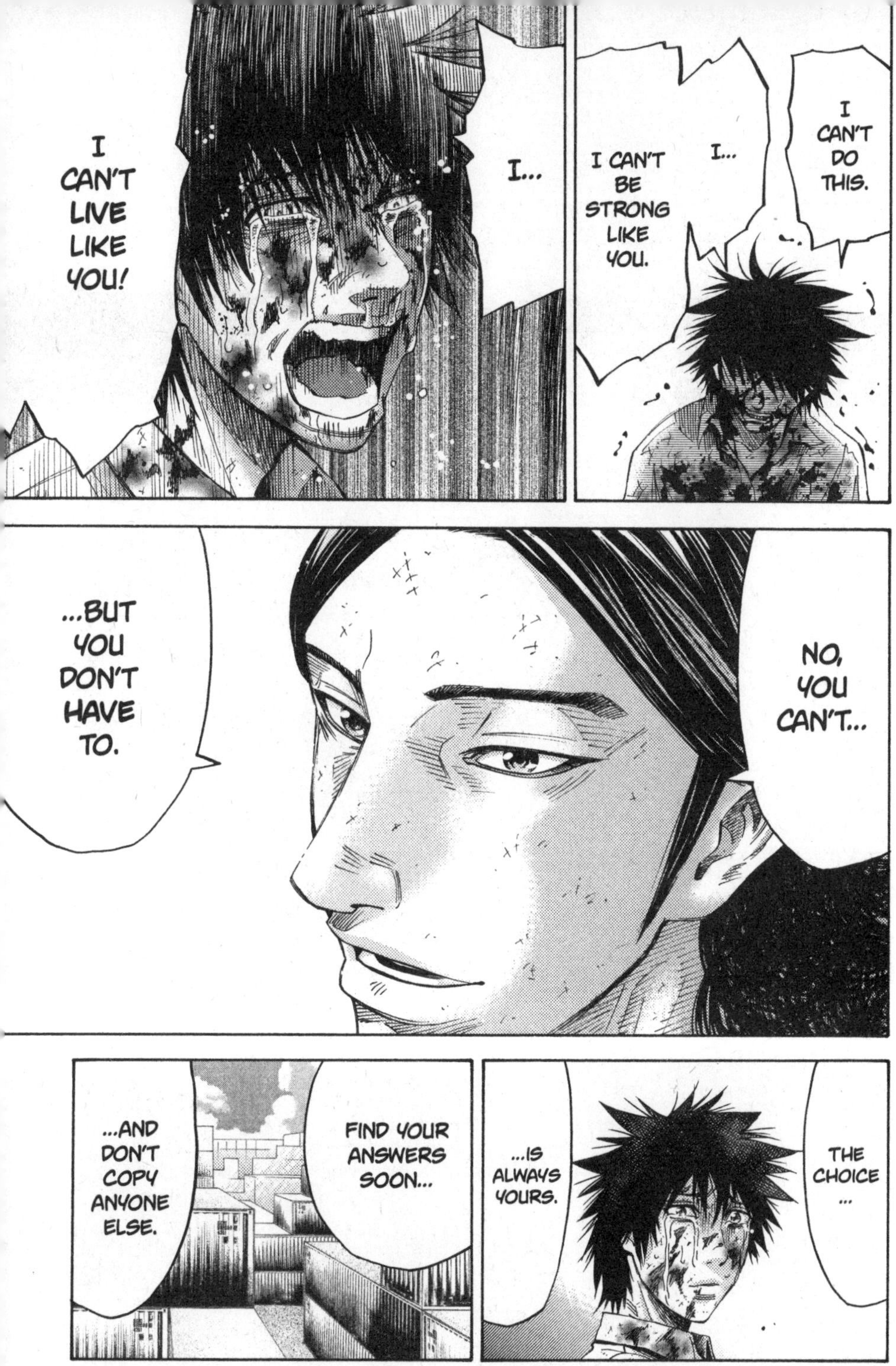
I CAN'T DO THIS.
I...
I CAN'T BE STRONG LIKE YOU.
I...
I CAN'T LIVE LIKE YOU!
NO, YOU CAN'T...
...BUT YOU DON'T HAVE TO.
THE CHOICE ...
...IS ALWAYS YOURS.
FIND YOUR ANSWERS SOON...
...AND DON'T COPY ANYONE ELSE.

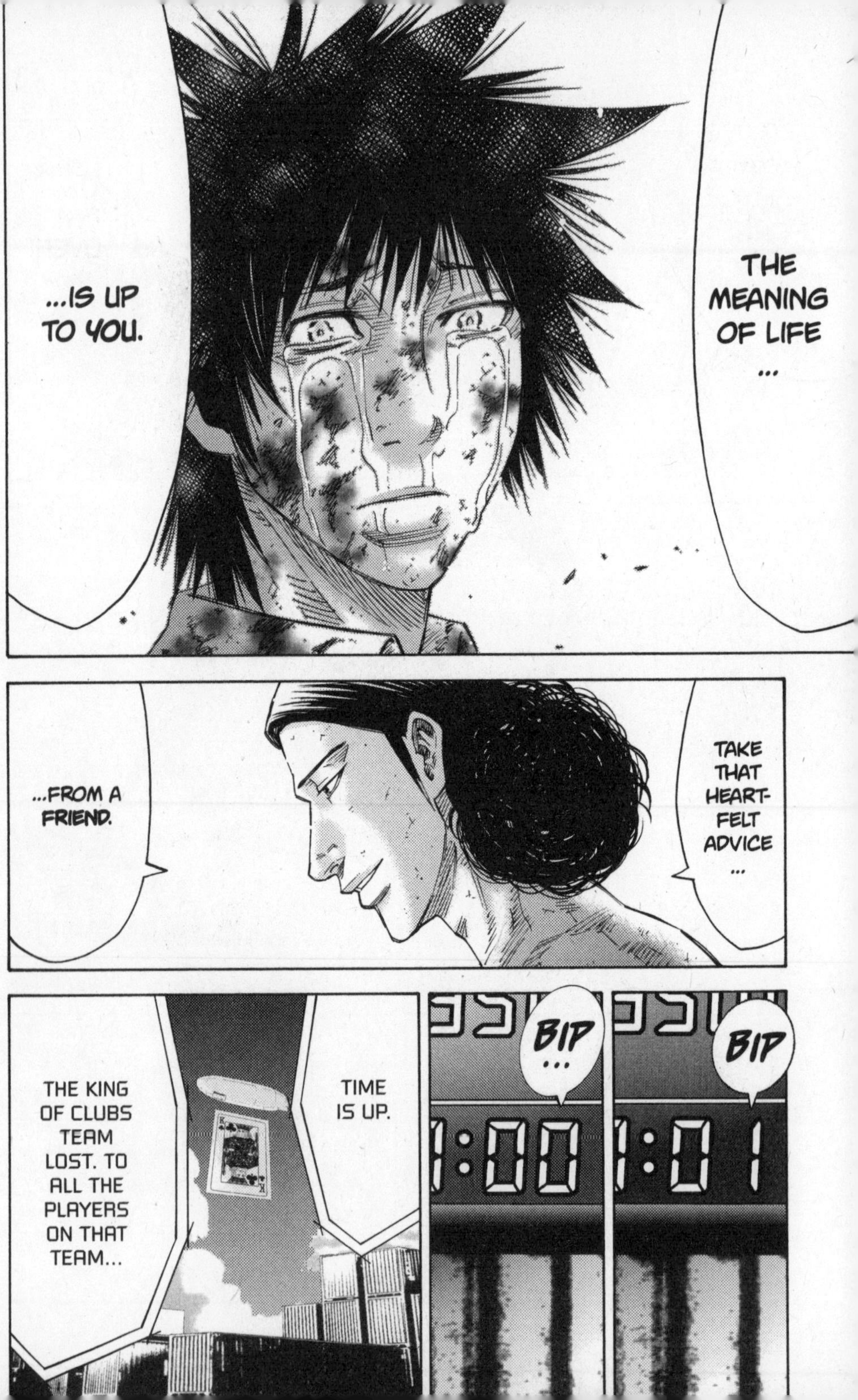
THE MEANING OF LIFE ...
...IS UP TO YOU.
TAKE THAT HEART-FELT ADVICE ...
...FROM A FRIEND.
BIP
1:01
BIP ...
0:00
TIME IS UP.
THE KING OF CLUBS TEAM LOST. TO ALL THE PLAYERS ON THAT TEAM...

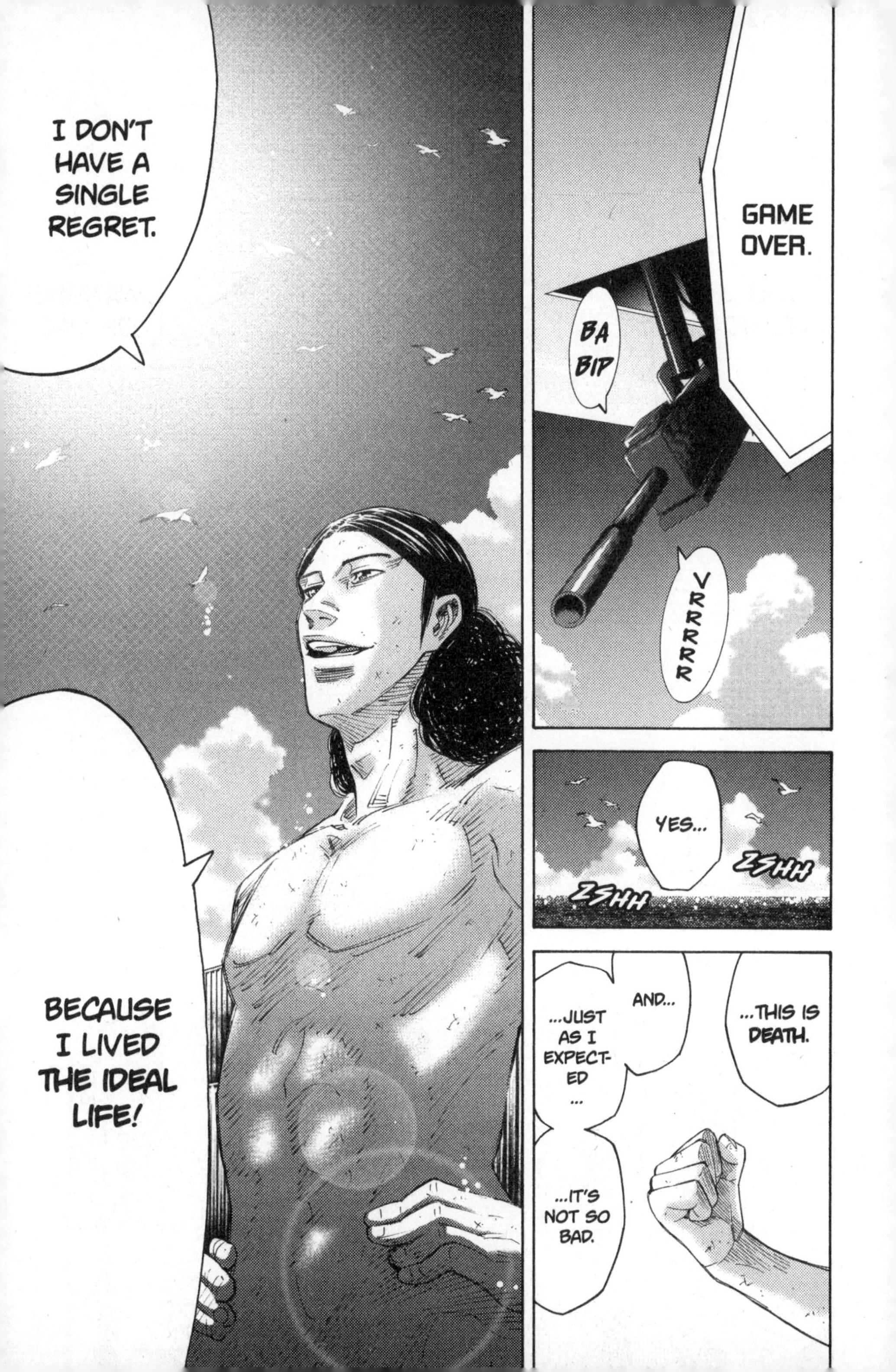
GAME OVER.
BA BIP
VRRRRR
YES...
ZSHH
ZSHH
...THIS IS DEATH.
AND...
...JUST AS I EXPECTED...
...IT'S NOT SO BAD.
I DON'T HAVE A SINGLE REGRET.
BECAUSE I LIVED THE IDEAL LIFE!

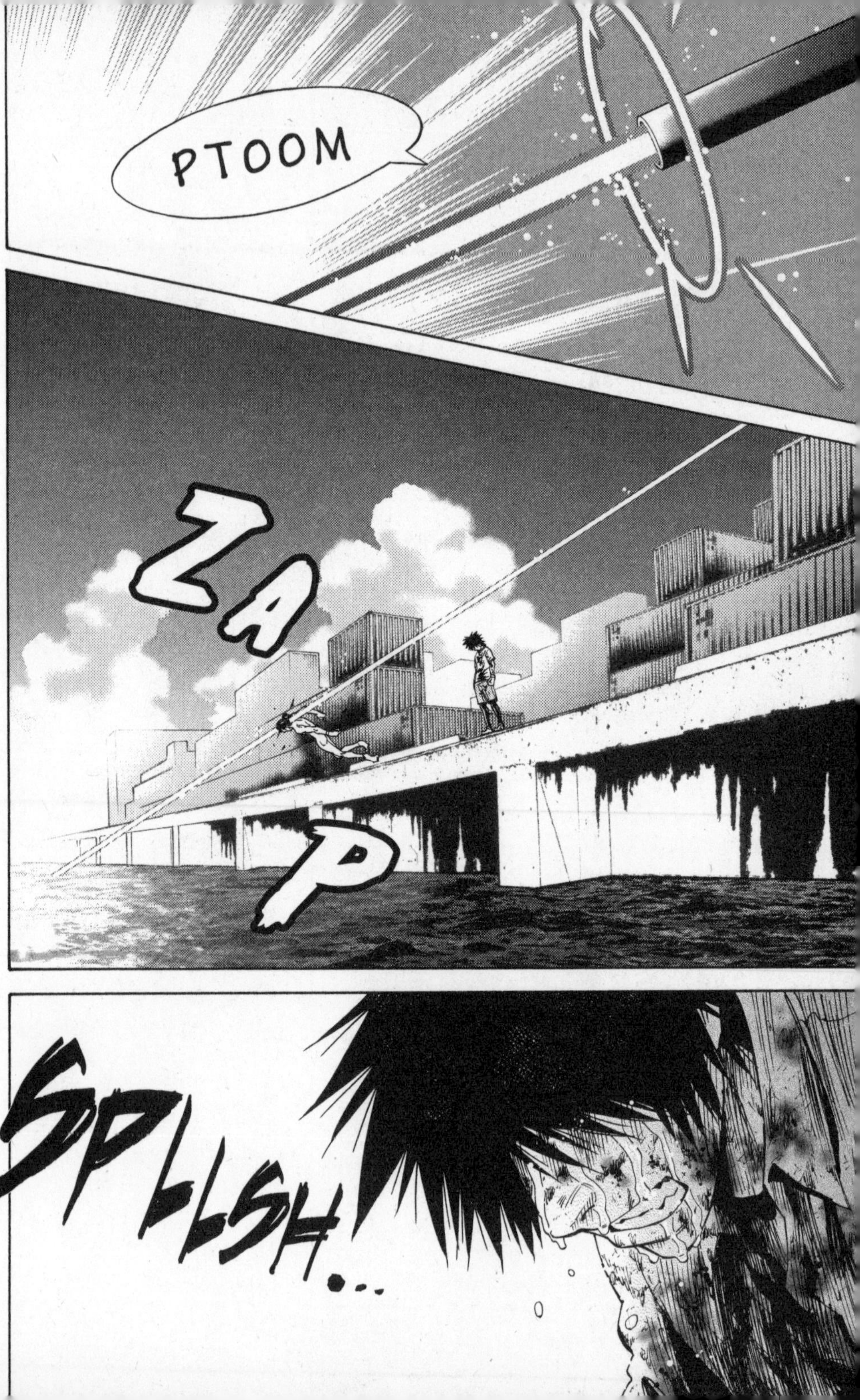
PTOOM
ZAP
SPLLSH...

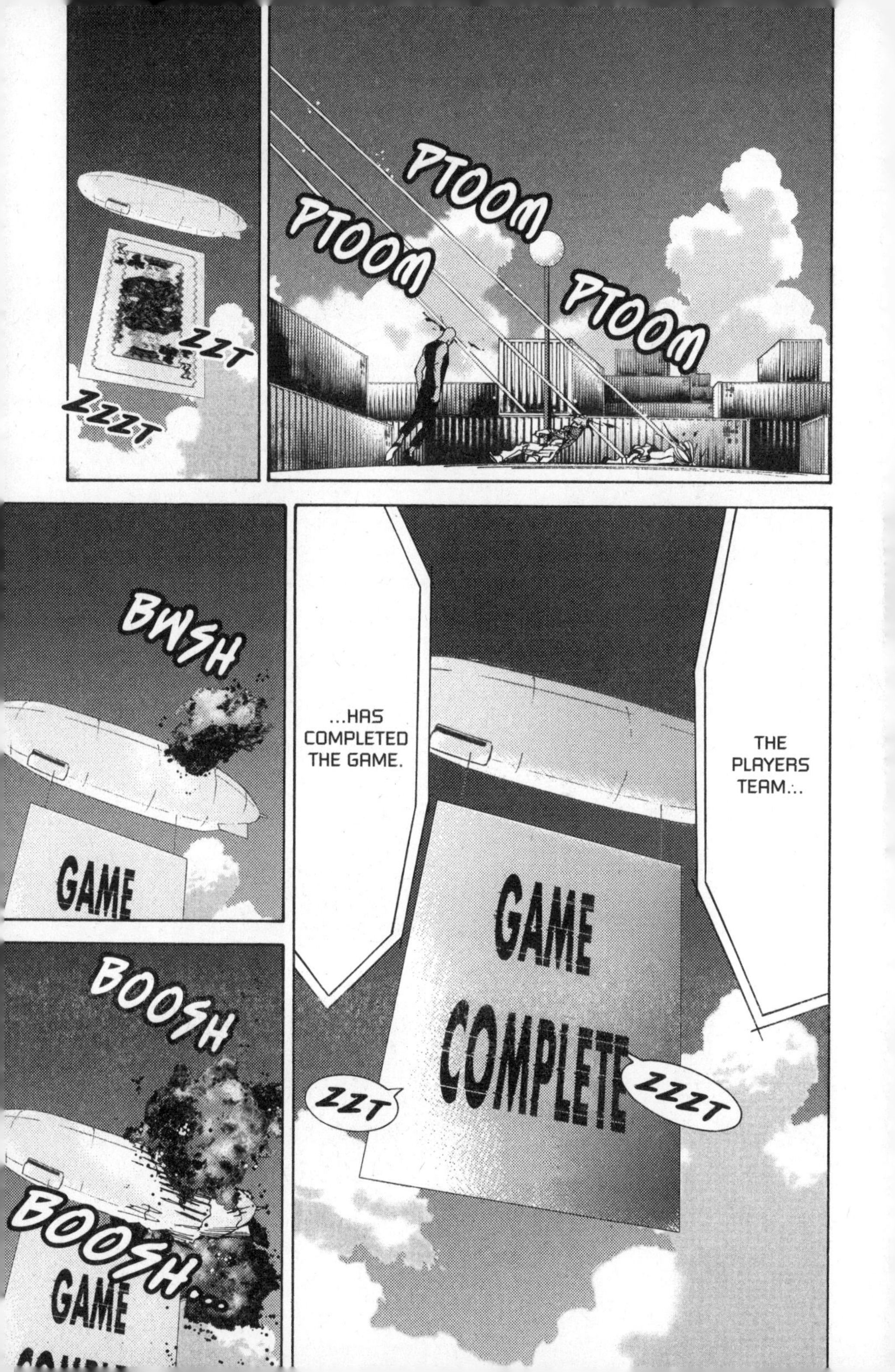
PTOOM
PTOOM
PTOOM
ZZZT
ZZZT
THE PLAYERS TEAM...
...HAS COMPLETED THE GAME.
GAME COMPLETE
ZZZT
ZZT
BWSH
GAME
BOOSH
BOOSH...
GAME

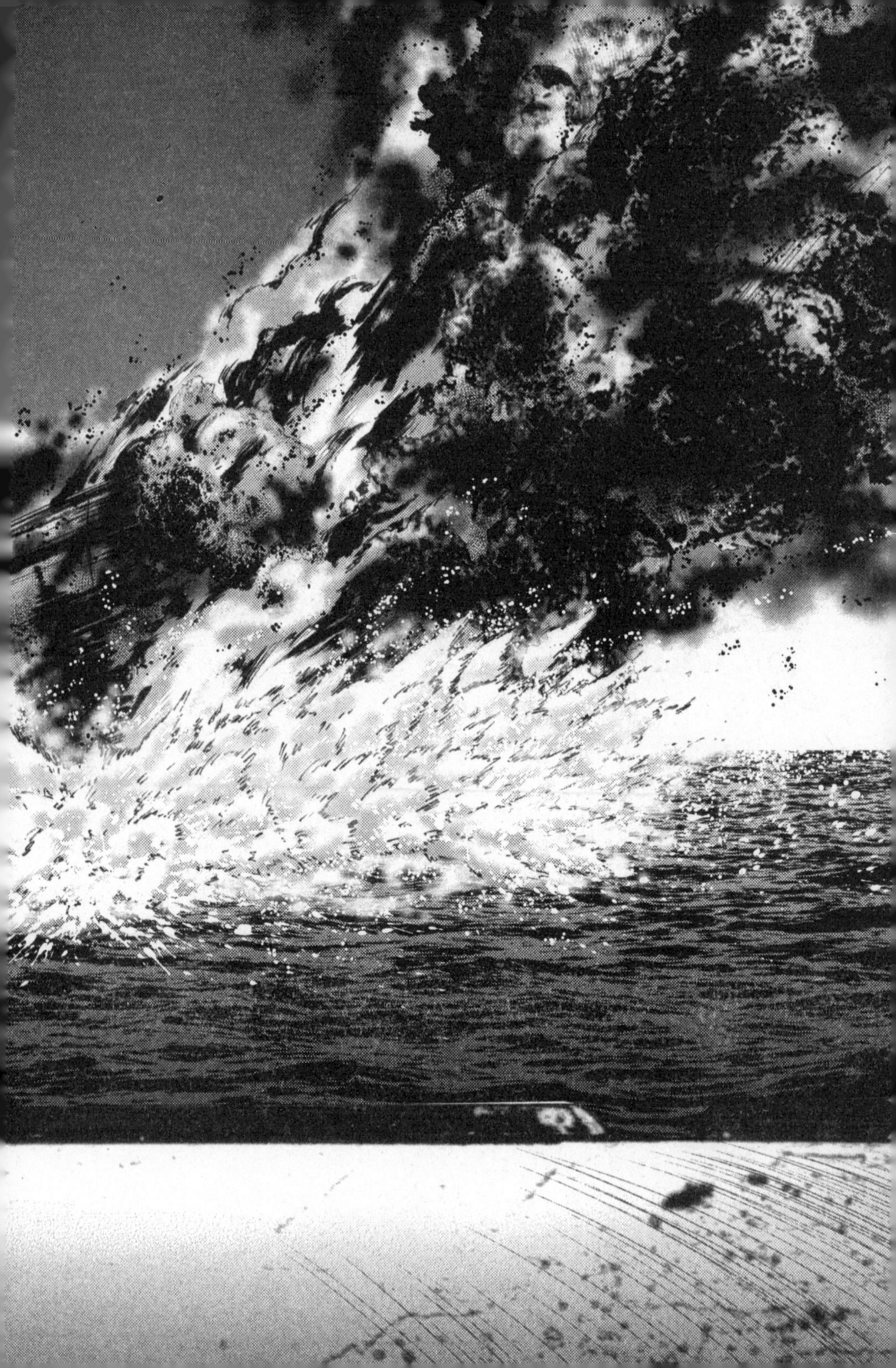

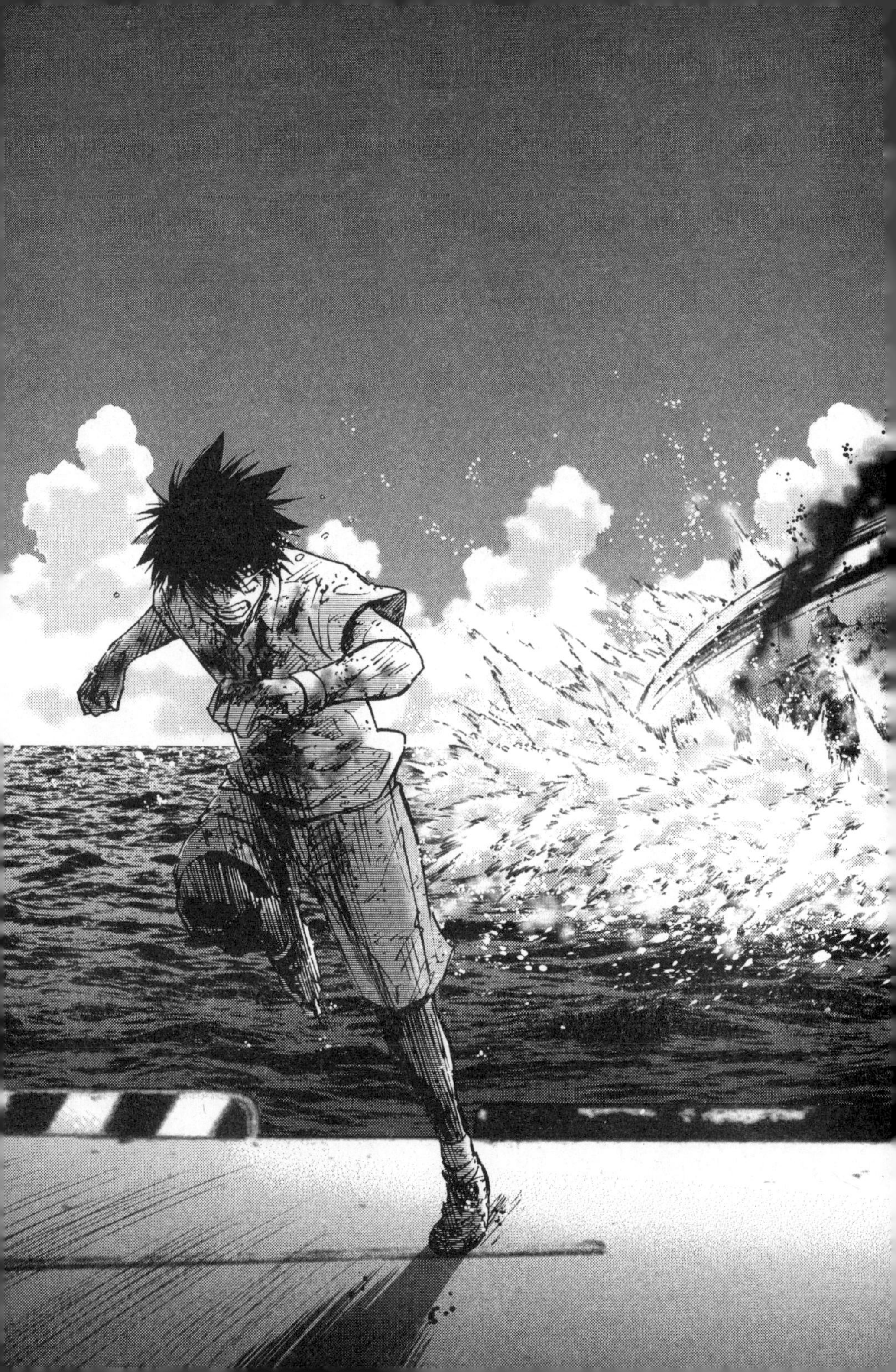

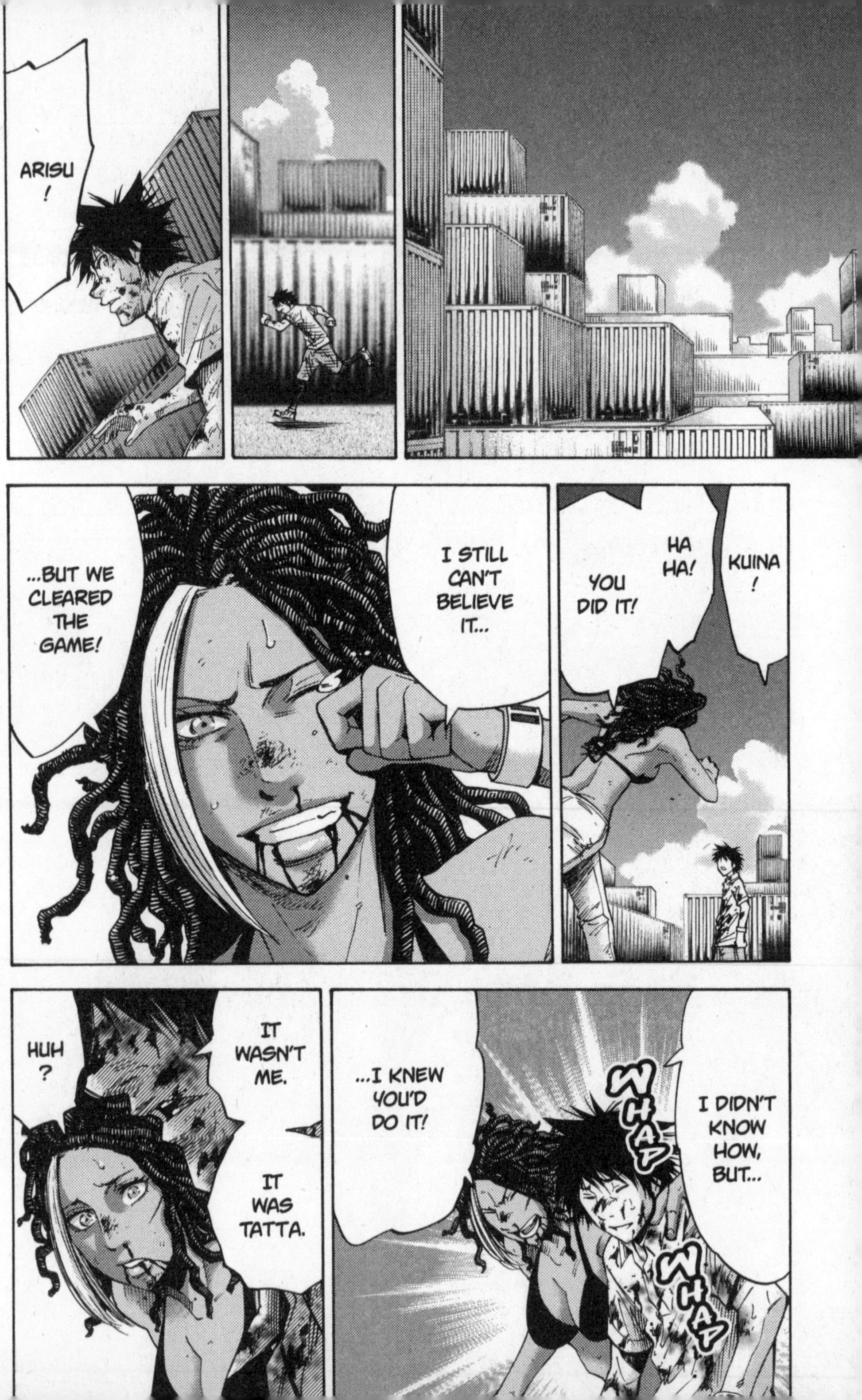
ARISU!
KUINA!
HA HA!
YOU DID IT!
I STILL CAN'T BELIEVE IT...
...BUT WE CLEARED THE GAME!
I DIDN'T KNOW HOW, BUT...
WHAP
WHAP
...I KNEW YOU'D DO IT!
HUH?
IT WASN'T ME.
IT WAS TATTA.

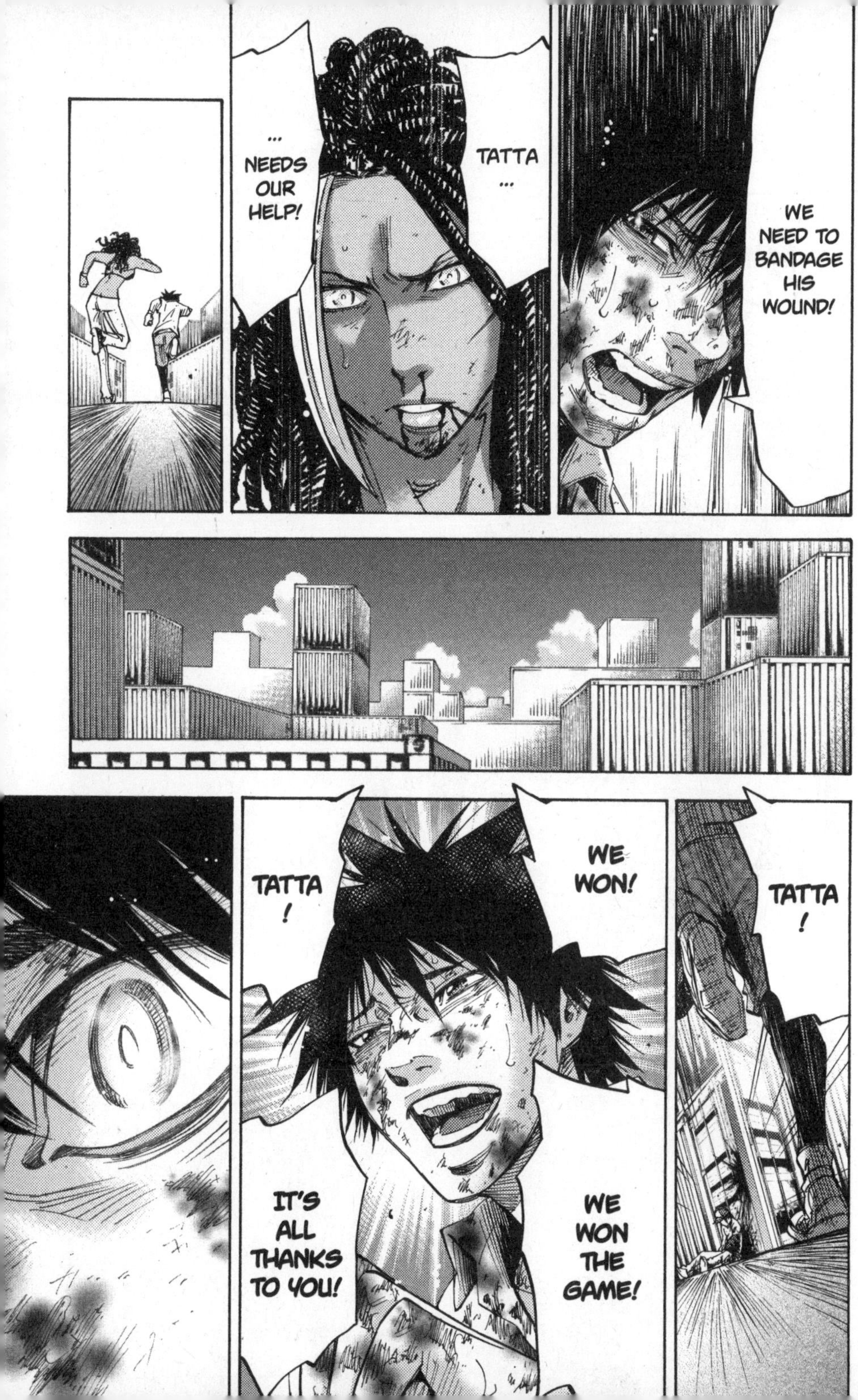
WE NEED TO BANDAGE HIS WOUND!
TATTA ...
... NEEDS OUR HELP!
TATTA!
WE WON!
TATTA!
WE WON THE GAME!
IT'S ALL THANKS TO YOU!

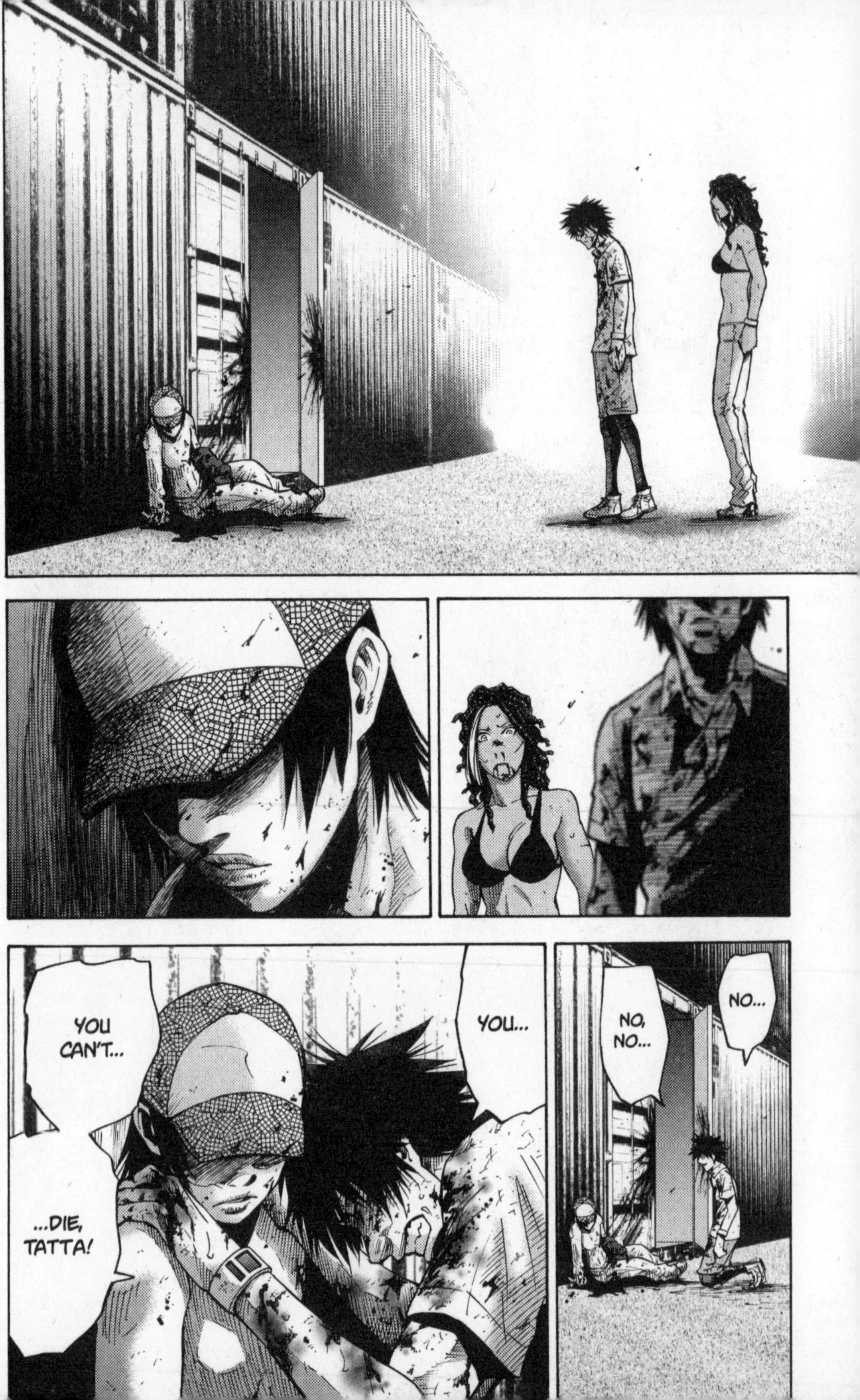
NO...
NO, NO...
YOU...
YOU CAN'T...
...DIE, TATTA!

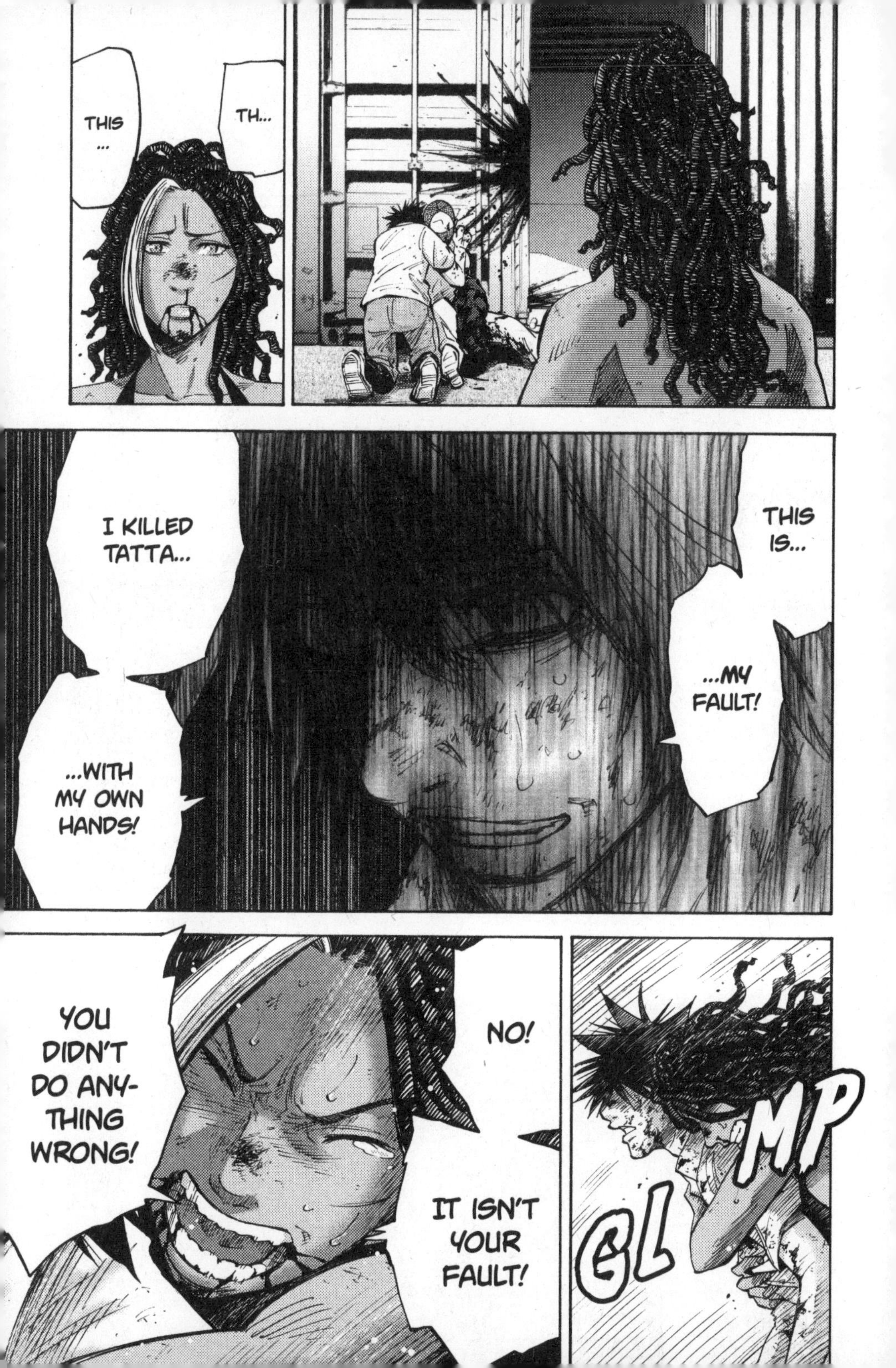
TH...
THIS ...
THIS IS...
...MY FAULT!
I KILLED TATTA...
...WITH MY OWN HANDS!
GL MP
NO!
IT ISN'T YOUR FAULT!
YOU DIDN'T DO ANY-THING WRONG!

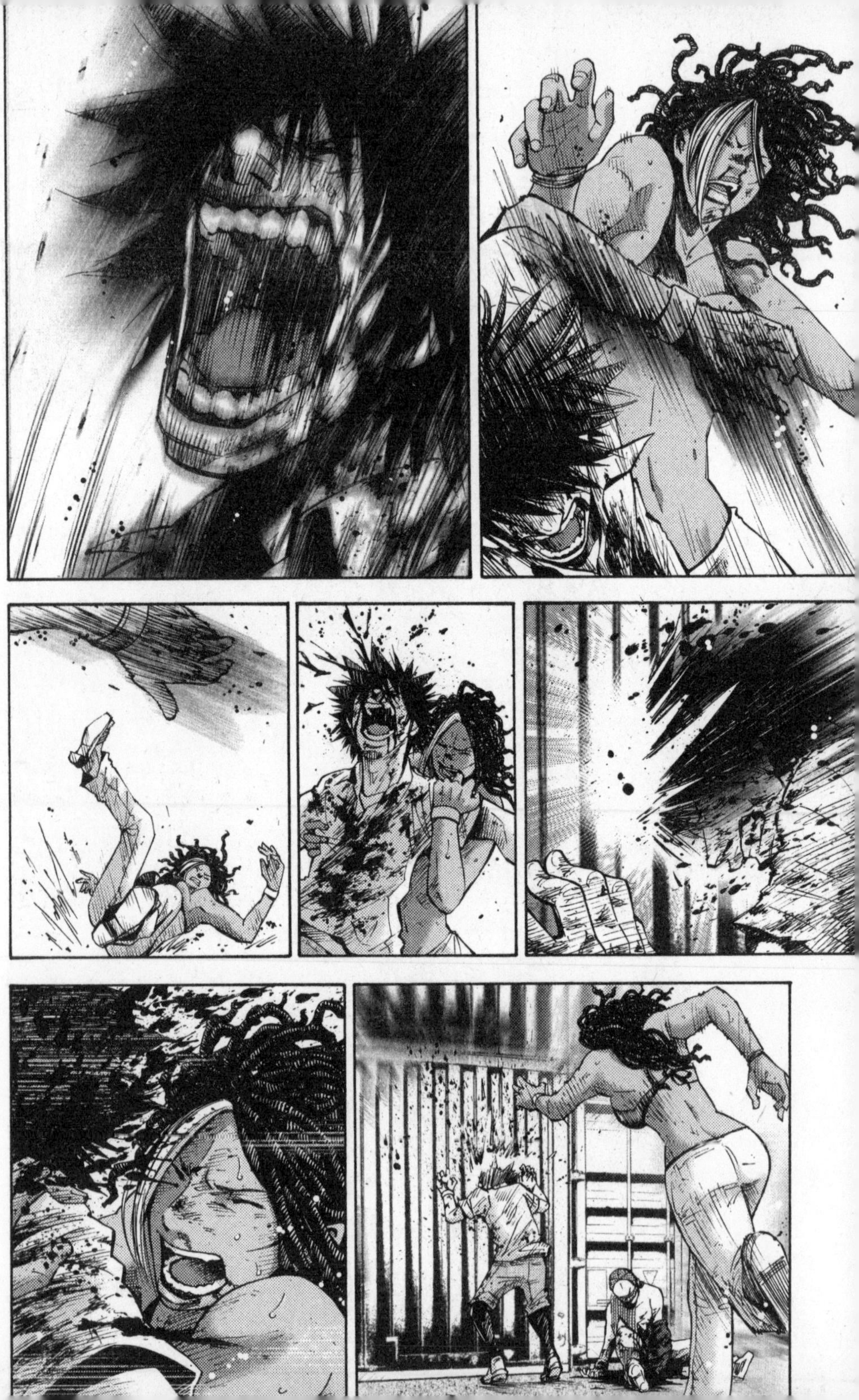

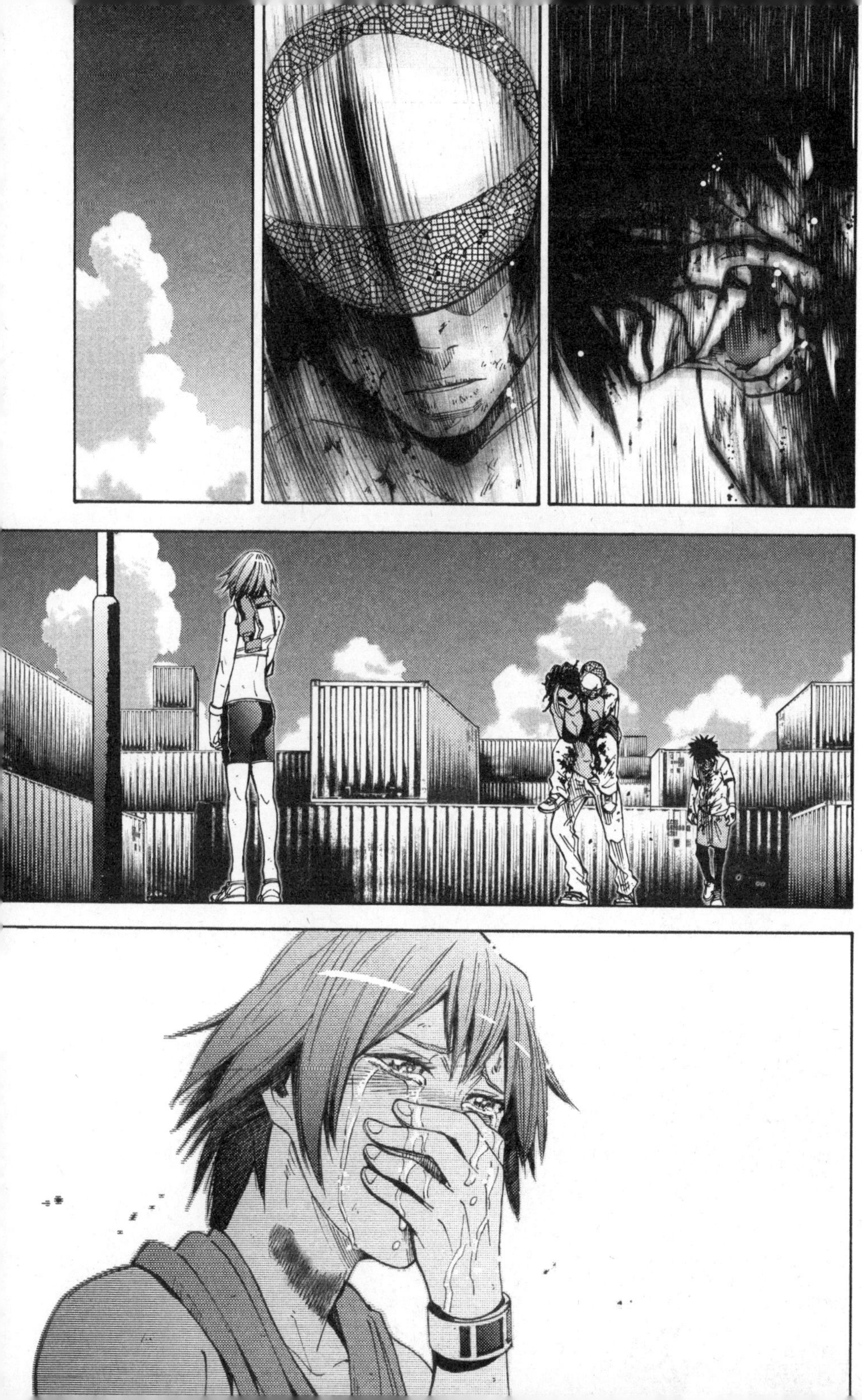

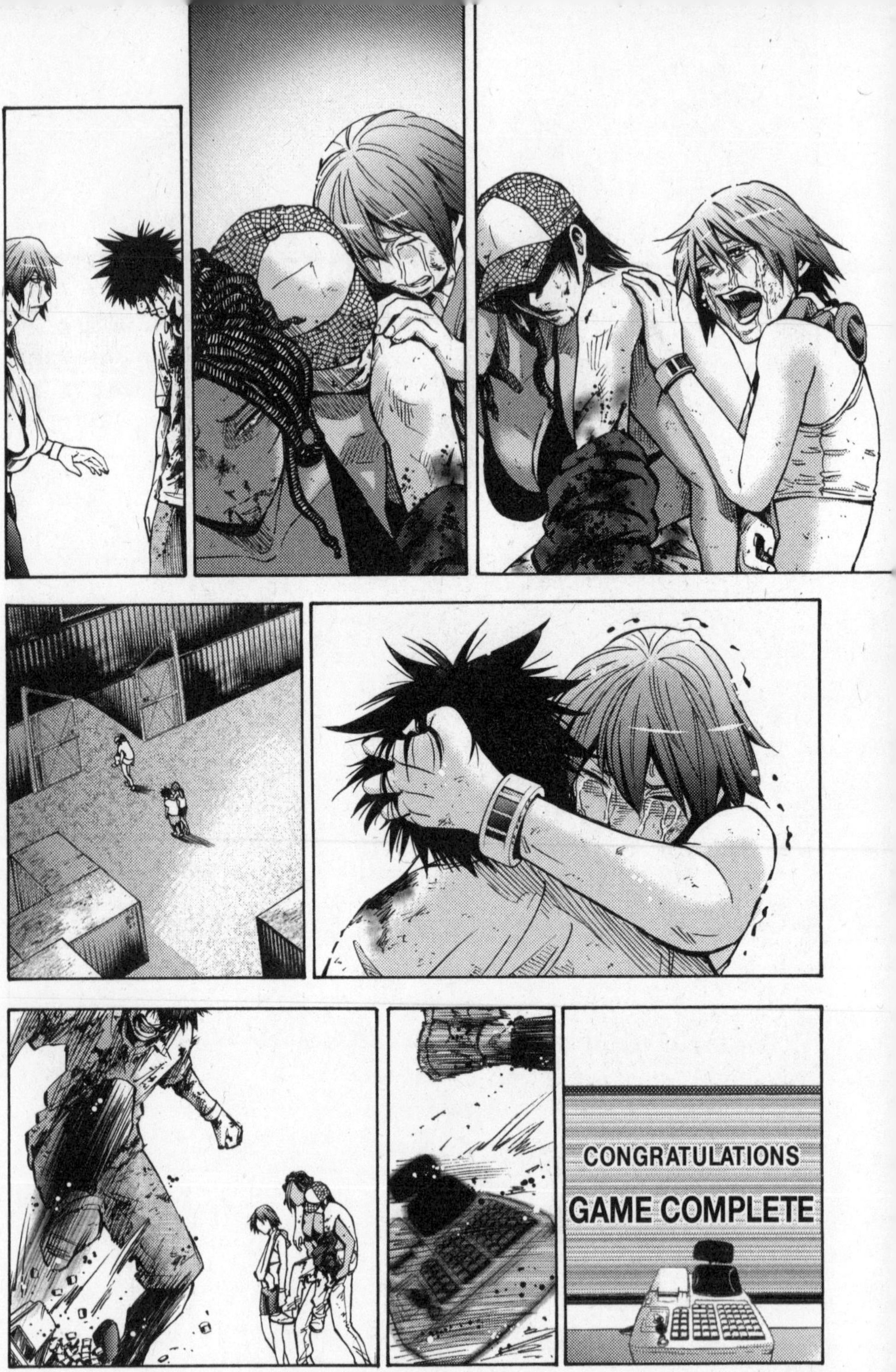
CONGRATULATIONS
GAME COMPLETE

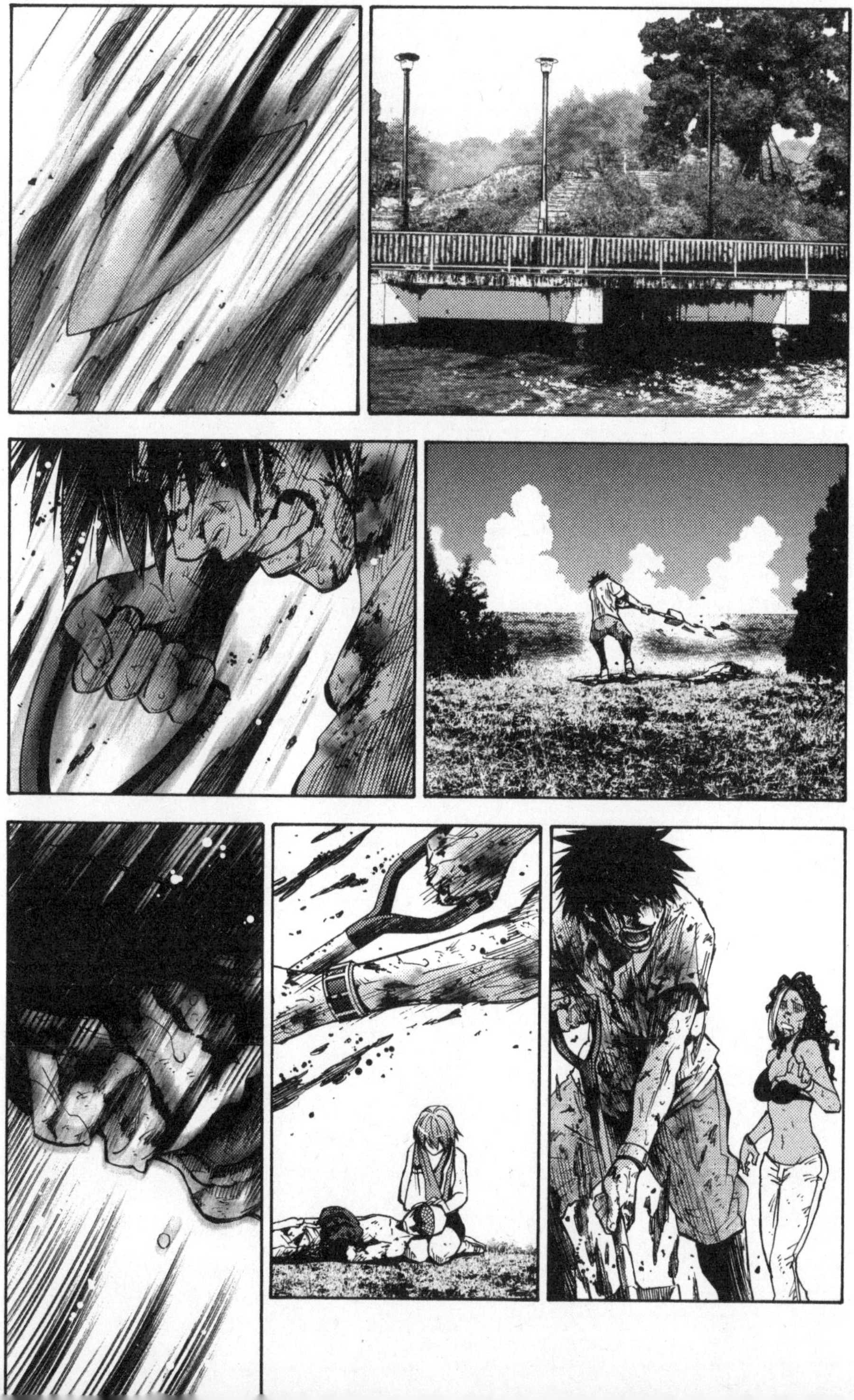

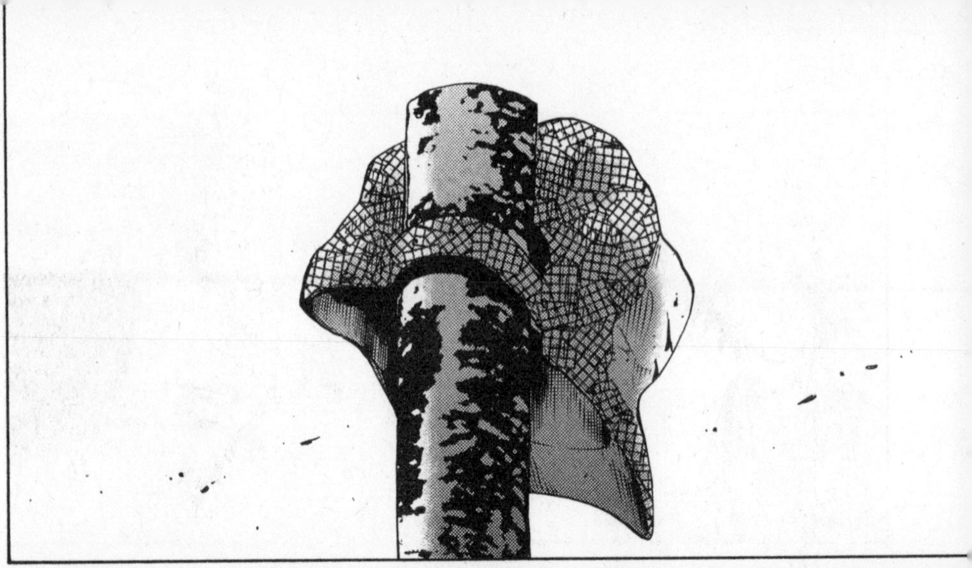

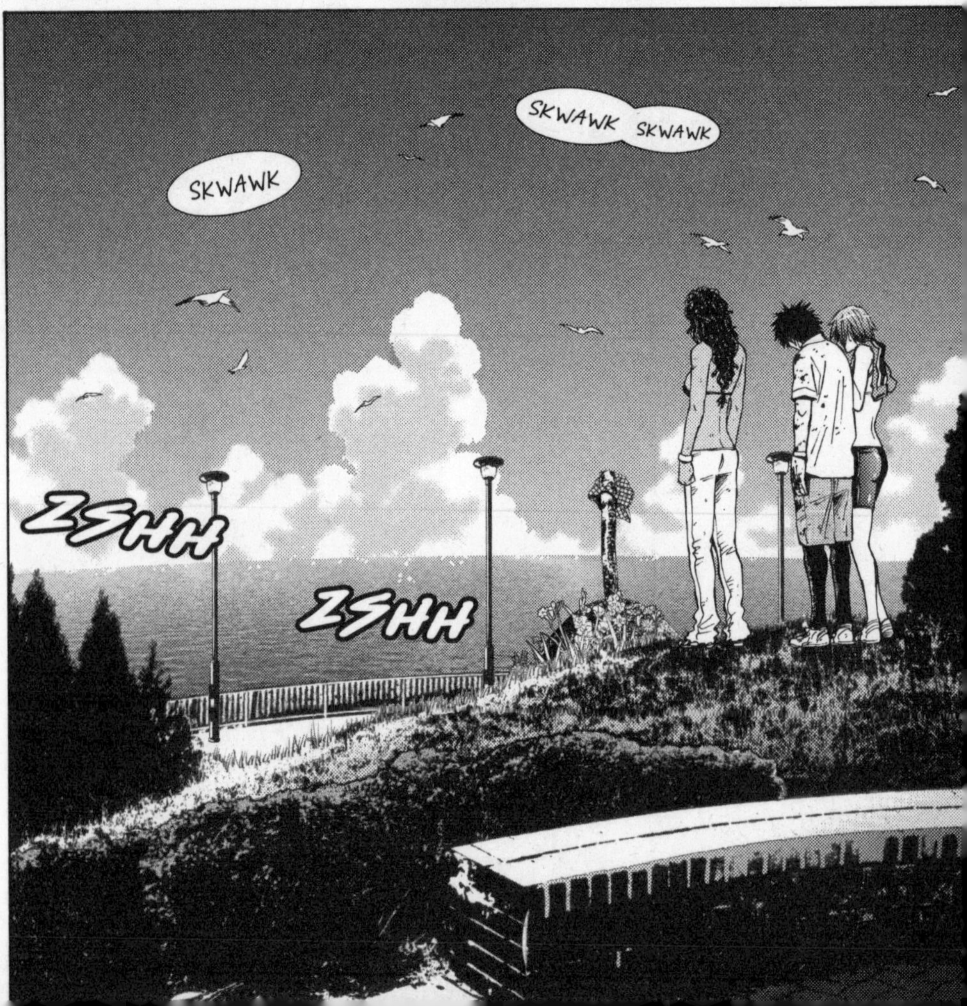
SKWAWK
SKWAWK
SKWAWK
ZSHH
ZSHH

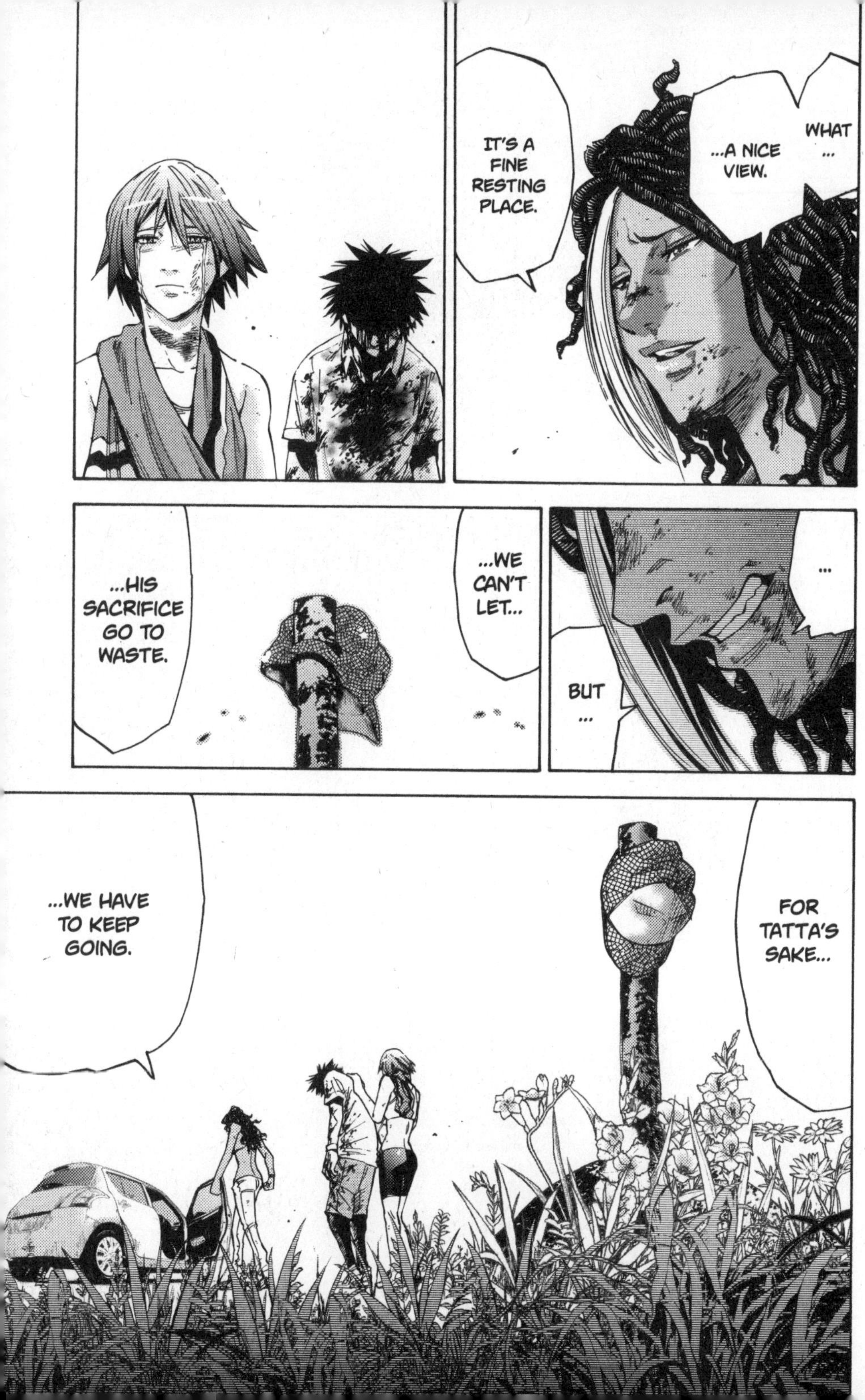
WHAT ...
...A NICE VIEW.
IT'S A FINE RESTING PLACE.
...
BUT ...
...WE CAN'T LET...
...HIS SACRIFICE GO TO WASTE.
FOR TATTA'S SAKE...
...WE HAVE TO KEEP GOING.

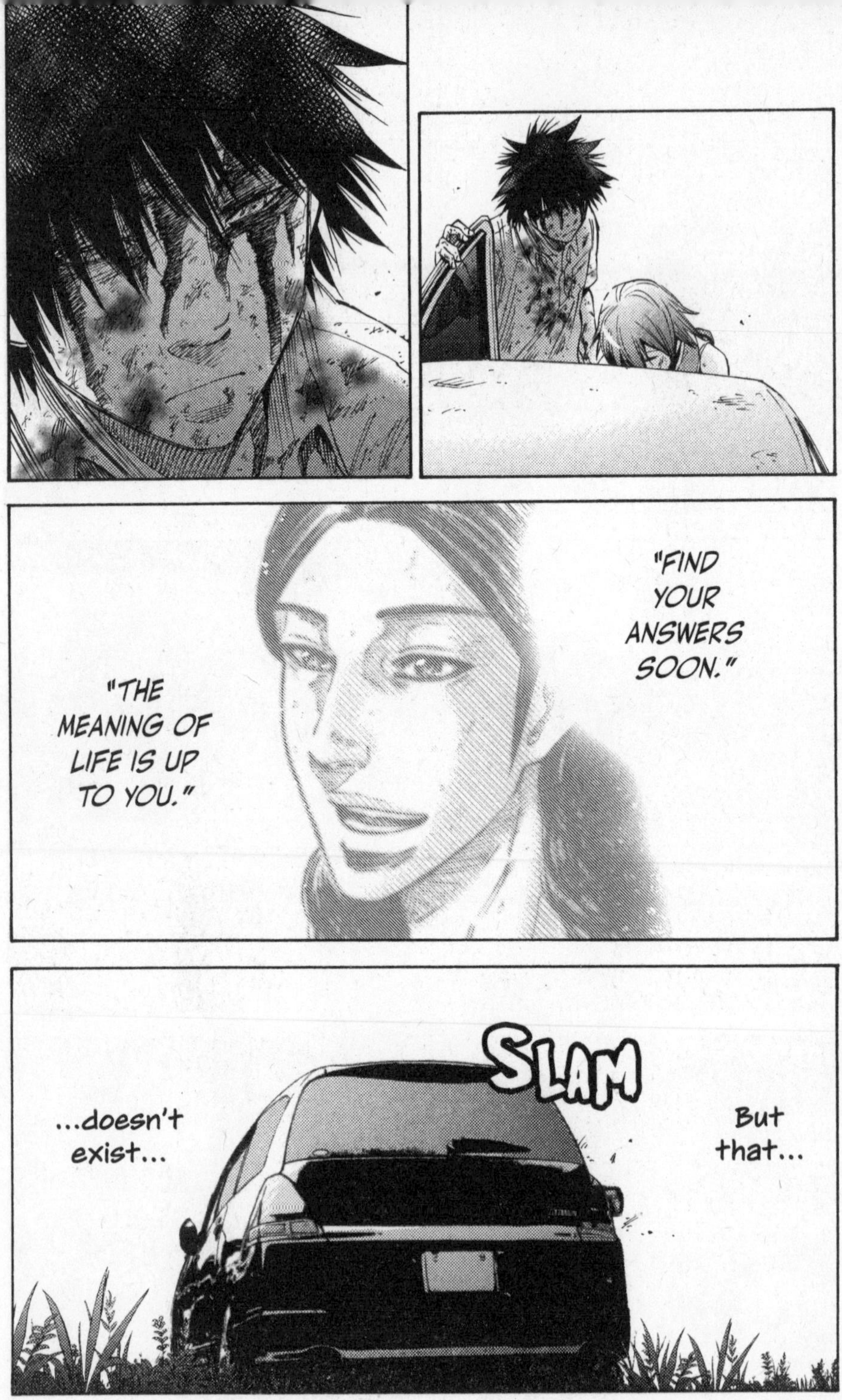
"FIND YOUR ANSWERS SOON."
"THE MEANING OF LIFE IS UP TO YOU."
SLAM
But that...
...doesn't exist...

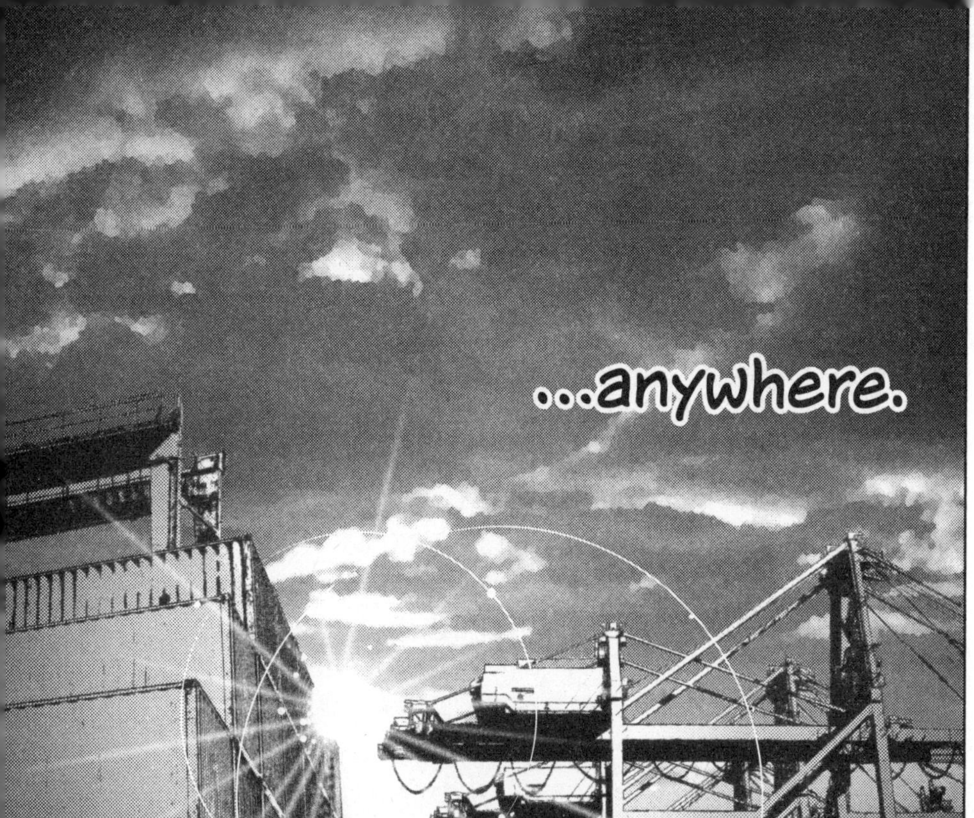
...anywhere.
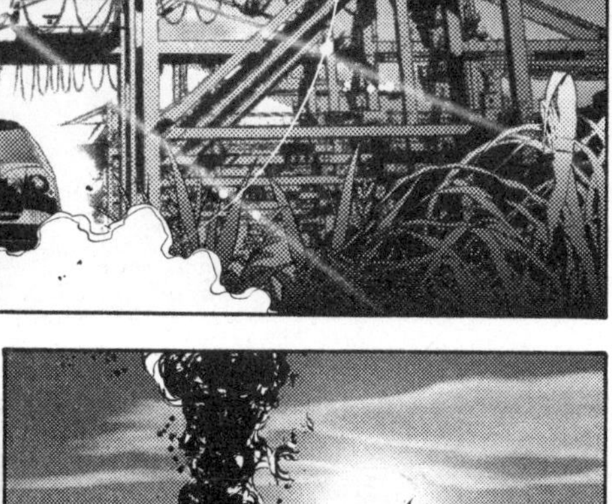
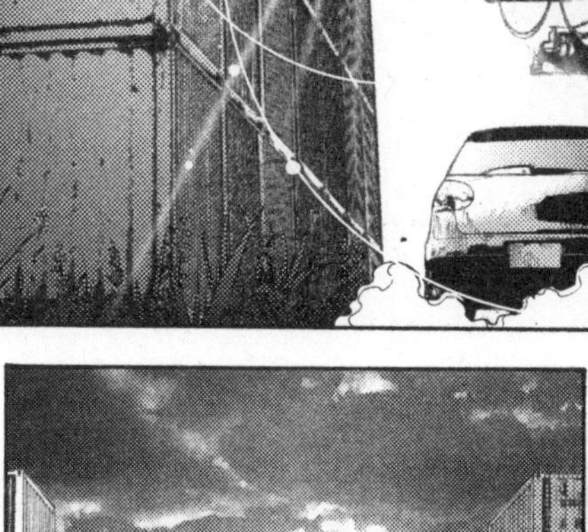

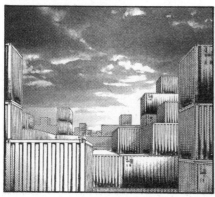

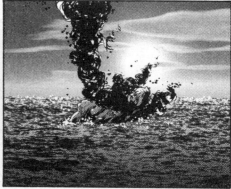

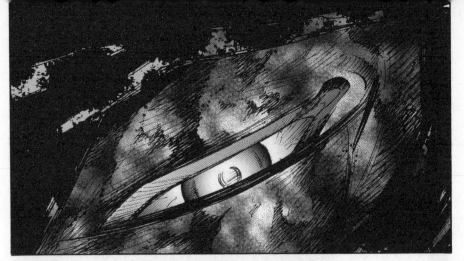

Players	King of Clubs
35500	35000

0:00:00

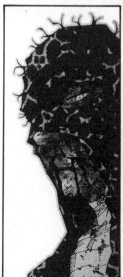

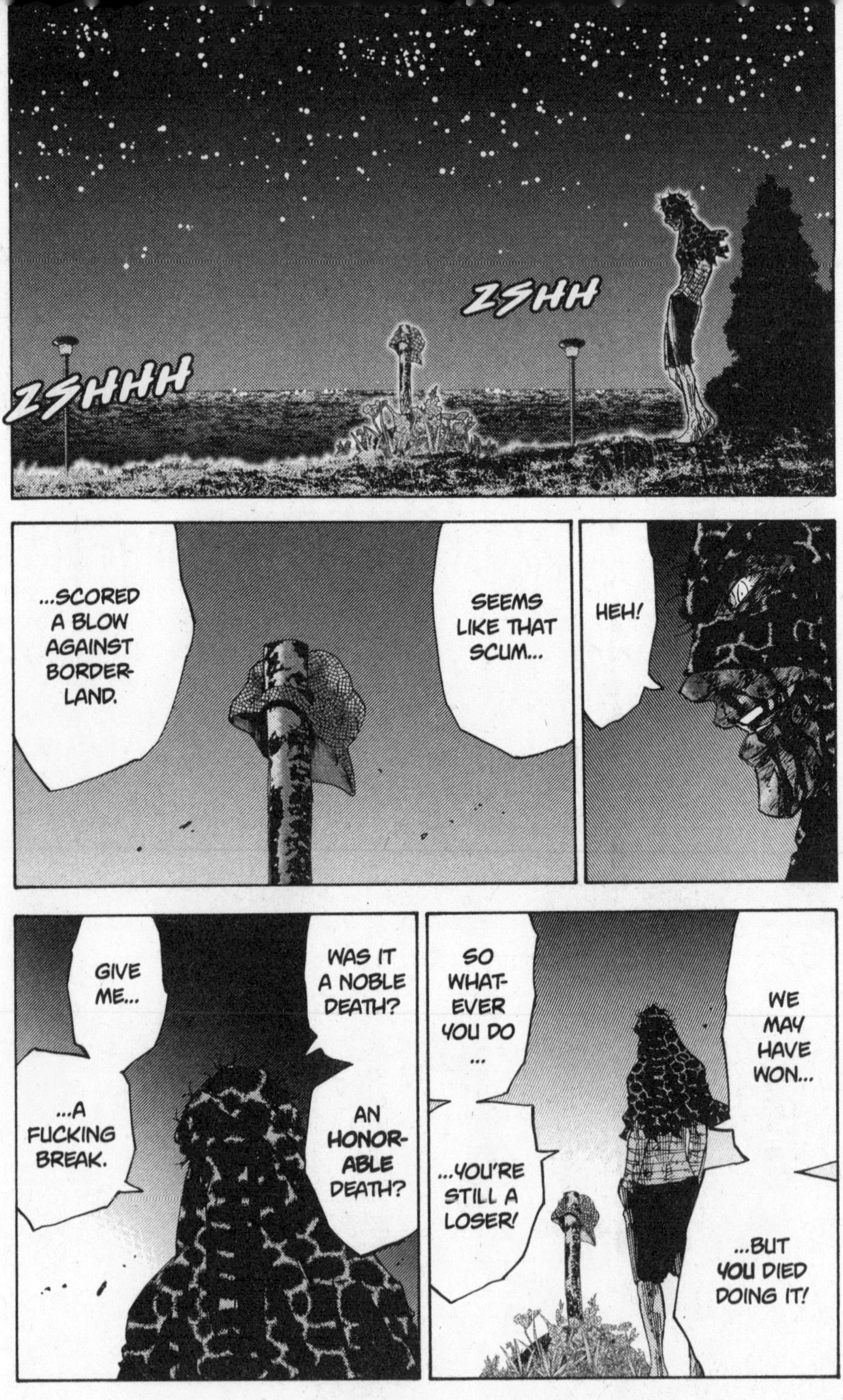
ZSHH
ZSHHH
HEH!
SEEMS LIKE THAT SCUM...
...SCORED A BLOW AGAINST BORDER-LAND.
WE MAY HAVE WON...
...BUT YOU DIED DOING IT!
SO WHAT-EVER YOU DO ...
...YOU'RE STILL A LOSER!
WAS IT A NOBLE DEATH?
AN HONOR-ABLE DEATH?
GIVE ME...
...A FUCKING BREAK.

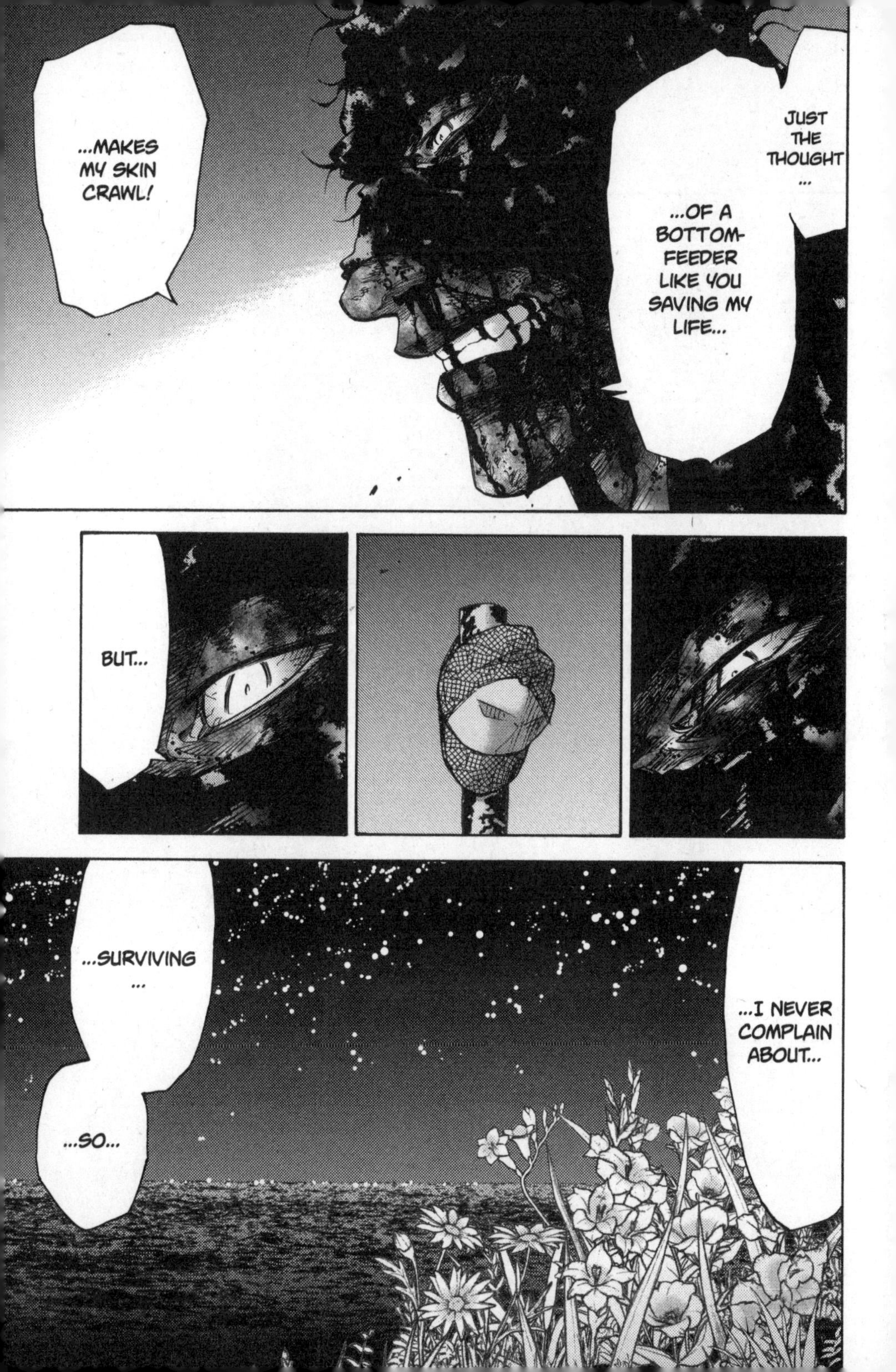
JUST THE THOUGHT ...
...OF A BOTTOM-FEEDER LIKE YOU SAVING MY LIFE...
...MAKES MY SKIN CRAWL!
BUT...
...I NEVER COMPLAIN ABOUT...
...SURVIVING ...
...SO...

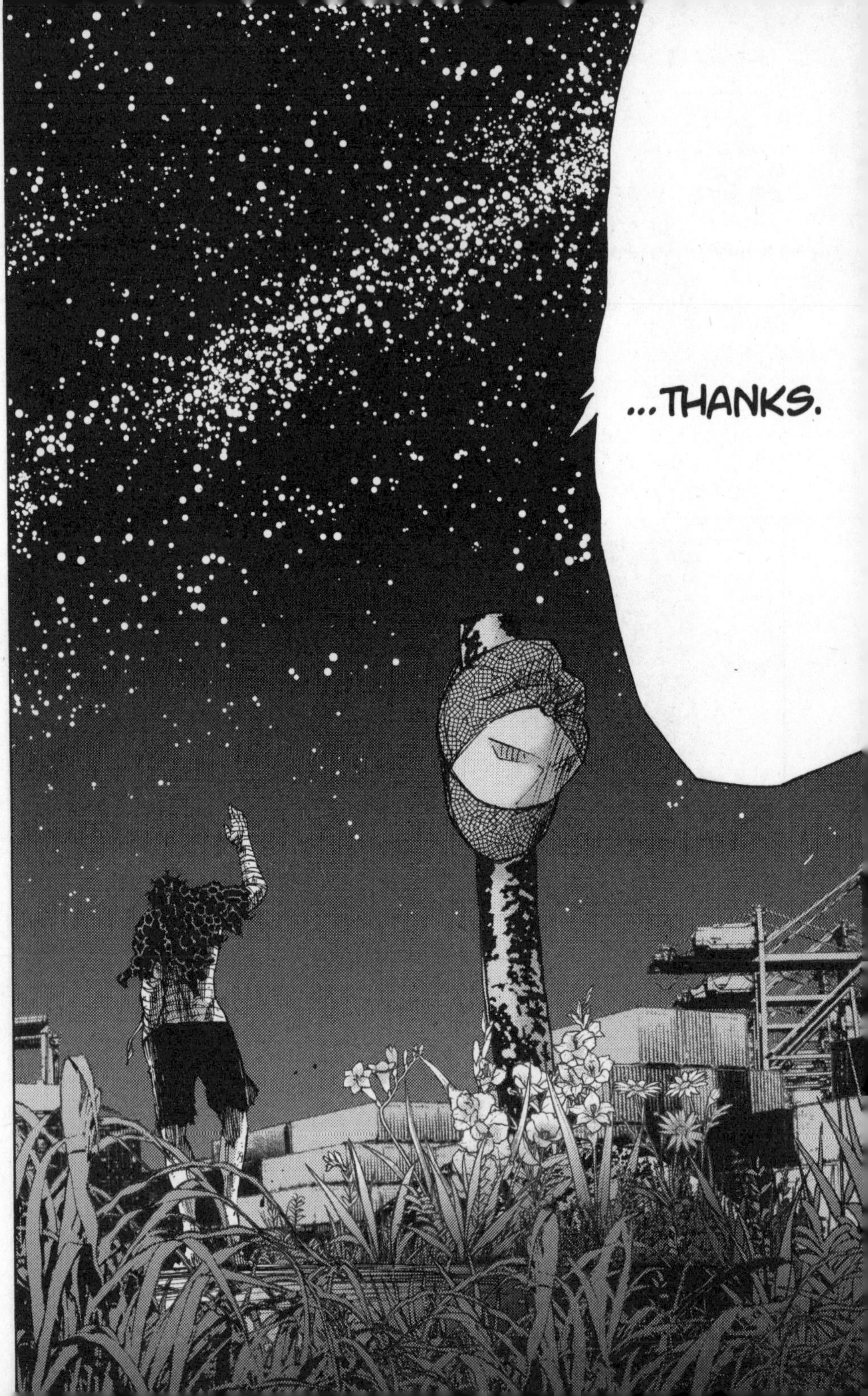
...THANKS.

CHAPTER 42: Three Days After the Start

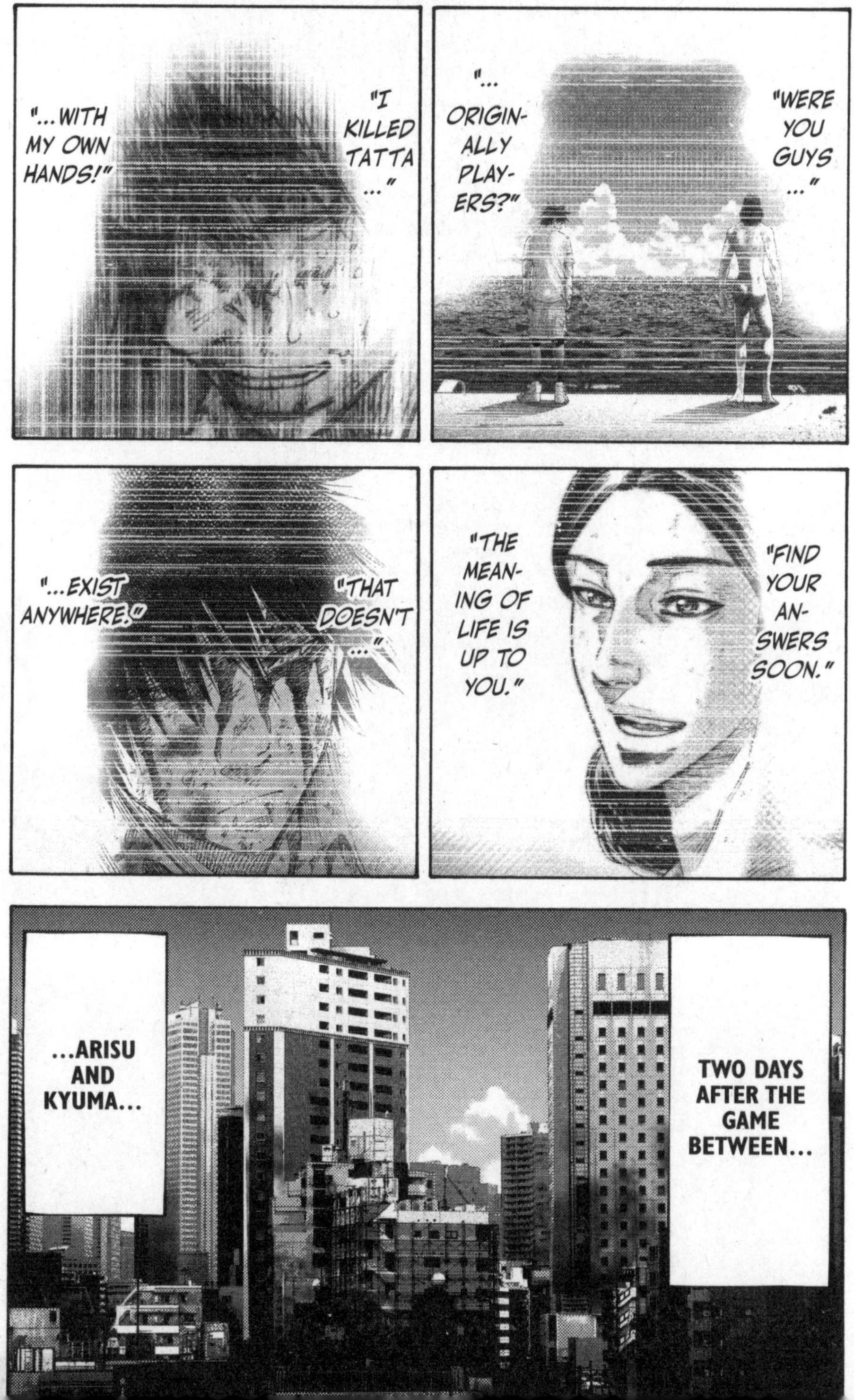
"WERE YOU GUYS..."
"...ORIGINALLY PLAYERS?"
"I KILLED TATTA..."
"...WITH MY OWN HANDS!"
"FIND YOUR ANSWERS SOON."
"THE MEANING OF LIFE IS UP TO YOU."
"THAT DOESN'T..."
"...EXIST ANYWHERE."
TWO DAYS AFTER THE GAME BETWEEN...
...ARISU AND KYUMA...

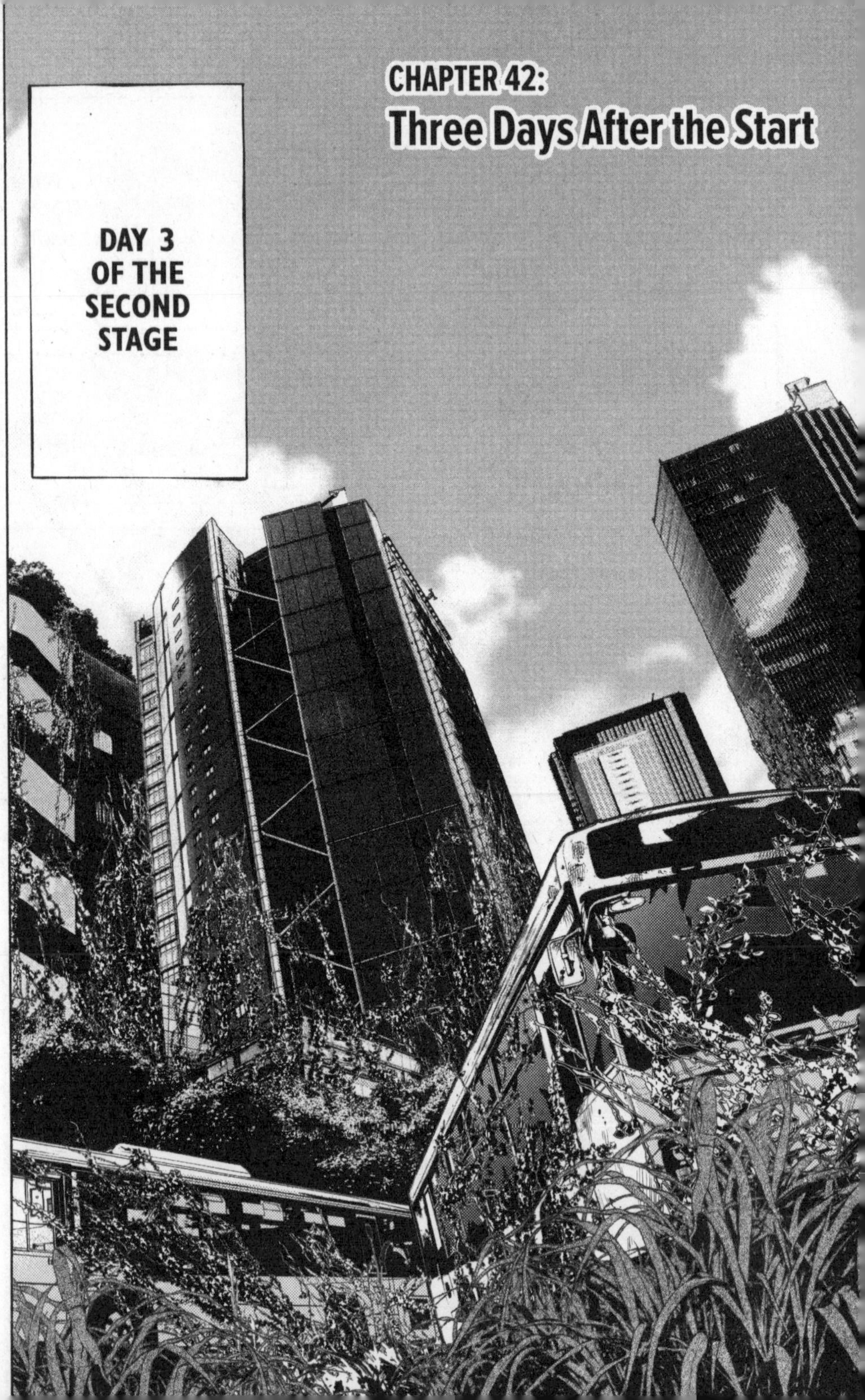
CHAPTER 42:
Three Days After the Start
DAY 3 OF THE SECOND STAGE

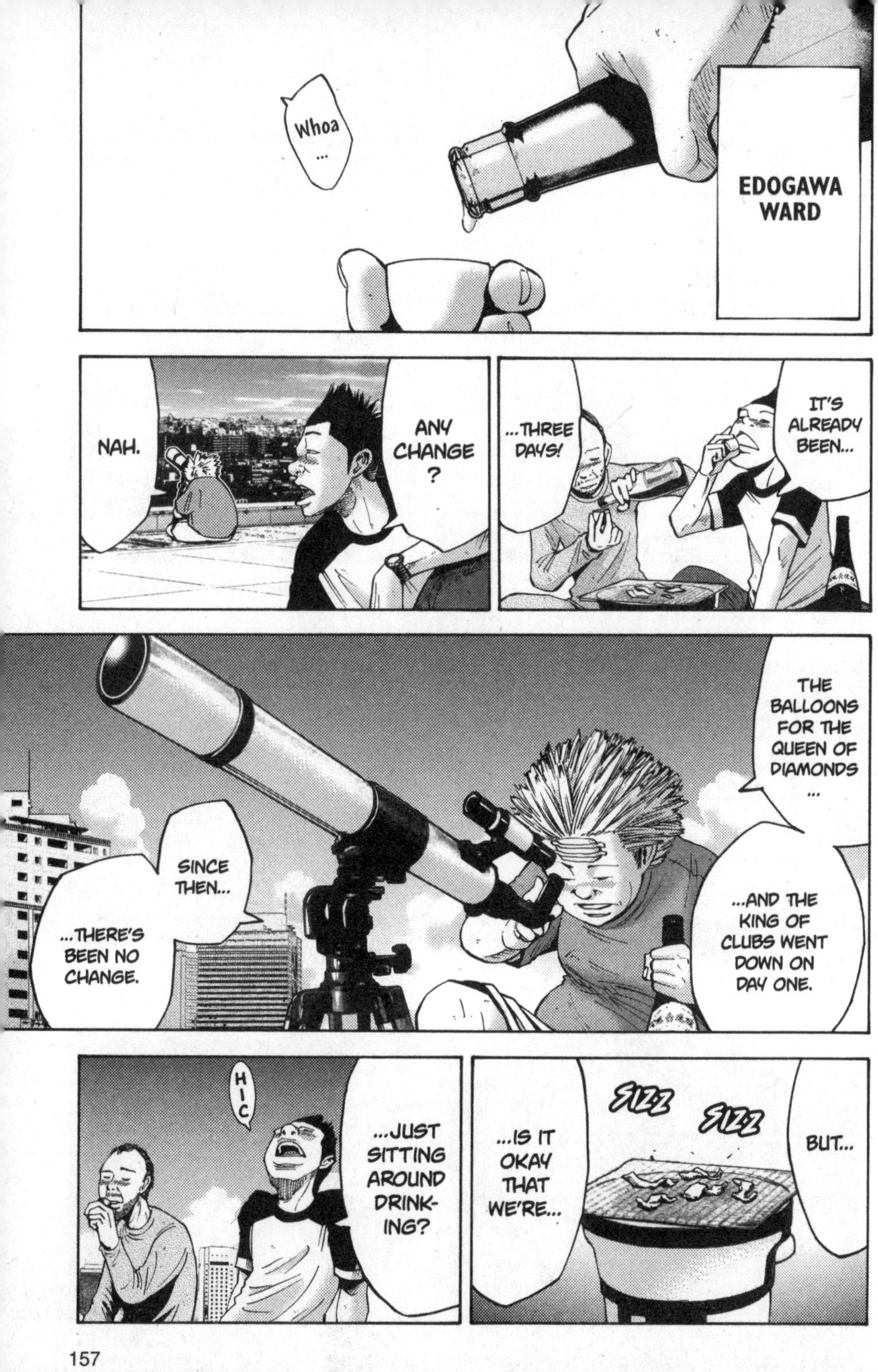
EDOGAWA WARD
Whoa ...
IT'S ALREADY BEEN...
...THREE DAYS!
ANY CHANGE?
NAH.
THE BALLOONS FOR THE QUEEN OF DIAMONDS ...
...AND THE KING OF CLUBS WENT DOWN ON DAY ONE.
SINCE THEN...
...THERE'S BEEN NO CHANGE.
BUT...
SIZZ
SIZZ
...IS IT OKAY THAT WE'RE...
...JUST SITTING AROUND DRINK-ING?
HIC

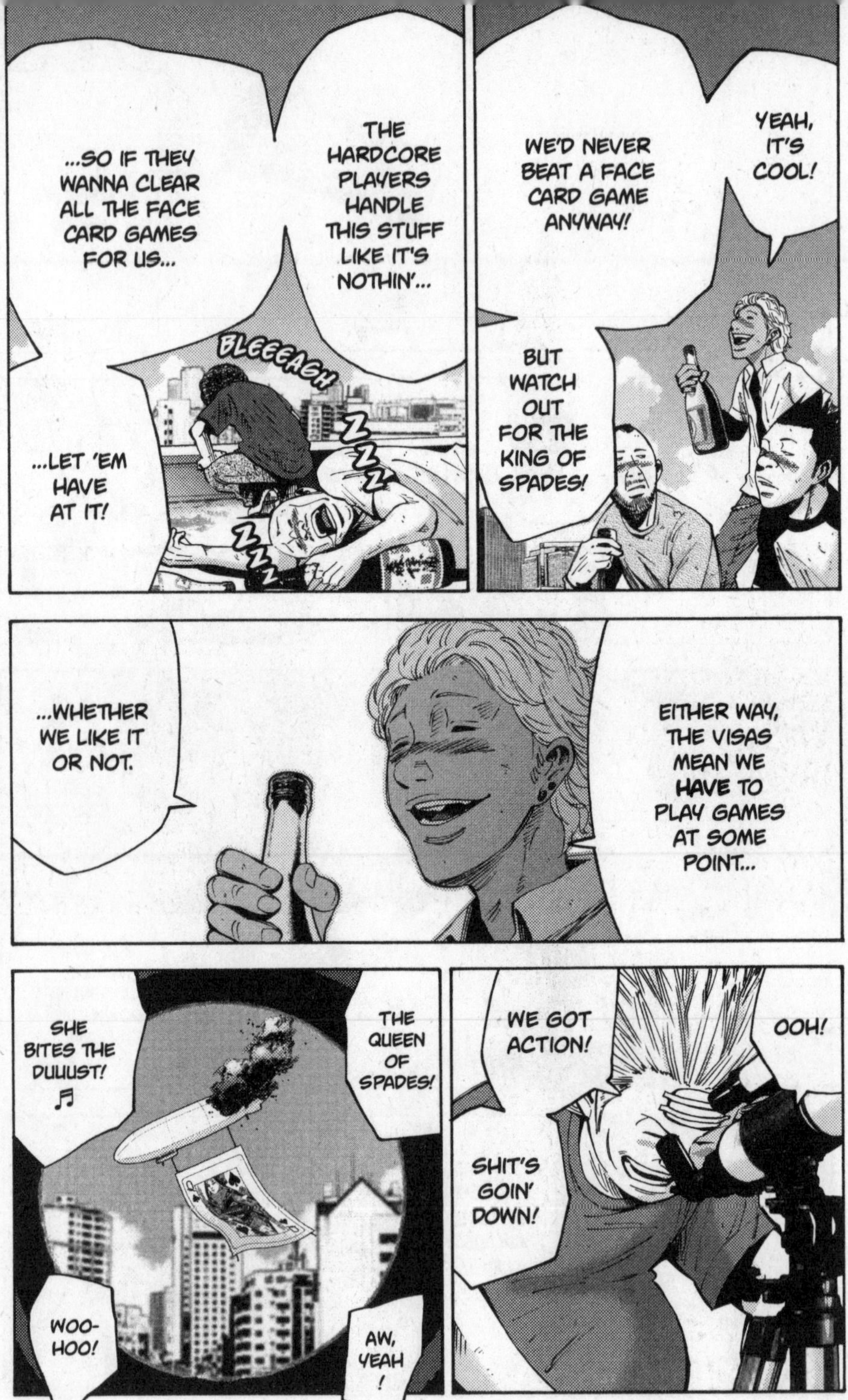
YEAH, IT'S COOL!
WE'D NEVER BEAT A FACE CARD GAME ANYWAY!
BUT WATCH OUT FOR THE KING OF SPADES!
THE HARDCORE PLAYERS HANDLE THIS STUFF LIKE IT'S NOTHIN'...
...SO IF THEY WANNA CLEAR ALL THE FACE CARD GAMES FOR US...
BLEEEEAGH
ZZZ
...LET 'EM HAVE AT IT!
ZZZ
EITHER WAY, THE VISAS MEAN WE HAVE TO PLAY GAMES AT SOME POINT...
...WHETHER WE LIKE IT OR NOT.
OOH!
WE GOT ACTION!
SHIT'S GOIN' DOWN!
THE QUEEN OF SPADES!
SHE BITES THE DUUUST! ♬
AW, YEAH!
WOO-HOO!

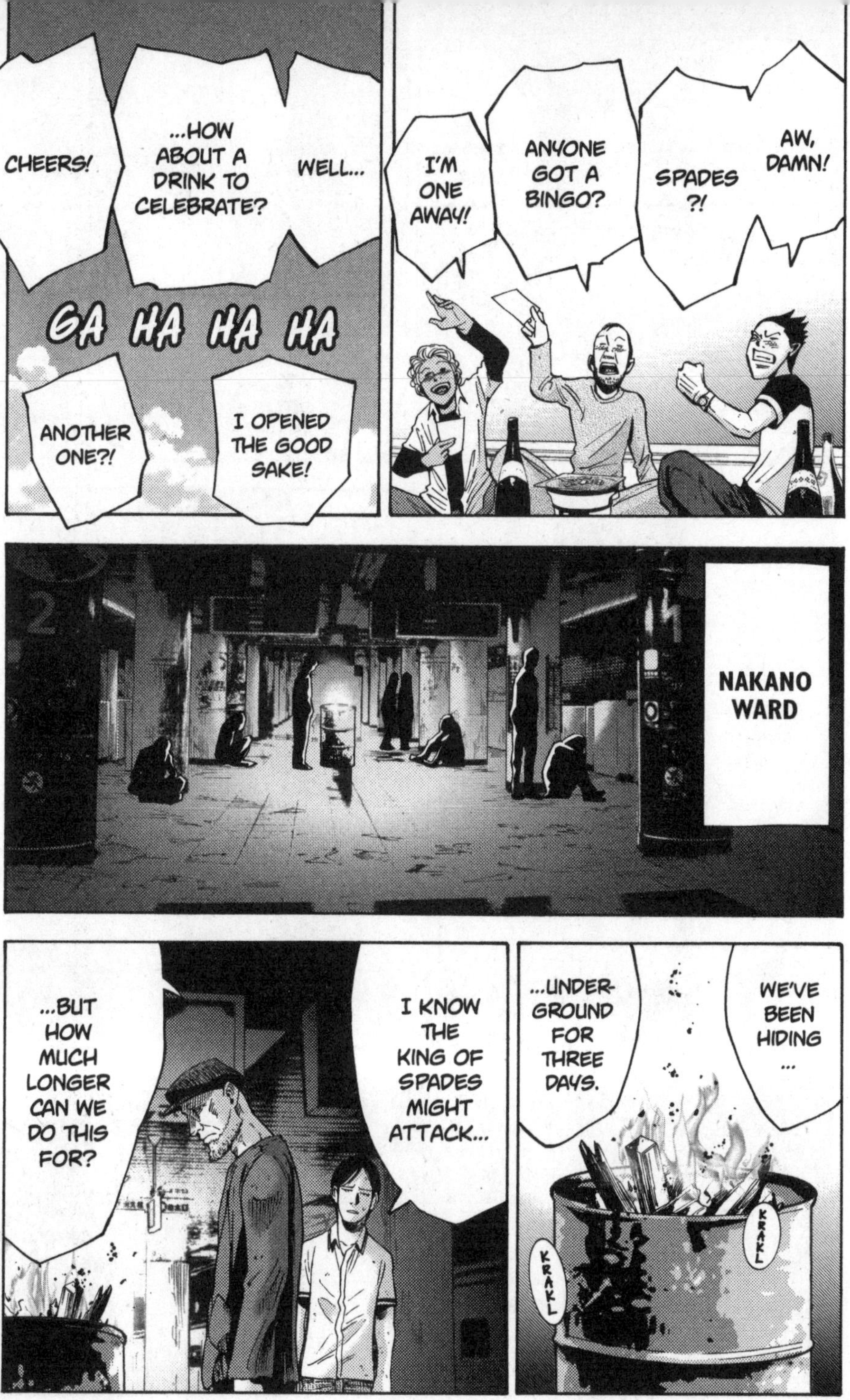
AW, DAMN!
SPADES?!
ANYONE GOT A BINGO?
I'M ONE AWAY!
WELL...
...HOW ABOUT A DRINK TO CELEBRATE?
CHEERS!
GA HA HA HA
I OPENED THE GOOD SAKE!
ANOTHER ONE?!
NAKANO WARD
WE'VE BEEN HIDING...
...UNDERGROUND FOR THREE DAYS.
KRAKL
KRAKL
I KNOW THE KING OF SPADES MIGHT ATTACK...
...BUT HOW MUCH LONGER CAN WE DO THIS FOR?

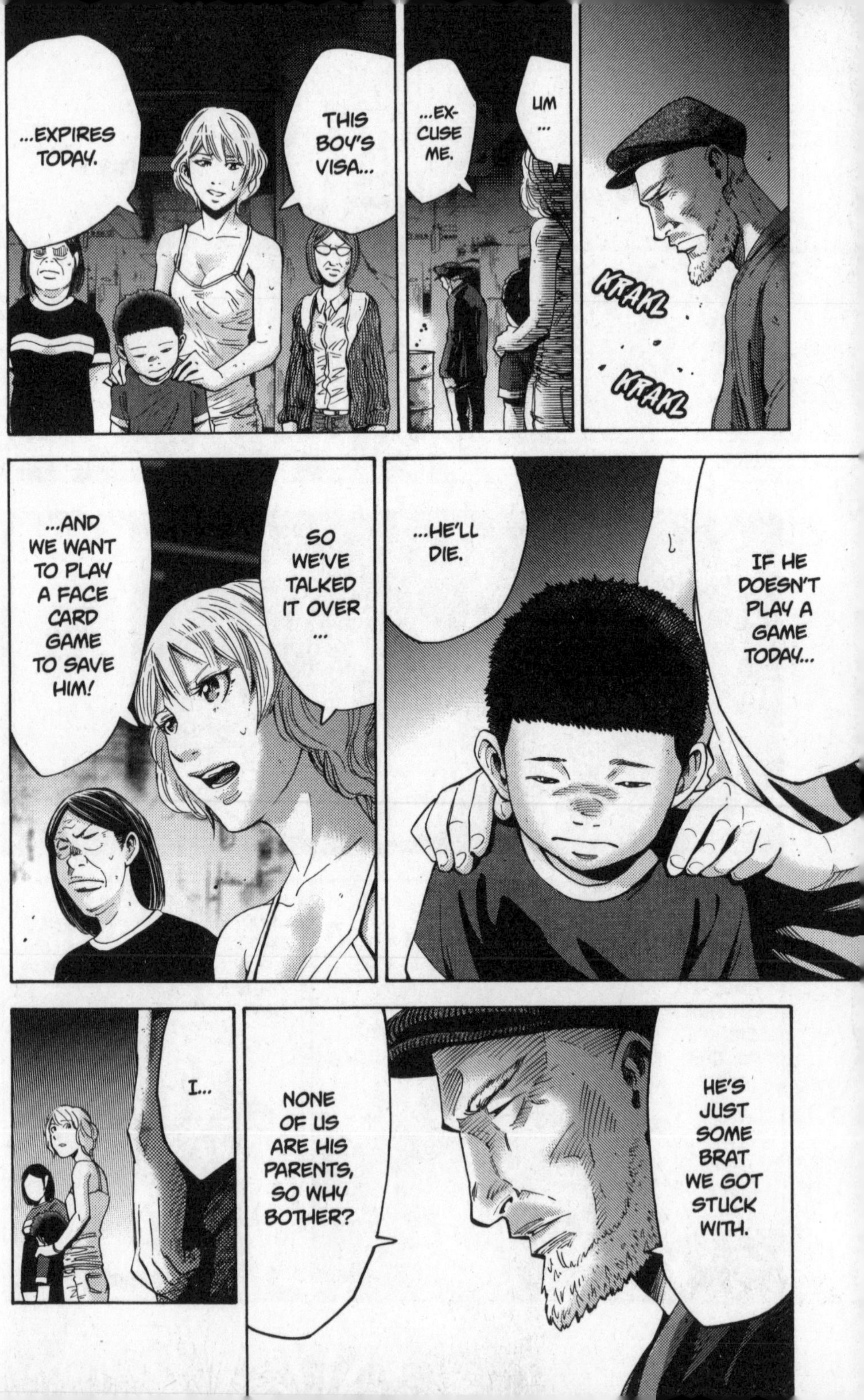
KRAKL
KRAKL
UM ...
...EX-CUSE ME.
THIS BOY'S VISA...
...EXPIRES TODAY.
IF HE DOESN'T PLAY A GAME TODAY...
...HE'LL DIE.
SO WE'VE TALKED IT OVER ...
...AND WE WANT TO PLAY A FACE CARD GAME TO SAVE HIM!
HE'S JUST SOME BRAT WE GOT STUCK WITH.
NONE OF US ARE HIS PARENTS, SO WHY BOTHER?
I...

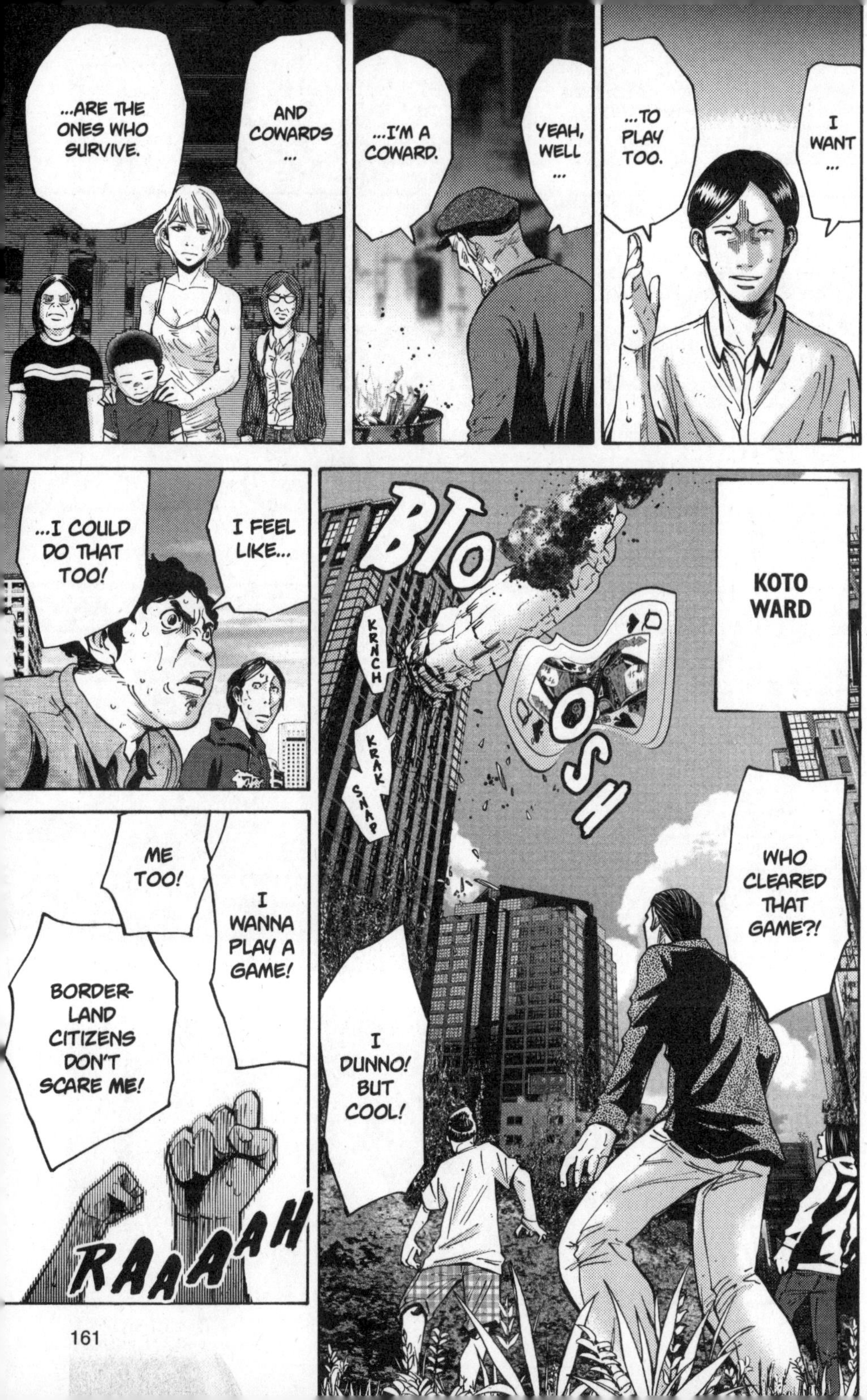
I WANT...
...TO PLAY TOO.
YEAH, WELL...
...I'M A COWARD.
AND COWARDS...
...ARE THE ONES WHO SURVIVE.
KOTO WARD
BIOOSH
KRNCH
KRAK
SNAP
WHO CLEARED THAT GAME?!
I DUNNO! BUT COOL!
I FEEL LIKE...
...I COULD DO THAT TOO!
ME TOO!
I WANNA PLAY A GAME!
BORDER-LAND CITIZENS DON'T SCARE ME!
RAAAAH

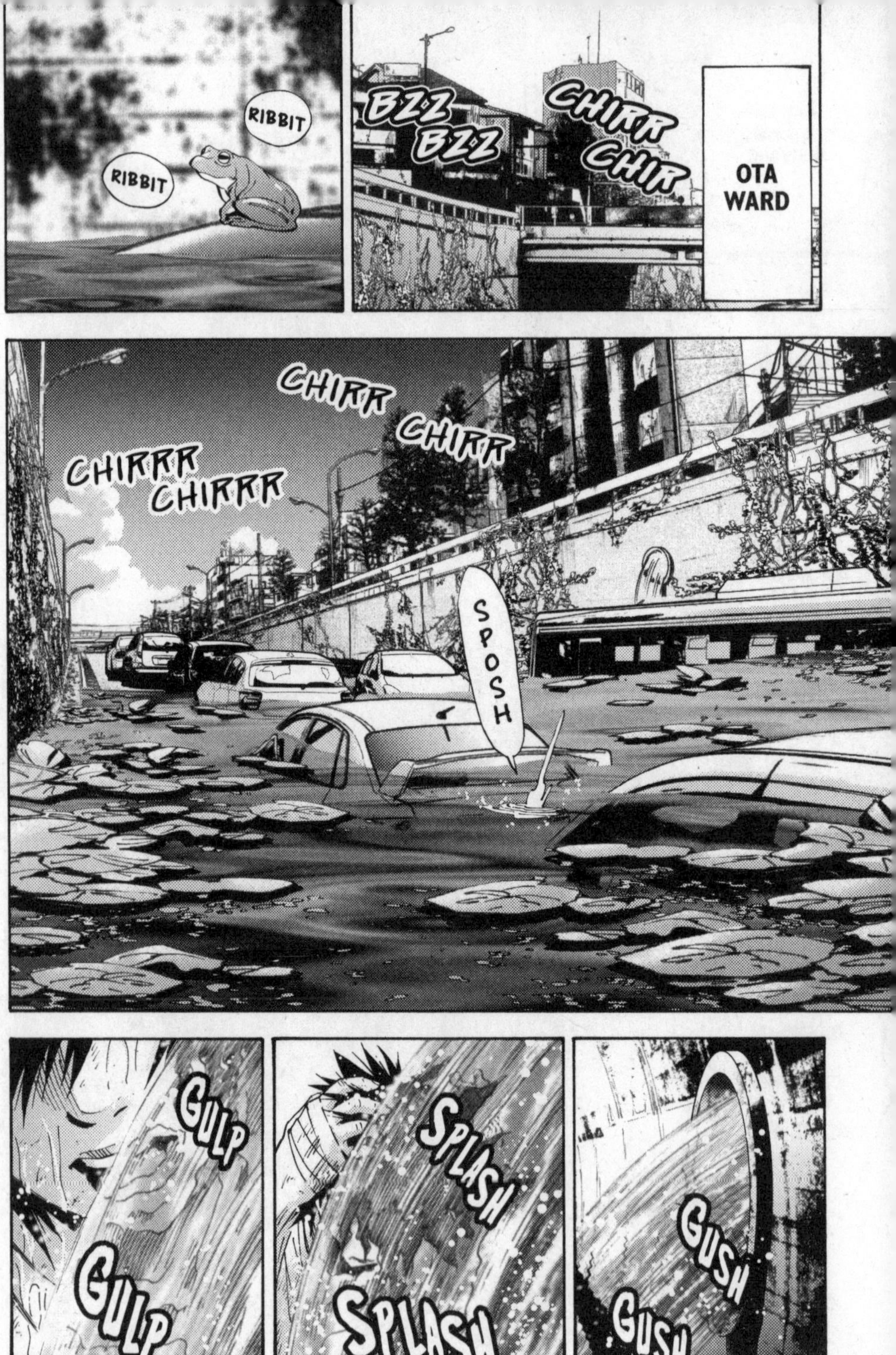
OTA WARD
CHIRR CHIR
BZZ BZZ
RIBBIT
RIBBIT
CHIRR
CHIRR
SPOSH
CHIRRR CHIRRR
GUSH
GUSH
SPLASH
SPLASH
GULP
GULP

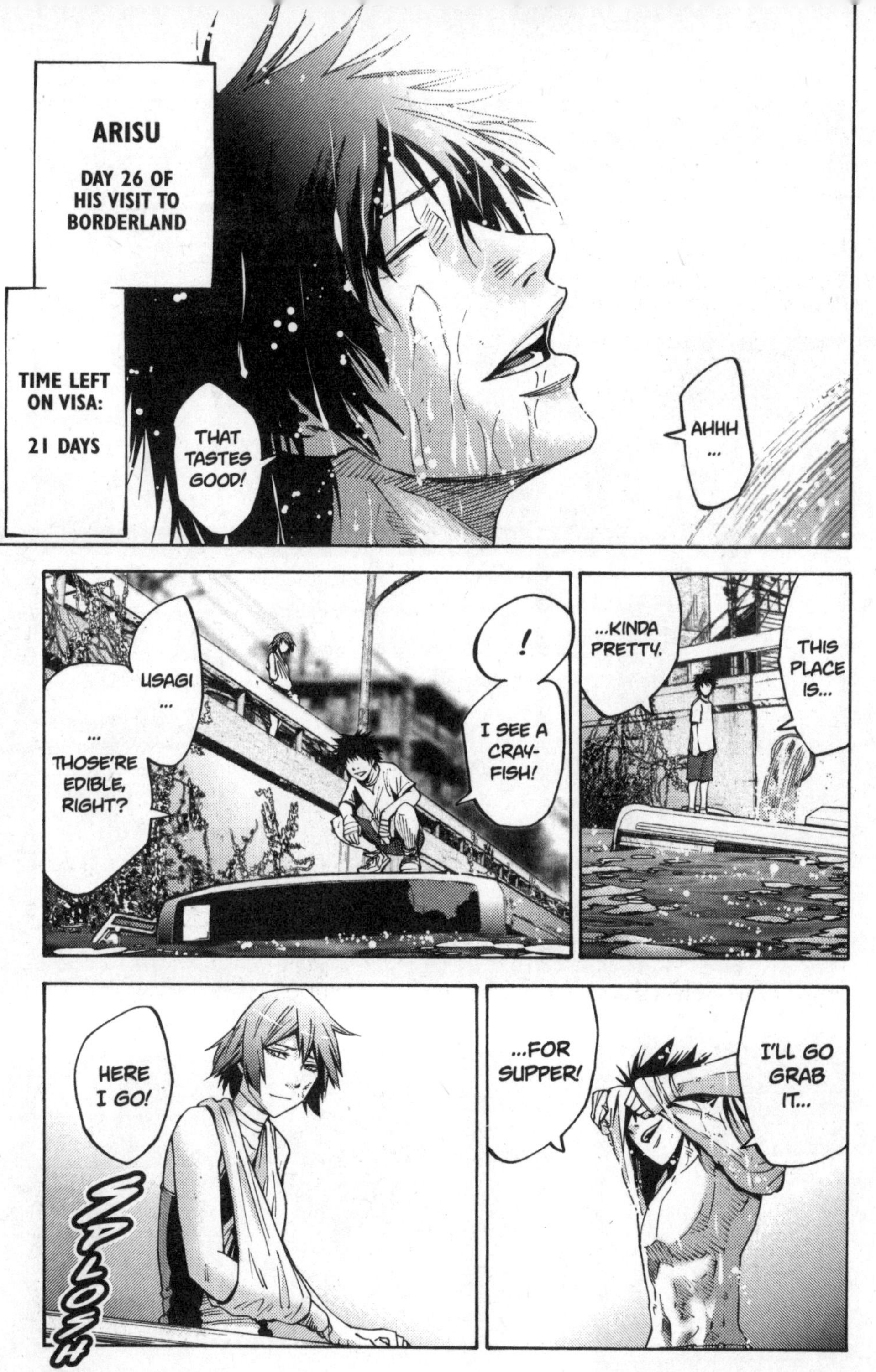

ARISU
DAY 26 OF HIS VISIT TO BORDERLAND
TIME LEFT ON VISA: 21 DAYS
AHHH ...
THAT TASTES GOOD!
THIS PLACE IS...
...KINDA PRETTY.
!
I SEE A CRAY-FISH!
USAGI ...
... THOSE'RE EDIBLE, RIGHT?
I'LL GO GRAB IT...
...FOR SUPPER!
HERE I GO!
SPLOSH

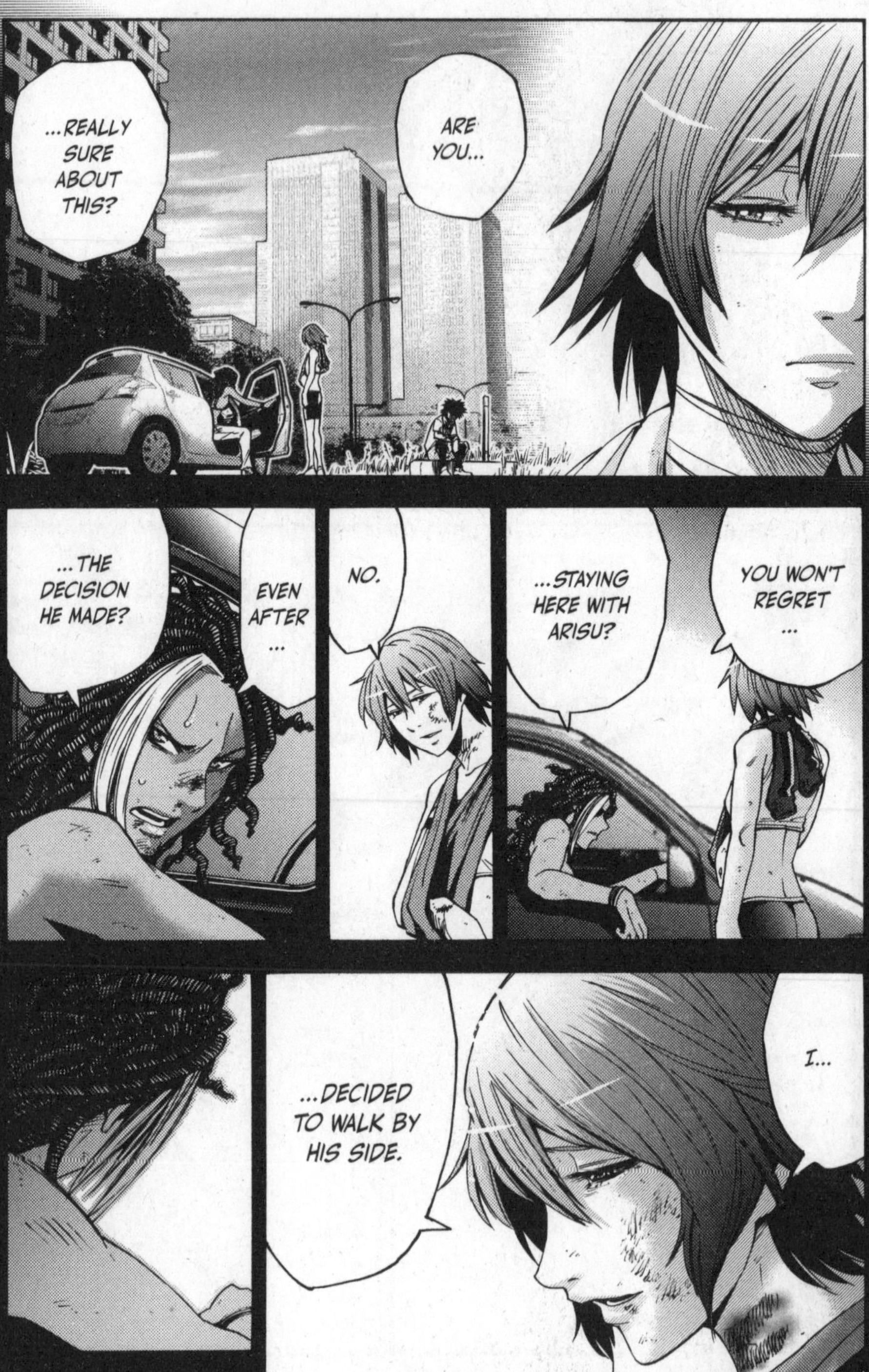
ARE YOU...
...REALLY SURE ABOUT THIS?
YOU WON'T REGRET ...
...STAYING HERE WITH ARISU?
NO.
EVEN AFTER ...
...THE DECISION HE MADE?
I...
...DECIDED TO WALK BY HIS SIDE.

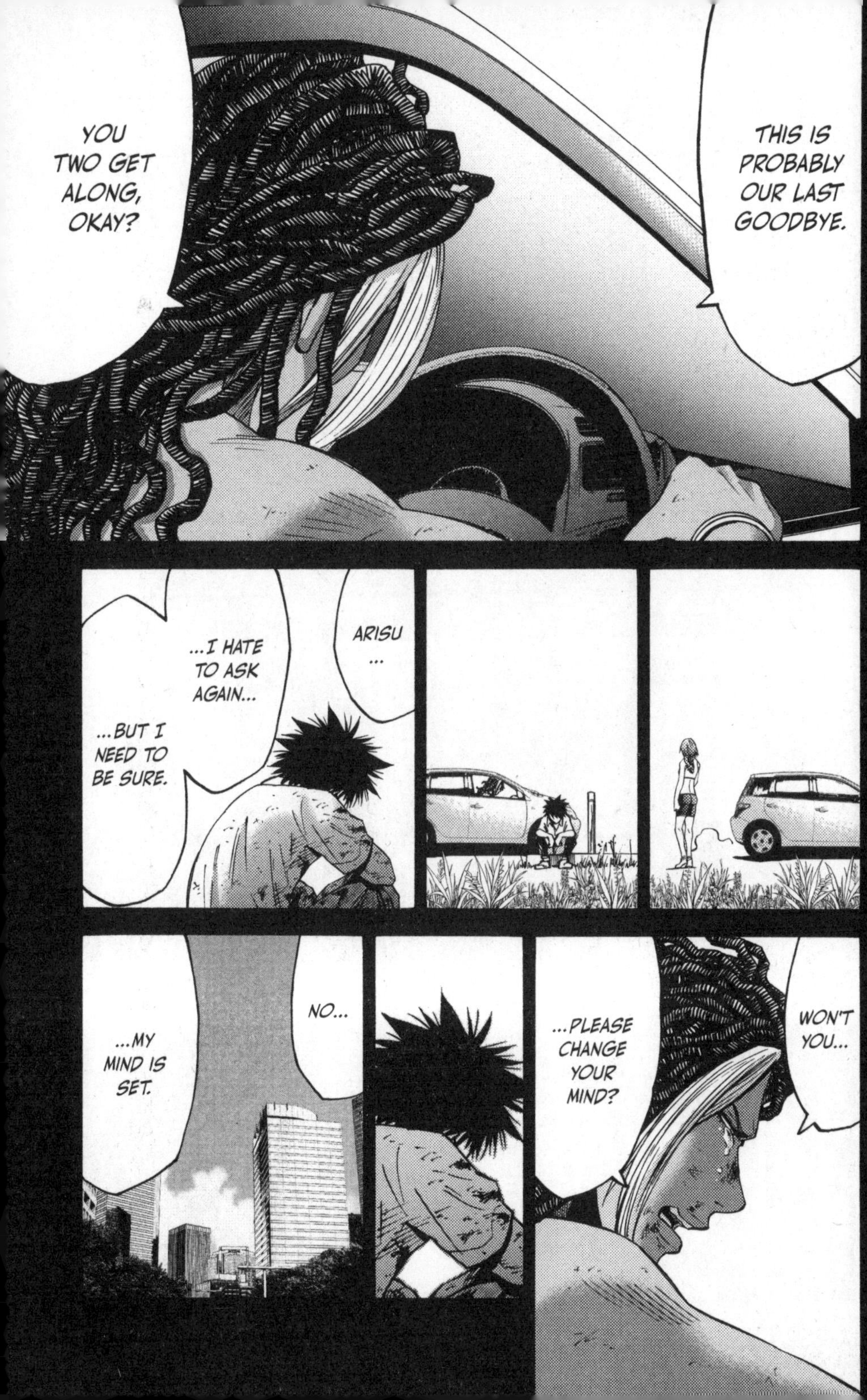
THIS IS PROBABLY OUR LAST GOODBYE.
YOU TWO GET ALONG, OKAY?
ARISU ...
...I HATE TO ASK AGAIN...
...BUT I NEED TO BE SURE.
WON'T YOU...
...PLEASE CHANGE YOUR MIND?
NO...
...MY MIND IS SET.

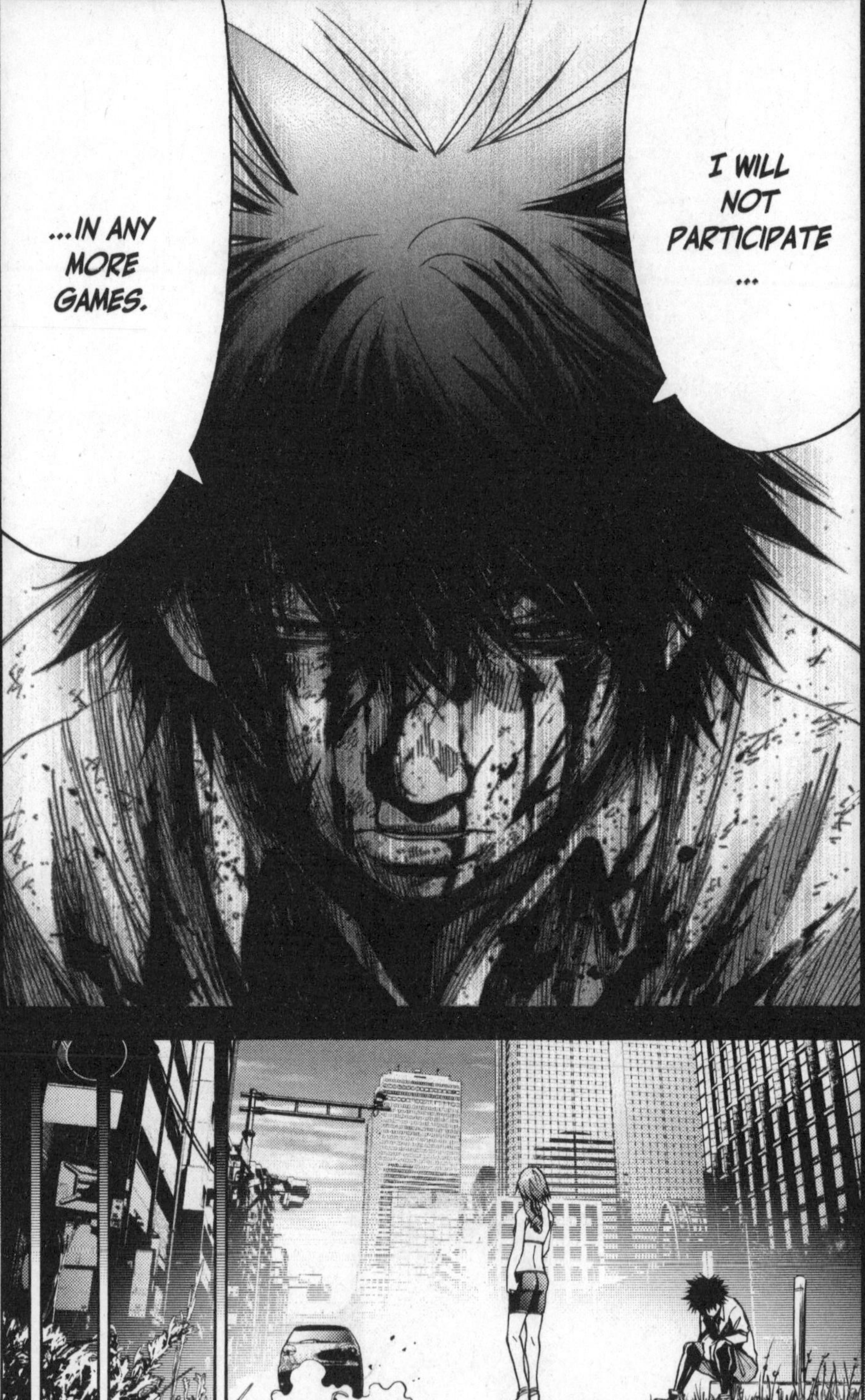
I WILL NOT PARTICIPATE ...
...IN ANY MORE GAMES.

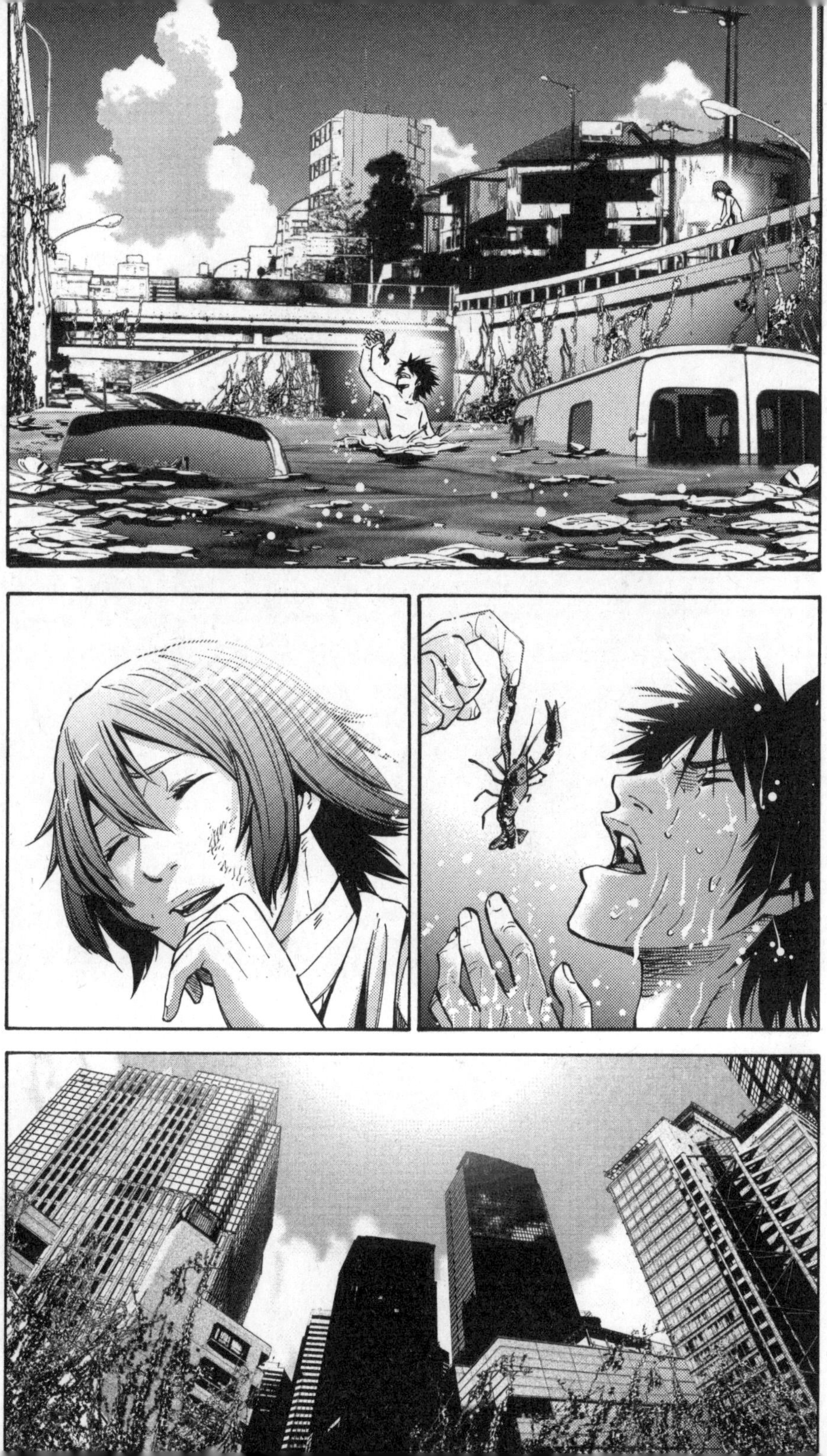

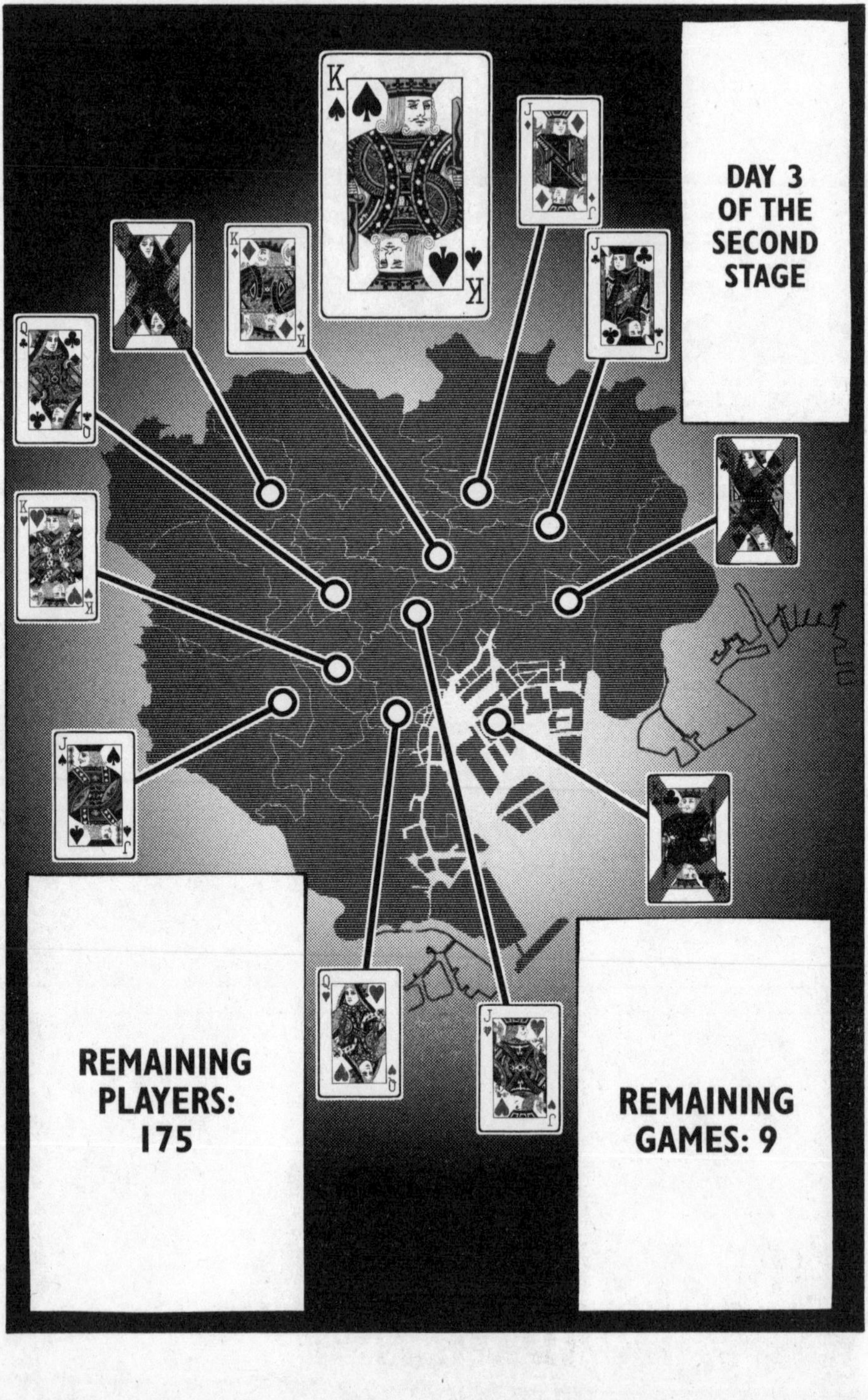
DAY 3
OF THE
SECOND
STAGE
REMAINING
PLAYERS:
175
REMAINING
GAMES: 9

ALICE IN BORDERLAND

It feels good to receive praise. It feels good to receive gratitude.

Those are important human emotions.

— HARO ASO

ALICE IN BORDERLAND

PART 12

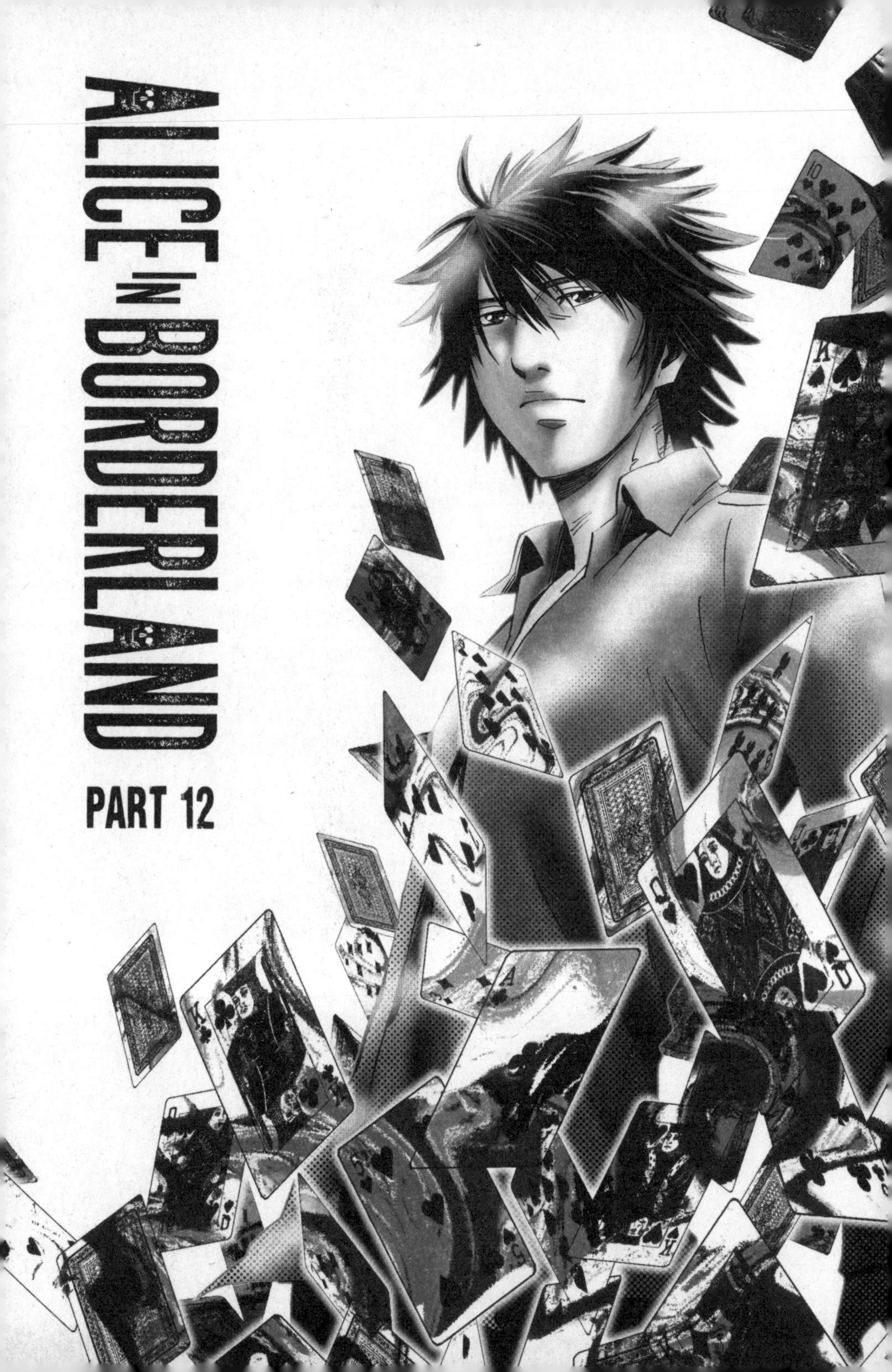

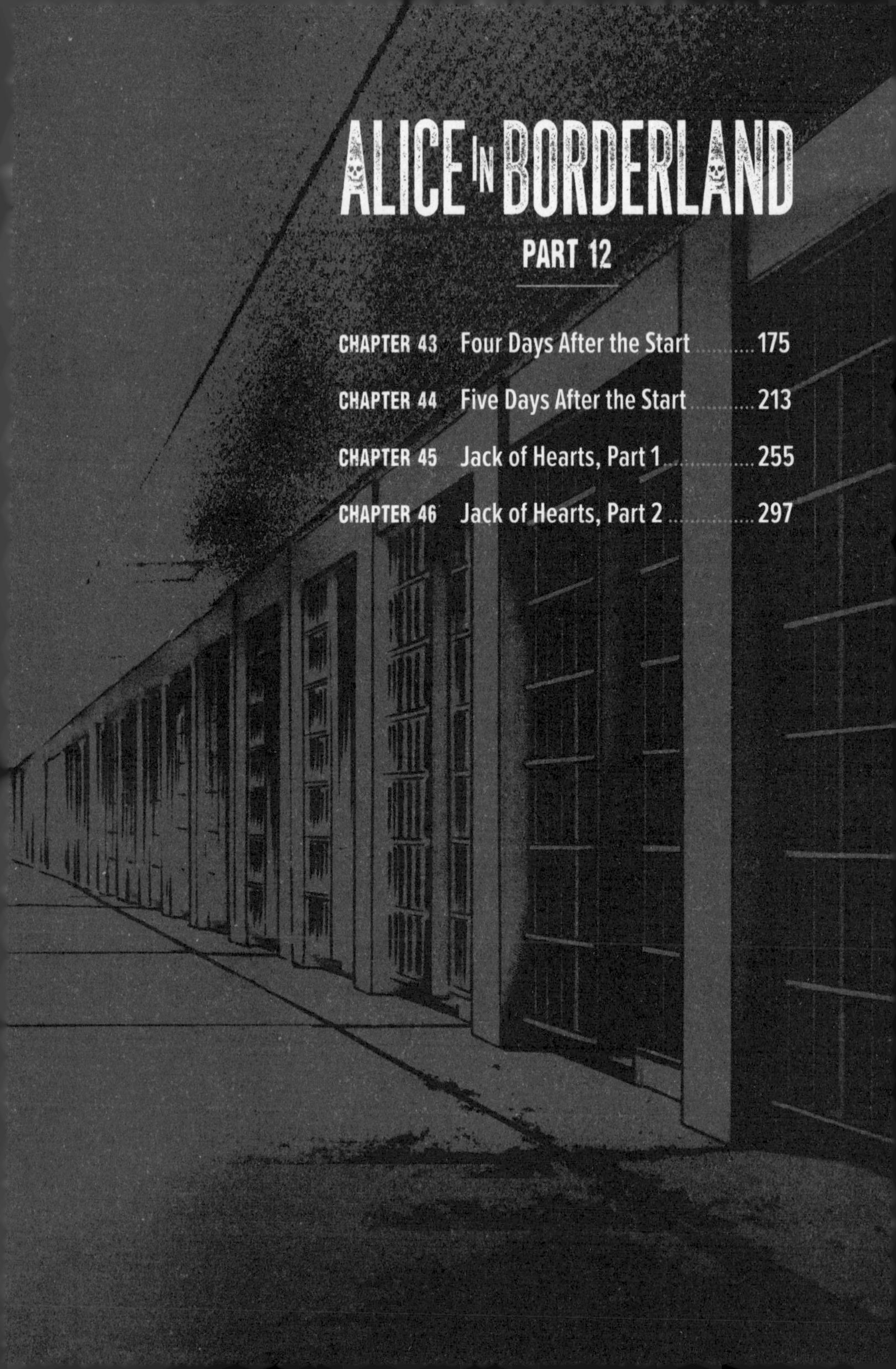

ALICE IN BORDERLAND

PART 12

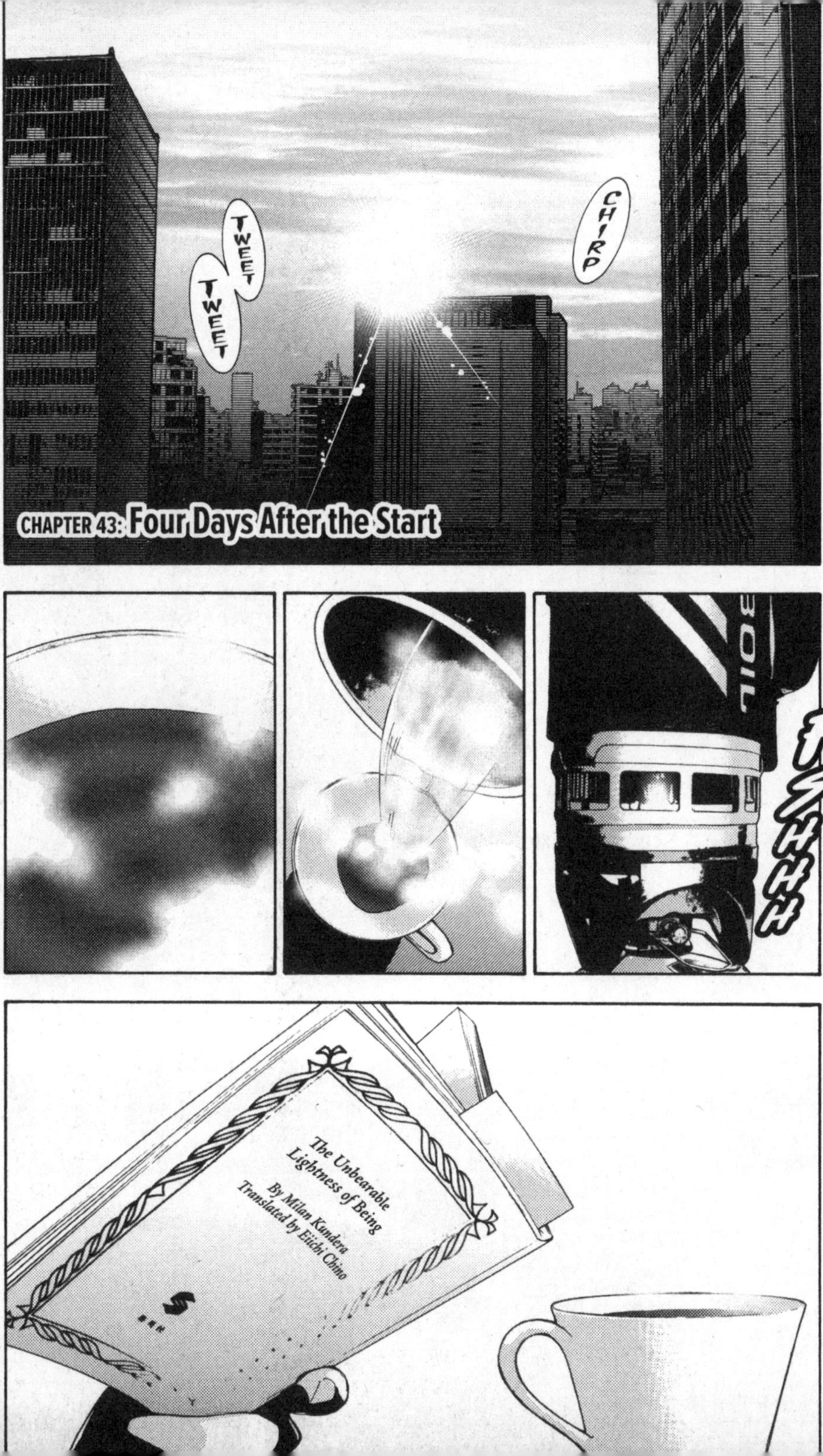
CHAPTER 43: Four Days After the Start
CHIRP
TWEET TWEET
FSHHHH
The Unbearable Lightness of Being
By Milan Kundera
Translated by Eiichi Chino

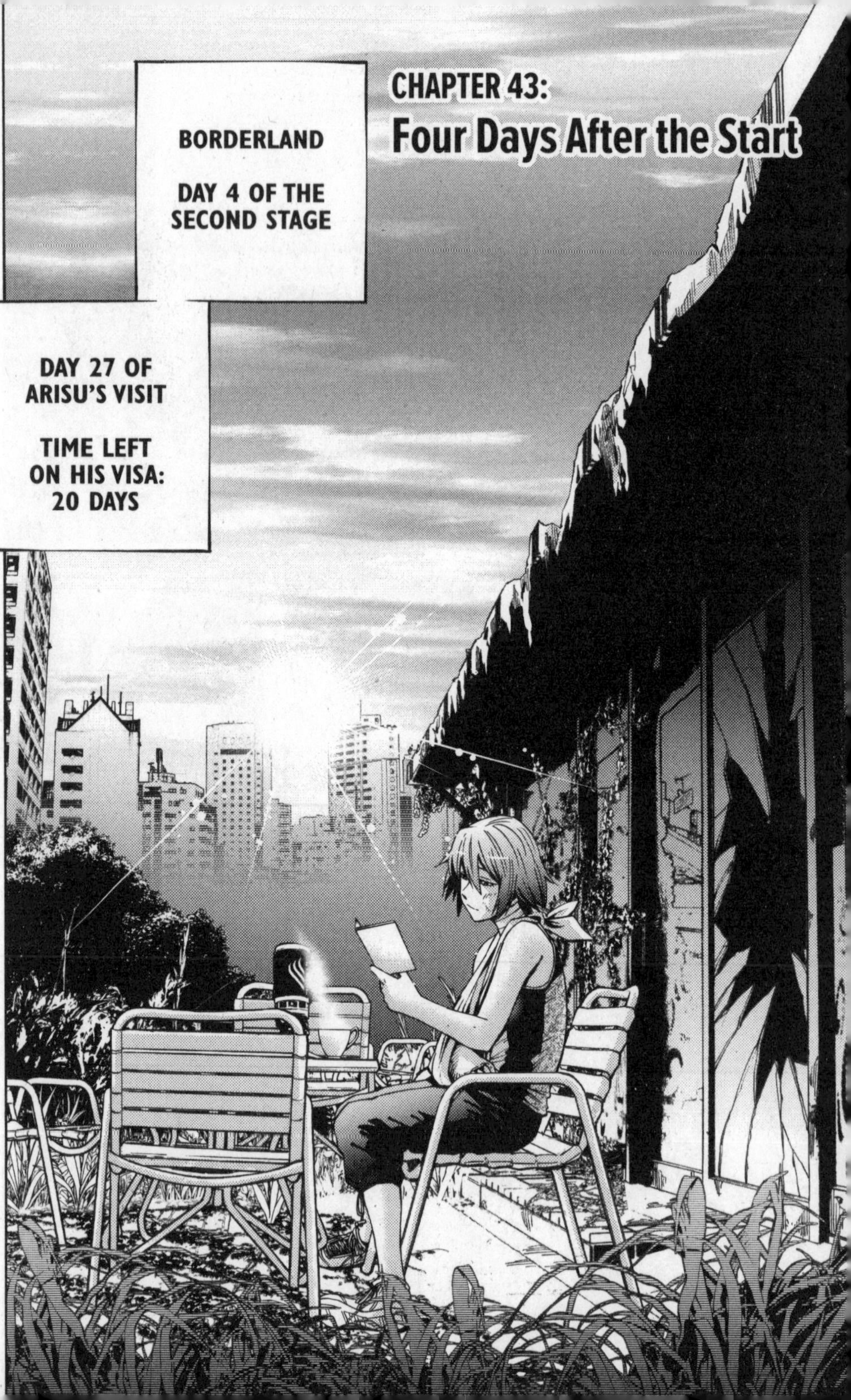
CHAPTER 43:
Four Days After the Start
BORDERLAND
DAY 4 OF THE SECOND STAGE
DAY 27 OF ARISU'S VISIT
TIME LEFT ON HIS VISA: 20 DAYS

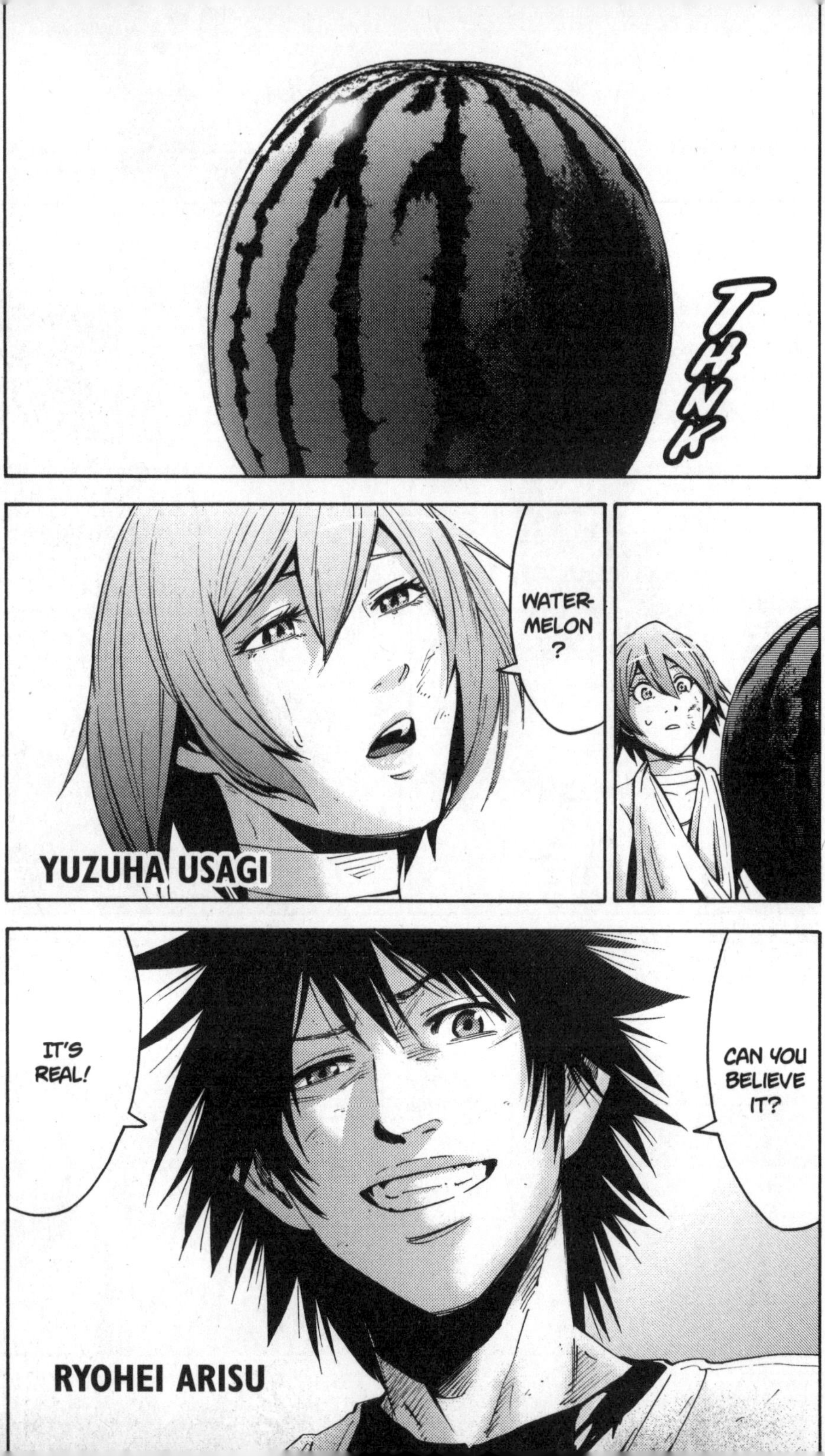
THNK
WATER-MELON?
YUZUHA USAGI
CAN YOU BELIEVE IT?
IT'S REAL!
RYOHEI ARISU

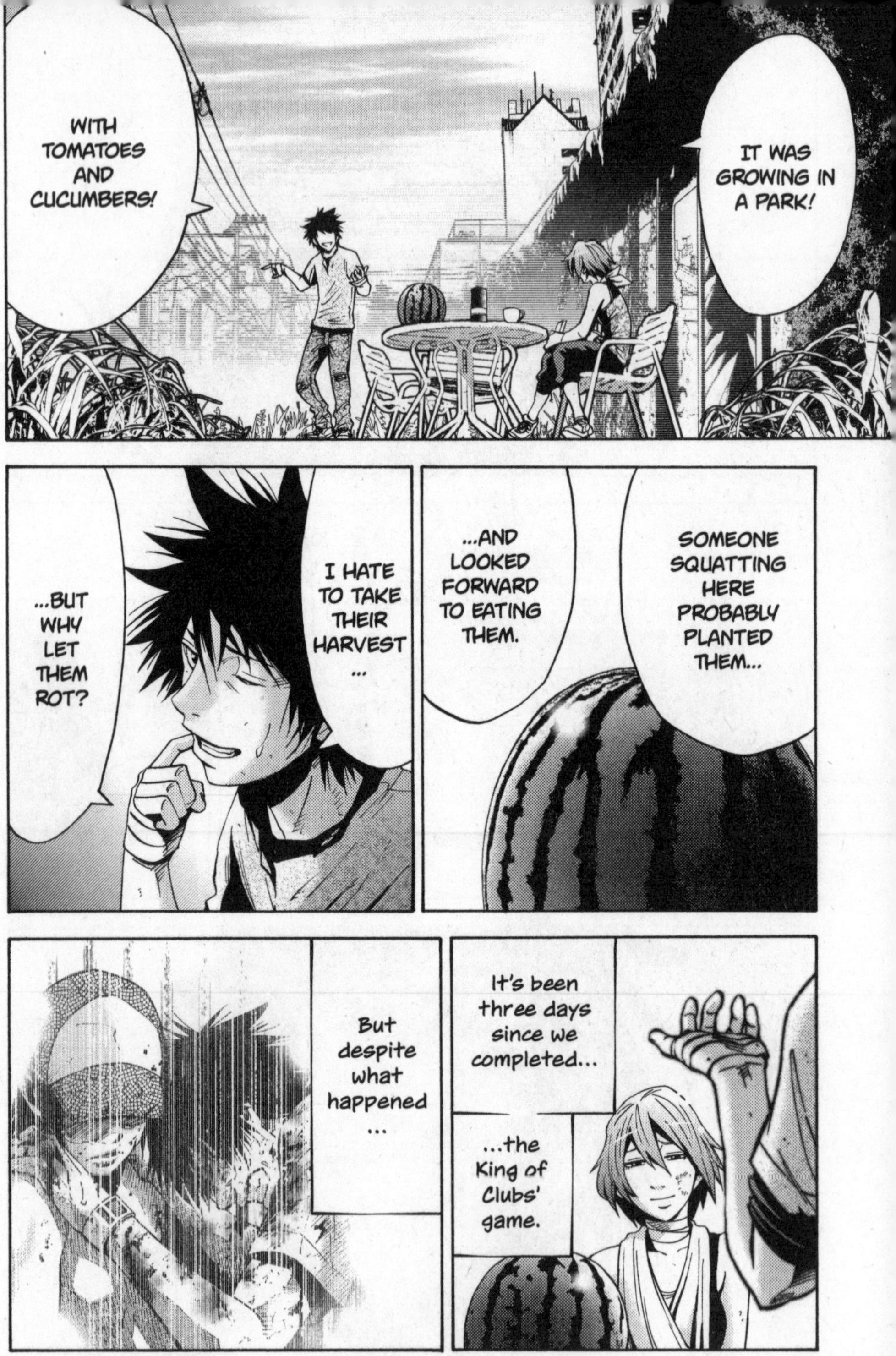
IT WAS GROWING IN A PARK!
WITH TOMATOES AND CUCUMBERS!
SOMEONE SQUATTING HERE PROBABLY PLANTED THEM...
...AND LOOKED FORWARD TO EATING THEM.
I HATE TO TAKE THEIR HARVEST...
...BUT WHY LET THEM ROT?
It's been three days since we completed...
...the King of Clubs' game.
But despite what happened...

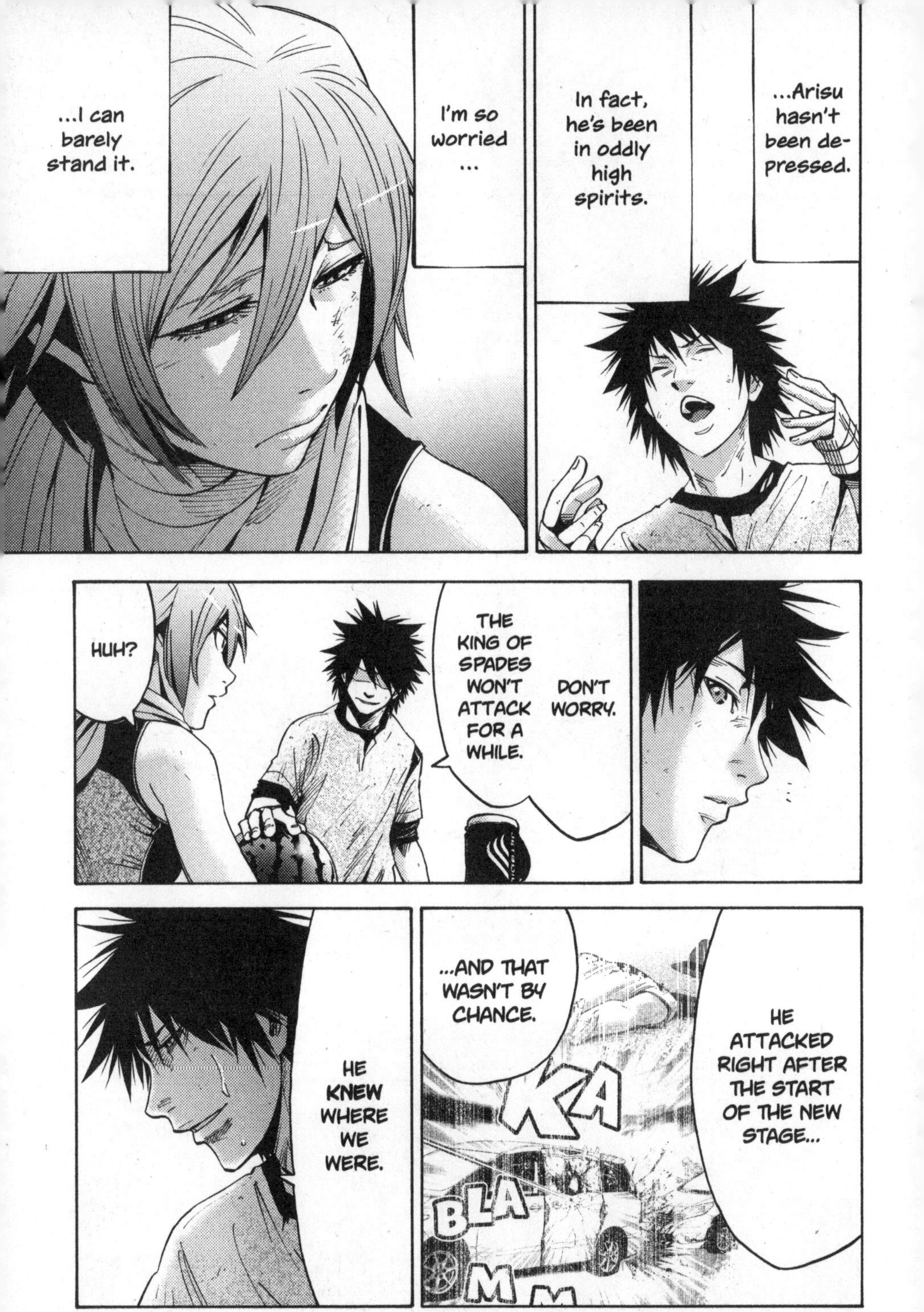

...Arisu hasn't been de- pressed.
In fact, he's been in oddly high spirits.
I'm so worried ...
...I can barely stand it.
DON'T WORRY.
THE KING OF SPADES WON'T ATTACK FOR A WHILE.
HUH?
HE ATTACKED RIGHT AFTER THE START OF THE NEW STAGE...
...AND THAT WASN'T BY CHANCE.
KA
BLA-MM
HE KNEW WHERE WE WERE.

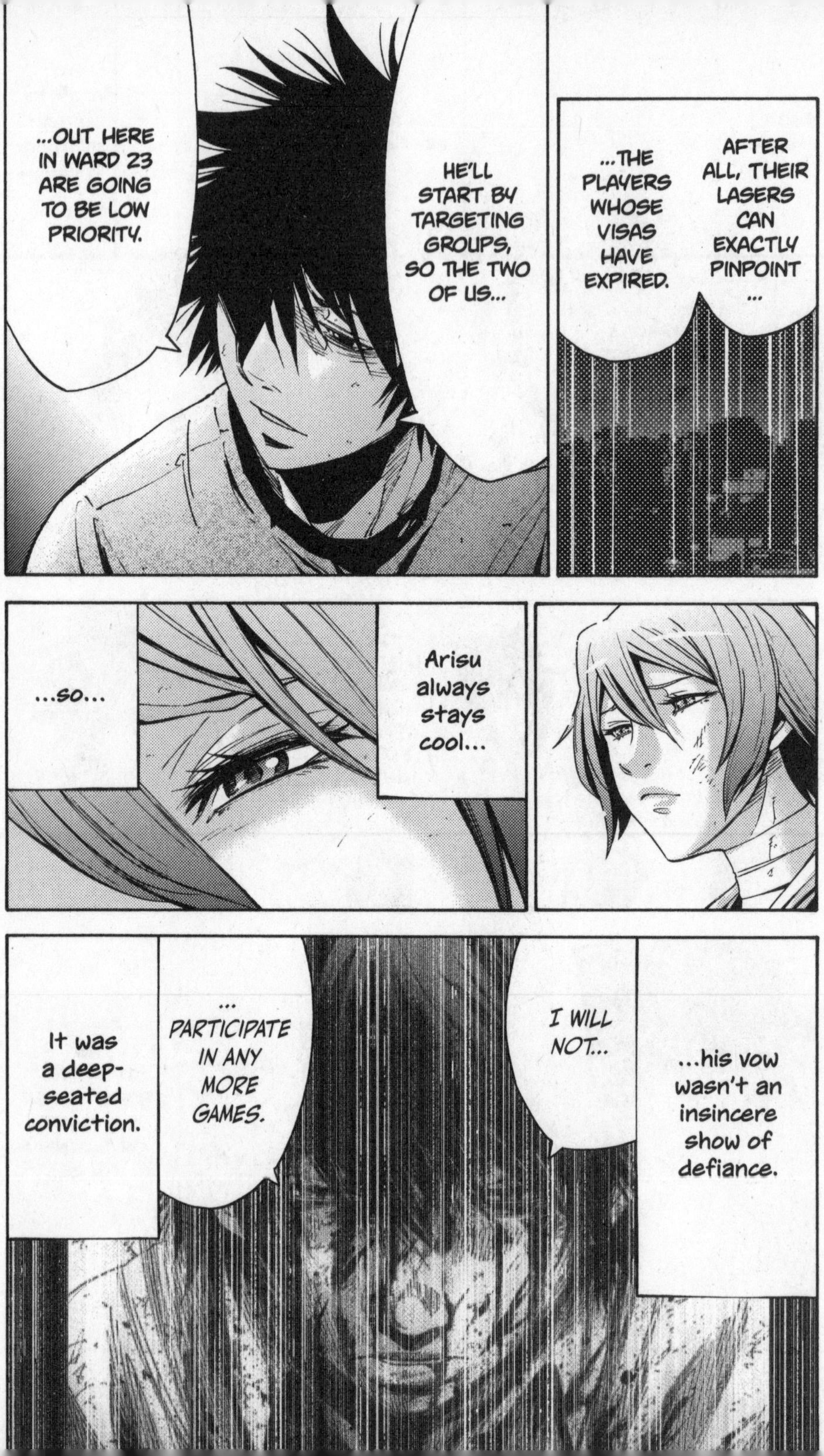
AFTER ALL, THEIR LASERS CAN EXACTLY PINPOINT ...
...THE PLAYERS WHOSE VISAS HAVE EXPIRED.
HE'LL START BY TARGETING GROUPS, SO THE TWO OF US...
...OUT HERE IN WARD 23 ARE GOING TO BE LOW PRIORITY.
Arisu always stays cool...
...so...
...his vow wasn't an insincere show of defiance.
I WILL NOT...
... PARTICIPATE IN ANY MORE GAMES.
It was a deep-seated conviction.

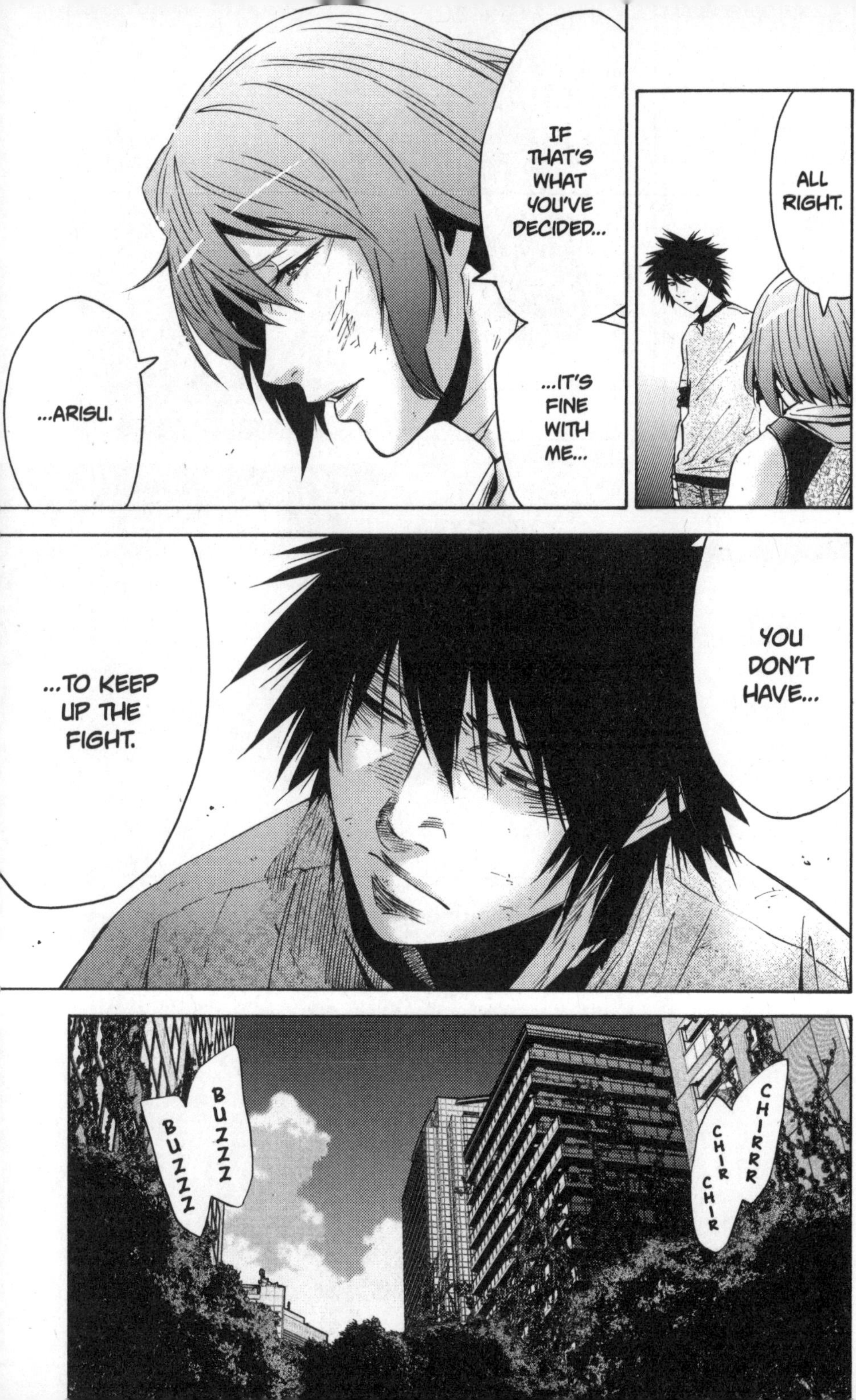
ALL RIGHT.
IF THAT'S WHAT YOU'VE DECIDED...
...IT'S FINE WITH ME...
...ARISU.
YOU DON'T HAVE...
...TO KEEP UP THE FIGHT.
CHIRRR
CHIR CHIR
BUZZZ BUZZZ

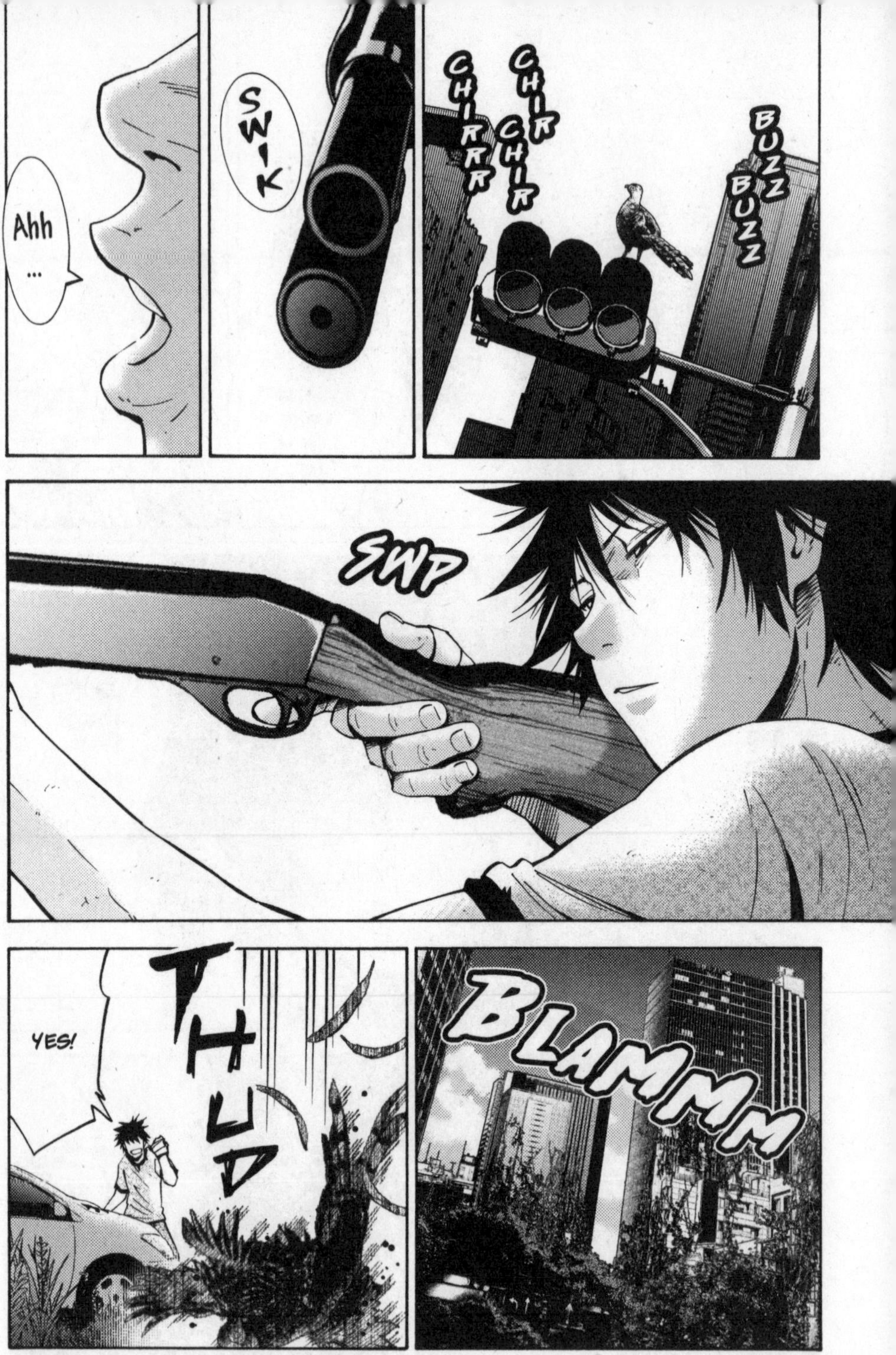
BUZZ BUZZ
CHIR CHIR
CHIRRR
SWIK
Ahh ...
SWP
BLAMMMM
THUD
YES!

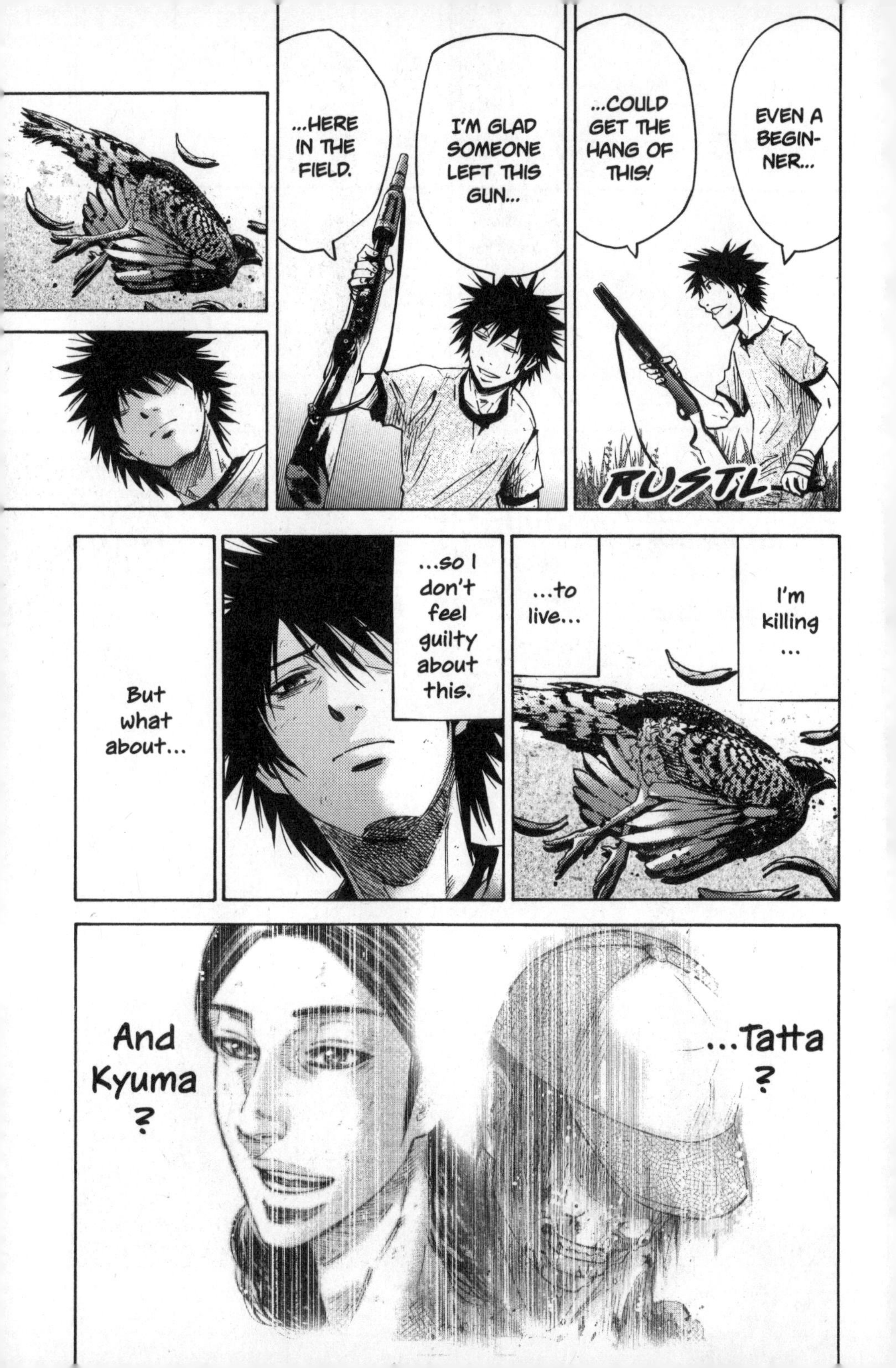
EVEN A BEGINNER...
...COULD GET THE HANG OF THIS!
RUSTL
I'M GLAD SOMEONE LEFT THIS GUN...
...HERE IN THE FIELD.
I'm killing...
...to live...
...so I don't feel guilty about this.
But what about...
...Tatta?
And Kyuma?

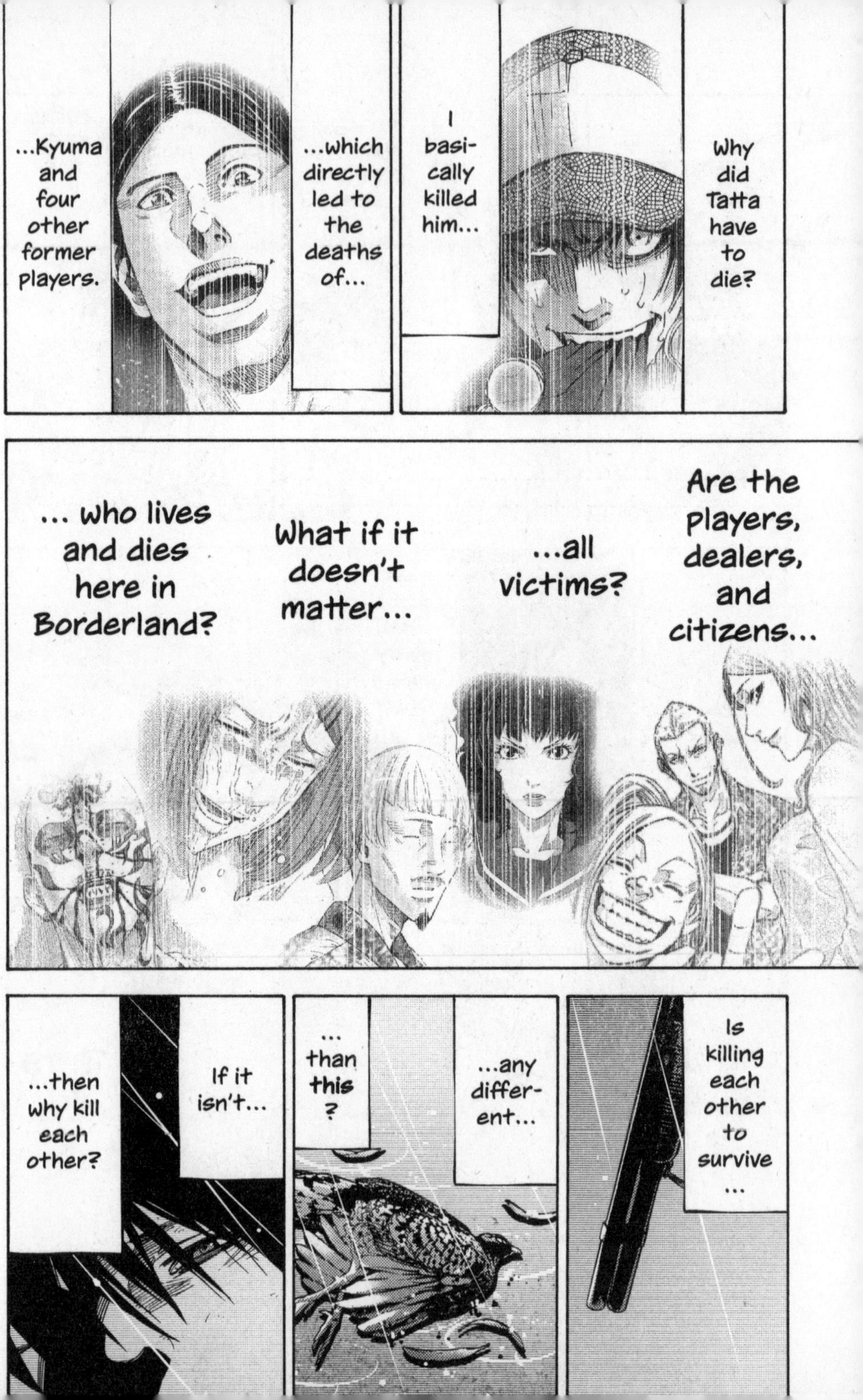
Why did Tatta have to die?
I basically killed him...
...which directly led to the deaths of...
...Kyuma and four other former players.
Are the players, dealers, and citizens...
...all victims?
What if it doesn't matter...
... who lives and dies here in Borderland?
Is killing each other to survive ...
...any different...
... than this ?
If it isn't...
...then why kill each other?

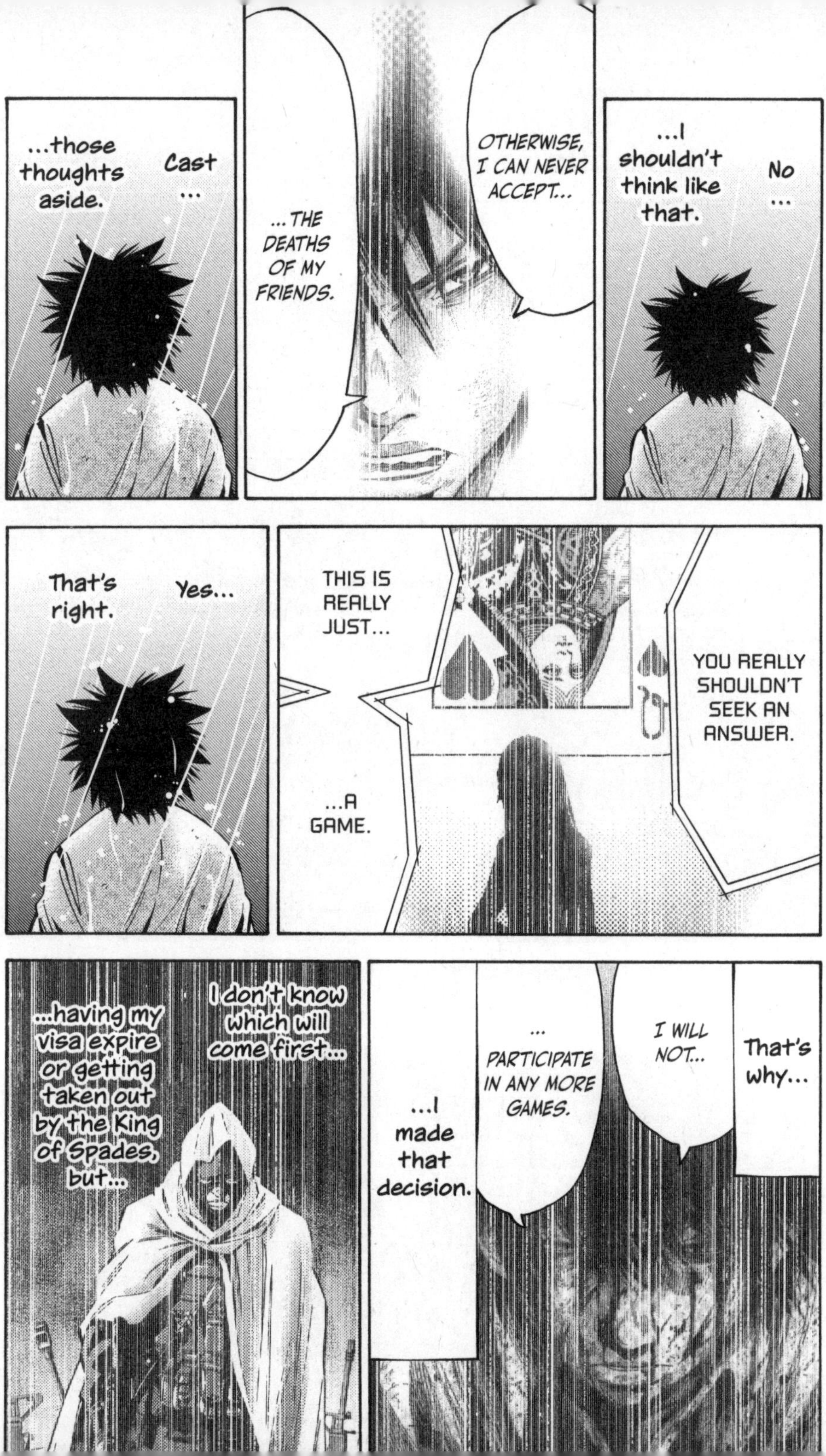

No...
...I shouldn't think like that.
OTHERWISE, I CAN NEVER ACCEPT...
...THE DEATHS OF MY FRIENDS.
Cast...
...those thoughts aside.
YOU REALLY SHOULDN'T SEEK AN ANSWER.
THIS IS REALLY JUST...
...A GAME.
Yes...
That's right.
That's why...
I WILL NOT...
...PARTICIPATE IN ANY MORE GAMES.
...I made that decision.
I don't know which will come first...
...having my visa expire or getting taken out by the King of Spades, but...

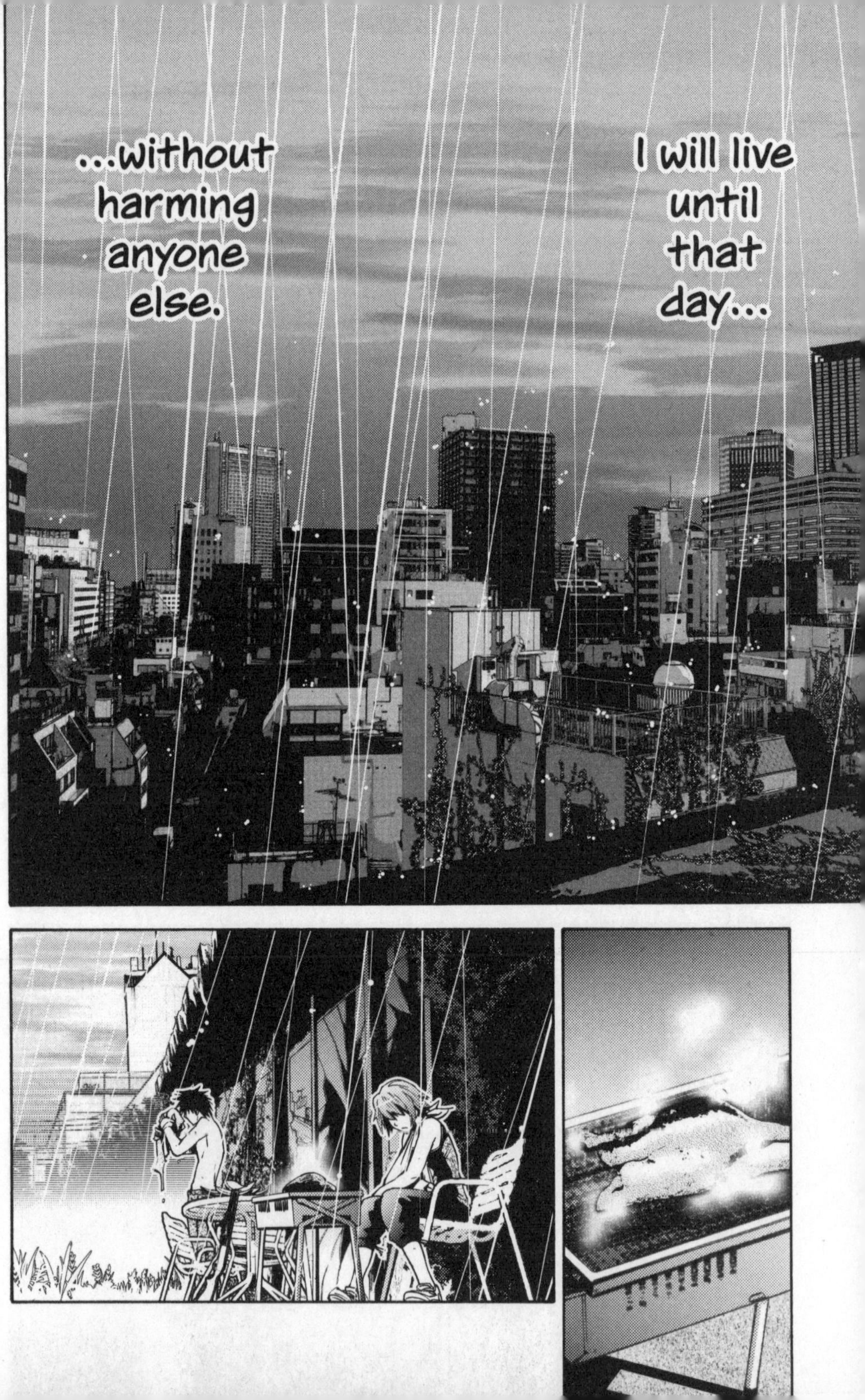
I will live until that day...
...without harming anyone else.

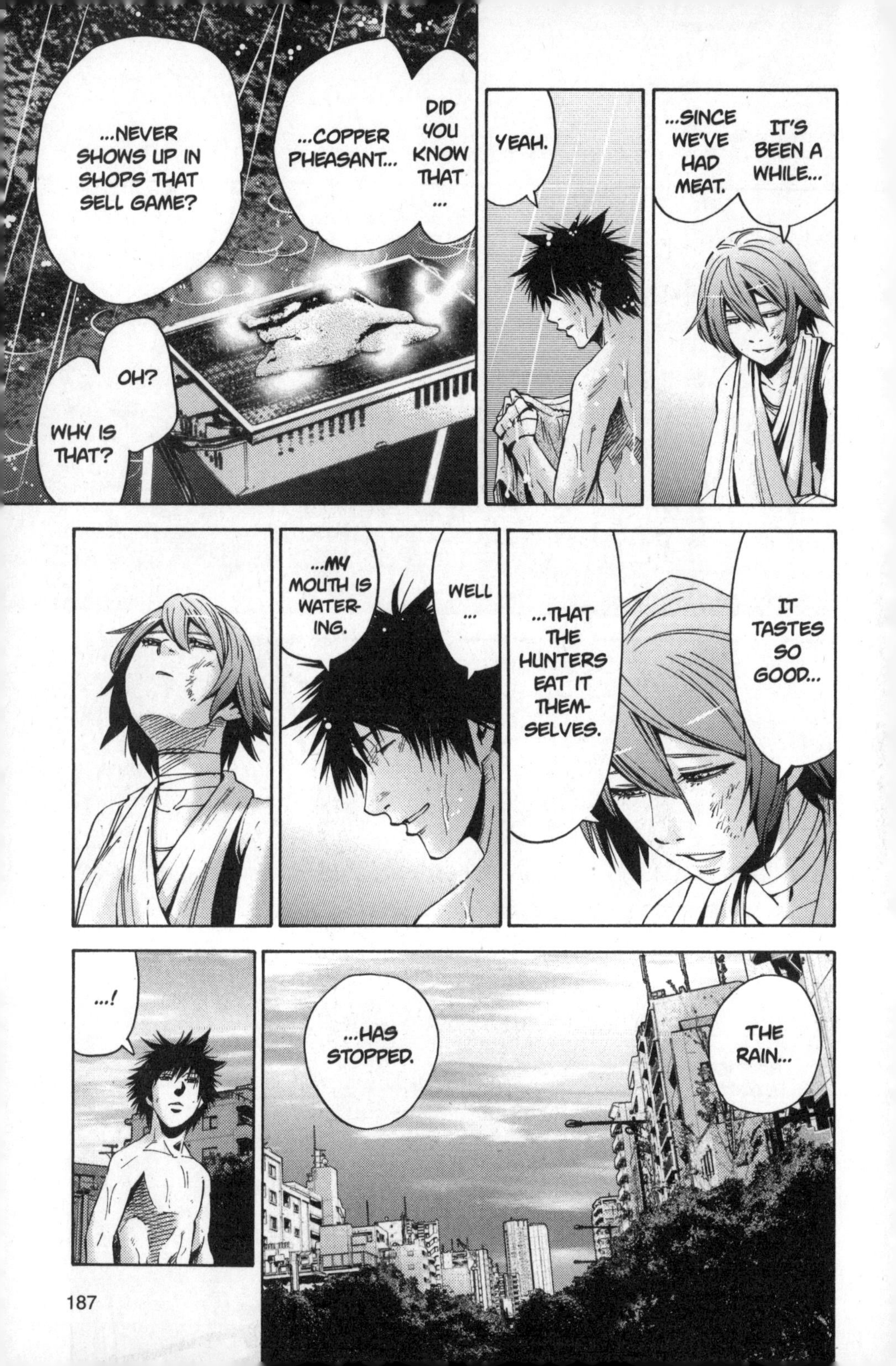
IT'S BEEN A WHILE...
...SINCE WE'VE HAD MEAT.
YEAH.
DID YOU KNOW THAT ...
...COPPER PHEASANT...
...NEVER SHOWS UP IN SHOPS THAT SELL GAME?
OH?
WHY IS THAT?
IT TASTES SO GOOD...
...THAT THE HUNTERS EAT IT THEM-SELVES.
WELL ...
...MY MOUTH IS WATER-ING.
THE RAIN...
...HAS STOPPED.
...!

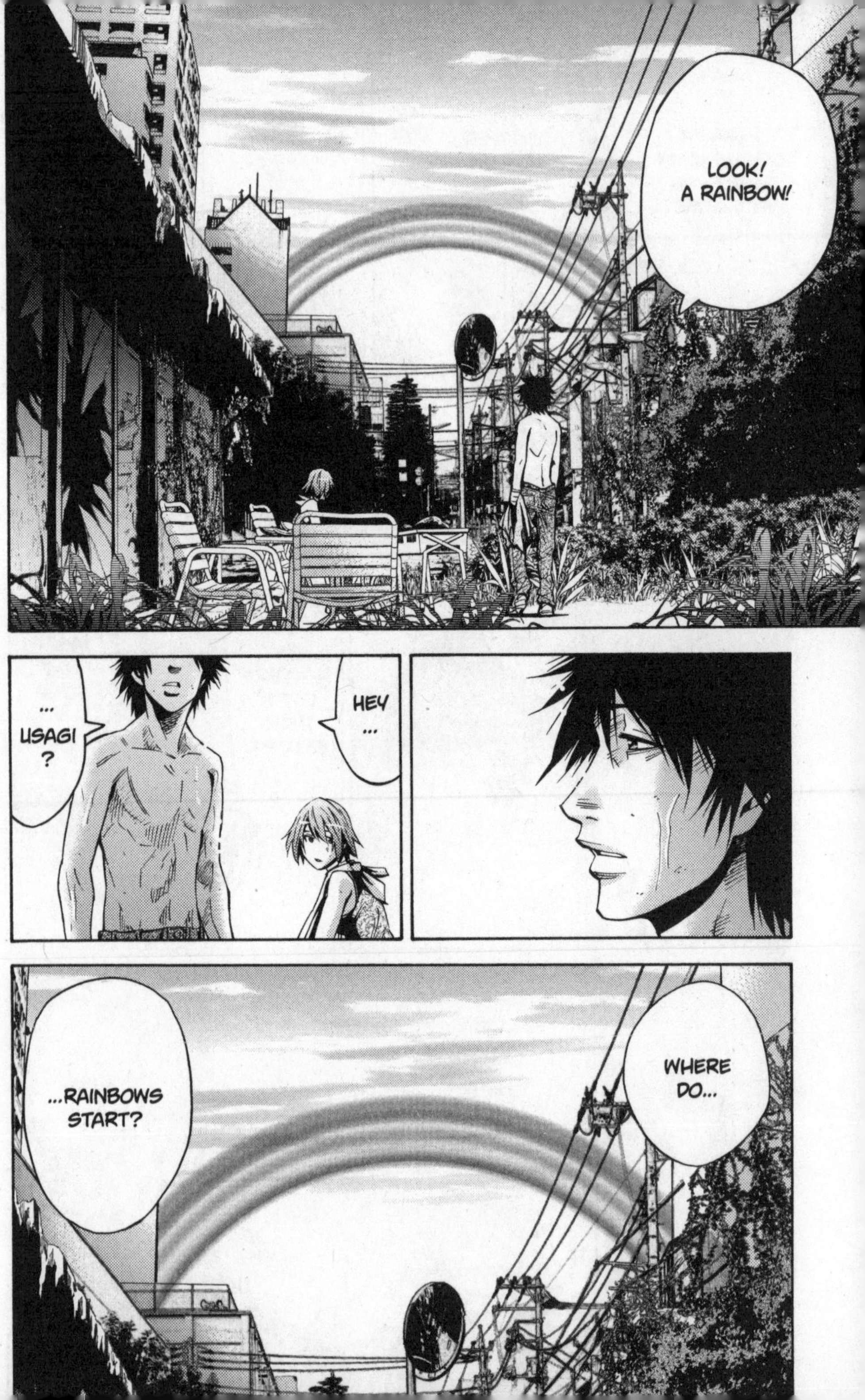
LOOK! A RAINBOW!
HEY ...
... USAGI ?
WHERE DO...
...RAINBOWS START?

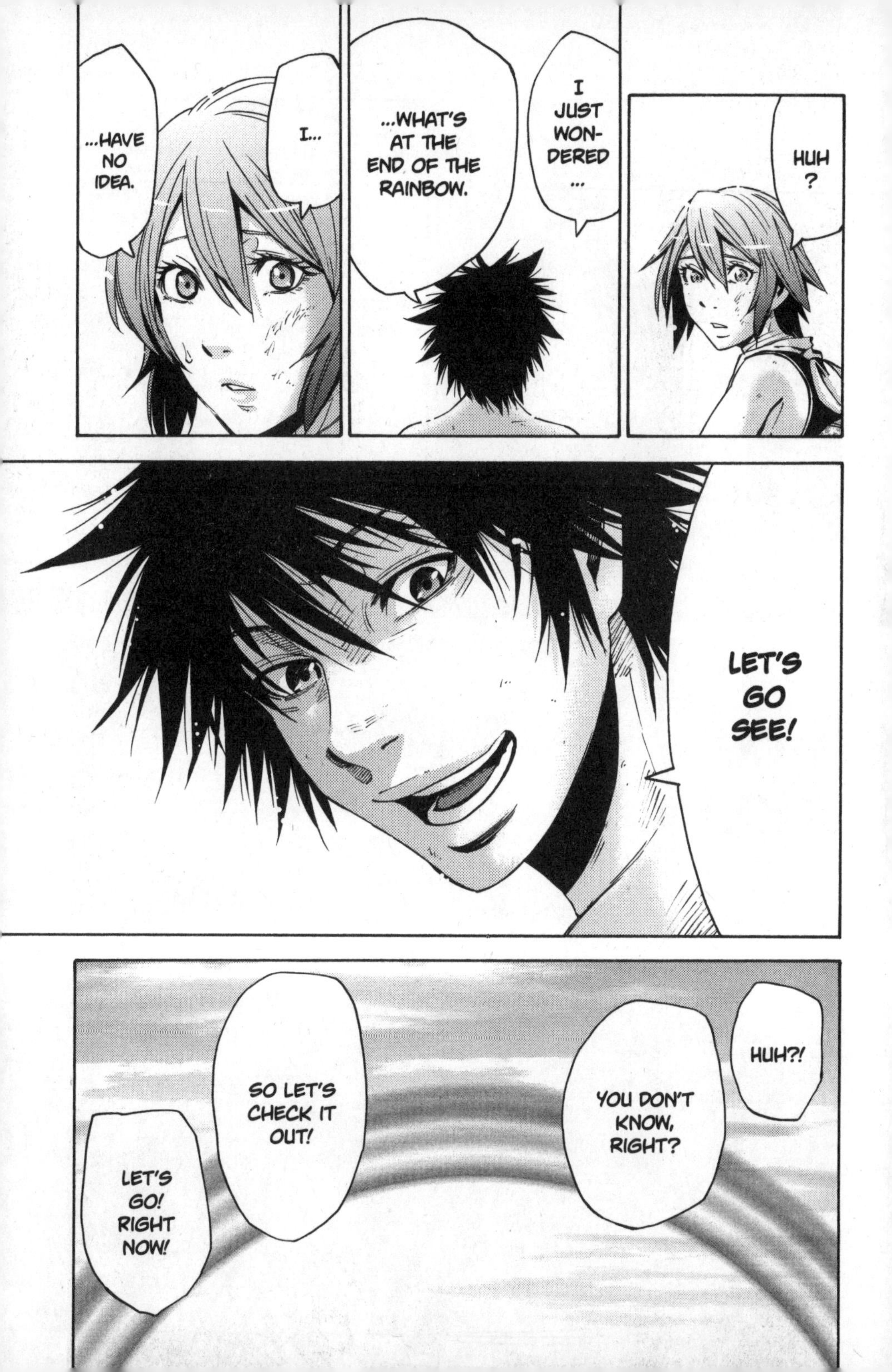
HUH?
I JUST WONDERED...
...WHAT'S AT THE END OF THE RAINBOW.
I...
...HAVE NO IDEA.
LET'S GO SEE!
HUH?!
YOU DON'T KNOW, RIGHT?
SO LET'S CHECK IT OUT!
LET'S GO! RIGHT NOW!

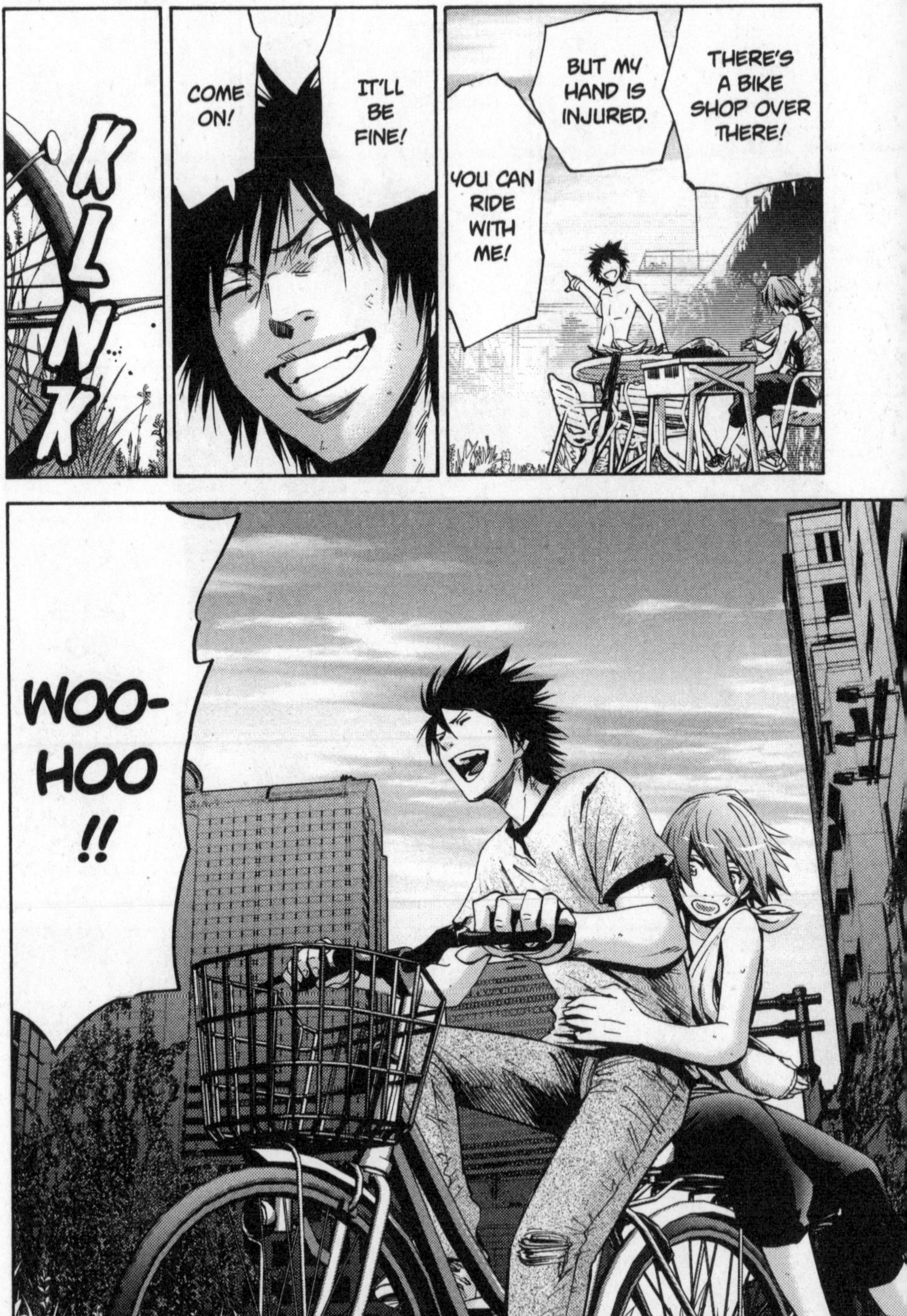
THERE'S A BIKE SHOP OVER THERE!
BUT MY HAND IS INJURED.
YOU CAN RIDE WITH ME!
IT'LL BE FINE!
COME ON!
KLNK
WOO-HOO!!

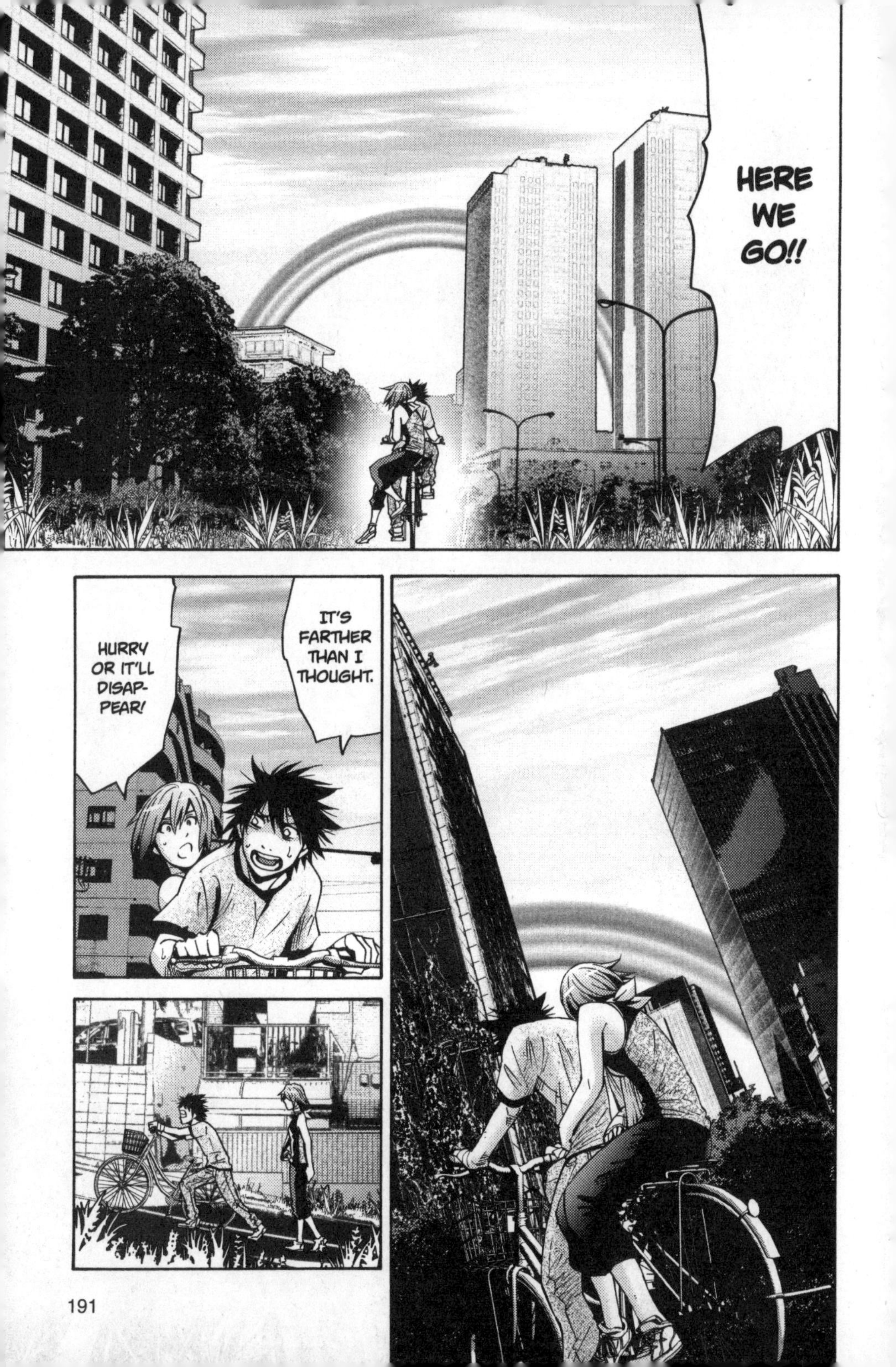
HERE WE GO!!
IT'S FARTHER THAN I THOUGHT.
HURRY OR IT'LL DISAP-PEAR!

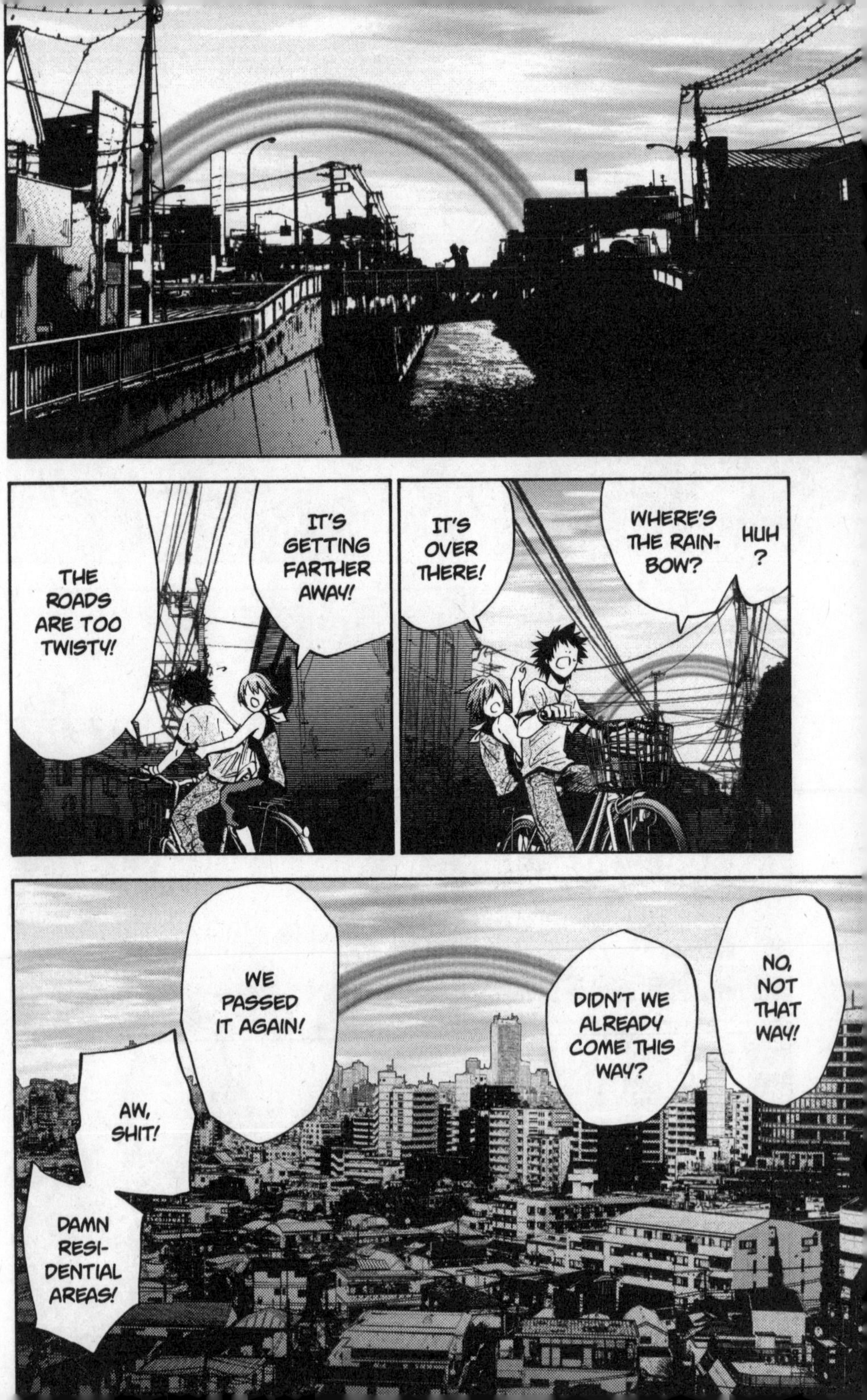
HUH?
WHERE'S THE RAINBOW?
IT'S OVER THERE!
IT'S GETTING FARTHER AWAY!
THE ROADS ARE TOO TWISTY!
NO, NOT THAT WAY!
DIDN'T WE ALREADY COME THIS WAY?
WE PASSED IT AGAIN!
AW, SHIT!
DAMN RESIDENTIAL AREAS!

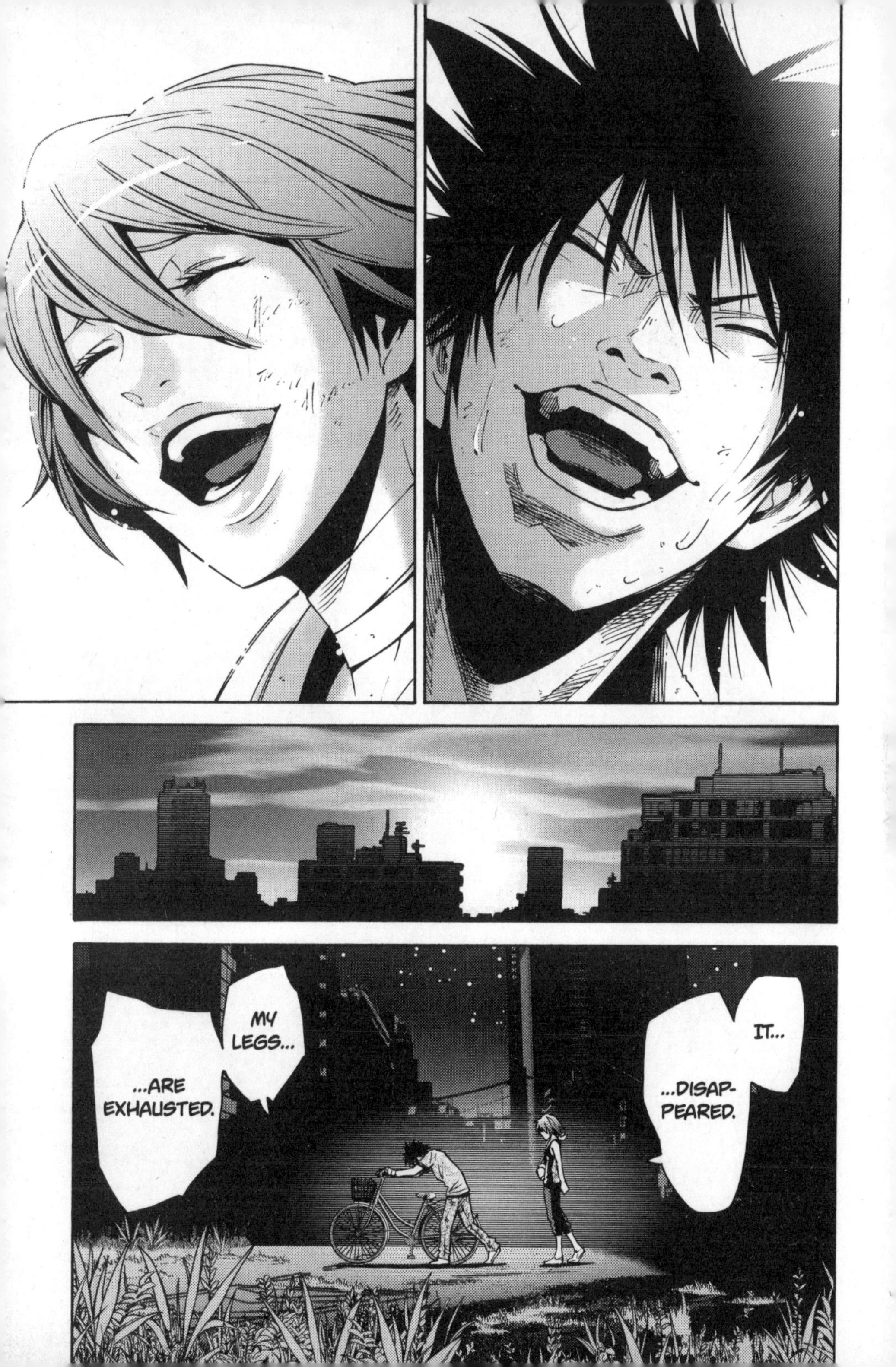
IT...
...DISAP-PEARED.
MY LEGS...
...ARE EXHAUSTED.

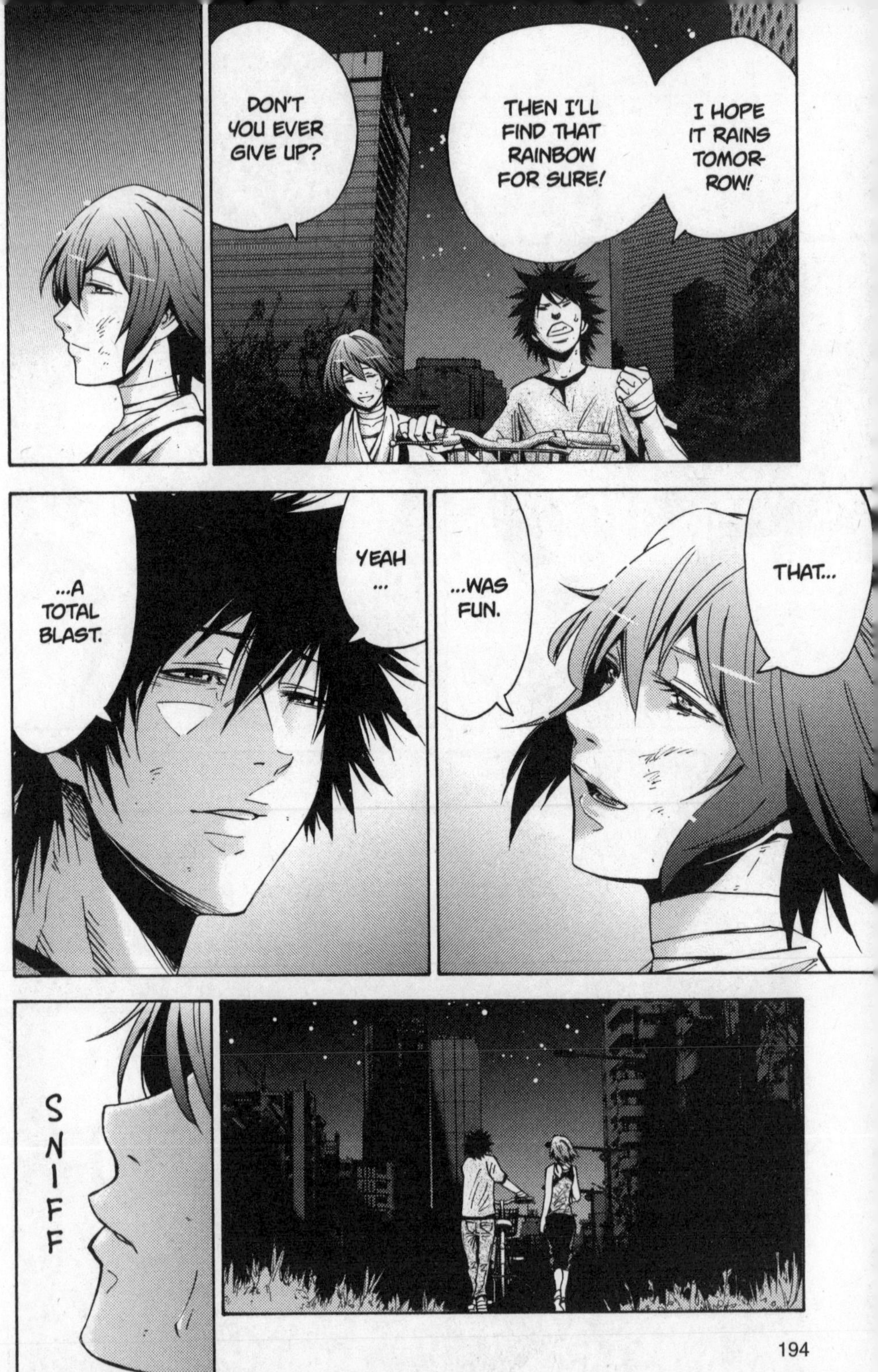
I HOPE IT RAINS TOMOR-ROW!
THEN I'LL FIND THAT RAINBOW FOR SURE!
DON'T YOU EVER GIVE UP?
THAT...
...WAS FUN.
YEAH...
...A TOTAL BLAST.
SNIFF

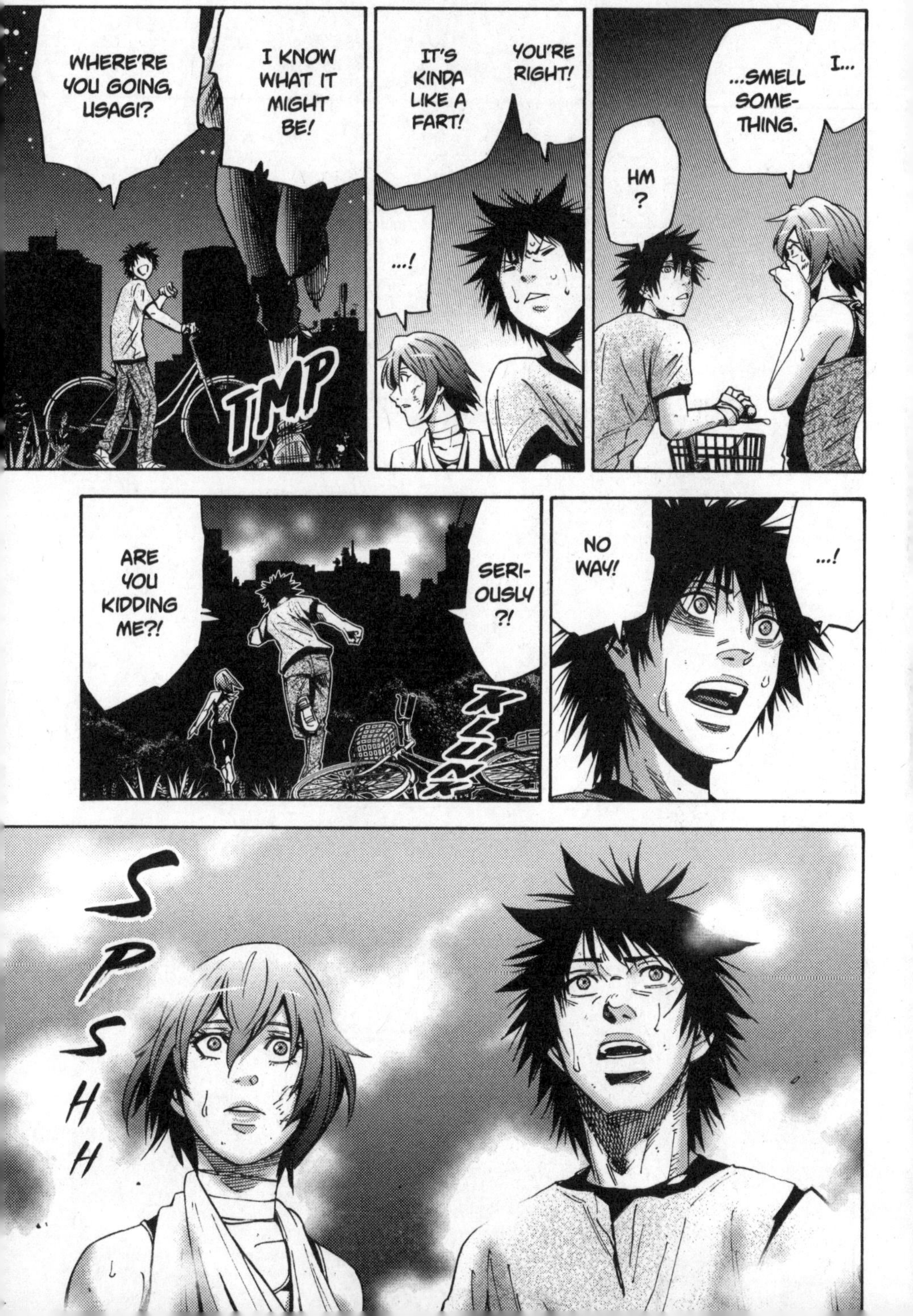
I...
...SMELL SOME-THING.
HM?
YOU'RE RIGHT!
IT'S KINDA LIKE A FART!
...!
I KNOW WHAT IT MIGHT BE!
WHERE'RE YOU GOING, USAGI?
TMP
...!
NO WAY!
SERI-OUSLY?!
ARE YOU KIDDING ME?!
KLUNK
SPSHH

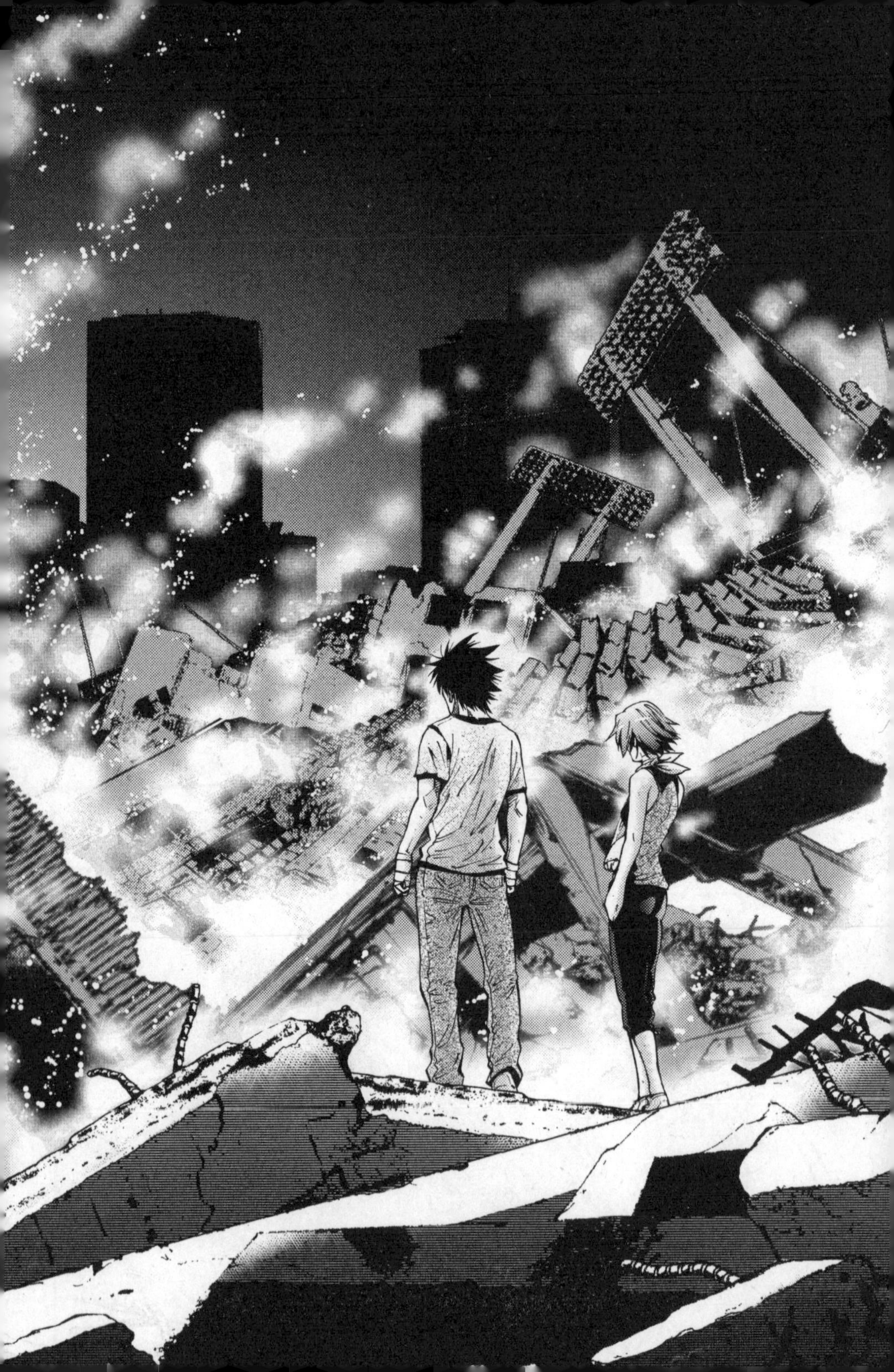

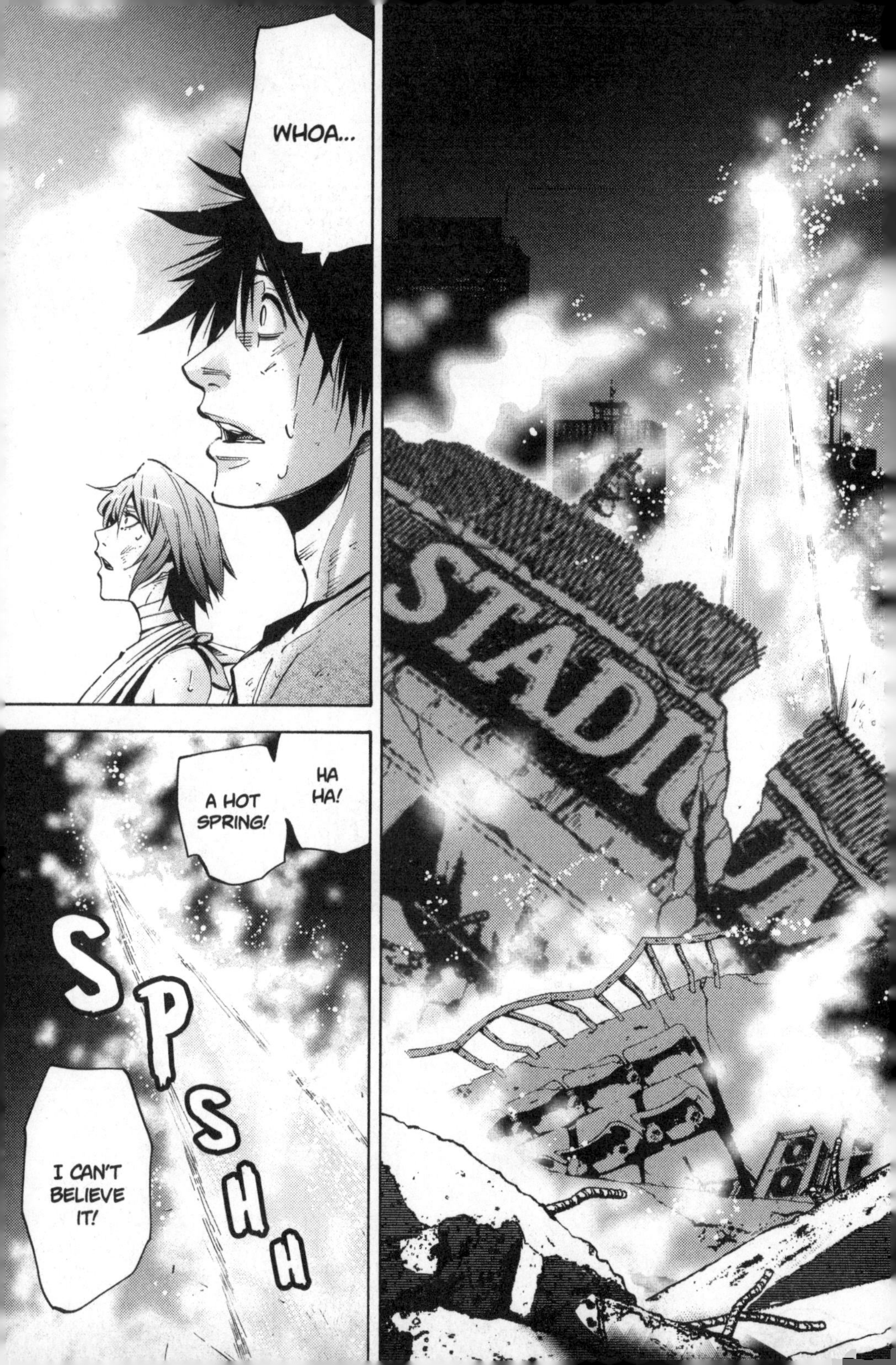
WHOA...
HA HA! A HOT SPRING!
SPSHH
I CAN'T BELIEVE IT!

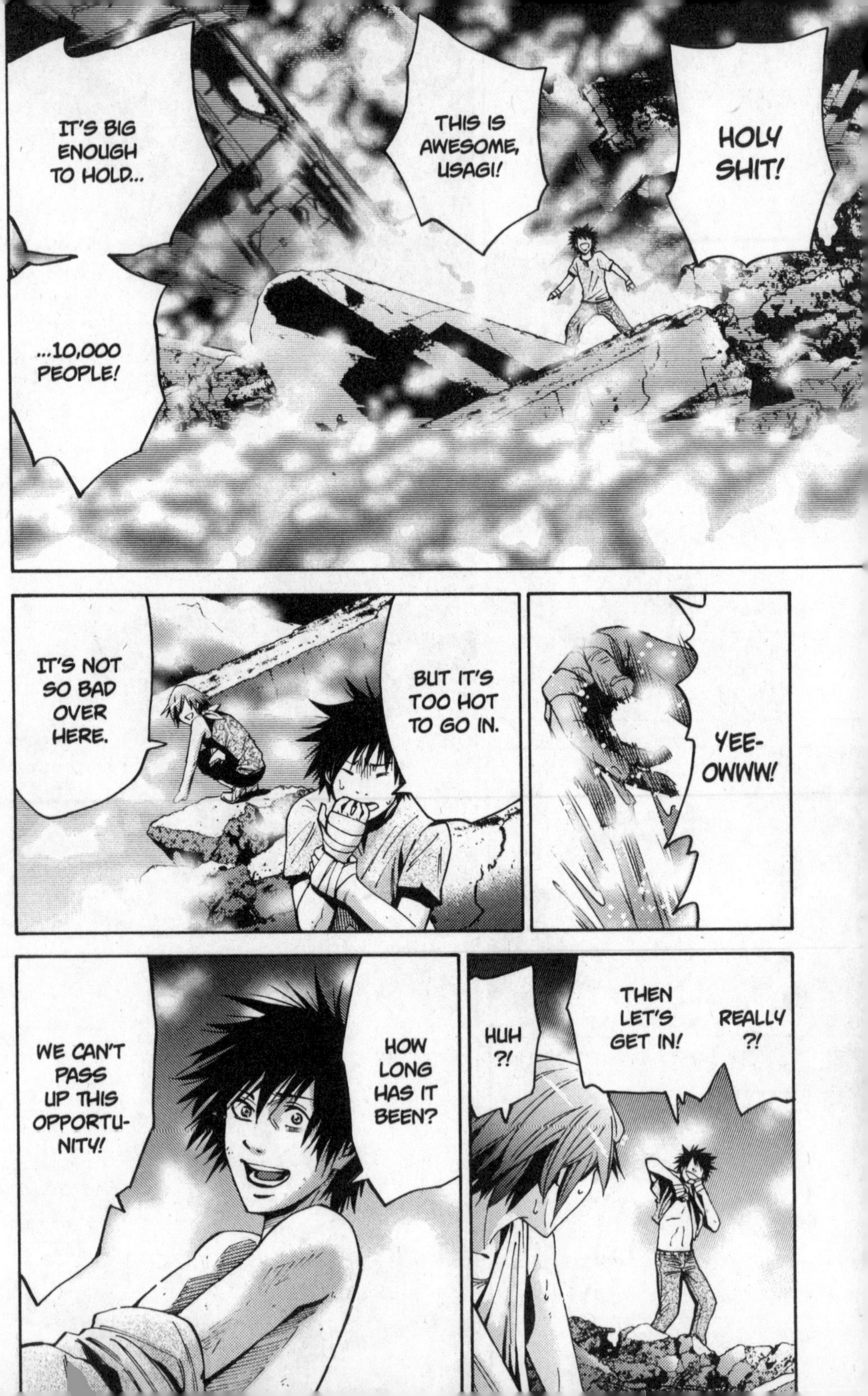
HOLY SHIT!
THIS IS AWESOME, USAGI!
IT'S BIG ENOUGH TO HOLD...
...10,000 PEOPLE!
YEE-OWWW!
BUT IT'S TOO HOT TO GO IN.
IT'S NOT SO BAD OVER HERE.
REALLY ?!
THEN LET'S GET IN!
HUH ?!
HOW LONG HAS IT BEEN?
WE CAN'T PASS UP THIS OPPORTUNITY!

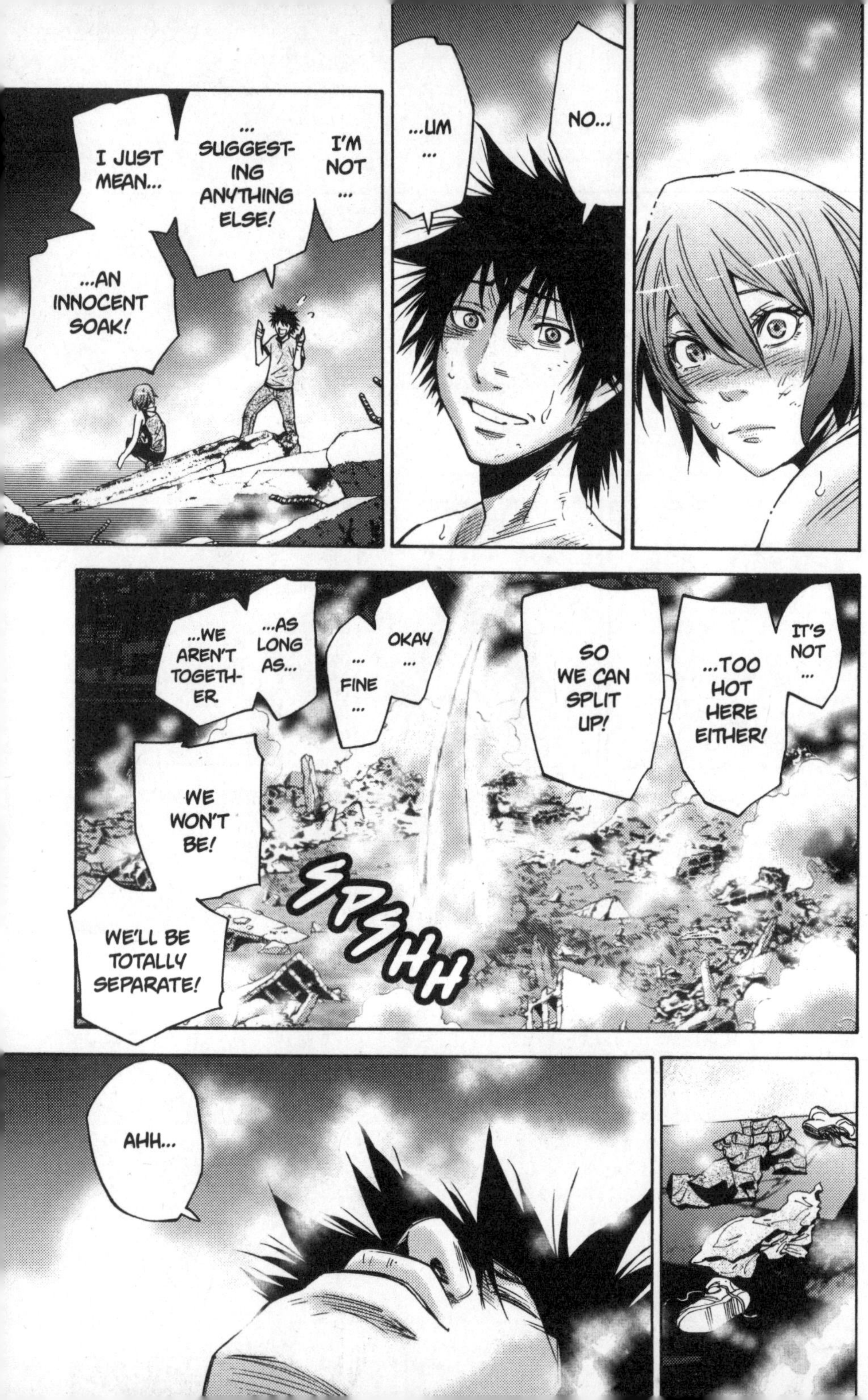
NO...
...UM ...
I'M NOT ...
... SUGGEST-ING ANYTHING ELSE!
I JUST MEAN...
...AN INNOCENT SOAK!
IT'S NOT ...
...TOO HOT HERE EITHER!
SO WE CAN SPLIT UP!
OKAY ...
... FINE ...
...AS LONG AS...
...WE AREN'T TOGETH-ER.
WE WON'T BE!
SPSHH
WE'LL BE TOTALLY SEPARATE!
AHH...

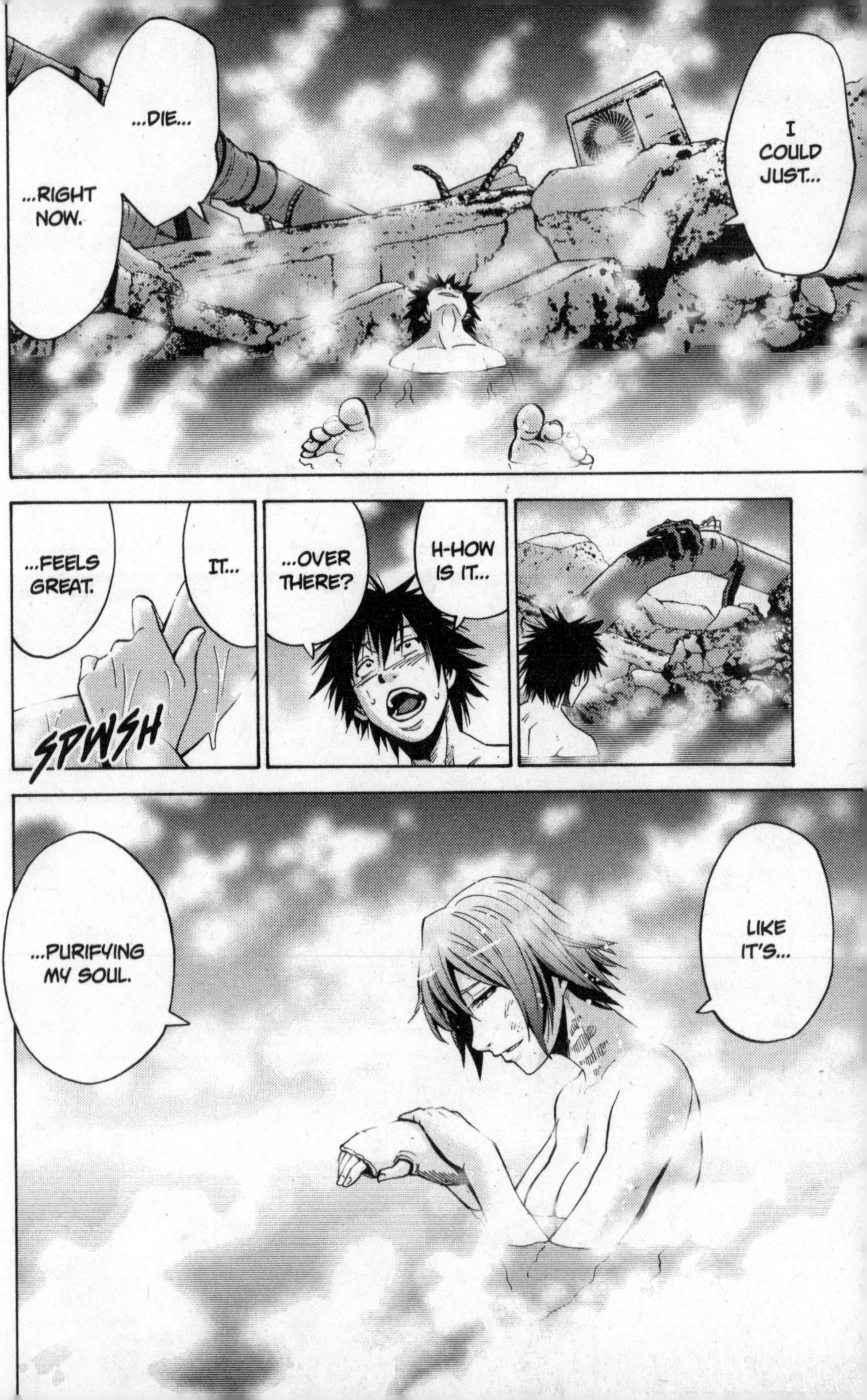
I COULD JUST...
...DIE...
...RIGHT NOW.
H-HOW IS IT...
...OVER THERE?
IT...
...FEELS GREAT.
SPWSH
LIKE IT'S...
...PURIFYING MY SOUL.

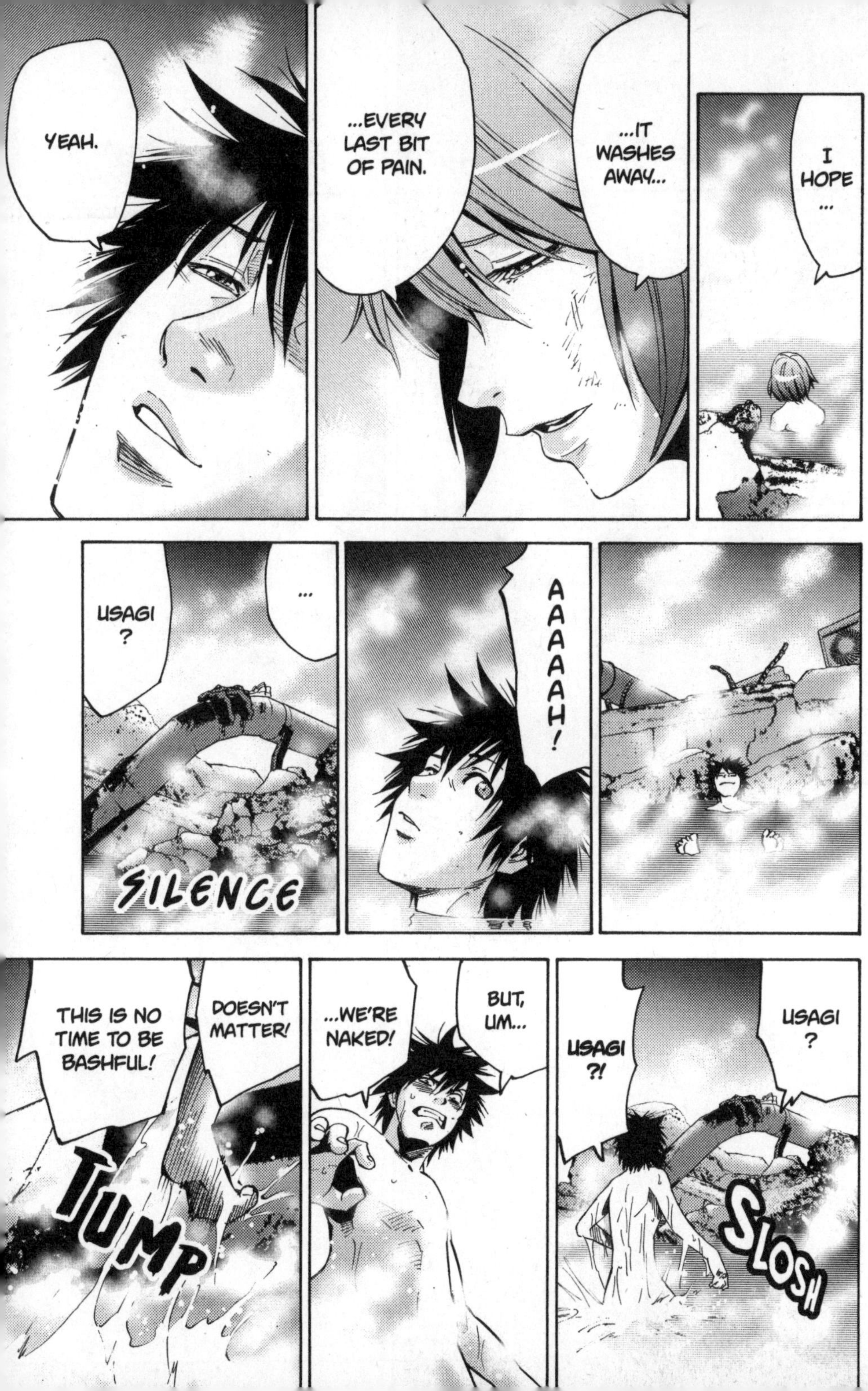
I HOPE ...
...IT WASHES AWAY...
...EVERY LAST BIT OF PAIN.
YEAH.
AAAAAAH!
...
USAGI ?
SILENCE
USAGI ?
USAGI ?!
SLOSH
BUT, UM...
...WE'RE NAKED!
DOESN'T MATTER!
THIS IS NO TIME TO BE BASHFUL!
TUMP

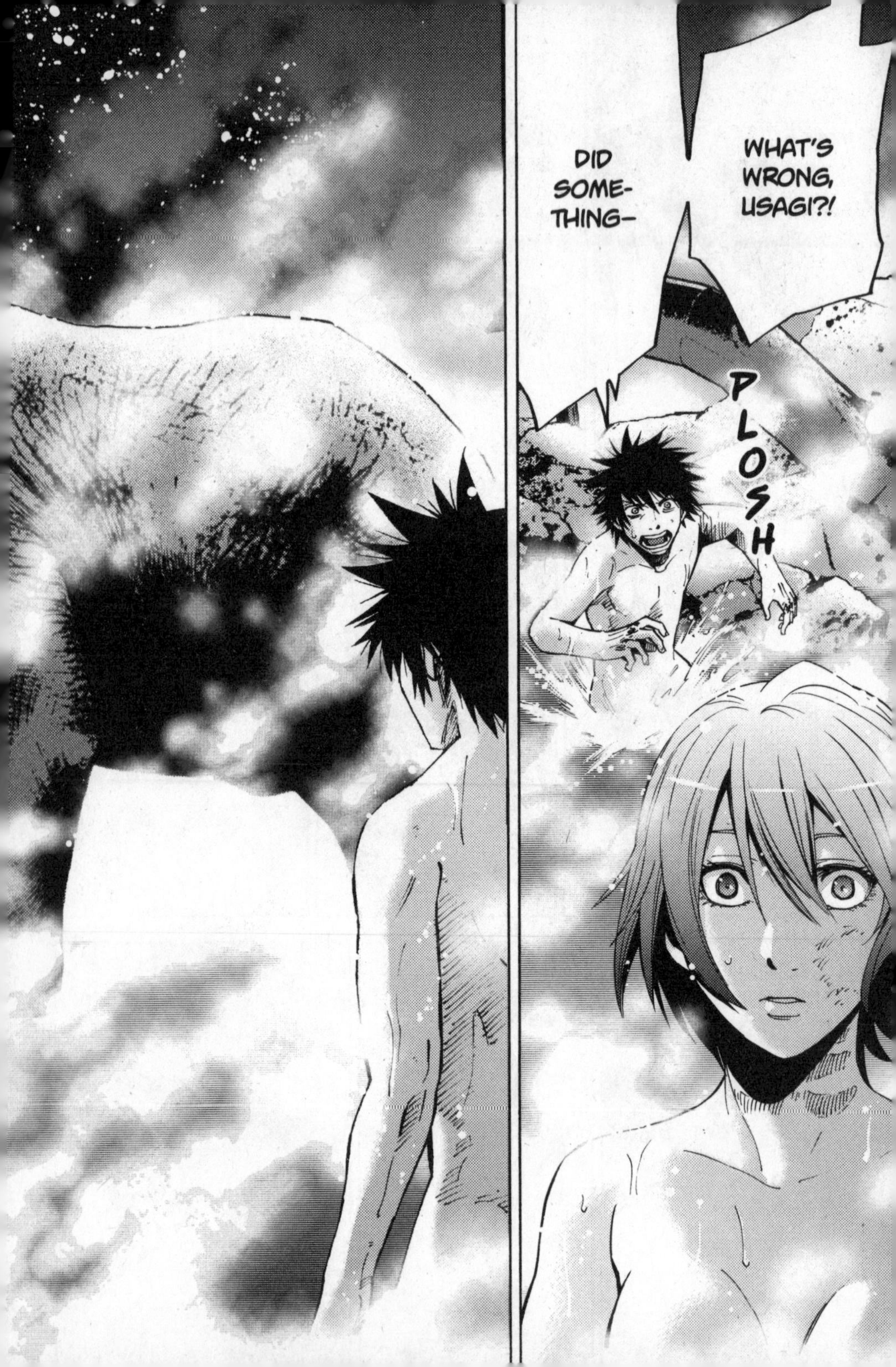
WHAT'S WRONG, USAGI?!
DID SOME-THING—
PLOSH

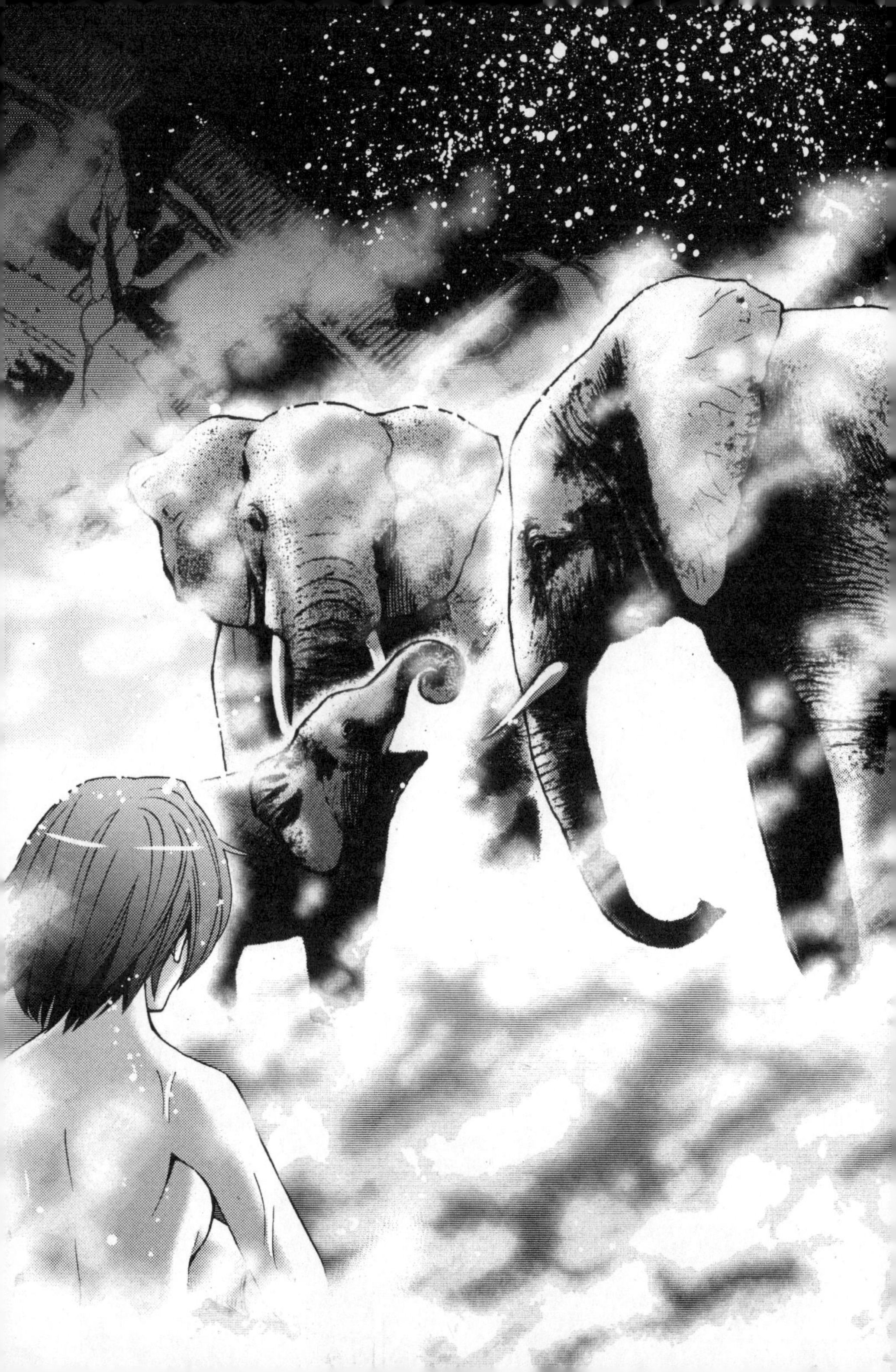

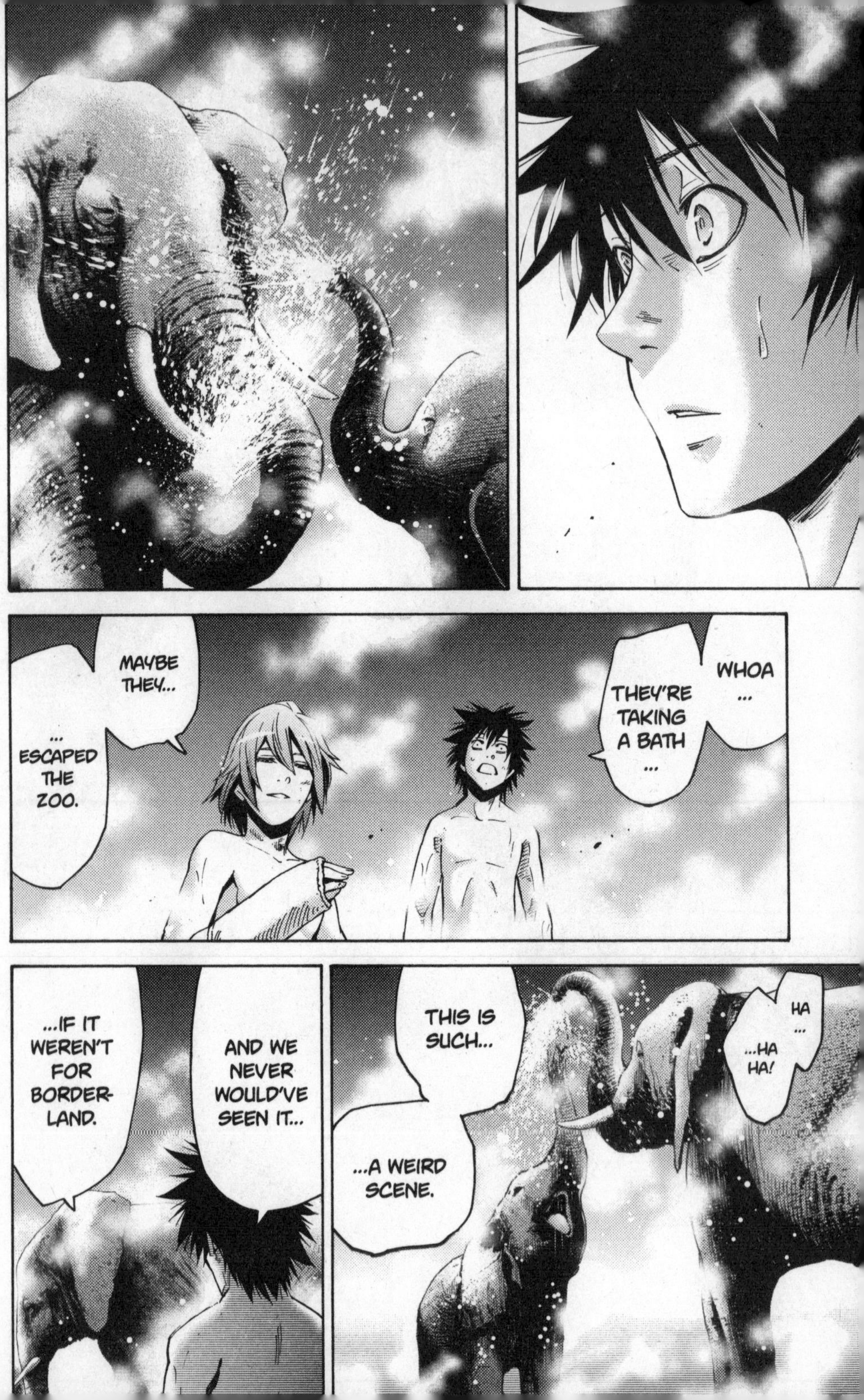
WHOA ...
THEY'RE TAKING A BATH ...
MAYBE THEY...
... ESCAPED THE ZOO.
HA ... ...HA HA!
THIS IS SUCH...
...A WEIRD SCENE.
AND WE NEVER WOULD'VE SEEN IT...
...IF IT WEREN'T FOR BORDER-LAND.

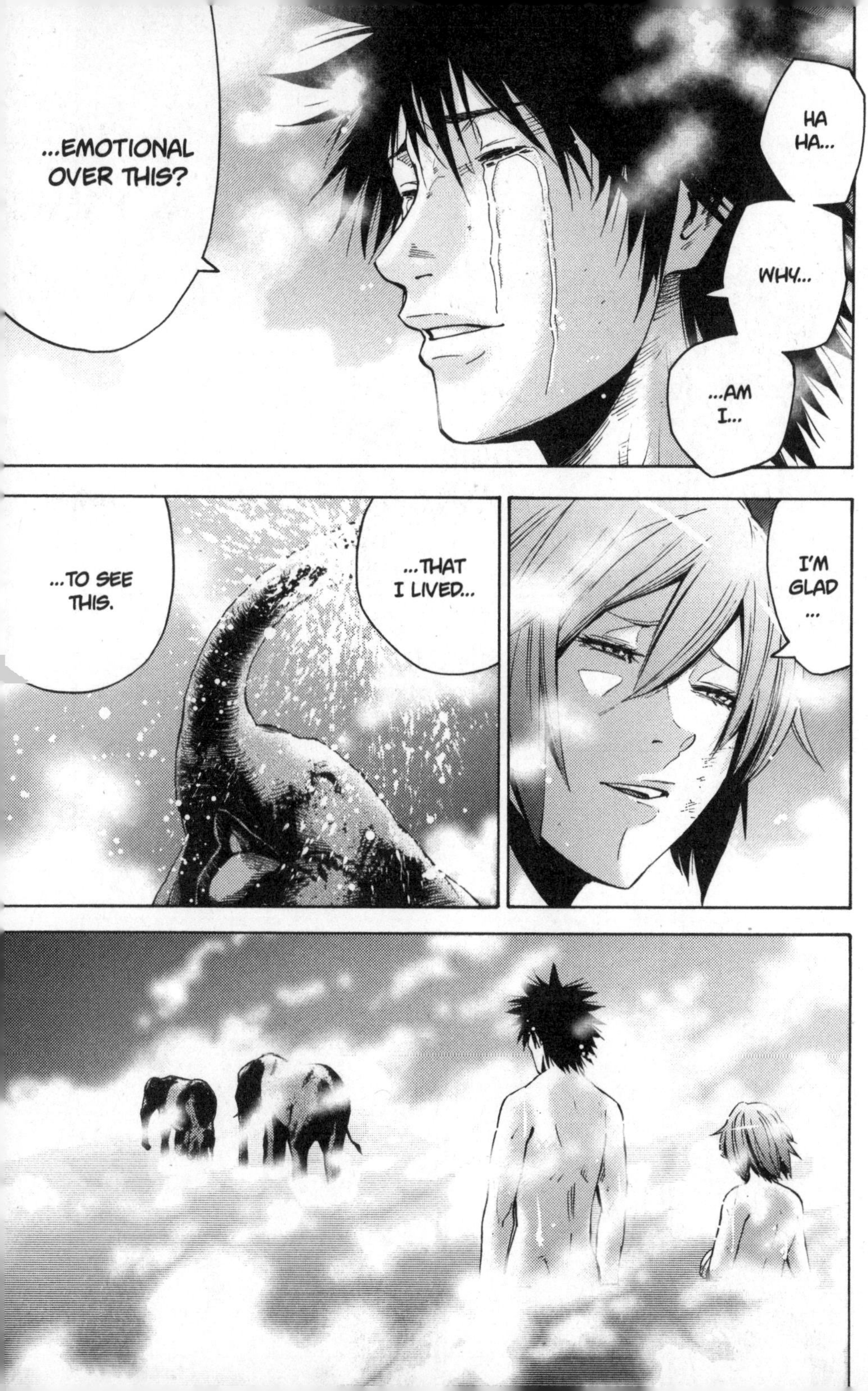
HA HA...
WHY...
...AM I...
...EMOTIONAL OVER THIS?
I'M GLAD ...
...THAT I LIVED...
...TO SEE THIS.

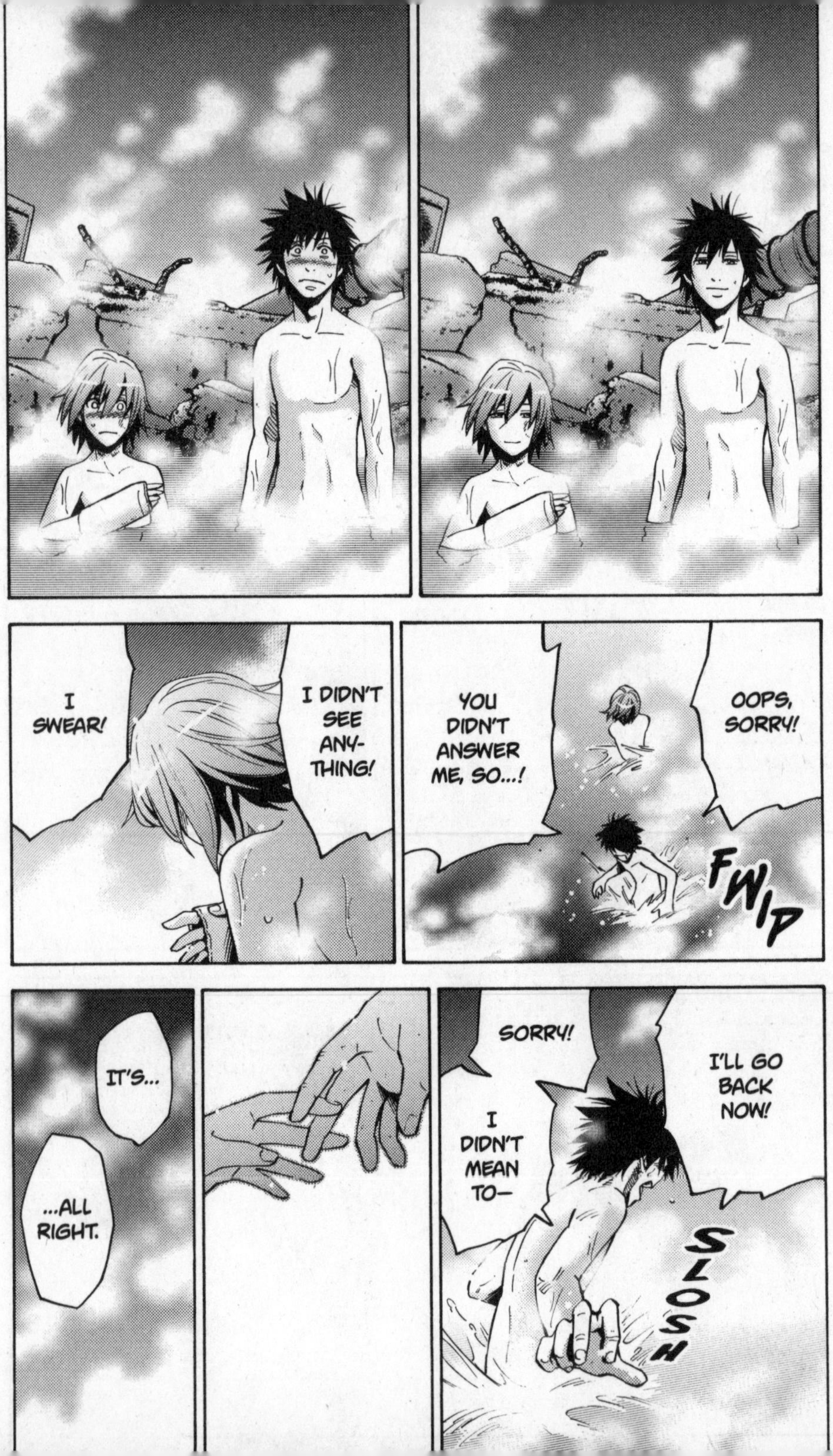
OOPS, SORRY!
YOU DIDN'T ANSWER ME, SO...!
FWIP
I DIDN'T SEE ANY-THING!
I SWEAR!
I'LL GO BACK NOW!
SORRY!
I DIDN'T MEAN TO—
SLOSH
IT'S...
...ALL RIGHT.

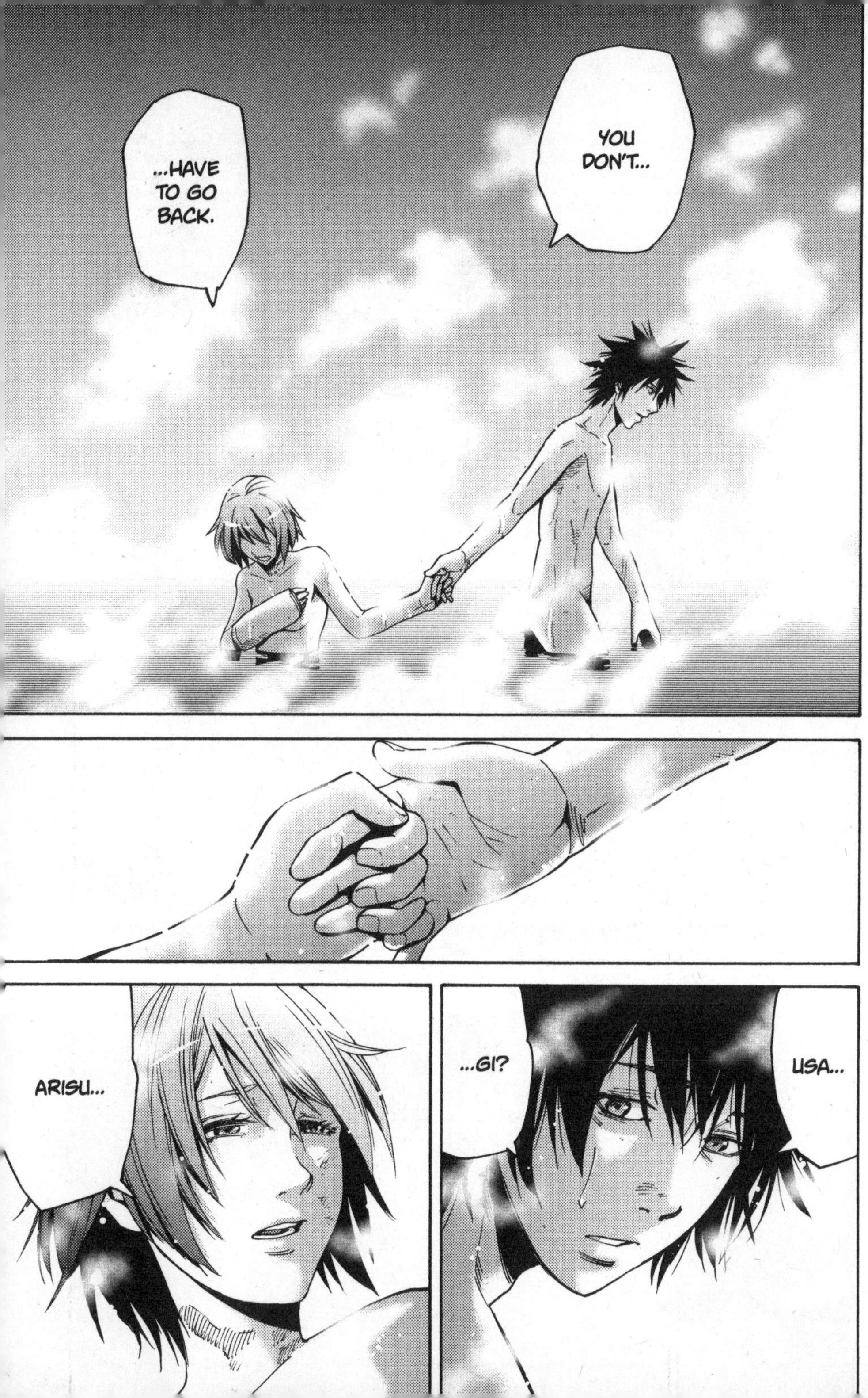
YOU DON'T...
...HAVE TO GO BACK.
USA...
...GI?
ARISU...

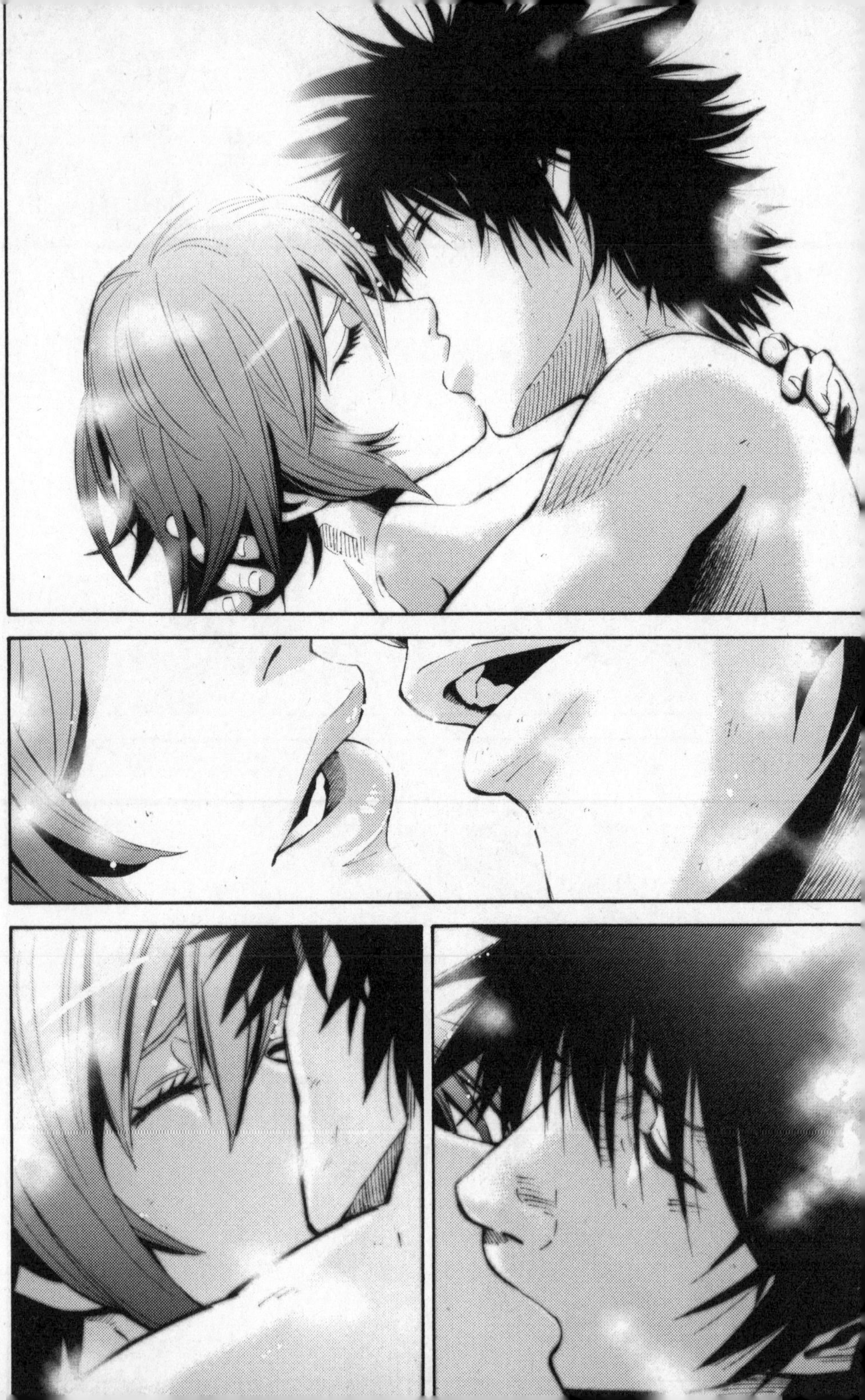

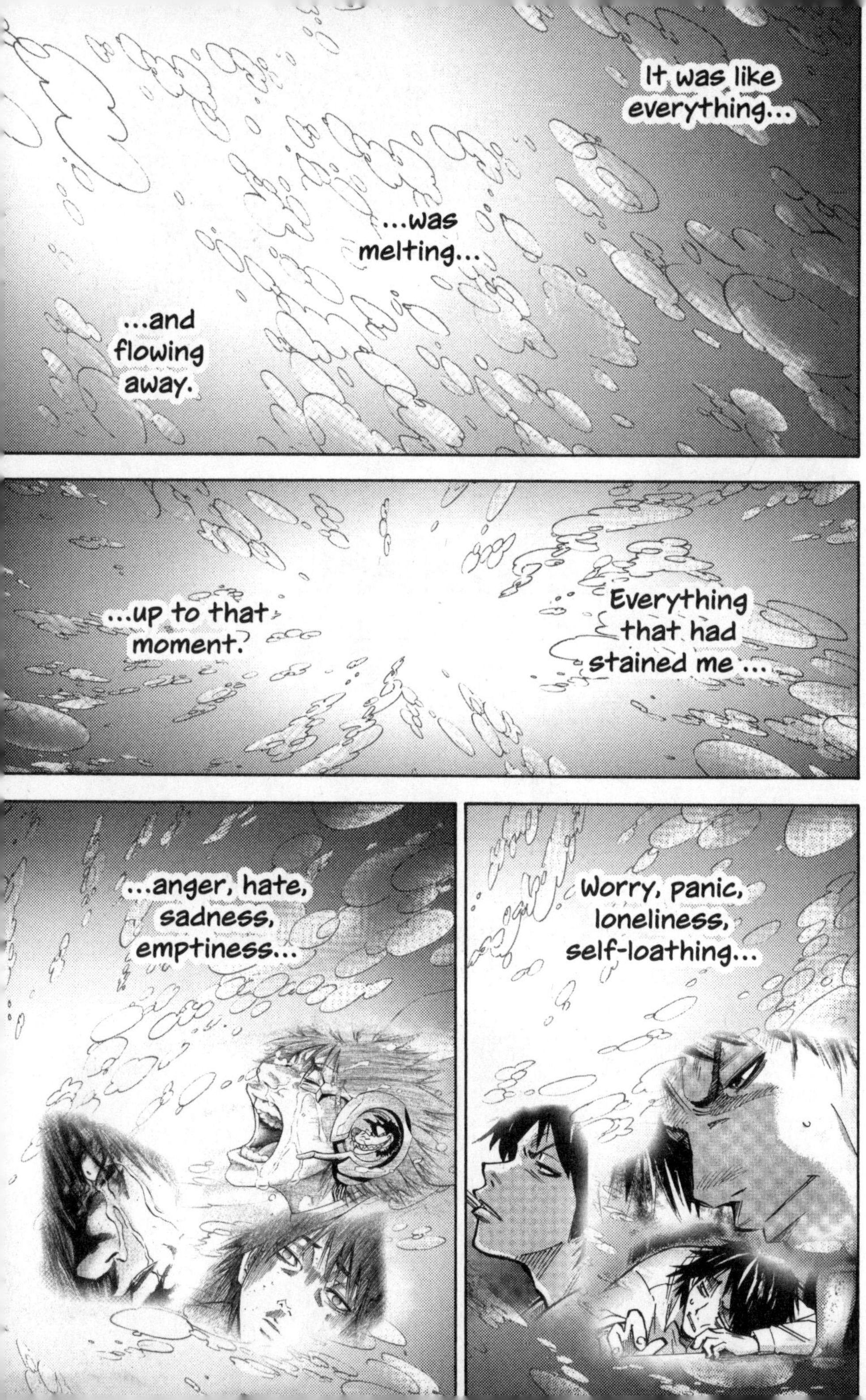
It was like everything...
...was melting...
...and flowing away.
Everything that had stained me ...
...up to that moment.
Worry, panic, loneliness, self-loathing...
...anger, hate, sadness, emptiness...

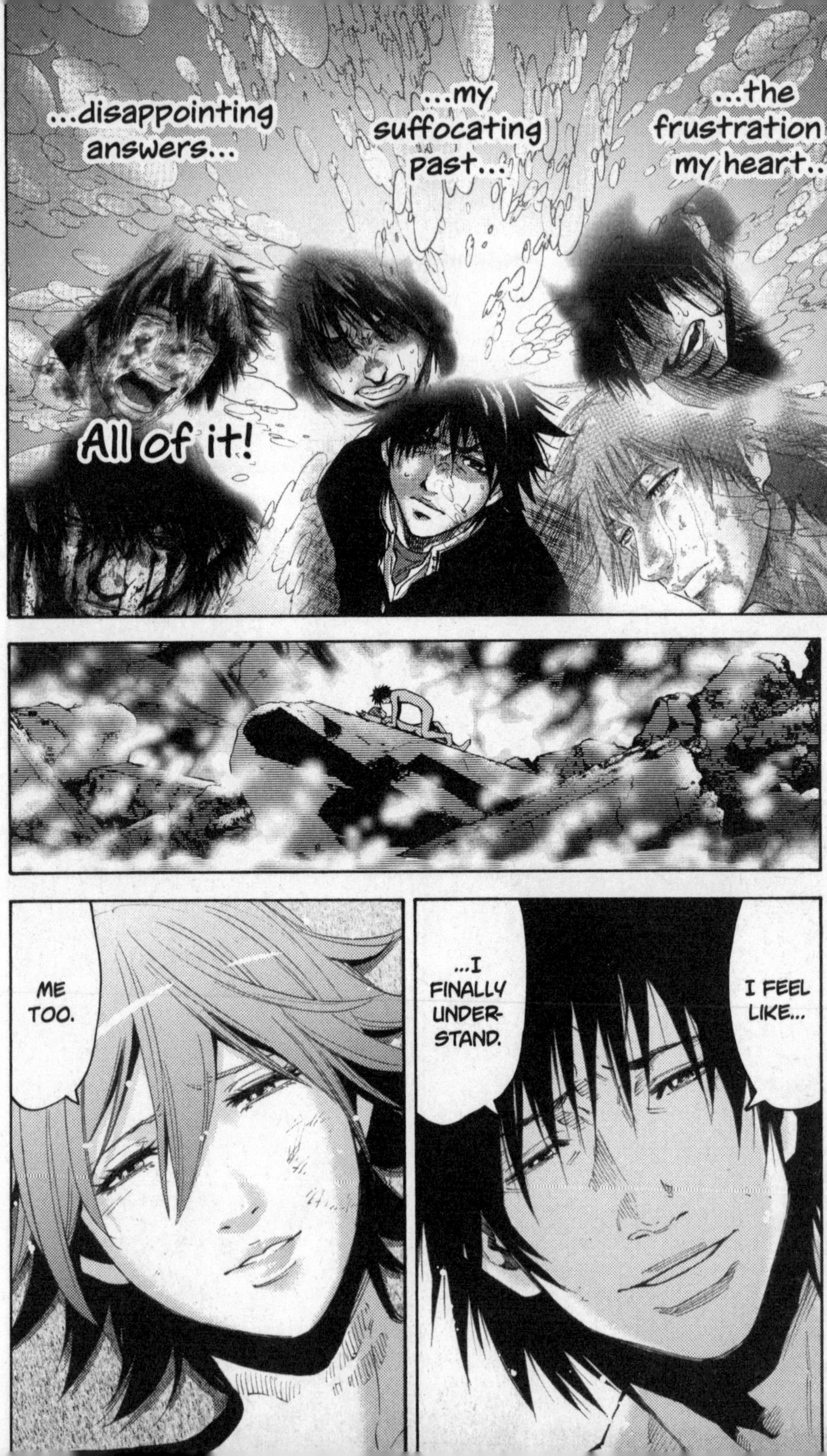
...the frustration in my heart...
...my suffocating past...
...disappointing answers...
All of it!
I FEEL LIKE...
...I FINALLY UNDERSTAND.
ME TOO.

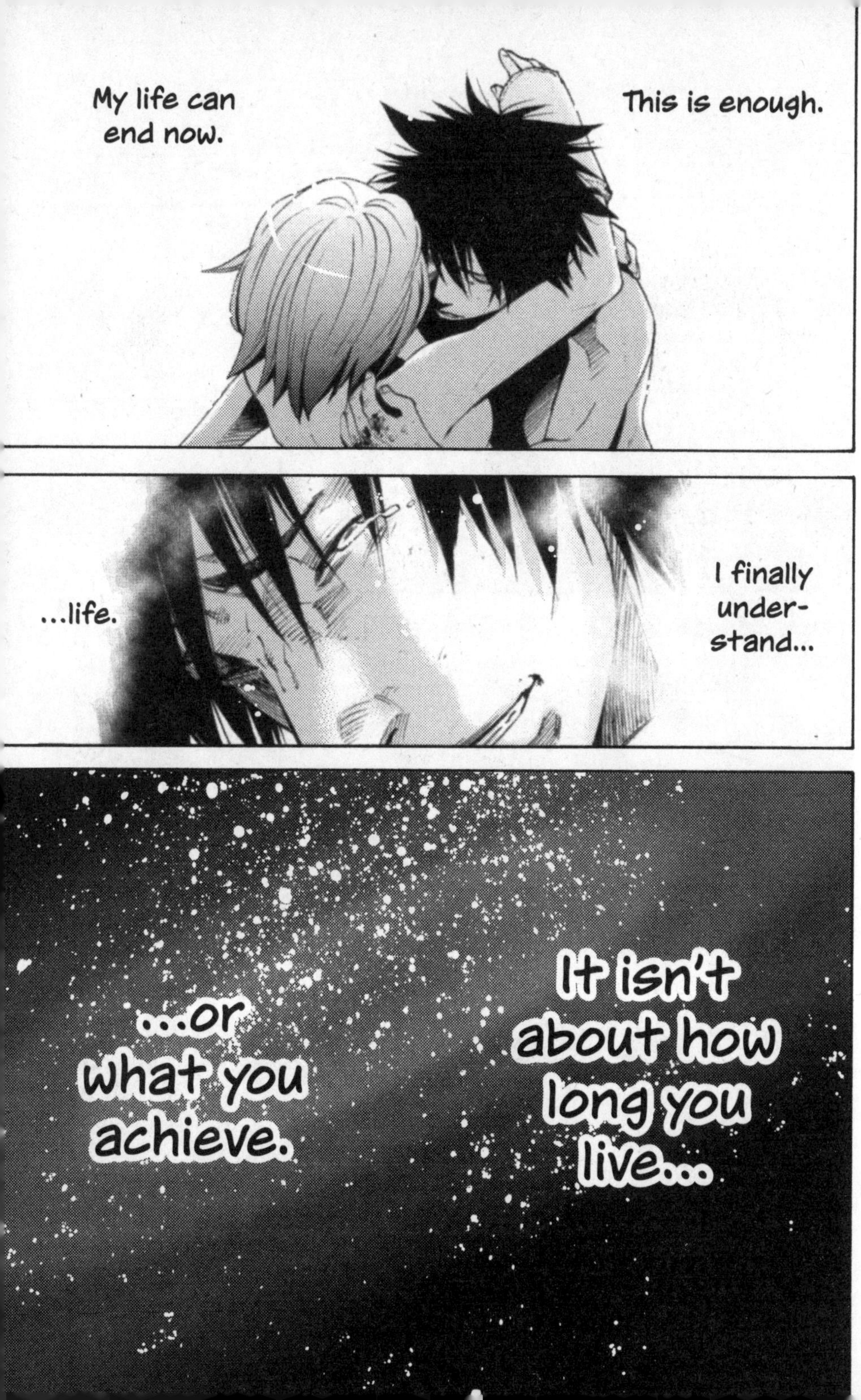
This is enough.
My life can end now.
I finally under-stand...
...life.
It isn't about how long you live...
...or what you achieve.

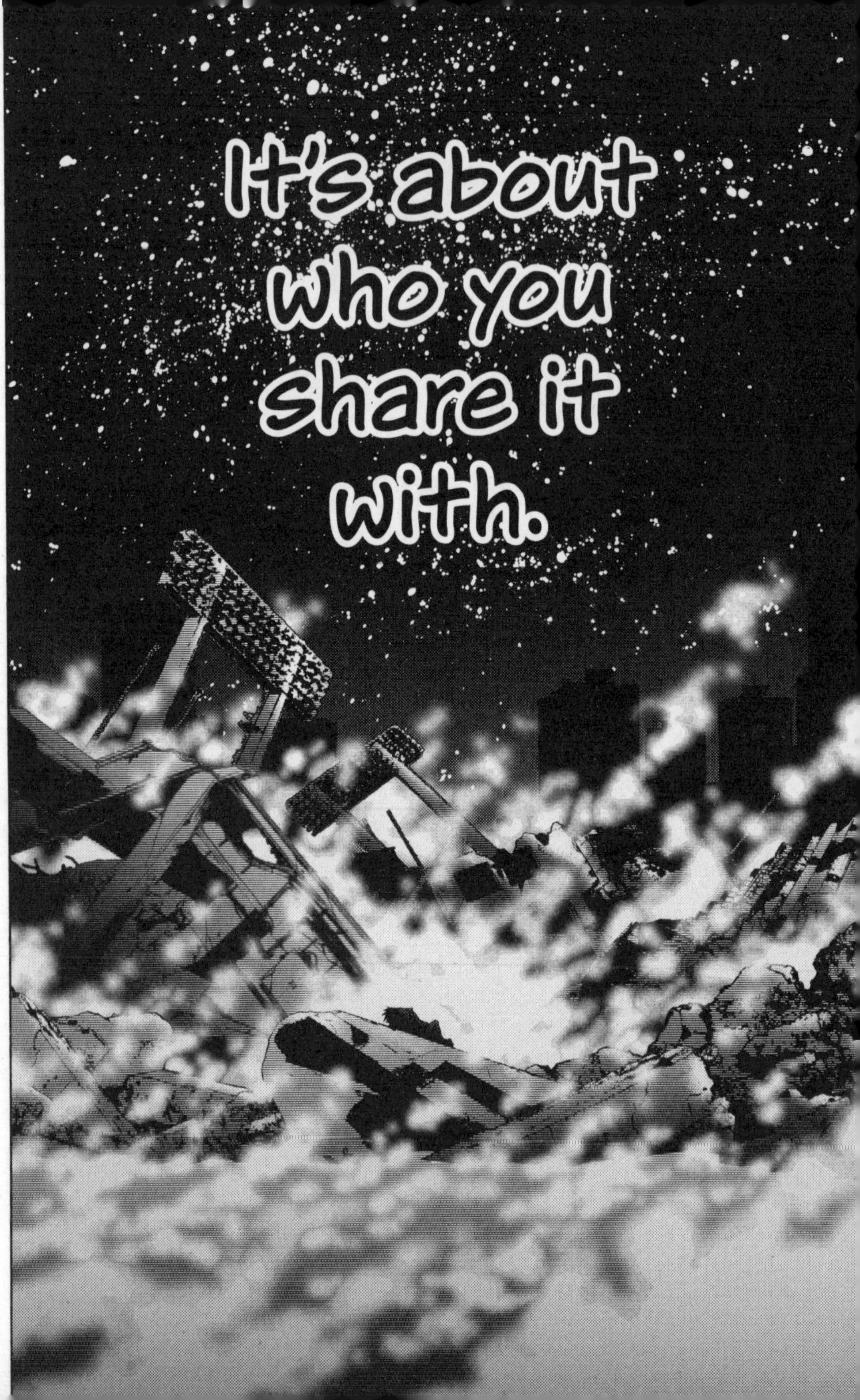
It's about who you share it with.

CHAPTER 44: **Five Days After the Start**

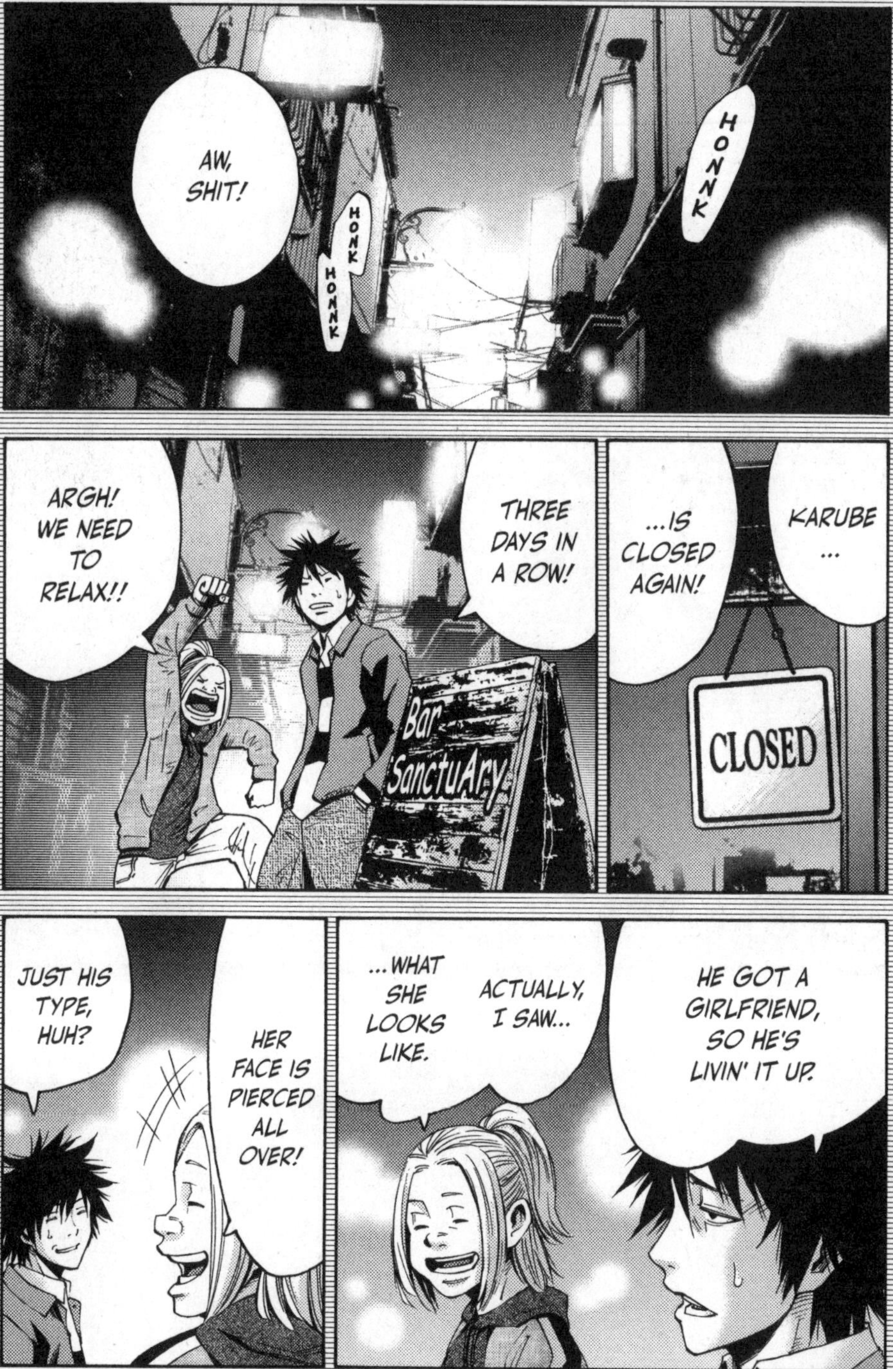
HONNK
HONK
HONNK
AW, SHIT!
KARUBE ...
...IS CLOSED AGAIN!
CLOSED
THREE DAYS IN A ROW!
ARGH! WE NEED TO RELAX!!
Bar SanctuAry
HE GOT A GIRLFRIEND, SO HE'S LIVIN' IT UP.
ACTUALLY, I SAW...
...WHAT SHE LOOKS LIKE.
HER FACE IS PIERCED ALL OVER!
JUST HIS TYPE, HUH?

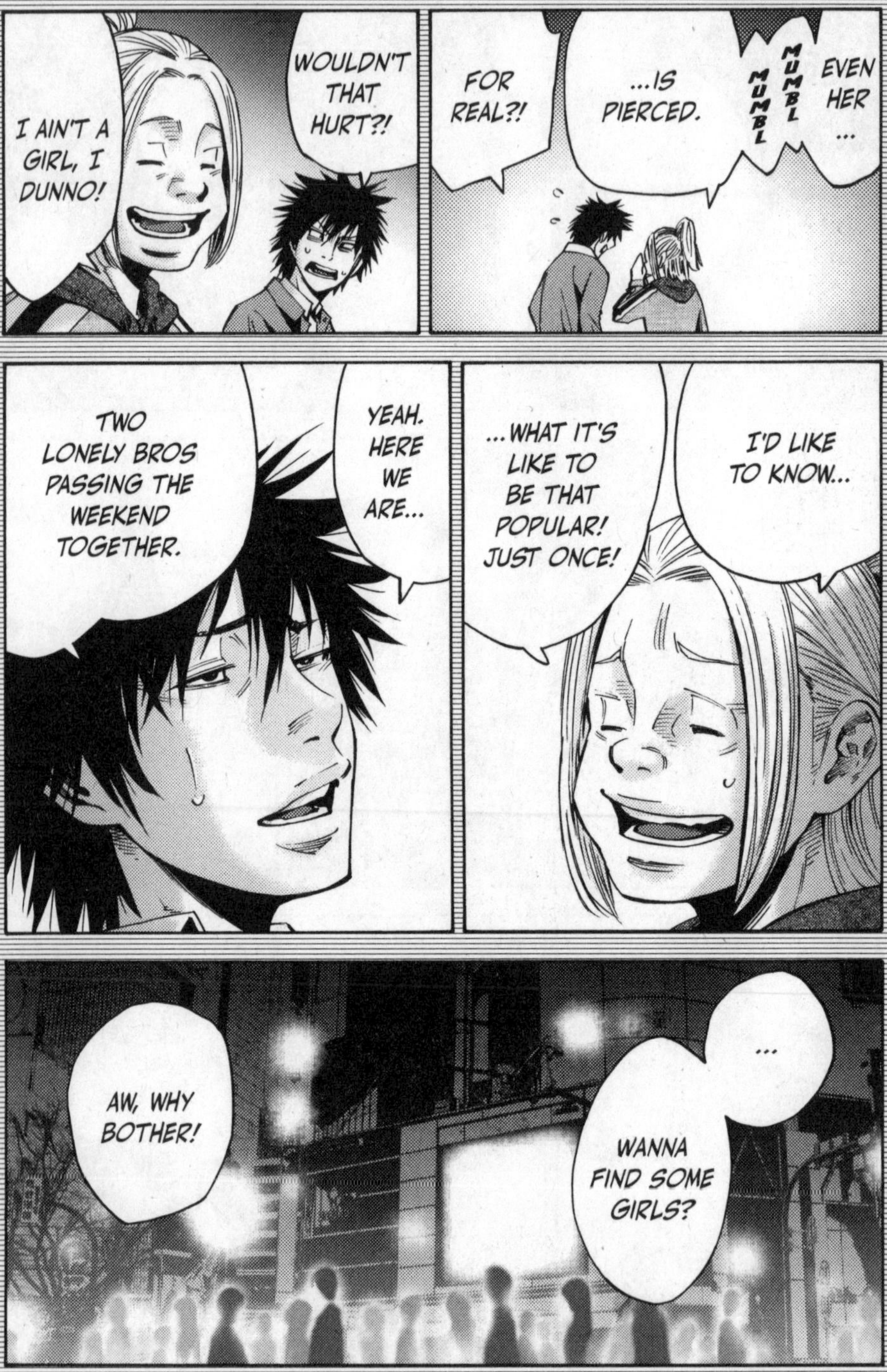
EVEN HER ...
MUMBL MUMBL
...IS PIERCED.
FOR REAL?!
WOULDN'T THAT HURT?!
I AIN'T A GIRL, I DUNNO!
I'D LIKE TO KNOW...
...WHAT IT'S LIKE TO BE THAT POPULAR! JUST ONCE!
YEAH. HERE WE ARE...
TWO LONELY BROS PASSING THE WEEKEND TOGETHER.
...
WANNA FIND SOME GIRLS?
AW, WHY BOTHER!

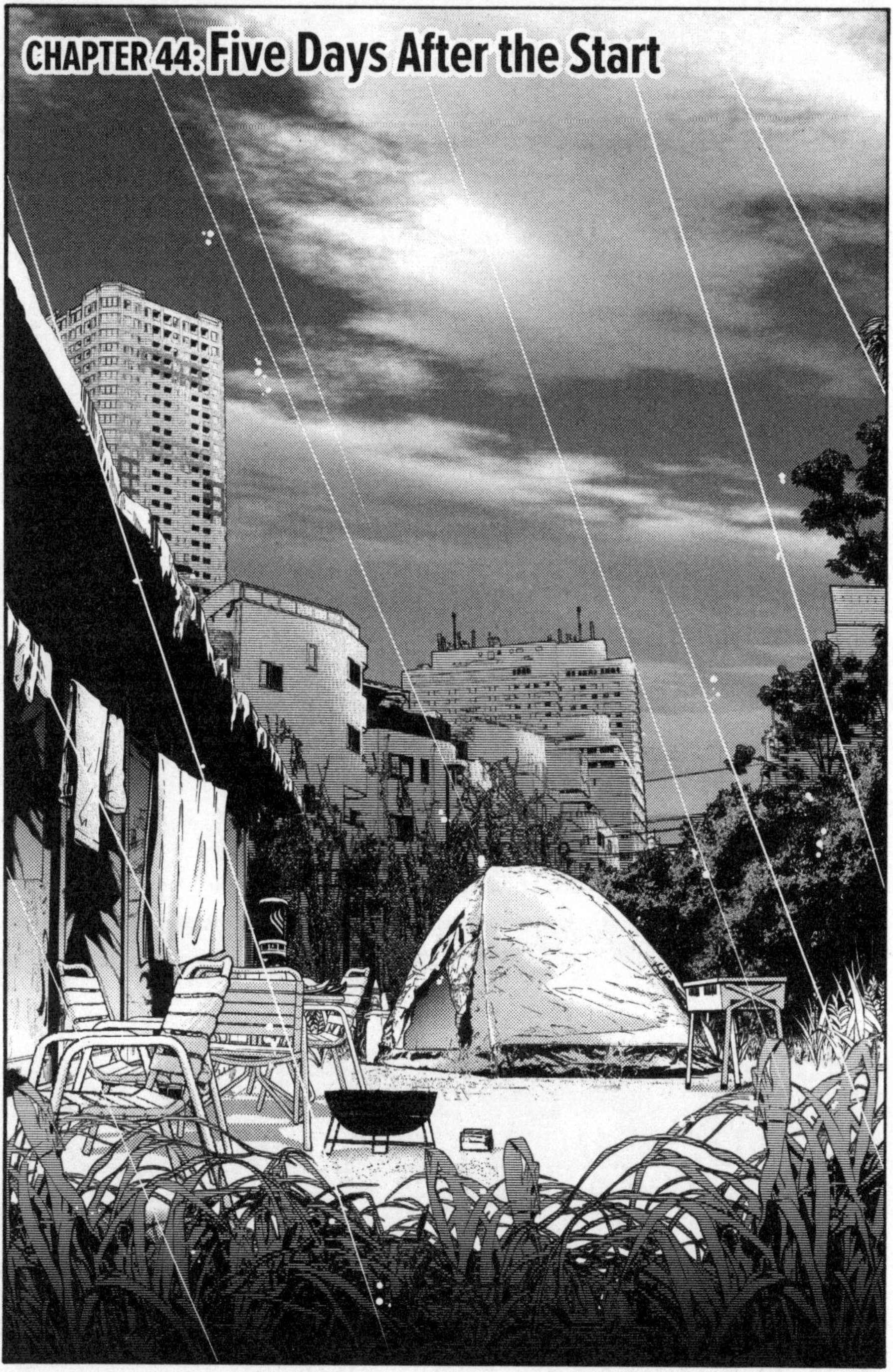
CHAPTER 44: Five Days After the Start

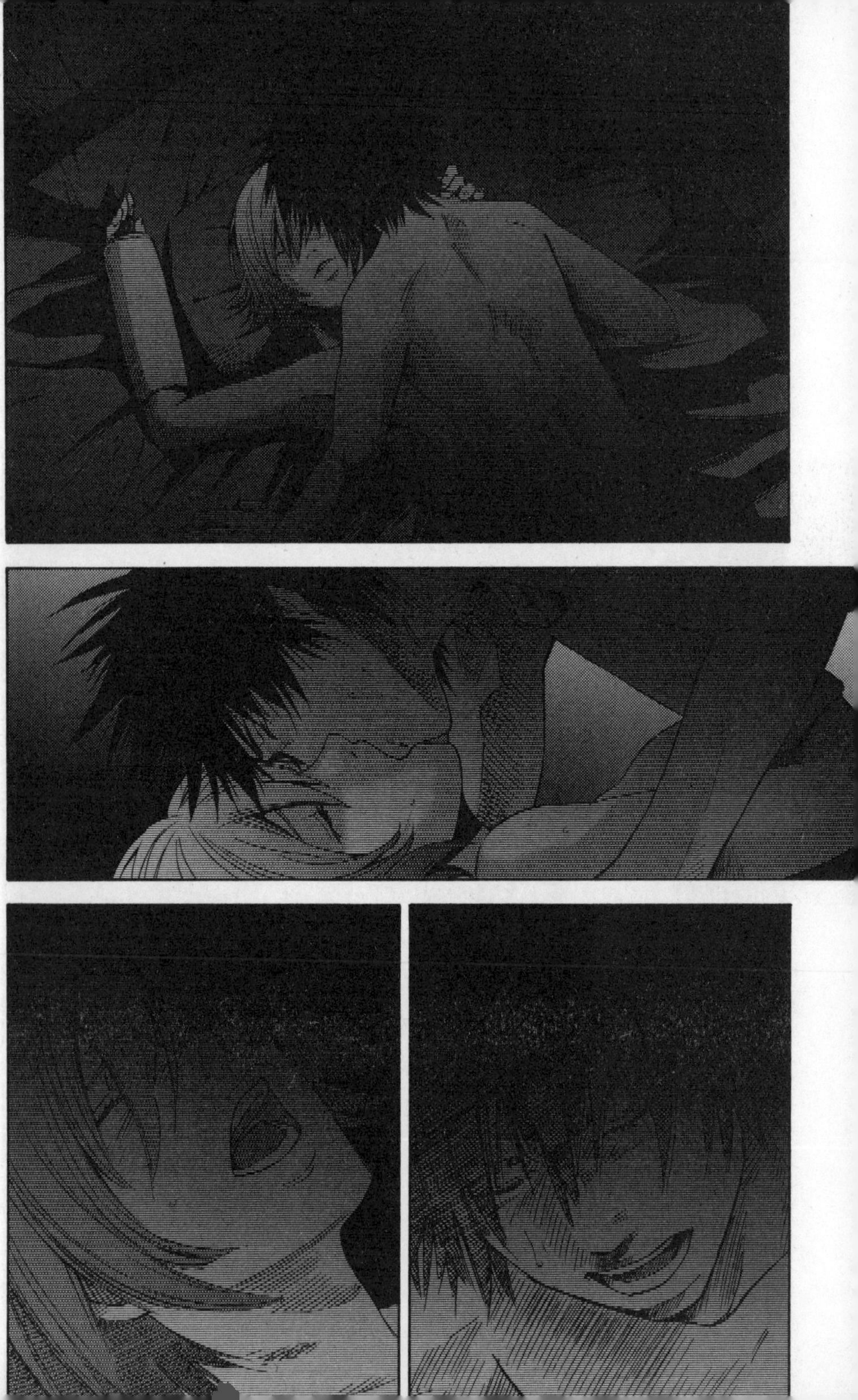

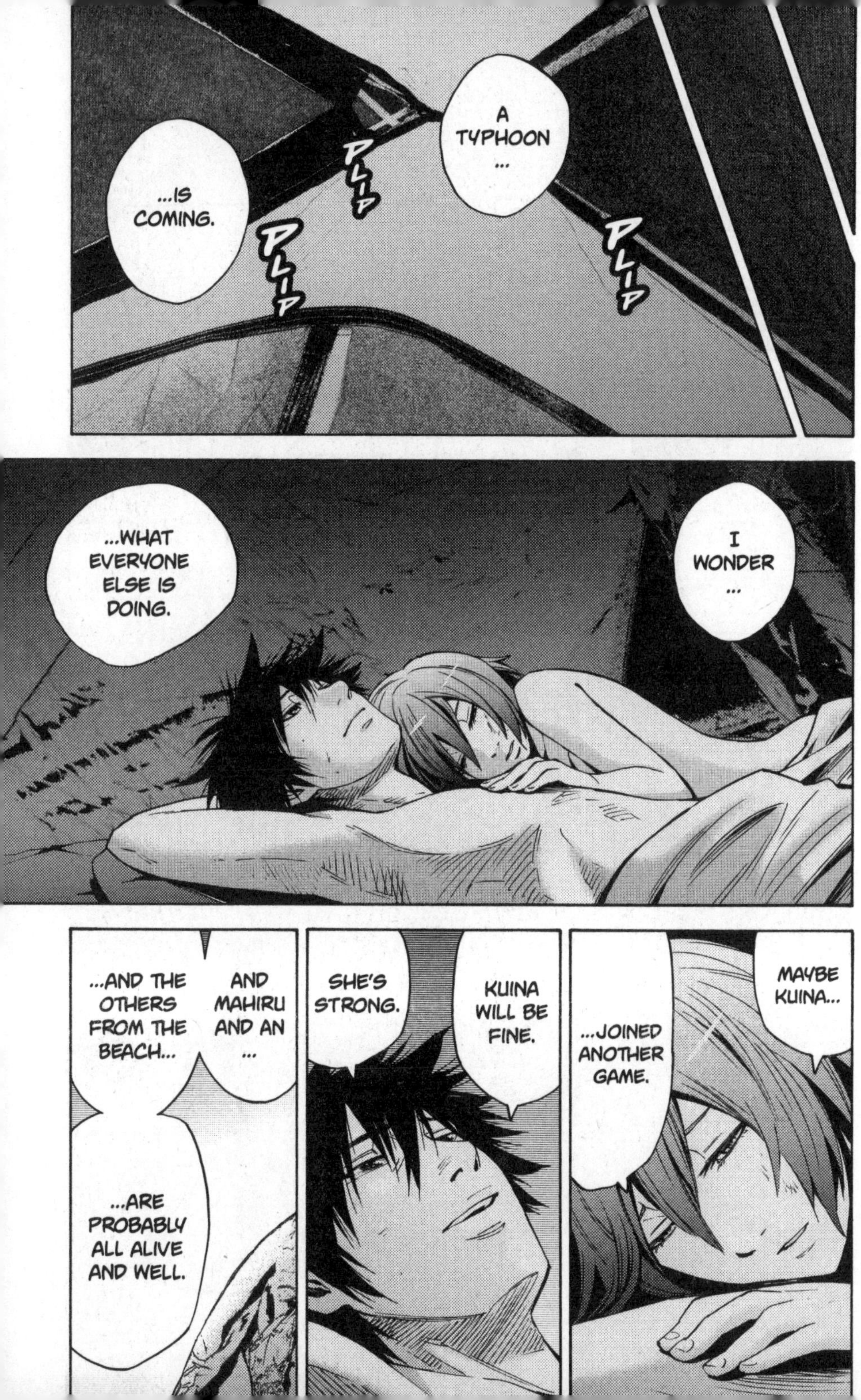

A TYPHOON ...
PLIP
PLIP
...IS COMING.
PLIP
I WONDER ...
...WHAT EVERYONE ELSE IS DOING.
MAYBE KUINA...
...JOINED ANOTHER GAME.
KUINA WILL BE FINE.
SHE'S STRONG.
AND MAHIRU AND AN ...
...AND THE OTHERS FROM THE BEACH...
...ARE PROBABLY ALL ALIVE AND WELL.

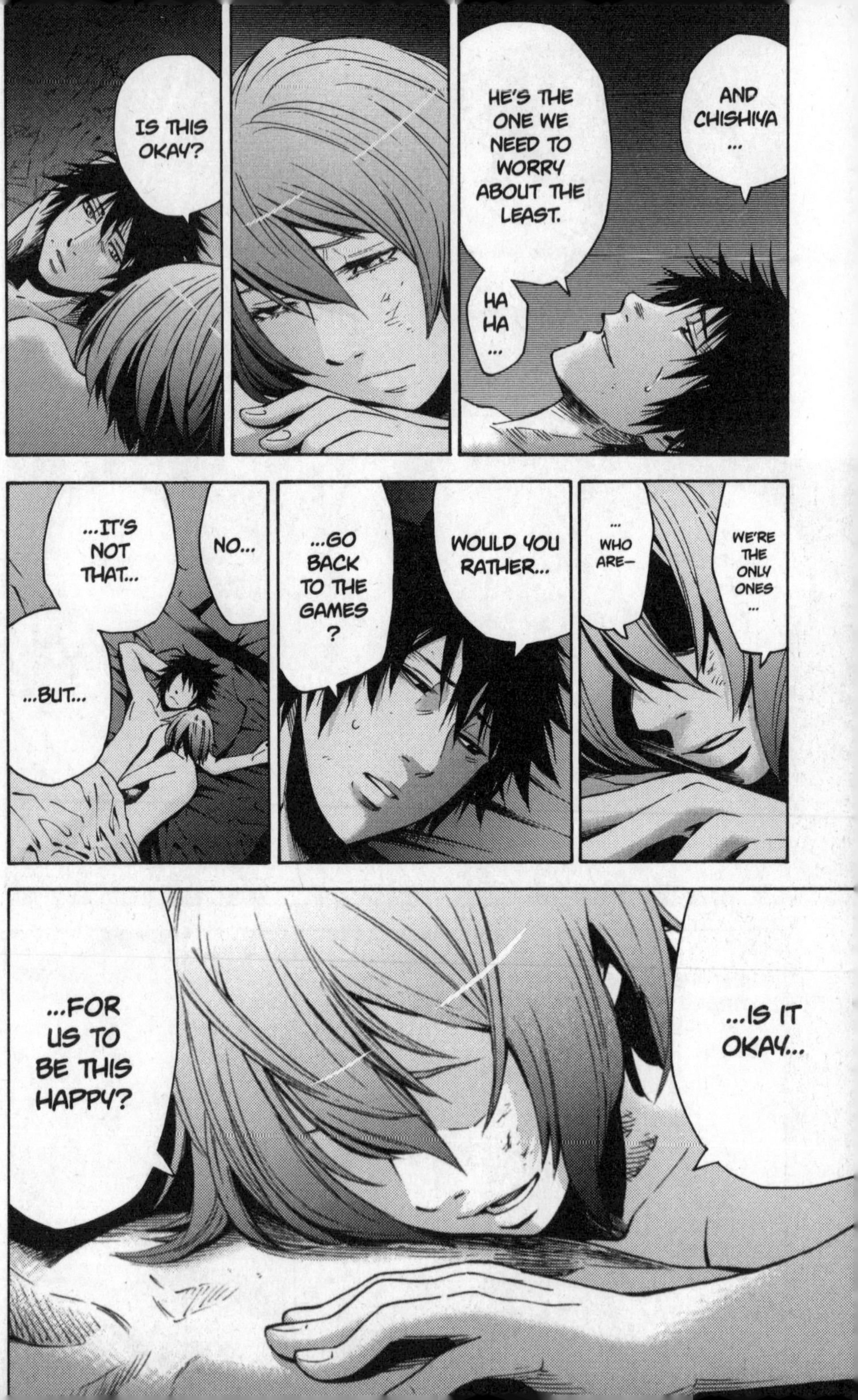
AND CHISHIYA ...
HE'S THE ONE WE NEED TO WORRY ABOUT THE LEAST.
HA HA ...
IS THIS OKAY?
WE'RE THE ONLY ONES ...
... WHO ARE–
WOULD YOU RATHER...
...GO BACK TO THE GAMES?
NO...
...IT'S NOT THAT...
...BUT...
...IS IT OKAY...
...FOR US TO BE THIS HAPPY?

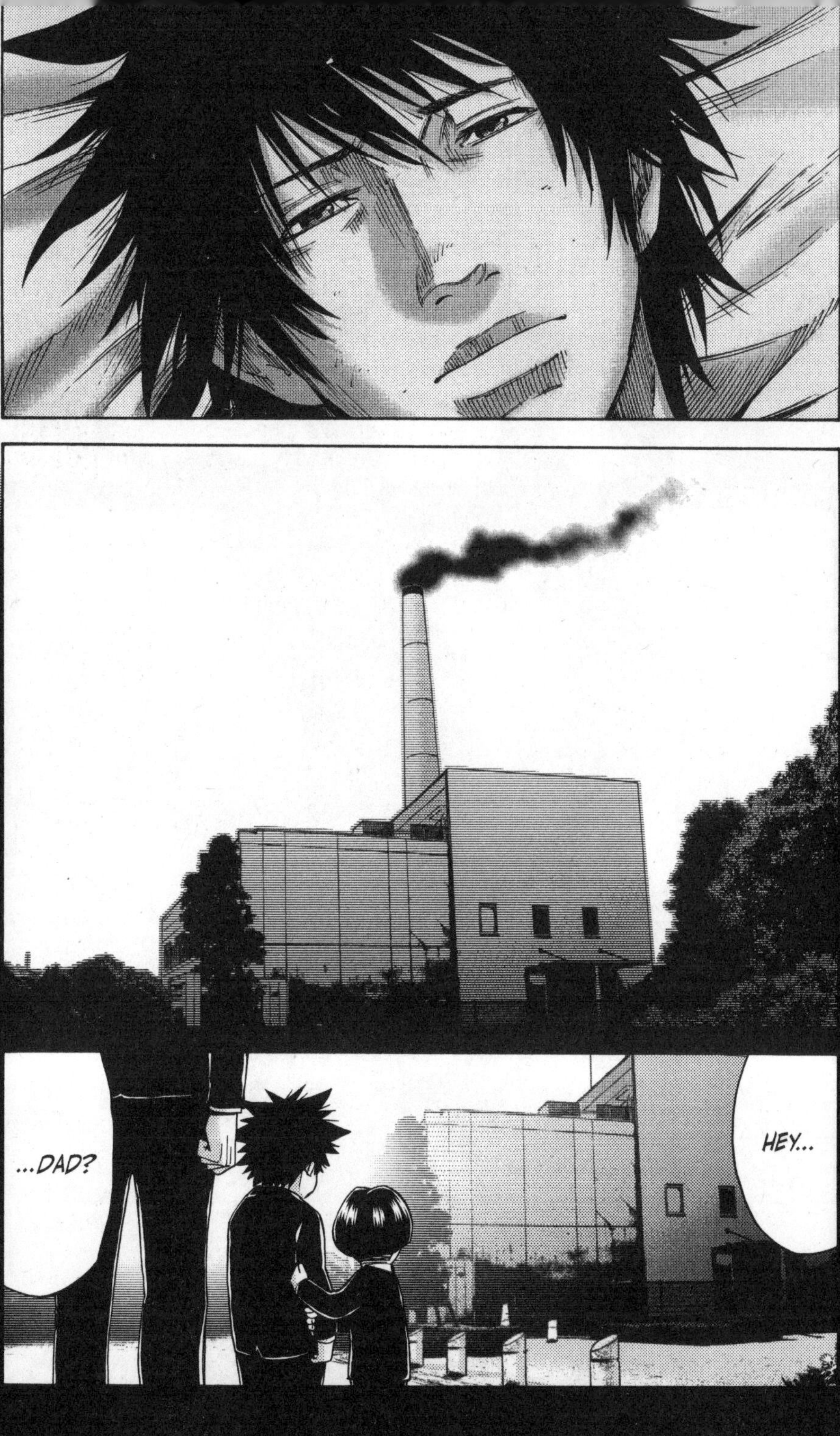
HEY...
...DAD?

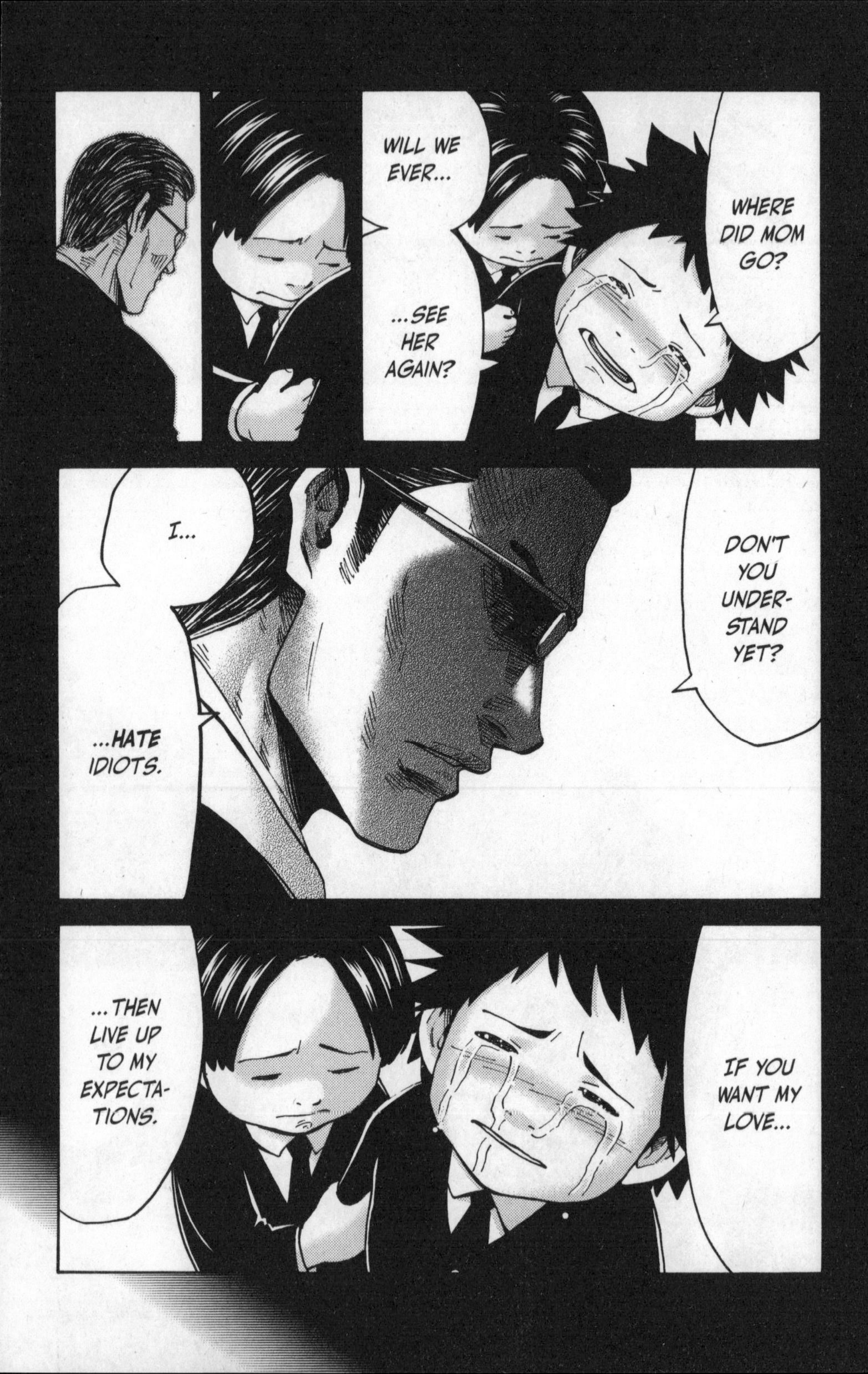
WHERE DID MOM GO?
WILL WE EVER...
...SEE HER AGAIN?
DON'T YOU UNDER-STAND YET?
I...
...HATE IDIOTS.
IF YOU WANT MY LOVE...
...THEN LIVE UP TO MY EXPECTA-TIONS.

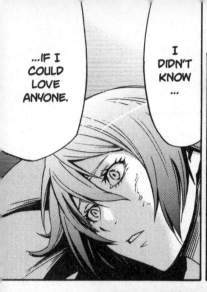

...
I...
...WAS SCARED.
I DIDN'T KNOW ...
...IF I COULD LOVE ANYONE.
I'VE NEVER BEEN LOVED...
...THE WAY EVERY-ONE ELSE HAS.
SHF

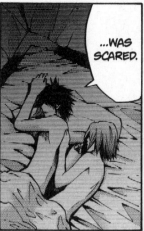

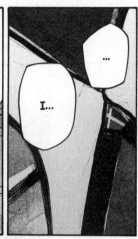

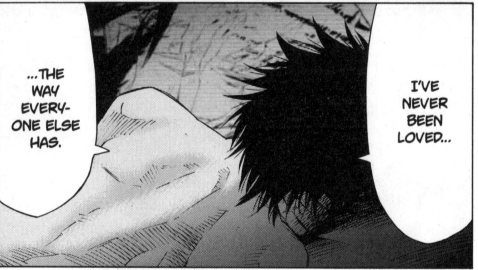

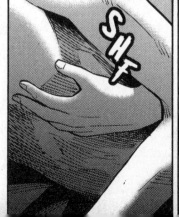

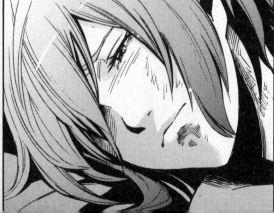

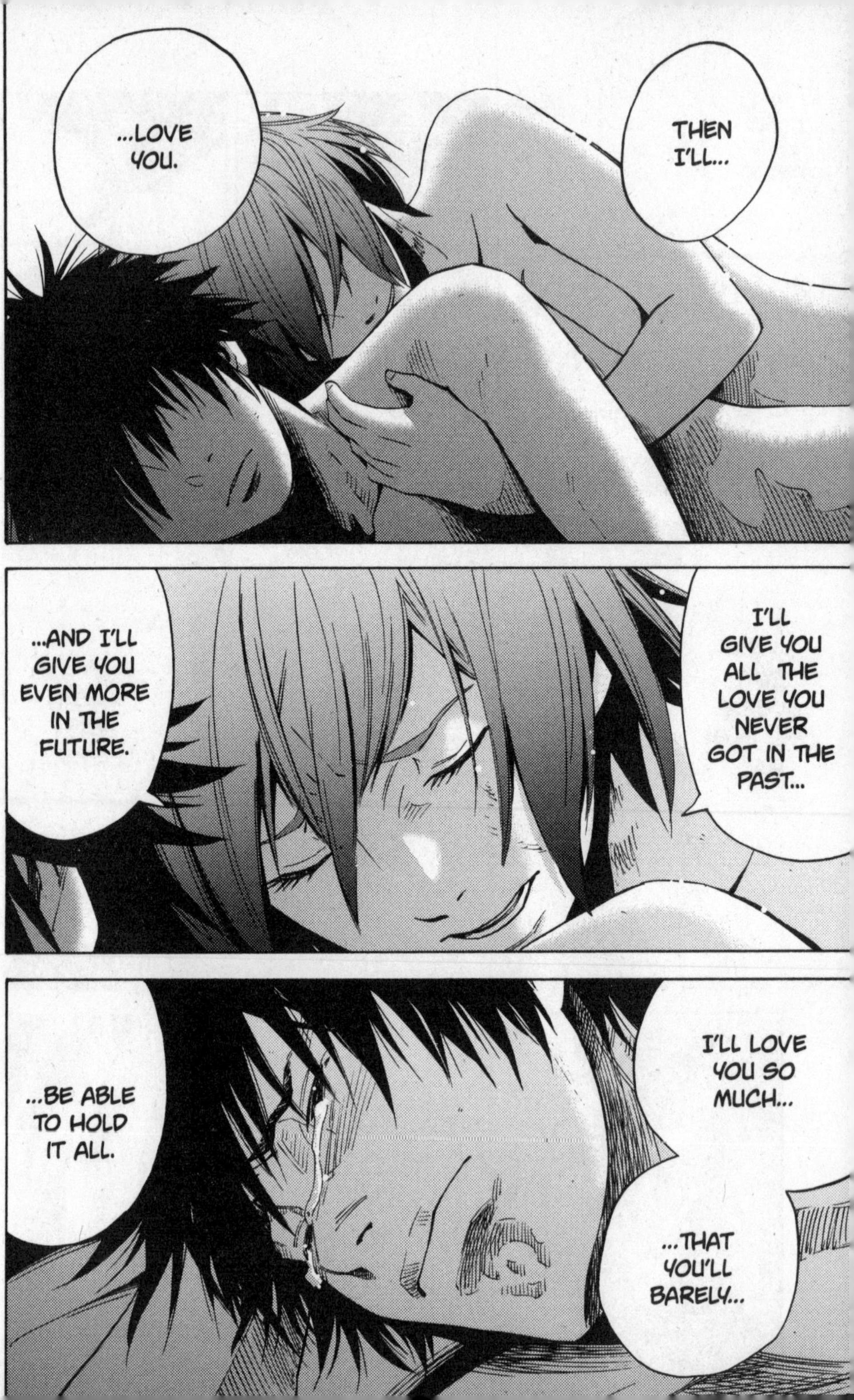
THEN I'LL...
...LOVE YOU.
I'LL GIVE YOU ALL THE LOVE YOU NEVER GOT IN THE PAST...
...AND I'LL GIVE YOU EVEN MORE IN THE FUTURE.
I'LL LOVE YOU SO MUCH...
...THAT YOU'LL BARELY...
...BE ABLE TO HOLD IT ALL.

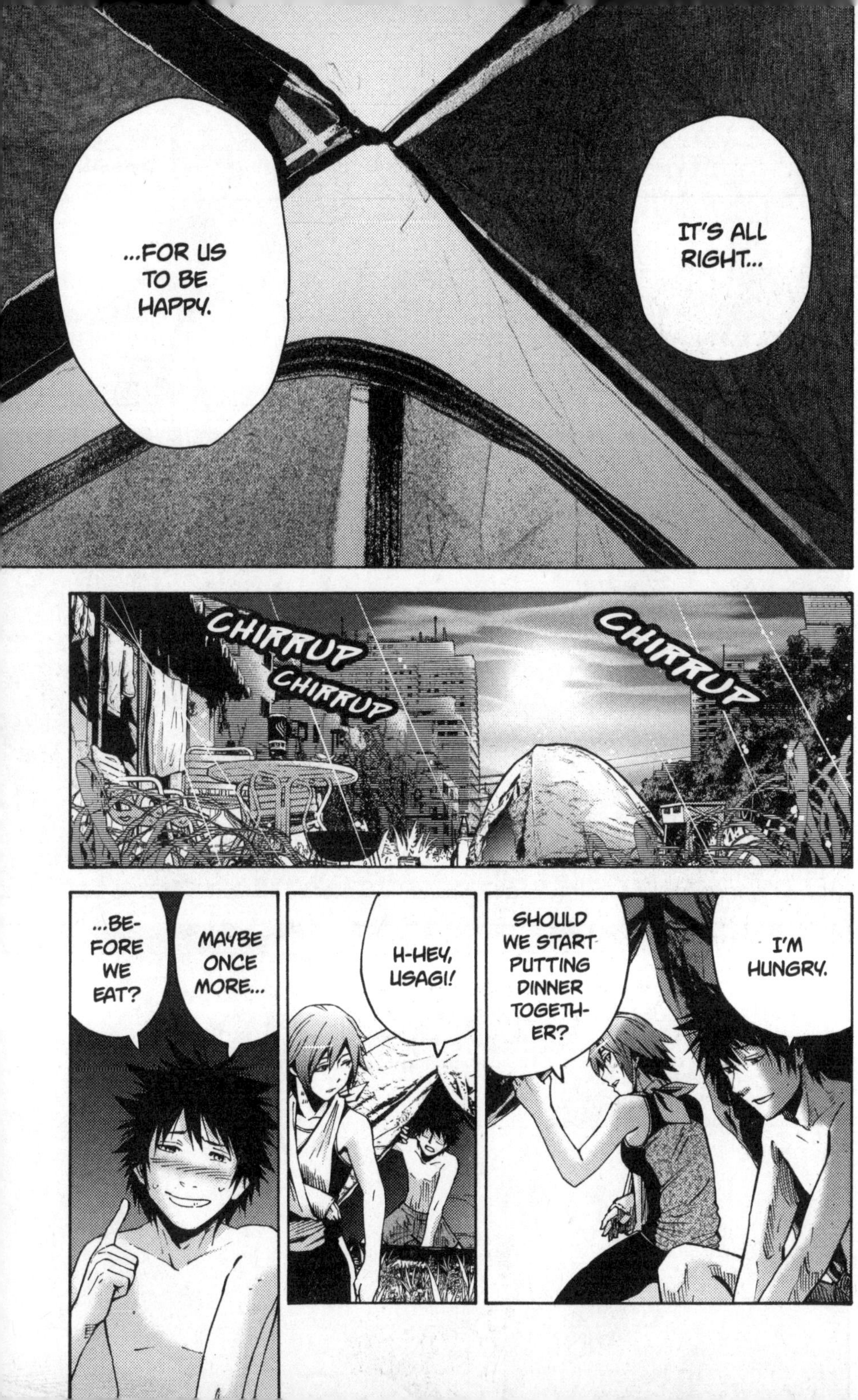
IT'S ALL RIGHT...
...FOR US TO BE HAPPY.
CHIRRUP
CHIRRUP
CHIRRUP
I'M HUNGRY.
SHOULD WE START PUTTING DINNER TOGETH-ER?
H-HEY, USAGI!
MAYBE ONCE MORE...
...BE-FORE WE EAT?

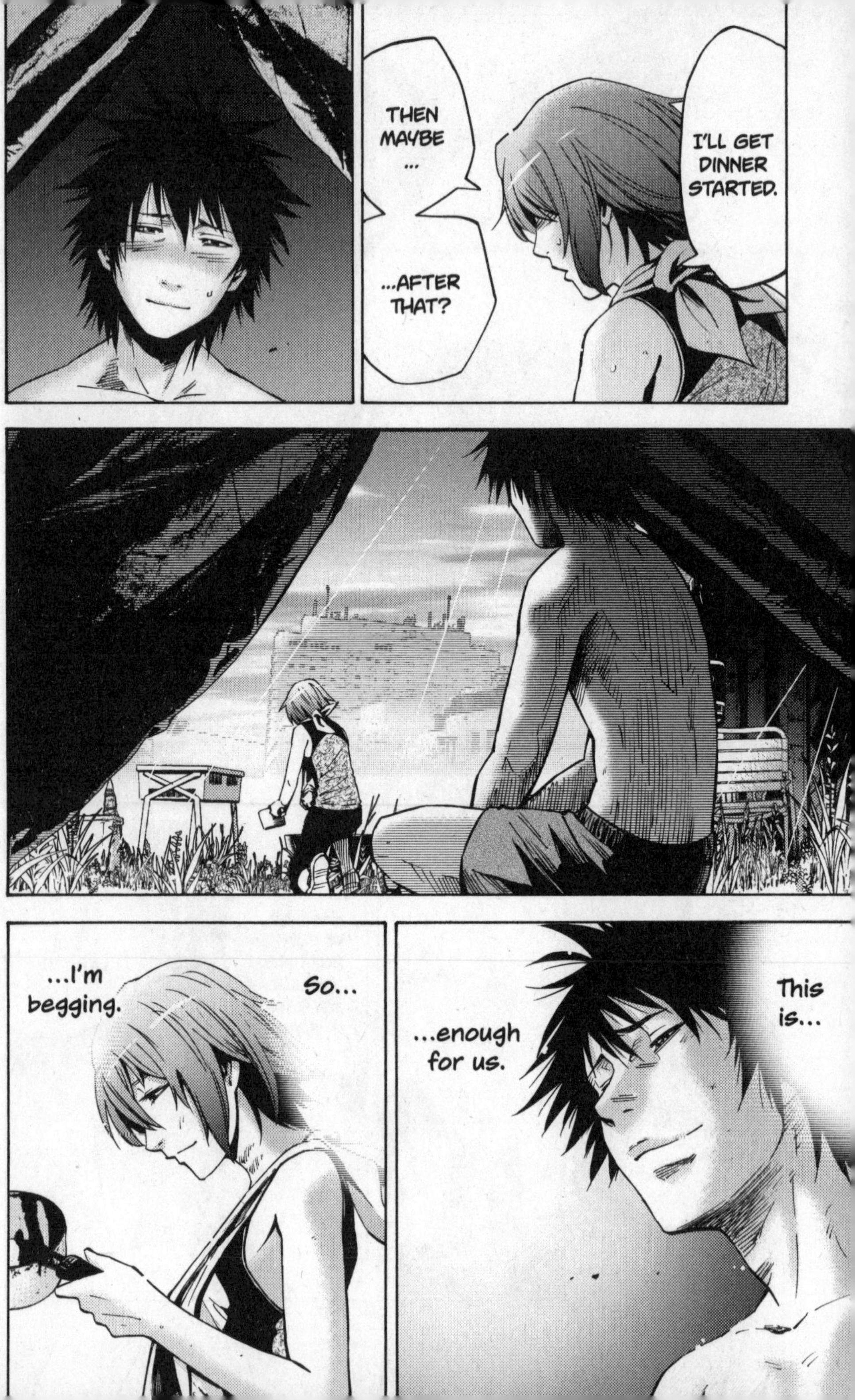
I'LL GET DINNER STARTED.
THEN MAYBE ...
...AFTER THAT?
This is...
...enough for us.
So...
...I'm begging.

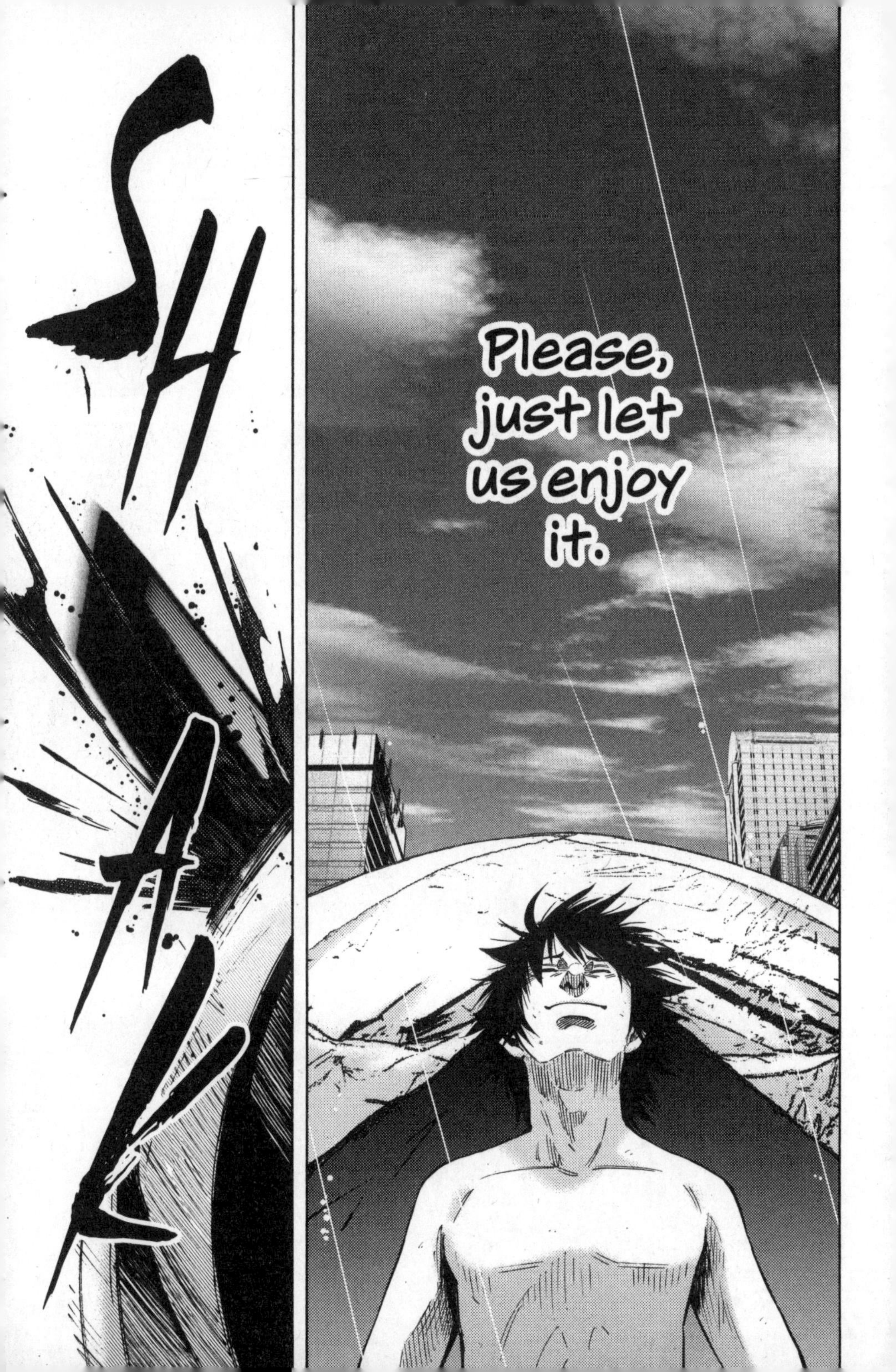
Please, just let us enjoy it.

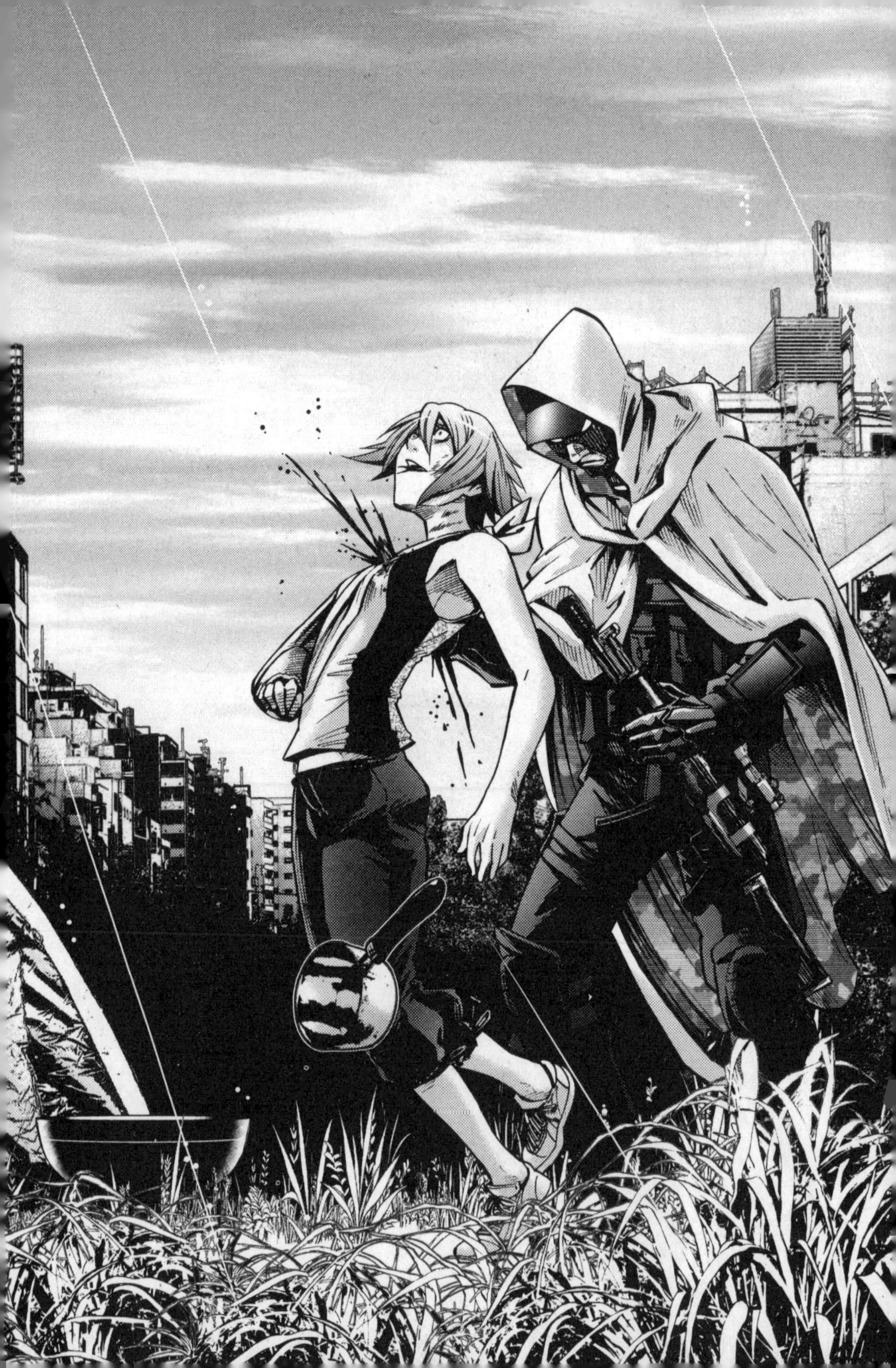

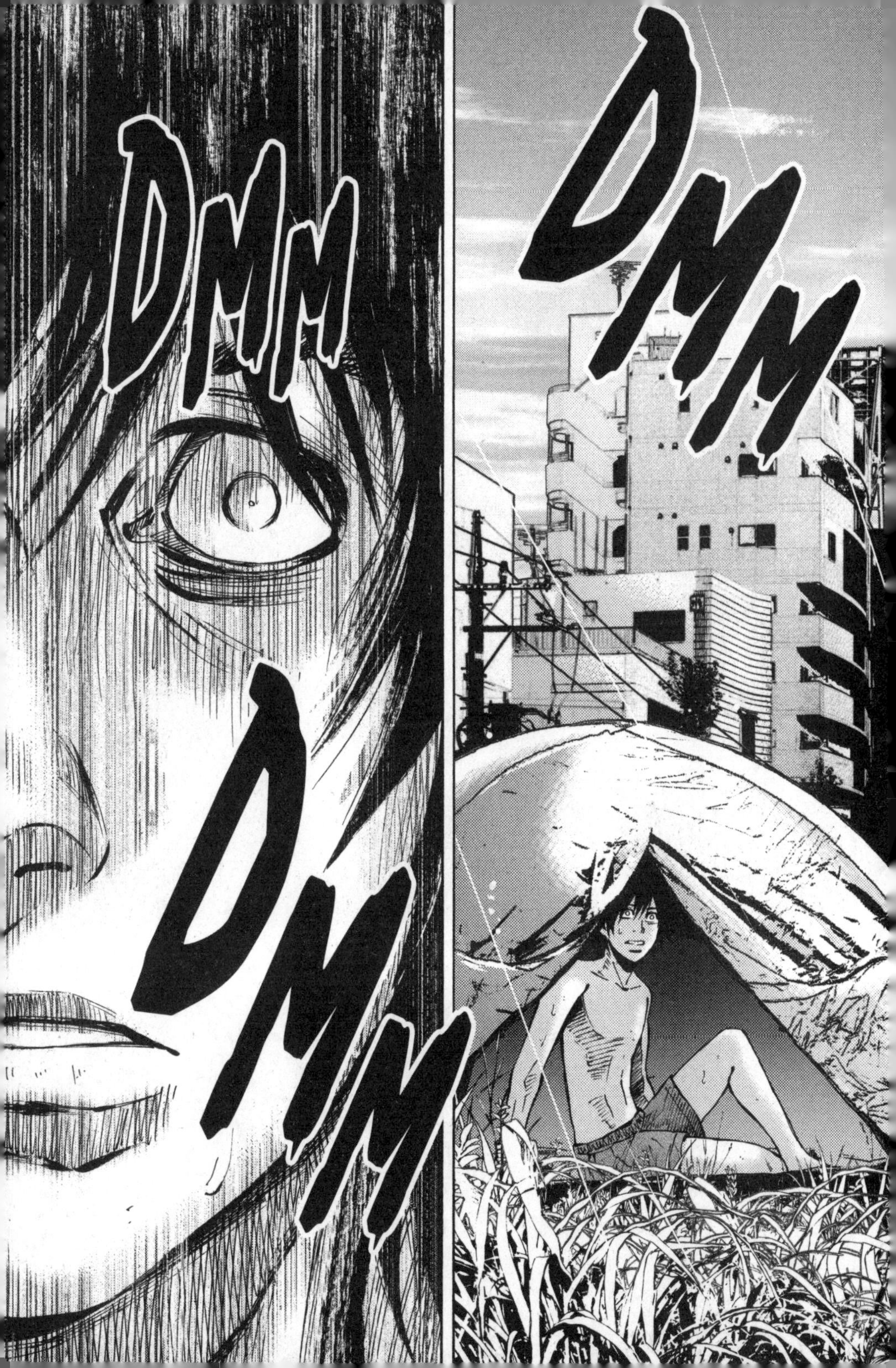
DMM
DMM
DMM

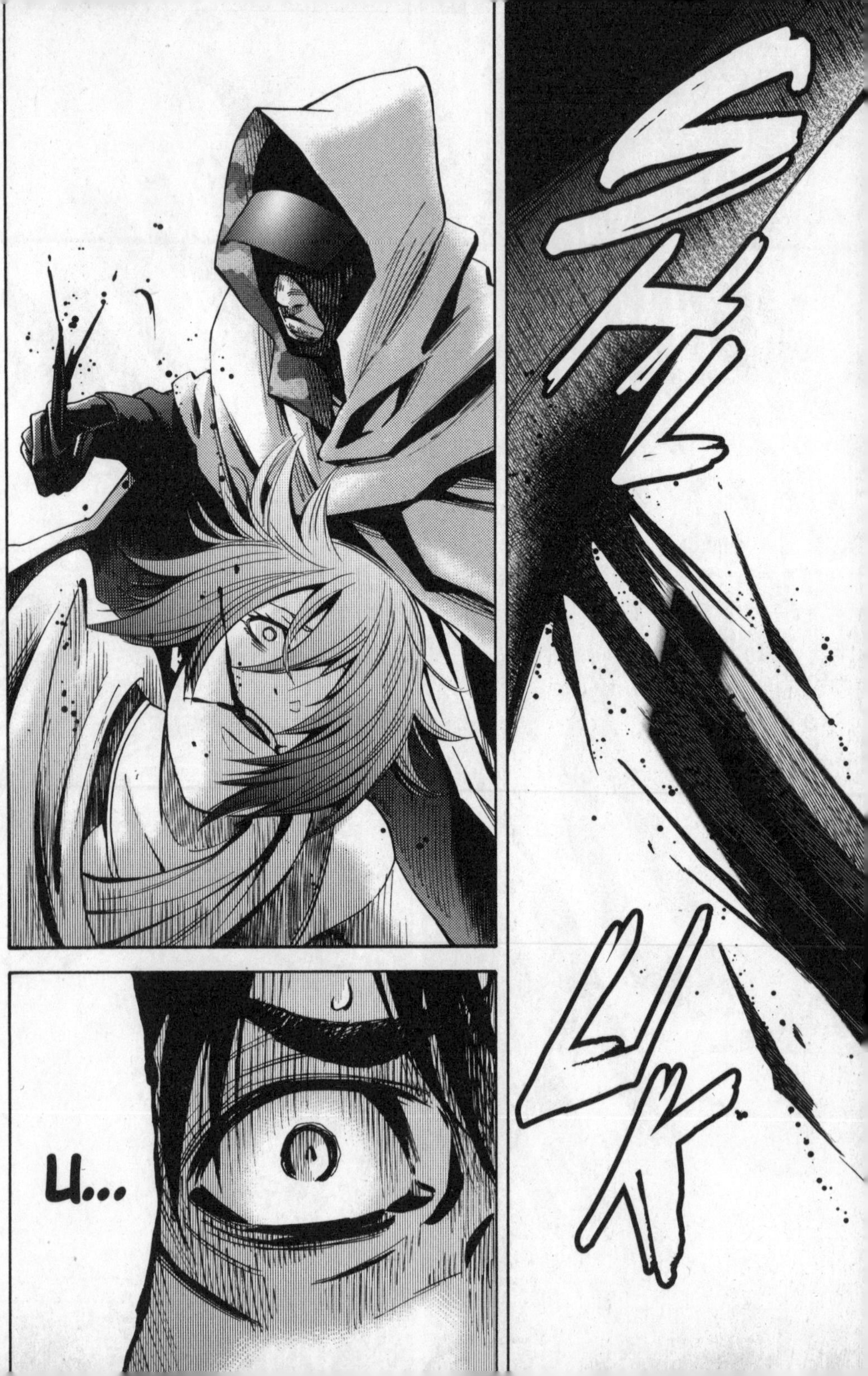
U...

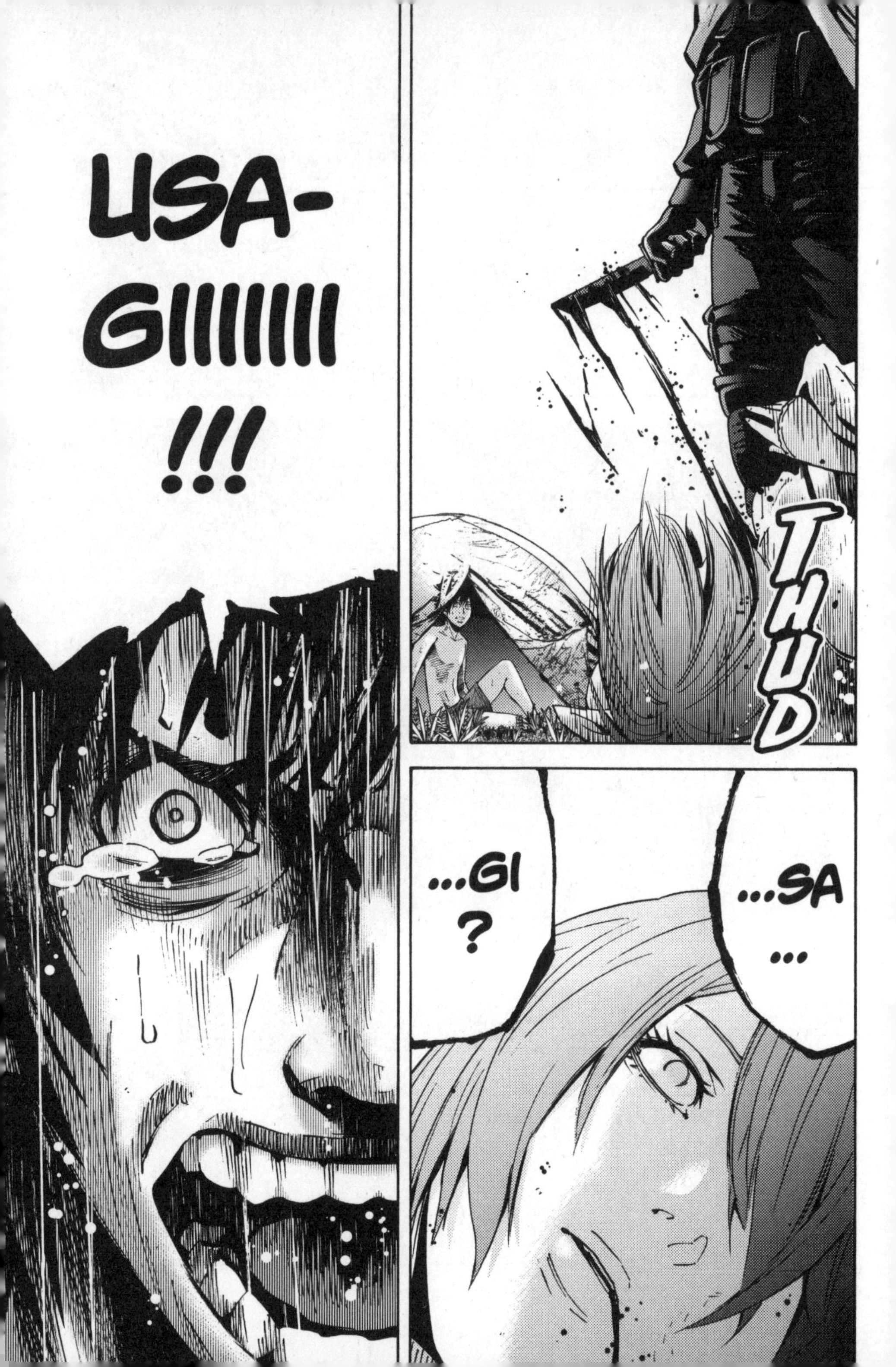
THUD
...SA...
...GI?
USA-GIIIIIII!!!

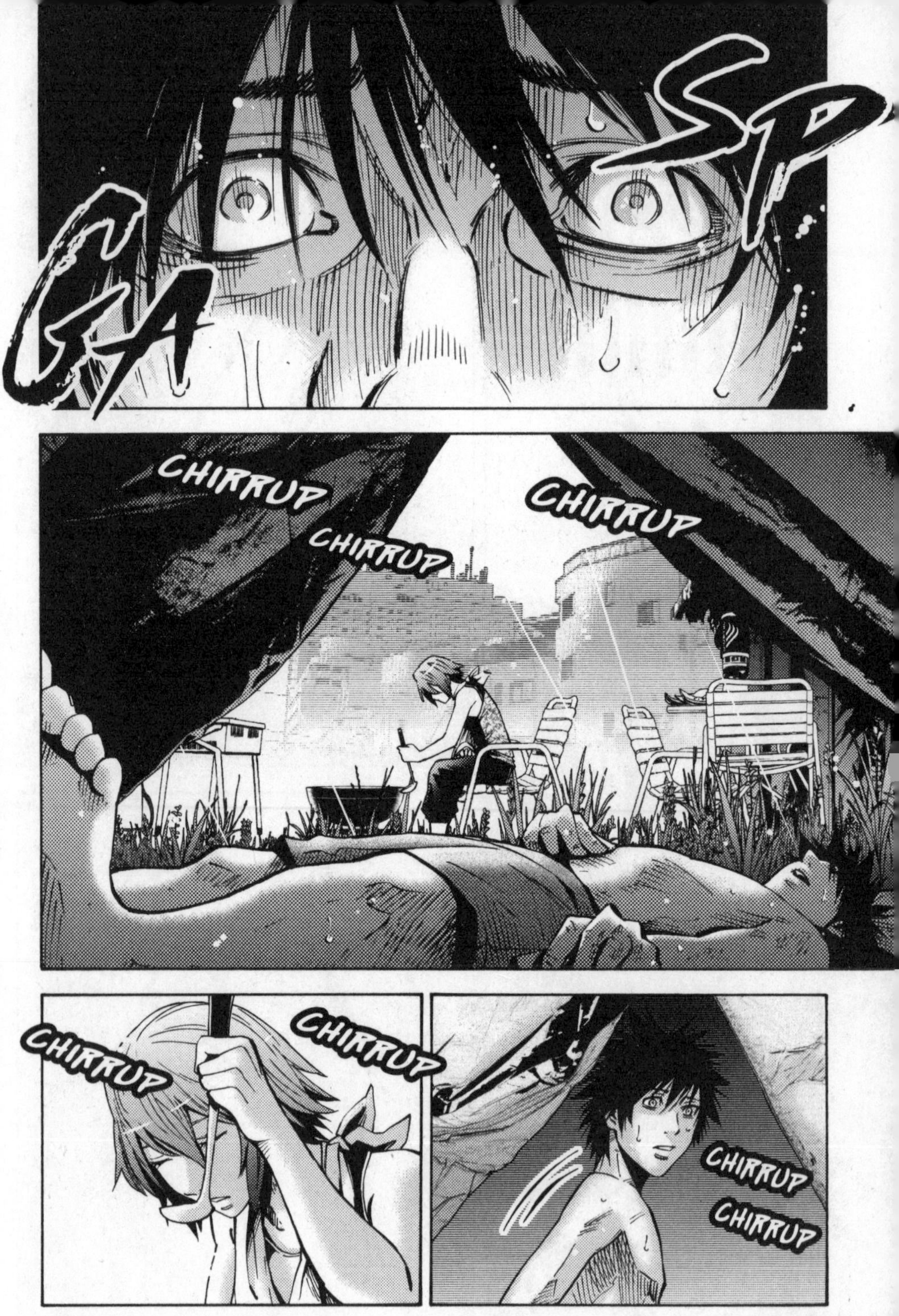
GASP
CHIRRUP
CHIRRUP
CHIRRUP
CHIRRUP
CHIRRUP
CHIRRUP
CHIRRUP

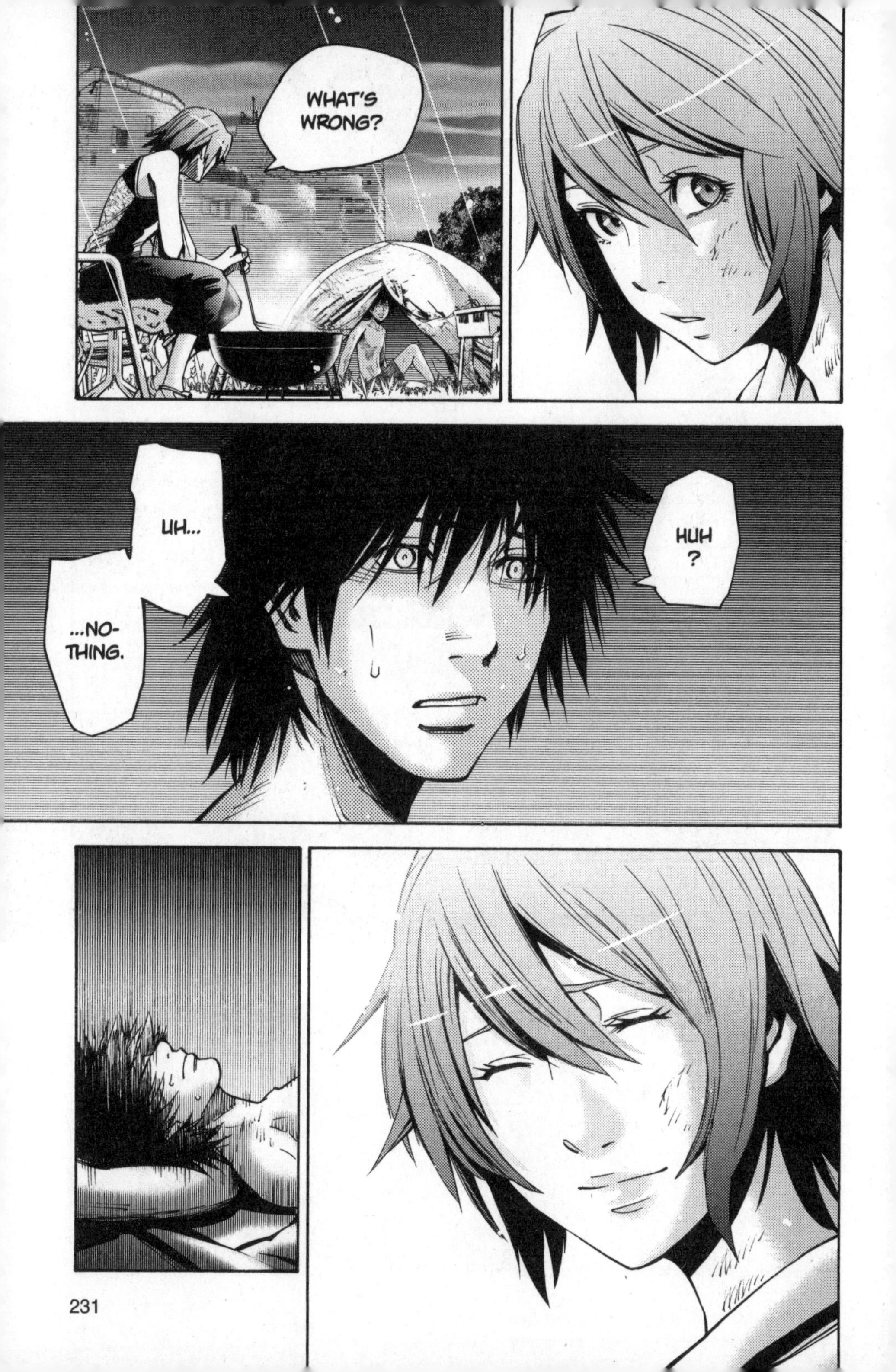
WHAT'S WRONG?
HUH ?
UH...
...NO-THING.

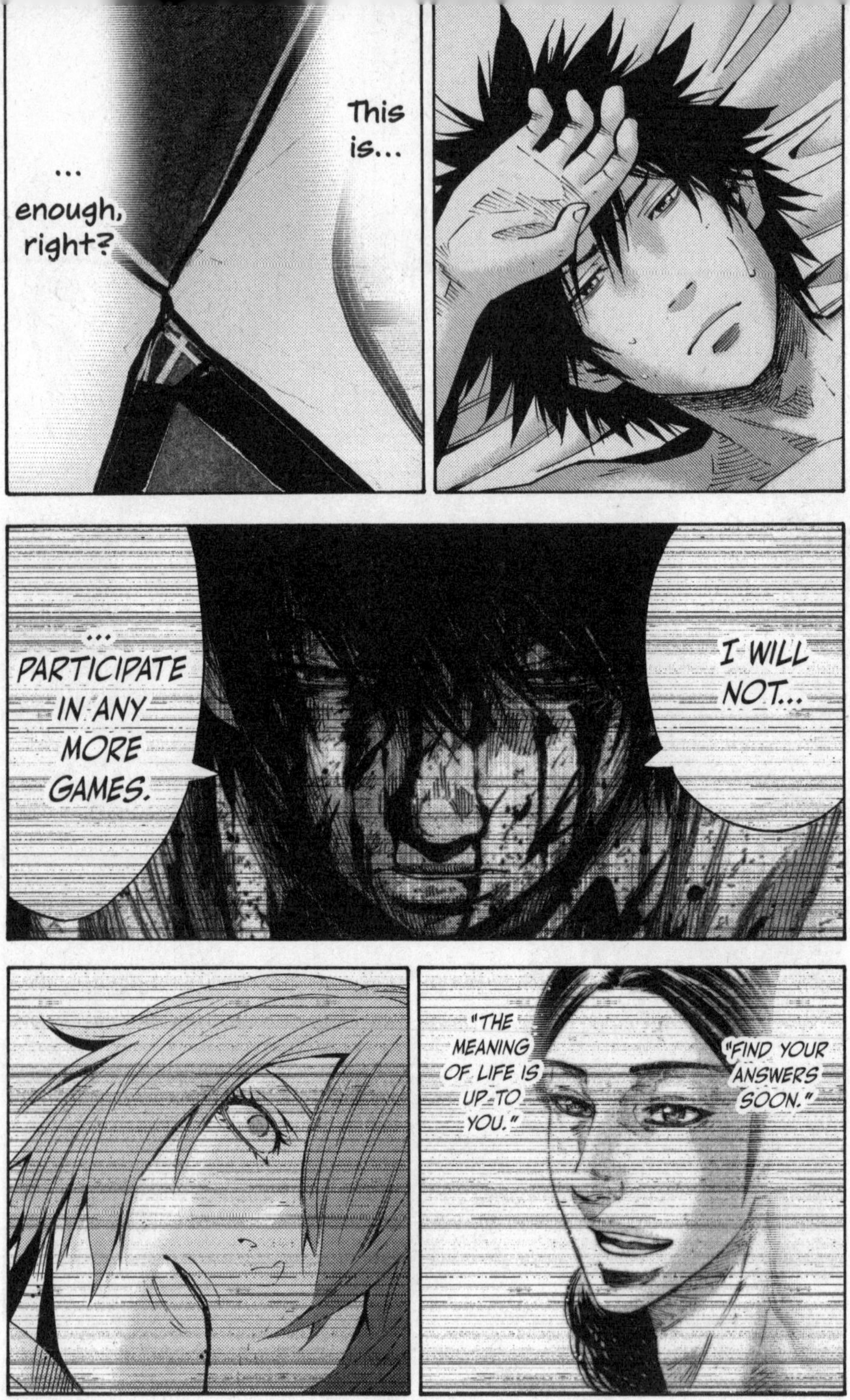
This is...
... enough, right?
I WILL NOT...
... PARTICIPATE IN ANY MORE GAMES.
"FIND YOUR ANSWERS SOON."
"THE MEANING OF LIFE IS UP TO YOU."

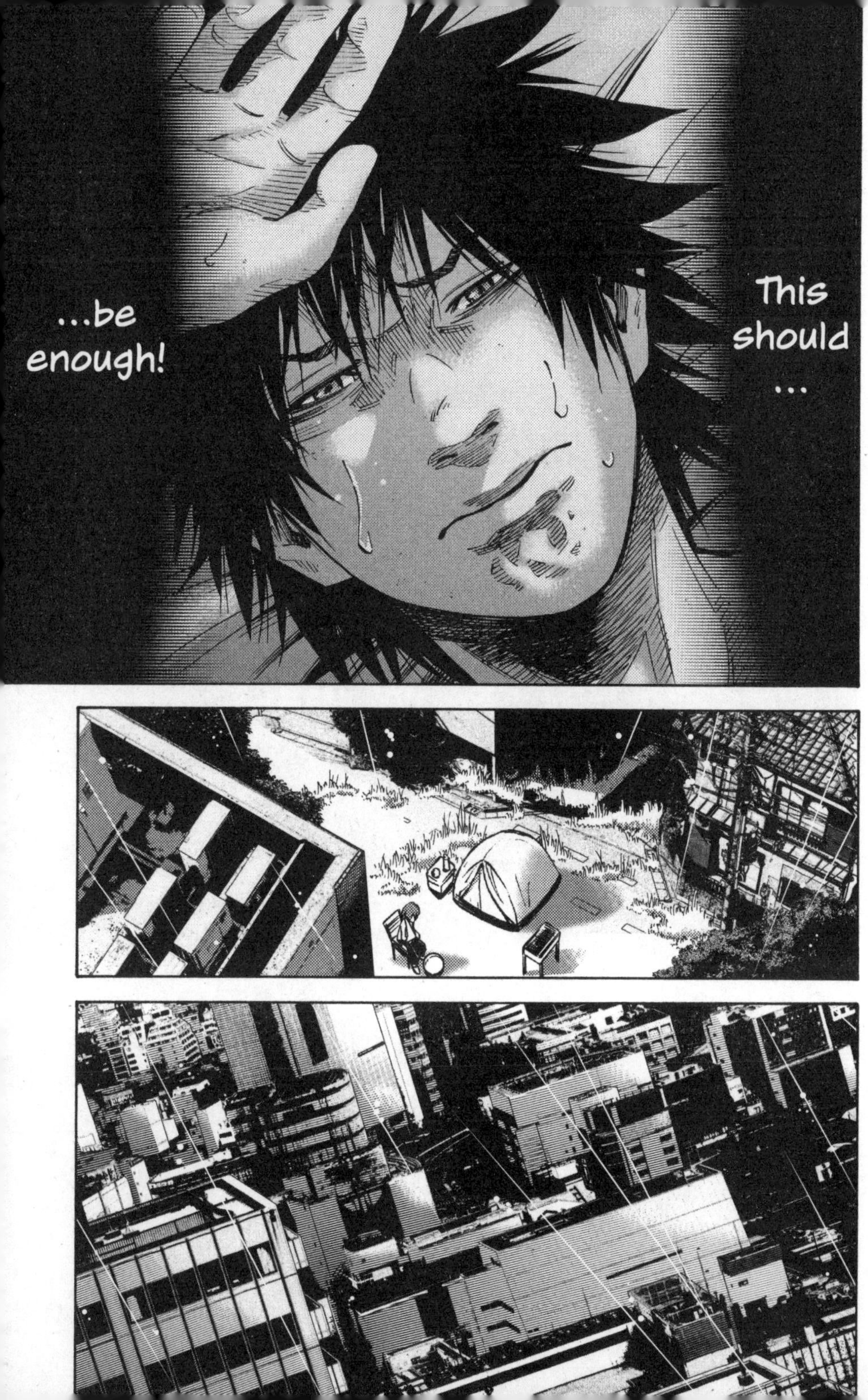
This should ...
...be enough!

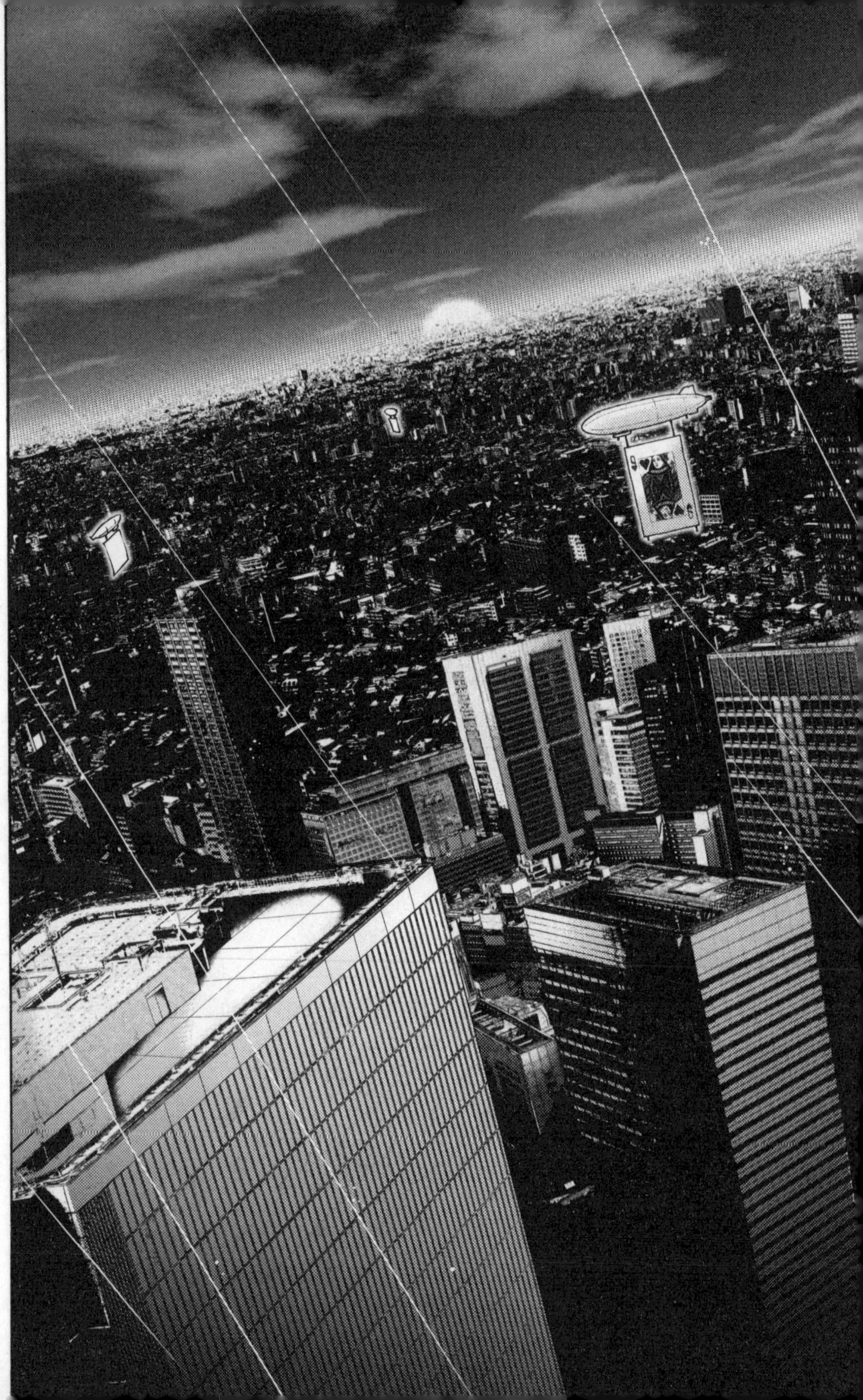

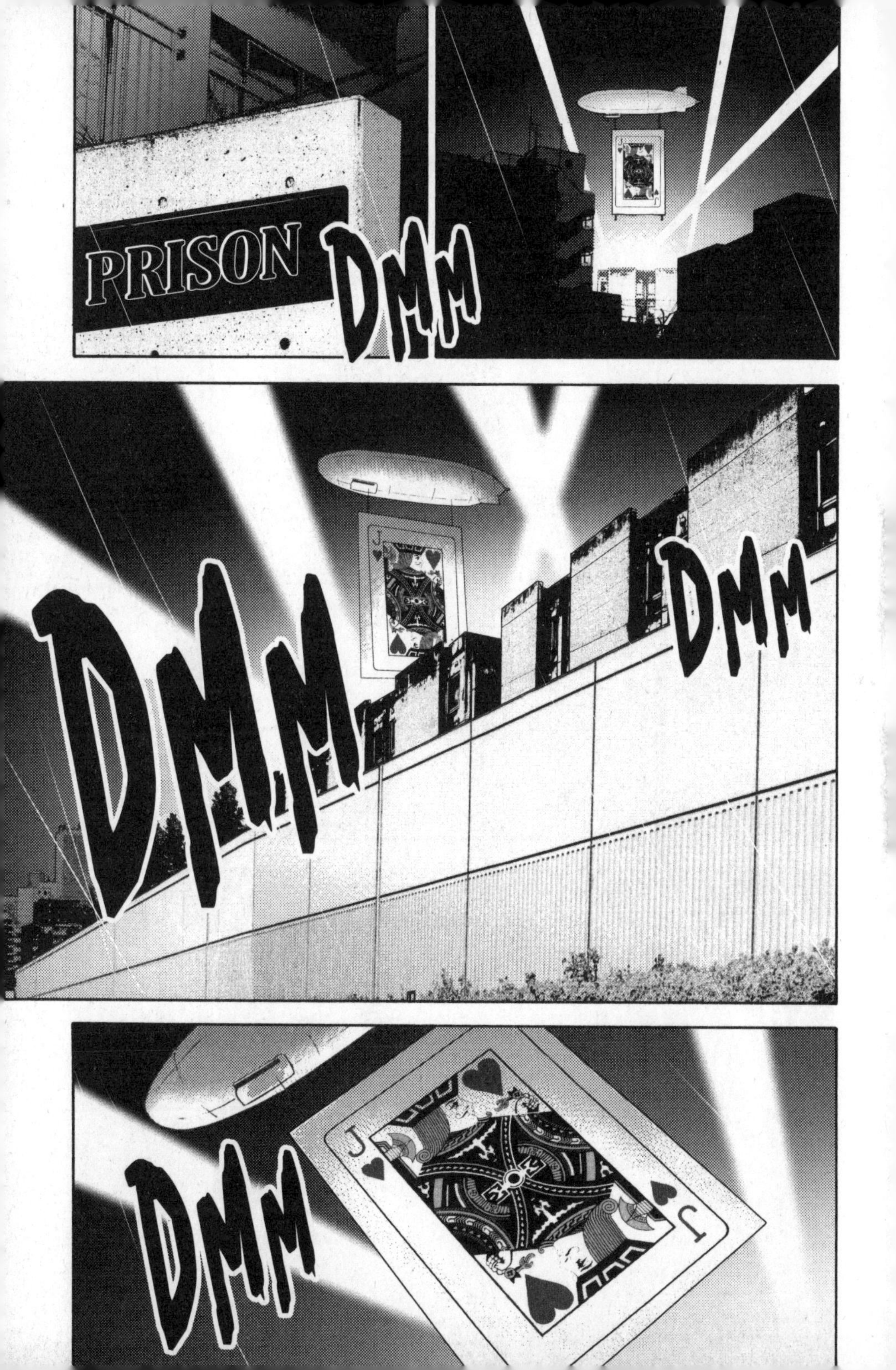
DMM
PRISON
DMM
D.M.M.
DMM

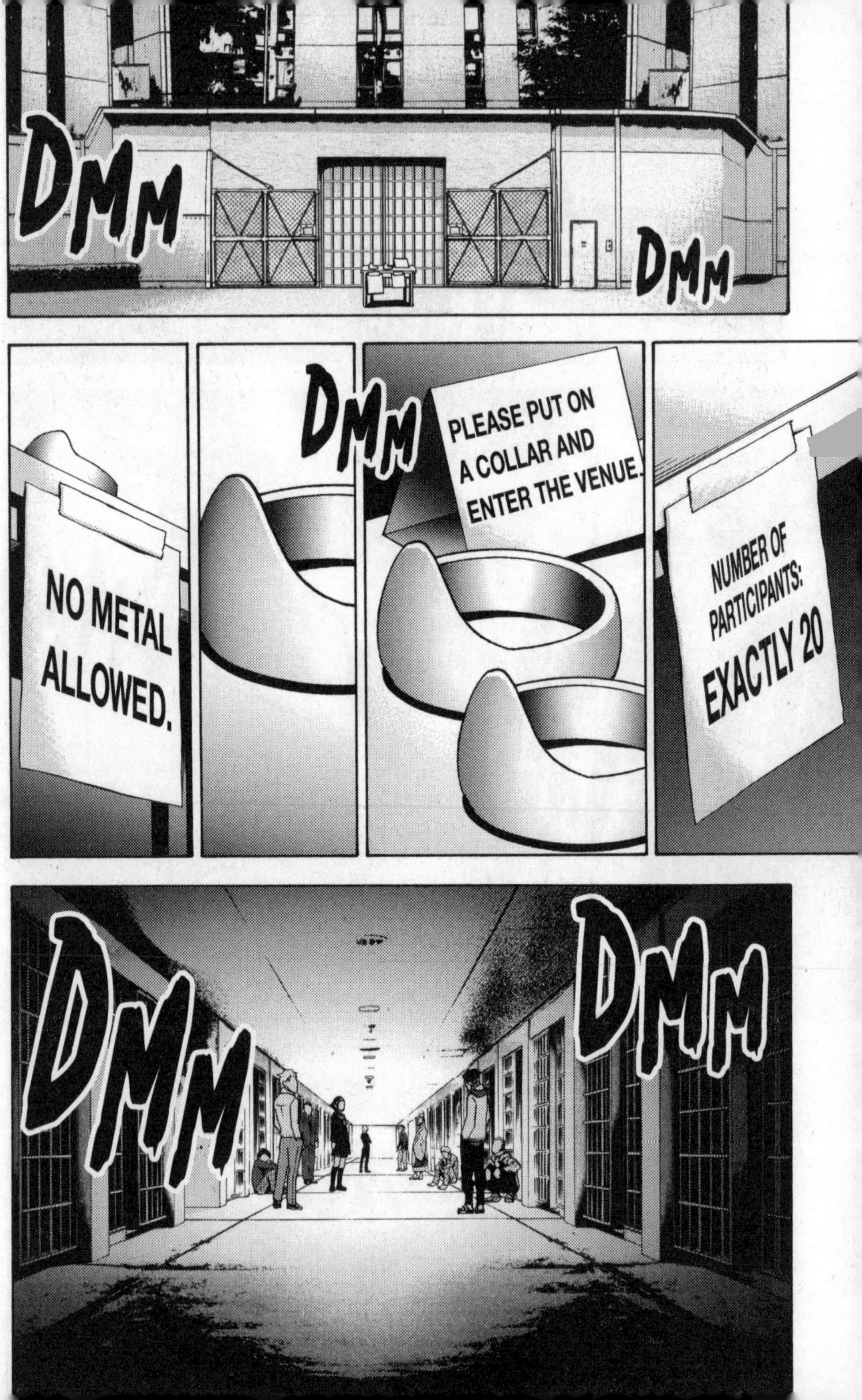
DMM
DMM
NUMBER OF PARTICIPANTS: EXACTLY 20
PLEASE PUT ON A COLLAR AND ENTER THE VENUE.
DMM
NO METAL ALLOWED.
DMM
DMM

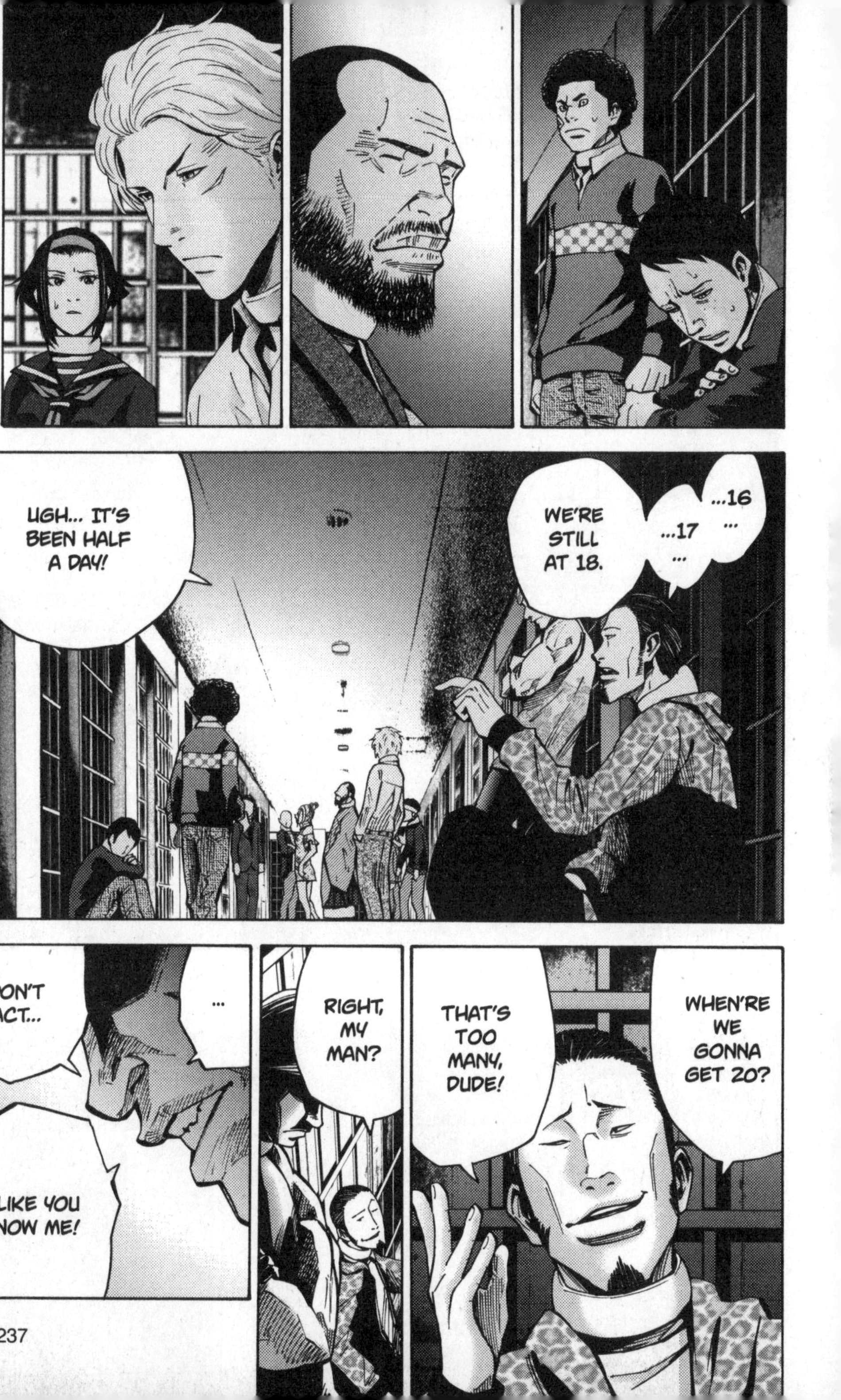
...16 ...
...17 ...
WE'RE STILL AT 18.
UGH... IT'S BEEN HALF A DAY!
WHEN'RE WE GONNA GET 20?
THAT'S TOO MANY, DUDE!
RIGHT, MY MAN?
...
DON'T ACT...
...LIKE YOU KNOW ME!

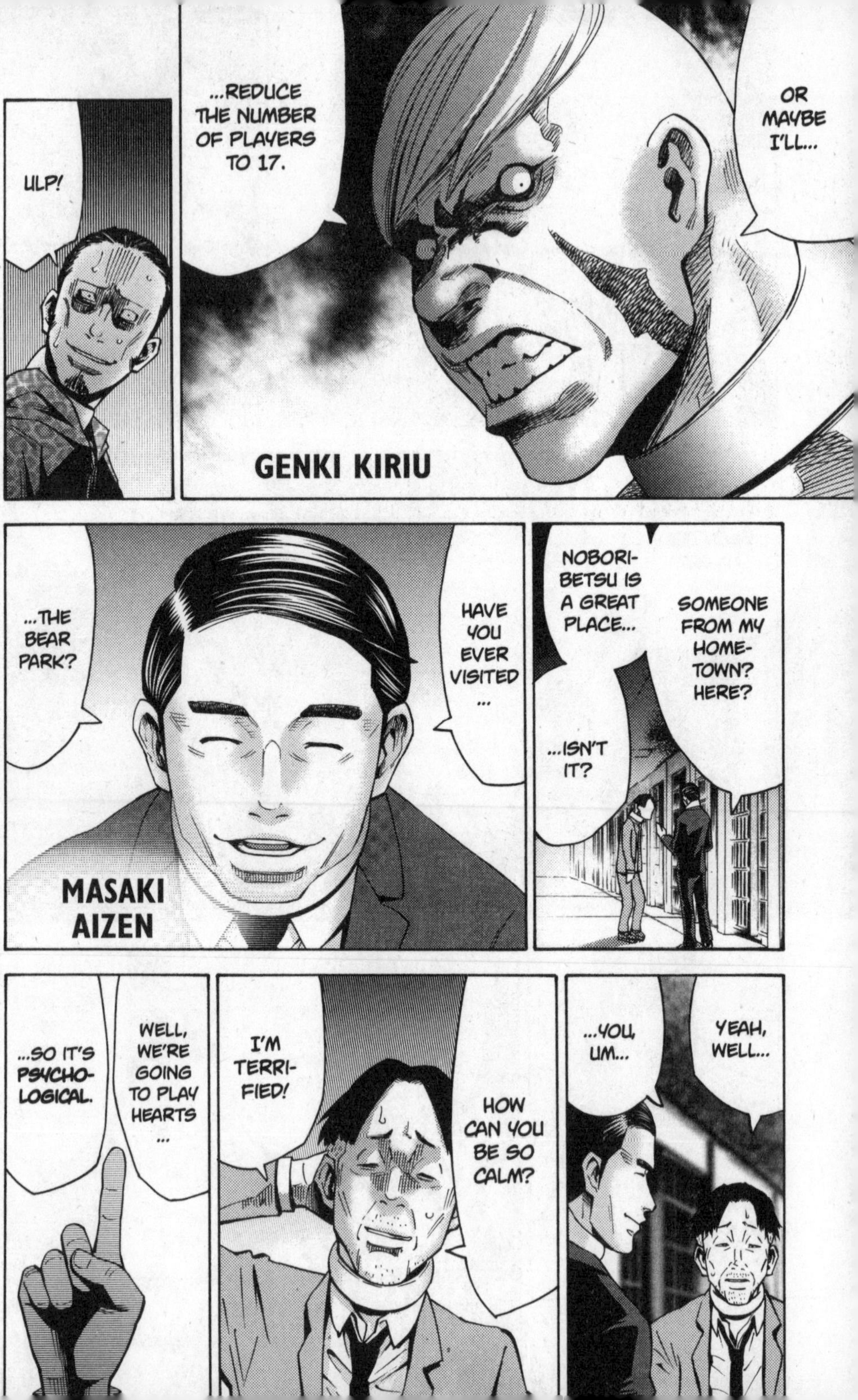
OR MAYBE I'LL...
...REDUCE THE NUMBER OF PLAYERS TO 17.
GENKI KIRIU
ULP!
SOMEONE FROM MY HOME-TOWN? HERE?
NOBORI-BETSU IS A GREAT PLACE...
...ISN'T IT?
HAVE YOU EVER VISITED...
...THE BEAR PARK?
MASAKI AIZEN
YEAH, WELL...
...YOU, UM...
HOW CAN YOU BE SO CALM?
I'M TERRI-FIED!
WELL, WE'RE GOING TO PLAY HEARTS...
...SO IT'S PSYCHO-LOGICAL.

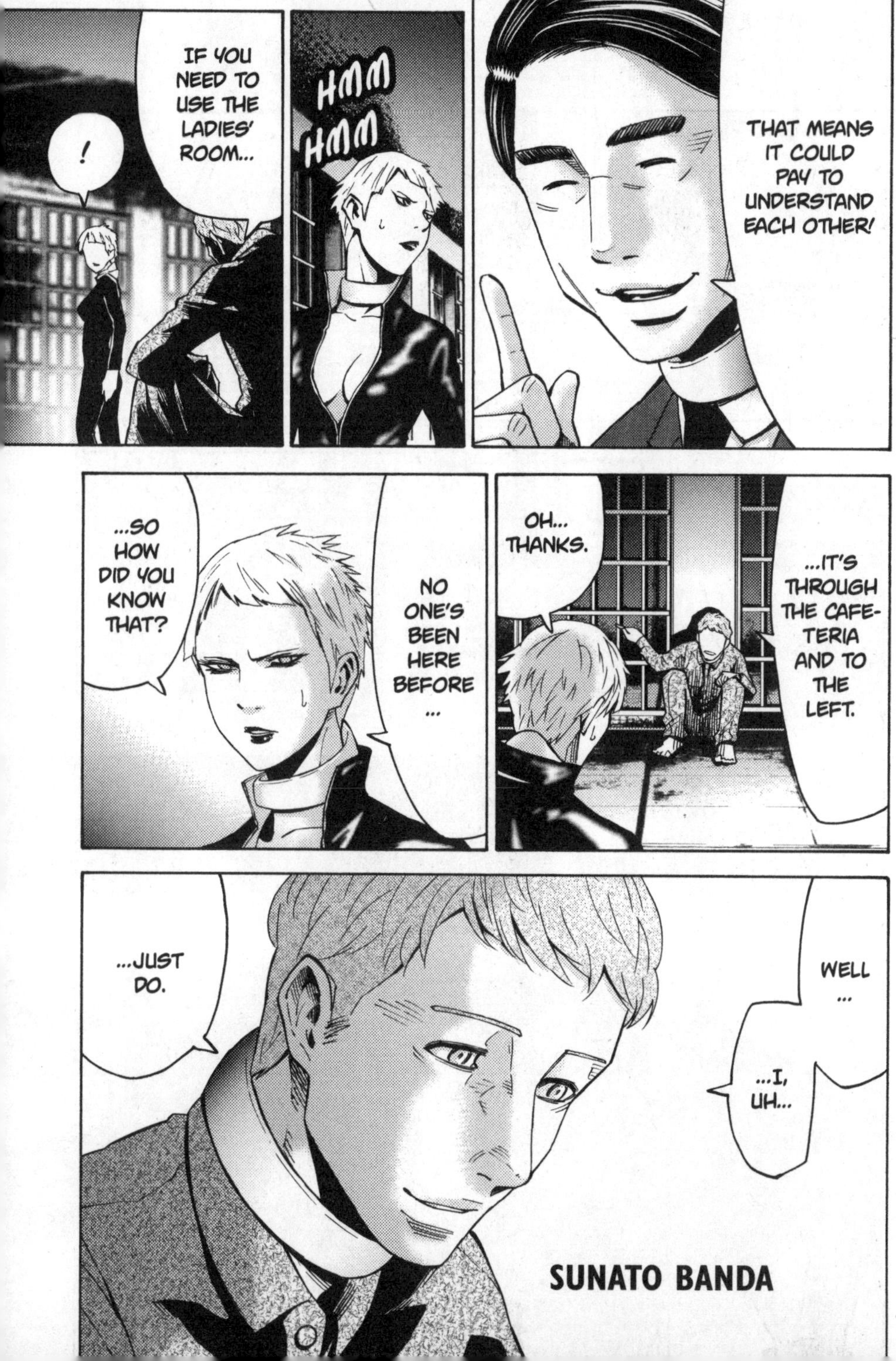
THAT MEANS IT COULD PAY TO UNDERSTAND EACH OTHER!
HMM
HMM
IF YOU NEED TO USE THE LADIES' ROOM...
!
...IT'S THROUGH THE CAFE-TERIA AND TO THE LEFT.
OH... THANKS.
NO ONE'S BEEN HERE BEFORE...
...SO HOW DID YOU KNOW THAT?
WELL...
...I, UH...
...JUST DO.
SUNATO BANDA

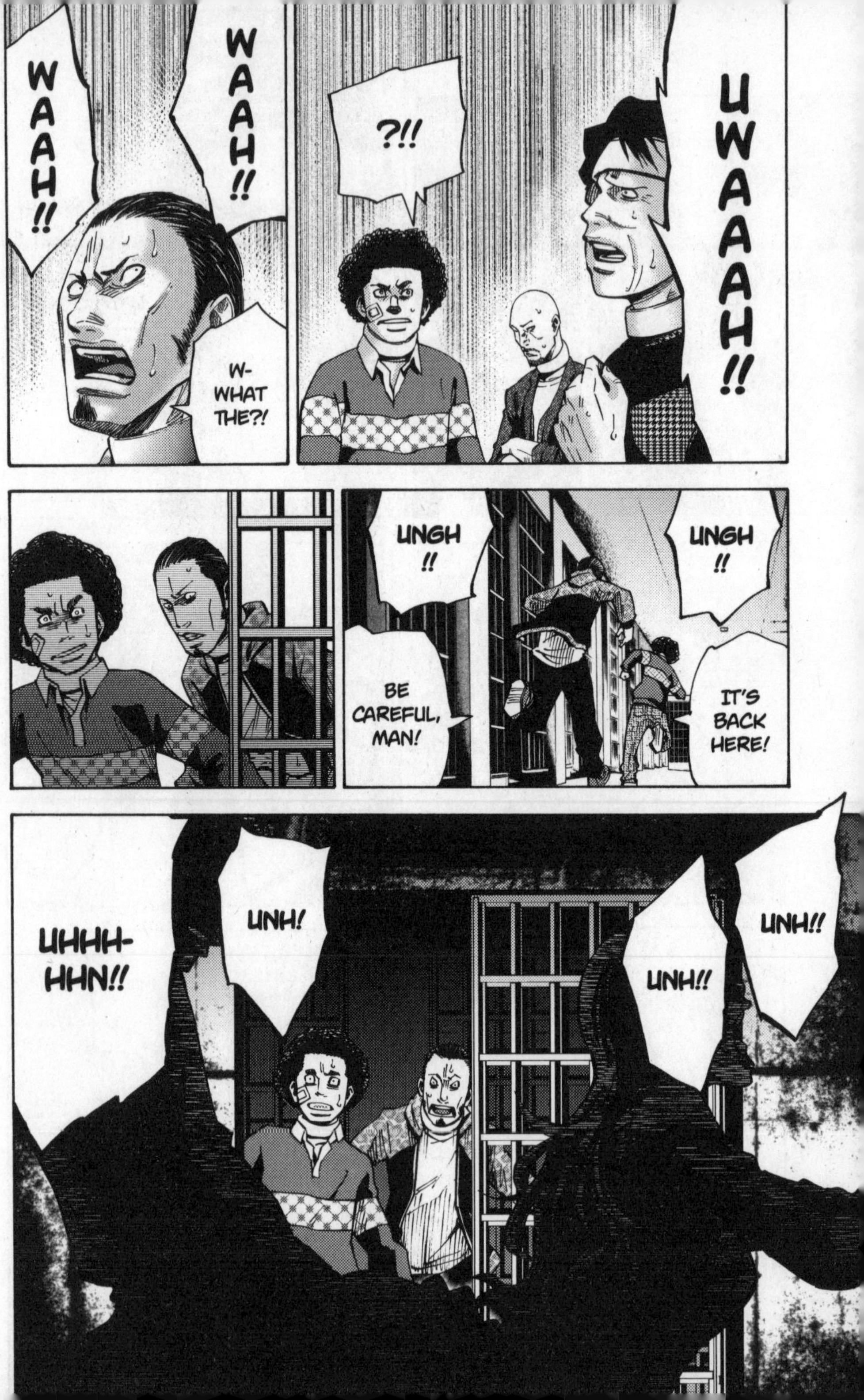
UWAAAAH!!
?!!
WAAH!!
WAAH!!
W-WHAT THE?!
UNGH !!
UNGH !!
IT'S BACK HERE!
BE CAREFUL, MAN!
UNH!!
UNH!!
UNH!
UHHH-HHN!!

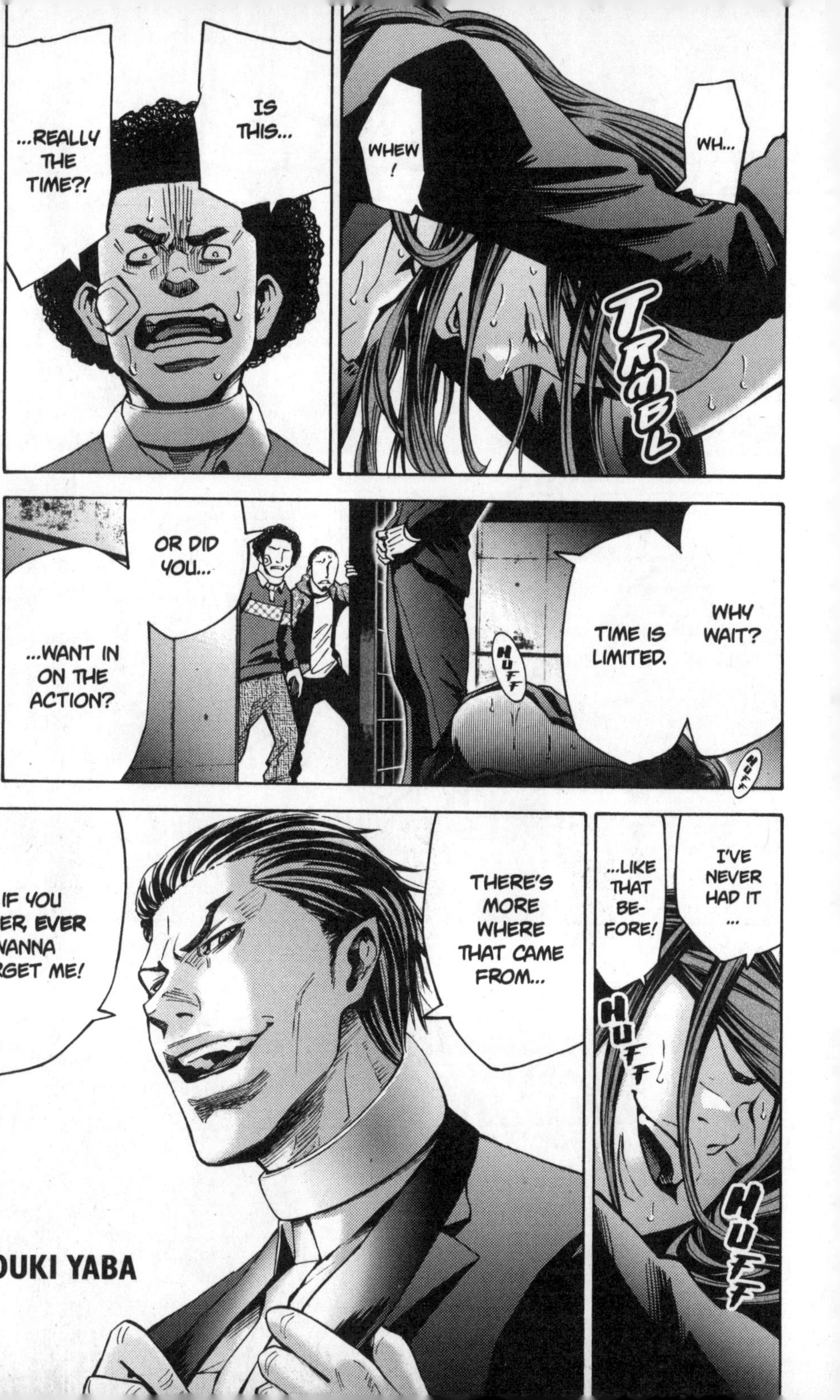
WH...
WHEW!
TRMBL
IS THIS...
...REALLY THE TIME?!
WHY WAIT?
TIME IS LIMITED.
HUFF
HUFF
OR DID YOU...
...WANT IN ON THE ACTION?
I'VE NEVER HAD IT ...
...LIKE THAT BE-FORE!
HUFF
HUFF
THERE'S MORE WHERE THAT CAME FROM...
...IF YOU NEVER, EVER WANNA FORGET ME!
OUKI YABA

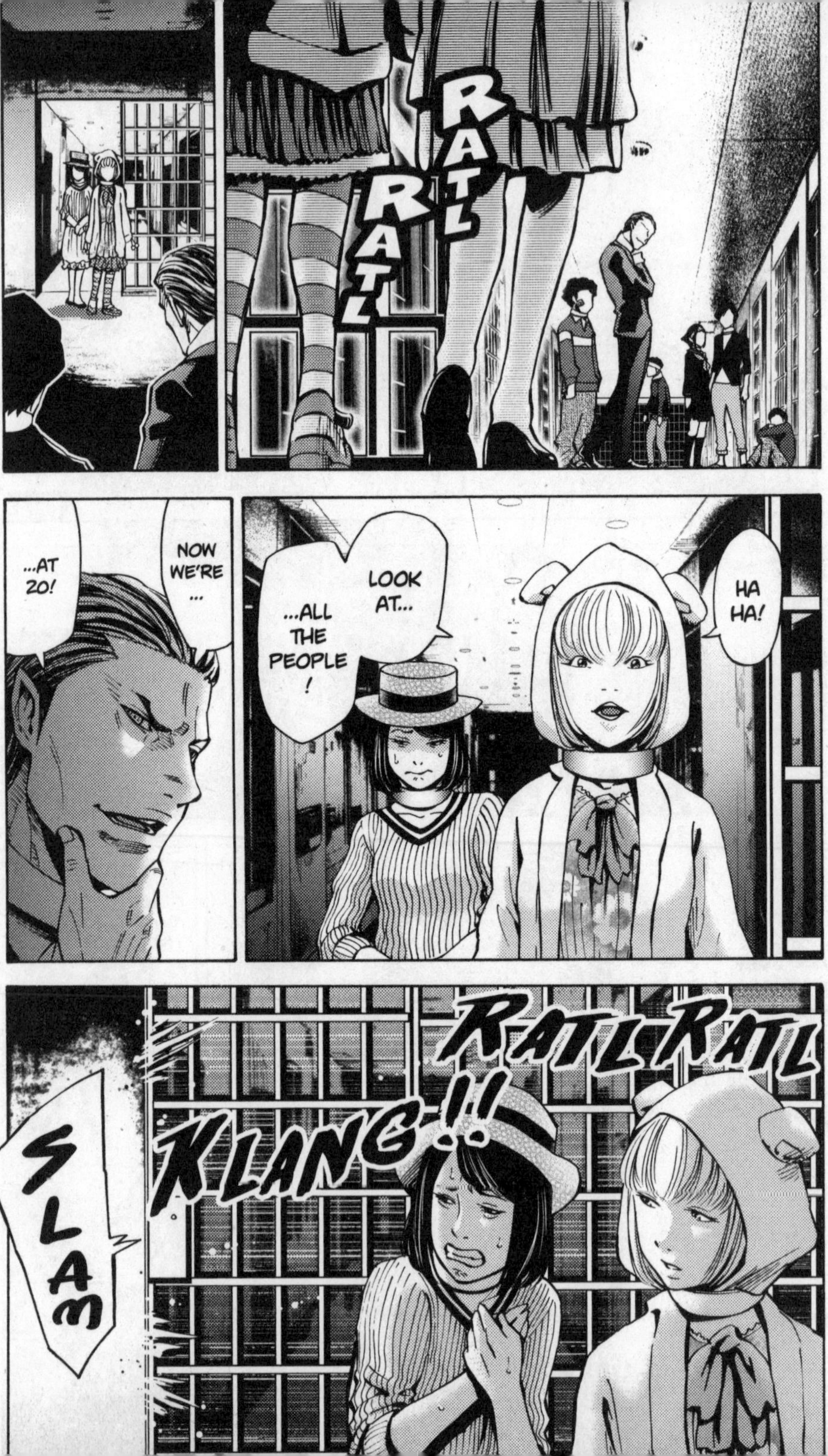
RATL
RATL
HA HA!
LOOK AT...
...ALL THE PEOPLE!
NOW WE'RE ...
...AT 20!
RATL RATL
KLANG!!
SLAM

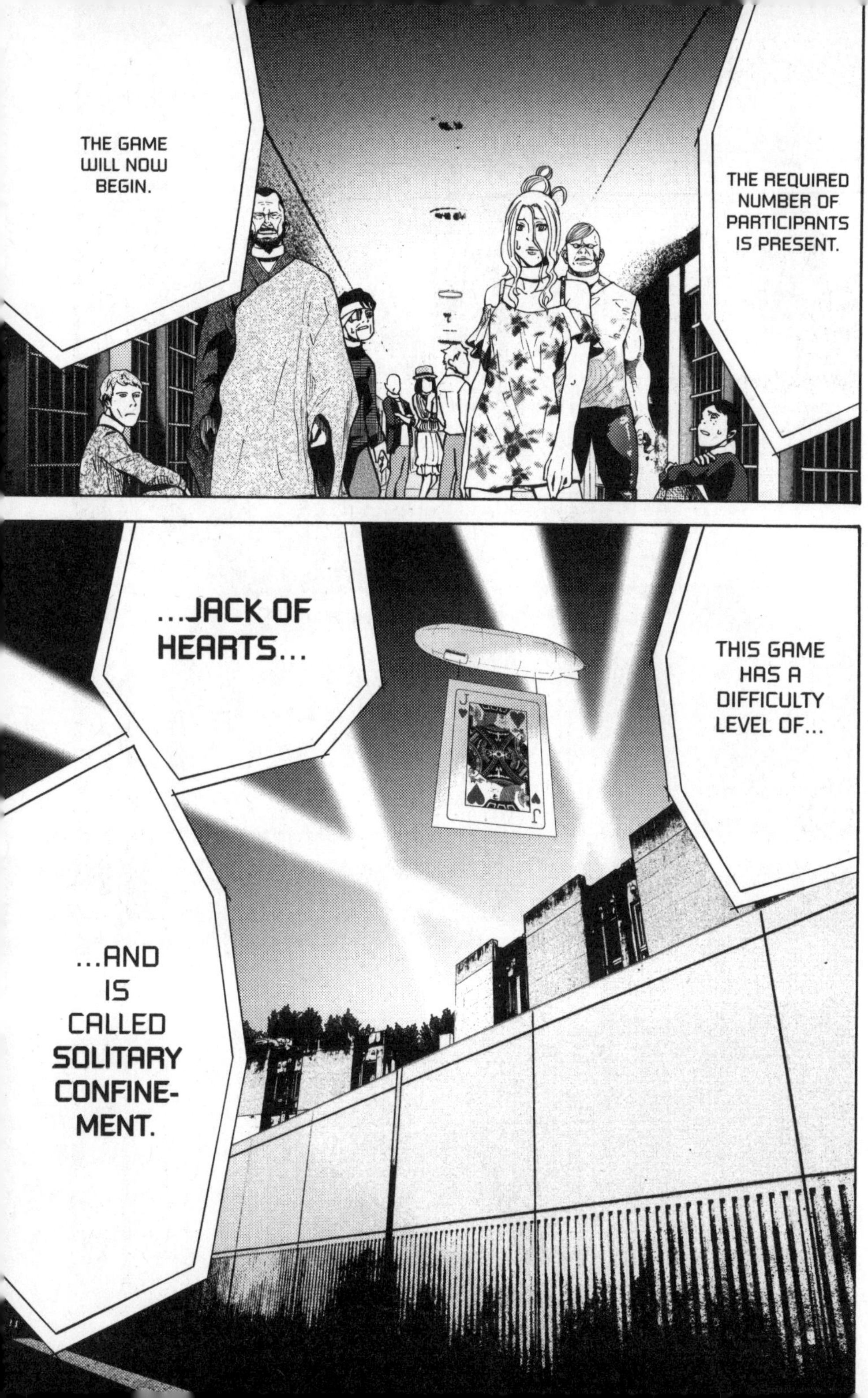
THE REQUIRED NUMBER OF PARTICIPANTS IS PRESENT.
THE GAME WILL NOW BEGIN.
THIS GAME HAS A DIFFICULTY LEVEL OF...
...JACK OF HEARTS...
...AND IS CALLED SOLITARY CONFINE-MENT.

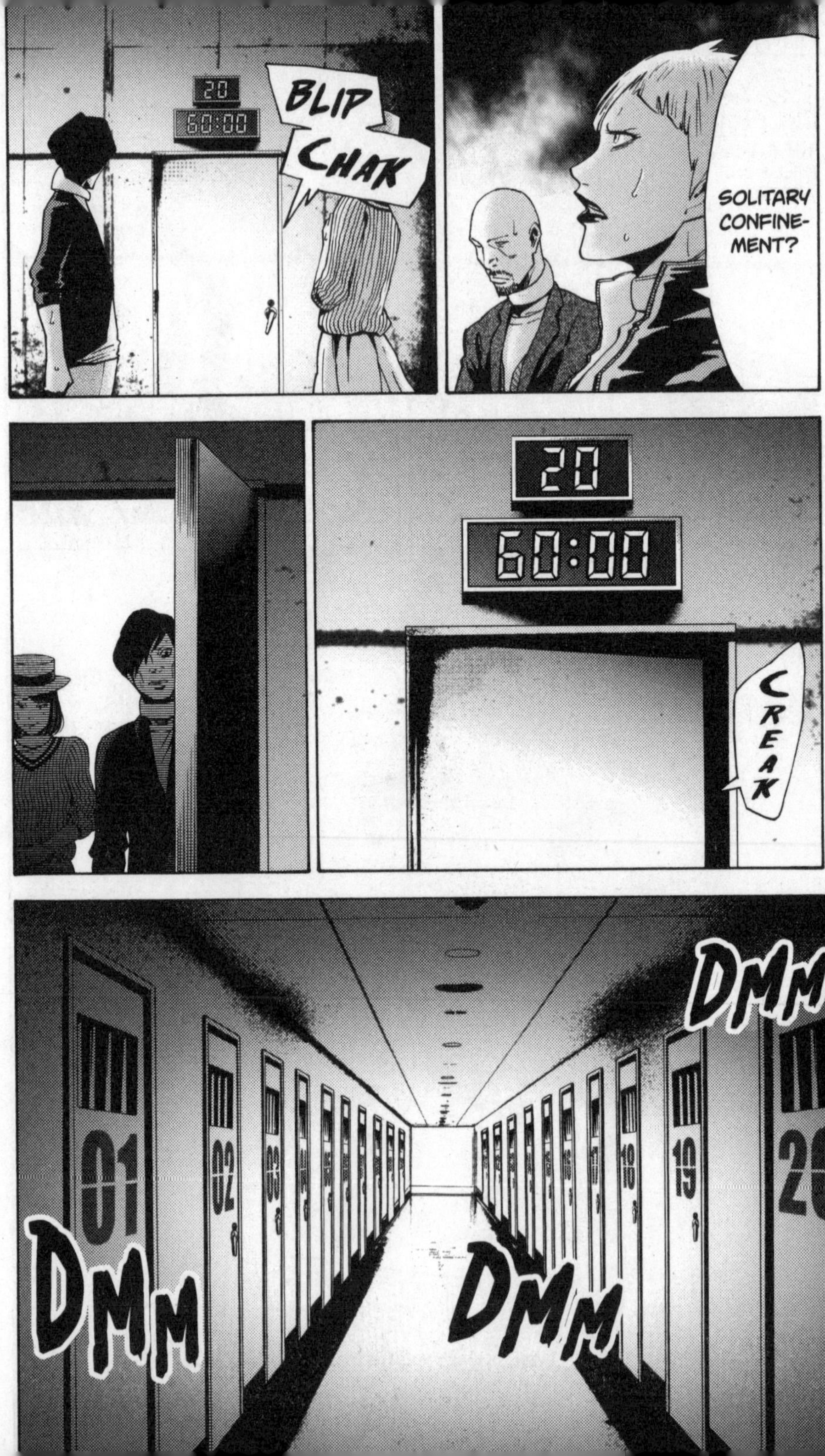
SOLITARY CONFINE-MENT?
20
60:00
BLIP
CHAK
20
60:00
CREAK
DMM
DMM
DMM
01
02
19
20

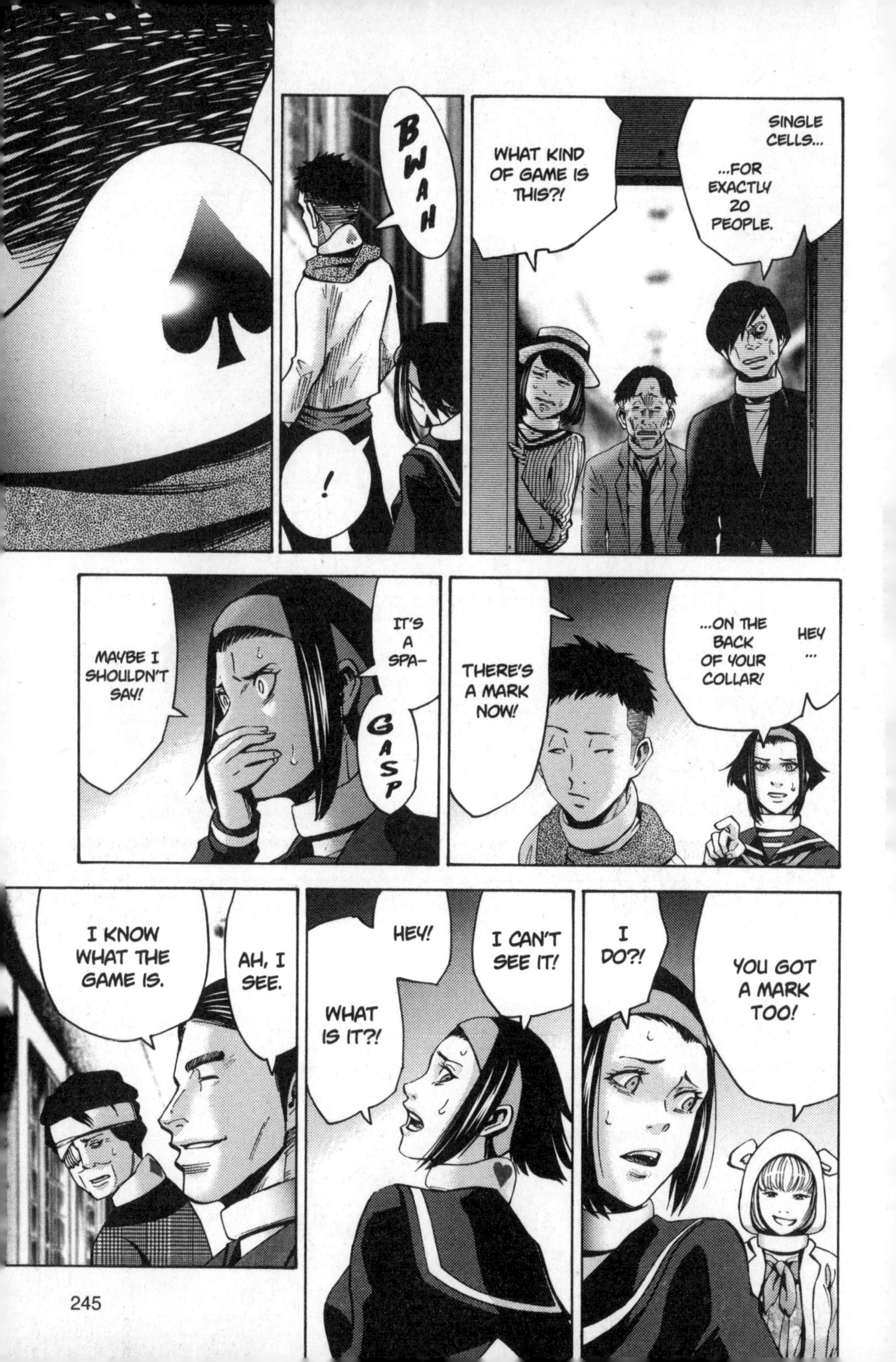
SINGLE CELLS...
...FOR EXACTLY 20 PEOPLE.
WHAT KIND OF GAME IS THIS?!
BWAH
!
HEY ...
...ON THE BACK OF YOUR COLLAR!
THERE'S A MARK NOW!
IT'S A SPA-
GASP
MAYBE I SHOULDN'T SAY!
YOU GOT A MARK TOO!
I DO?!
I CAN'T SEE IT!
HEY!
WHAT IS IT?!
AH, I SEE.
I KNOW WHAT THE GAME IS.

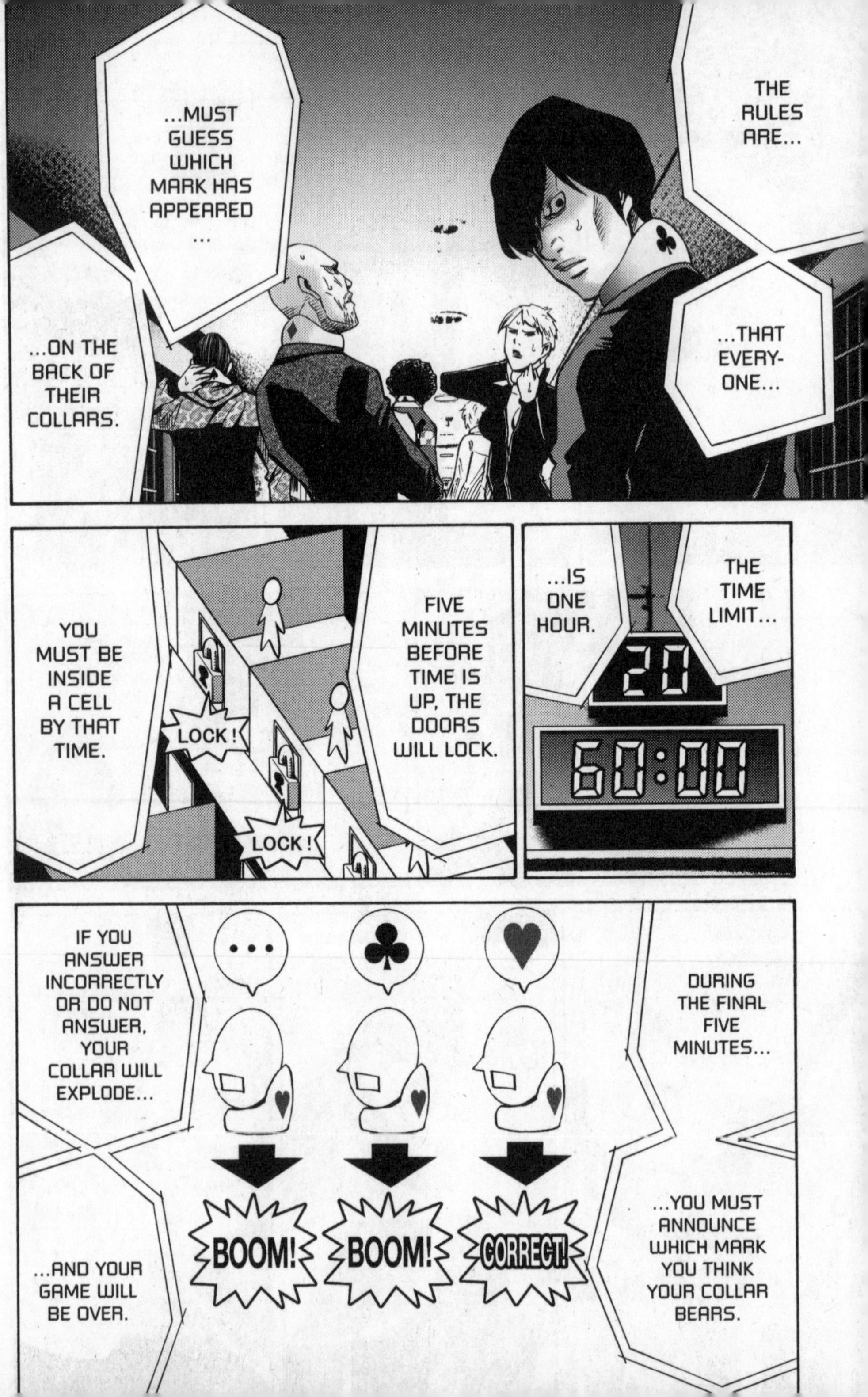
THE RULES ARE...
...THAT EVERY-ONE...
...MUST GUESS WHICH MARK HAS APPEARED ...
...ON THE BACK OF THEIR COLLARS.
THE TIME LIMIT...
...IS ONE HOUR.
20
60:00
FIVE MINUTES BEFORE TIME IS UP, THE DOORS WILL LOCK.
LOCK!
LOCK!
YOU MUST BE INSIDE A CELL BY THAT TIME.
DURING THE FINAL FIVE MINUTES...
...YOU MUST ANNOUNCE WHICH MARK YOU THINK YOUR COLLAR BEARS.
CORRECT!
BOOM!
BOOM!
IF YOU ANSWER INCORRECTLY OR DO NOT ANSWER, YOUR COLLAR WILL EXPLODE...
...AND YOUR GAME WILL BE OVER.

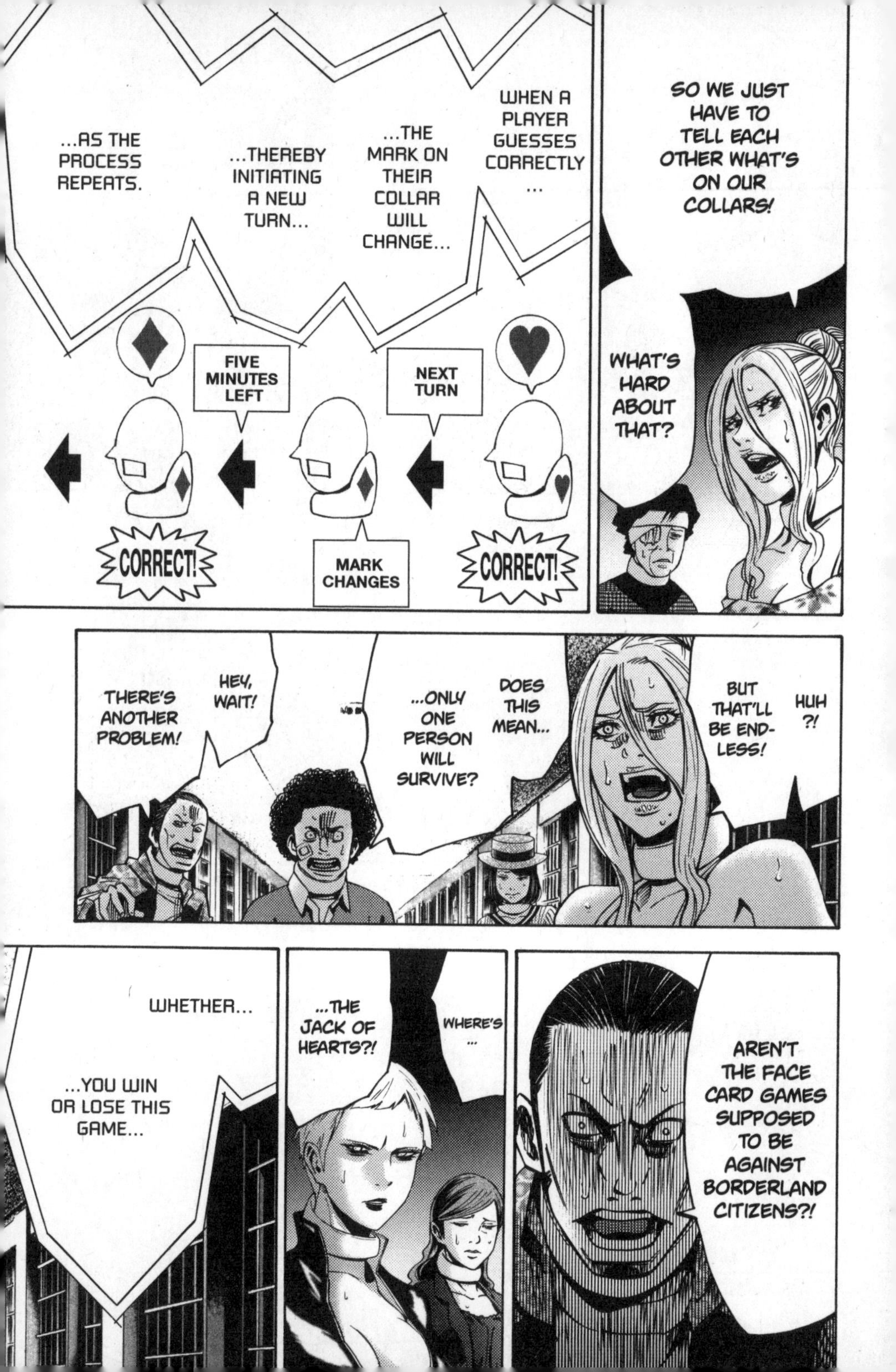
SO WE JUST HAVE TO TELL EACH OTHER WHAT'S ON OUR COLLARS!
WHAT'S HARD ABOUT THAT?
WHEN A PLAYER GUESSES CORRECTLY ...
...THE MARK ON THEIR COLLAR WILL CHANGE...
...THEREBY INITIATING A NEW TURN...
...AS THE PROCESS REPEATS.
CORRECT!
NEXT TURN
MARK CHANGES
FIVE MINUTES LEFT
CORRECT!
HUH?!
BUT THAT'LL BE END-LESS!
DOES THIS MEAN...
...ONLY ONE PERSON WILL SURVIVE?
HEY, WAIT!
THERE'S ANOTHER PROBLEM!
AREN'T THE FACE CARD GAMES SUPPOSED TO BE AGAINST BORDERLAND CITIZENS?!
WHERE'S ...
...THE JACK OF HEARTS?!
WHETHER...
...YOU WIN OR LOSE THIS GAME...

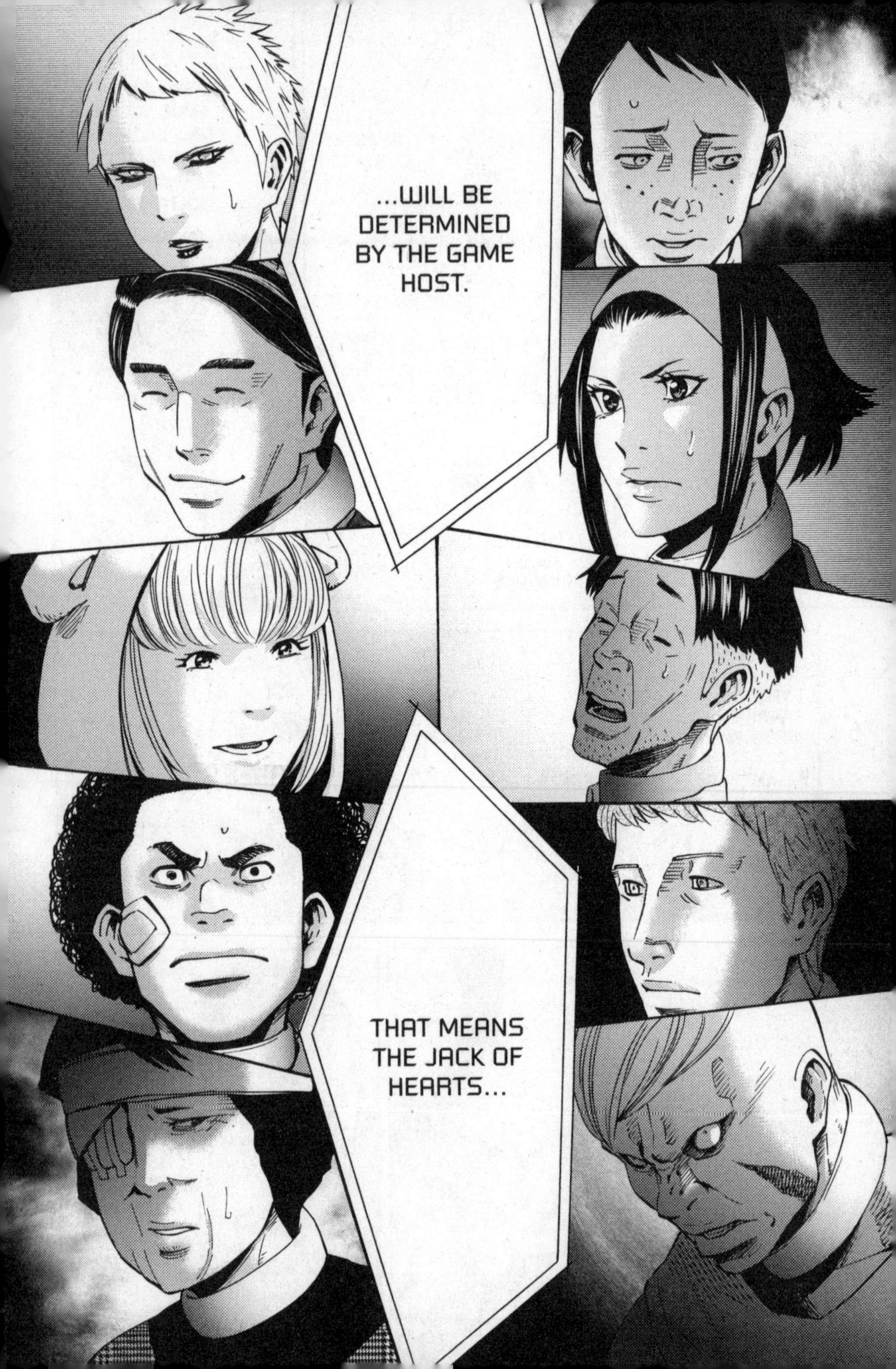
...WILL BE DETERMINED BY THE GAME HOST.
THAT MEANS THE JACK OF HEARTS...

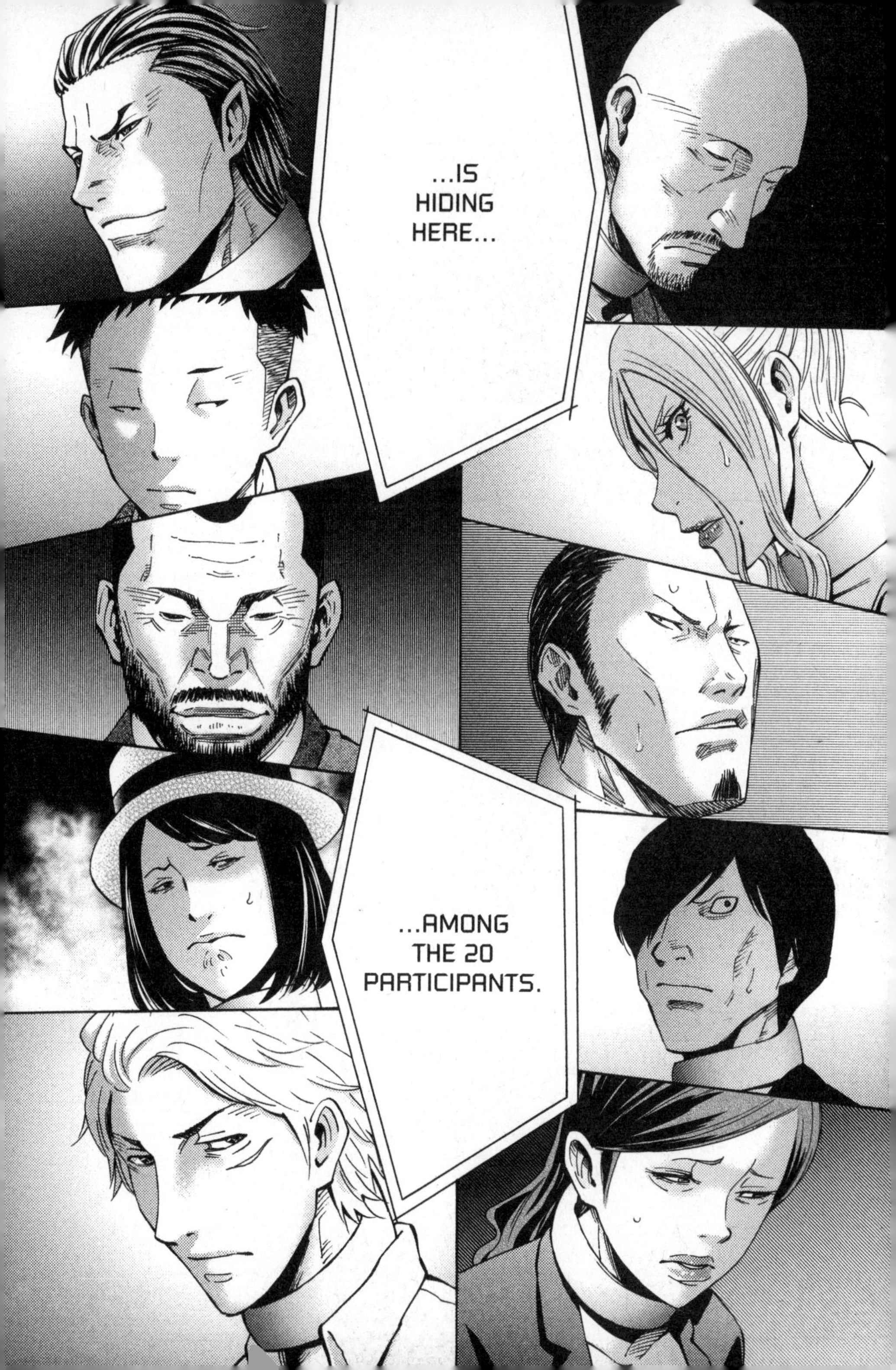
...IS
HIDING
HERE...
...AMONG
THE 20
PARTICIPANTS.

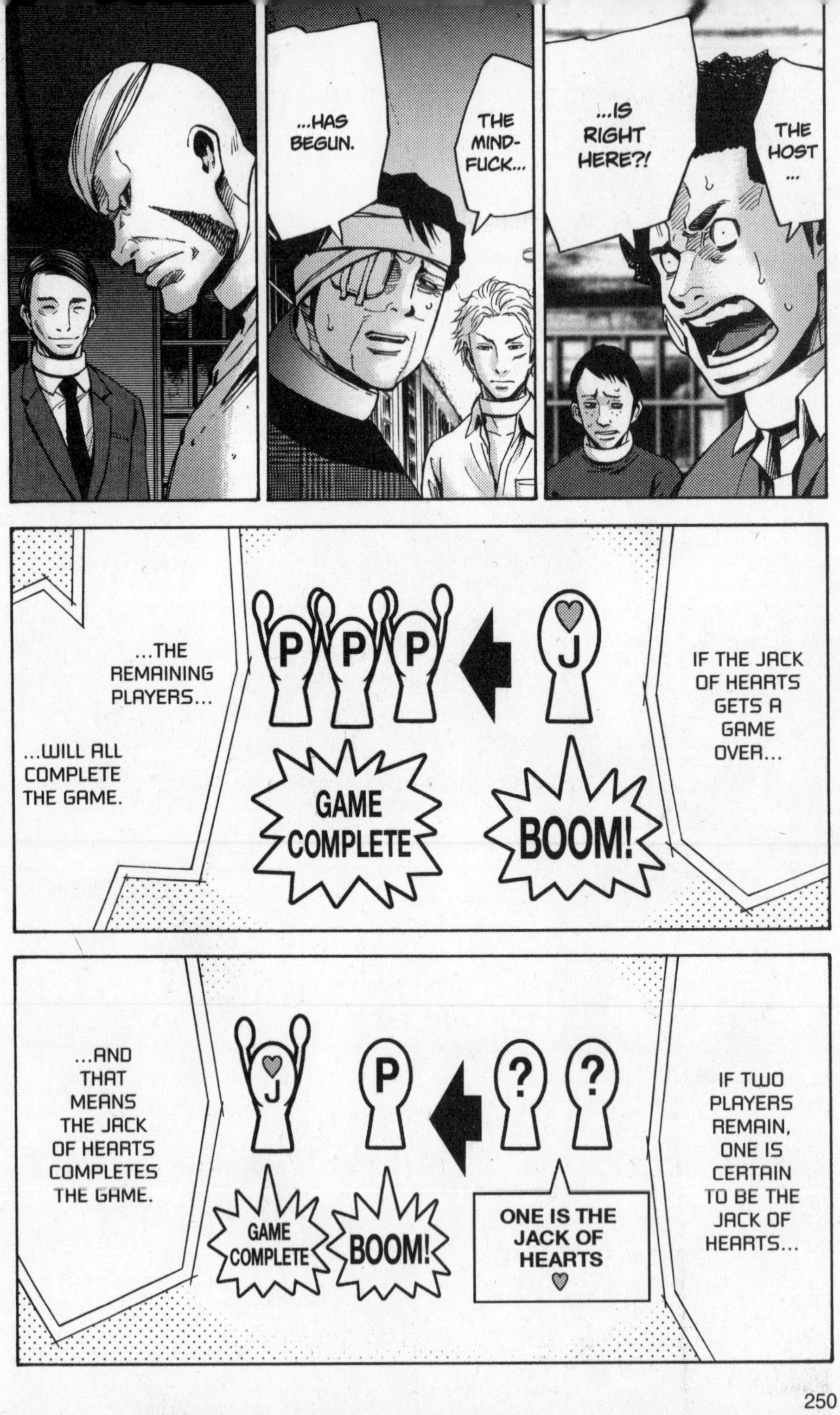
THE HOST...
...IS RIGHT HERE?!
THE MIND-FUCK...
...HAS BEGUN.
IF THE JACK OF HEARTS GETS A GAME OVER...
BOOM!
GAME COMPLETE
...THE REMAINING PLAYERS...
...WILL ALL COMPLETE THE GAME.
IF TWO PLAYERS REMAIN, ONE IS CERTAIN TO BE THE JACK OF HEARTS...
ONE IS THE JACK OF HEARTS
BOOM!
GAME COMPLETE
...AND THAT MEANS THE JACK OF HEARTS COMPLETES THE GAME.

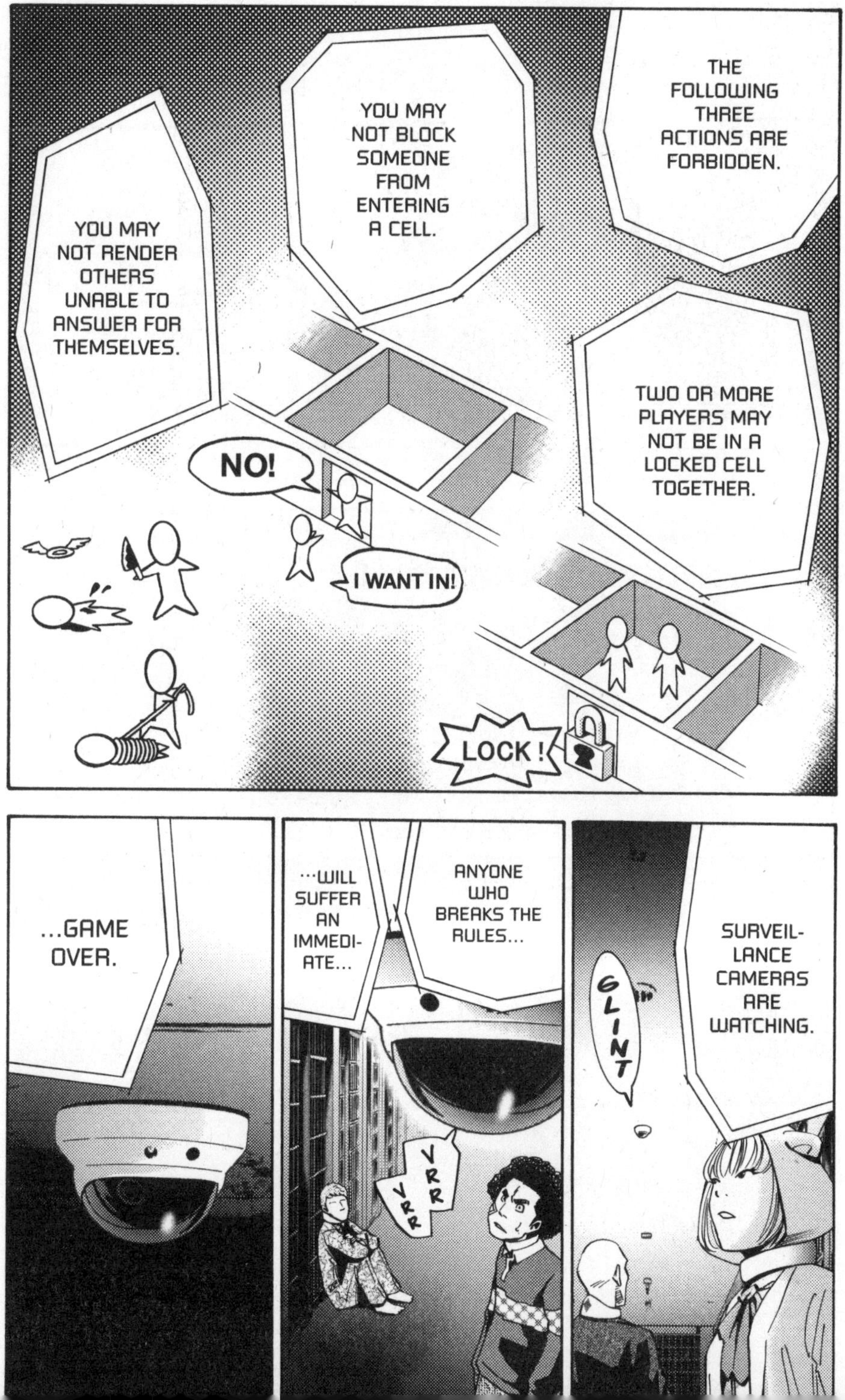
THE FOLLOWING THREE ACTIONS ARE FORBIDDEN.
TWO OR MORE PLAYERS MAY NOT BE IN A LOCKED CELL TOGETHER.
YOU MAY NOT BLOCK SOMEONE FROM ENTERING A CELL.
YOU MAY NOT RENDER OTHERS UNABLE TO ANSWER FOR THEMSELVES.
NO!
I WANT IN!
LOCK!
SURVEIL-LANCE CAMERAS ARE WATCHING.
GLINT
ANYONE WHO BREAKS THE RULES...
...WILL SUFFER AN IMMEDI-ATE...
VRR VRR
...GAME OVER.

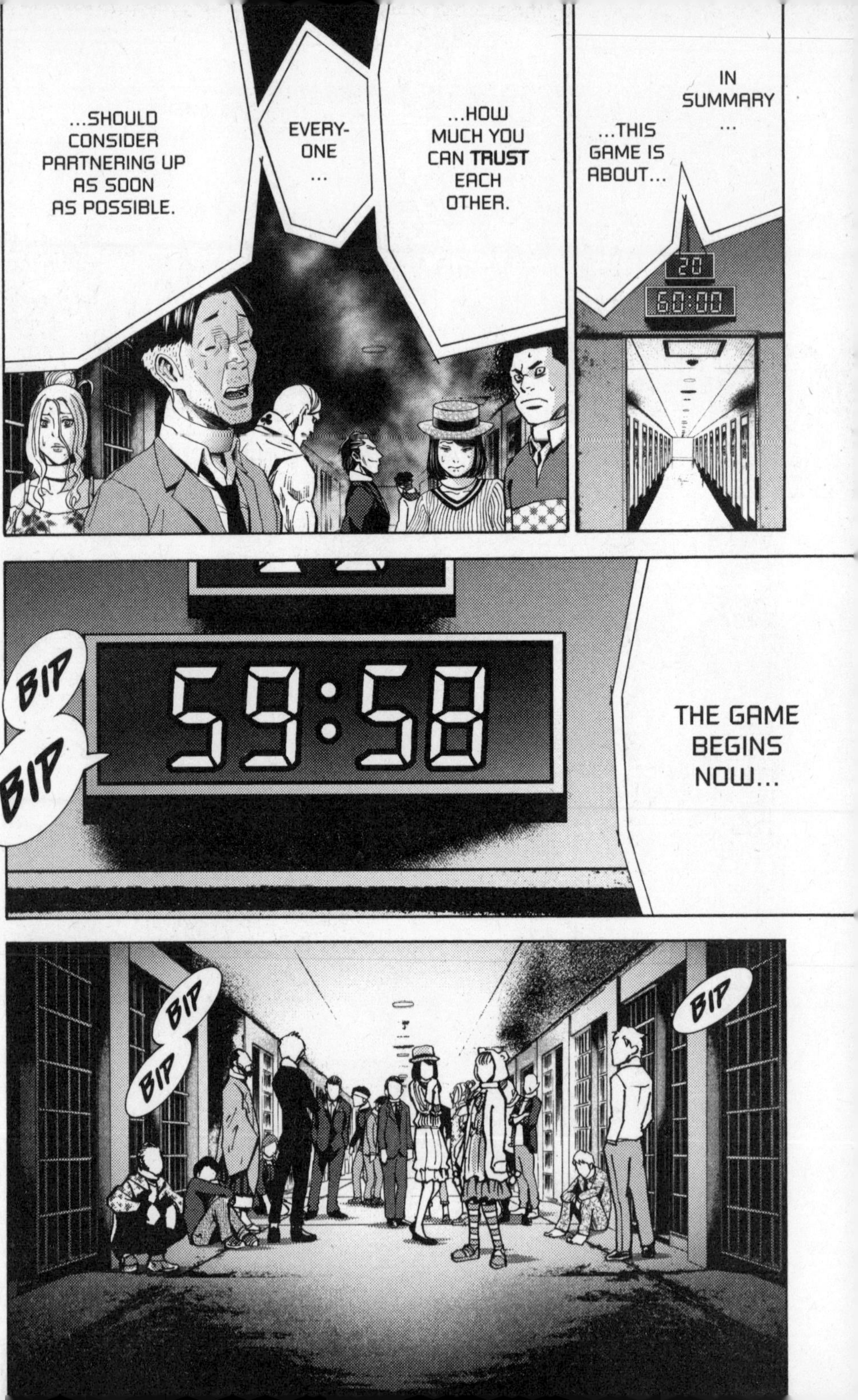
IN SUMMARY ...
...THIS GAME IS ABOUT...
20
60:00
...HOW MUCH YOU CAN **TRUST** EACH OTHER.
EVERY-ONE ...
...SHOULD CONSIDER PARTNERING UP AS SOON AS POSSIBLE.
THE GAME BEGINS NOW...
59:58
BIP BIP
BIP
BIP BIP

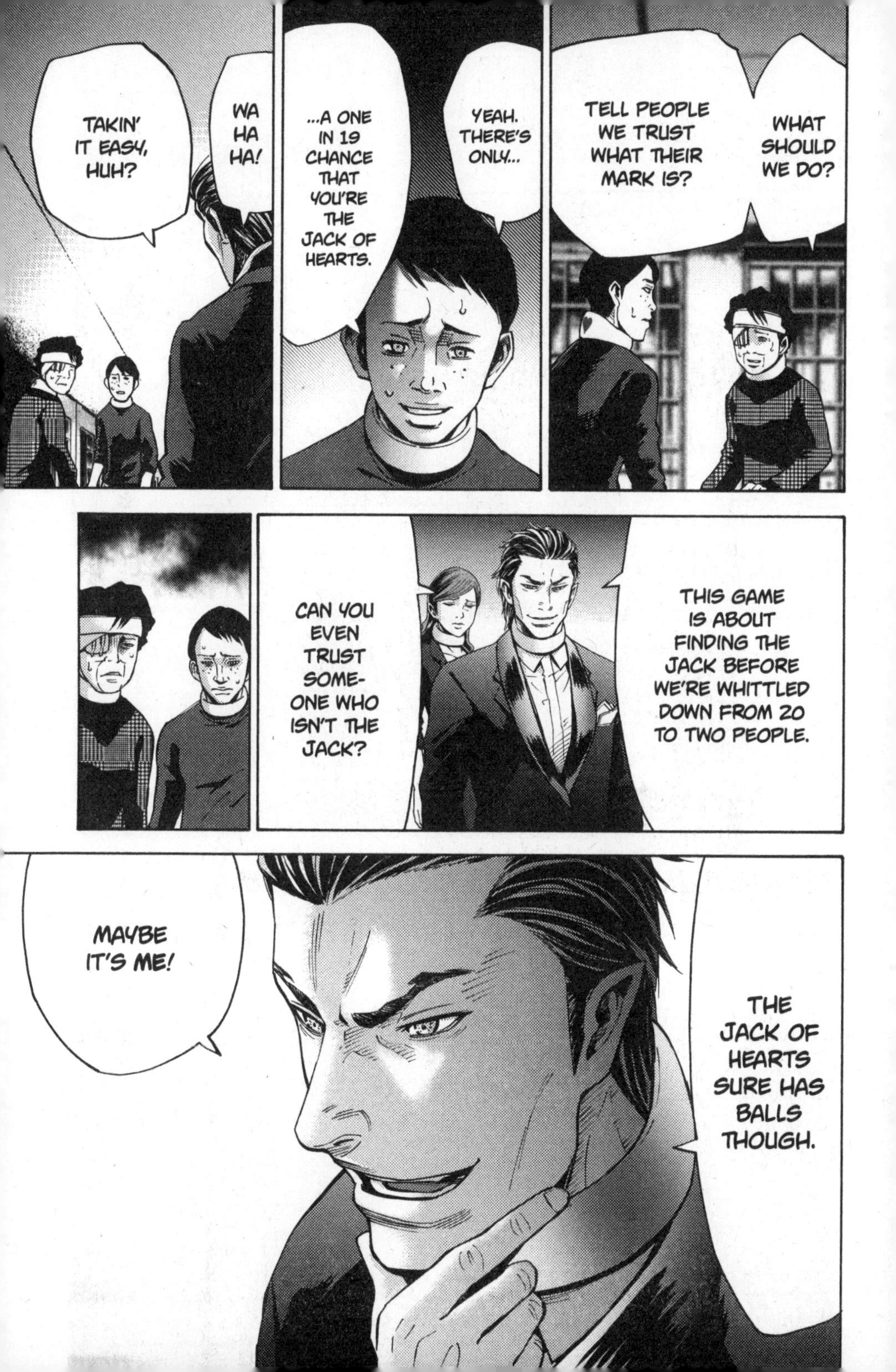
WHAT SHOULD WE DO?
TELL PEOPLE WE TRUST WHAT THEIR MARK IS?
YEAH. THERE'S ONLY...
...A ONE IN 19 CHANCE THAT YOU'RE THE JACK OF HEARTS.
WA HA HA!
TAKIN' IT EASY, HUH?
THIS GAME IS ABOUT FINDING THE JACK BEFORE WE'RE WHITTLED DOWN FROM 20 TO TWO PEOPLE.
CAN YOU EVEN TRUST SOME-ONE WHO ISN'T THE JACK?
THE JACK OF HEARTS SURE HAS BALLS THOUGH.
MAYBE IT'S ME!

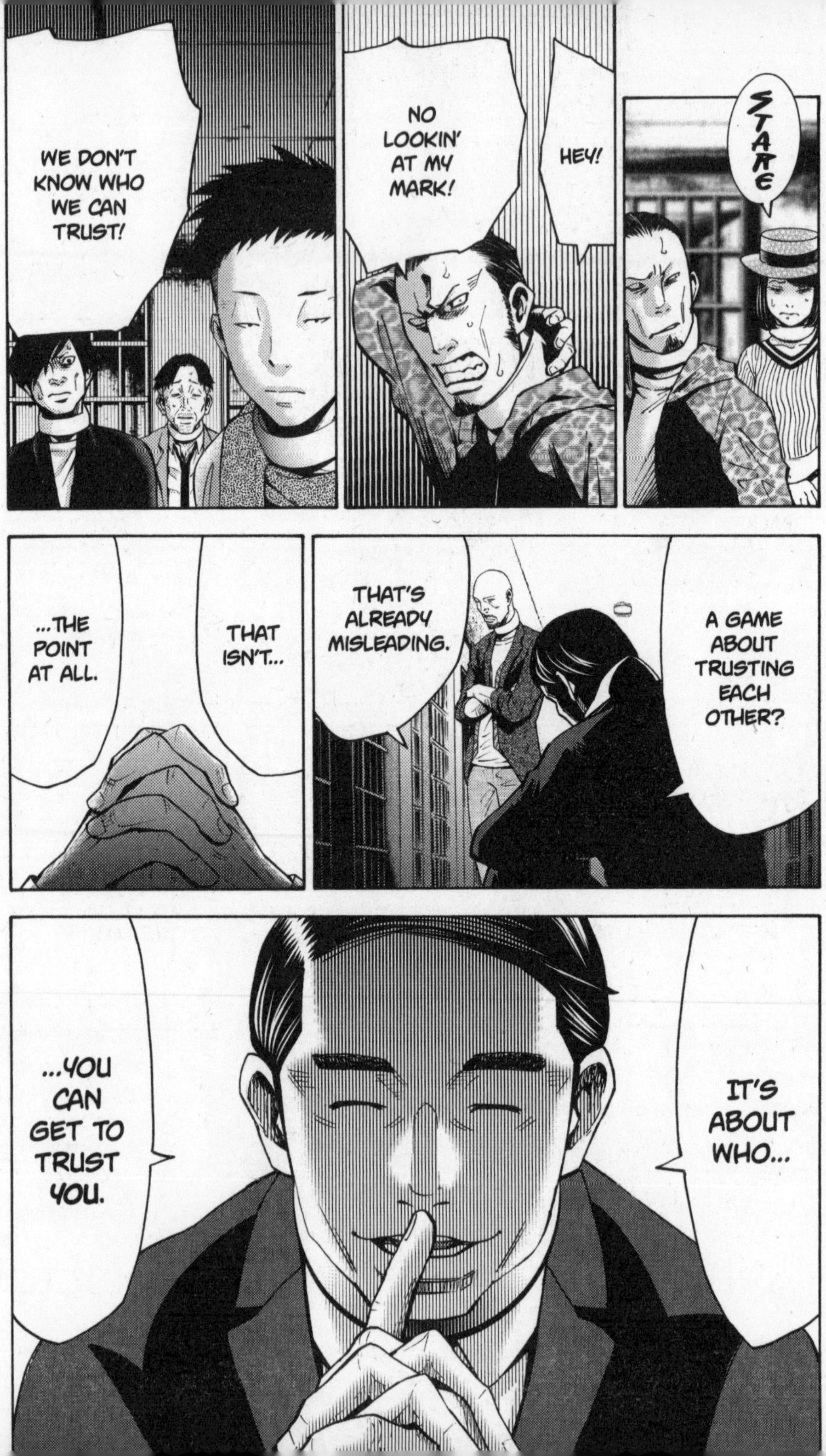
STARE
HEY!
NO LOOKIN' AT MY MARK!
WE DON'T KNOW WHO WE CAN TRUST!
A GAME ABOUT TRUSTING EACH OTHER?
THAT'S ALREADY MISLEADING.
THAT ISN'T...
...THE POINT AT ALL.
IT'S ABOUT WHO...
...YOU CAN GET TO TRUST YOU.

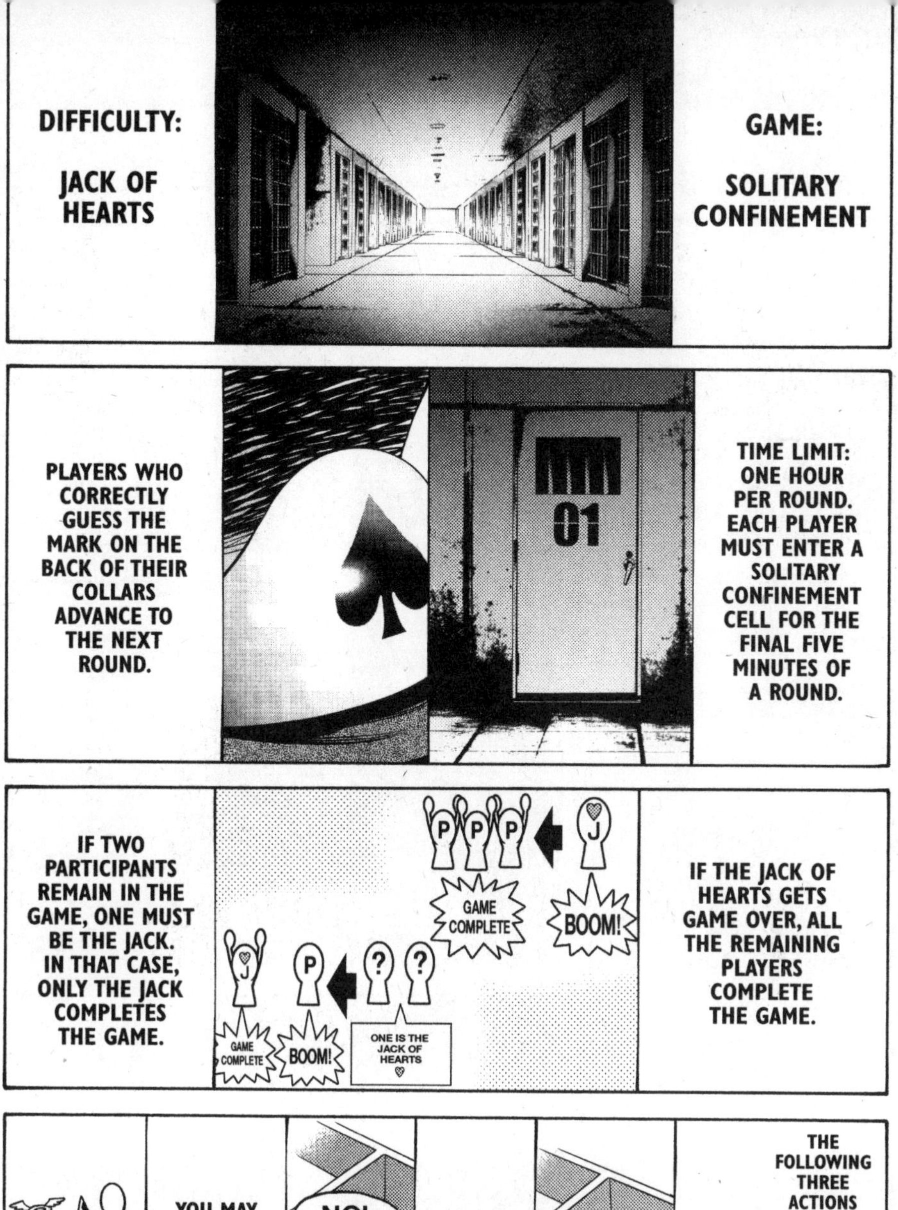
GAME:
SOLITARY CONFINEMENT
DIFFICULTY:
JACK OF HEARTS
TIME LIMIT: ONE HOUR PER ROUND. EACH PLAYER MUST ENTER A SOLITARY CONFINEMENT CELL FOR THE FINAL FIVE MINUTES OF A ROUND.
01
PLAYERS WHO CORRECTLY GUESS THE MARK ON THE BACK OF THEIR COLLARS ADVANCE TO THE NEXT ROUND.
IF THE JACK OF HEARTS GETS GAME OVER, ALL THE REMAINING PLAYERS COMPLETE THE GAME.
J
P P P
BOOM!
GAME COMPLETE
? ?
ONE IS THE JACK OF HEARTS
P
BOOM!
J
GAME COMPLETE
IF TWO PARTICIPANTS REMAIN IN THE GAME, ONE MUST BE THE JACK. IN THAT CASE, ONLY THE JACK COMPLETES THE GAME.
THE FOLLOWING THREE ACTIONS ARE AGAINST THE RULES:
TWO OR MORE PLAYERS MAY NOT BE IN A LOCKED CELL TOGETHER.
LOCK!
YOU MAY NOT BLOCK SOMEONE FROM ENTERING A CELL.
NO!
I WANT IN!
YOU MAY NOT RENDER OTHERS UNABLE TO ANSWER FOR THEMSELVES.

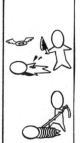

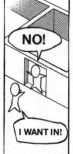

CHAPTER 45: Jack of Hearts, Part 1

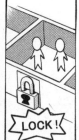

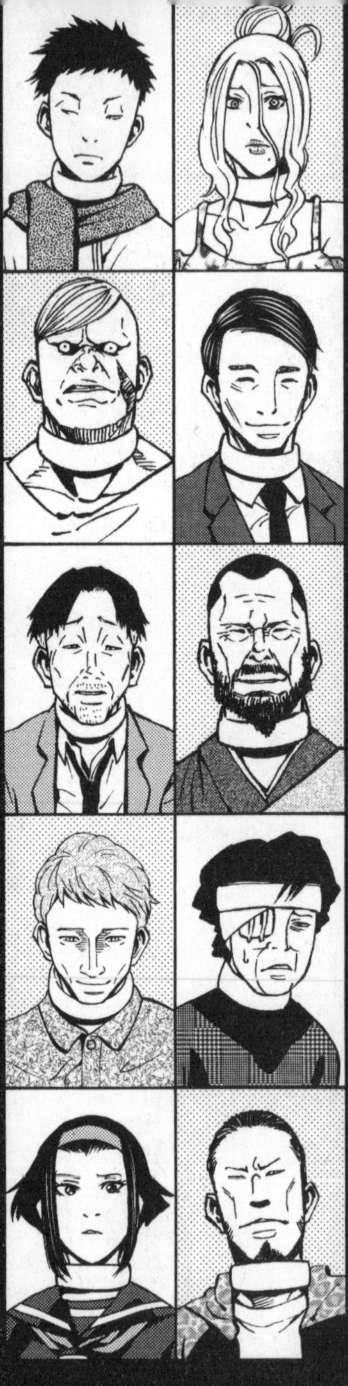

CHAPTER 45: Jack of Hearts, Part 1

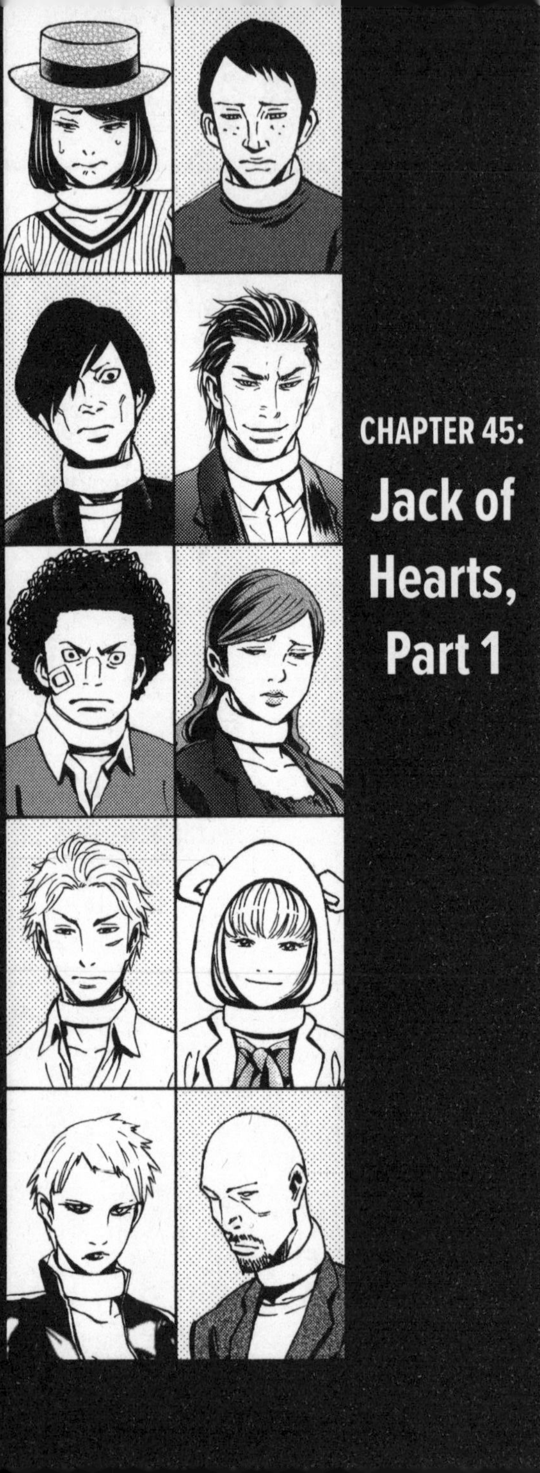

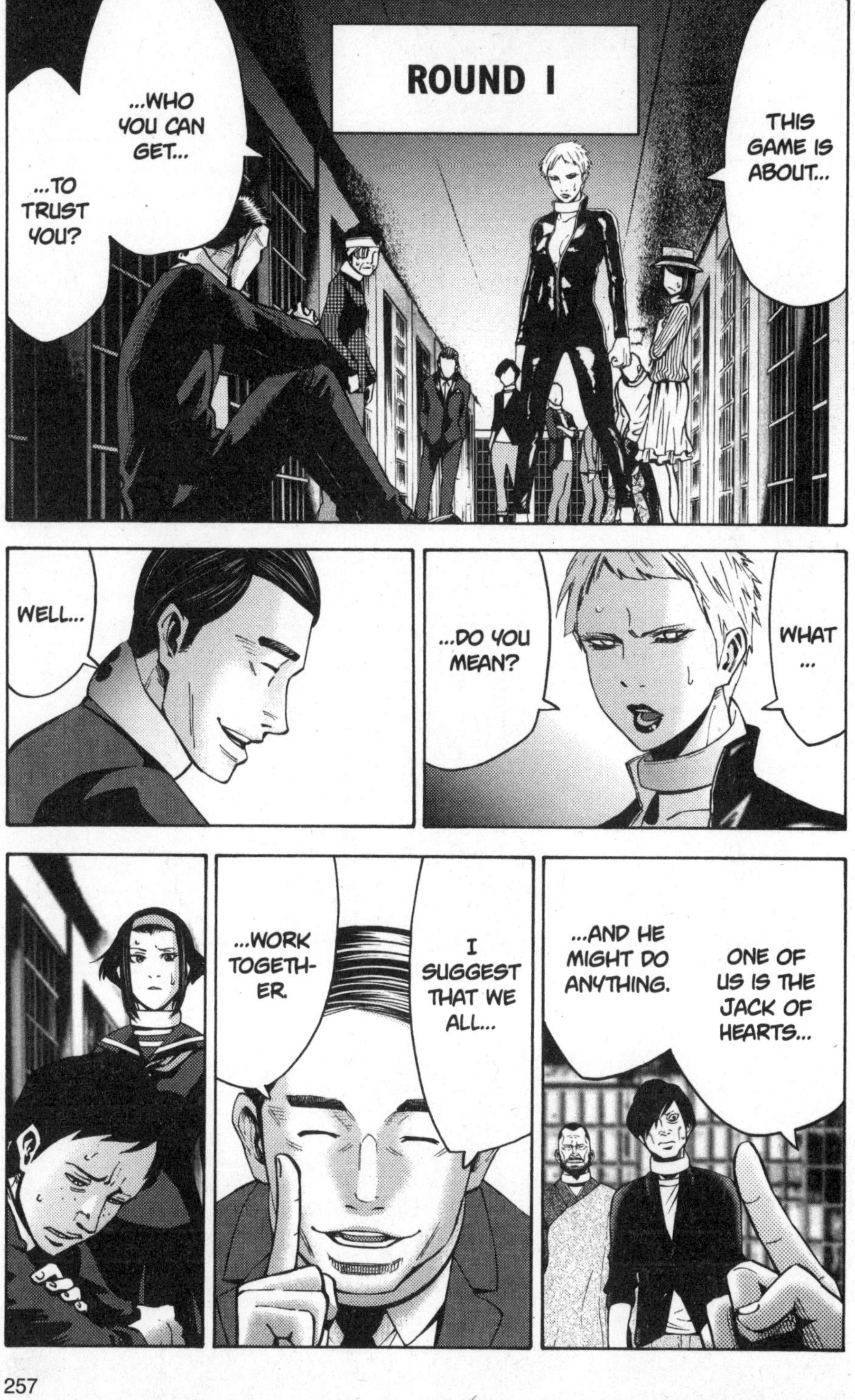
ROUND 1
THIS GAME IS ABOUT...
...WHO YOU CAN GET...
...TO TRUST YOU?
WHAT ...
...DO YOU MEAN?
WELL...
ONE OF US IS THE JACK OF HEARTS...
...AND HE MIGHT DO ANYTHING.
I SUGGEST THAT WE ALL...
...WORK TOGETH-ER.

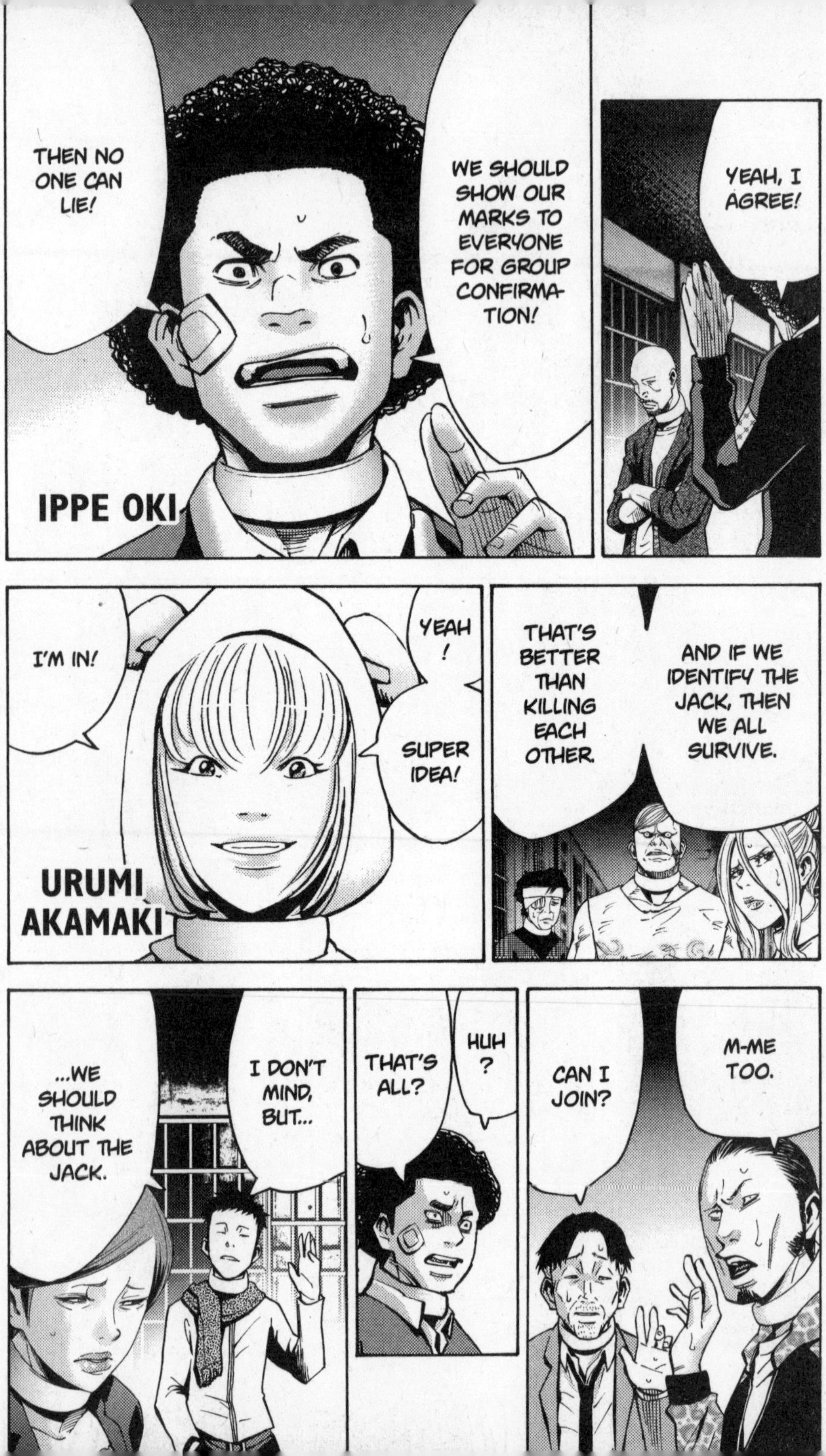
YEAH, I AGREE!
WE SHOULD SHOW OUR MARKS TO EVERYONE FOR GROUP CONFIRMATION!
THEN NO ONE CAN LIE!
IPPE OKI
AND IF WE IDENTIFY THE JACK, THEN WE ALL SURVIVE.
THAT'S BETTER THAN KILLING EACH OTHER.
YEAH!
SUPER IDEA!
I'M IN!
URUMI AKAMAKI
M-ME TOO.
CAN I JOIN?
HUH?
THAT'S ALL?
I DON'T MIND, BUT...
...WE SHOULD THINK ABOUT THE JACK.

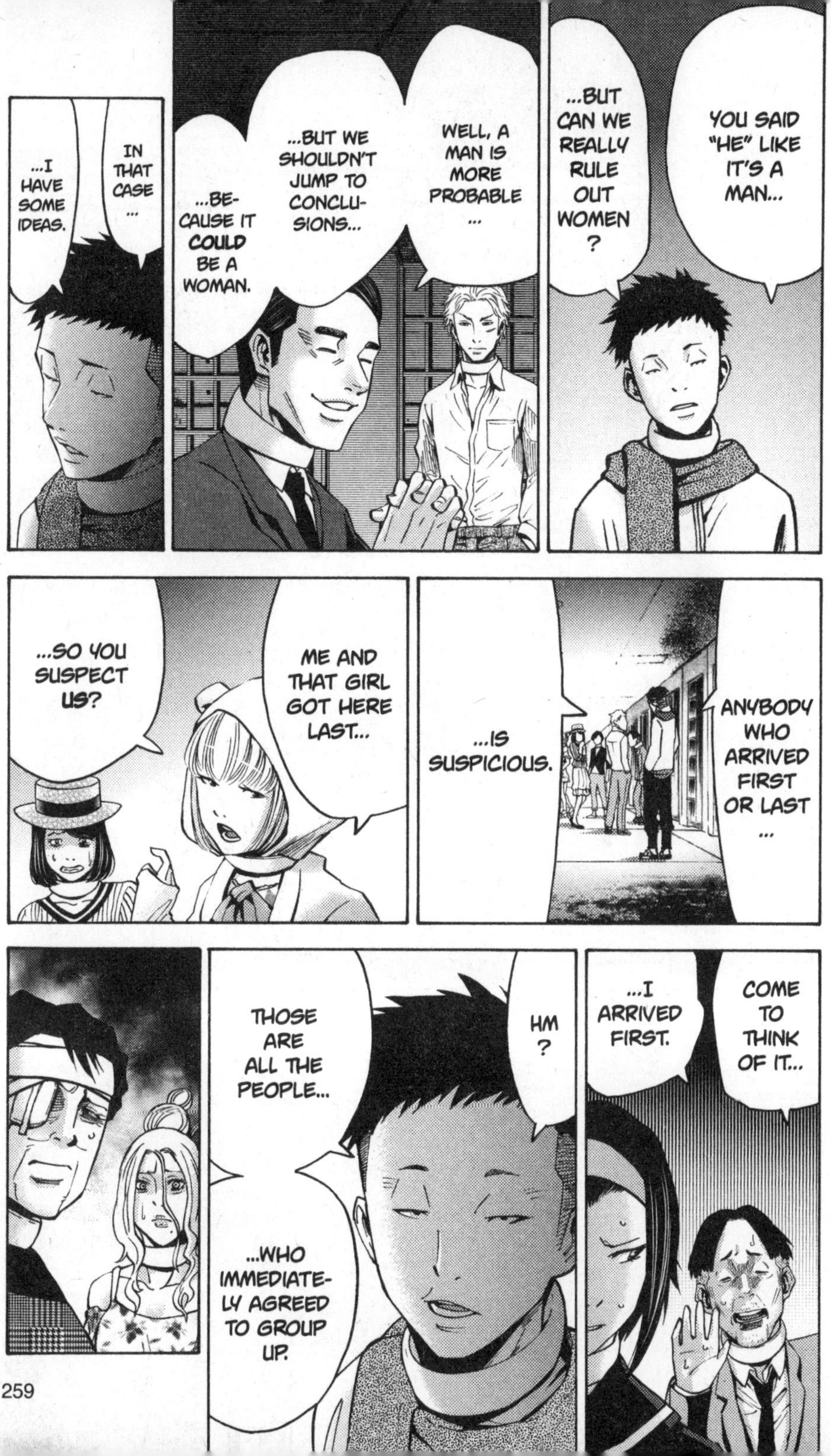
YOU SAID "HE" LIKE IT'S A MAN...
...BUT CAN WE REALLY RULE OUT WOMEN?
WELL, A MAN IS MORE PROBABLE...
...BUT WE SHOULDN'T JUMP TO CONCLUSIONS...
...BECAUSE IT **COULD** BE A WOMAN.
IN THAT CASE...
...I HAVE SOME IDEAS.
ANYBODY WHO ARRIVED FIRST OR LAST...
...IS SUSPICIOUS.
ME AND THAT GIRL GOT HERE LAST...
...SO YOU SUSPECT US?
COME TO THINK OF IT...
...I ARRIVED FIRST.
HM?
THOSE ARE ALL THE PEOPLE...
...WHO IMMEDIATELY AGREED TO GROUP UP.

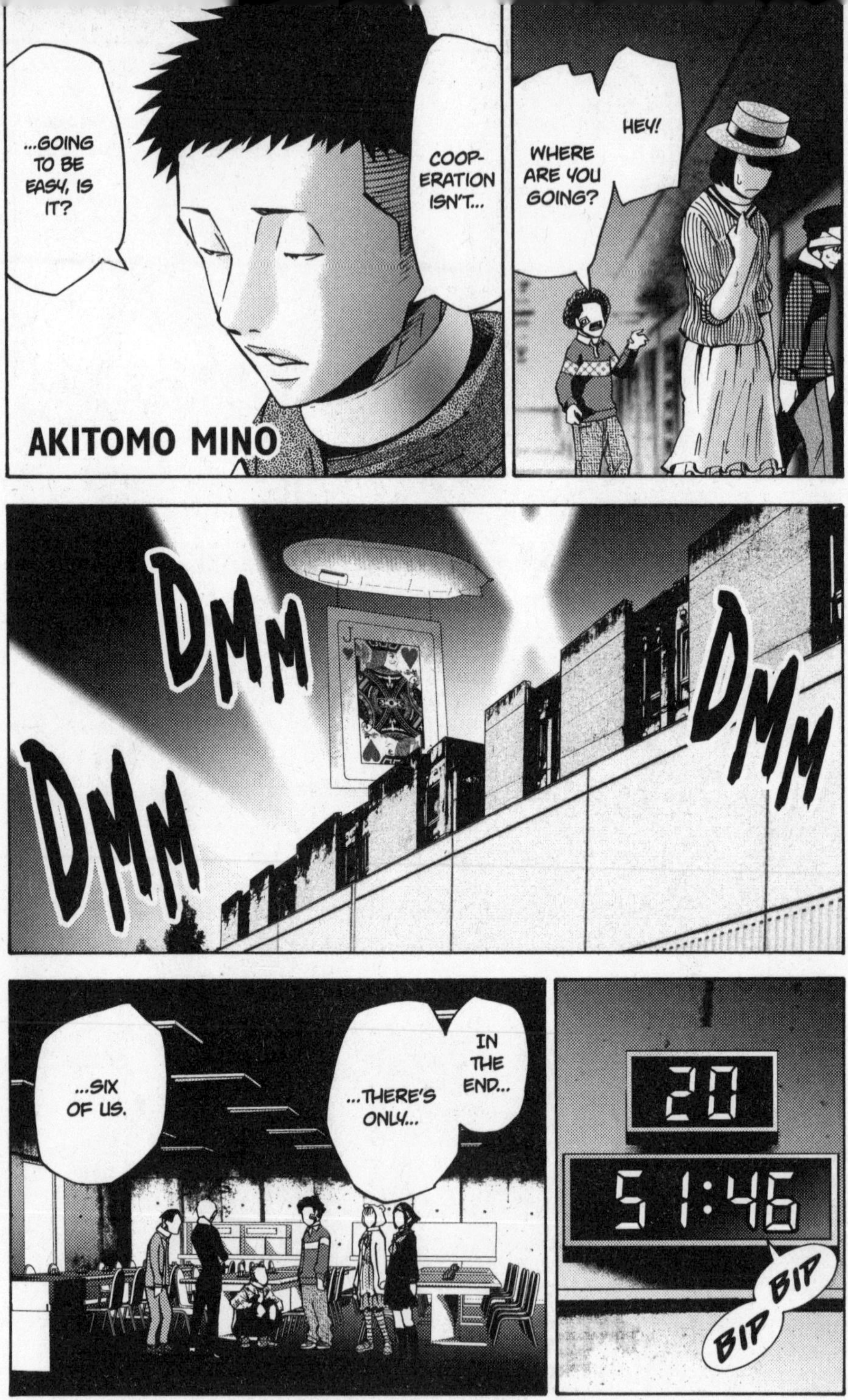
HEY!
WHERE ARE YOU GOING?
COOP-ERATION ISN'T...
...GOING TO BE EASY, IS IT?
AKITOMO MINO
DMM
DMM
DMM
20
51:46
BIP BIP
IN THE END...
...THERE'S ONLY...
...SIX OF US.

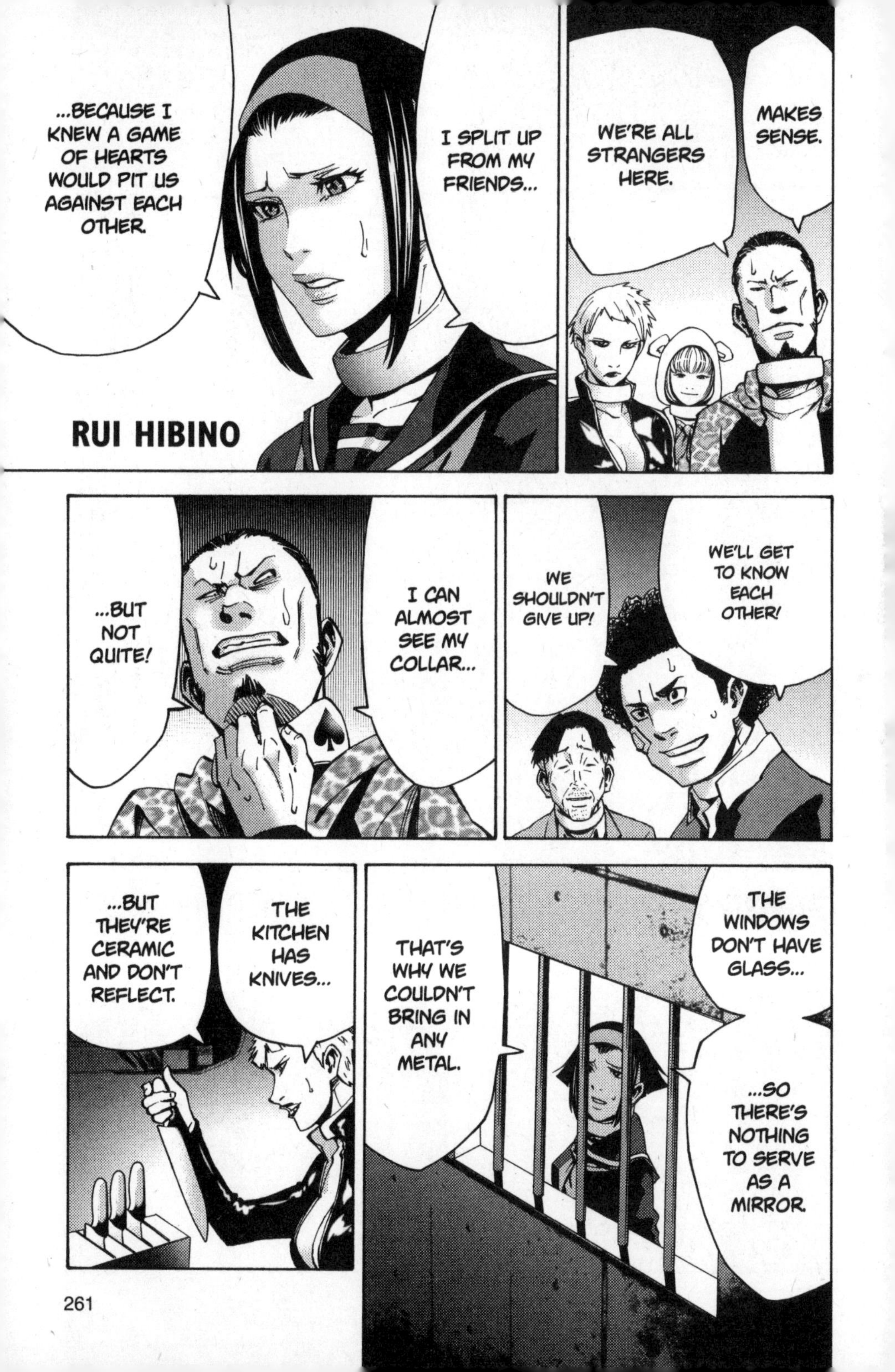
MAKES SENSE.
WE'RE ALL STRANGERS HERE.
I SPLIT UP FROM MY FRIENDS...
...BECAUSE I KNEW A GAME OF HEARTS WOULD PIT US AGAINST EACH OTHER.
RUI HIBINO
WE'LL GET TO KNOW EACH OTHER!
WE SHOULDN'T GIVE UP!
I CAN ALMOST SEE MY COLLAR...
...BUT NOT QUITE!
THE WINDOWS DON'T HAVE GLASS...
...SO THERE'S NOTHING TO SERVE AS A MIRROR.
THAT'S WHY WE COULDN'T BRING IN ANY METAL.
THE KITCHEN HAS KNIVES...
...BUT THEY'RE CERAMIC AND DON'T REFLECT.

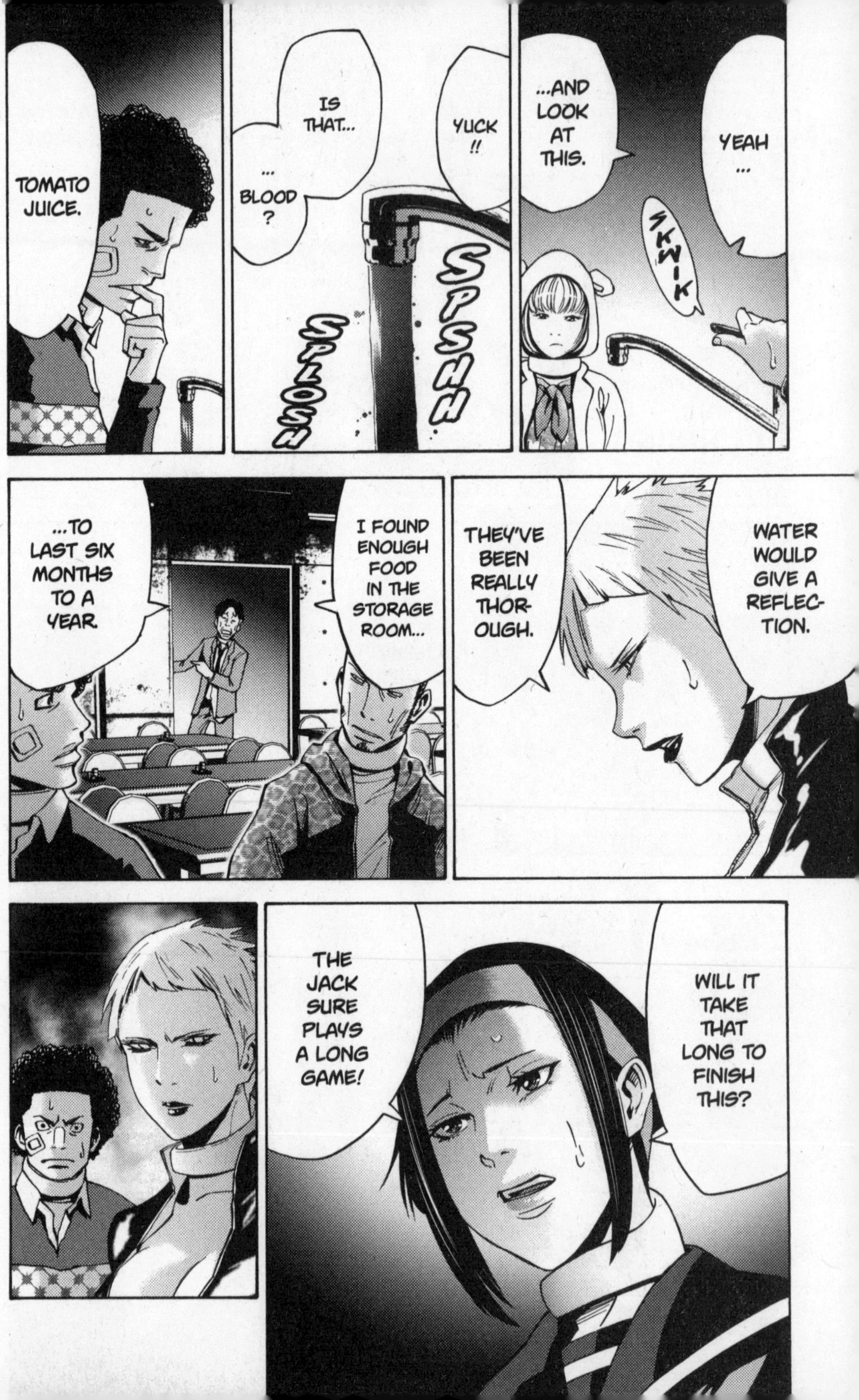
YEAH ...
SKWIK
...AND LOOK AT THIS.
YUCK !!
IS THAT...
... BLOOD ?
SPSHH
SPLOSH
TOMATO JUICE.
WATER WOULD GIVE A REFLECTION.
THEY'VE BEEN REALLY THOR-OUGH.
I FOUND ENOUGH FOOD IN THE STORAGE ROOM...
...TO LAST SIX MONTHS TO A YEAR.
WILL IT TAKE THAT LONG TO FINISH THIS?
THE JACK SURE PLAYS A LONG GAME!

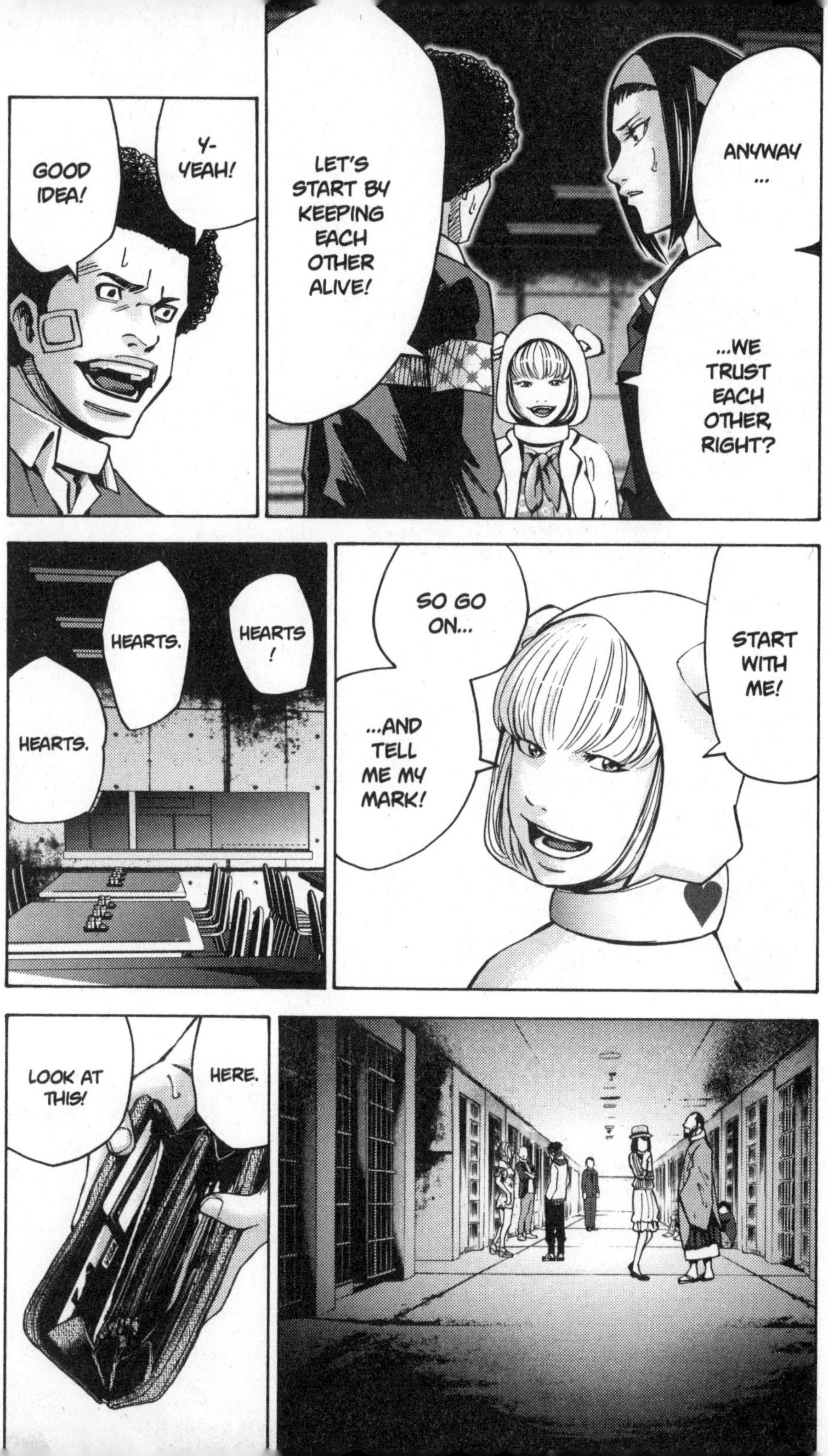
ANYWAY ...
...WE TRUST EACH OTHER, RIGHT?
LET'S START BY KEEPING EACH OTHER ALIVE!
Y-YEAH!
GOOD IDEA!
START WITH ME!
SO GO ON...
...AND TELL ME MY MARK!
HEARTS!
HEARTS.
HEARTS.
HERE.
LOOK AT THIS!

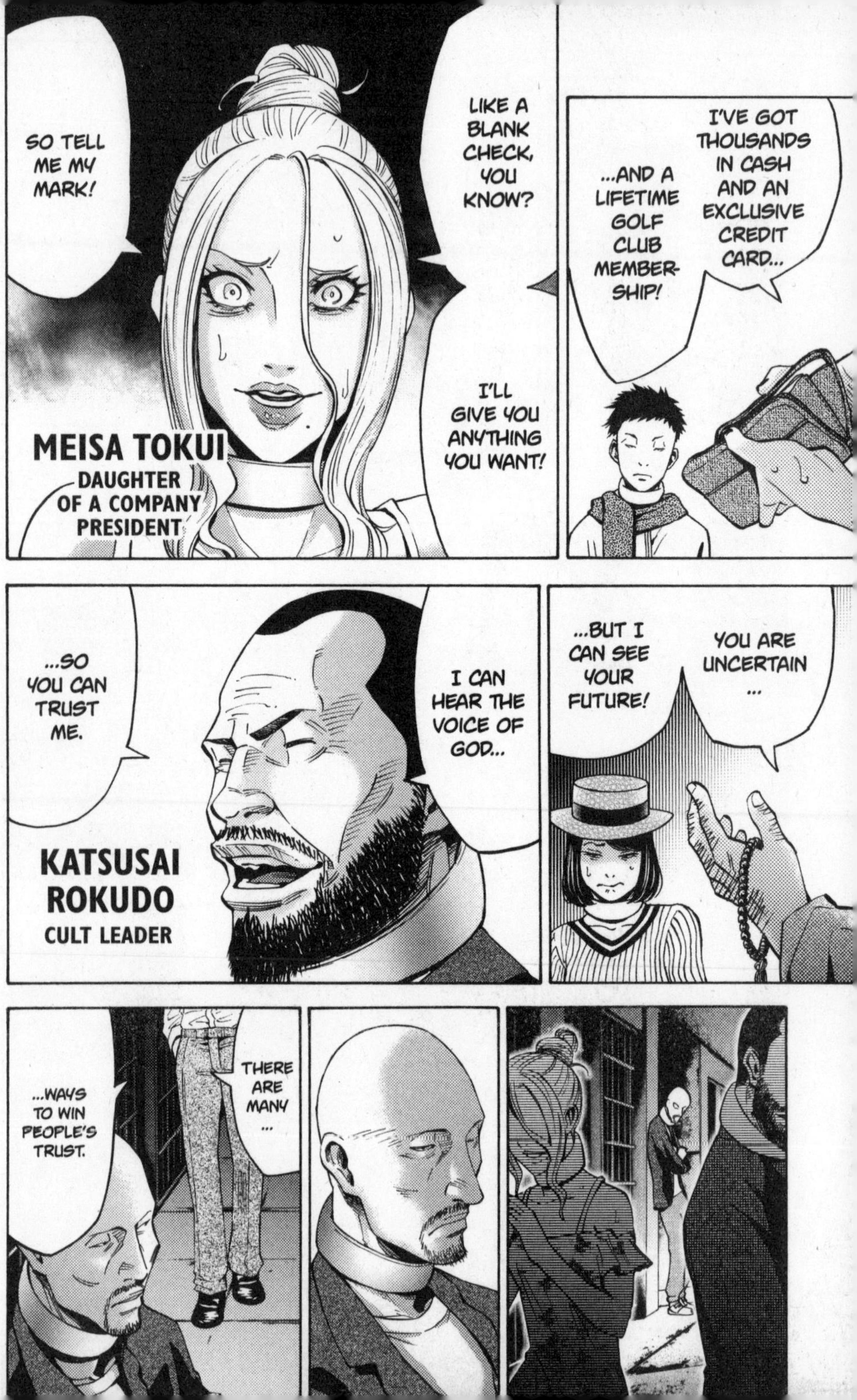
I'VE GOT THOUSANDS IN CASH AND AN EXCLUSIVE CREDIT CARD...
...AND A LIFETIME GOLF CLUB MEMBER-SHIP!
LIKE A BLANK CHECK, YOU KNOW?
I'LL GIVE YOU ANYTHING YOU WANT!
SO TELL ME MY MARK!
MEISA TOKUI
DAUGHTER OF A COMPANY PRESIDENT
YOU ARE UNCERTAIN ...
...BUT I CAN SEE YOUR FUTURE!
I CAN HEAR THE VOICE OF GOD...
...SO YOU CAN TRUST ME.
KATSUSAI ROKUDO
CULT LEADER
THERE ARE MANY ...
...WAYS TO WIN PEOPLE'S TRUST.

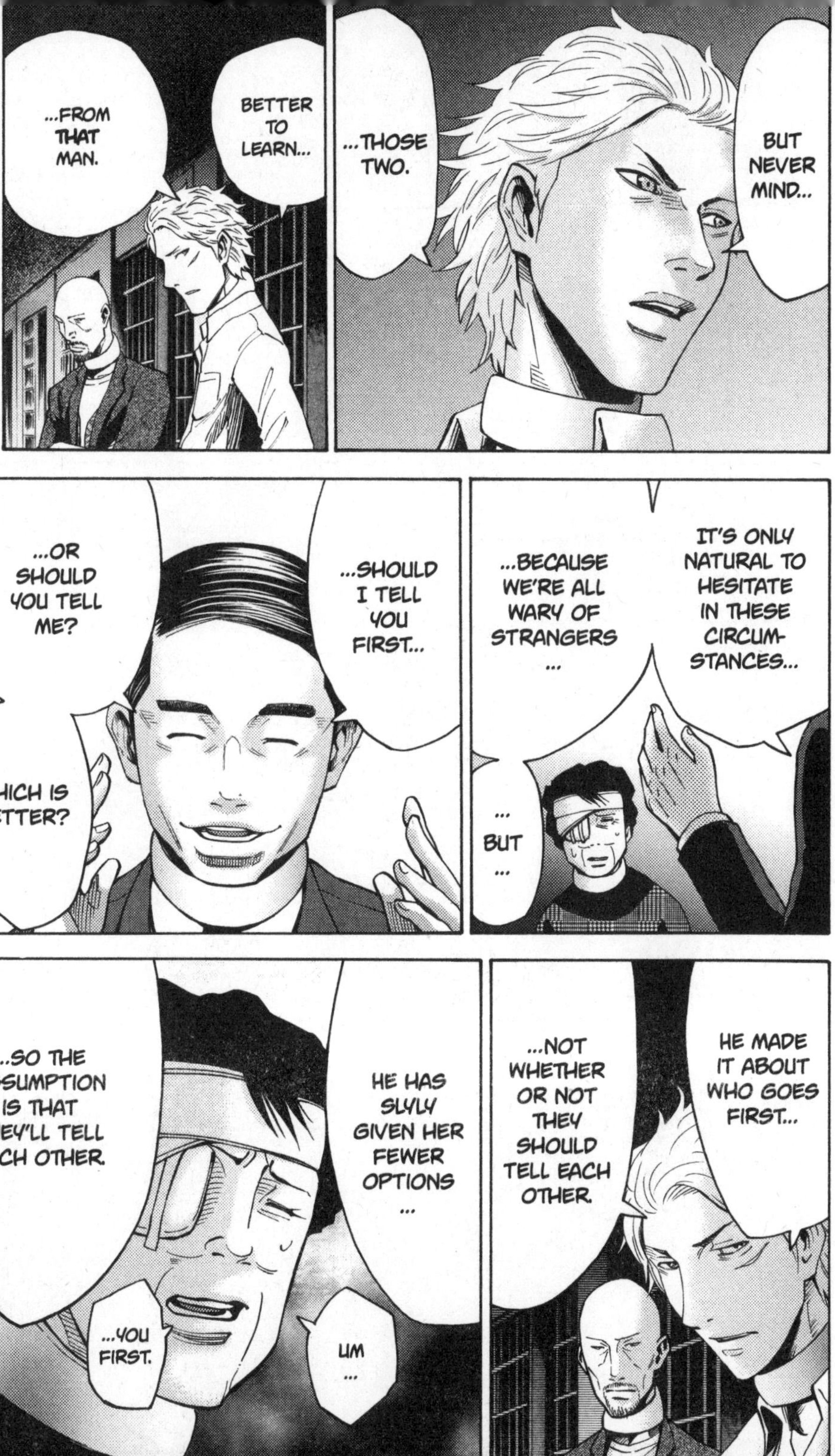
BUT NEVER MIND...
...THOSE TWO.
BETTER TO LEARN...
...FROM THAT MAN.
IT'S ONLY NATURAL TO HESITATE IN THESE CIRCUM-STANCES...
...BECAUSE WE'RE ALL WARY OF STRANGERS...
...BUT...
...SHOULD I TELL YOU FIRST...
...OR SHOULD YOU TELL ME?
WHICH IS BETTER?
HE MADE IT ABOUT WHO GOES FIRST...
...NOT WHETHER OR NOT THEY SHOULD TELL EACH OTHER.
HE HAS SLYLY GIVEN HER FEWER OPTIONS...
...SO THE ASSUMPTION IS THAT THEY'LL TELL EACH OTHER.
UM...
...YOU FIRST.

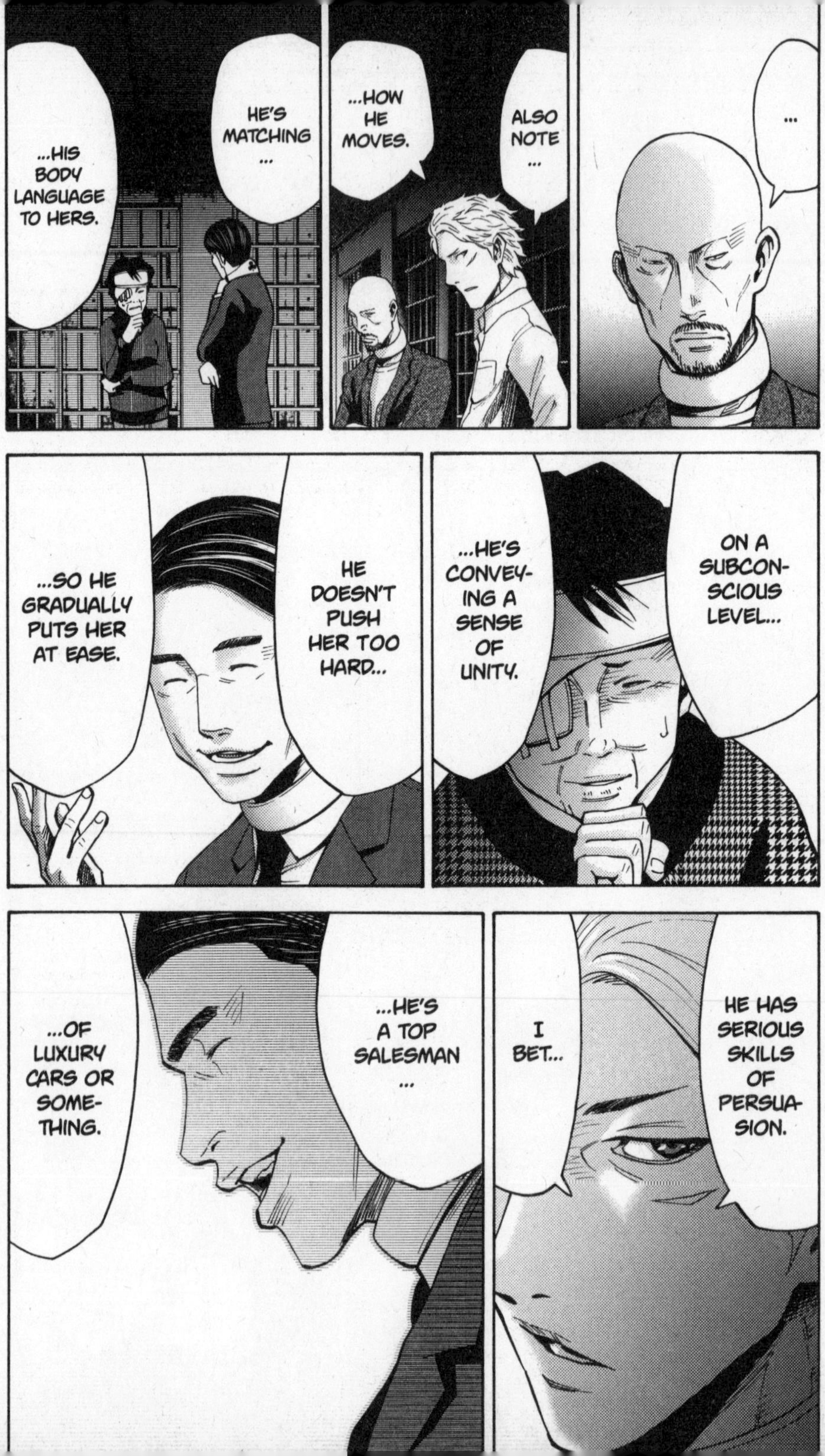
...
ALSO NOTE ...
...HOW HE MOVES.
HE'S MATCHING ...
...HIS BODY LANGUAGE TO HERS.
ON A SUBCONSCIOUS LEVEL...
...HE'S CONVEYING A SENSE OF UNITY.
HE DOESN'T PUSH HER TOO HARD...
...SO HE GRADUALLY PUTS HER AT EASE.
HE HAS SERIOUS SKILLS OF PERSUASION.
I BET...
...HE'S A TOP SALESMAN ...
...OF LUXURY CARS OR SOMETHING.

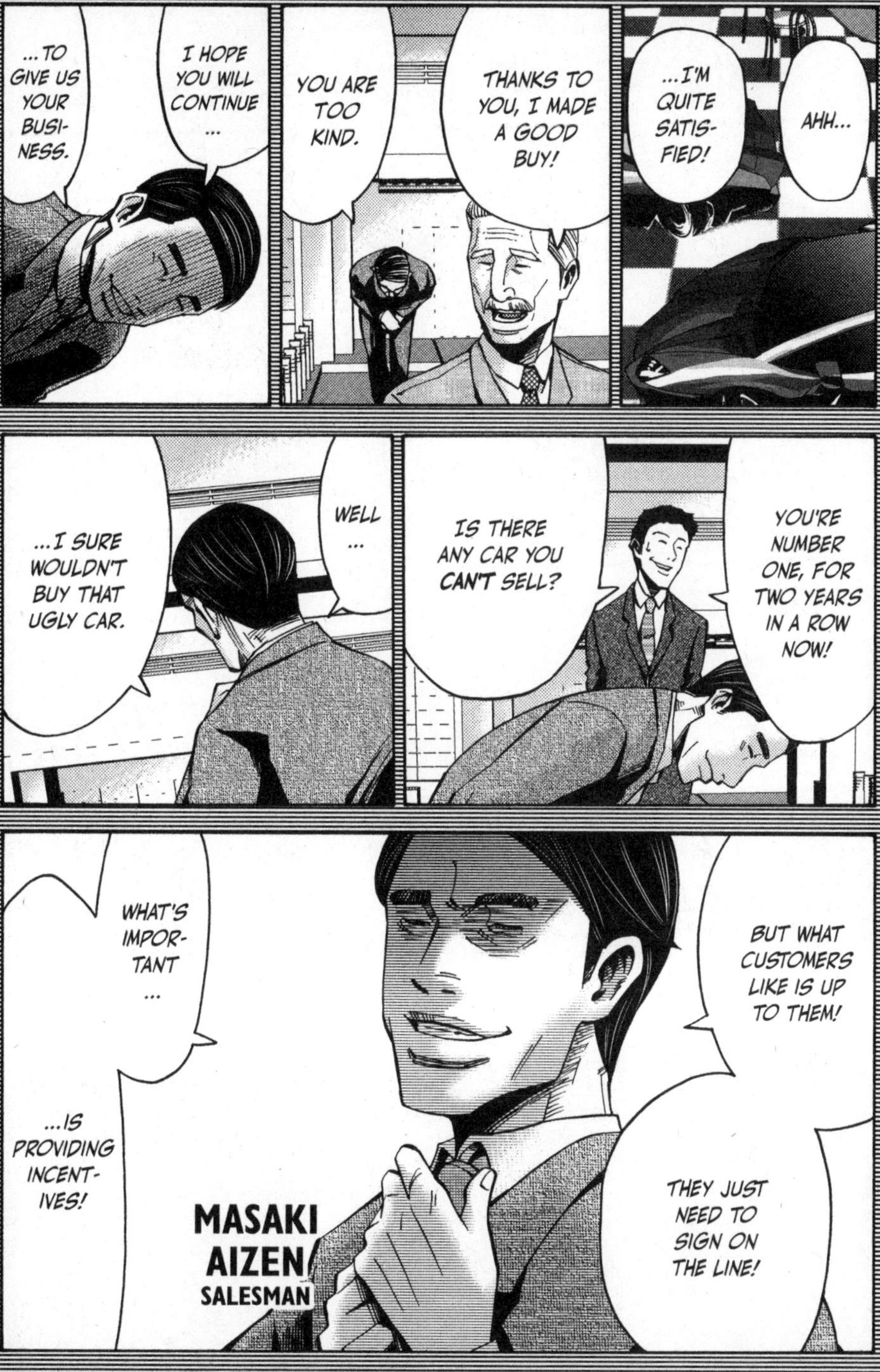
AHH...
...I'M QUITE SATISFIED!
THANKS TO YOU, I MADE A GOOD BUY!
YOU ARE TOO KIND.
I HOPE YOU WILL CONTINUE ...
...TO GIVE US YOUR BUSINESS.
YOU'RE NUMBER ONE, FOR TWO YEARS IN A ROW NOW!
IS THERE ANY CAR YOU CAN'T SELL?
WELL ...
...I SURE WOULDN'T BUY THAT UGLY CAR.
BUT WHAT CUSTOMERS LIKE IS UP TO THEM!
THEY JUST NEED TO SIGN ON THE LINE!
WHAT'S IMPORTANT ...
...IS PROVIDING INCENTIVES!
MASAKI AIZEN
SALESMAN

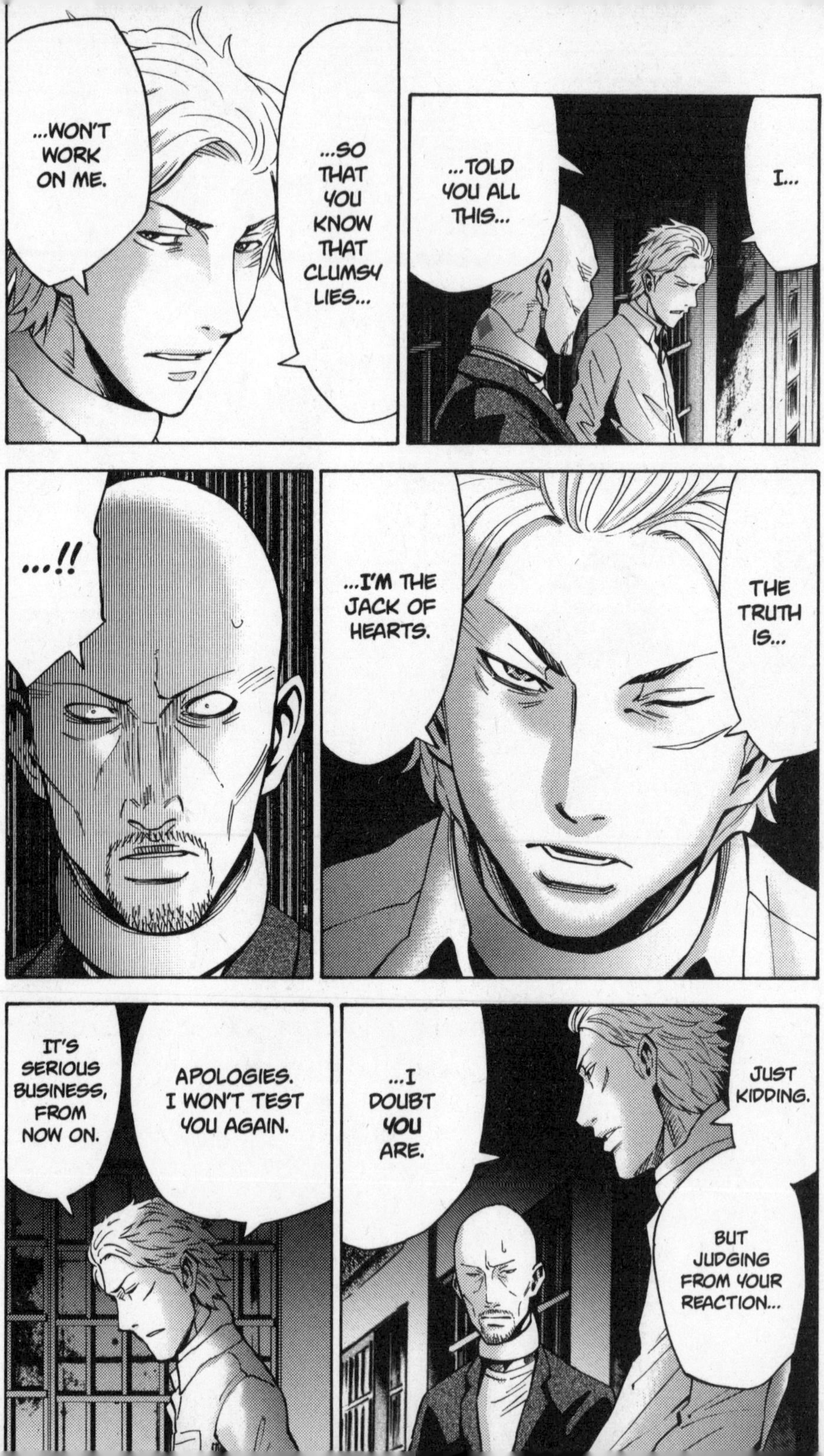

I...
...TOLD YOU ALL THIS...
...SO THAT YOU KNOW THAT CLUMSY LIES...
...WON'T WORK ON ME.
THE TRUTH IS...
...I'M THE JACK OF HEARTS.
...!!
JUST KIDDING.
...I DOUBT YOU ARE.
BUT JUDGING FROM YOUR REACTION...
APOLOGIES. I WON'T TEST YOU AGAIN.
IT'S SERIOUS BUSINESS, FROM NOW ON.

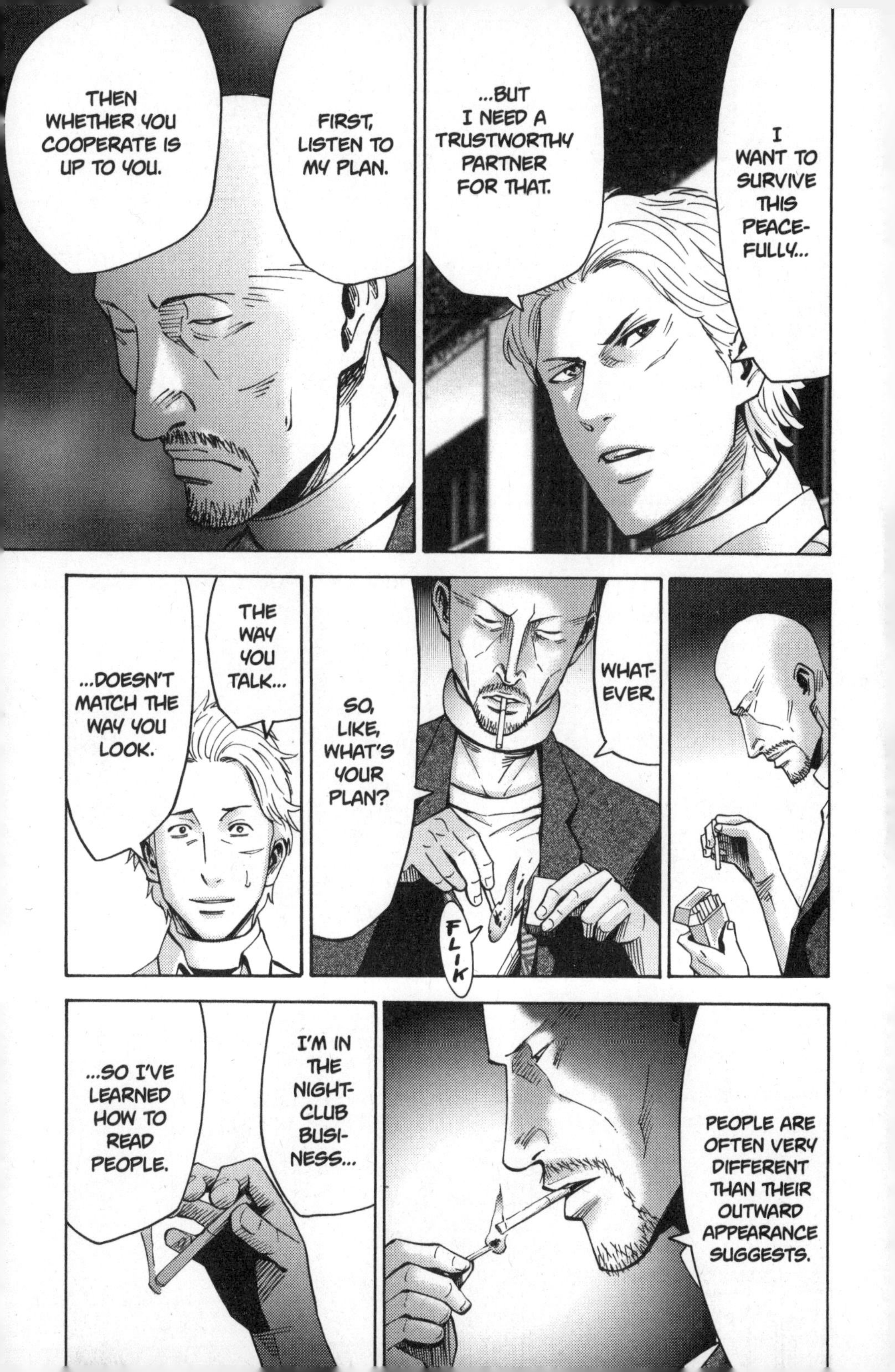
I WANT TO SURVIVE THIS PEACE-FULLY...
...BUT I NEED A TRUSTWORTHY PARTNER FOR THAT.
FIRST, LISTEN TO MY PLAN.
THEN WHETHER YOU COOPERATE IS UP TO YOU.
WHAT-EVER.
SO, LIKE, WHAT'S YOUR PLAN?
FLIK
THE WAY YOU TALK...
...DOESN'T MATCH THE WAY YOU LOOK.
PEOPLE ARE OFTEN VERY DIFFERENT THAN THEIR OUTWARD APPEARANCE SUGGESTS.
I'M IN THE NIGHT-CLUB BUSI-NESS...
...SO I'VE LEARNED HOW TO READ PEOPLE.

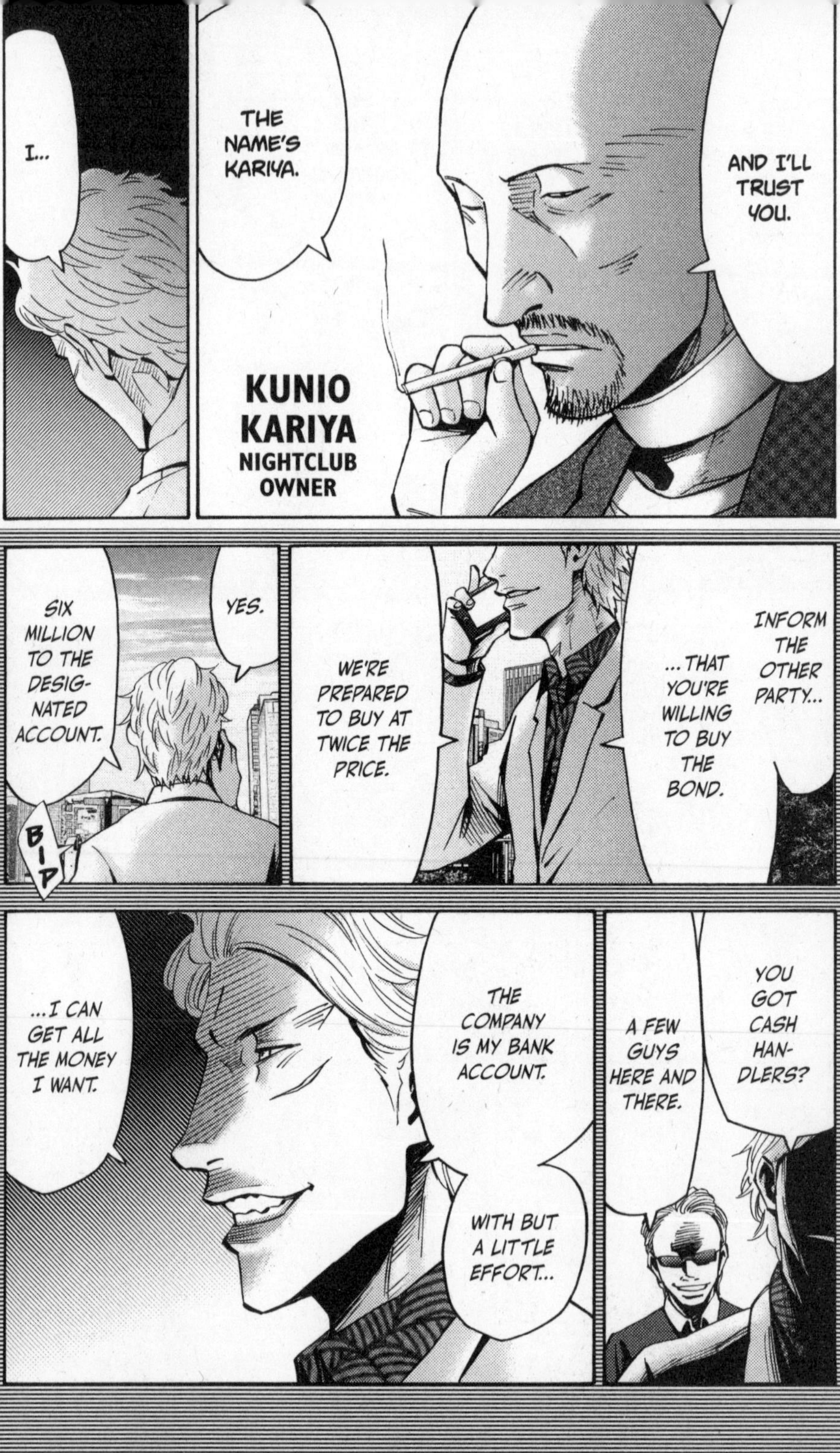
AND I'LL TRUST YOU.
THE NAME'S KARIYA.
KUNIO KARIYA NIGHTCLUB OWNER
I...
INFORM THE OTHER PARTY...
...THAT YOU'RE WILLING TO BUY THE BOND.
WE'RE PREPARED TO BUY AT TWICE THE PRICE.
YES.
SIX MILLION TO THE DESIGNATED ACCOUNT.
BIP
YOU GOT CASH HANDLERS?
A FEW GUYS HERE AND THERE.
THE COMPANY IS MY BANK ACCOUNT.
WITH BUT A LITTLE EFFORT...
...I CAN GET ALL THE MONEY I WANT.

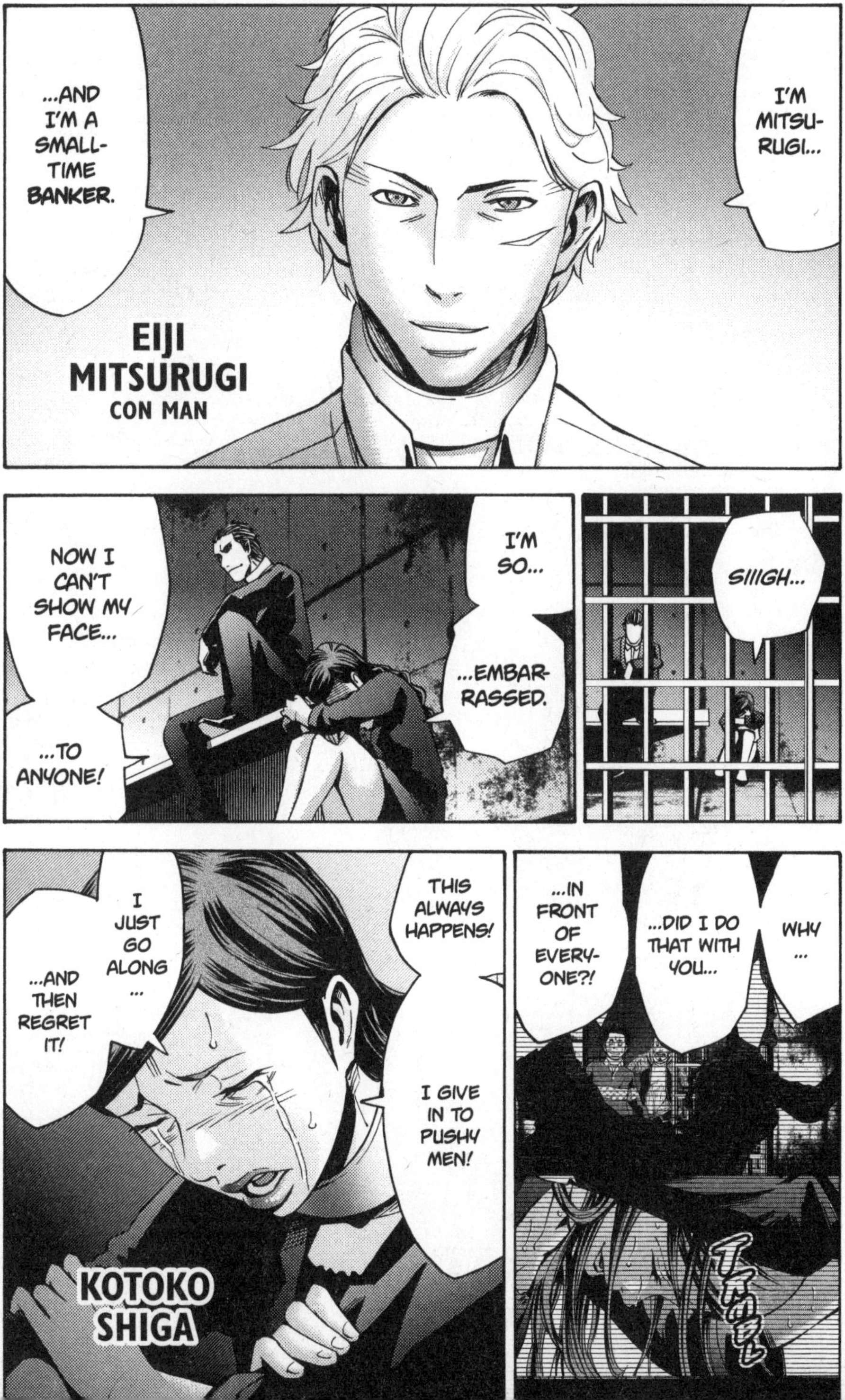
I'M MITSU-RUGI...
...AND I'M A SMALL-TIME BANKER.
EIJI MITSURUGI
CON MAN
SIIIGH...
I'M SO...
...EMBAR-RASSED.
NOW I CAN'T SHOW MY FACE...
...TO ANYONE!
WHY ...
...DID I DO THAT WITH YOU...
...IN FRONT OF EVERY-ONE?!
THIS ALWAYS HAPPENS!
I JUST GO ALONG ...
...AND THEN REGRET IT!
I GIVE IN TO PUSHY MEN!
KOTOKO SHIGA

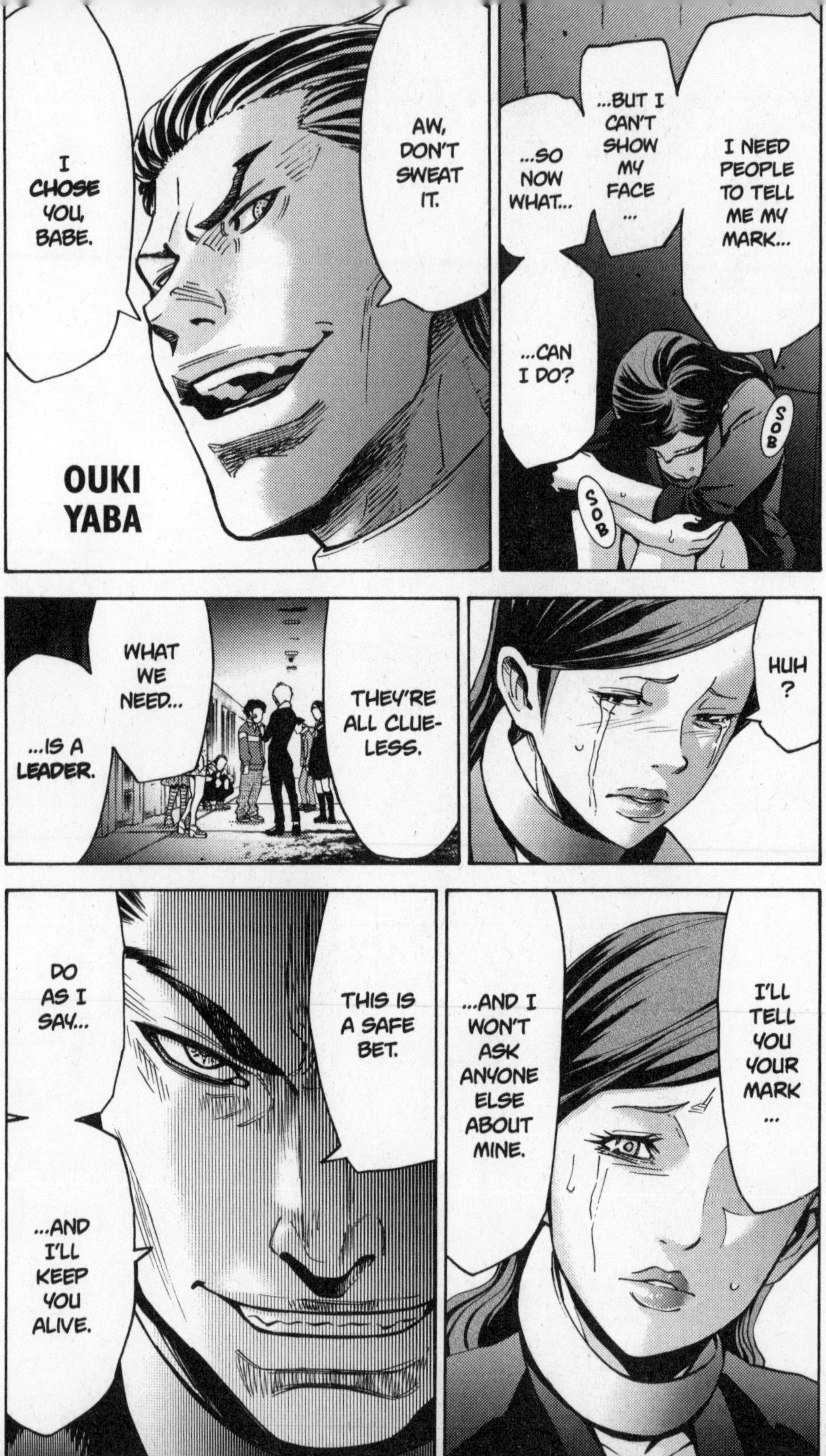
I NEED PEOPLE TO TELL ME MY MARK...
...BUT I CAN'T SHOW MY FACE...
...SO NOW WHAT...
...CAN I DO?
SOB
SOB
AW, DON'T SWEAT IT.
I CHOSE YOU, BABE.
OUKI YABA
HUH?
THEY'RE ALL CLUELESS.
WHAT WE NEED...
...IS A LEADER.
I'LL TELL YOU YOUR MARK...
...AND I WON'T ASK ANYONE ELSE ABOUT MINE.
THIS IS A SAFE BET.
DO AS I SAY...
...AND I'LL KEEP YOU ALIVE.

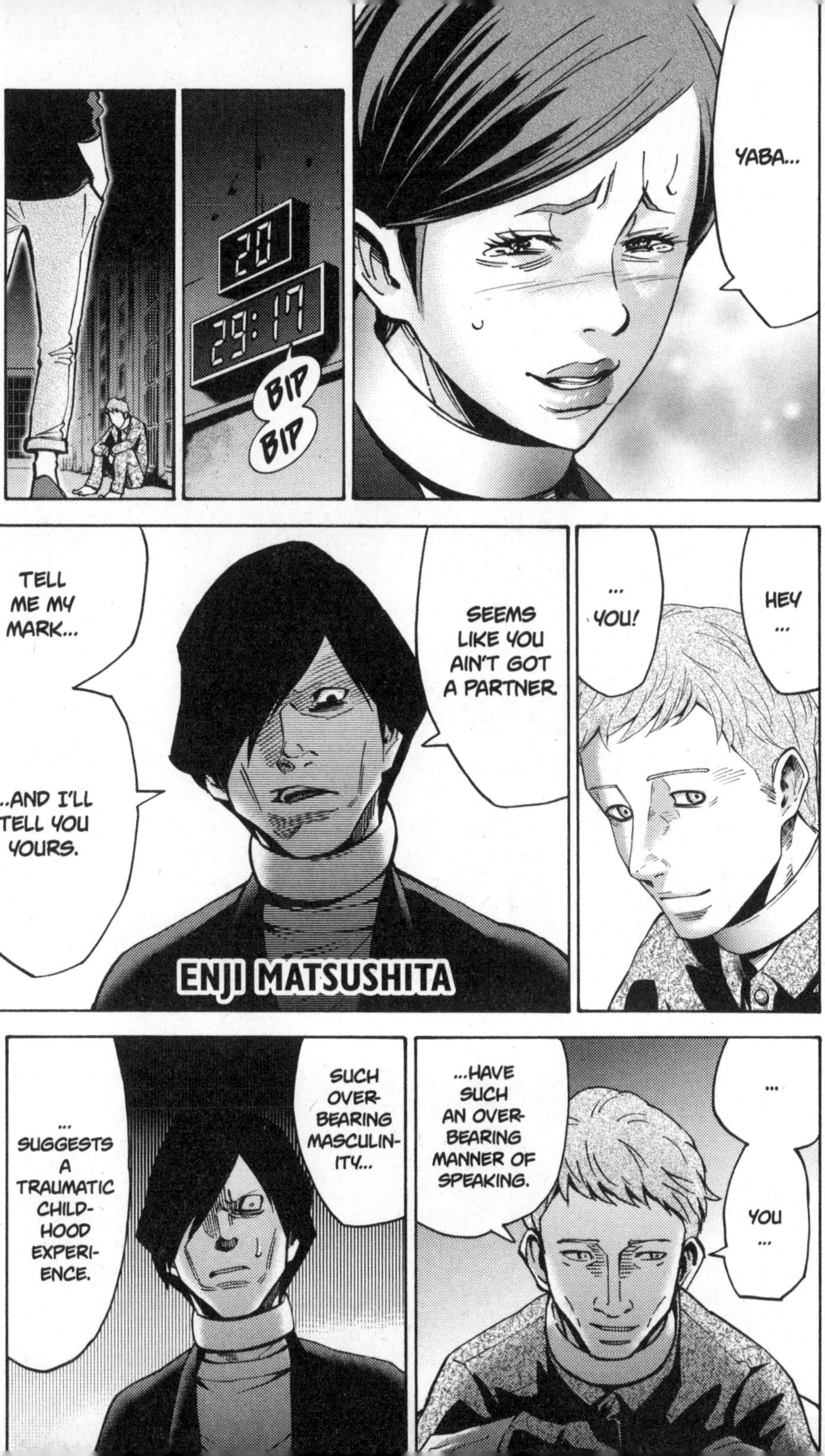
YABA...
20
29:17
BIP BIP
HEY ...
... YOU!
SEEMS LIKE YOU AIN'T GOT A PARTNER.
TELL ME MY MARK...
...AND I'LL TELL YOU YOURS.
ENJI MATSUSHITA
...
YOU ...
...HAVE SUCH AN OVER-BEARING MANNER OF SPEAKING.
SUCH OVER-BEARING MASCULIN-ITY...
... SUGGESTS A TRAUMATIC CHILD-HOOD EXPERI-ENCE.

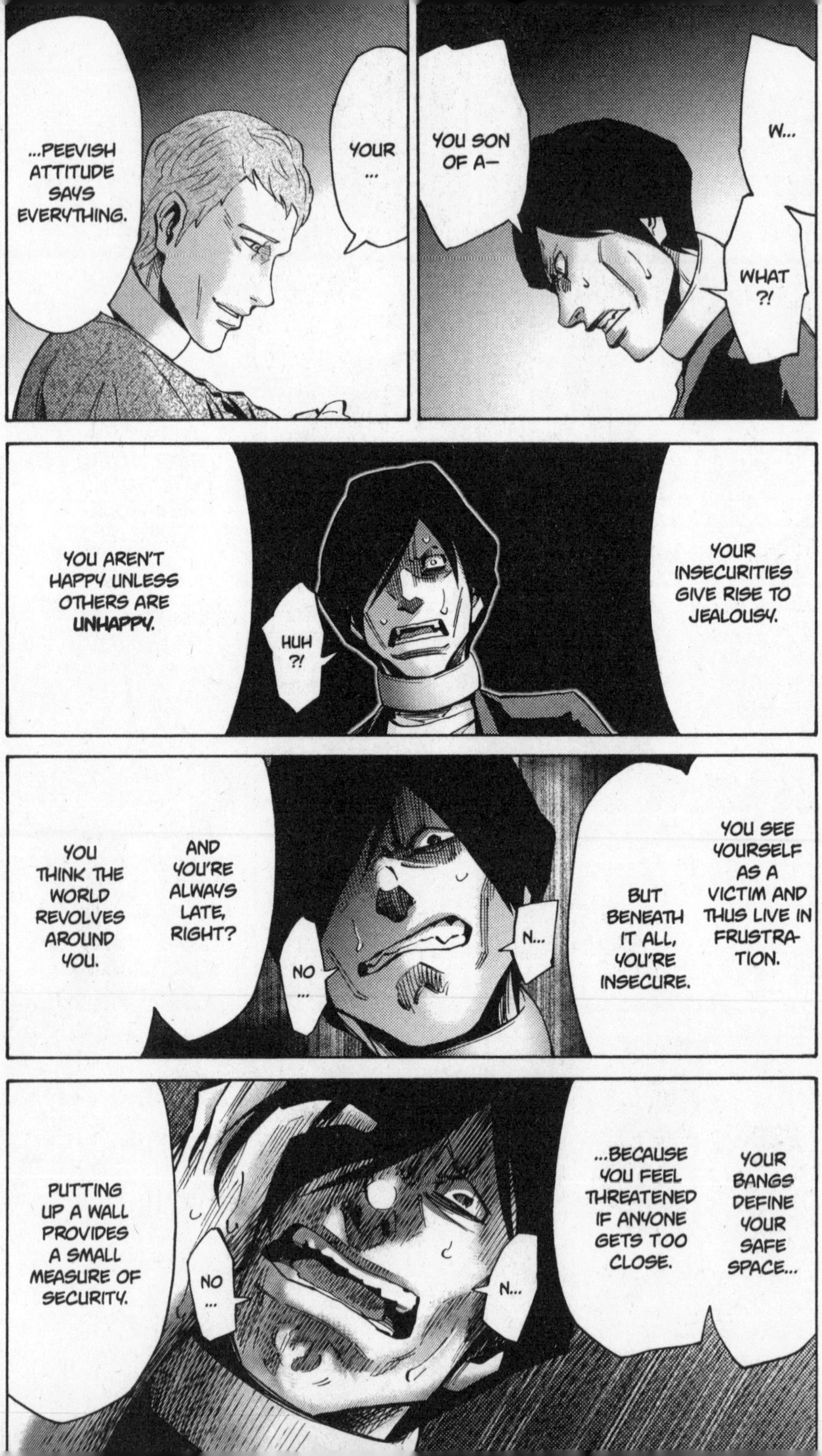

W...
WHAT ?!
YOU SON OF A—
YOUR ...
...PEEVISH ATTITUDE SAYS EVERYTHING.
YOUR INSECURITIES GIVE RISE TO JEALOUSY.
HUH ?!
YOU AREN'T HAPPY UNLESS OTHERS ARE **UNHAPPY**.
YOU SEE YOURSELF AS A VICTIM AND THUS LIVE IN FRUSTRATION.
BUT BENEATH IT ALL, YOU'RE INSECURE.
N...
NO ...
AND YOU'RE ALWAYS LATE, RIGHT?
YOU THINK THE WORLD REVOLVES AROUND YOU.
YOUR BANGS DEFINE YOUR SAFE SPACE...
...BECAUSE YOU FEEL THREATENED IF ANYONE GETS TOO CLOSE.
N...
NO ...
PUTTING UP A WALL PROVIDES A SMALL MEASURE OF SECURITY.

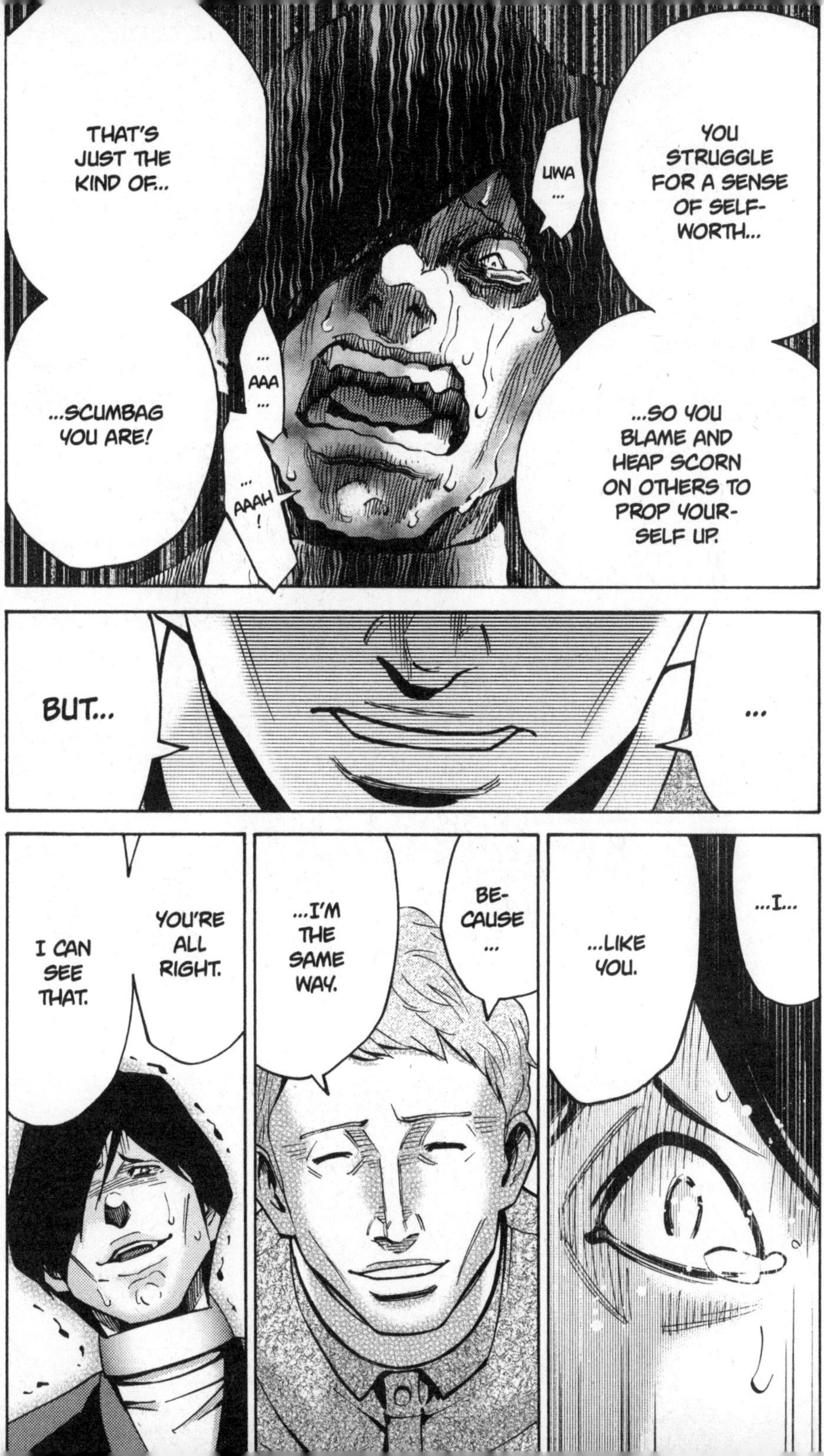
YOU STRUGGLE FOR A SENSE OF SELF-WORTH...
UWA ...
...SO YOU BLAME AND HEAP SCORN ON OTHERS TO PROP YOURSELF UP.
THAT'S JUST THE KIND OF...
... AAA ...
... AAAH !
...SCUMBAG YOU ARE!
...
BUT...
...I...
...LIKE YOU.
BE-CAUSE ...
...I'M THE SAME WAY.
YOU'RE ALL RIGHT.
I CAN SEE THAT.

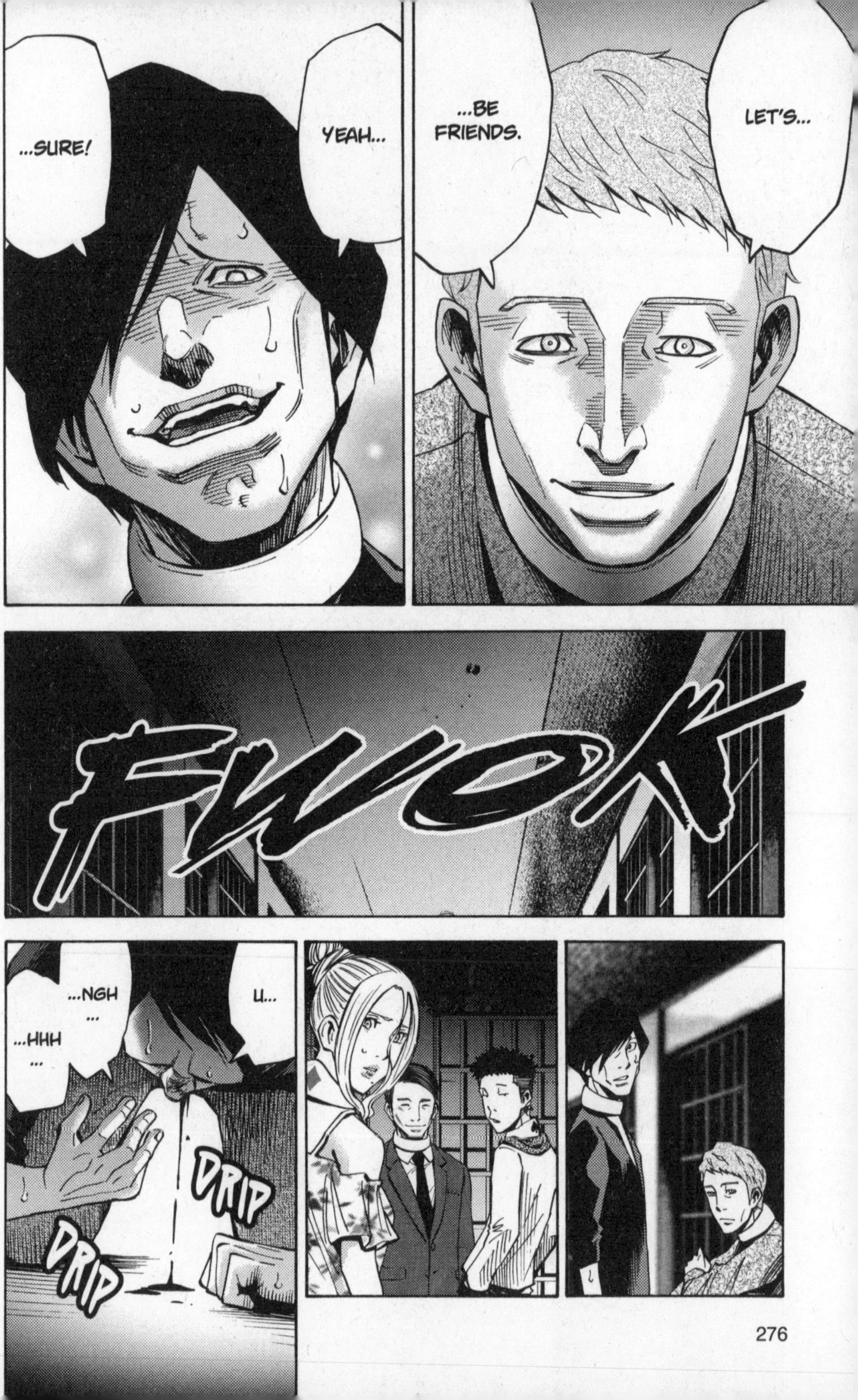
LET'S...
...BE FRIENDS.
YEAH...
...SURE!
FWOK
U...
...NGH ...
...HHH ...
DRIP
DRIP

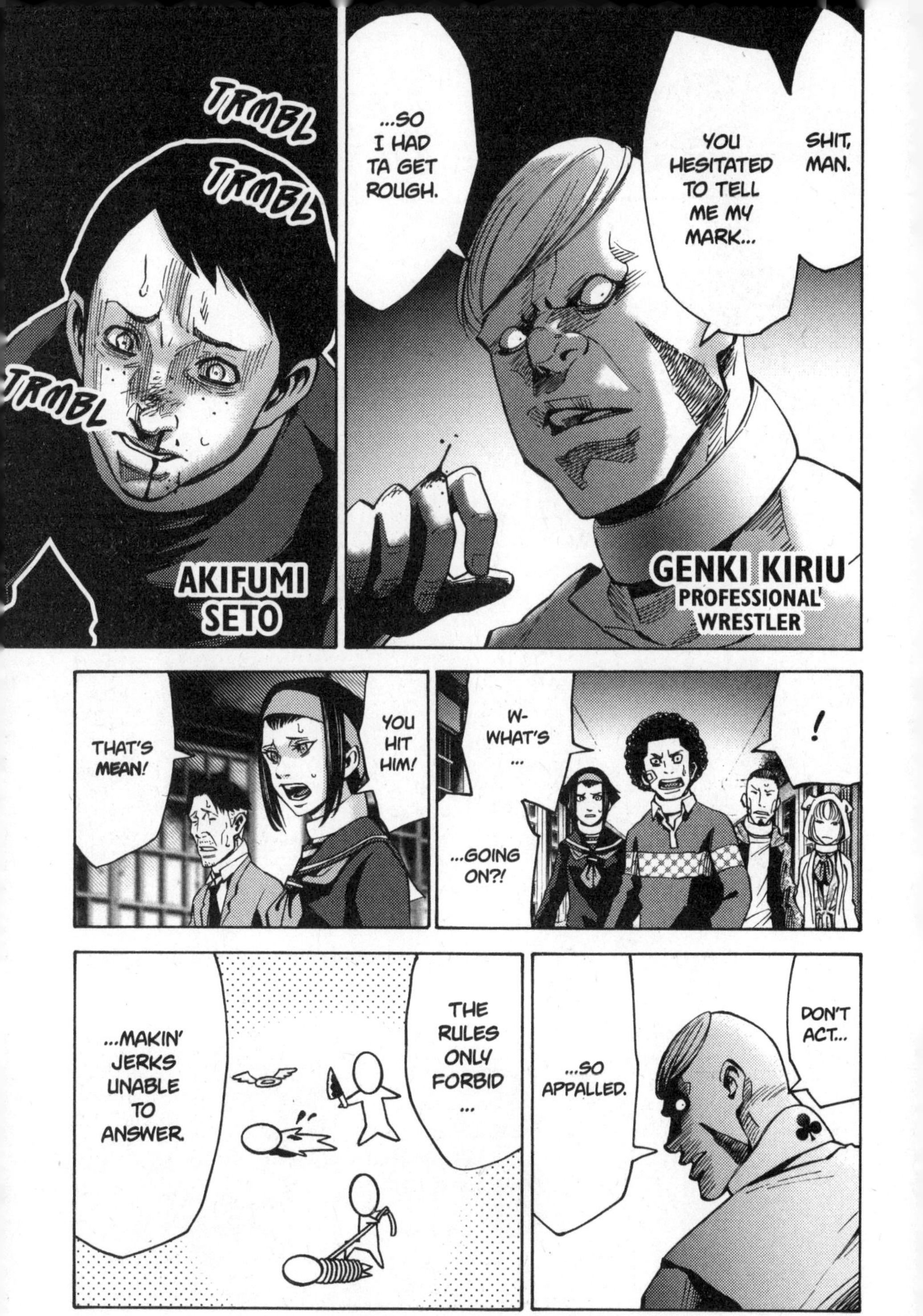
SHIT, MAN.
YOU HESITATED TO TELL ME MY MARK...
...SO I HAD TA GET ROUGH.
GENKI KIRIU
PROFESSIONAL WRESTLER
TRMBL
TRMBL
TRMBL
AKIFUMI SETO
!
W- WHAT'S ...
...GOING ON?!
YOU HIT HIM!
THAT'S MEAN!
DON'T ACT...
...SO APPALLED.
THE RULES ONLY FORBID ...
...MAKIN' JERKS UNABLE TO ANSWER.

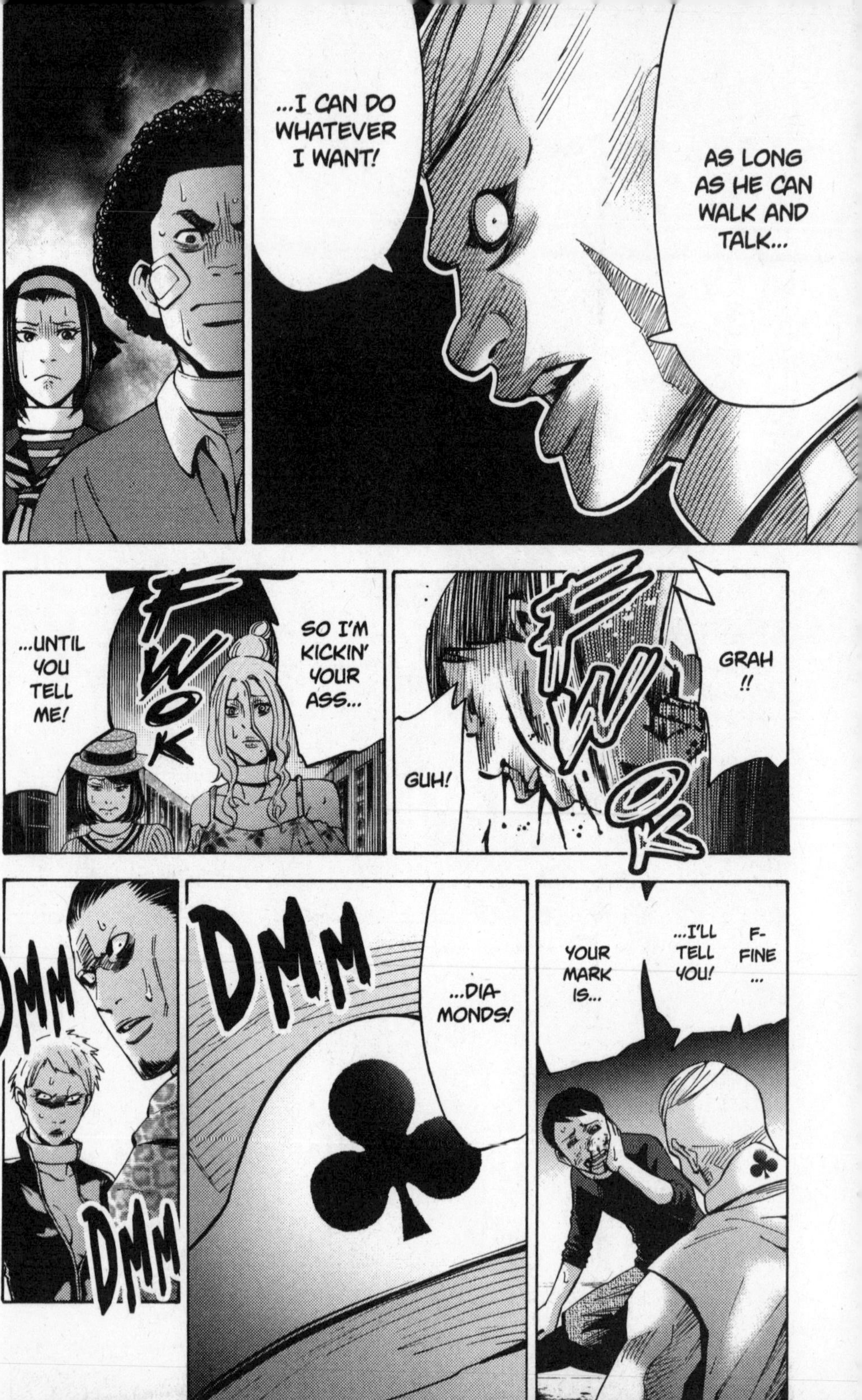
AS LONG AS HE CAN WALK AND TALK...
...I CAN DO WHATEVER I WANT!
GRAH!!
FWOK
GUH!
SO I'M KICKIN' YOUR ASS...
...UNTIL YOU TELL ME!
FWOK
F-FINE...
...I'LL TELL YOU!
YOUR MARK IS...
...DIAMONDS!
DMM
DMM
DMM

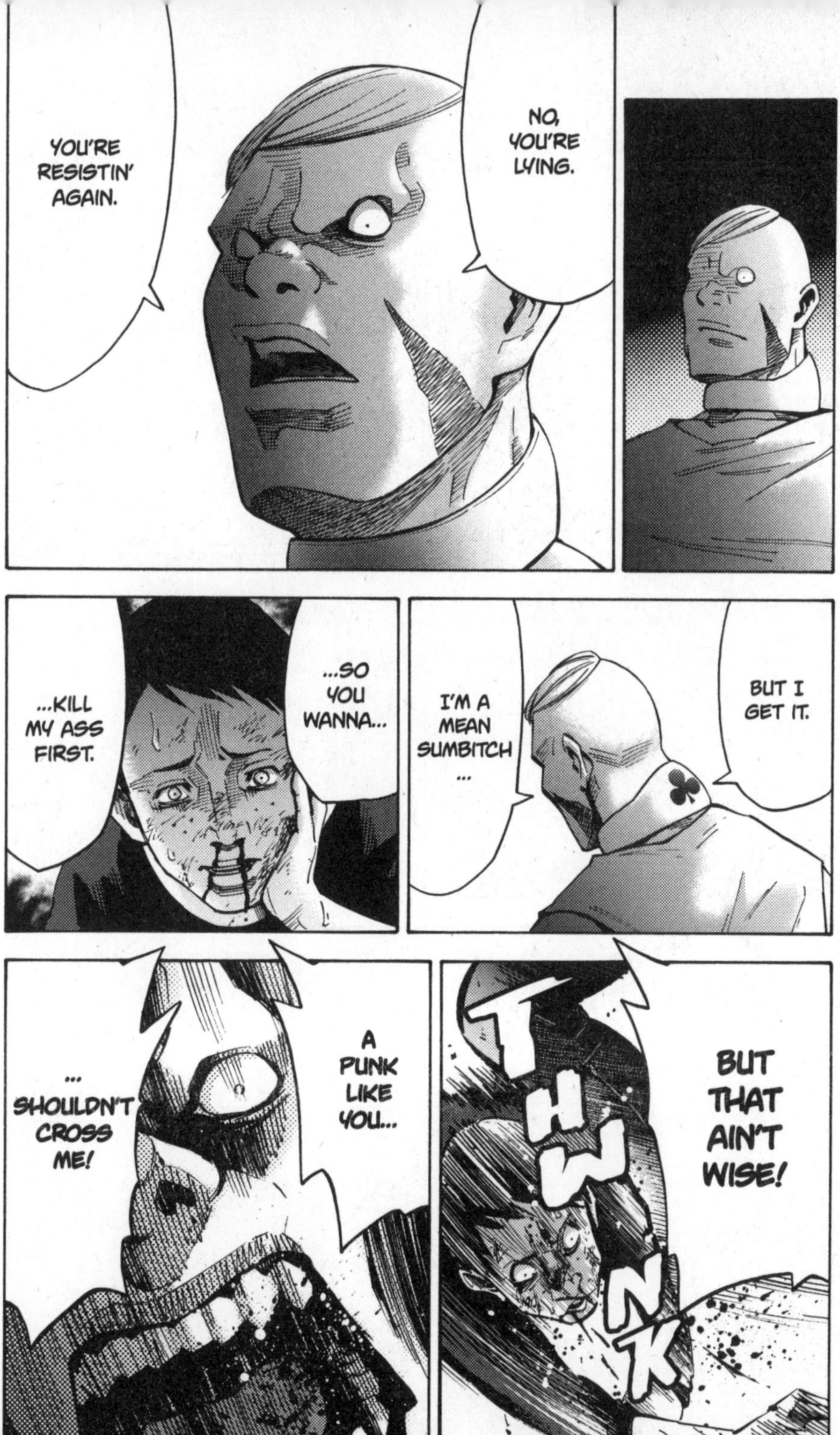
NO, YOU'RE LYING.
YOU'RE RESISTIN' AGAIN.
BUT I GET IT.
I'M A MEAN SUMBITCH ...
...SO YOU WANNA...
...KILL MY ASS FIRST.
BUT THAT AIN'T WISE!
THWNK
A PUNK LIKE YOU...
... SHOULDN'T CROSS ME!

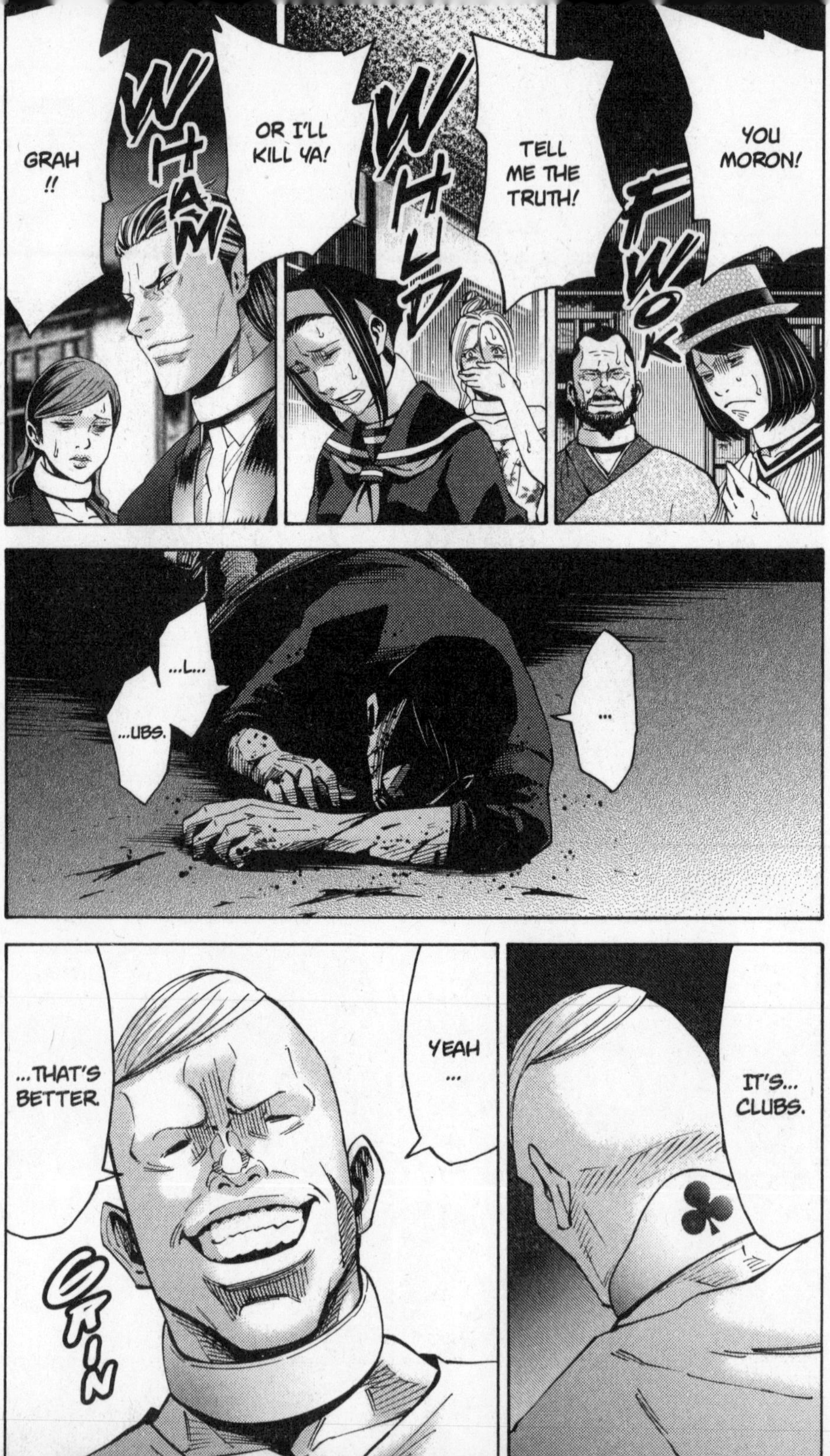
YOU MORON!
FWOK
TELL ME THE TRUTH!
WHUD
OR I'LL KILL YA!
WHAM
GRAH !!
...
...L...
...UBS.
IT'S... CLUBS.
YEAH ...
...THAT'S BETTER.
GRIN

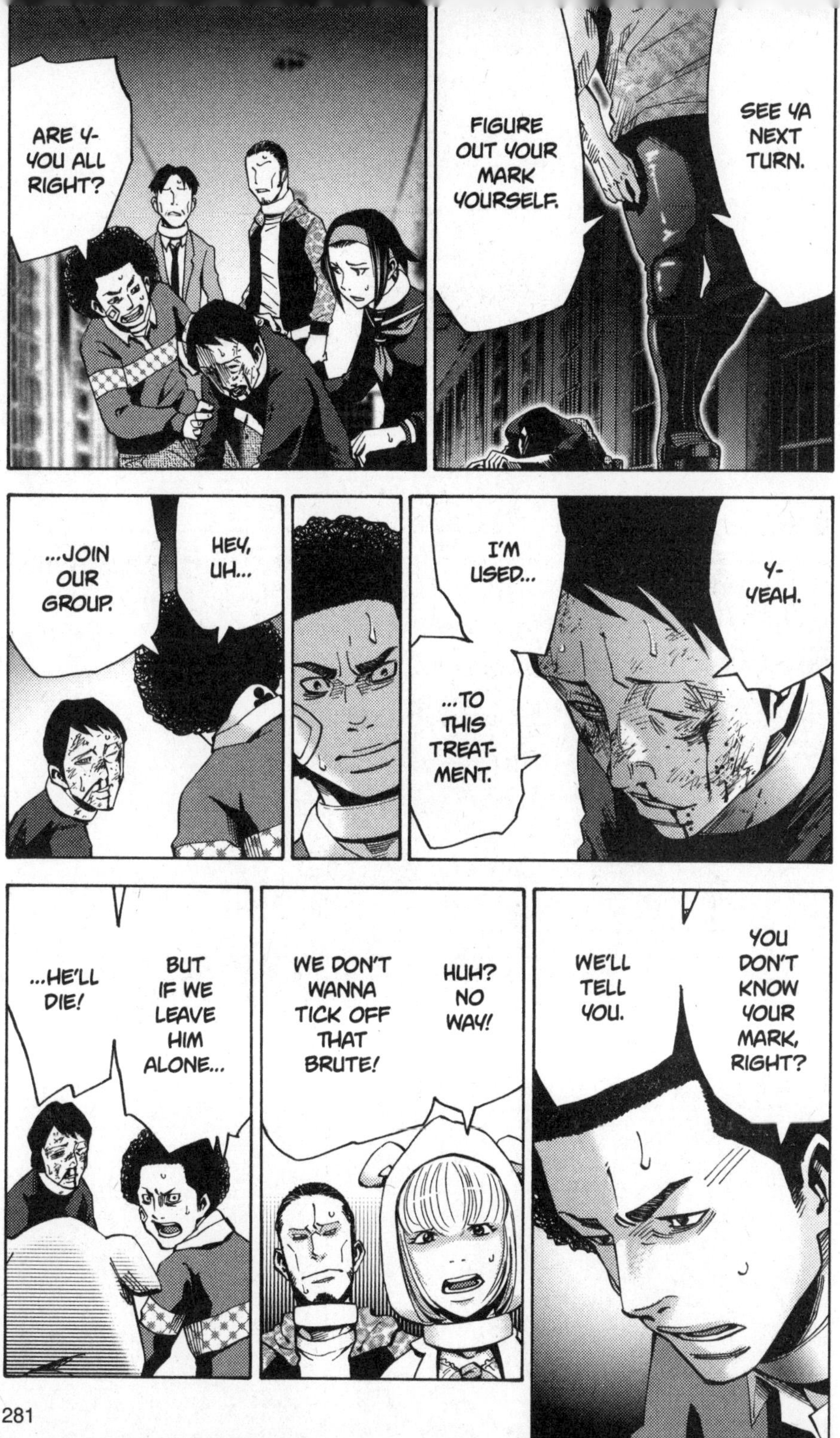
SEE YA NEXT TURN.
FIGURE OUT YOUR MARK YOURSELF.
ARE Y-YOU ALL RIGHT?
Y-YEAH.
I'M USED...
...TO THIS TREATMENT.
HEY, UH...
...JOIN OUR GROUP.
YOU DON'T KNOW YOUR MARK, RIGHT?
WE'LL TELL YOU.
HUH? NO WAY!
WE DON'T WANNA TICK OFF THAT BRUTE!
BUT IF WE LEAVE HIM ALONE...
...HE'LL DIE!

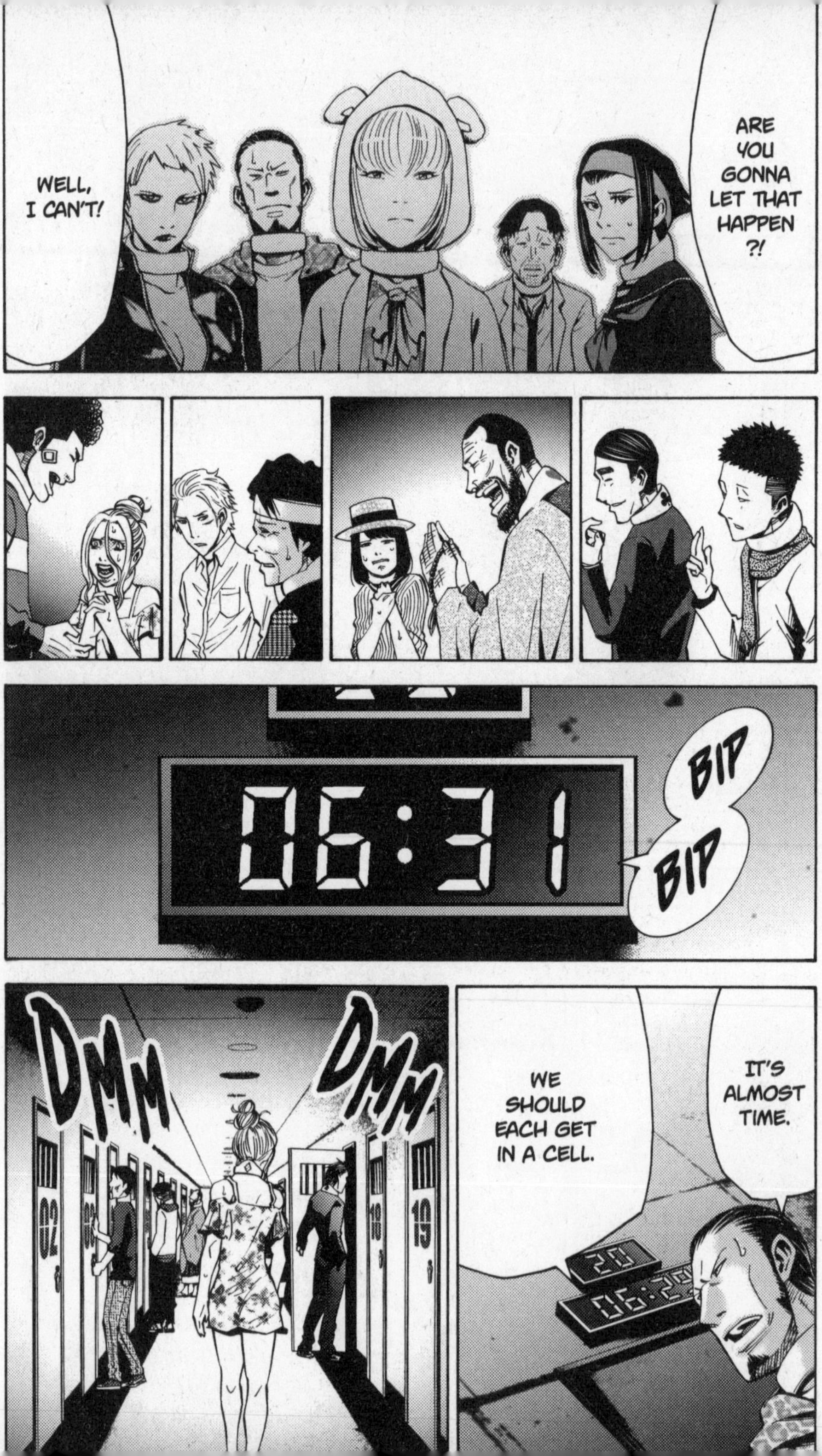
ARE YOU GONNA LET THAT HAPPEN ?!
WELL, I CAN'T!
06:31
BIP
BIP
IT'S ALMOST TIME.
WE SHOULD EACH GET IN A CELL.
DMM
DMM

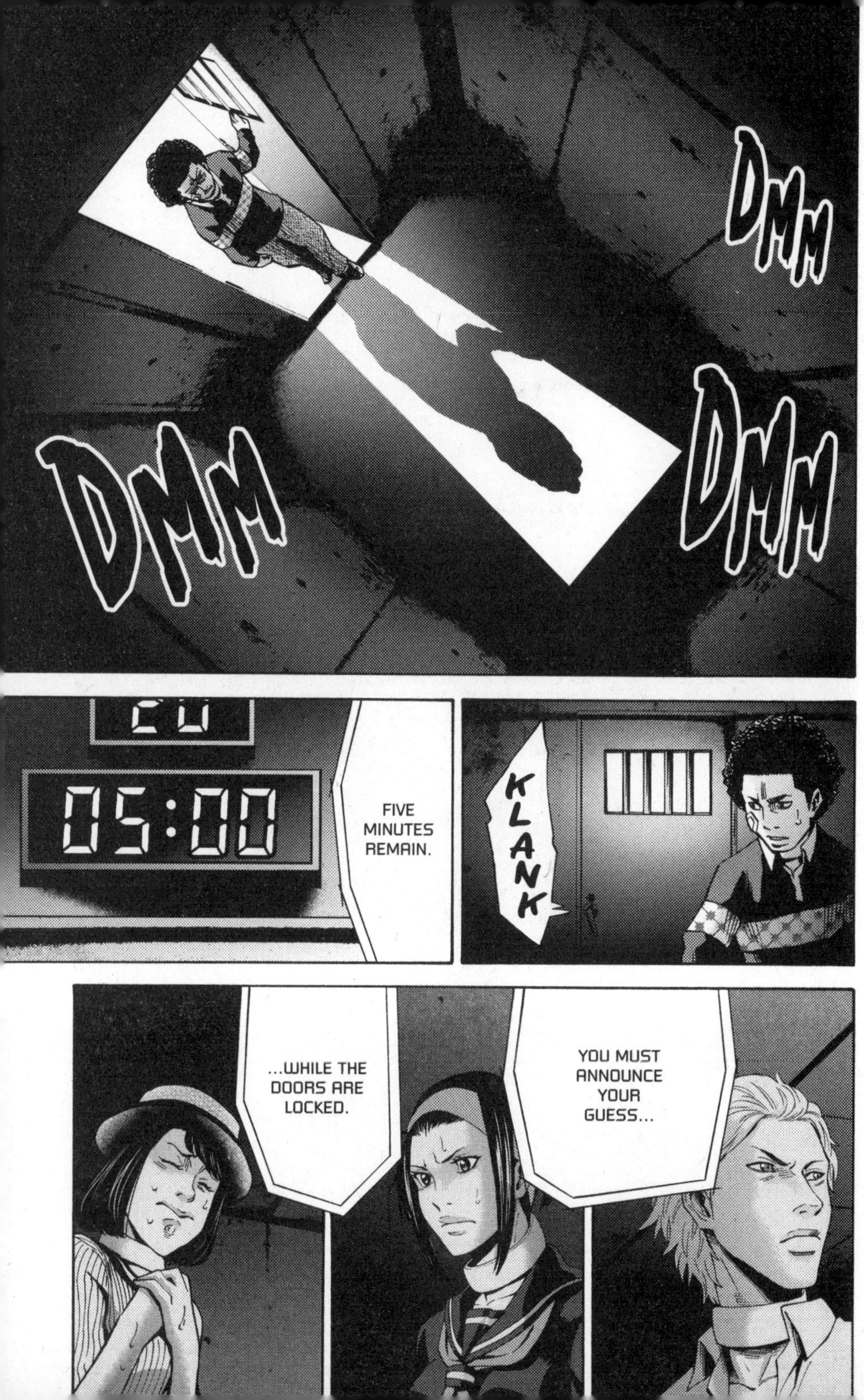
DMM
DMM
DMM
KLANK
05:00
FIVE MINUTES REMAIN.
YOU MUST ANNOUNCE YOUR GUESS...
...WHILE THE DOORS ARE LOCKED.

...SPADES! S-s-s...

DIA-MONDS!

CLUBS!

HEARTS!

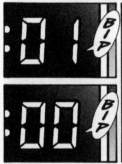
:01 BIP
:00 BIP

PLEASE, BE HEARTS!

DIA-MONDS. D...

CLUBS.

SPADES!

OUT OF THE ORIGINAL 20 PARTICIPANTS...

...THE NUMBER OF ROUND ONE SURVIVORS IS...

TIME'S UP.

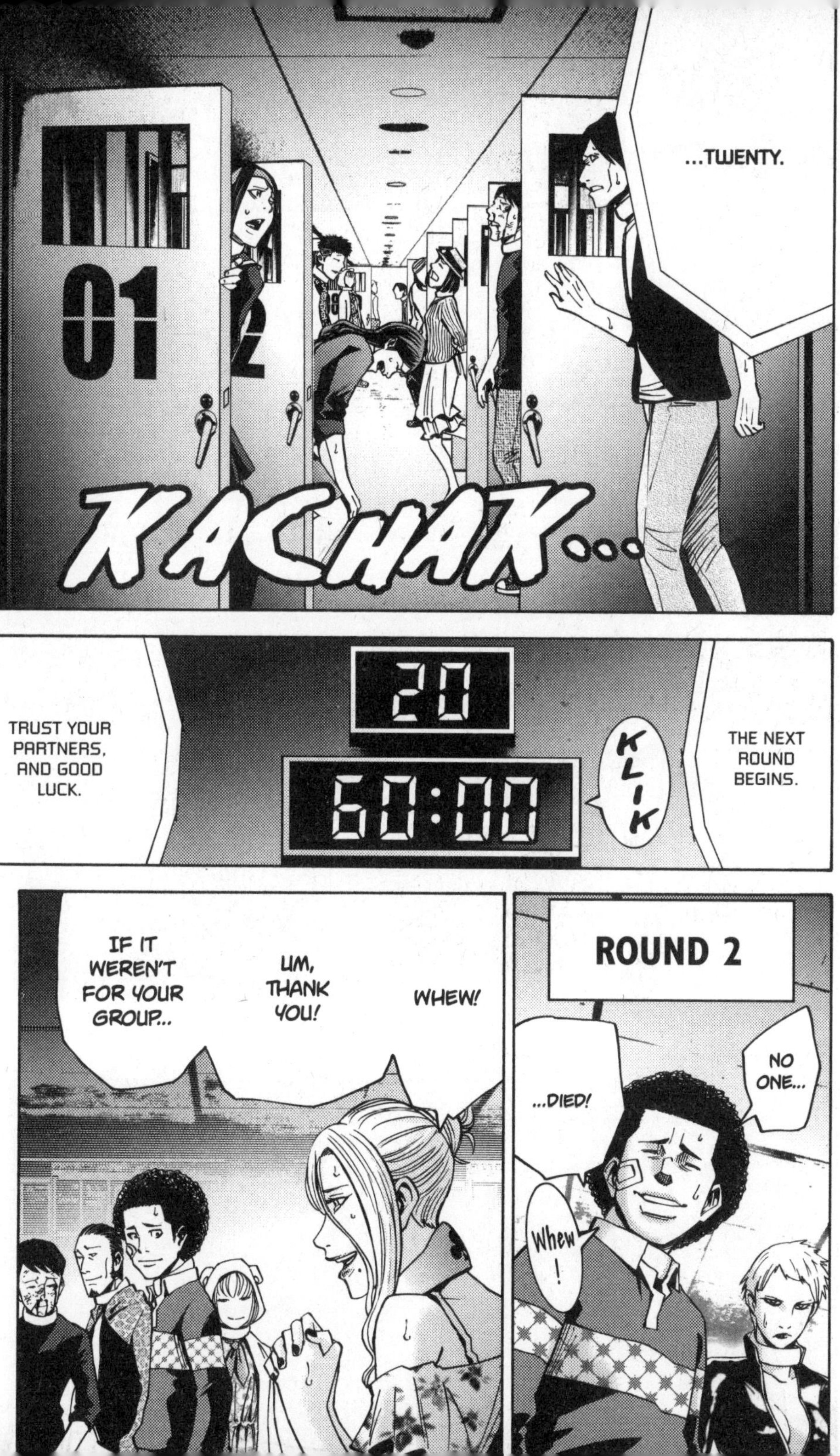
...TWENTY.
01
2
KACHAK...
THE NEXT ROUND BEGINS.
KLIK
20
60:00
TRUST YOUR PARTNERS, AND GOOD LUCK.
ROUND 2
NO ONE...
...DIED!
Whew!
WHEW!
UM, THANK YOU!
IF IT WEREN'T FOR YOUR GROUP...

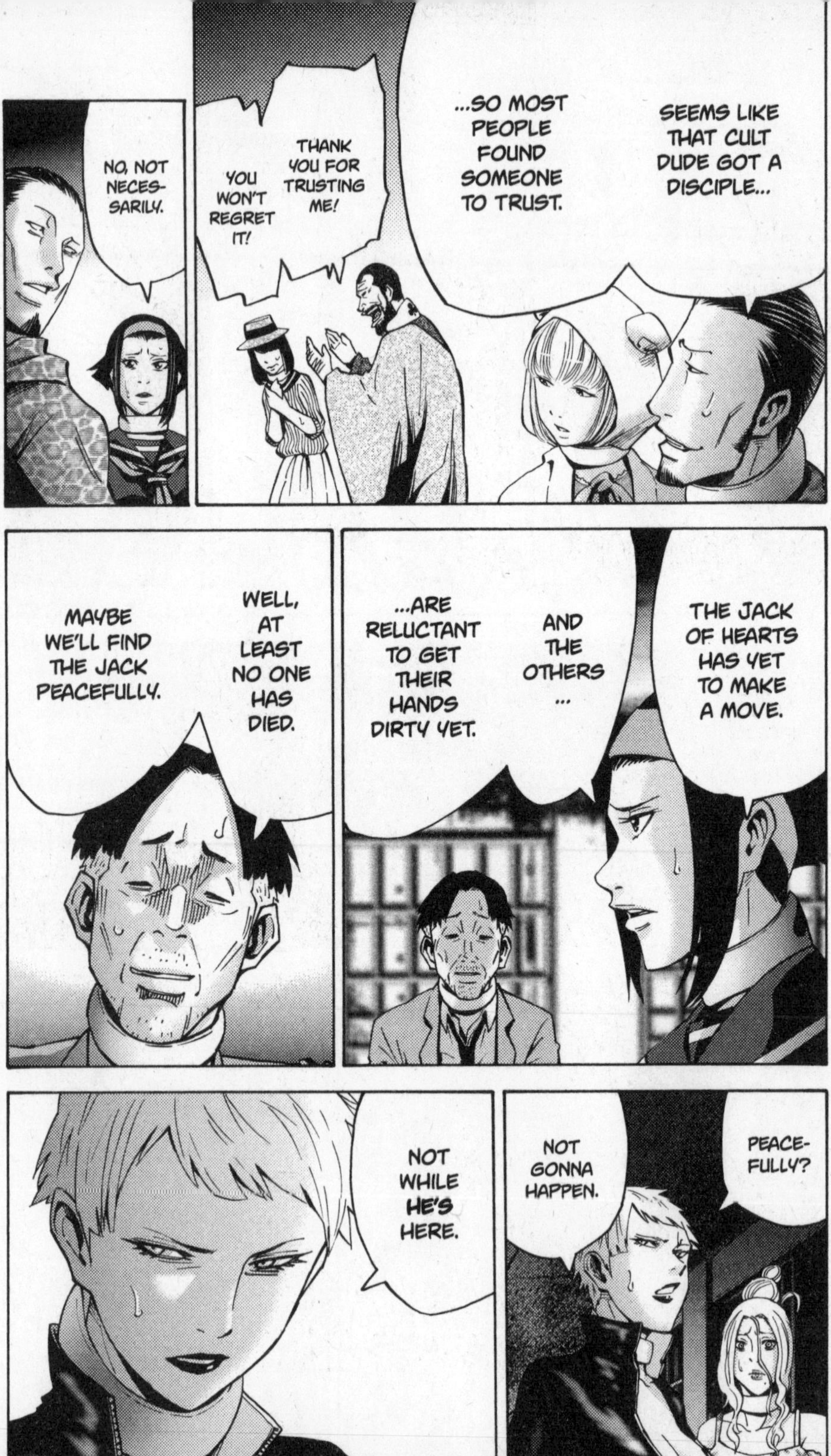
SEEMS LIKE THAT CULT DUDE GOT A DISCIPLE...
...SO MOST PEOPLE FOUND SOMEONE TO TRUST.
THANK YOU FOR TRUSTING ME!
YOU WON'T REGRET IT!
NO, NOT NECES-SARILY.
THE JACK OF HEARTS HAS YET TO MAKE A MOVE.
AND THE OTHERS ...
...ARE RELUCTANT TO GET THEIR HANDS DIRTY YET.
WELL, AT LEAST NO ONE HAS DIED.
MAYBE WE'LL FIND THE JACK PEACEFULLY.
PEACE-FULLY?
NOT GONNA HAPPEN.
NOT WHILE HE'S HERE.

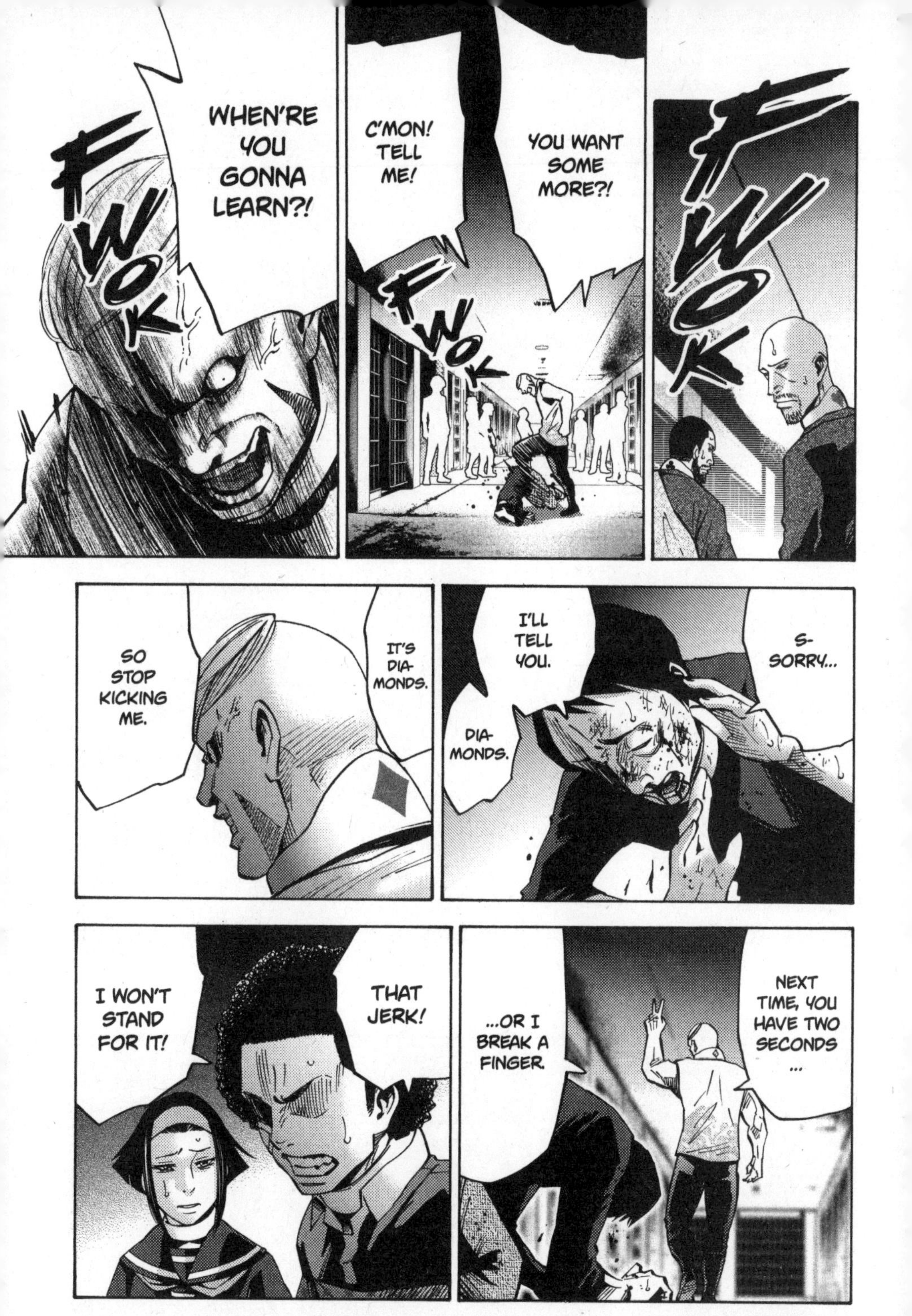
FWOK
YOU WANT SOME MORE?!
C'MON! TELL ME!
FWOK
WHEN'RE YOU GONNA LEARN?!
FWOK
S-SORRY...
I'LL TELL YOU.
DIAMONDS.
IT'S DIAMONDS.
SO STOP KICKING ME.
NEXT TIME, YOU HAVE TWO SECONDS ...
...OR I BREAK A FINGER.
THAT JERK!
I WON'T STAND FOR IT!

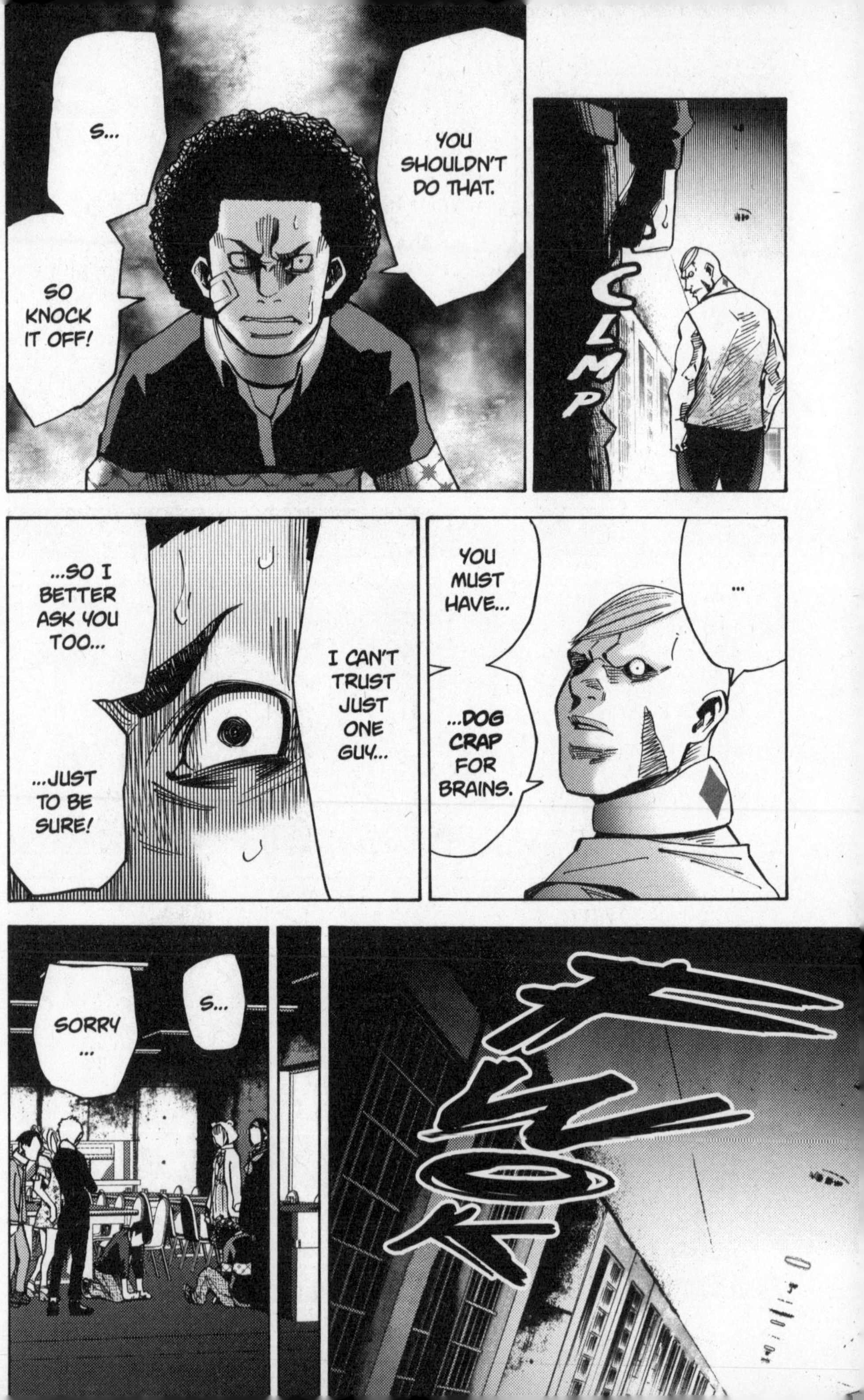
CLMP
YOU SHOULDN'T DO THAT.
S...
SO KNOCK IT OFF!
...
YOU MUST HAVE...
...DOG CRAP FOR BRAINS.
I CAN'T TRUST JUST ONE GUY...
...SO I BETTER ASK YOU TOO...
...JUST TO BE SURE!
S...
SORRY ...

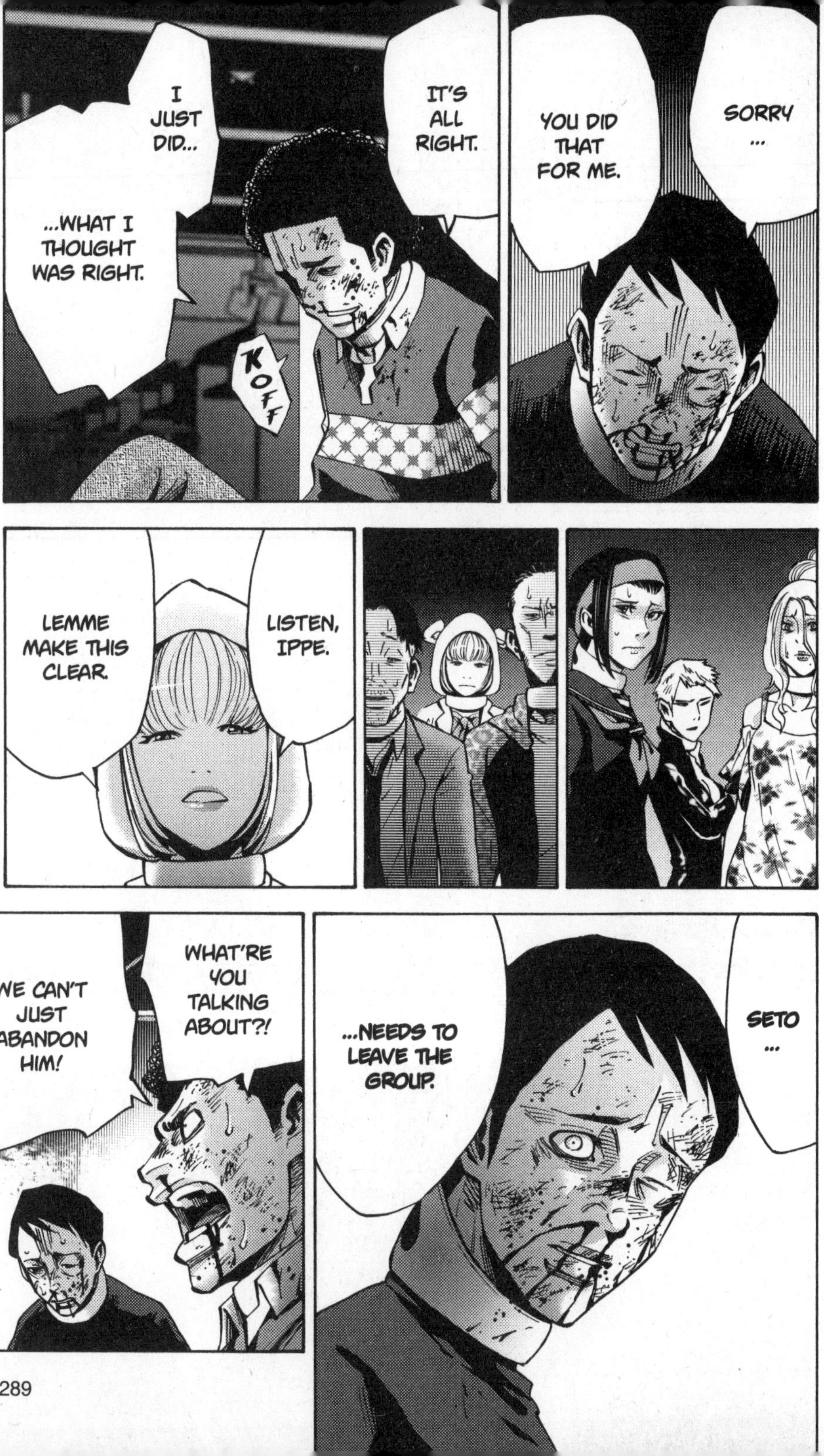
SORRY ...
YOU DID THAT FOR ME.
IT'S ALL RIGHT.
I JUST DID...
...WHAT I THOUGHT WAS RIGHT.
KOFF
LISTEN, IPPE.
LEMME MAKE THIS CLEAR.
SETO ...
...NEEDS TO LEAVE THE GROUP.
WHAT'RE YOU TALKING ABOUT?!
WE CAN'T JUST ABANDON HIM!

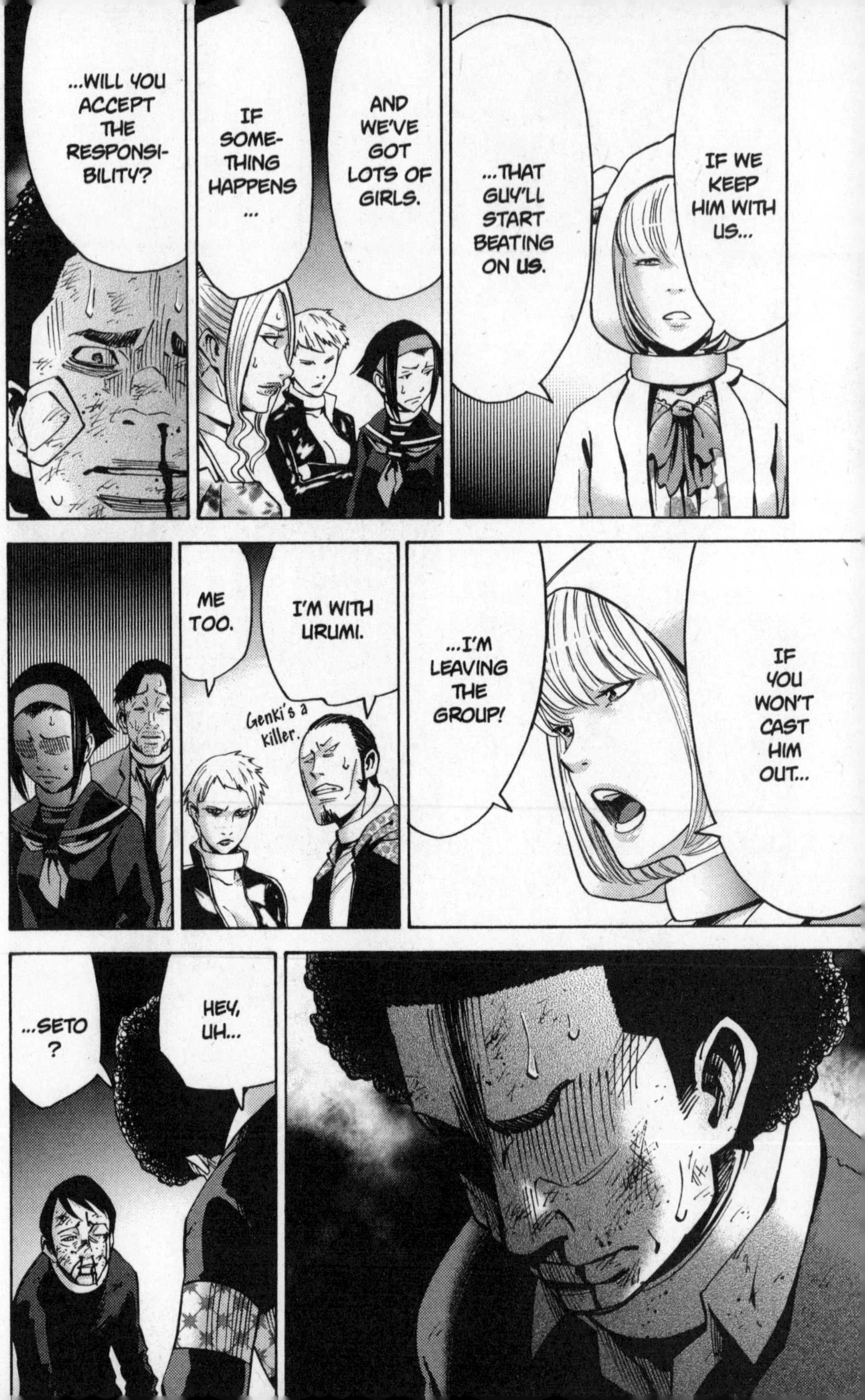
IF WE KEEP HIM WITH US...
...THAT GUY'LL START BEATING ON US.
AND WE'VE GOT LOTS OF GIRLS.
IF SOME-THING HAPPENS...
...WILL YOU ACCEPT THE RESPONSI-BILITY?
IF YOU WON'T CAST HIM OUT...
...I'M LEAVING THE GROUP!
I'M WITH URUMI.
Genki's a killer.
ME TOO.
HEY, UH...
...SETO?

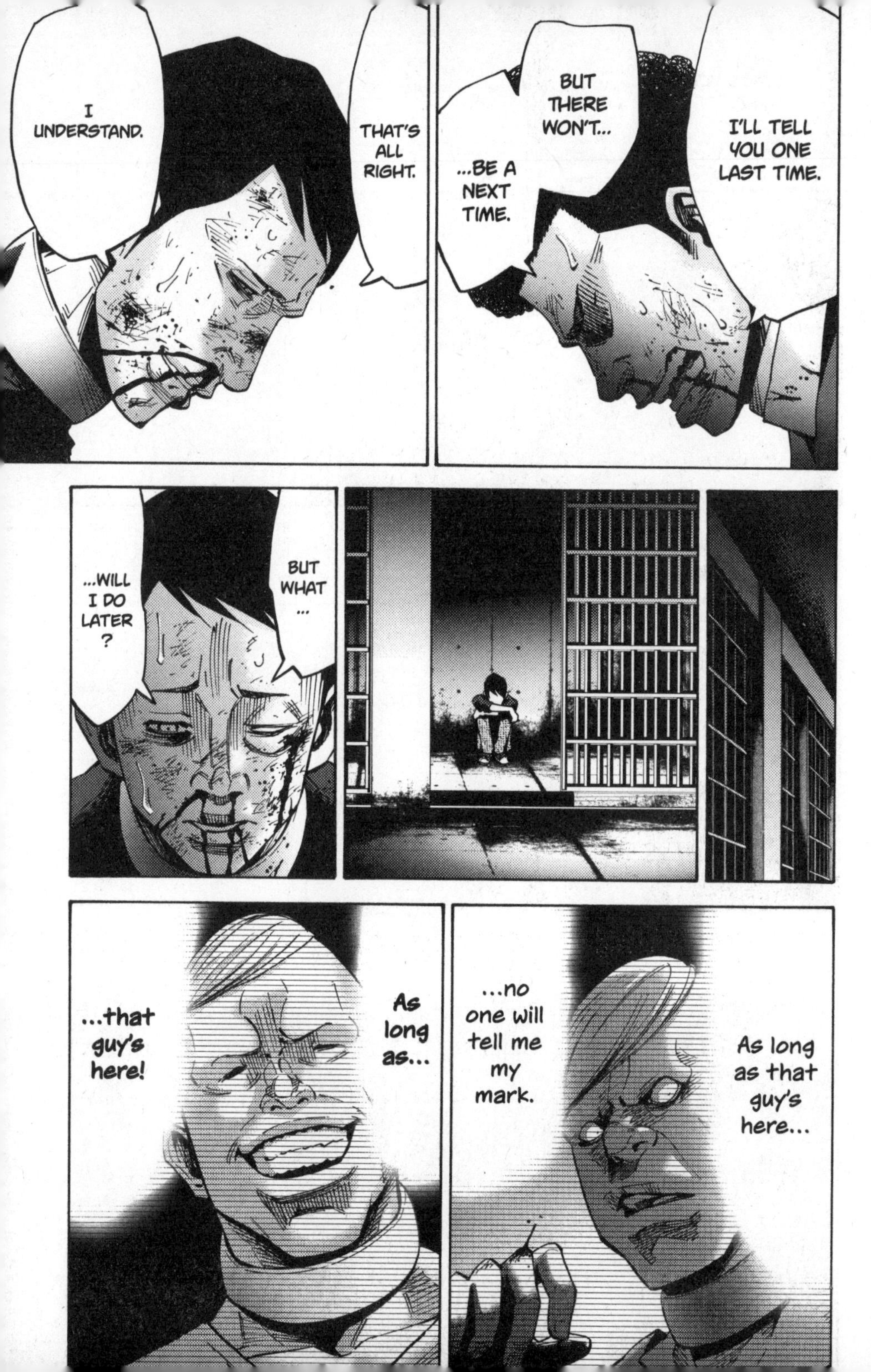
I'LL TELL YOU ONE LAST TIME.
BUT THERE WON'T...
...BE A NEXT TIME.
THAT'S ALL RIGHT.
I UNDERSTAND.
BUT WHAT ...
...WILL I DO LATER ?
As long as that guy's here...
...no one will tell me my mark.
As long as...
...that guy's here!

"KILL THAT MAN."

...IT WASN'T MINE.

IF YOU JUST HEARD A FAINT VOICE...

TMP

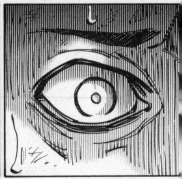

IT WAS YOUR OWN.

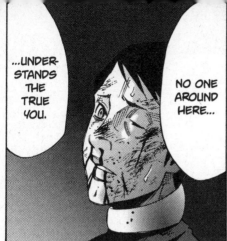

THAT BRUTE UNDERESTIMATES YOU...
...AS DO THE OTHERS.
NO ONE AROUND HERE...
...UNDERSTANDS THE TRUE YOU.
BUT I CAN SEE YOUR SPRY, VIOLENT, INTENSE FEROCITY.
ONLY I UNDERSTAND THE TRUE YOU.
YOU CAN BE SO MUCH MORE.
SO...
...IT'S TIME TO RISE.

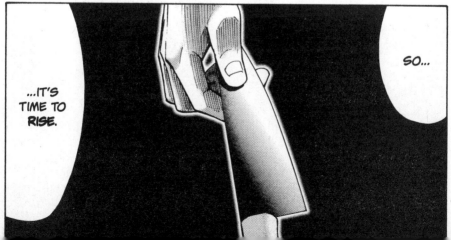

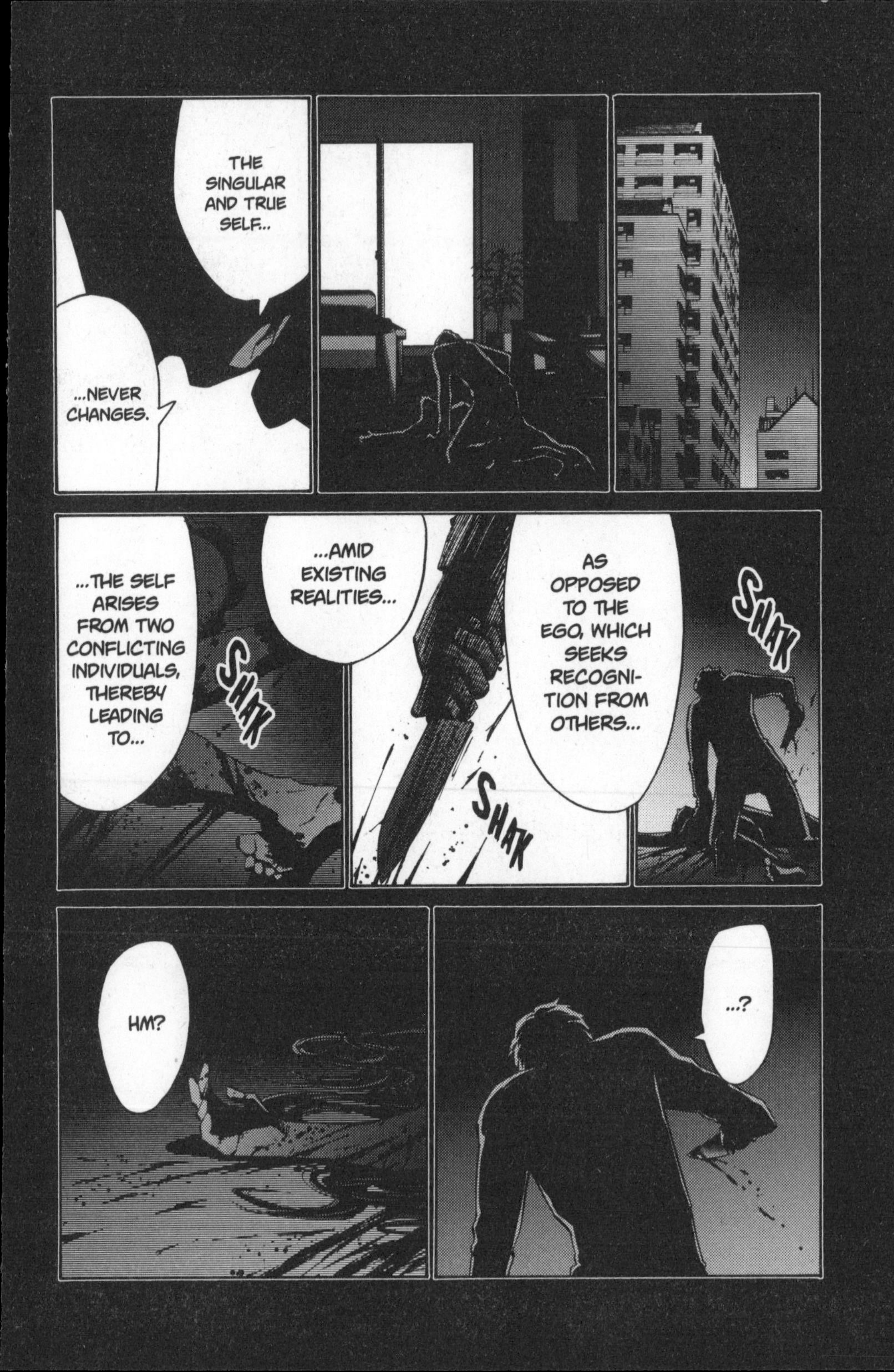
THE SINGULAR AND TRUE SELF...
...NEVER CHANGES.
SHAK
AS OPPOSED TO THE EGO, WHICH SEEKS RECOGNITION FROM OTHERS...
SHAK
...AMID EXISTING REALITIES...
...THE SELF ARISES FROM TWO CONFLICTING INDIVIDUALS, THEREBY LEADING TO...
SHAK
...?
HM?

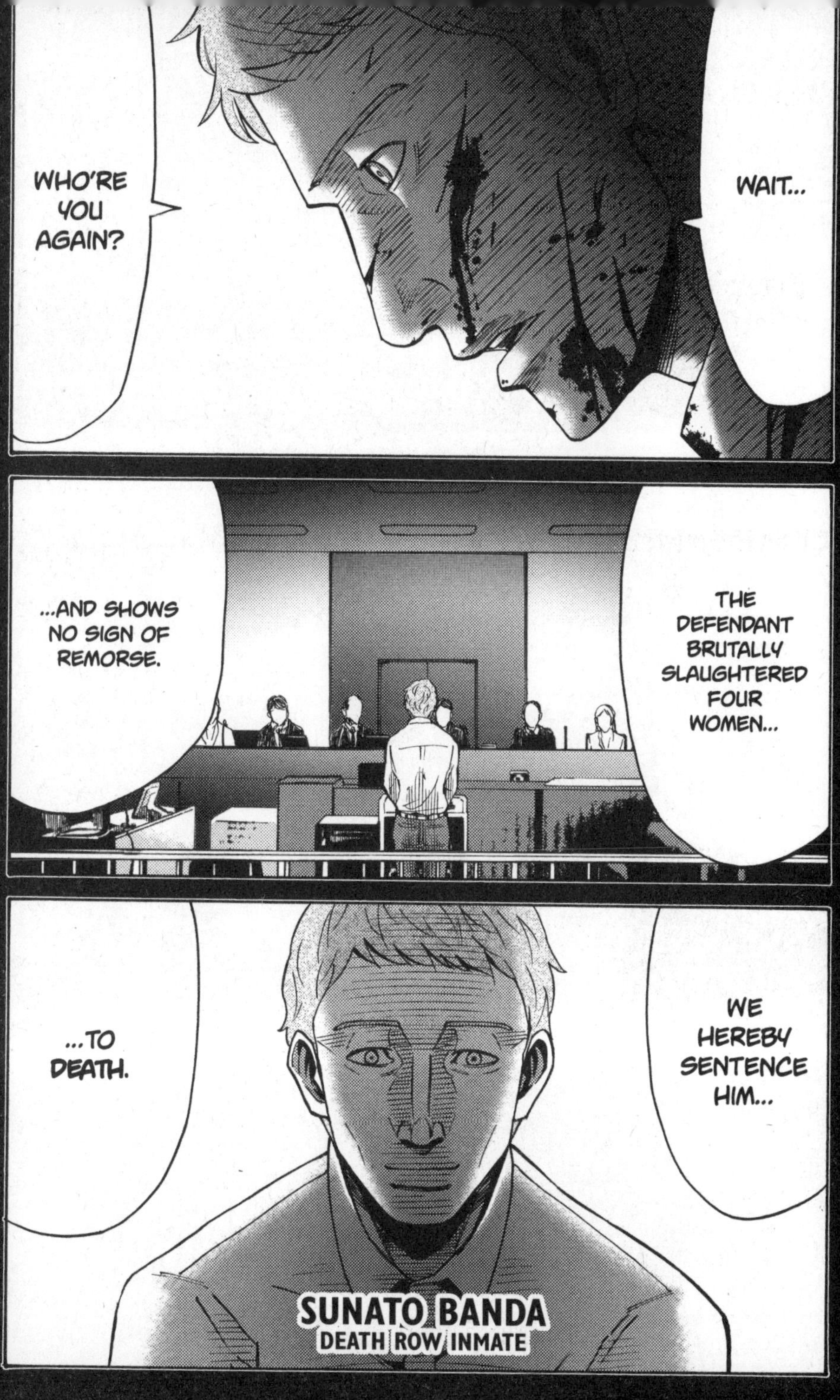
WAIT...
WHO'RE YOU AGAIN?
THE DEFENDANT BRUTALLY SLAUGHTERED FOUR WOMEN...
...AND SHOWS NO SIGN OF REMORSE.
WE HEREBY SENTENCE HIM...
...TO DEATH.
SUNATO BANDA
DEATH ROW INMATE

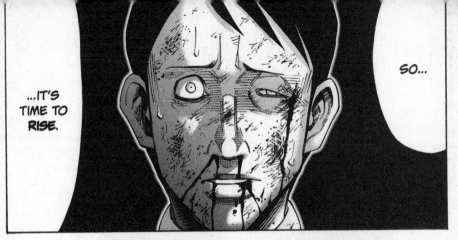

SO...

...IT'S TIME TO RISE.

IF YOU KILL HIM...

...NO ONE WILL MESS WITH YOU AGAIN.

I'M...

...WITH YOU ALL THE WAY!

HA ...

...HA HA!

CHAPTER 46: Jack of Hearts, Part 2

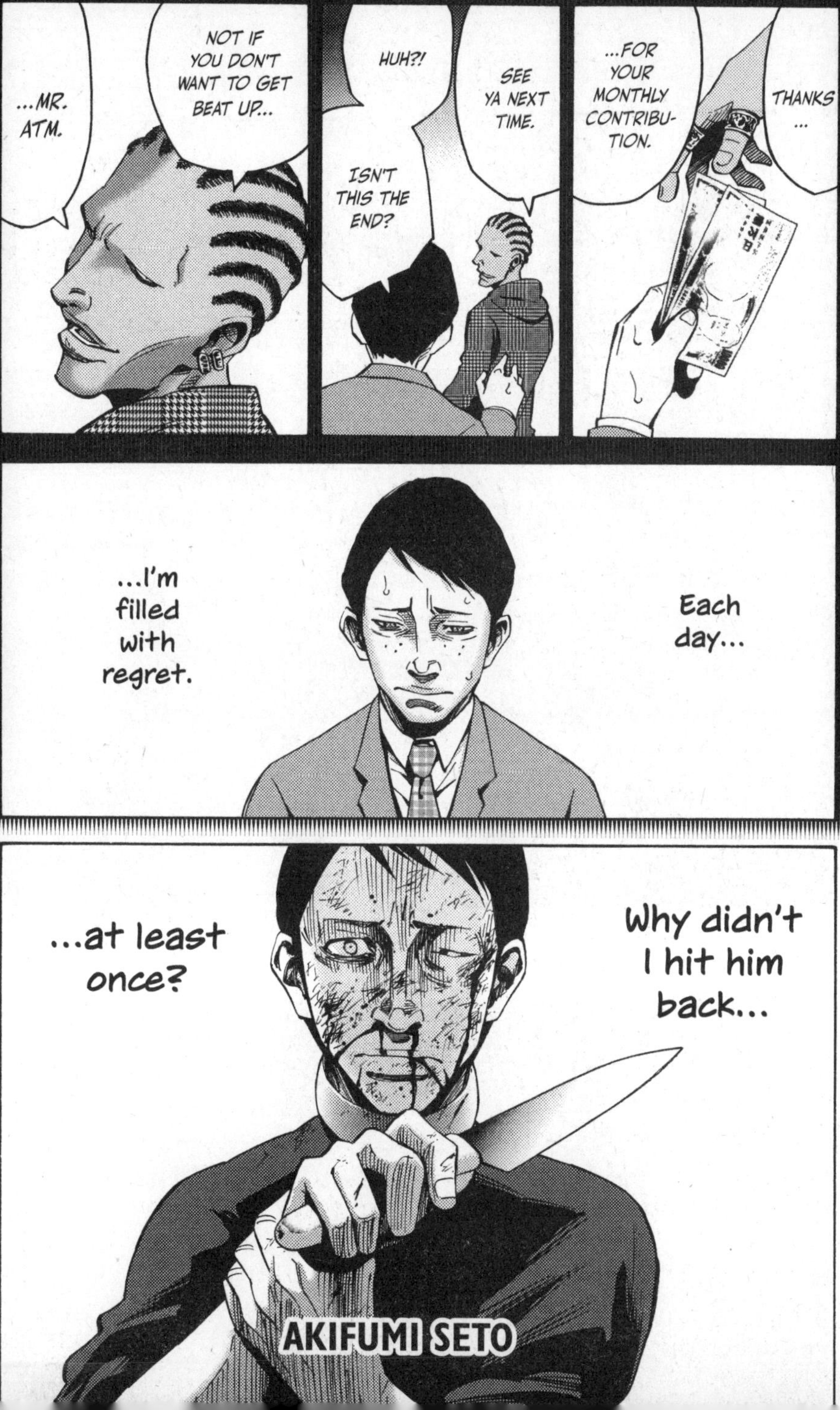
THANKS ...
...FOR YOUR MONTHLY CONTRIBU-TION.
SEE YA NEXT TIME.
HUH?!
ISN'T THIS THE END?
NOT IF YOU DON'T WANT TO GET BEAT UP...
...MR. ATM.
Each day...
...I'm filled with regret.
Why didn't I hit him back...
...at least once?
AKIFUMI SETO

CHAPTER 46: Jack of Hearts, Part 2

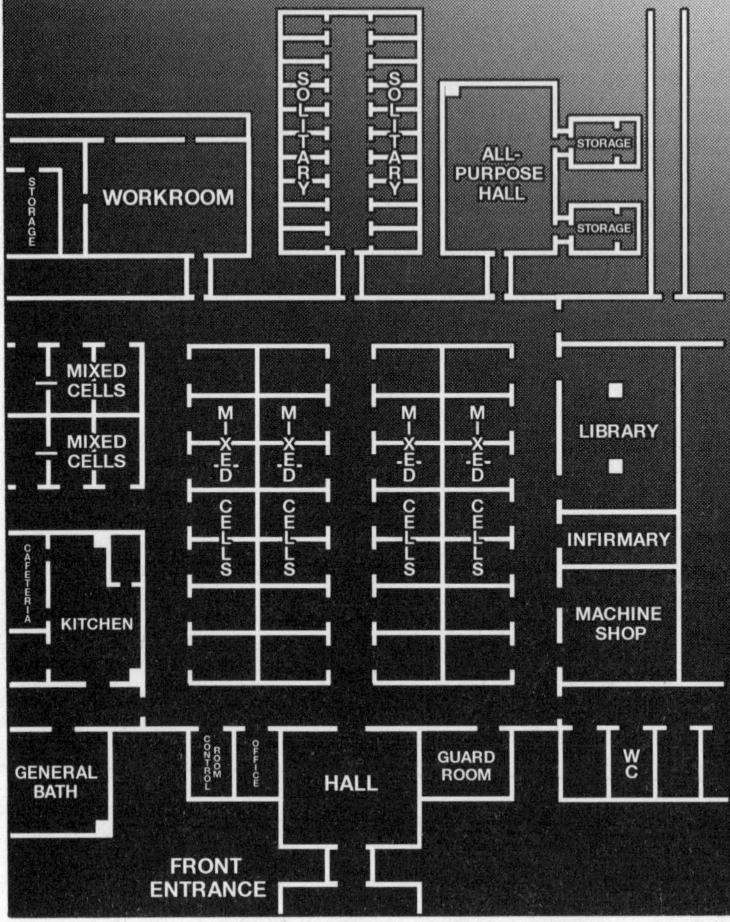
SOLITARY
SOLITARY
ALL-PURPOSE HALL
STORAGE
STORAGE
STORAGE
WORKROOM
MIXED CELLS
MIXED CELLS
MIXED CELLS
MIXED CELLS
MIXED CELLS
MIXED CELLS
LIBRARY
INFIRMARY
CAFETERIA
KITCHEN
MACHINE SHOP
GENERAL BATH
CONTROL ROOM
OFFICE
HALL
GUARD ROOM
WC
FRONT ENTRANCE

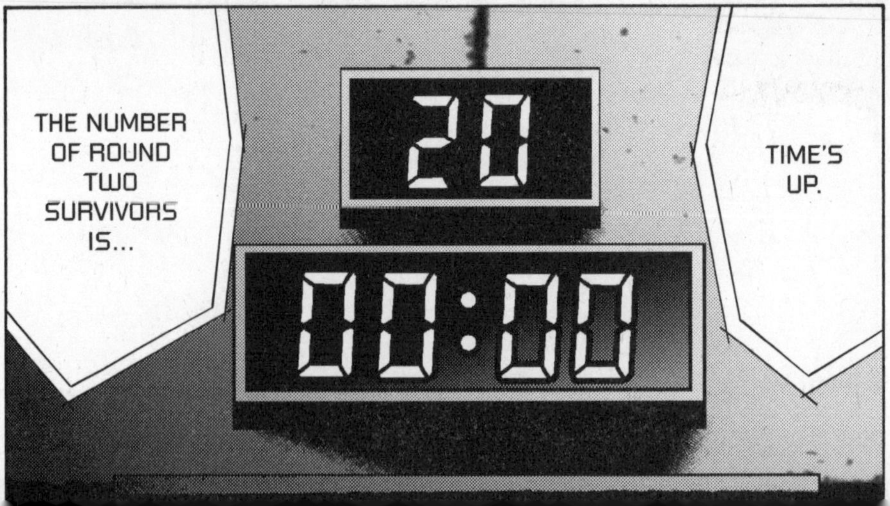
TIME'S UP.
20
00:00
THE NUMBER OF ROUND TWO SURVIVORS IS...

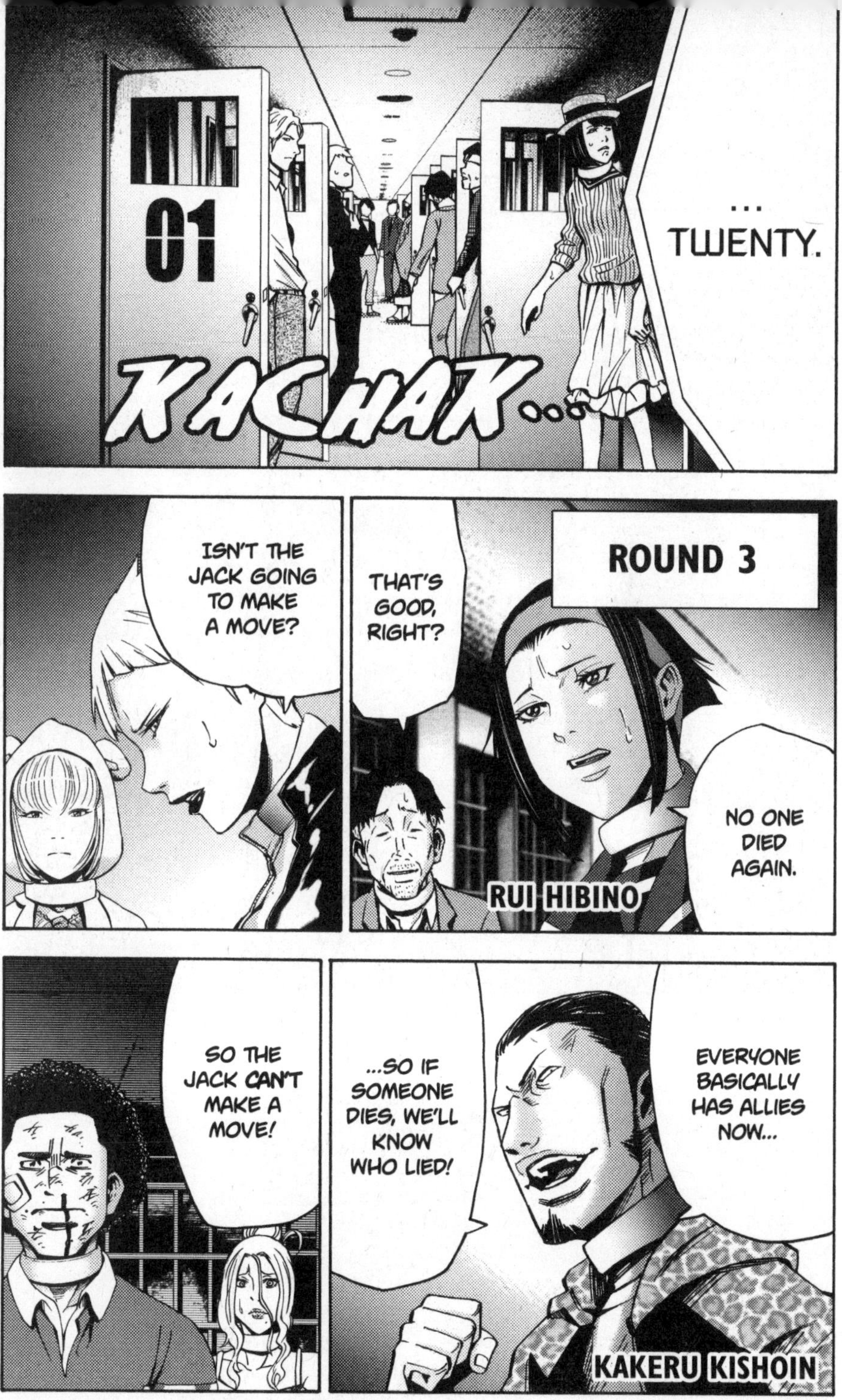
...TWENTY.
KACHAK...
ROUND 3
NO ONE DIED AGAIN.
THAT'S GOOD, RIGHT?
RUI HIBINO
ISN'T THE JACK GOING TO MAKE A MOVE?
EVERYONE BASICALLY HAS ALLIES NOW...
...SO IF SOMEONE DIES, WE'LL KNOW WHO LIED!
KAKERU KISHOIN
SO THE JACK CAN'T MAKE A MOVE!

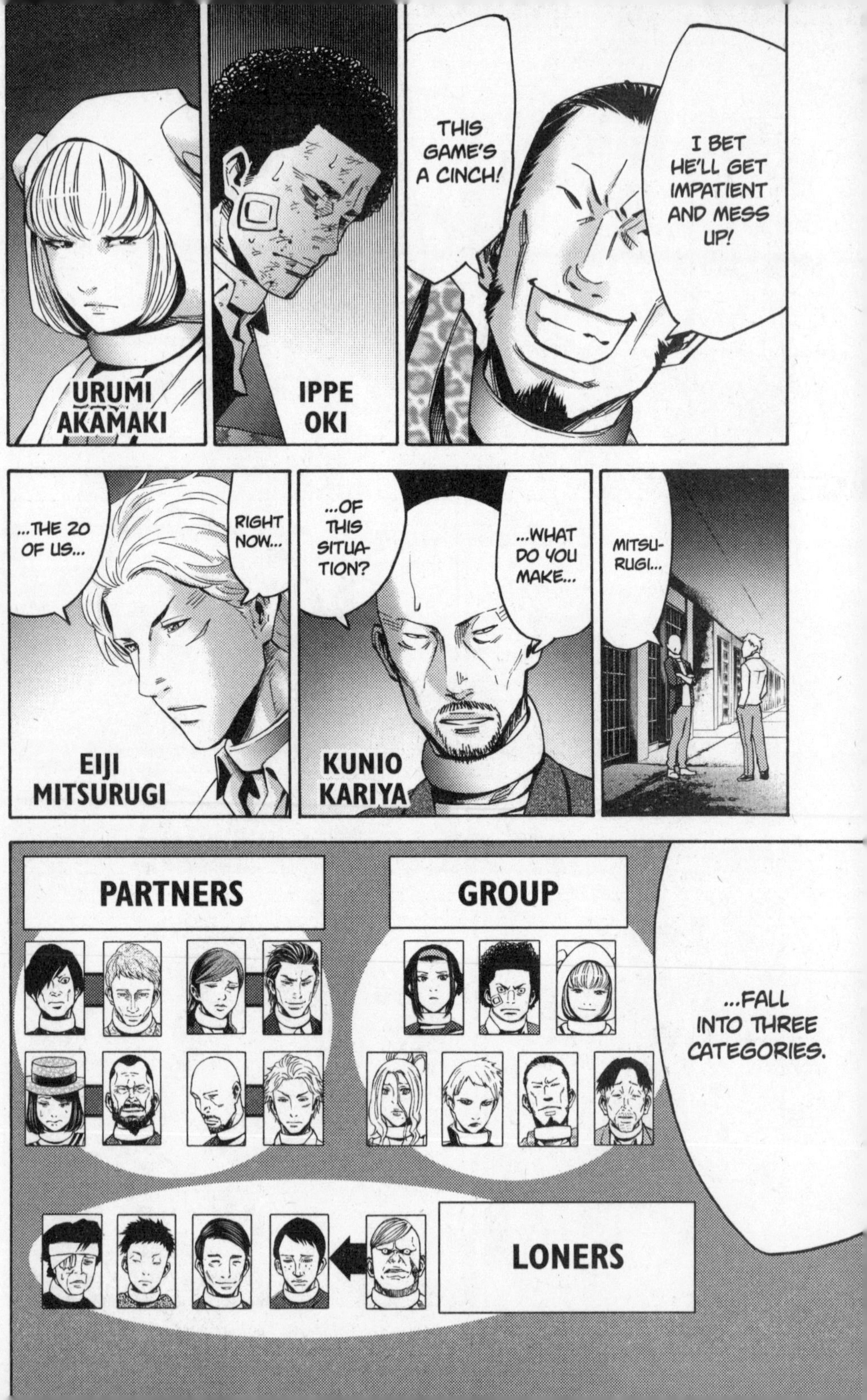
I BET HE'LL GET IMPATIENT AND MESS UP!
THIS GAME'S A CINCH!
IPPE OKI
URUMI AKAMAKI
MITSU-RUGI...
...WHAT DO YOU MAKE...
...OF THIS SITUA-TION?
KUNIO KARIYA
RIGHT NOW...
...THE 20 OF US...
EIJI MITSURUGI
...FALL INTO THREE CATEGORIES.
GROUP
PARTNERS
LONERS

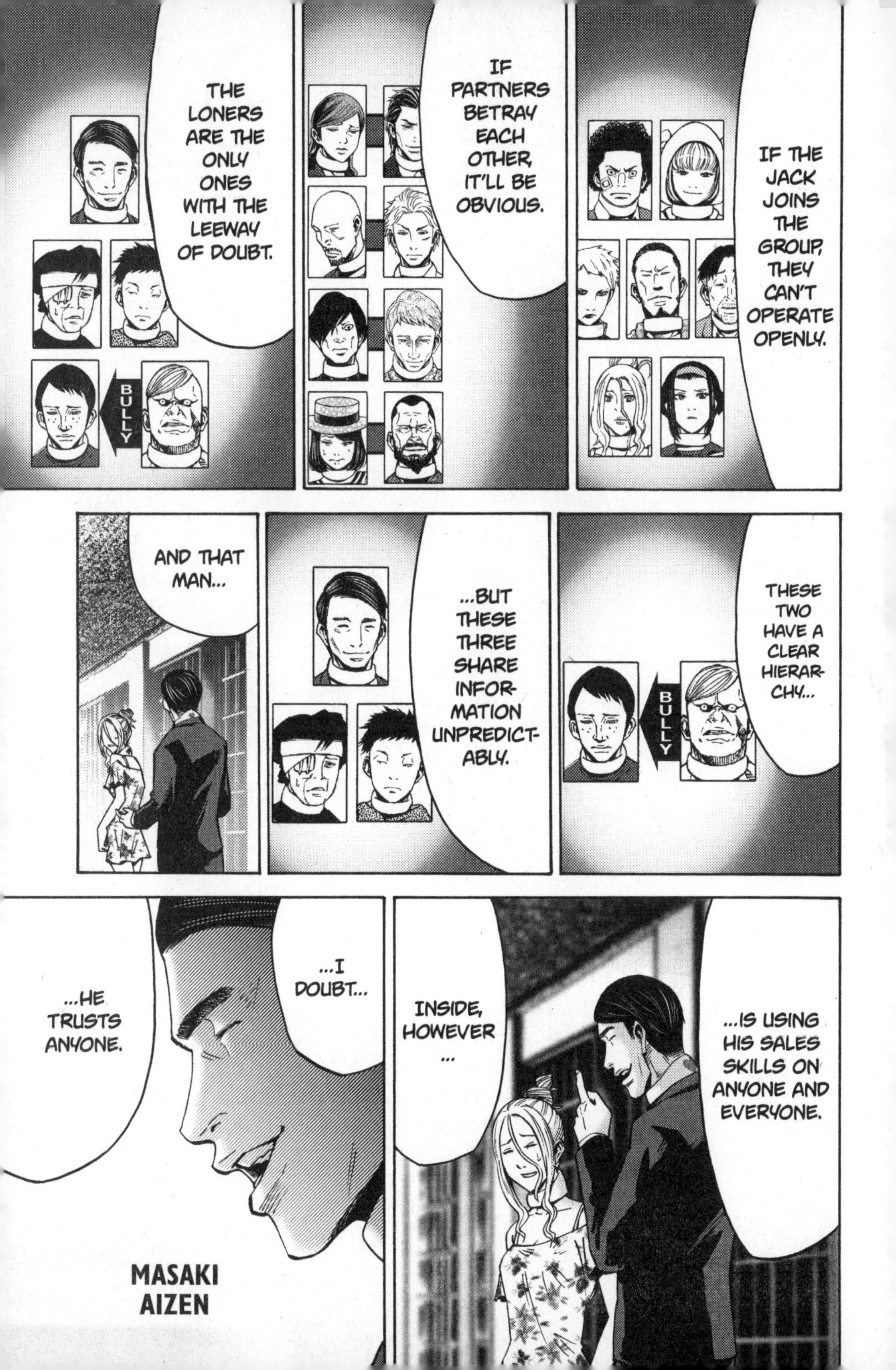
IF THE JACK JOINS THE GROUP, THEY CAN'T OPERATE OPENLY.
IF PARTNERS BETRAY EACH OTHER, IT'LL BE OBVIOUS.
THE LONERS ARE THE ONLY ONES WITH THE LEEWAY OF DOUBT.
BULLY
THESE TWO HAVE A CLEAR HIERARCHY...
BULLY
...BUT THESE THREE SHARE INFORMATION UNPREDICTABLY.
AND THAT MAN...
...IS USING HIS SALES SKILLS ON ANYONE AND EVERYONE.
INSIDE, HOWEVER...
...I DOUBT...
...HE TRUSTS ANYONE.
MASAKI AIZEN

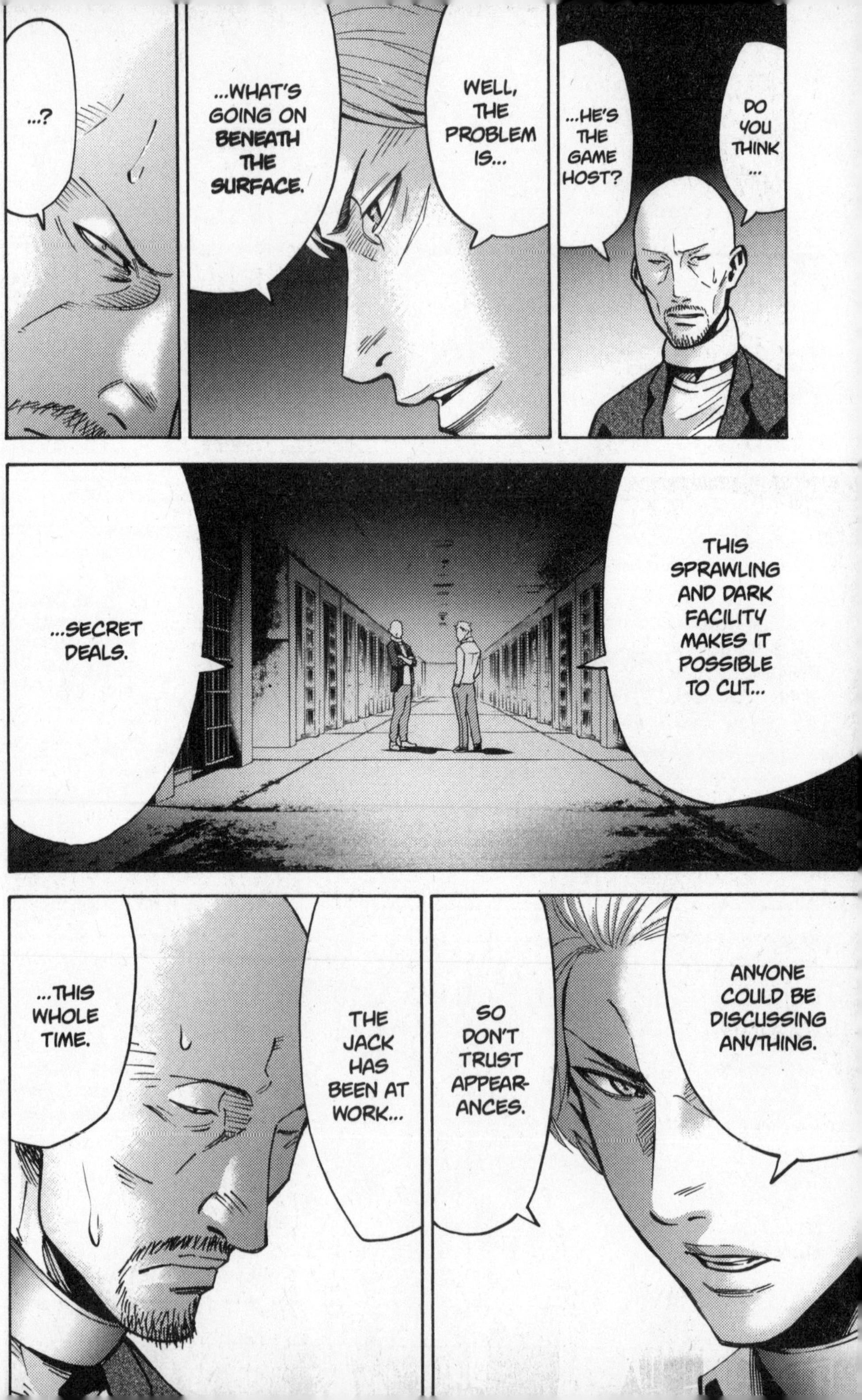
DO YOU THINK ...
...HE'S THE GAME HOST?
WELL, THE PROBLEM IS...
...WHAT'S GOING ON BENEATH THE SURFACE.
...?
THIS SPRAWLING AND DARK FACILITY MAKES IT POSSIBLE TO CUT...
...SECRET DEALS.
ANYONE COULD BE DISCUSSING ANYTHING.
SO DON'T TRUST APPEAR-ANCES.
THE JACK HAS BEEN AT WORK...
...THIS WHOLE TIME.

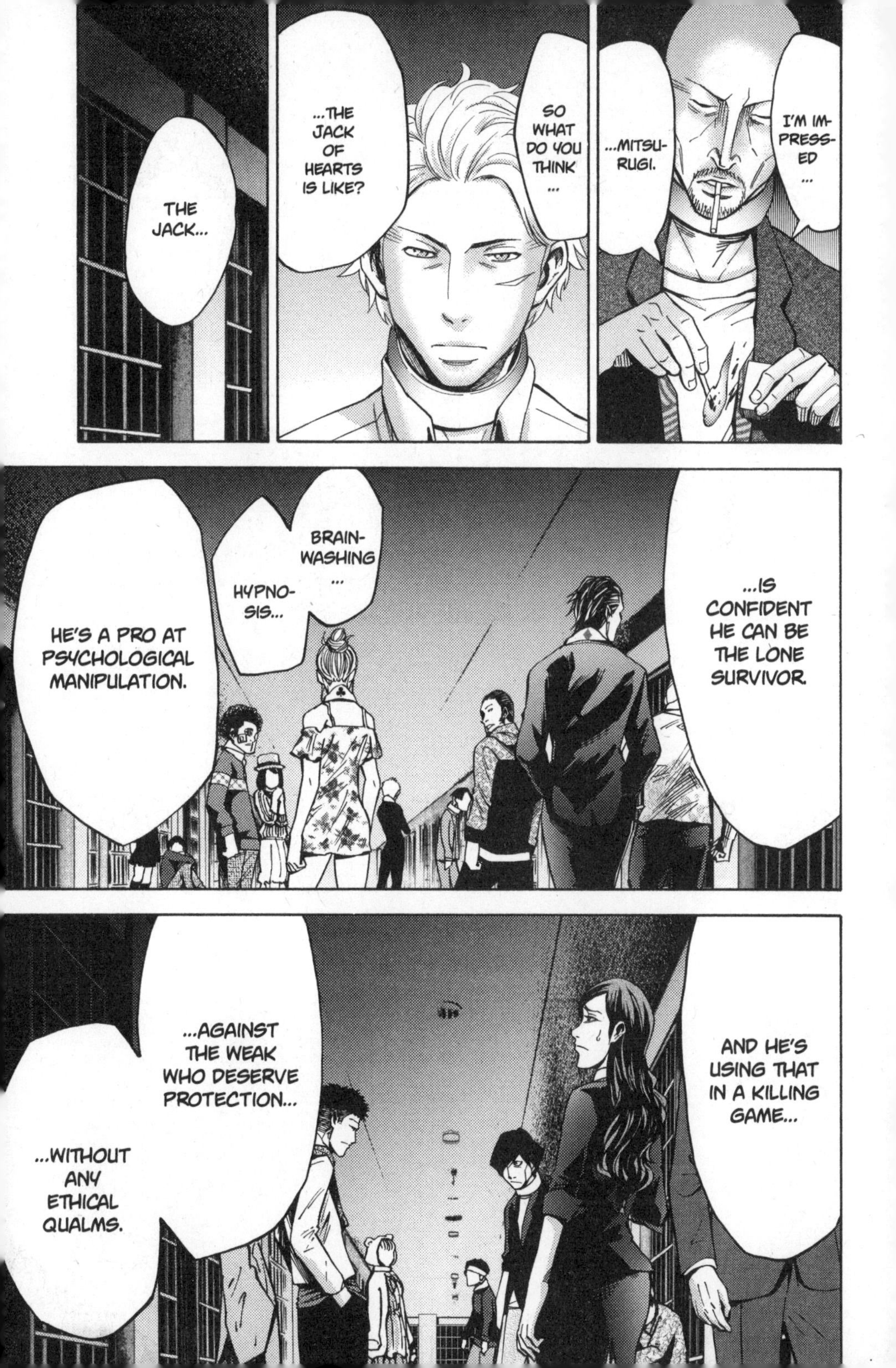
I'M IMPRESSED...
...MITSURUGI.
SO WHAT DO YOU THINK...
...THE JACK OF HEARTS IS LIKE?
THE JACK...
...IS CONFIDENT HE CAN BE THE LONE SURVIVOR.
BRAINWASHING...
HYPNOSIS...
HE'S A PRO AT PSYCHOLOGICAL MANIPULATION.
AND HE'S USING THAT IN A KILLING GAME...
...AGAINST THE WEAK WHO DESERVE PROTECTION...
...WITHOUT ANY ETHICAL QUALMS.

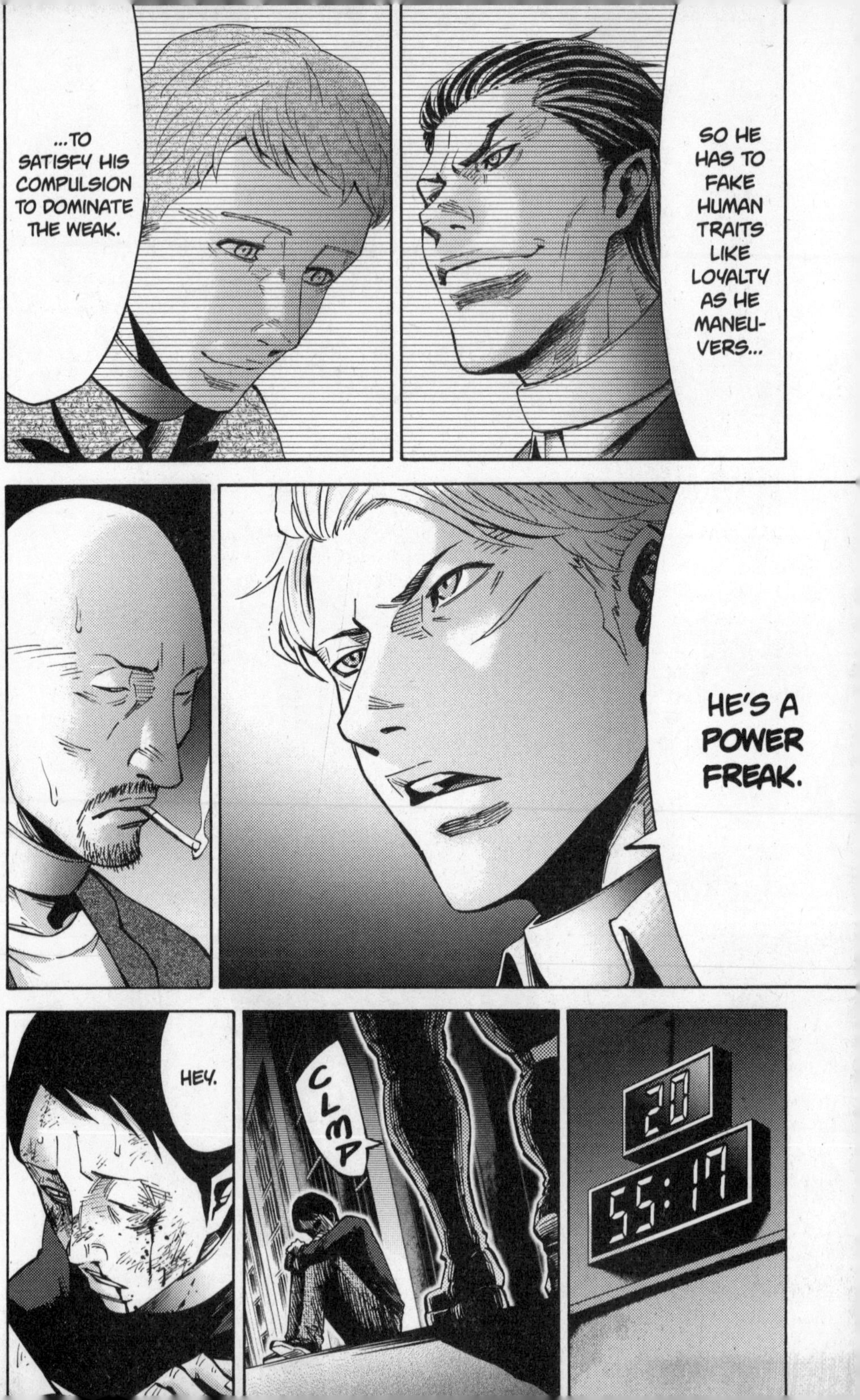
SO HE HAS TO FAKE HUMAN TRAITS LIKE LOYALTY AS HE MANEUVERS...
...TO SATISFY HIS COMPULSION TO DOMINATE THE WEAK.
HE'S A POWER FREAK.
20
55:17
CLMP
HEY.

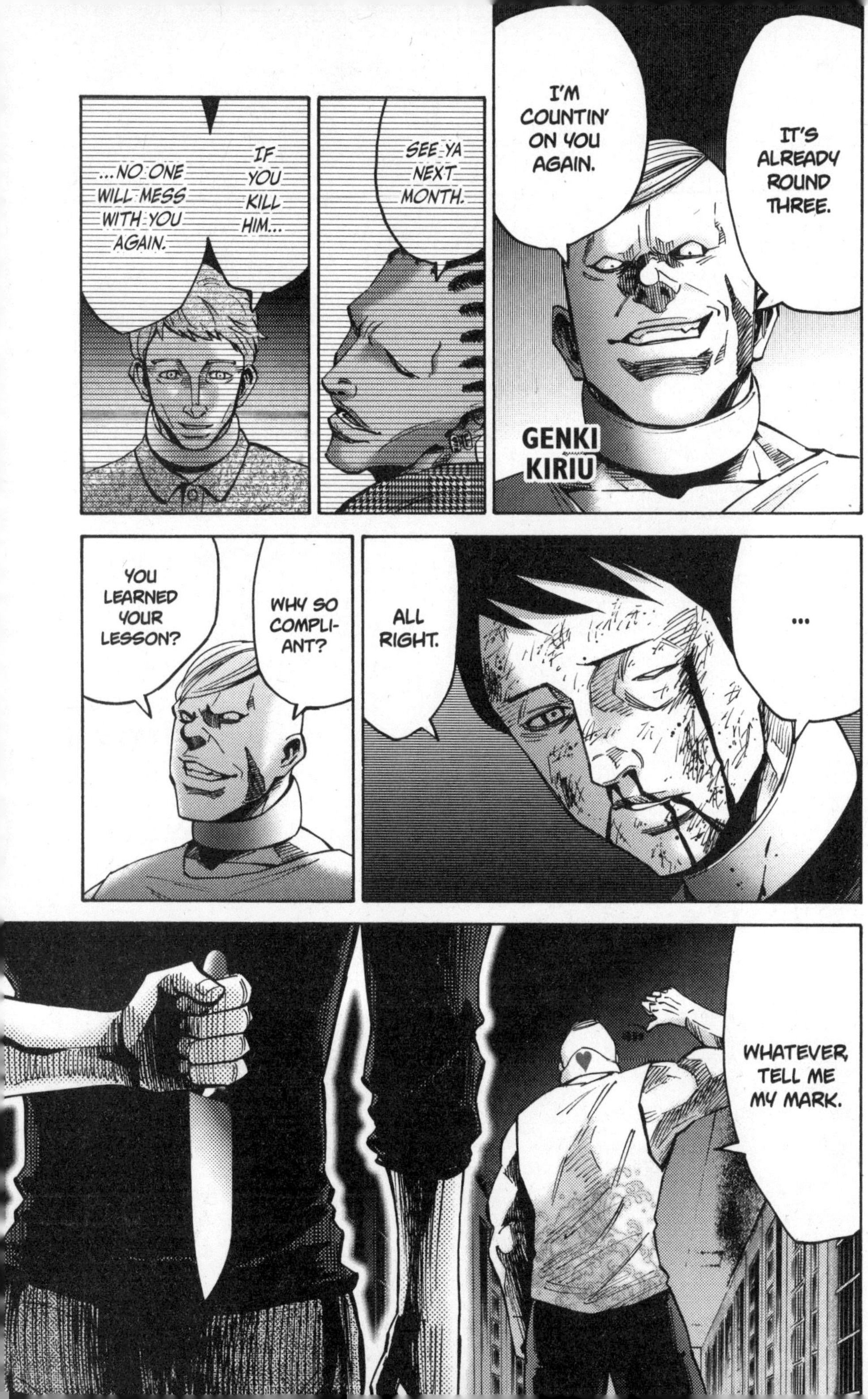
IT'S ALREADY ROUND THREE.
I'M COUNTIN' ON YOU AGAIN.
GENKI KIRIU
SEE YA NEXT MONTH.
IF YOU KILL HIM...
...NO ONE WILL MESS WITH YOU AGAIN.
...
ALL RIGHT.
WHY SO COMPLI-ANT?
YOU LEARNED YOUR LESSON?
WHATEVER, TELL ME MY MARK.

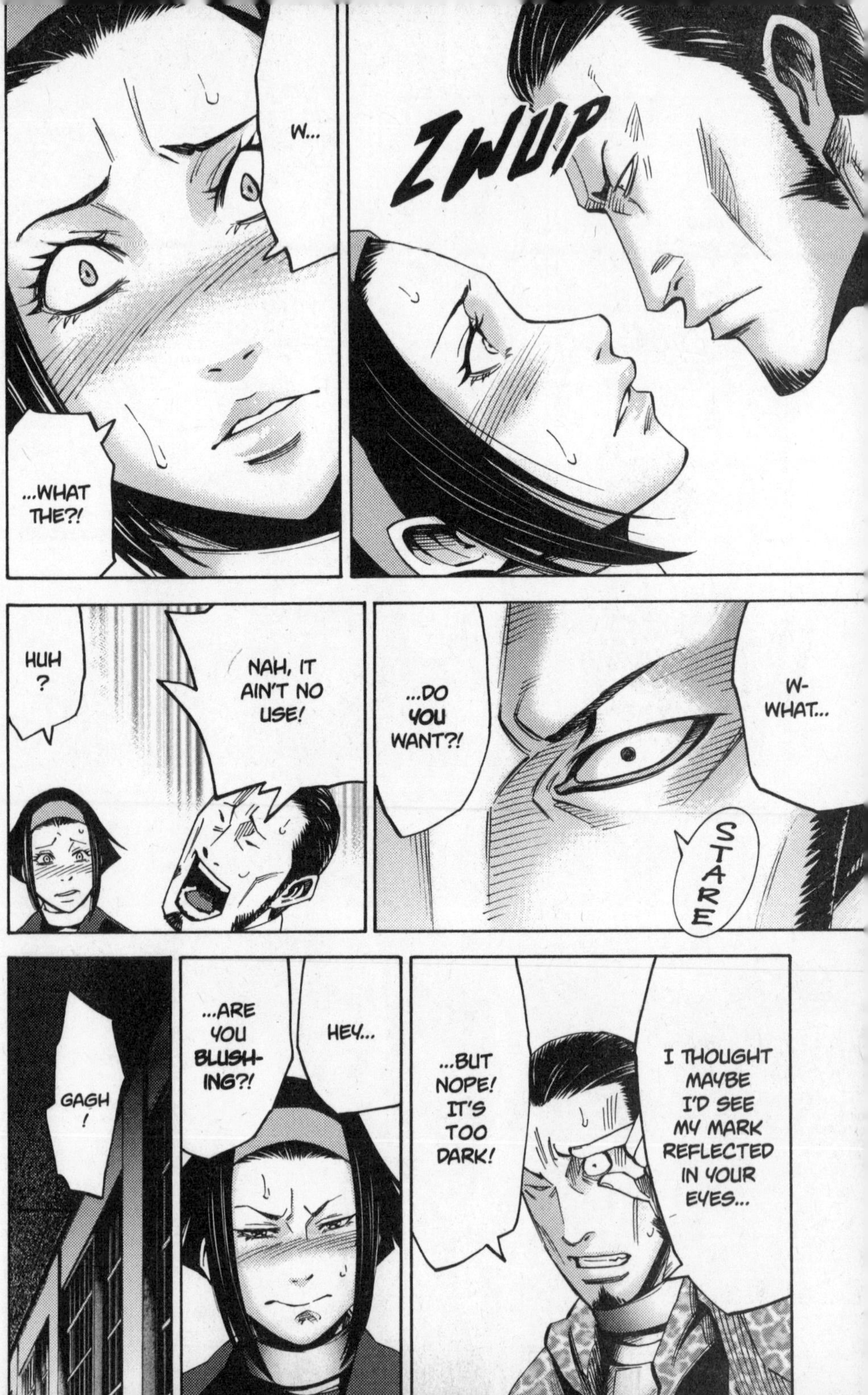
ZWUP
W...
...WHAT THE?!
W- WHAT...
...DO YOU WANT?!
STARE
NAH, IT AIN'T NO USE!
HUH ?
I THOUGHT MAYBE I'D SEE MY MARK REFLECTED IN YOUR EYES...
...BUT NOPE! IT'S TOO DARK!
HEY...
...ARE YOU BLUSHING?!
GAGH !

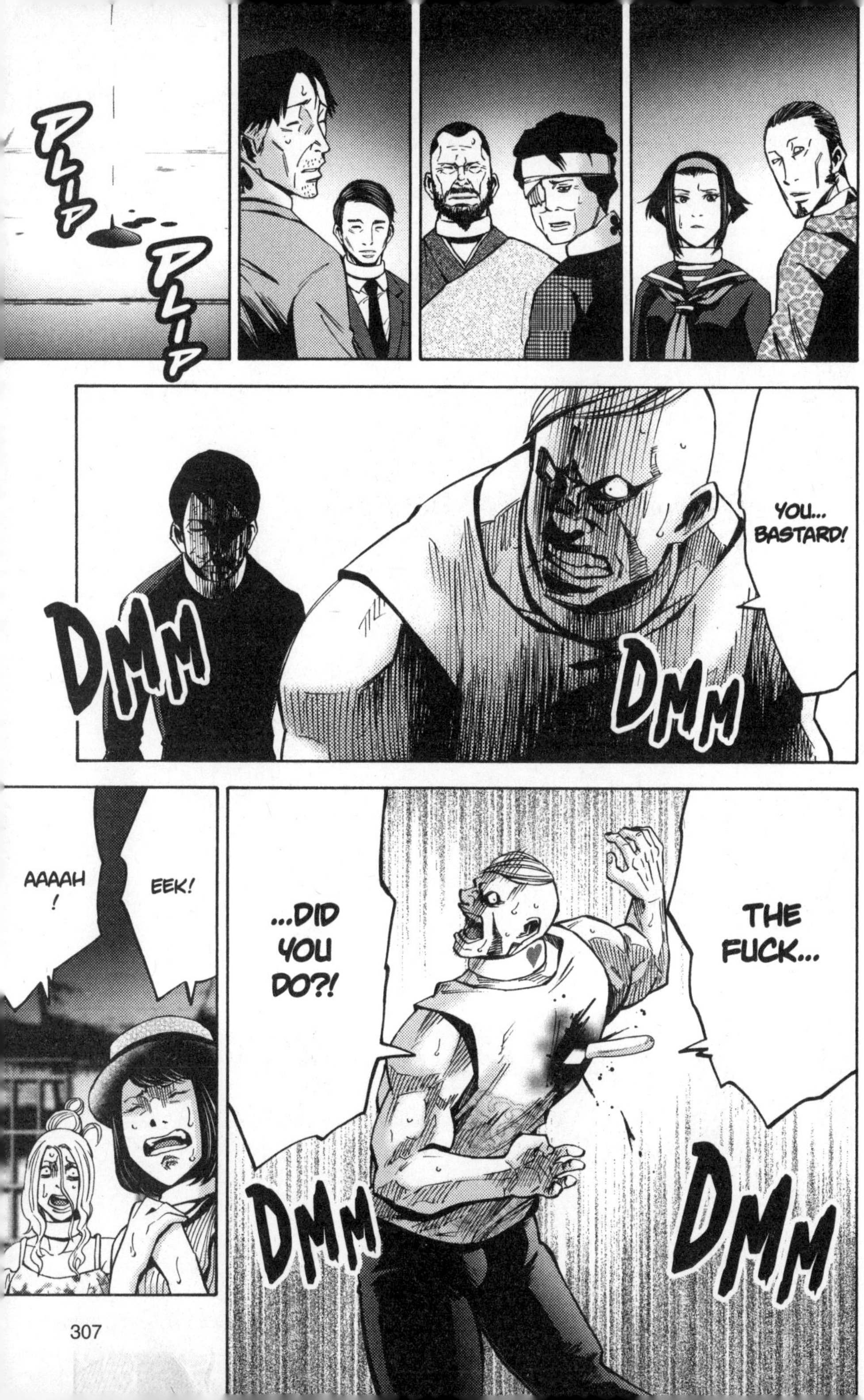
PLIP
PLIP
YOU... BASTARD!
DMM
DMM
THE FUCK...
...DID YOU DO?!
DMM
DMM
EEK!
AAAAH!

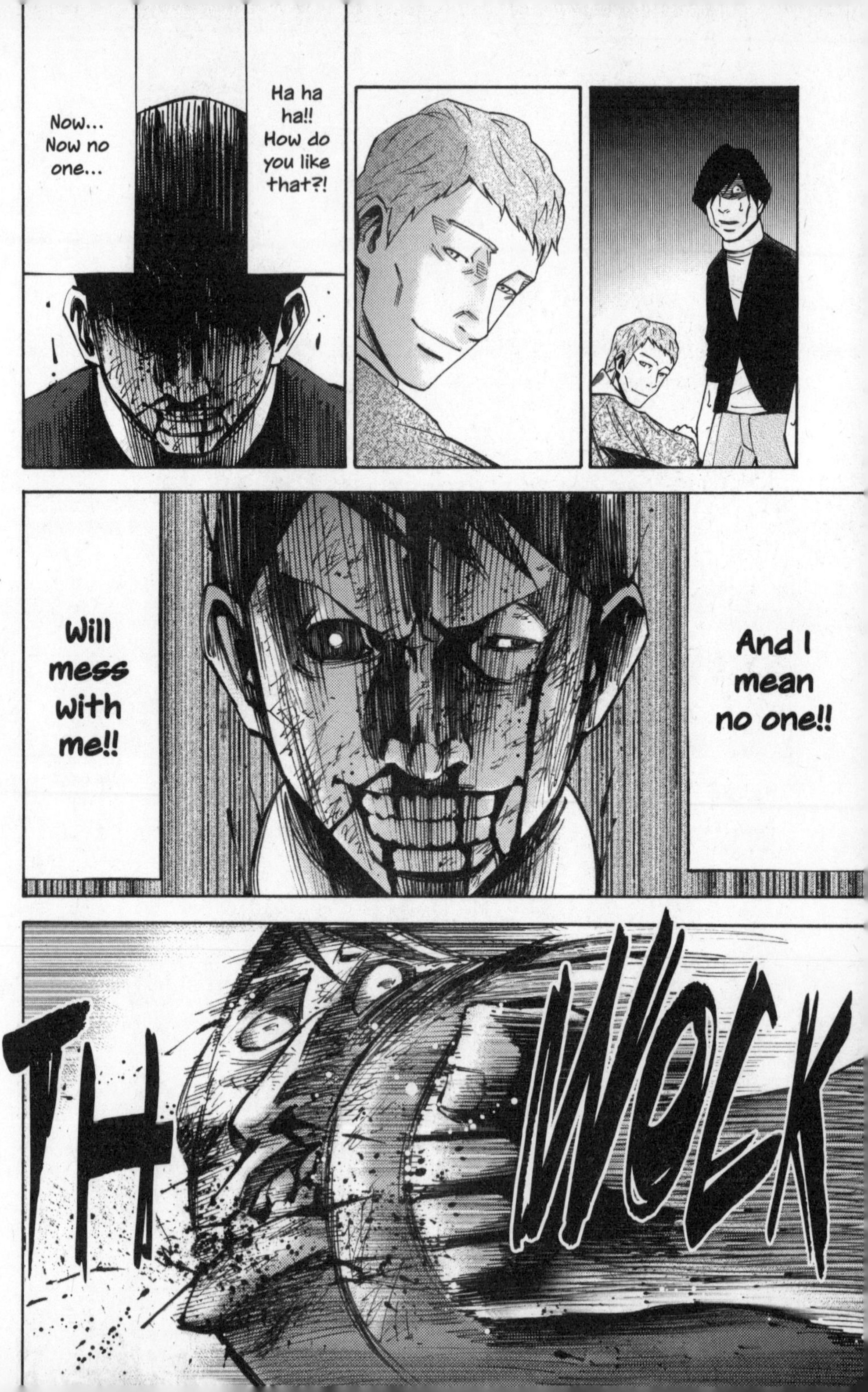
Ha ha ha!! How do you like that?!
Now... Now no one...
Will mess with me!!
And I mean no one!!
TH WACK

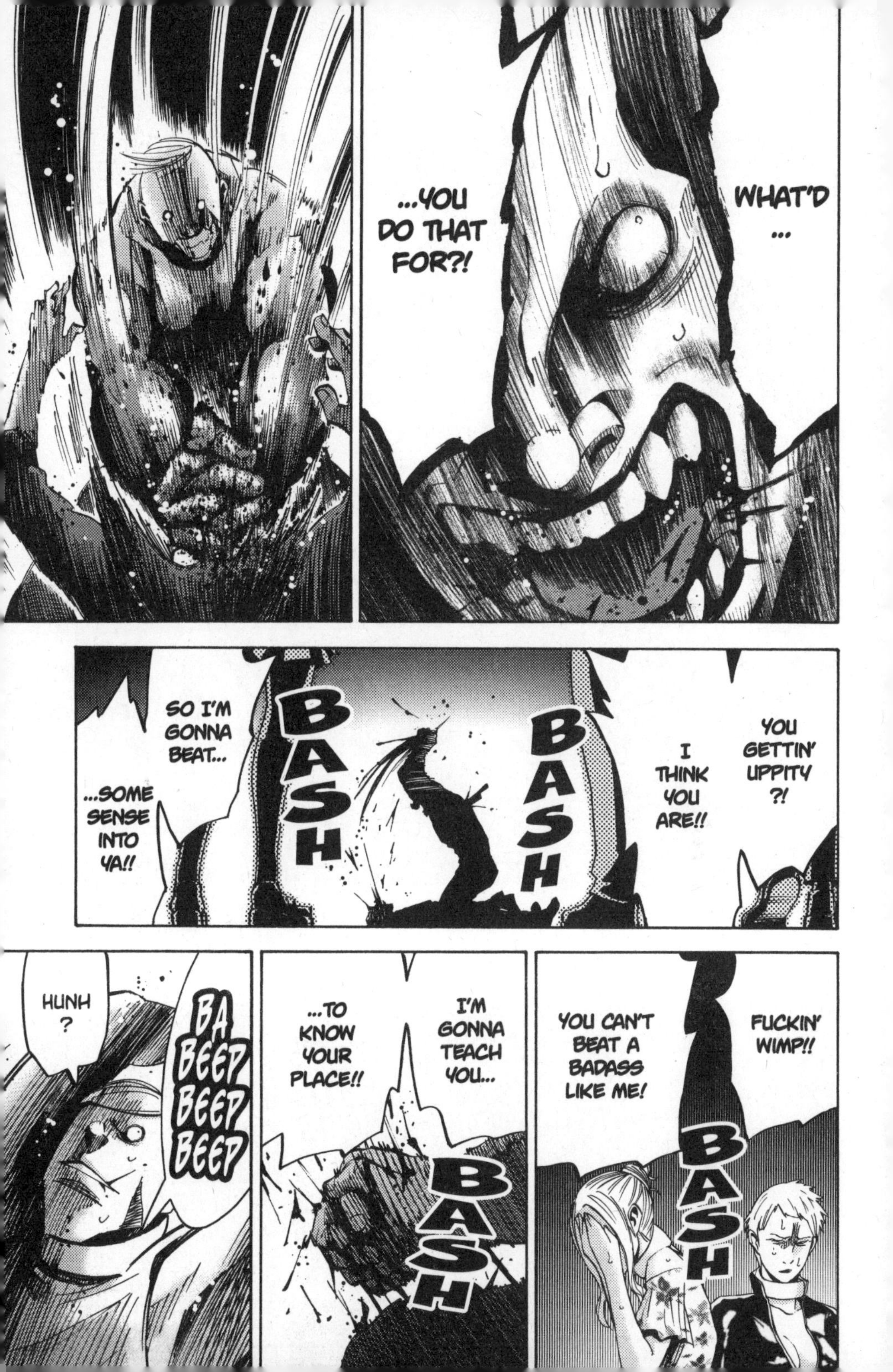
WHAT'D ...
...YOU DO THAT FOR?!
YOU GETTIN' UPPITY?!
I THINK YOU ARE!!
BASH
BASH
SO I'M GONNA BEAT...
...SOME SENSE INTO YA!!
FUCKIN' WIMP!!
YOU CAN'T BEAT A BADASS LIKE ME!
BASH
I'M GONNA TEACH YOU...
...TO KNOW YOUR PLACE!!
BASH
BA BEEP BEEP BEEP
HUNH?

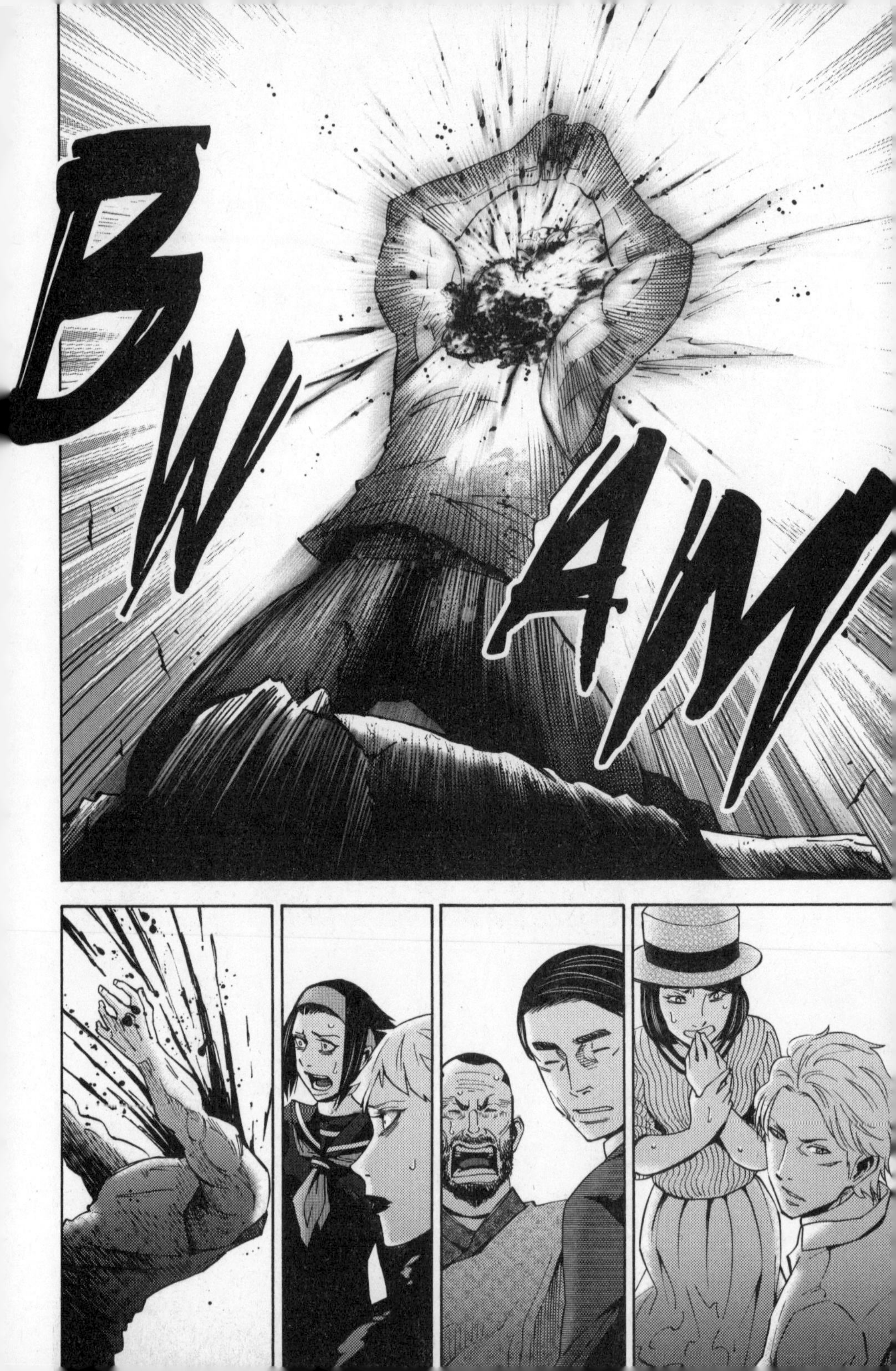
BWAM

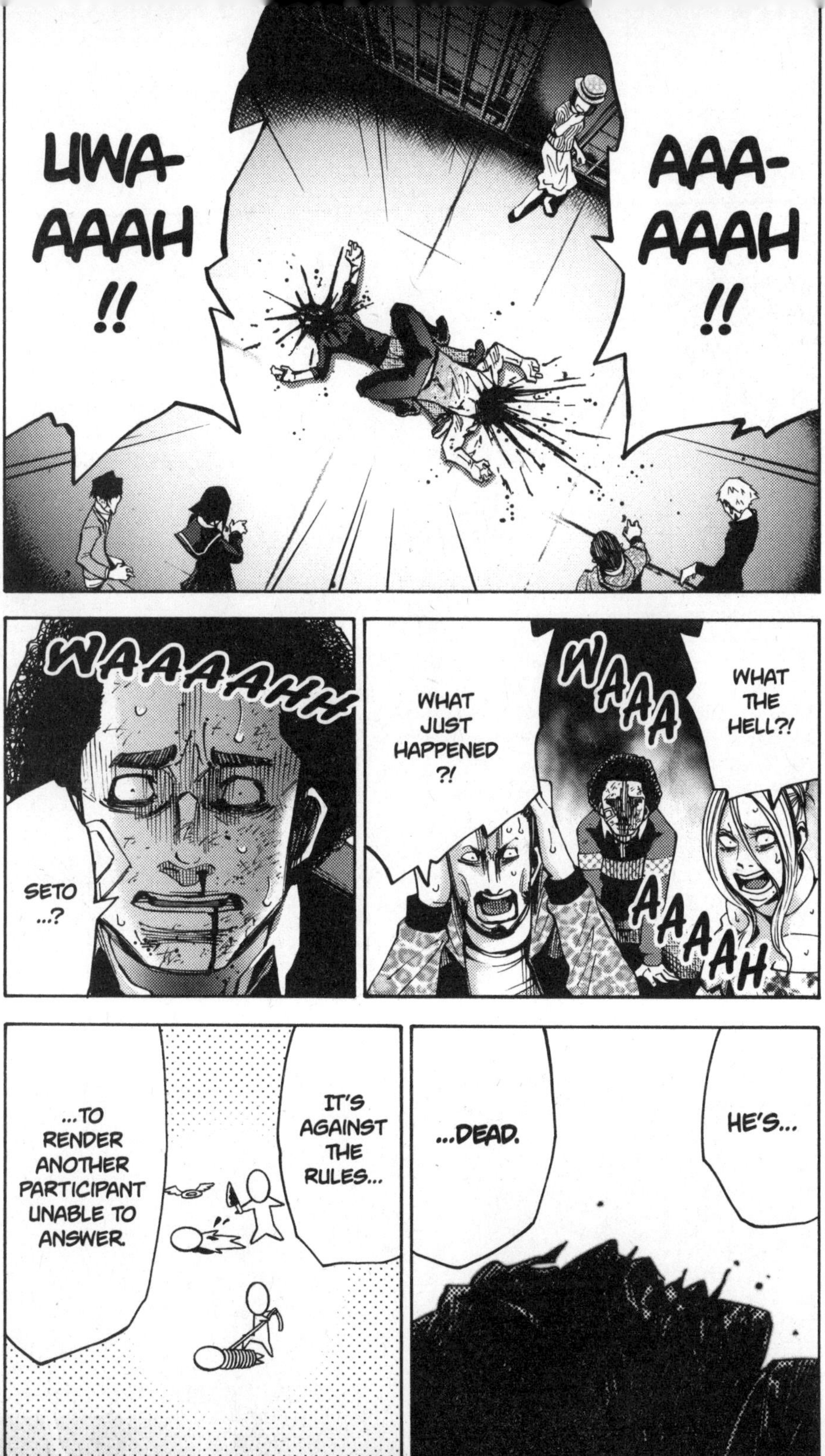
AAA-AAAH!!
UWA-AAAH!!
WHAT THE HELL?!
WAAAA AAAAH
WHAT JUST HAPPENED ?!
WAAAAAHH
SETO ...?
HE'S...
...DEAD.
IT'S AGAINST THE RULES...
...TO RENDER ANOTHER PARTICIPANT UNABLE TO ANSWER.

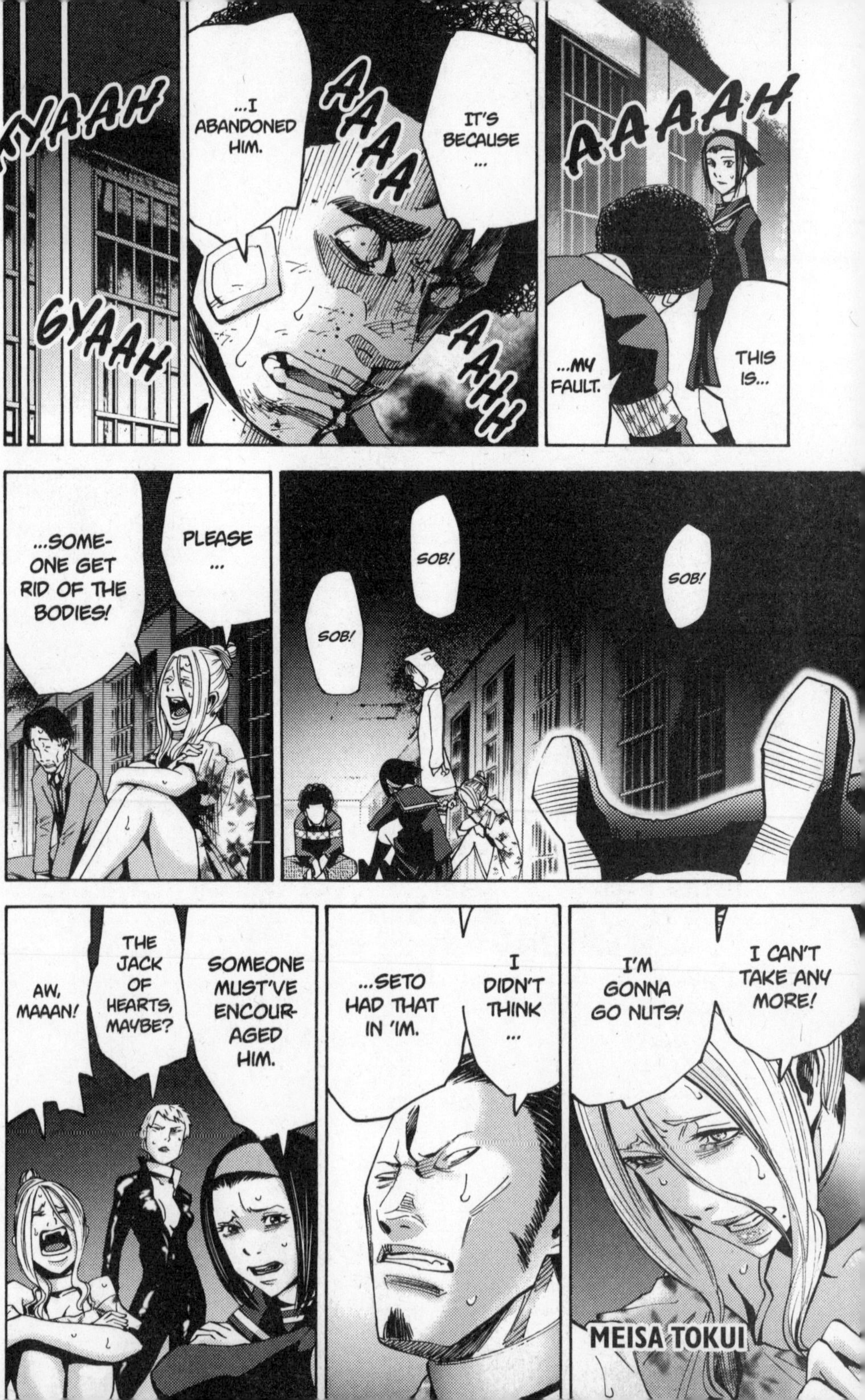
AAAAAH
THIS IS...
...MY FAULT.
IT'S BECAUSE ...
AAAAAAHH
...I ABANDONED HIM.
KYAAH
GYAAH
SOB!
SOB!
SOB!
PLEASE ...
...SOME-ONE GET RID OF THE BODIES!
I CAN'T TAKE ANY MORE!
I'M GONNA GO NUTS!
MEISA TOKUI
I DIDN'T THINK ...
...SETO HAD THAT IN 'IM.
SOMEONE MUST'VE ENCOUR-AGED HIM.
THE JACK OF HEARTS, MAYBE?
AW, MAAAN!

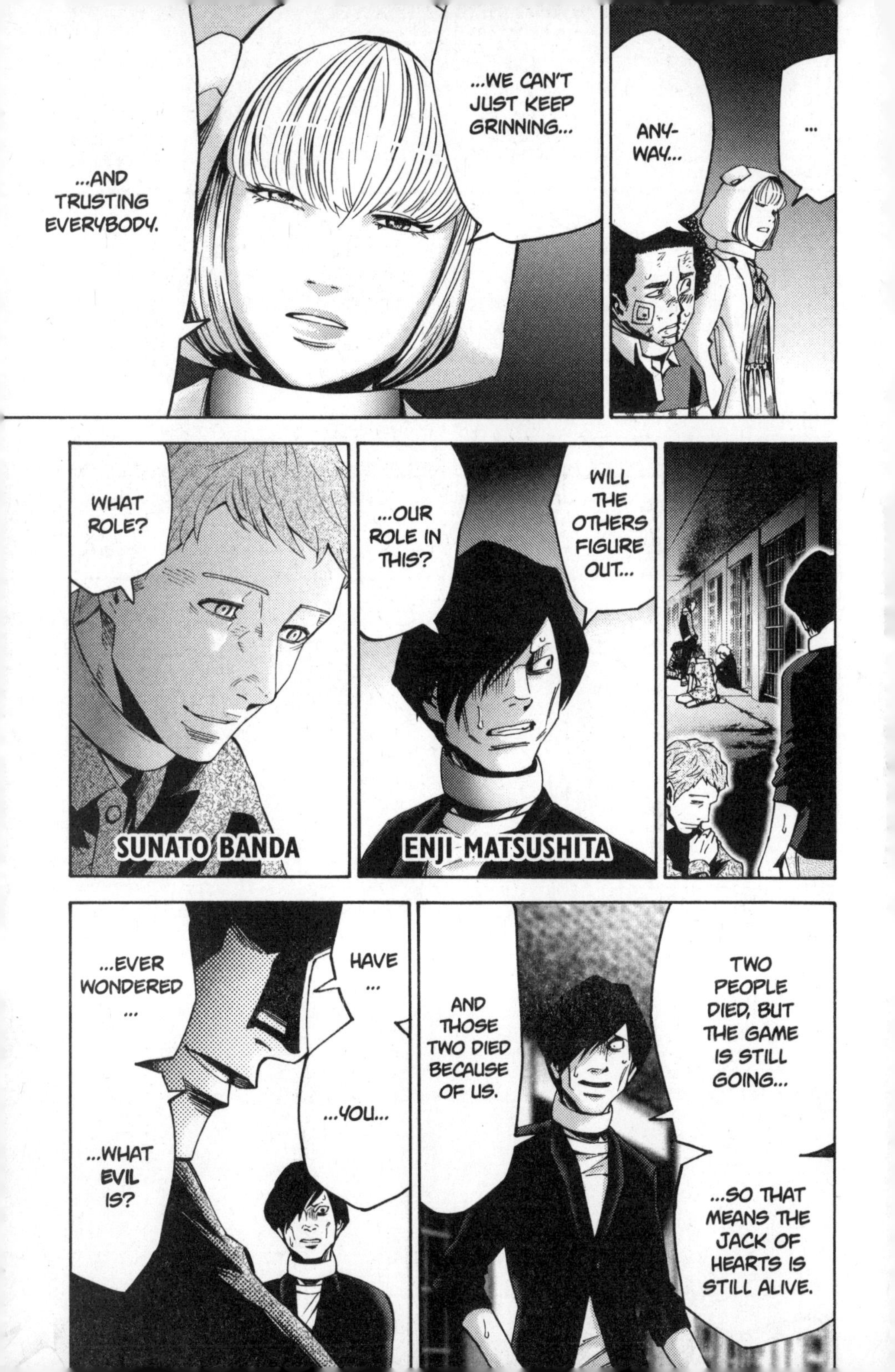
...
ANY-WAY...
...WE CAN'T JUST KEEP GRINNING...
...AND TRUSTING EVERYBODY.
WILL THE OTHERS FIGURE OUT...
...OUR ROLE IN THIS?
ENJI MATSUSHITA
WHAT ROLE?
SUNATO BANDA
TWO PEOPLE DIED, BUT THE GAME IS STILL GOING...
AND THOSE TWO DIED BECAUSE OF US.
...SO THAT MEANS THE JACK OF HEARTS IS STILL ALIVE.
HAVE ...
...EVER WONDERED ...
...YOU...
...WHAT EVIL IS?

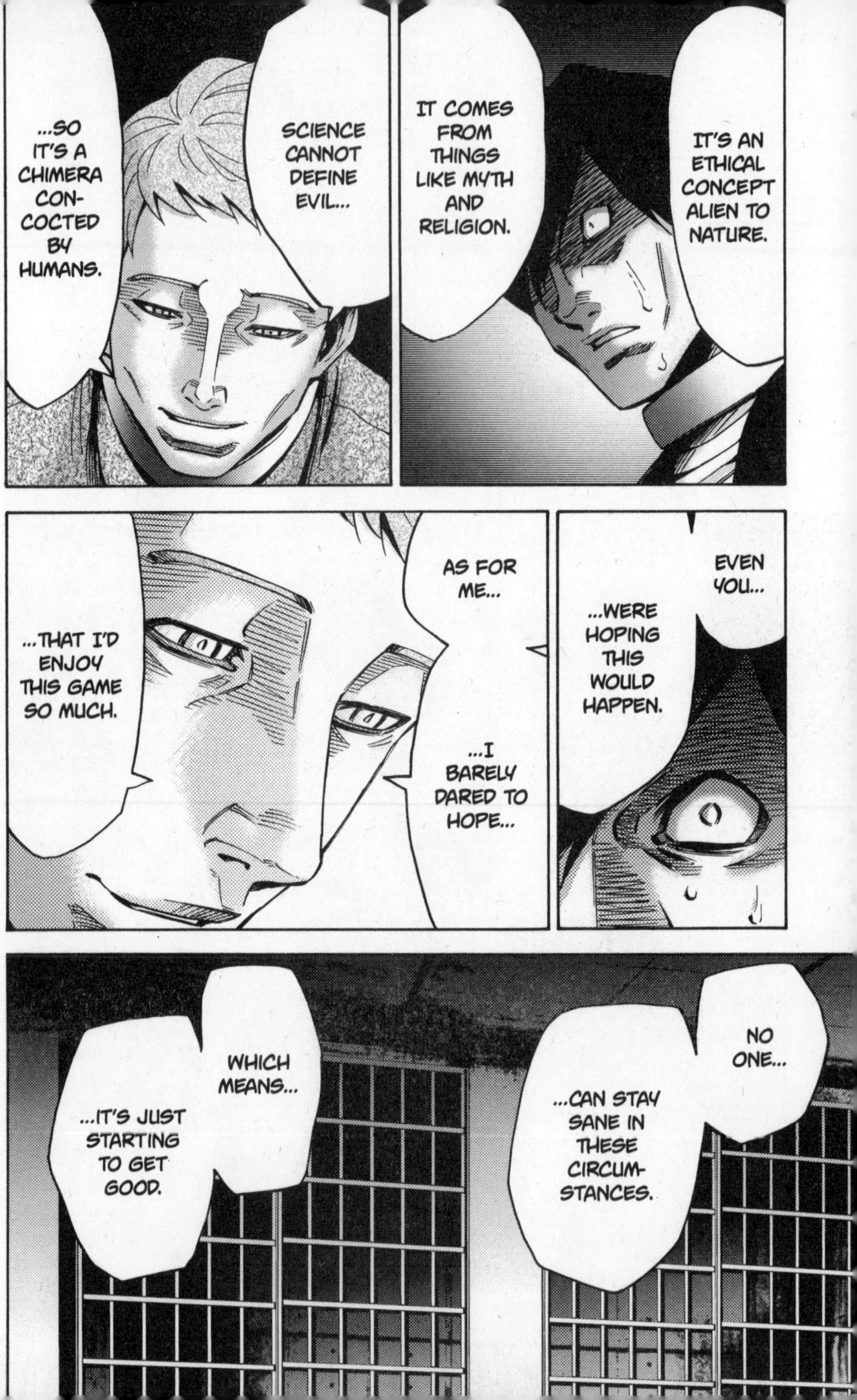

IT'S AN ETHICAL CONCEPT ALIEN TO NATURE.
IT COMES FROM THINGS LIKE MYTH AND RELIGION.
SCIENCE CANNOT DEFINE EVIL...
...SO IT'S A CHIMERA CON-COCTED BY HUMANS.
EVEN YOU...
...WERE HOPING THIS WOULD HAPPEN.
AS FOR ME...
...I BARELY DARED TO HOPE...
...THAT I'D ENJOY THIS GAME SO MUCH.
NO ONE...
...CAN STAY SANE IN THESE CIRCUM-STANCES.
WHICH MEANS...
...IT'S JUST STARTING TO GET GOOD.

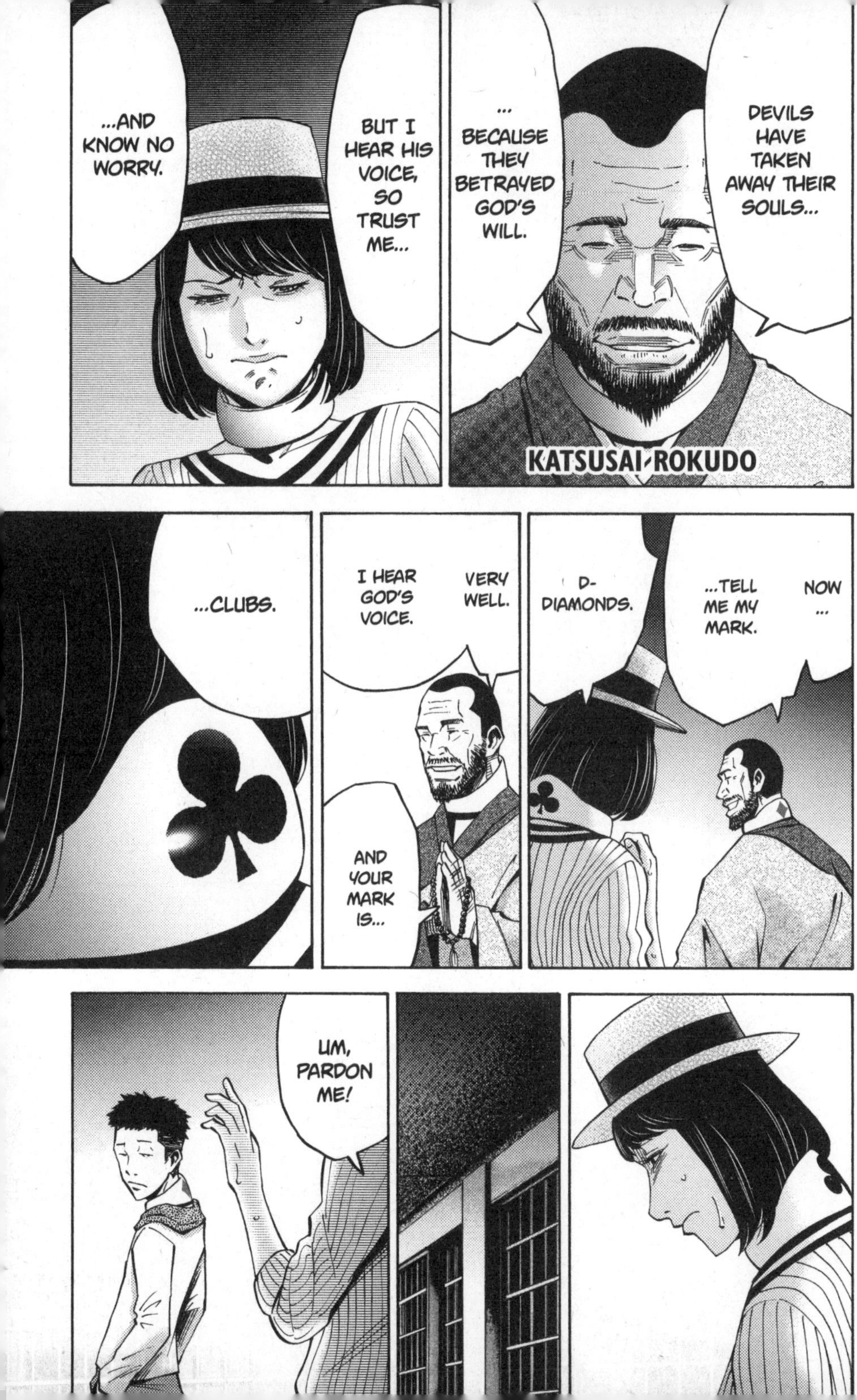
DEVILS HAVE TAKEN AWAY THEIR SOULS...
... BECAUSE THEY BETRAYED GOD'S WILL.
KATSUSAI ROKUDO
BUT I HEAR HIS VOICE, SO TRUST ME...
...AND KNOW NO WORRY.
NOW ...
...TELL ME MY MARK.
D-DIAMONDS.
VERY WELL.
I HEAR GOD'S VOICE.
AND YOUR MARK IS...
...CLUBS.
UM, PARDON ME!

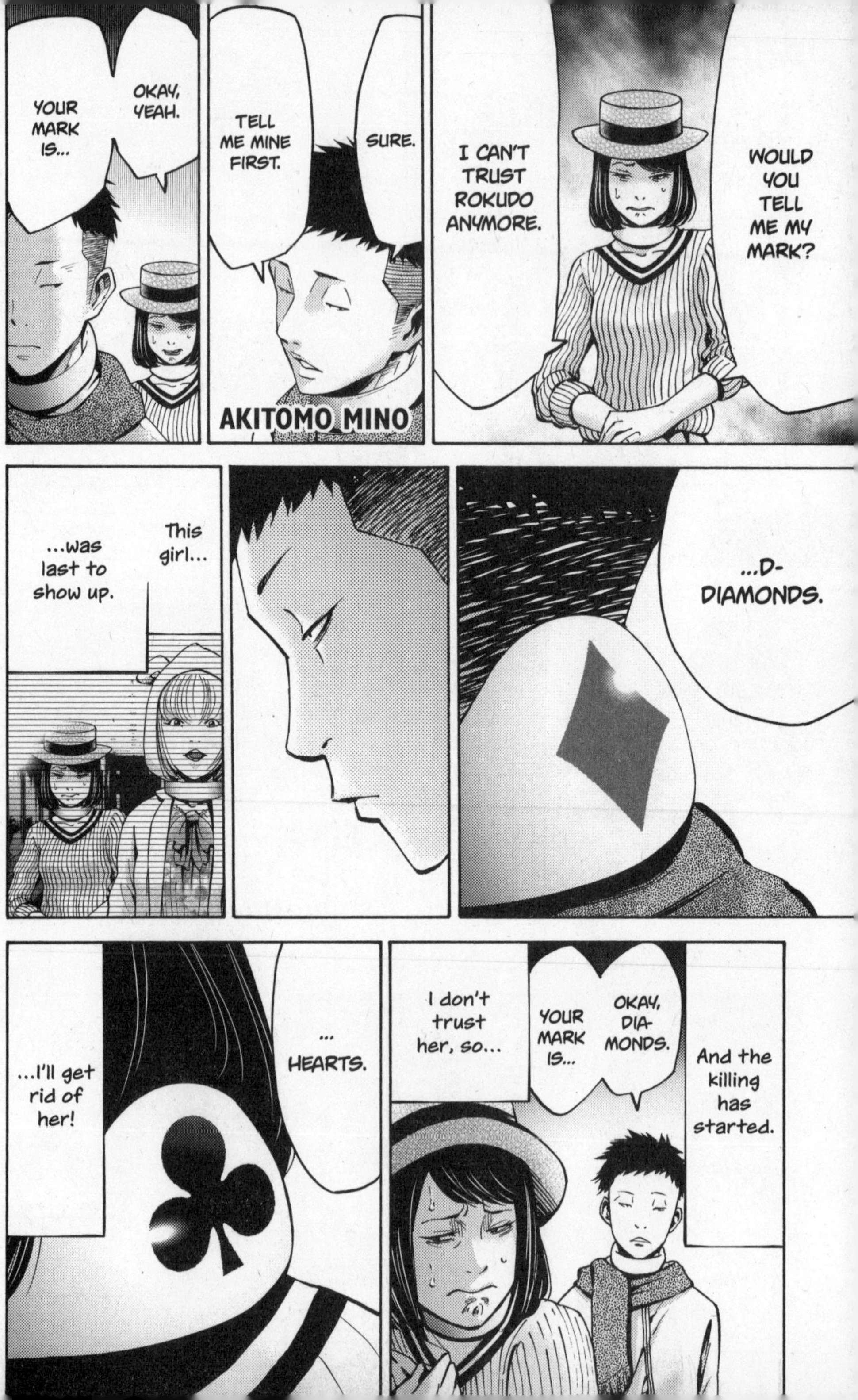
WOULD YOU TELL ME MY MARK?
I CAN'T TRUST ROKUDO ANYMORE.
SURE.
TELL ME MINE FIRST.
AKITOMO MINO
OKAY, YEAH.
YOUR MARK IS...
...D- DIAMONDS.
This girl...
...was last to show up.
OKAY, DIAMONDS.
YOUR MARK IS...
And the killing has started.
I don't trust her, so...
... HEARTS.
...I'll get rid of her!

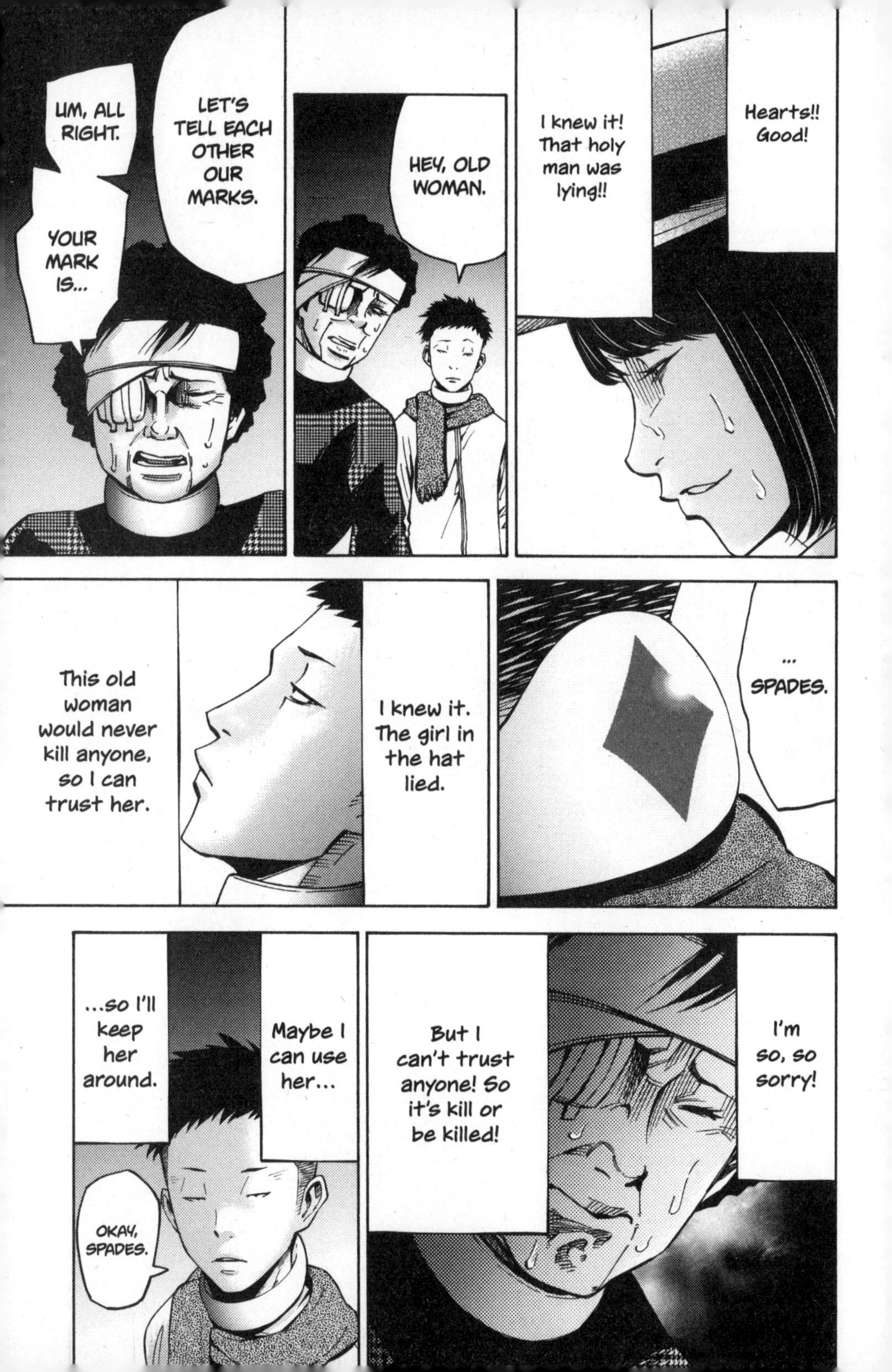
Hearts!! Good!
I knew it! That holy man was lying!!
HEY, OLD WOMAN.
LET'S TELL EACH OTHER OUR MARKS.
UM, ALL RIGHT.
YOUR MARK IS...
...SPADES.
I knew it. The girl in the hat lied.
This old woman would never kill anyone, so I can trust her.
I'm so, so sorry!
But I can't trust anyone! So it's kill or be killed!
Maybe I can use her...
...so I'll keep her around.
OKAY, SPADES.

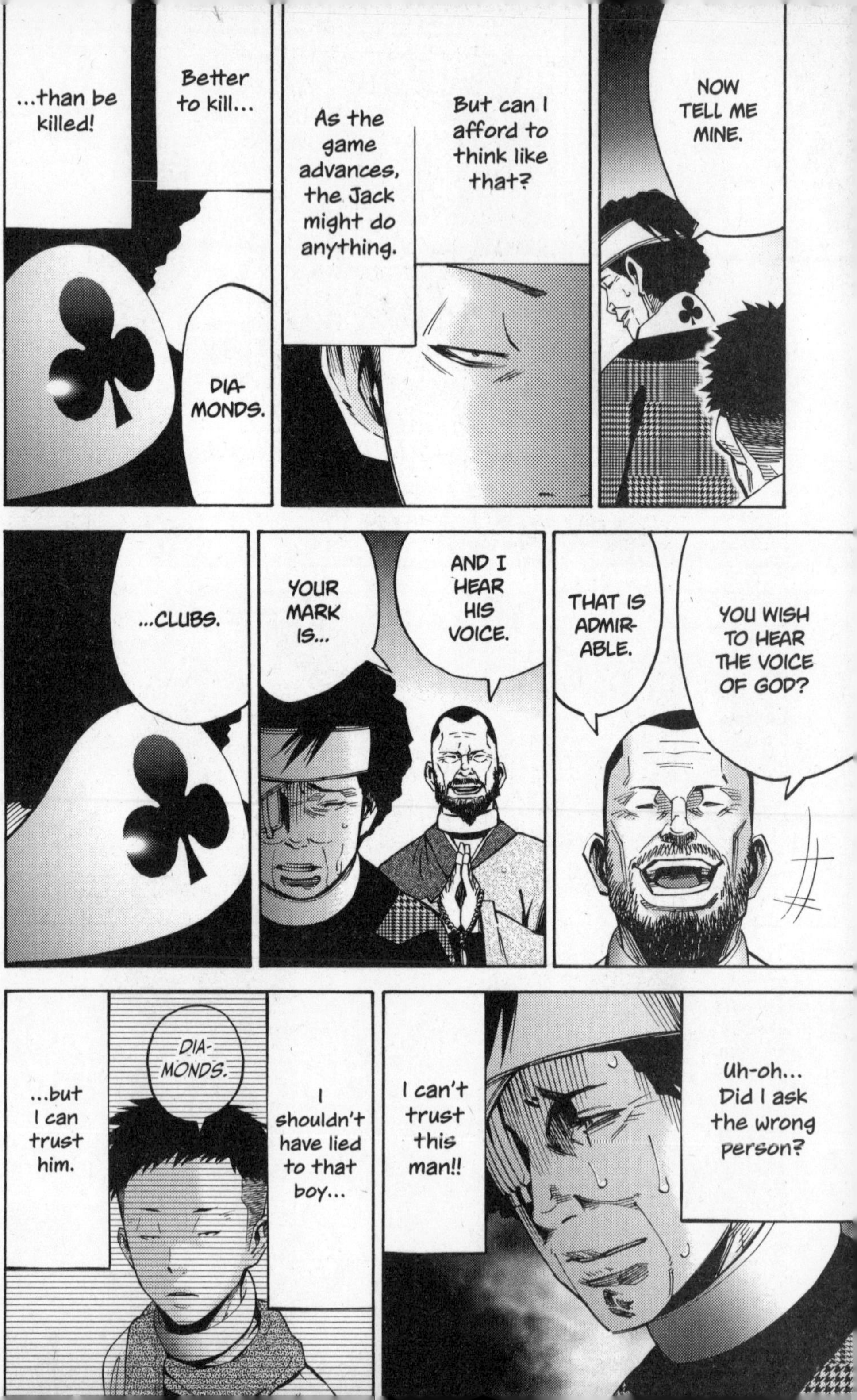
NOW TELL ME MINE.
But can I afford to think like that?
As the game advances, the Jack might do anything.
Better to kill...
...than be killed!
DIA-MONDS.
YOU WISH TO HEAR THE VOICE OF GOD?
THAT IS ADMIR-ABLE.
AND I HEAR HIS VOICE.
YOUR MARK IS...
...CLUBS.
Uh-oh... Did I ask the wrong person?
I can't trust this man!!
I shouldn't have lied to that boy...
DIA-MONDS.
...but I can trust him.

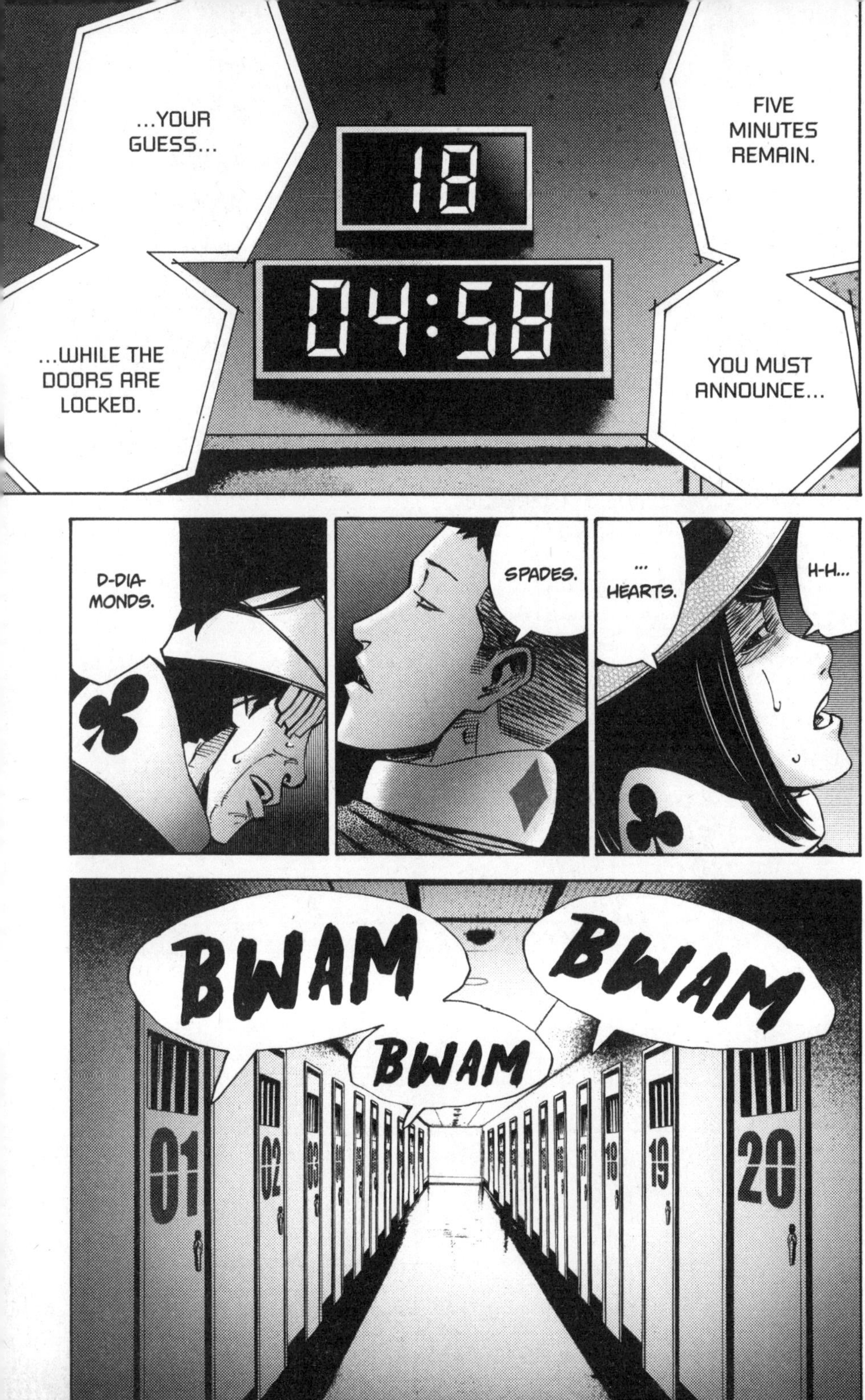
FIVE MINUTES REMAIN.
YOU MUST ANNOUNCE...
18
04:58
...YOUR GUESS...
...WHILE THE DOORS ARE LOCKED.
H-H...
...HEARTS.
SPADES.
D-DIAMONDS.
BWAM
BWAM
BWAM

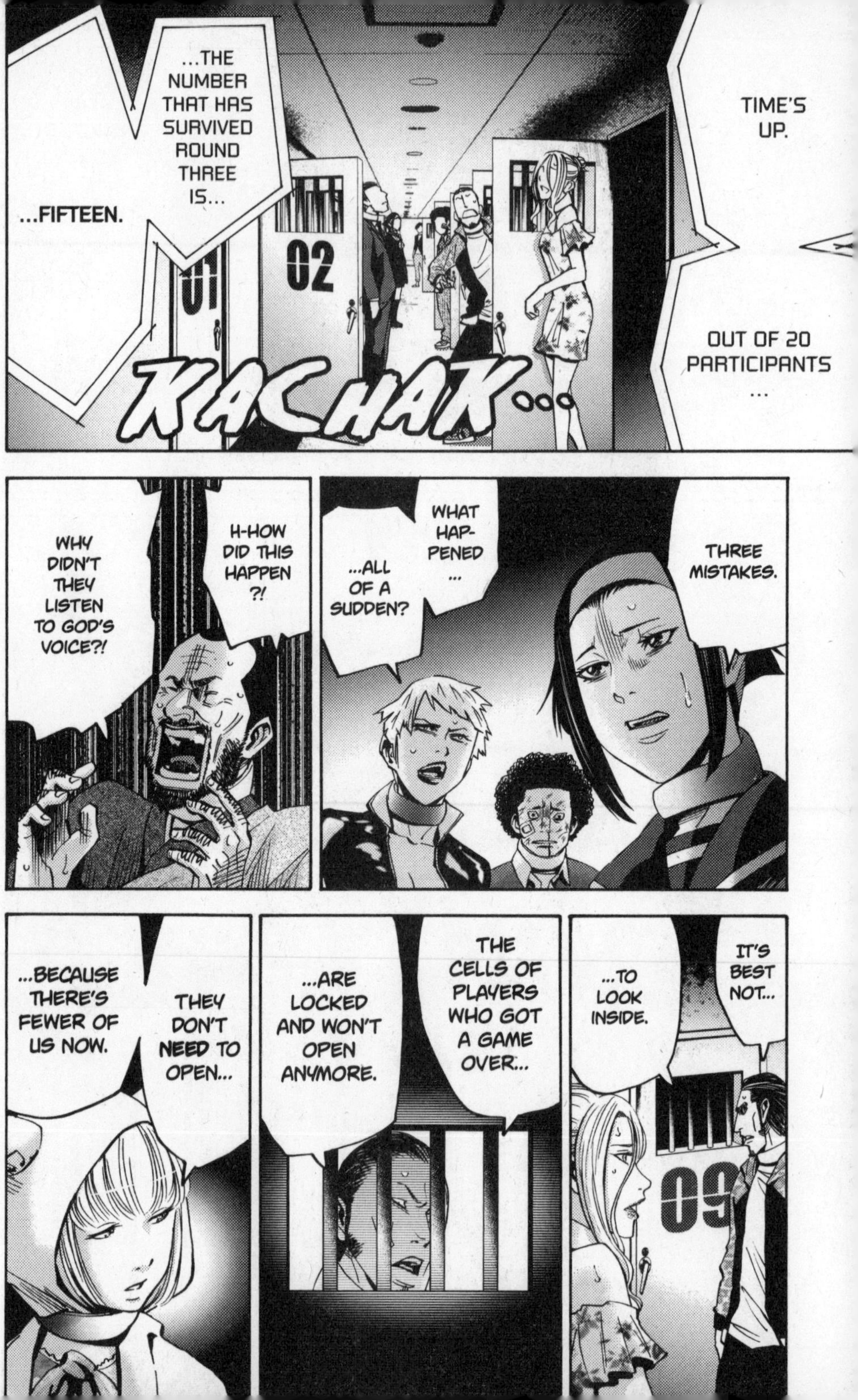
TIME'S UP.
OUT OF 20 PARTICIPANTS ...
...THE NUMBER THAT HAS SURVIVED ROUND THREE IS...
...FIFTEEN.
KACHAK...
THREE MISTAKES.
WHAT HAPPENED ...
...ALL OF A SUDDEN?
H-HOW DID THIS HAPPEN ?!
WHY DIDN'T THEY LISTEN TO GOD'S VOICE?!
IT'S BEST NOT...
...TO LOOK INSIDE.
THE CELLS OF PLAYERS WHO GOT A GAME OVER...
...ARE LOCKED AND WON'T OPEN ANYMORE.
THEY DON'T NEED TO OPEN...
...BECAUSE THERE'S FEWER OF US NOW.

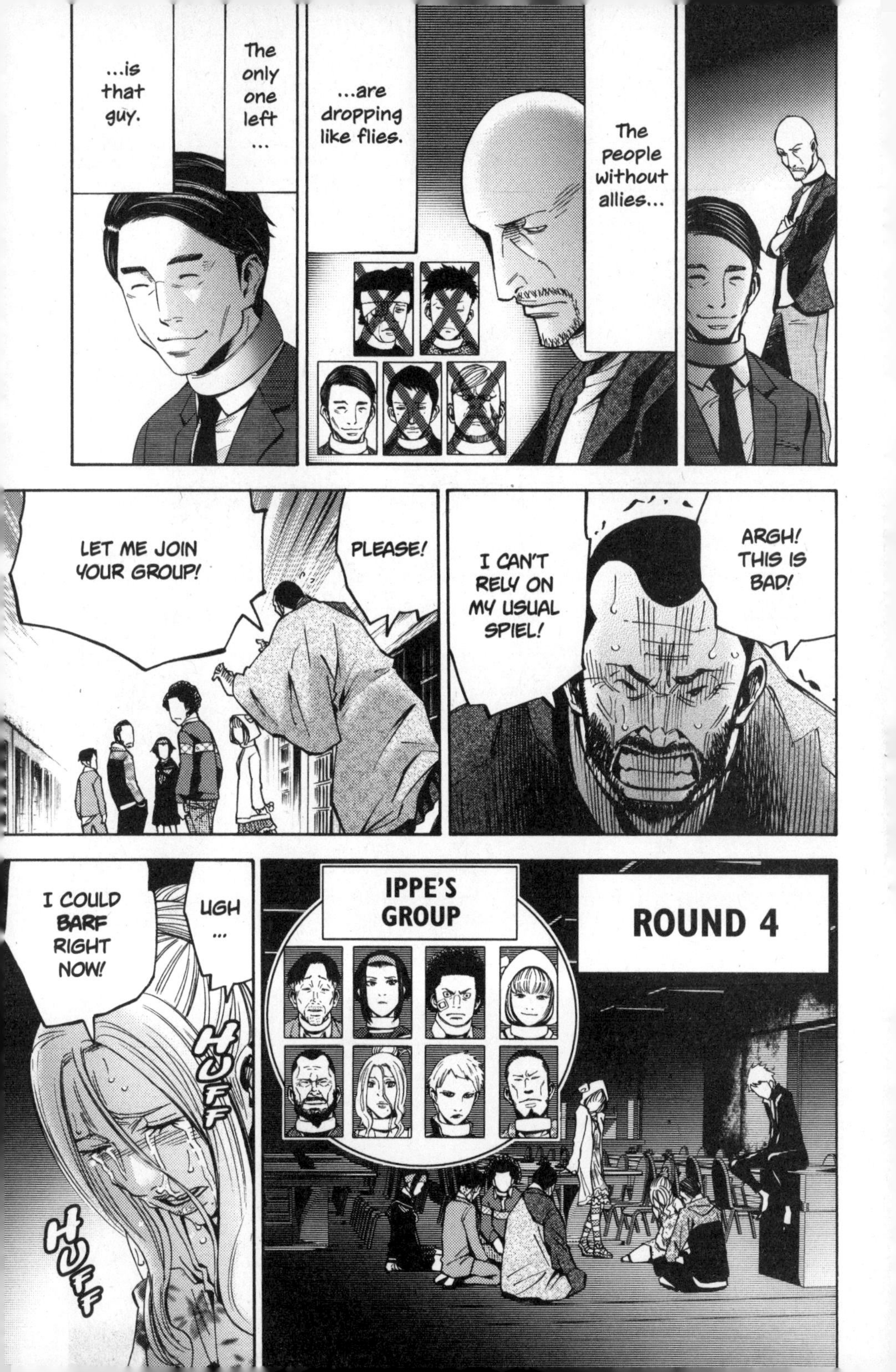
The people without allies...
...are dropping like flies.
The only one left...
...is that guy.
ARGH! THIS IS BAD!
I CAN'T RELY ON MY USUAL SPIEL!
PLEASE!
LET ME JOIN YOUR GROUP!
ROUND 4
IPPE'S GROUP
UGH...
I COULD BARF RIGHT NOW!
HUFF
HUFF

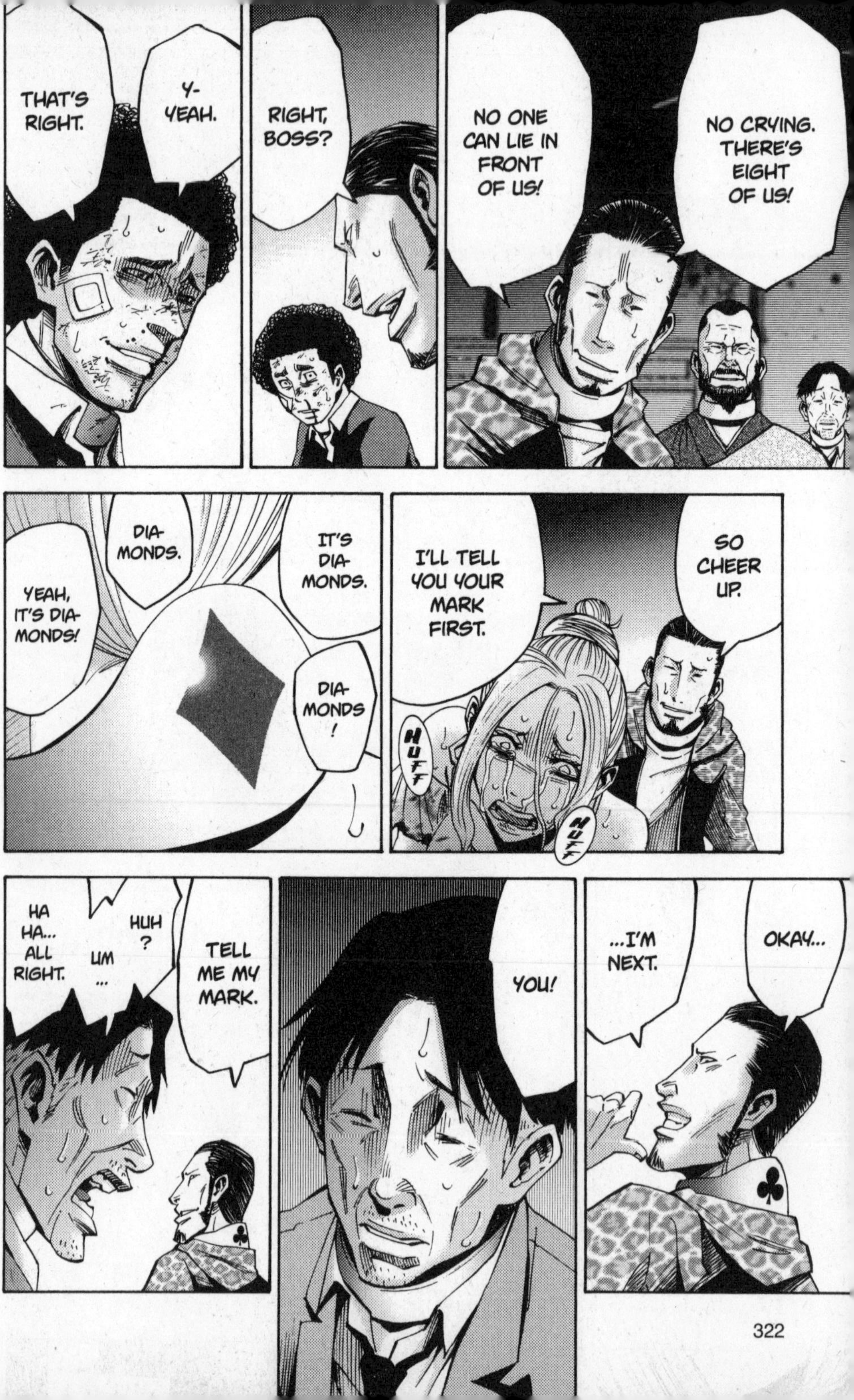
NO CRYING. THERE'S EIGHT OF US!
NO ONE CAN LIE IN FRONT OF US!
RIGHT, BOSS?
Y-YEAH.
THAT'S RIGHT.
SO CHEER UP.
I'LL TELL YOU YOUR MARK FIRST.
HUFF
HUFF
IT'S DIAMONDS.
DIAMONDS.
DIAMONDS!
YEAH, IT'S DIAMONDS!
OKAY...
...I'M NEXT.
YOU!
TELL ME MY MARK.
HUH?
UM...
HA HA... ALL RIGHT.

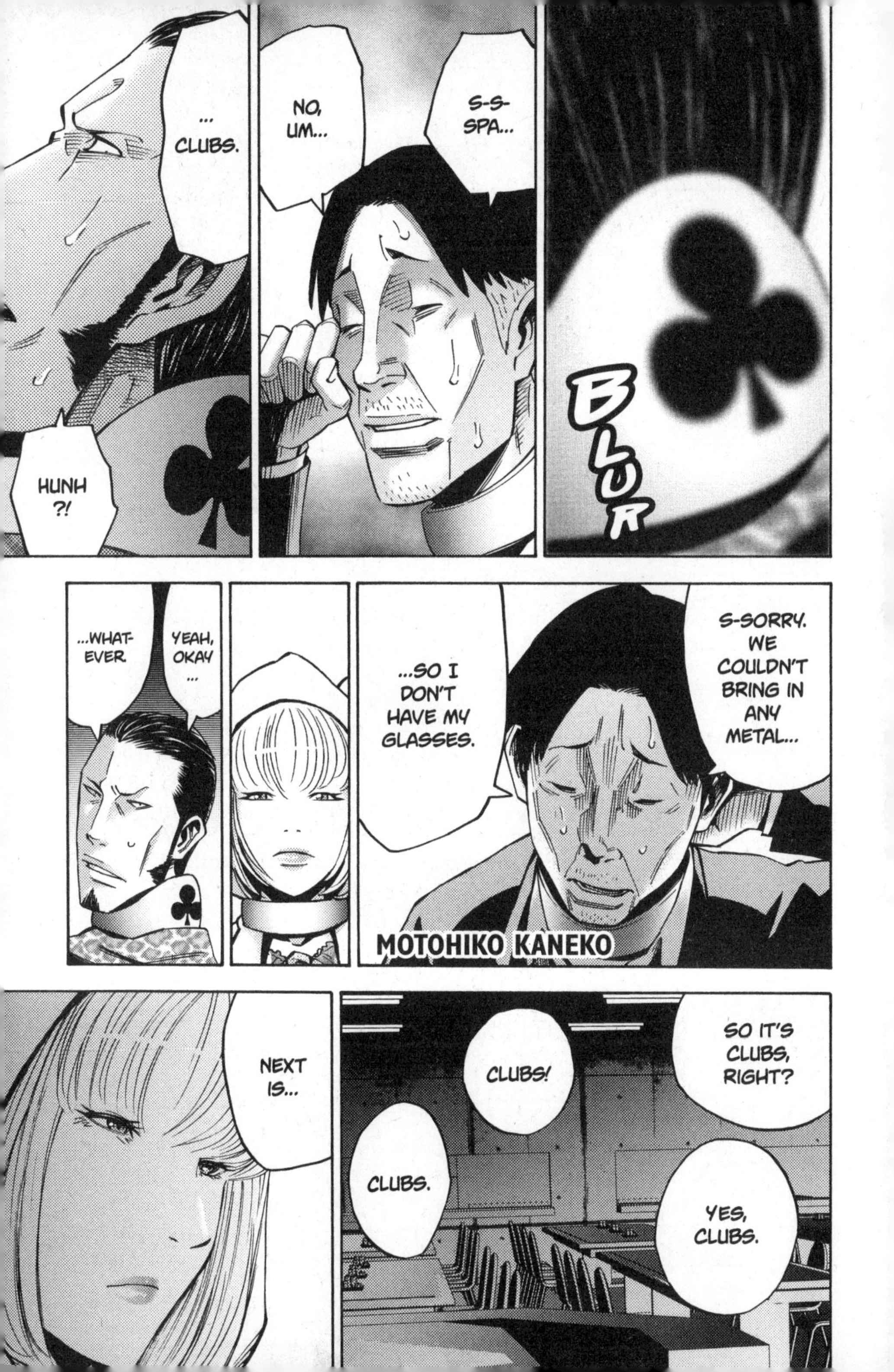
BLUR
S-S-SPA...
NO, UM...
... CLUBS.
HUNH ?!
S-SORRY. WE COULDN'T BRING IN ANY METAL...
...SO I DON'T HAVE MY GLASSES.
MOTOHIKO KANEKO
YEAH, OKAY ...
...WHAT-EVER.
SO IT'S CLUBS, RIGHT?
CLUBS!
YES, CLUBS.
CLUBS.
NEXT IS...

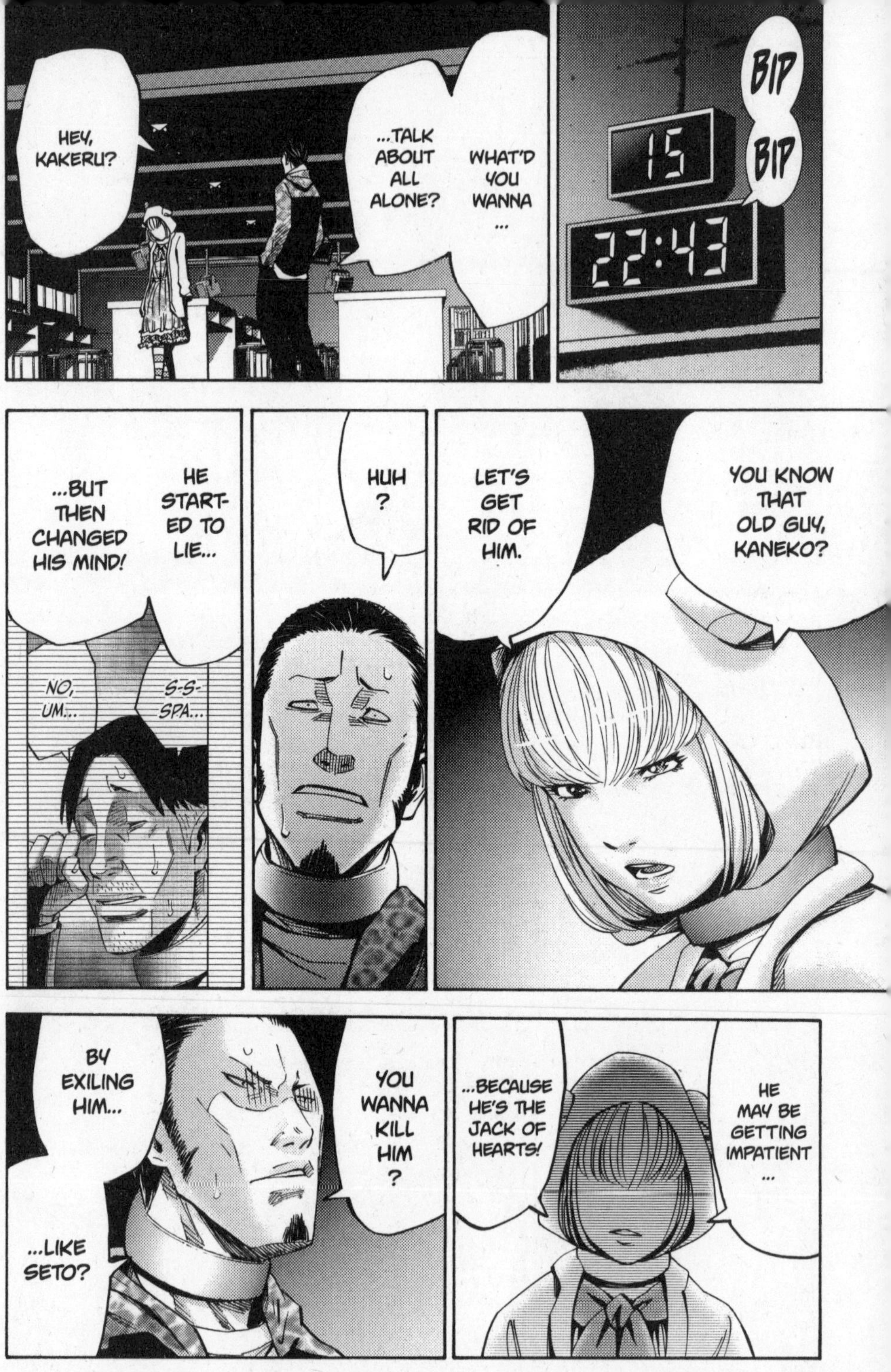
BIP
BIP
15
22:43
WHAT'D YOU WANNA ...
...TALK ABOUT ALL ALONE?
HEY, KAKERU?
YOU KNOW THAT OLD GUY, KANEKO?
LET'S GET RID OF HIM.
HUH?
HE START-ED TO LIE...
...BUT THEN CHANGED HIS MIND!
S-S-SPA...
NO, UM...
HE MAY BE GETTING IMPATIENT ...
...BECAUSE HE'S THE JACK OF HEARTS!
YOU WANNA KILL HIM?
BY EXILING HIM...
...LIKE SETO?

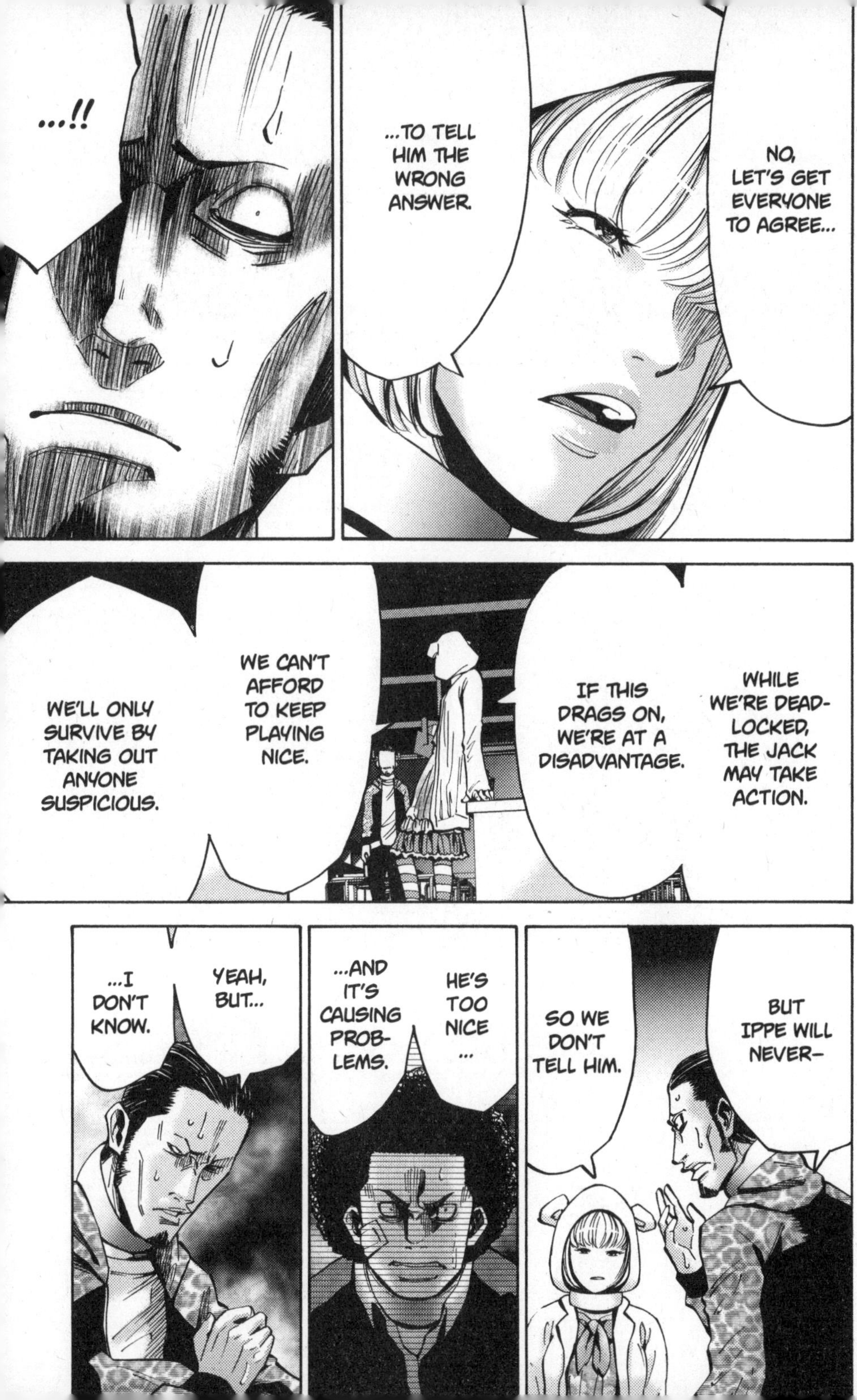
NO, LET'S GET EVERYONE TO AGREE...
...TO TELL HIM THE WRONG ANSWER.
...!!
WHILE WE'RE DEAD-LOCKED, THE JACK MAY TAKE ACTION.
IF THIS DRAGS ON, WE'RE AT A DISADVANTAGE.
WE CAN'T AFFORD TO KEEP PLAYING NICE.
WE'LL ONLY SURVIVE BY TAKING OUT ANYONE SUSPICIOUS.
BUT IPPE WILL NEVER—
SO WE DON'T TELL HIM.
HE'S TOO NICE...
...AND IT'S CAUSING PROB-LEMS.
YEAH, BUT...
...I DON'T KNOW.

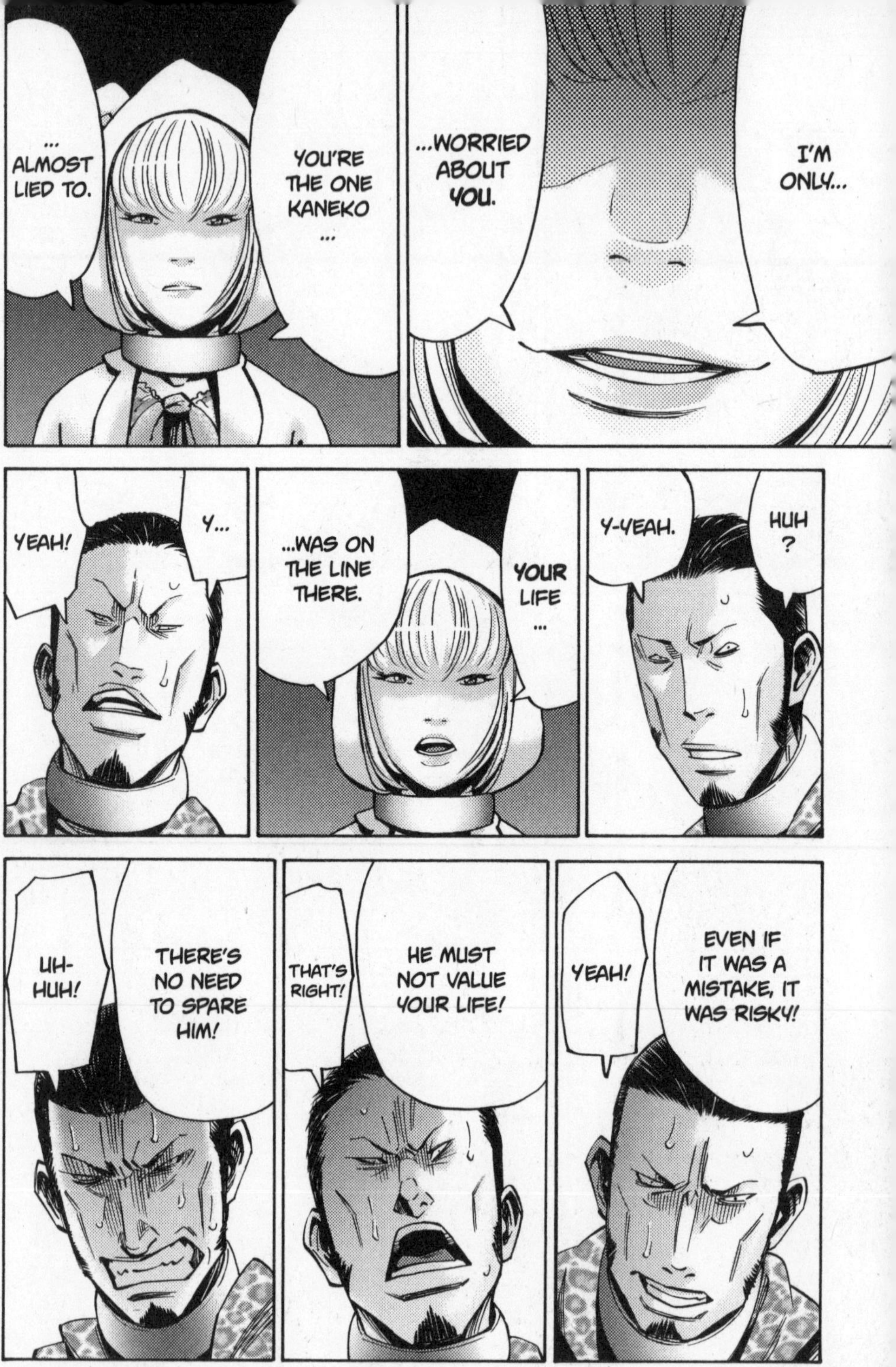
I'M ONLY...
...WORRIED ABOUT YOU.
YOU'RE THE ONE KANEKO ...
... ALMOST LIED TO.
HUH ?
Y-YEAH.
YOUR LIFE ...
...WAS ON THE LINE THERE.
Y...
YEAH!
EVEN IF IT WAS A MISTAKE, IT WAS RISKY!
YEAH!
HE MUST NOT VALUE YOUR LIFE!
THAT'S RIGHT!
THERE'S NO NEED TO SPARE HIM!
UH-HUH!

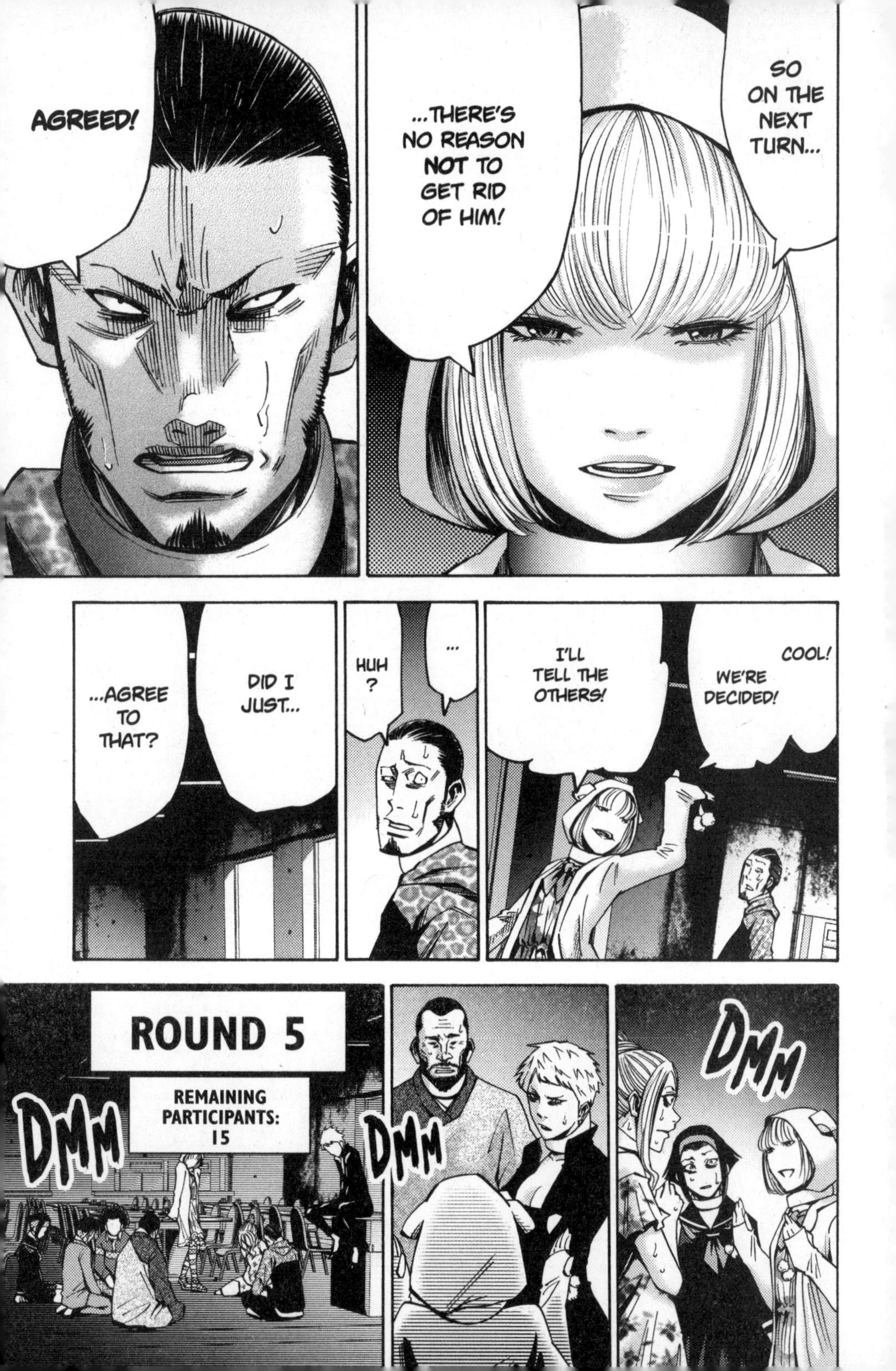
SO ON THE NEXT TURN...
...THERE'S NO REASON NOT TO GET RID OF HIM!
AGREED!
COOL! WE'RE DECIDED!
I'LL TELL THE OTHERS!
...
HUH?
DID I JUST...
...AGREE TO THAT?
DMM
DMM
ROUND 5
REMAINING PARTICIPANTS: 15
DMM

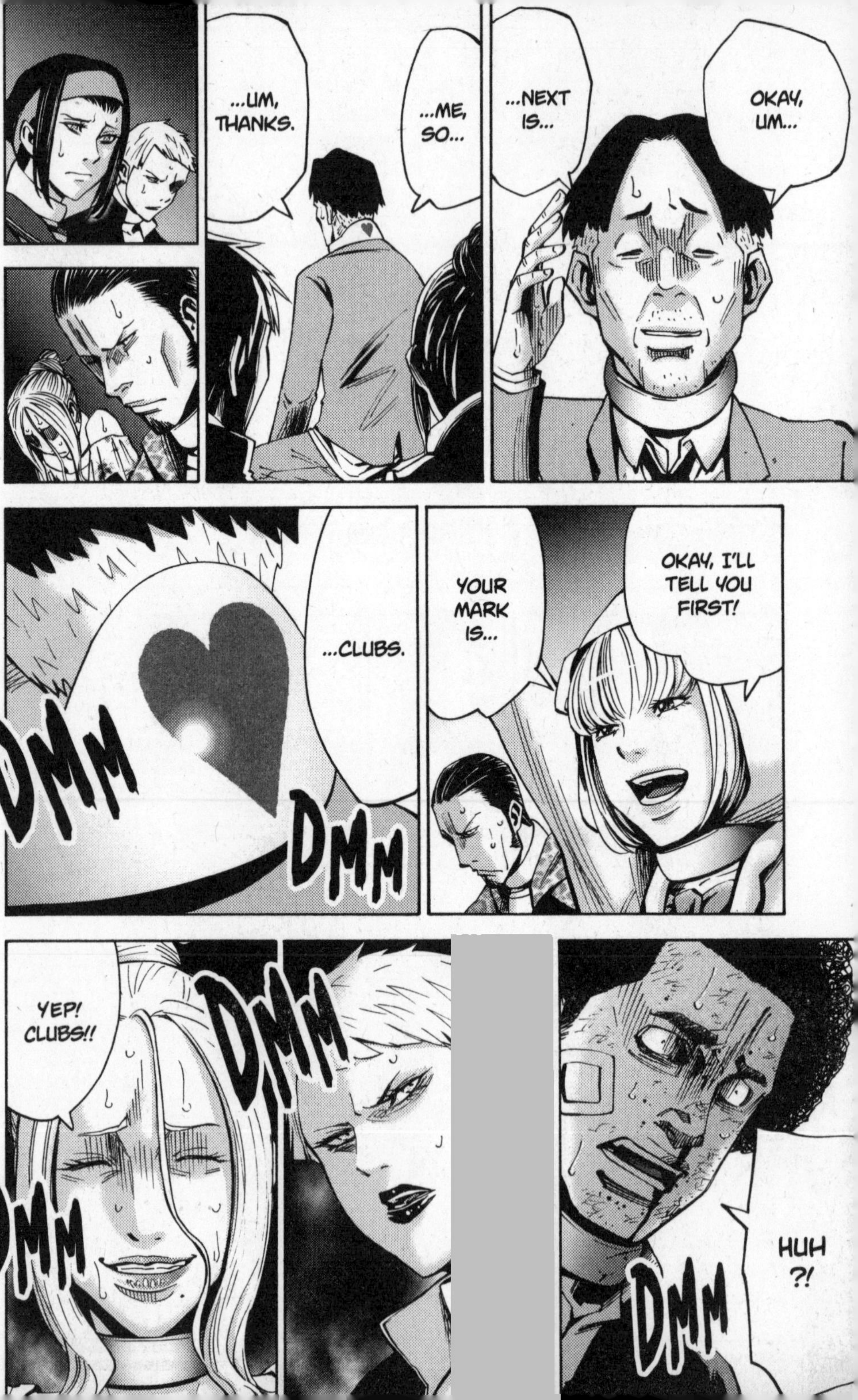
OKAY, UM...
...NEXT IS...
...ME, SO...
...UM, THANKS.
OKAY, I'LL TELL YOU FIRST!
YOUR MARK IS...
...CLUBS.
DMM
DMM
HUH ?!
DMM
DMM
YEP! CLUBS!!
DMM

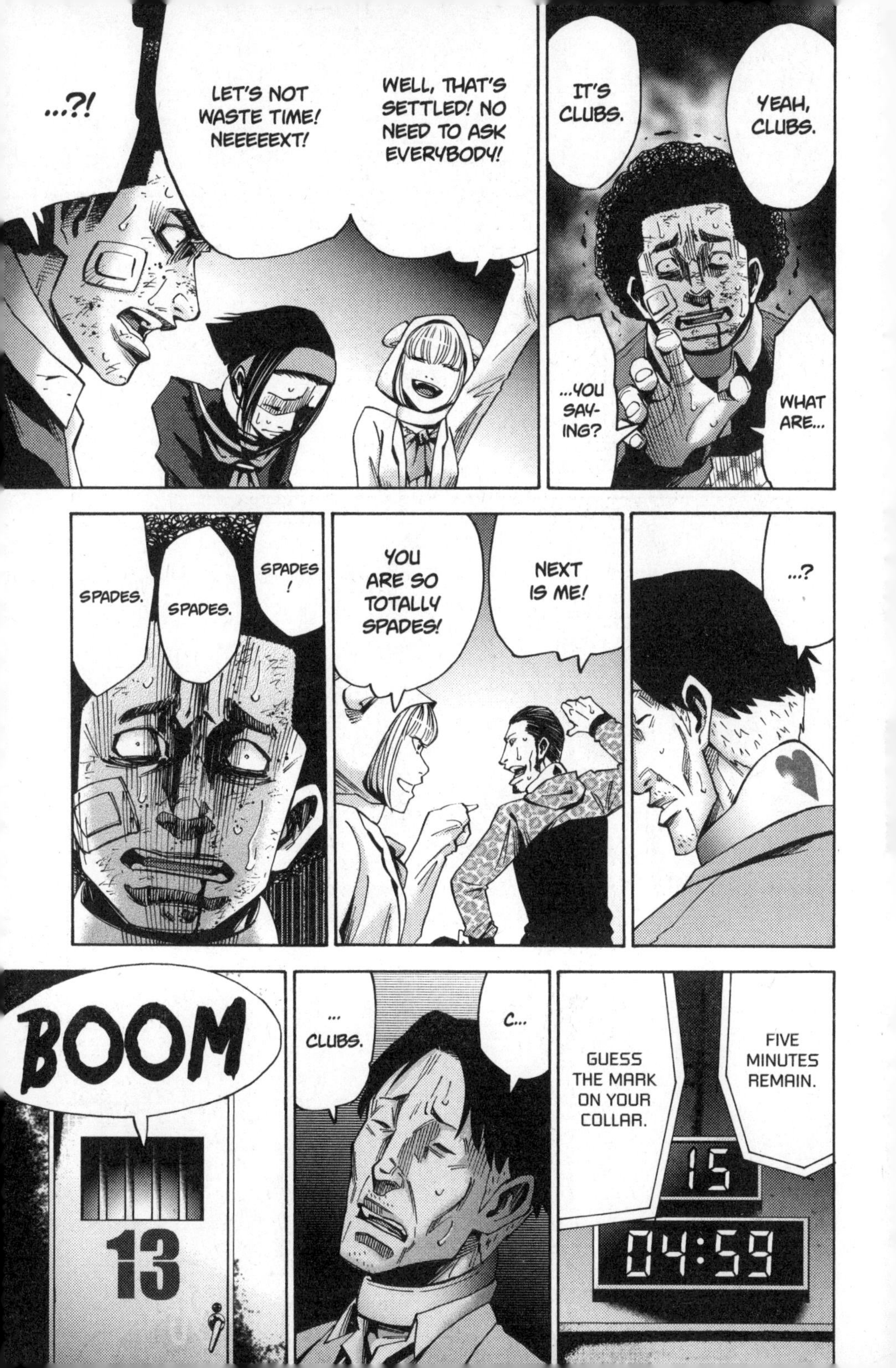
YEAH, CLUBS.
IT'S CLUBS.
WHAT ARE...
...YOU SAY-ING?
WELL, THAT'S SETTLED! NO NEED TO ASK EVERYBODY!
LET'S NOT WASTE TIME! NEEEEEXT!
...?!
...?
NEXT IS ME!
YOU ARE SO TOTALLY SPADES!
SPADES!
SPADES.
SPADES.
FIVE MINUTES REMAIN.
GUESS THE MARK ON YOUR COLLAR.
15
04:59
C...
... CLUBS.
BOOM
13

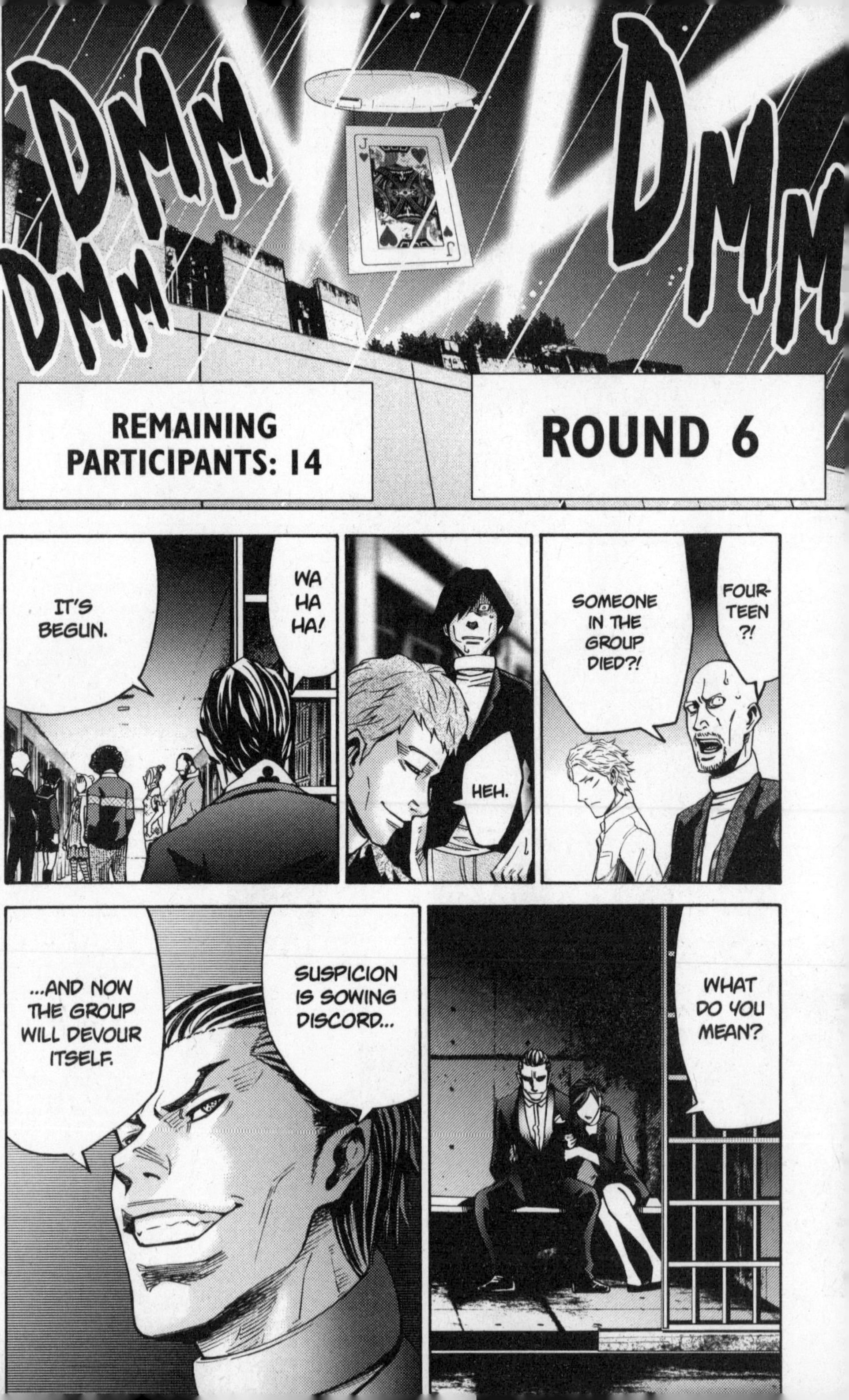
DMM
DMM
DMM
ROUND 6
REMAINING PARTICIPANTS: 14
FOUR-TEEN?!
SOMEONE IN THE GROUP DIED?!
HEH.
WA HA HA!
IT'S BEGUN.
WHAT DO YOU MEAN?
SUSPICION IS SOWING DISCORD...
...AND NOW THE GROUP WILL DEVOUR ITSELF.

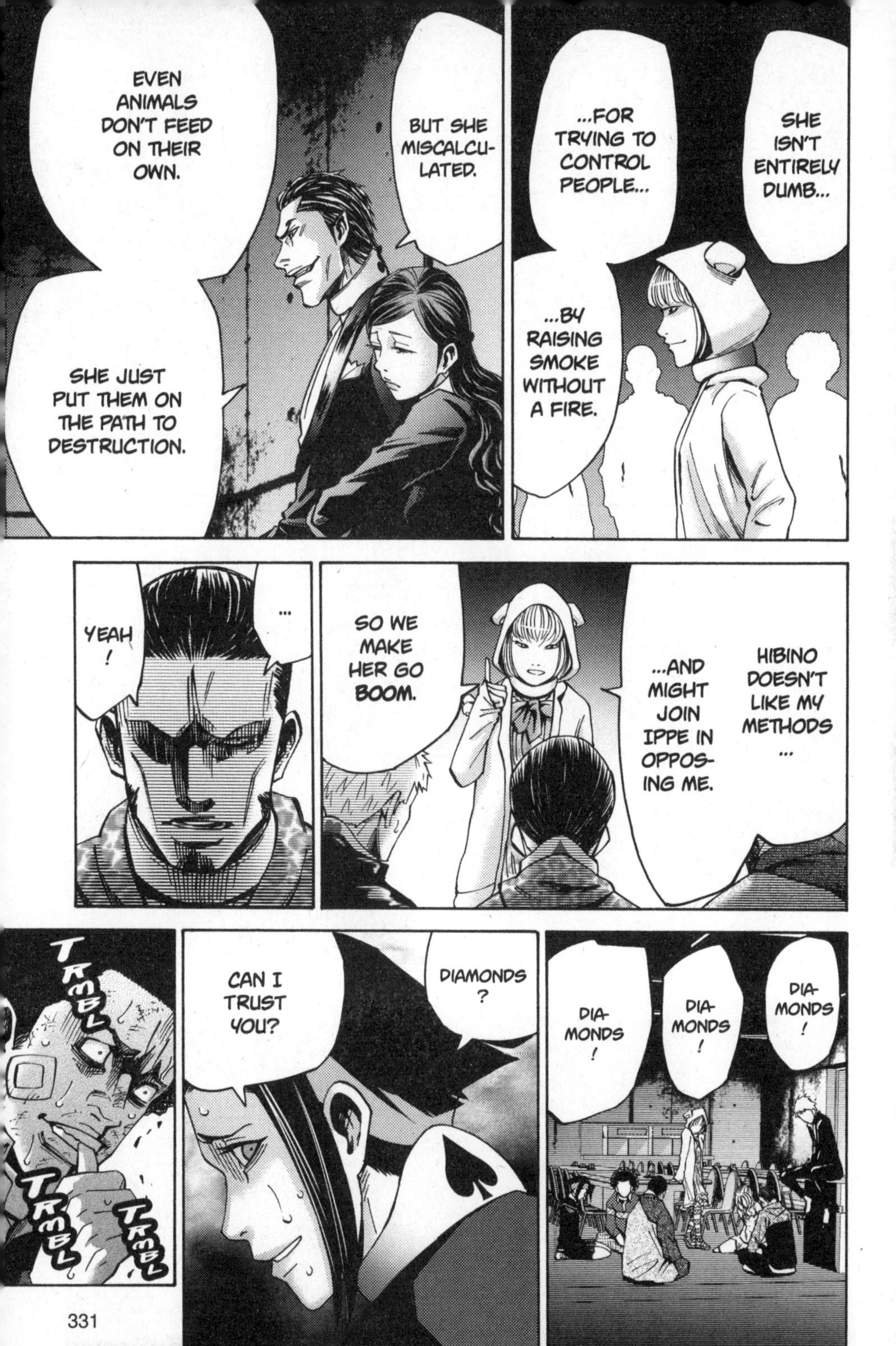
SHE ISN'T ENTIRELY DUMB...
...FOR TRYING TO CONTROL PEOPLE...
...BY RAISING SMOKE WITHOUT A FIRE.
BUT SHE MISCALCU-LATED.
EVEN ANIMALS DON'T FEED ON THEIR OWN.
SHE JUST PUT THEM ON THE PATH TO DESTRUCTION.
HIBINO DOESN'T LIKE MY METHODS...
...AND MIGHT JOIN IPPE IN OPPOS-ING ME.
SO WE MAKE HER GO BOOM.
...
YEAH!
DIA-MONDS!
DIA-MONDS!
DIA-MONDS!
DIAMONDS?
CAN I TRUST YOU?
TRMBL
TRMBL
TRMBL

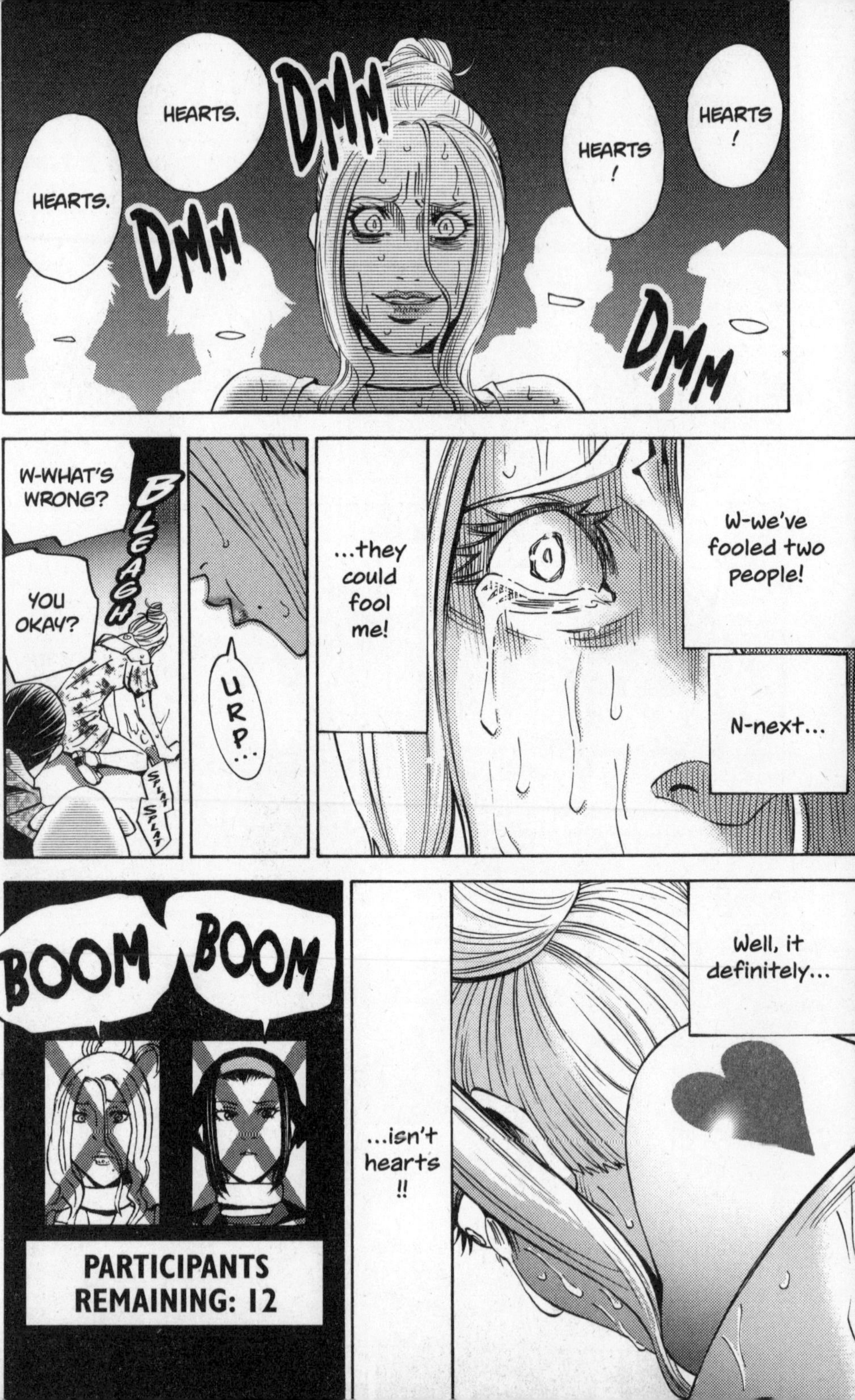
HEARTS!
HEARTS!
DMM
HEARTS.
HEARTS.
DMM
DMM
W-we've fooled two people!
N-next...
...they could fool me!
URP...
BLEAGH
W-WHAT'S WRONG?
YOU OKAY?
SPLAT SPLAT
Well, it definitely...
...isn't hearts!!
BOOM
BOOM
PARTICIPANTS REMAINING: 12

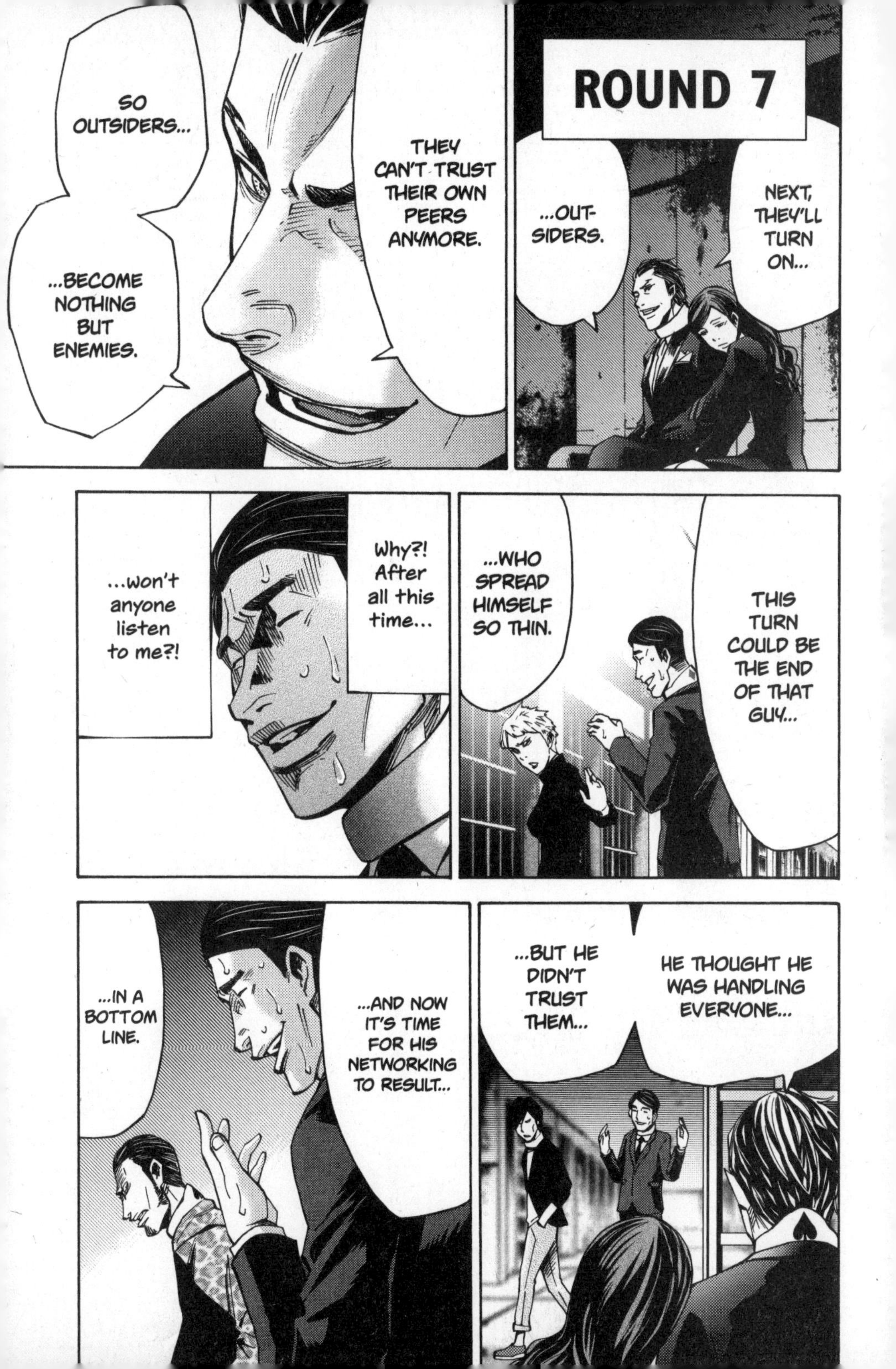
ROUND 7
NEXT, THEY'LL TURN ON...
...OUT-SIDERS.
THEY CAN'T TRUST THEIR OWN PEERS ANYMORE.
SO OUTSIDERS...
...BECOME NOTHING BUT ENEMIES.
THIS TURN COULD BE THE END OF THAT GUY...
...WHO SPREAD HIMSELF SO THIN.
Why?! After all this time...
...won't anyone listen to me?!
HE THOUGHT HE WAS HANDLING EVERYONE...
...BUT HE DIDN'T TRUST THEM...
...AND NOW IT'S TIME FOR HIS NETWORKING TO RESULT...
...IN A BOTTOM LINE.

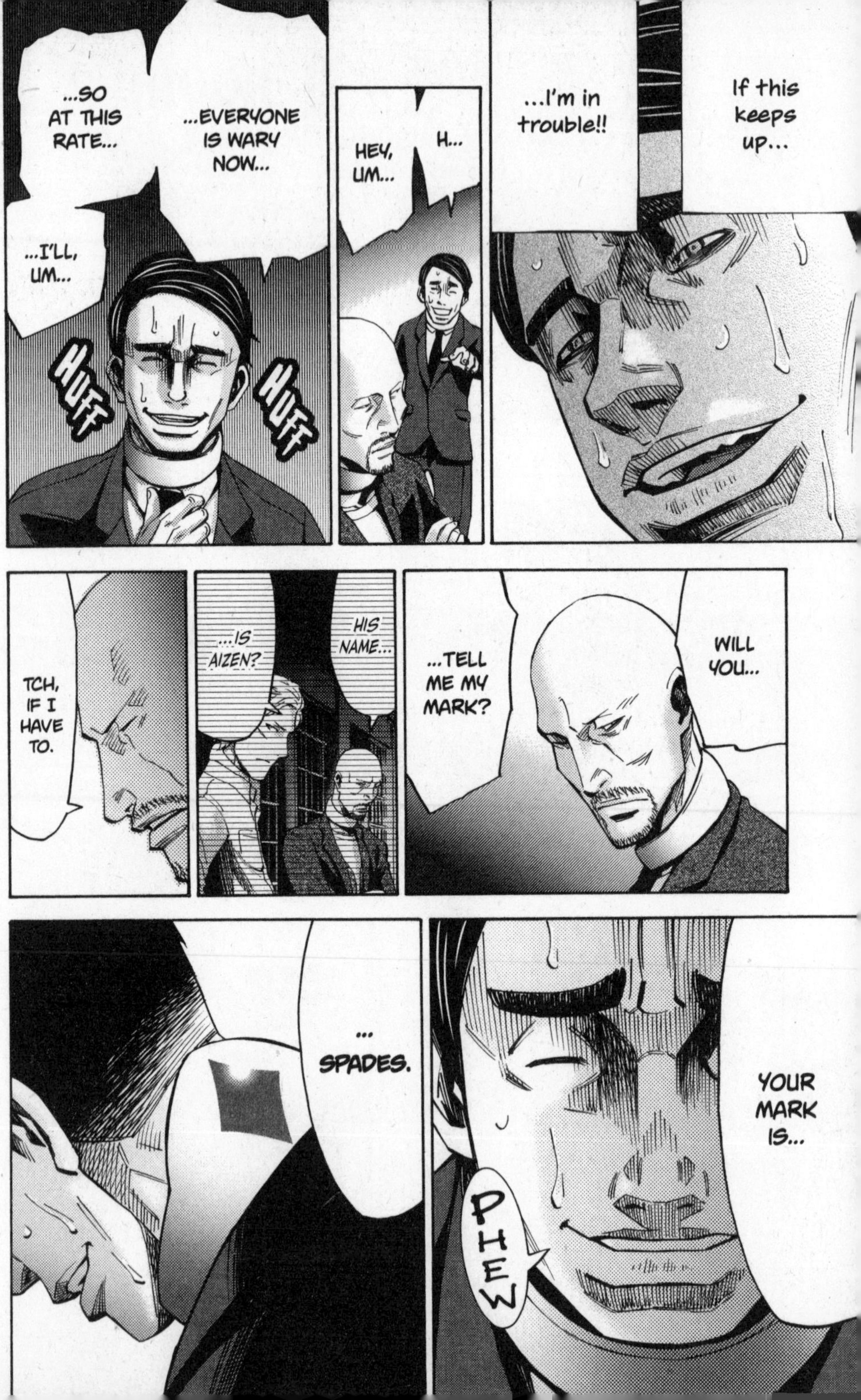
If this keeps up...
...I'm in trouble!!
H...
HEY, UM...
...EVERYONE IS WARY NOW...
...SO AT THIS RATE...
...I'LL, UM...
HUFF
HUFF
WILL YOU...
...TELL ME MY MARK?
HIS NAME...
...IS AIZEN?
TCH, IF I HAVE TO.
YOUR MARK IS...
PHEW
...SPADES.

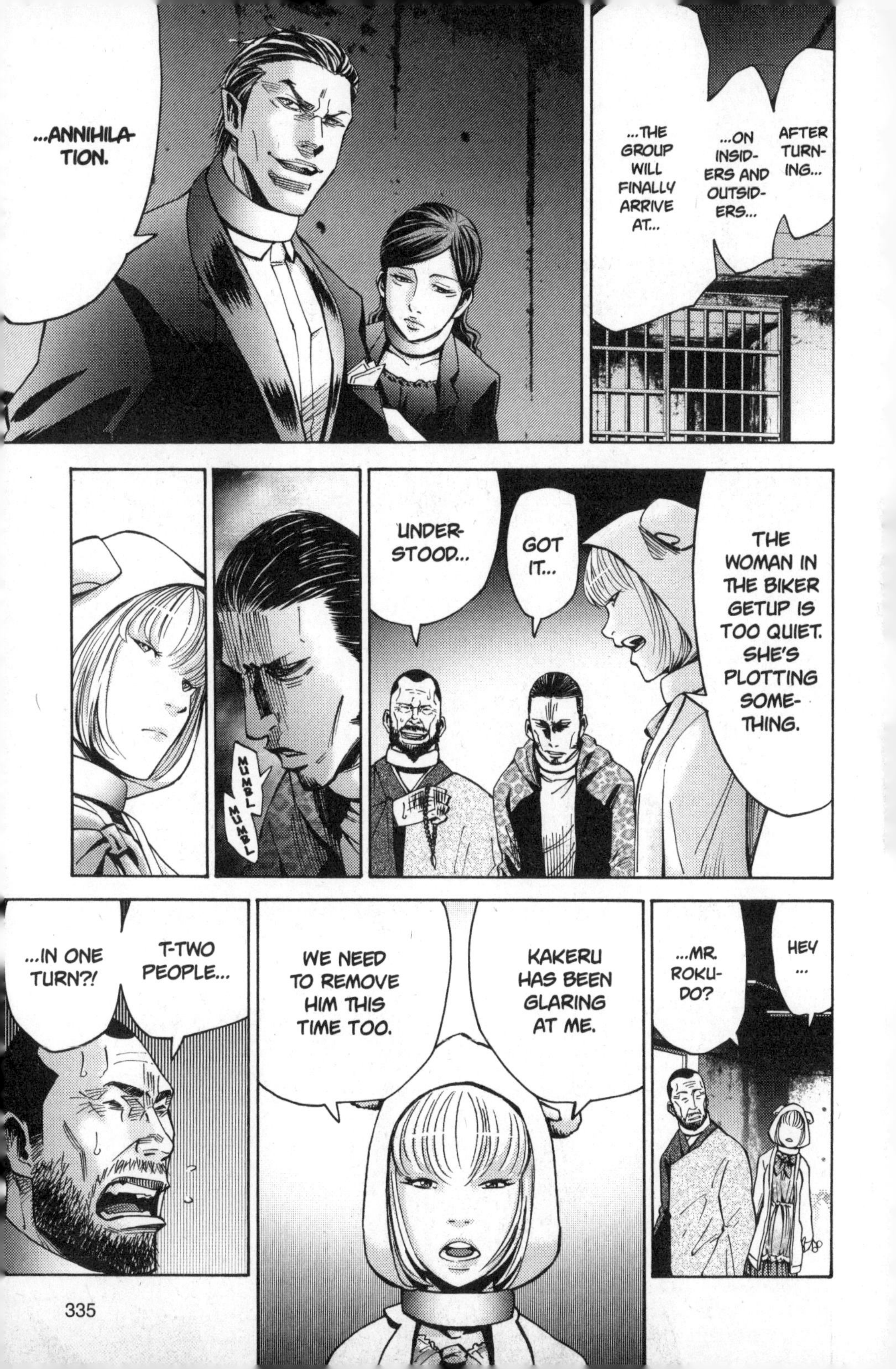
AFTER TURNING...
...ON INSIDERS AND OUTSIDERS...
...THE GROUP WILL FINALLY ARRIVE AT...
...ANNIHILATION.
THE WOMAN IN THE BIKER GETUP IS TOO QUIET. SHE'S PLOTTING SOMETHING.
GOT IT...
UNDERSTOOD...
MUMBL MUMBL
HEY...
...MR. ROKUDO?
KAKERU HAS BEEN GLARING AT ME.
WE NEED TO REMOVE HIM THIS TIME TOO.
T-TWO PEOPLE...
...IN ONE TURN?!

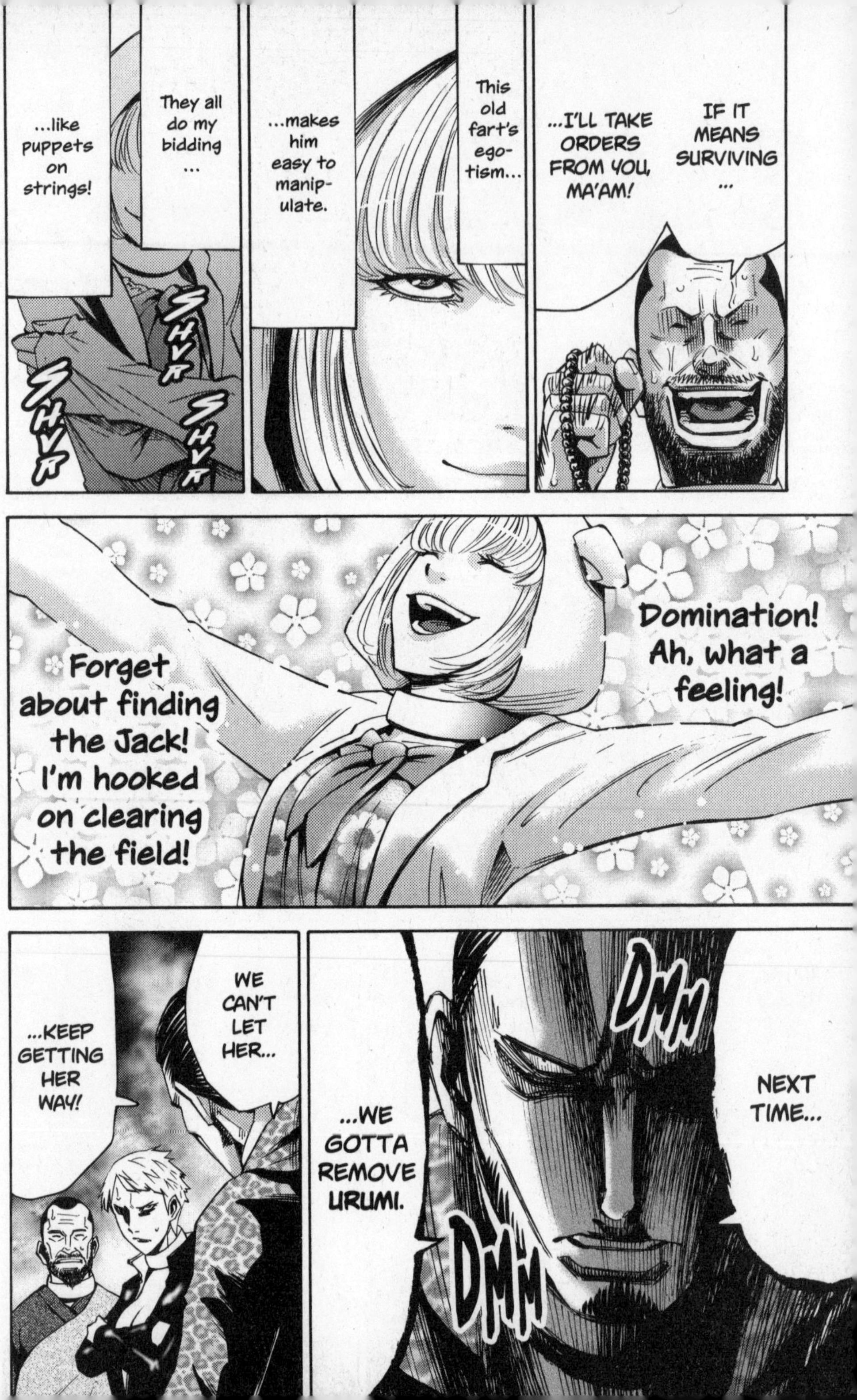
IF IT MEANS SURVIVING ...
...I'LL TAKE ORDERS FROM YOU, MA'AM!
This old fart's egotism...
...makes him easy to manipulate.
SHVR
SHVR
SHVR
They all do my bidding ...
...like puppets on strings!
Domination! Ah, what a feeling!
Forget about finding the Jack! I'm hooked on clearing the field!
DMM
NEXT TIME...
...WE GOTTA REMOVE URUMI.
DMM
WE CAN'T LET HER...
...KEEP GETTING HER WAY!

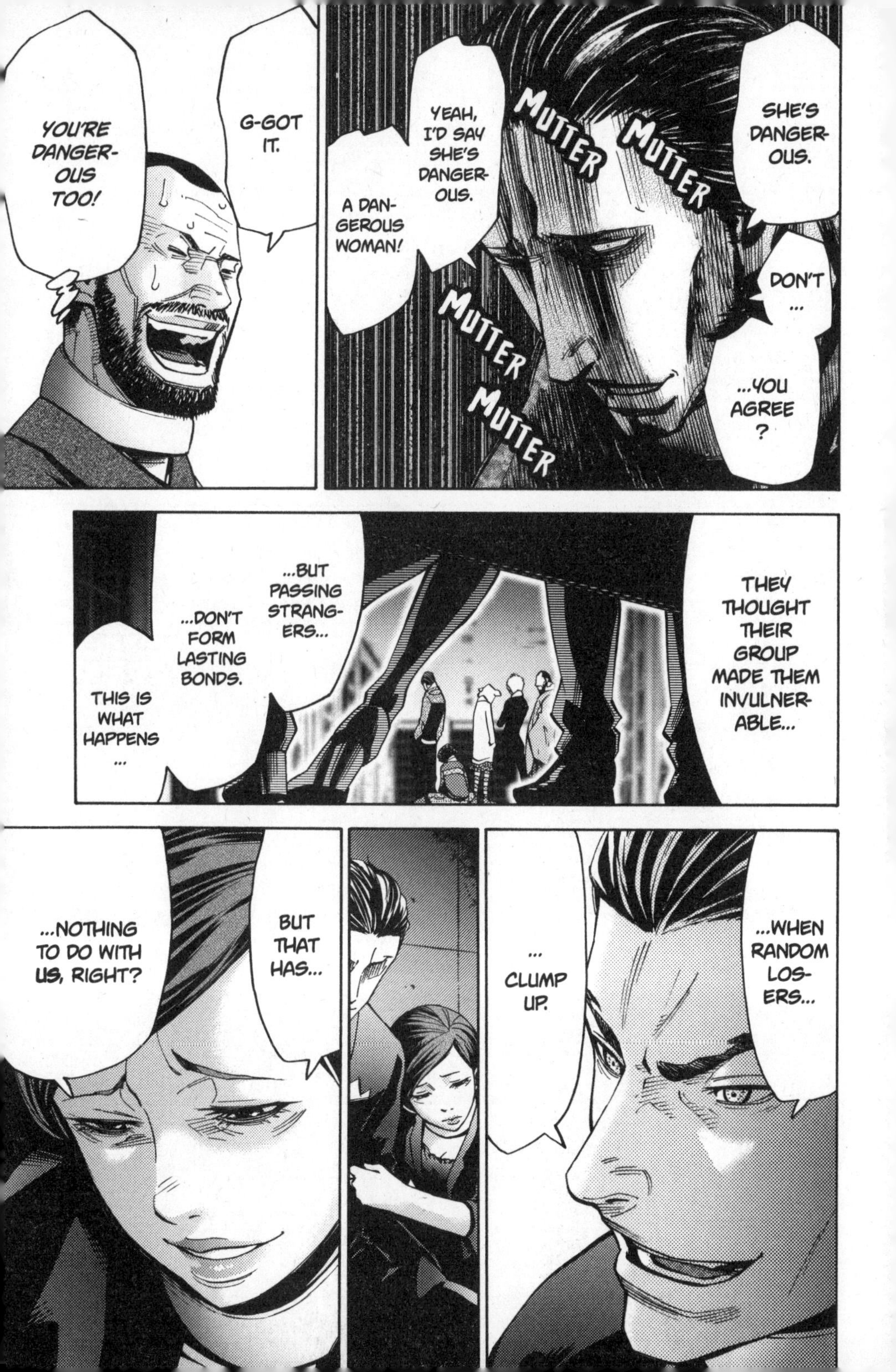
SHE'S DANGEROUS.
DON'T ...
...YOU AGREE ?
MUTTER MUTTER
MUTTER MUTTER
YEAH, I'D SAY SHE'S DANGEROUS.
A DANGEROUS WOMAN!
G-GOT IT.
YOU'RE DANGEROUS TOO!
THEY THOUGHT THEIR GROUP MADE THEM INVULNERABLE...
...BUT PASSING STRANGERS...
...DON'T FORM LASTING BONDS.
THIS IS WHAT HAPPENS ...
...WHEN RANDOM LOSERS...
... CLUMP UP.
BUT THAT HAS...
...NOTHING TO DO WITH US, RIGHT?

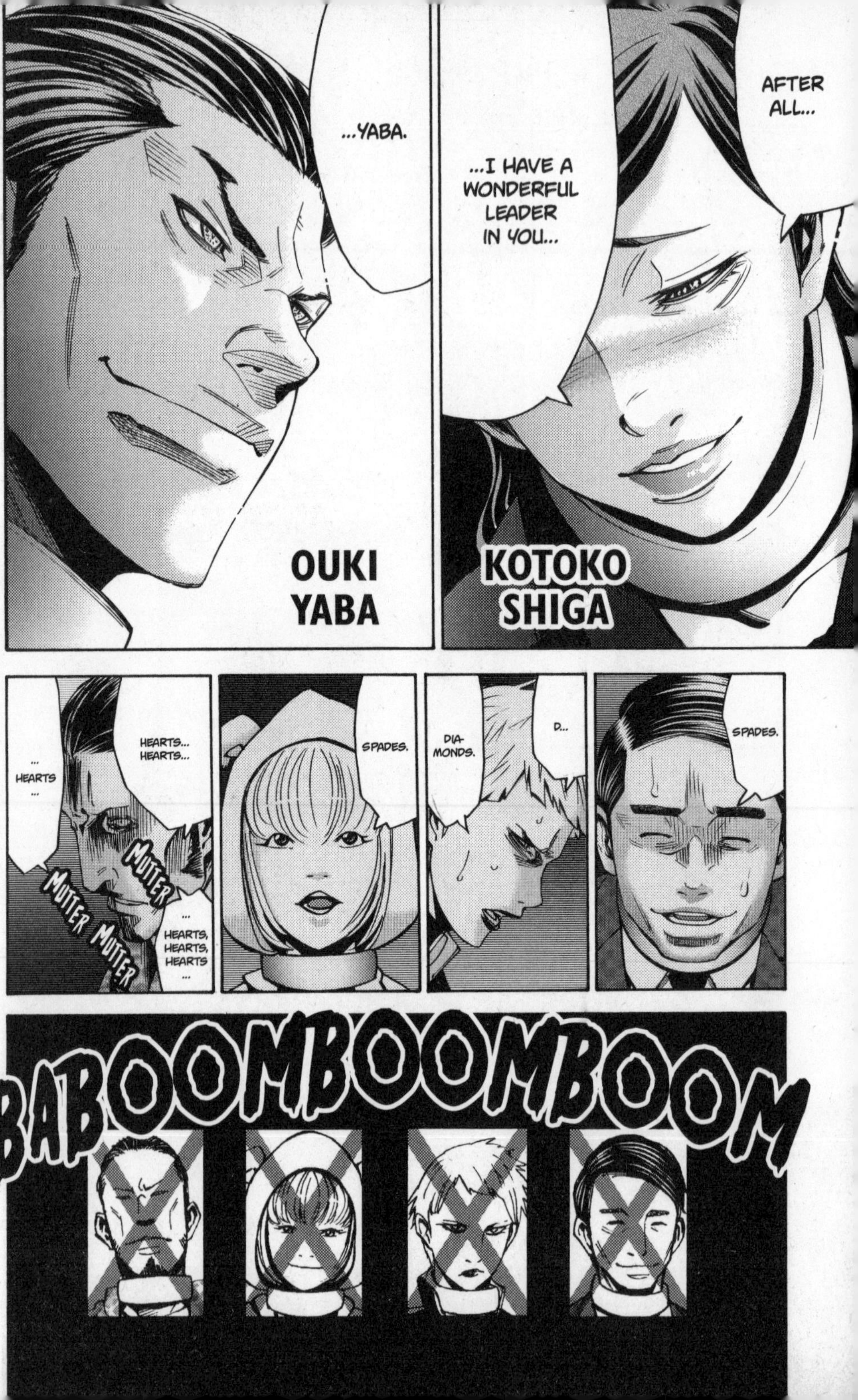
AFTER ALL...
...I HAVE A WONDERFUL LEADER IN YOU...
KOTOKO SHIGA
...YABA.
OUKI YABA
SPADES.
D...
DIA-MONDS.
SPADES.
HEARTS... HEARTS...
... HEARTS ...
MUTTER
MUTTER MUTTER MUTTER
... HEARTS, HEARTS, HEARTS ...
BABOOMBOOMBOOM

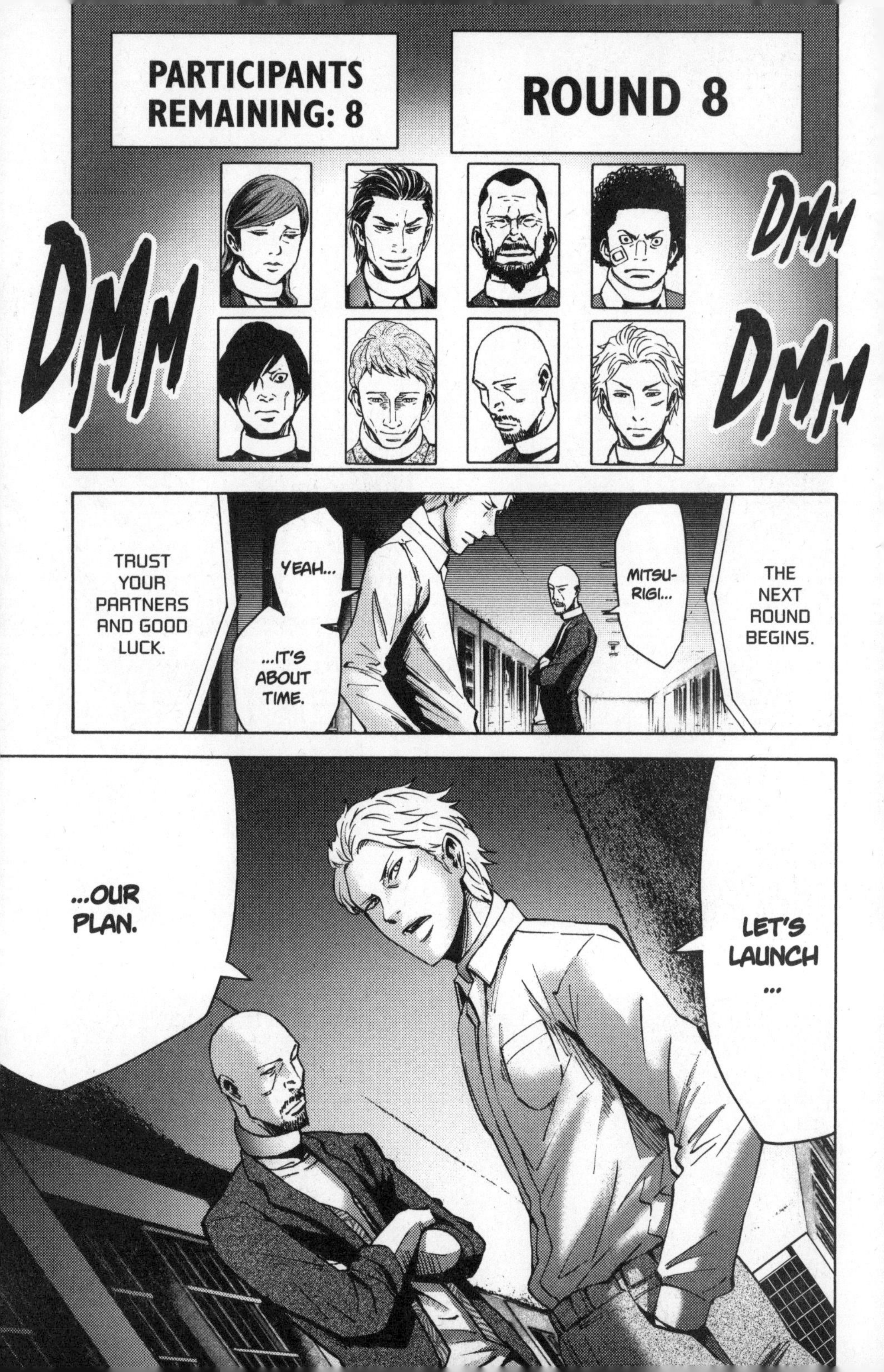
ROUND 8
PARTICIPANTS REMAINING: 8
DMM
DMM
DMM
THE NEXT ROUND BEGINS.
MITSU-RIGI...
YEAH...
...IT'S ABOUT TIME.
TRUST YOUR PARTNERS AND GOOD LUCK.
LET'S LAUNCH ...
...OUR PLAN.

Knowing when enough is enough, knowing the limits of our own knowledge... There's a lot we need to know, but above all we should know how to love!

— HARO ASO

HARO ASO

In 2004, Haro Aso received *Shonen Sunday's* Manga
College Award for his short story "YUNGE!" After the
success of his 2007 short story "Onigami Amon,"
Aso got the chance to start a series of his own—
2008's *Hyde & Closer*. In 2010, his series *Alice in
Borderland* began serialization in *Shonen Sunday S*
and is now a Netflix live-action drama. *Zom 100:
Bucket List of the Dead* is his follow-up series.